Mrs Beeton's A–Z of Everyday Cookery

MRS BEETON'S A–Z OF EVERYDAY COOKERY

Consultant Editor
Bridget Jones

BROCKHAMPTON PRESS
LONDON

A WARD LOCK BOOK

First published in 1995 by Ward Lock, Wellington House,
125 Strand, London WC2R OBB

A Cassell Imprint

This edition published 1998 by Brockhampton Press,
a member of Hodder Headline PLC Group

ISBN 1 86019 866 X

Copyright © Ward Lock 1995

Mrs Beeton's is a registered trademark of Ward Lock Ltd

Edited by Jenni Fleetwood

Photography by Sue Atkinson and Clive Streeter

Home Economists Jacqui Hine, Sarah Maxwell and
Lyn Rutherford

British Library Cataloguing-in-Publication Data

A catalogue record of this book is available from the British
Library

Printed at Oriental Press, Dubai, U.A.E.

CONTENTS

USEFUL WEIGHTS AND MEASURES

USING METRIC OR IMPERIAL MEASURES

Throughout the book, all weights and measures are given first in metric, then in Imperial. For example 100 g/4 oz, 150 ml/¼ pint or 15 ml/1 tbsp.

When following any of the recipes use either metric or Imperial – do not combine the two sets of measures as they are not interchangeable.

EQUIVALENT METRIC/IMPERIAL MEASURES

WEIGHTS

The chart that follows lists some of the metric/Imperial weights used in the recipes.

METRIC	IMPERIAL	METRIC	IMPERIAL
15 g	½ oz	375 g	13 oz
25 g	1 oz	400 g	14 oz
50 g	2 oz	425 g	15oz
75 g	3 oz	450 g	1 lb
100 g	4 oz	575 g	1¼ lb
150 g	5 oz	675 g	1½ lb
175 g	6 oz	800 g	1¾ lb
200 g	7 oz	900 g	2 lb
225 g	8 oz	1 kg	2¼ lb
250 g	9 oz	1.4 kg	3 lb
275 g	10 oz	1.6 kg	3½ lb
300 g	11 oz	1.8 kg	4 lb
350 g	12 oz	2.25 kg	5 lb

LIQUID MEASURES

The following chart lists some metric/Imperial equivalents for liquids. Millilitres (ml), litres and fluid ounces (fl oz) or pints are used throughout.

METRIC	IMPERIAL
50 ml	2 fl oz
125 ml	4 fl oz
150 ml	¼ pint
300 ml	½ pint
450 ml	¾ pint
600 ml	1 pint

SPOON MEASURES

Both metric and Imperial equivalents are given for all spoon measures, expressed as millilitres (ml) and teaspoons (tsp) or tablespoons (tbsp).

All spoon measures refer to British standard measuring spoons and the quantities given are always for level spoons.

Do not use ordinary kitchen cutlery instead of proper measuring spoons as they will hold different quantities.

METRIC	IMPERIAL
1.25 ml	¼ tsp
2.5 ml	½ tsp
5 ml	1 tsp
15 ml	1 tbsp

LENGTH

All linear measures are expressed in millimetres (mm), centimetres (cm) or metres (m) and inches or feet. The following list gives examples of typical conversions.

METRIC	IMPERIAL
5 mm	¼ inch
1 cm	½ inch
2.5 cm	1 inch
5 cm	2 inches
15 cm	6 inches
30 cm	12 inches (1 foot)

OVEN TEMPERATURES

Whenever the oven is used, the required setting is given as three alternatives: degrees Celsius (°C), degrees Fahrenheit (°F) and gas.

The temperature settings given are for conventional ovens. If you have a fan oven, adjust the temperature according to the manufacturer's instructions.

°C	°F	Gas
110	225	¼
120	250	½
140	275	1
150	300	2
160	325	3
180	350	4
190	375	5
200	400	6
220	425	7
230	450	8
240	475	9

MICROWAVE INFORMATION

Occasional microwave hints and instructions are included for certain recipes, as appropriate. All the information given is for microwave ovens rated at 650–700 watts.

The following terms have been used for the microwave settings: High, Medium, Defrost and Low. For each setting, the power input is as follows: High = 100% power, Medium = 50% power, Defrost = 30% power and Low = 20% power.

All microwave notes and timings are for guidance only: always read and follow the manufacturer's instructions for your particular appliance. Remember to avoid putting any metal in the microwave and never operate the microwave empty.

A GUIDE TO INGREDIENTS AND COOKING TECHNIQUES

In this, the first part of Mrs Beeton's A–Z of Everyday Cookery, a wide variety of basic ingredients are listed with notes on buying, storing and using them. Guidelines on food preparation are accompanied, where appropriate, by step-by-step illustrations and information on basic cooking methods includes brief charts giving temperatures and times.

In addition to essential information, the sections on different foods also provide standard recipes for pastries, breads and other basics, such as how to cook rice and eggs. Composite recipes for these ingredients will be found at the back of the book, in the A–Z of Recipes.

The secret of a good soup lies in the stock, which should marry the various components without in itself dominating the flavour. This chapter therefore begins with recipes and suggestions for essential stocks, which are then used to advantage in a selection of classic recipes.

In Mrs Beeton's day, stock-making and the preparation of vast quantities of soup was a standard household task, requiring many hours of gentle simmering and arm-aching sieving to achieve a smooth result. Nowadays, pressure cookers reduce the simmering time for stock while food processors and blenders make short work of puréeing ingredients.

Making your own stock is still the best way to obtain a fine soup and it is essential if you intend serving a high-quality consommé; however, some bought stocks are of good quality. Bouillon cubes or chilled stocks can be a useful base for certain soups, as can certain canned consommés. If a good quality stock is not available, it is preferable to use water with additional flavouring ingredients such as celery, onions, carrots and parsley than to crumble in powerful stock cubes with poor flavour which may dominate the soup.

TIPS FOR MAKING STOCKS AND SOUPS

- Use good quality boiling or stewing cuts of meat, trimmings and bones for making stock. Trim off excess fat before you begin, and when the stock has cooled, skim off all surface fat.
- Leftovers from a roast give excellent flavour to stocks. For the richest flavour and a good dark stock, use uncooked bones. These should be roasted in the oven until well browned, then simmered with flavouring ingredients as described in the recipe for Rich Strong Stock on page 376. This method is not suitable for a light stock.
- Bones, cut or chopped into pieces, should be used whenever possible. (Ask the butcher to chop marrow bones.) However, on their own, bones do not give sufficient flavour, so use a meaty carcass or add some raw meat.
- To extract the maximum flavour, heat the ingredients gently and cook for long periods. Rapid boiling is not recommended except at the end of cooking, when it may be desirable to reduce and concentrate the stock.
- Do not add salt and pepper to stock at the beginning of cooking. The cooked stock should be seasoned according to the requirements of the finished dish and only after it has been reduced and concentrated as required. Remove scum as it rises to the surface of the stock.
- When making a meat stock, bring the water and meat trimmings to simmering point and skim the liquid before adding vegetables and other flavouring ingredients.

- Ask the fishmonger for bones and trimmings for making fish stock, but do not add gills, which can make the stock bitter.
- Use herbs and spices sparingly and balance strong and delicate flavours with care. This is particularly important if the stock is to be frozen.
- When the stock reaches the desired strength, allow it to cool, then strain it well. The stock may be clarified, see below.
- Cool and chill stocks as quickly as possible after cooking and store them in the refrigerator for 1–2 days. Stock freezes well; to save space it may be further reduced and its flavour concentrated by boiling, but remember to label the pack with the estimated concentration. Reducing by half to three quarters is appropriate, depending on the original volume.
- Good beef or chicken stock can be made by substituting 450 g/1 lb lean minced beef or 1 chicken quarter for stewing meat or bones. Add the same vegetables and flavouring ingredients as for Rich Strong Stock (page 376). The result will be a lighter stock; a practical solution to the problem of making authentic stock when a meaty carcass or the remains of a joint are not available.

CLARIFYING STOCK

Scald a saucepan (not aluminium), a piece of muslin, a metal sieve and a whisk. Pour the strained stock into the pan. Lightly whisk 2 egg whites and crush the shells from 2 eggs; add to the stock. Heat slowly to simmering point, whisking to form a thick white crust. Stop whisking, allow the stock to rise in the pan, then turn the heat off just before it boils. Repeat twice more. Line the sieve with the muslin and place it over a clean bowl. Strain the stock through the muslin. Try not to break the crust which acts as a filter.

PRESSURE COOKER TIP

Meat and poultry stocks, made with raw or cooked meat and bones, can be prepared in the pressure cooker in approximately 40 minutes at 15 lb pressure. Follow the manufacturer's recommendations regarding the maximum quantity of ingredients and liquid for the pan; failing this, make a concentrated stock by reducing the volume of water to ensure that the pan is no more than half to two-thirds full. Add extra water and simmer briefly in the open pan after the pressure has been reduced.

Home-made pâtés and potted foods have a character of their own, quite different from bought types and definitely superior to the majority of commercial varieties. With careful preparation, prompt cooling and chilling, they keep well in the refrigerator – ideal for impressing weekend guests, for picnics or holiday meals.

A pâté is a coarse or fine mixture, seasoned and flavoured for serving cold. Fish, meat, offal, poultry, game, cheese, vegetables or pulses may be potted or used to make pâtés. The term 'terrine' may be used to describe a lidded baking dish and, traditionally, a coarse pâté which is cooked in such a dish. Terrine is also now more broadly used for vegetable, fish or fruit recipes which are baked or set in a loaf-shaped container. Potted foods may be finely minced, cut up or whole, as in the case of shrimps, and served as for pâtés.

PREPARATION TECHNIQUES

Mincing or Puréeing When this is carried out depends on the recipe. Some pâtés require the raw meat, offal, onions and bread to be processed until smooth, then combined and cooked. In other recipes the meat or offal is parcooked before processing. Potted foods are usually cooked, if necessary, before being puréed.

A mincer is the best appliance for puréeing raw meat, whereas a food processor or blender may be used for parcooked or cooked meat. Use a coarse blade first, followed by a fine one. For a very smooth result, the purée may be sieved.

Stretching Bacon for Lining Some pâtés are cooked in a tin, terrine or dish which is first lined with bacon rashers. Streaky bacon should be used and the rashers should be stretched with the back of a knife. When they are thin and long, lay them in the dish, overlapping each rasher and leaving extra length overhanging the edge. When the dish is filled with pâté, the ends of the bacon should be folded over the top of the mixture.

Stretching bacon rashers

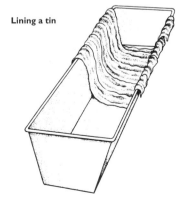

Lining a tin

Baking in a Bain Marie To prevent the outside of the pâté from overcooking before the centre has cooked, the dish or container is placed in a roasting tin. Hot water is poured into the roasting tin to just below its rim, and the pâté is then baked. The water should be topped up during cooking.

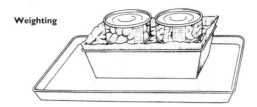

Weighting

Weighting To give the pâté its characteristic dense texture it should be weighted after cooking. Cover the top of the pâté with greaseproof paper and foil, then place a heavy weight on top. If the pâté has been cooked in a round dish, place a plate on top before adding the weight; the plate should be slightly smaller in diameter than the dish. Leave the pâté until cold, then chill overnight.

Cans of food, scale weights or other suitable heavy items may be used to weight the pâté. Remember to stand the dish in an outer container to catch any juices that spill over.

Storage and Usage Always keep pâtés and potted foods covered on a low shelf in the refrigerator. Remove slices or portions as required and return the rest to the refrigerator promptly.

Most pâtés improve if they are allowed to mature for 1–2 days, but they should be eaten within a week. Pâtés made from poultry livers are the exception; they should be made and eaten within 2 days. Always use perfectly fresh ingredients for making pâtés.

From humble herring to luxurious lobster, there is literally a fish for every occasion. The alphabetical list that follows includes advice on selection, size and seasonal availability.

ABALONE

A single-shelled relation of the limpet, this large shellfish has a reputation for being tough. It is beaten to tenderize the flesh, then cooked quickly to prevent it from toughening again. Soups and Oriental dishes incorporating abalone are available in cans; the frozen shellfish is sometimes sold at Oriental supermarkets.

ANCHOVY

A relation of the herring, the fresh anchovy is a small round fish, 7.5–15 cm/3–6 inches in length. Canned anchovy fillets are salted for at least a month before being packed in either olive or vegetable oil.

BRILL

A large flat fish, similar to turbot but slightly more oval and smaller, weighing up to 4.5 kg/10 lb. Small brill may be cooked whole but the fish is usually sold as fillets. Brill is available from June to February and is at its best during June and July.

CARP

There are many species of this round freshwater fish. Carp is popular in China and eastern Europe. Wild carp can have a muddy taste; the live fish should be kept in clean water for 24 hours before being killed. The carp available in specialist fish-mongers comes from fish farms. The two farmed varieties are mirror carp, which is covered in scales, and leather carp which has a tough skin and fewer, large scales. They are available from June to March but not in April and May, which is the breed-ing season.

You will have to order carp well in advance to be sure of obtaining a fish for a specific occasion. Fish weighing less than 900 g/2 lb are not worth preparing and those above 3.5–4 kg/8–9 lb are very coarse. Farmed fish usually weigh between 1–2.5 kg/2¼–5½ lb, the best weight for eating. The firm white flesh has large flakes and a distinctive taste which is not to everyone's liking. Although carp is very bony, the bones are long and large, therefore easy to avoid.

CATFISH

There are both sea and freshwater species. The sea fish is the most common and it is also known as rock fish, wolf fish or spotted catfish. This fish has a long body which tapers towards the tail to resemble a large tadpole. The skin is brown-beige with a mottled, dark pattern of inverted 'V' shapes along its length. A long dorsal fin extends from the head to the tail. The flesh is white and fine flavoured as the catfish feeds on mussels and whelks. It is usually sold as fillets between February and July.

Freshwater catfish has dark skin and whiskers on either side of the head. Its white flesh resembles that of pike.

CAVIAR

The soft roe, or eggs of sturgeon which are processed with speed and care. They are lightly salted to flavour and preserve them, then vacuum packed. Cans of Russian caviar are marked 'malassol', indicating that the contents are lightly salted.

Beluga caviar – the most expensive – is grey in colour; the eggs are large. It comes from the largest variety of sturgeon, the beluga, which can live for up to a century and may grow to be a huge fish.

Pressed caviar is made of very small immature eggs or those that may have been slightly crushed or damaged in production.

CLAMS

There are many types of clam, ranging from the giant species to the small, striped Venus clam of the Mediterranean which is likely to be 2.5–4 cm/1–1½ inches long.

Fresh clams are available all year but you will have to order them in advance. Prepare as for mussels. Canned and frozen clams are also available.

COCKLES

Small molluscs with ridged shells which look heart-shaped when viewed from the side, cockles are usually cooked and shelled before being sold in local markets. Fresh cockles must be purged overnight and prepared as for mussels (see page 31). They are most readily available in jars, preserved in vinegar.

COD

Probably the most popular white fish, cod has firm, white flesh and a good flavour. This is a large fish which is sold prepared, either in fillets, cutlets or steaks. The fillets are thick and therefore versatile. Although the battered cod on sale at fish and chip shops is not often skinned, it is best to skin cod fillets before cooking. Codling are young cod.

Smoked cod fillet and smoked cod's roe are readily available from fishmongers and supermarket fish counters. See also Salt Cod.

COLEY

A relative of the cod, coley has thicker skin, darker flesh, a coarse texture and stronger taste. Although it is not much favoured as a fish for grilling or frying, it makes good pies, fish cakes or sauced dishes. Coley is usually sold in fillets. Frozen, pre-formed coley steaks are also popular and quick to prepare.

Pollock is an American term for coley. In Britain, the fish is also known as saithe or coalfish.

CONGER EEL

A sea eel which grows to great length (up to 3 metres/9 feet). Sold skinned and cut in steaks, conger is firm and meaty with large bones. Unlike most fish, conger requires comparatively long cooking in sauce until tender, otherwise it can be tough. Conger steaks are used in Mediterranean fish stews, such as bouillabaisse or bourride.

CRAB

World-wide, there is an enormous variety of edible crabs. The brown crab is the species most often sold in Britain, both live and cooked. As with all live crustaceans, crabs should be lively when bought. Avoid limp-clawed specimens with little sign of life. Live crabs should feel heavy for their size. Give the crabs a shake and avoid any that make swishing noises; a sign that they contain water.

When buying a cooked crab, make sure that it looks clean and fresh and that the legs and claws are tight against the body. Cooked crab is also sold ready dressed, with all meat removed and presented in the cleaned shell. Buy from a reputable source.

Soft shell crabs are small shore crabs that have shed their hard covering in spring or autumn and have not had time to acquire new ones. These are cooked and eaten whole.

CRAWFISH

Also known as langouste or spiny lobster, this is a marine crustacean which looks rather like a large lobster without claws. It differs from the lobster in that the shell of the live animal is red, although some species are darker than others. A prized seafood, crawfish is not often found on the supermarket fish counter, although it may be available at a large wholesale fish market. The American use of the term crawfish to describe crayfish is confusing. Crayfish, a freshwater species, is not readily available.

DAB

A small flat fish of the plaice family, in season all year. Dabs are cleaned (gutted), trimmed and cooked whole by grilling or frying.

DOVER SOLE

Dover sole has a fine flavour and firm delicate flesh. The fish yields small fillets, so it is usually grilled or fried whole. The fishmonger will clean and skin the fish for you – the tough skin is slit at the tail end and easily pulled away from the flesh.

EEL

Freshwater eel are considered superior to conger eel as they have rich, oily flesh. Although they are available all year, they are best during the winter months when fully mature, dark-skinned specimens are on sale. Young, yellow-coloured eels are inferior.

Since eels have to be cooked absolutely fresh, they are usually sold live. Fishmongers selling eels keep them in tanks or buckets of water and kill, then skin them as required. They should be cooked on the day of purchase.

Elvers, tiny eels resembling short spaghetti and measuring about 5 cm/2 inches in length, are a traditional West Country speciality, fried with bacon. Cold elver cake consists of cooked, pressed elvers, and is served in slices.

Smoked eel fillets are a speciality from the Netherlands and Scandinavian countries. They are also an East Anglian delicacy. Available from delicatessens and larger supermarkets, smoked eel is skinned and ready to serve. It has a delicate flavour and is good served very simply with soured cream and chives, and thin, buttered bread.

FLOUNDER

A flat fish which is similar in size to plaice. It has brown and yellow blotchy markings and a rough patch on its head. Flounder is available from March to November and it may be cooked whole or as fillets. The flesh is delicate but not outstanding.

GRAYLING

A freshwater fish of the salmon and trout family. Grayling is seldom sold commercially but the firm white flesh and good flavour make for excellent eating.

GREY MULLET

A round fish with large scales, grey mullet is available from September to February. This fish is not related to red mullet and is different in size, appearance and taste.

Grey mullet vary in size, the largest farmed mullet being over 60 cm/24 inches long, although the majority are about 45 cm/18 inches long. The white flesh is of good quality but it bruises and becomes soft easily, so the fish should be handled and scaled with care. Mullet is usually cooked whole, by baking or poaching; it is also a good candidate for the barbecue.

GURNARD

These are a group of ugly-looking fish with bony, angular heads. Both red and grey gurnard are available, the latter being slightly more brown-beige in colour than grey. Red gurnard, available from July to February, is better quality than the grey fish. Red gurnard must not be confused with red mullet which is usually smaller and not as ugly.

The flesh is firm and the flakes are large with a fairly strong flavour. Gurnard may be cooked whole or filleted. Also known as gurnet.

HADDOCK

A firm white fish which is not as large as cod, yielding thinner fillets with smaller, slightly less firm flakes. Haddock is distinguished by a black line which runs along its length and a thumbprint mark behind the gills. Readily available as fillets, haddock may be grilled, fried, braised or used instead of cod.

Smoked haddock varies enormously in quality and colour. Some fillets are dyed a bright golden hue, others are naturally pale. Good fishmongers clearly distinguish between the different types.

Finnan haddock are small fish that are split and smoked on the bone over peat or oak. They are pale gold, with the tail still intact. They look slightly dry compared to smoked haddock fillets that are processed by other methods, but are actually superior in flavour. The name derives from the Scottish village, Findon, where the haddock were originally smoked by this method.

HAKE

From the same family as cod and haddock, hake is longer and slimmer in shape. It has a finer flavour than its relatives and firm, white flesh. Available from June to March, hake is most often sold as steaks or cutlets.

Available from June to March, halibut is the largest of the flat fish. It is sold fresh and frozen, as fillets or steaks. Its firm, white flesh has a fine flavour. Halibut may be cooked by almost any method but it should be kept moist during cooking, either by the addition of a sauce or by frequent basting.

An oily fish of silvery appearance which is known for its tasty flesh and multitude of bones, herring is similar in size to small or medium mackerel. It is best to bone the fish before cooking. Herrings may be grilled, fried, baked or soused and are also available preserved as rollmops in brine or in vinegar. Salted herring fillets packed in oil have an excellent flavour. Herring fillets are also canned in oil, mustard sauce or a variety of other sauces.

Kippers are smoked herrings, either split and opened out or filleted. Bloaters are whole, lightly smoked herrings.

Also known as dogfish, flake or tope, huss is a member of the shark family. It does not have bones but is a tough, cartilaginous fish with a characteristic, slightly chewy texture which is not to everyone's taste. Huss often appears on fish and chip shop menus; in some areas the battered and deep-fried form is greatly favoured.

At the wet fish shop it is usually sold skinned and prepared for cooking. The flesh has a very slight pink tinge. Huss may be barbecued or grilled on kebabs, but is also suitable for braising.

A deep-bodied fish which looks alarming, mainly because of its large mouth and long, prickle-like fins. When headless and cleaned, the fish is reduced to two-thirds of its original weight. The flesh has a good flavour and texture. Available all year, the fish is good grilled, poached or baked and served cold.

Cooked and puréed laver seaweed, a Welsh speciality. It resembles spinach in flavour but has a dark, almost black, colour. Oatmeal is added to thicken the purée which is coated in more oatmeal and fried in the shape of soft cakes. Laver bread is usually served with bacon.

This is not related to true sole (referred to as Dover sole in this book). Lemon sole is a flat fish, larger than Dover sole and not as expensive. Lemon sole has good flavour which, as the name suggests, has a hint of lemon. It may be cooked whole but it is also large enough to yield good fillets. Available from April to February.

Live lobsters are dark in colour – almost black – and turn red on cooking. Although cooked lobsters are available both fresh and frozen in ice, live ones are only stocked by the busiest and most cosmopolitan fishmongers. However, most good fishmongers or fish counters at large supermarkets will order a live lobster on request.

HALIBUT

HERRING

HUSS

JOHN DORY

LAVER BREAD

LEMON SOLE

LOBSTER

Lobster meat, extracted from the tail and claws, is firm, white and sweet. If you are buying a live lobster, look for one which is quite perky and heavy for its size.

Cooked lobster should be clean and bright in appearance with a tightly curled tail. Follow the instructions on the packaging for thawing and using frozen lobster.

MACKEREL
An oily fish with distinctive green-blue markings, mackerel are available all year.

Tasty dark flesh and large bones are typical of this fish which may be grilled, fried, poached, soused, baked or barbecued. The fish may be cooked whole, split or filleted.

Smoked mackerel fillets or whole smoked mackerel are widely available, sometimes with additional seasonings.

MEGRIM
A small flat fish which is pale brown-gold in colour. Available from May to March. The fillets are not exceptionally flavoursome; they tend to be slightly dry as well as rather bland.

MONKFISH
This weird-looking fish has a huge ugly head, so the tail flesh is usually sold skinned and prepared for cooking. The flesh is firm and has an excellent flavour; it is also expensive. It may be cooked by all methods and served either hot or cold. Available all year, it is also known as angler fish or angel fish.

MUSSELS
Dark, oval bivalves, these shellfish are in season from September to March. Apart from the familiar dark-shelled mussels, there are also brown-shelled species and very large New Zealand mussels with green shells.

Smoked mussels vary in quality from small, shrunken offerings, sometimes canned in oil, to lightly smoked, large mussels that retain a delicate texture.

Pickled mussels in vinegar or brine are a poor substitute for fresh mussels; however frozen mussels are a good alternative. These are available frozen on the half shell.

OCTOPUS
These molluscs are popular in Mediterranean countries where they may be served stewed or fried whole when small. They are not so readily available as squid which is more versatile.

OYSTERS
There are many varieties of oyster and they vary in size. In Britain, Colchester and Whitstable are known for their oyster beds and for the excellent quality of their shellfish. British oysters are known as 'native' to distinguish them from imported types.

Oysters are, of course, known for the fact that they are eaten raw, with a squeeze of lemon or perhaps a dash of Tabasco. To be served this way, they must be absolutely fresh and newly opened, displayed on ice.

Smoked oysters vary enormously in quality. The best are succulent and lightly smoked; the worst are strong, synthetic in flavour and oily.

A freshwater fish, olive-green in colour with vertical black stripes. Good to eat but bony, perch is usually filleted, then poached or fried.

PERCH

A large, fierce freshwater fish of medium size. Those weighing up to 3 kg/6½ lb are best for cooking. Pike flesh is soft, with many fine bones. The flavour is valued for making traditional dishes such as quenelles, when the flesh is puréed and sieved. Not readily available.

PIKE

These are usually large sardines.

PILCHARDS

A familiar flat fish which is available either whole or as fillets. Fine, slightly soft flesh and a delicate flavour are characteristic of plaice. The fish may be fried, grilled, baked, stuffed or poached.

PLAICE

Not to be confused with the pollock (the American name for coley), pollack is a white-fleshed member of the cod family. Its flesh is slightly watery and not such good quality as cod.

POLLACK

See also Shrimps. Good fishmongers usually sell two varieties of this crustacean: cold water prawns and Mediterranean prawns, also known as king prawns or jumbo prawns. The smaller, more familiar cold water prawns are available cooked, either peeled or in their shells. They are also readily available frozen. Mediterranean prawns are usually sold cooked and in their shells. Uncooked Mediterranean prawns are sometimes available. They are a grey colour and turn pink on cooking. The usual way of buying uncooked Mediterranean prawns is peeled and frozen.

Confusion arises over the terms prawn and shrimp because Americans use only the latter. American cooks refer to shrimp and jumbo shrimp; both are larger than those available in Britain.

PRAWNS

Available all year, the redfish can grow up to 1 metre/3¼ feet long. Another ugly-looking specimen, the redfish is often displayed whole or filleted. The flesh is not noted for exceptional flavour.

REDFISH

Roes are the testes of a male fish or the ovaries of the female.

Soft roes come from the herring. They are often cooked in butter and served on toast. Pressed roes are sold canned, for slicing and frying or grilling.

Smoked cod's roe is used for making Taramasalata.

Lumpfish roe is served in the same way as caviar. It is salted and usually dyed. Norwegian types are less salty than some others.

ROE

SALMON

Both farmed and wild salmon are available. Wild salmon, caught in rivers and lochs, is in season from February to the end of August. Excellent farmed salmon is available all year, as steaks, fillet portions or whole fish. From June to the beginning of August small one-year-old farmed salmon are available.

Sea trout or salmon trout are in season from March to July. Smaller than salmon, these are caught in the sea. The flesh is similar in colour to salmon but has the flaky texture of trout. The bone structure is the same as for trout.

SALT COD

Also known as *bacalao*, this is cod fillet which is preserved by salting. Available from continental delicatessens, it is widely used in Mediterranean countries. The salted fillets must be soaked in cold water for 24 hours before use. Not to be confused with Italian dried cod (stockfish) which is unsalted.

SARDINES

These small flavoursome fish are available from February to July. They are also frozen and are of good quality. Usually cooked whole by grilling, sardines taste delicious barbecued. They may also be stuffed either whole or boned and rolled.

SCALLOPS

These shellfish are usually sold separated from their shells. They have a nugget of firm white flesh and a bright moon-shaped coral which should be a good red colour. Unopened scallops should be placed in a warm oven for a few moments until their shells begin to open. Place rounded shell down to catch precious juices. Carefully prise the white flesh and coral away from the shell, discarding the grey-brown frill and dark intestine.

Queen scallops are a small species, sold without roes as small rounds of very pale pink muscle. Canned queen scallops are also available but the flavour tends to be very disappointing.

Frozen scallops are often available from delicatessens or Oriental stores and they can be excellent. Scallops should be cooked gently and briefly; otherwise they become leathery.

SCAMPI

Also known as langoustine, Dublin Bay prawns or Norway lobsters, these are orange-red crustaceans which look like miniature lobsters. They have long claws and curled tails. They must not be confused with Mediterranean prawns or crawfish, neither of which has claws. Remember, too, that uncooked Mediterranean prawns are grey rather than pink. Scampi are bright red-pink when alive; they retain this colour when cooked. The tail contains the meat. They are not readily available but an advance order at a good fishmonger may secure them.

Breaded scampi tails are available frozen. Check the wording on the packet to ensure that they are exactly that and not 'scampi-style' portions which are not the real thing.

A fine-flavoured, large scaly fish which is grey in colour, sea bass is in season from August to March. The fish may be baked, poached or barbecued whole. Although a fishmonger will fillet the fish, the fillets are surprisingly small.

SEA BASS

Several types of bream (including a freshwater fish) are available from June to February. Known as porgy in America, bream has a good flavour. Look out for red bream, black bream and gilt head bream which is dark grey-blue with silvery lower sides. Also known as gilthead, the edge of the gill is scarlet and the fish has a bright golden stripe running across its forehead between the eyes.

SEA BREAM

See Salmon.

SEA TROUT

Although many of the fish described here belong to the shark family, you can also buy shark steaks as such. Larger fishmongers may even display whole shark.

SHARK

The tough, leather-like skin has to be removed before cooking as it shrinks and spoils the flesh. The flesh is firm, meaty and rather cartilaginous, a texture which not everyone likes. The flavour is not particularly noteworthy.

Both brown and pink shrimps are available, although the brown ones are usually a regional speciality. They resemble very small prawns and are sold cooked in their shells. Peeling shrimps is a time-consuming task but the excellent flavour is ample reward. Shrimps are available canned but not frozen.

SHRIMPS

A member of the shark family, also known as ray. Wings of skate are available from May to February. The flesh is cartilaginous and characteristically has a faint odour of ammonia which disappears when the fish is rinsed or blanched in acidulated water. Any strong smell of ammonia indicates that the fish is not as fresh as it should be.

SKATE

While snails are not, strictly speaking, seafood, they are members of the same family as periwinkles, limpets and whelks and are habitually classified alongside these related molluscs. There are many types of snail. They are now commercially farmed. The wild snail (or 'garden snail') was traditionally collected but today the favoured variety is the Burgundy or Roman snail.

SNAILS

Processing live snails is a complicated business. They must be kept in a basket or ventilated box for a week to purge their systems. The next stage is salting, to remove all the slime. They are then washed, boiled, removed from their shells and boiled again until tender.

Prepared snails are sold in cans, often with clean shells as part of the packaging. The snails are placed in the shells, then topped with garlic butter. They are heated through in the oven and served in dimpled snail dishes with tongs to hold the shells and special forks for extracting the snails. The shells can be thoroughly washed, dried and used again and again.

SPRATS

Available from October to March, these small fish may be grilled or deep fried. They are usually gutted and their backbones are removed.

SQUID

Squid is sold prepared or whole from May to September. Many supermarkets sell battered squid rings, or calamari, ready for baking or frying.

SWORDFISH

Available all year, swordfish steaks are firm and meaty. They have a good flavour and are ideal for grilling or barbecuing. Since it can become rather dry during cooking, swordfish benefits from frequent basting or cooking in butter or oil.

TROUT

A freshwater fish that is now inexpensive due to extensive farming. Available fresh and frozen, also as prepared fillets. Rainbow trout has pale pink, delicately flavoured flesh. For sea trout or salmon trout, see Salmon.

TUNA

There are several different species of tuna, all large. It is available throughout the year, either fresh or frozen. The dark, sculptured flesh is dry; it benefits from marinating and frequent basting during cooking. Tuna is sold as portions or steaks and is ideal for barbecuing and for cooking in a sauce.

Canned tuna in oil or brine is a familiar – and useful – storecupboard item.

TURBOT

A large flat fish, turbot has firm white meat with a good flavour. It is available from April to February and is usually sold as steaks or fillets. Special turbot kettles are available for cooking whole fish.

WHELKS AND WINKLES

These are both sea snails. Whelks are carnivores and winkles are herbivores. Winkles, the smaller of the two, are traditionally picked from their shells by using a pin. Both are usually sold cooked and shelled. Whelks are available from February to August; winkles from September to April.

WHITEBAIT

Small young herrings and sprat fry, whitebait is available fresh from February to June. Frozen whitebait is on sale throughout the year. They are cooked whole by deep frying. The fish are eaten whole.

WHITING

A member of the cod family, whiting has slightly soft white flesh which tends to be rather bland and uninteresting. It is usually sold filleted but is sometimes available whole. It is available from June to February.

The following are just a few examples of the exotic fish which are sometimes available. Many are from tropical regions including the west coast of Africa, the Seychelles, the Pacific Ocean and the Indian Ocean. They make good eating and many look attractive when cooked and served whole.

Croakers or Drums Light brown fish with a red-tinged belly. Available all year.

Emperors or Emperor Bream A striking fish, available all year, this has golden fins, tail and nose on an otherwise grey-silver body.

Groupers A golden dorsal line, hints of orange-gold speckles and a bright orange-gold eye make this a decorative species. Available all year.

Jacks Colourful fish, tinged blue, yellow and red. Available all year.

Parrot Fish Striking coloured, either blue or brightly coloured fish. Available all year.

Pomfret Available all year, a deep-bodied fish with a small face. Tinged pale gold to grey.

Snappers Available all year. The red snapper is the most common.

PREPARATION TECHNIQUES

The basic techniques outlined below are, on the whole, interesting rather than essential because the majority of good fishmongers will prepare the fish for you. However, the advice on handling live crustaceans and shellfish should be followed carefully. If you are lucky enough to have a fisherman in the family, you may find the information on cleaning fish (page 32) useful.

SKINNING FLAT FISH
(Dover sole, plaice etc)

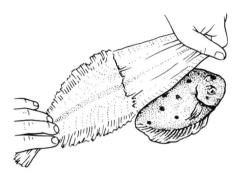

Lay the fish on a clean surface, light skin down. Cut through the skin at the tail end. Slip the point of a knife under the skin to separate a flap from the flesh. Dip your fingers in salt to prevent them from slipping and hold the fish down firmly by its tail, then pull the skin off, working towards the head. Cut the skin neatly around the head. Turn the fish over; repeat on the second side.

FILLETING FLAT FISH

1 Lay the fish on a clean surface with the tail towards you. Use a sharp pointed knife to cut the flesh down to the bone around the head. Cut straight down the middle of the back, from head to tail.

2 Starting at the head end of the fillet, cut the flesh off the bones, working from the middle towards the side of the fish. Slide the point of the knife down the bones, keeping it close to them all the time, and lift the fillet of fish away as it is cut free.

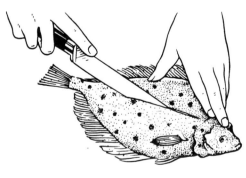

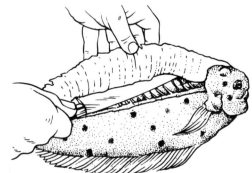

1 Cut a slit down the backbone, from head to tail. Carefully ease the point of the knife under the flesh, cutting it off the bones on one side. Work right against the bone down to the side but do not cut through to the skin of the fish. Repeat on the second side to reveal the bones.

2 Use a pair of kitchen scissors to snip the backbone at the head and tail ends. Make two more snips along its length. Use the point of a knife and scissors to remove all the bones from the cavity, leaving a pouch ready for stuffing.

BONING A POUCH IN FLAT FISH

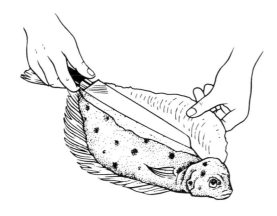

1 Cut the flesh down to the bone around the head. Hold the fish firmly with one hand and cut along its length down to the backbone.

2 Starting at the head again, cut the flesh away from the bones, easing the fillet back as you cut. Work close to the bones. Turn the fish over and repeat on the second side.

FILLETING ROUND FISH
(mackerel, herring etc)

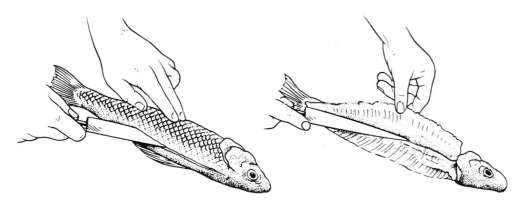

NOTE
If you ask the fishmonger to fillet a round fish, for example mackerel, you will often be given a flat, boned whole fish. Therefore, if you want two fillets from each fish, make this clear when you ask to have them filleted.

BONING ROUND FISH

1 Ensure that the cleaned fish has been slit right down to the tail. The head must be removed. Lay the fish, skin up, flat on a board. Press the flesh firmly along the backbone.

2 Turn the fish over and lift the backbone off from the head end. It should come away easily, lifting most of the bones with it. Remove any stray bones.

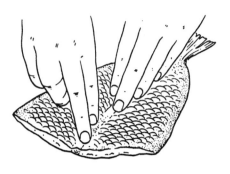
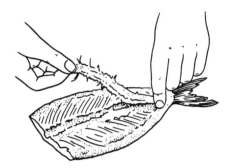

BONING WHOLE ROUND FISH

This is a technique for removing the bones while keeping the head and tail intact, for instance when stuffing the body cavity of a whole fish.

1 Make sure the body cavity of the fish is slit all along its length. Slide the point of a knife under each bone to free it from the flesh. Work from the backbone outwards.

2 Use a pair of kitchen scissors to snip through the backbone at the head end. Use the point of a knife to free the backbone, then snip through it at the tail end and lift it away. Remove any stray bones.

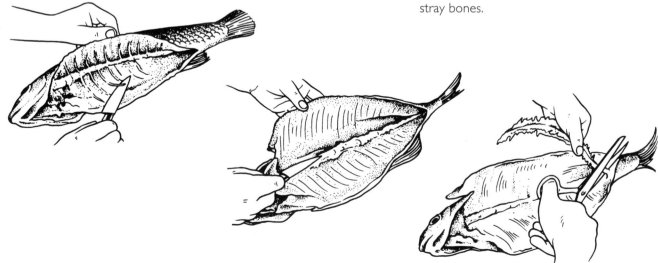

I Lay the fillet on a board, skin down. Rub your fingers in salt. Hold the tail end firmly, then cut the flesh away from the skin. Hold the knife at an acute angle and use a sawing motion to remove the flesh in one piece, folding it back as you cut from the tail end towards the head.

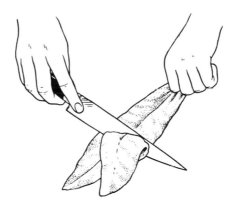

SKINNING FISH FILLETS

I Hold the fish in a clean sink and have cold water running slowly to wash away the scales as you work. Scrape off the scales from the tail towards the head, occasionally rinsing the knife and fish. A messy task, also known as descaling.

SCALING FISH

I Use a thin, pointed knife and cut down around the bone to free the flesh from it. In the case of fish cutlets, it is sometimes easier to snip the end of the bone free with kitchen scissors.

BONING FISH STEAKS OR CUTLETS

CLEANING COOKED CRAB

1 Twist off the claws and legs. Tap the edge of the shell firmly on a board to loosen the body slightly. Turn the crab upside down on a board with the mouth and eyes away from you. Pull off and discard the tail flap. Use both thumbs to ease the body up and out of the shell.

2 Discard the stomach sac, located just behind the mouth, and remove the soft gills around the body. The gills are known as dead men's fingers because of their appearance. Cut the body in half.

3 Pick out the white meat from the body and the brown meat from inside the shell. Crack the claws and legs, then pick out the white meat.

4 Trim the shell: tap away the shell edge around the groove and remove it. This gives a neat shell which should be thoroughly scrubbed in hot soapy water, rinsed with boiling water, then dried.

To dress crab, mix the brown meat with a small quantity of fresh breadcrumbs, a dash of lemon juice and salt and pepper to taste. Arrange it in the sides of the clean shell. Arrange the white meat in the middle. Chopped parsley, hard-boiled egg and lemon may be added as a garnish.

1 Twist off the claws and legs. Lay the lobster on a board with the shell down. Use a heavy, sharp knife and rolling pin or meat mallet to split the lobster down the middle.

2 Discard the dark intestinal tract which runs down the length of the body. Discard the spongy gills from the head end. Scoop out and save any red coral. The soft, brown liver may be saved and used to flavour a sauce. Remove the firm white tail meat.

CLEANING LOBSTER

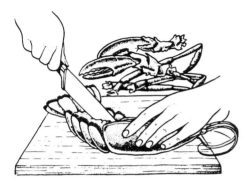

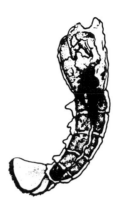

3 Clean out the head end of the shell, wash and dry it. The shell may be used to serve the cold dressed lobster, sauced lobster or lobster gratin. Crack the claws and pick out the meat.

PEELING PRAWNS

1 Break off and discard the head.

2 Pull the shell apart from underneath and slip it all off, leaving just the tail in place. Break off the tail.

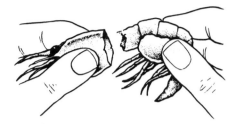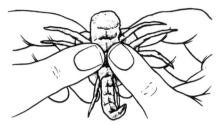

CLEANING SQUID

1 If the tentacles are to be used, cut them off first and set them aside. Cut off and discard the beak from the centre of the tentacles. Pull the head and the attached parts out of the sac: discard the head parts.

2 Remove the transparent 'pen' from inside the body.

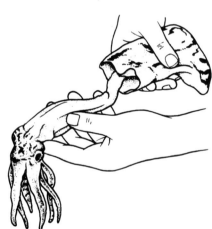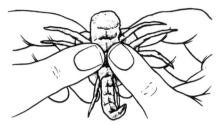

3 Rub off the mottled skin under cold running water, at the same time rubbing off the small flaps on either side of the body, leaving the body clean and white.

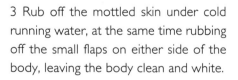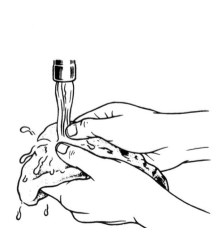

There are two acceptable options: freezing or cooking in cold water which is heated gradually.

Freezing Place the live crab or lobster in a clean polythene carrier bag in the freezer and leave it there for 5–7 hours or overnight.

Cover the frozen lobster with cold water in a large saucepan, add a little salt and bring slowly to the boil. Lower the heat and simmer for 15 minutes per 450 g/1 lb, plus 10 minutes. Lobster is cooked when the shell has turned a bright pink. Drain well and cool. Allow an extra 5 minutes for shellfish that are frozen hard right through.

Cooking from Live Place the crab or lobster in a large pan of cold salted water and put a tight-fitting lid on the pan. Heat gently to boiling point, then cook as above.

Killing by Stabbing The method of stabbing lobsters behind the head or crabs between the eyes is not to be recommended. Freezing is much more humane.

If empty shells are to be used for serving, they must first be thoroughly scrubbed and boiled in clean water for 5 minutes, then drained and dried. This applies particularly to shells from scallops or oysters which are not cooked with the shellfish.

Conger eel is sold skinned and cut into steaks. Freshwater eels are kept alive until they are prepared. The fishmonger will usually do this for you as it is not a pleasant task. If, however, you have to prepare an eel, the following may prove valuable.

First stun the eel by banging its head firmly against a hard surface. Then stab it through the back of the head to kill it.

Slit the skin around the head using a strong sharp knife. Using pliers, loosen the skin, then, holding the head firmly in a piece of cloth, pull back the skin from head to tail in one piece. Cut off and discard the head.

The eel may be hung by the head from a meat hook and the skin pulled off.

Thoroughly scrub the shells and scrape off any barnacles. Discard any open shells which do not close when tapped. Pull away the dark hairy 'beard' which protrudes slightly from the shell.

Cook mussels in a small amount of boiling liquid over high heat. Put a tight-fitting lid on the saucepan. Shake the pan occasionally and cook for about 5 minutes, until all the shells have opened. The mussels cook in the steam of the liquid. They should not be overcooked or they will toughen. Discard any shells that have not opened after cooking.

NOTE
The above method is also used for cockles and clams. Bought farmed shellfish should not be sandy; however, leaving the shellfish in a cold place in a bucket of salted water overnight allows time for them to expel any sand they may contain.

KILLING AND COOKING LIVE CRAB AND LOBSTER

PREPARATION OF SHELLS FOR SERVING

STUNNING AND SKINNING EELS

PREPARING MUSSELS

OPENING OYSTERS

Ideally a special, short-bladed, tough oyster knife should be used. Do not use your favourite light kitchen knife as the blade may break. Select a fairly blunt, short, strong knife or similar implement. Hold the oyster with the curved shell down. Insert the point of the knife into the hinged end of the shell and prise it open. Take care as the tough shell is difficult to open and the knife can slip easily.

OPENING SCALLOPS

Scallops are usually sold prepared. To open them at home place them in a warm oven for a few moments, until the shells part slightly. Then prise the shells apart and cut the nugget of white muscle and coral free.

ASK THE FISHMONGER

Knowing the basics of fish preparation makes it easier when shopping. Always ask the fishmonger to clean (gut) whole fish (trout, mackerel, bass, mullet and so on), stating clearly whether you want the head and tail on or off. Filleting is a task for the fishmonger. Most will also bone, scale and skin fish. Some may even cut large fillets into serving portions.

These are not attributes of the model fishmonger; they are services you should reasonably expect, for no extra charge, but you must be reasonable in making a request. At busy times, select your purchase, explain the preparation required and call back later. A polite request achieves a lot more than a haughty demand. Most fishmongers are highly skilled and only too ready to help.

SEAFISH QUALITY AWARD

Look out for the symbol (right). It is displayed by fishmongers who have satisfied the judges that they not only sell quality fish, but also score in terms of the quality and operation of premises, storage, equipment, staff, handling and presentation.

CLEANING FISH

If possible, ask the fishmonger or fisherman to clean (gut) fish for you. If you have to do this at home, lay several thicknesses of clean newspaper on the work surface and place the fish on greaseproof paper on top. Slit the fish down its belly, then scrape out the innards. Transfer the fish to a plate; repeat with other fish. Wrap the newspaper tightly around the innards at once, and place in an outdoor waste bin. Wash down all surfaces, utensils and your hands. Thoroughly rinse the fish, then pat it dry with absorbent kitchen paper.

Other methods Round fish may also be cleaned through the gills to avoid splitting the body open. Similarly, whole flat fish (plaice and Dover or lemon sole) have only small pockets of innards that are removed through a small slit below the head. The fishmonger will clean fish in this way for you but always remember to ask for a specific cleaning method, such as through the gills.

Buying fish and seafood

- Buy from a reputable source – the premises should look clean and smell perfectly fresh.
- Wet fish should look moist and bright. Eyes should be bright, gills red, markings on skin should be clear. Fish fillets should be moist, clean and unbroken.
- Ready-to-eat fish and seafood (for example, smoked mackerel) should never be handled immediately after raw fish. The fishmonger should pick up the ready-to-eat fish with an implement or in a bag. This rule is particularly important if the fishmonger has been cleaning raw fish. He should either wear gloves for this operation or wash his hands thoroughly when the fish has been cleaned.
- Make fish the last item you buy on a shopping trip, take it home quickly (in a chiller bag on hot days) and unpack it at once.
- Rinse and dry the fish, then put it in a dish and cover it with cling film. Place in the refrigerator and cook it within 24 hours.

Handling fish

- Use a clean board, preferably made of plastic material. Wooden boards should always be scrubbed and rinsed in boiling water, then allowed to dry, after use.
- Use a sharp, narrow-bladed, pointed knife for preparing fish.
- Kitchen scissors are useful for snipping off fins and for cutting bones. Wash them well after use.
- Never prepare raw fish and cooked food using the same utensils, unless the utensils have been thoroughly washed and dried.
- Always keep fish covered and chilled before cooking.

Freezing fish

- Bought frozen fish is frozen soon after it is taken from the sea. It is frozen speedily at low temperatures for best results.
- Fish for home freezing should be freshly caught or bought fresh from a reputable fishmonger. Do not freeze bought fish which has been frozen and thawed before sale. Freeze fish immediately after purchase. This applies particularly to oily fish such as mackerel.
- Always clean and prepare fish for cooking before freezing it.
- Pack fish in heavy polythene bags, excluding as much air as possible.
- White fish may be stored for 3–4 months; oily fish keep for 2–3 months in a domestic freezer at 18°C/0°F.

Rules to remember

COOKING FISH

A wide variety of cooking methods may be used for fish, including steaming, poaching, grilling, frying and baking. Whichever method is selected, it is vital to avoid overcooking.

STEAMING

Steaming is a method of cooking food in water vapour, producing moist results and retaining the maximum flavour of the food. The wealth of international ingredients now at our disposal means that this plain cooking technique can be used to produce exciting, flavoursome fish dishes. Delicate herbs and crisp vegetables transform steamed fish from invalid food to a gourmet treat.

EQUIPMENT

The traditional, and simplest, method of steaming fish and seafood is to sandwich it between two plates and to place it over a saucepan of boiling water; however, there are alternatives.

A saucepan-top steamer placed in or on a container over boiling water may be used to cook fish and seafood. Alternatively, foods such as rice may be cooked in the pan, with the seafood steamed directly on top so that its juices flavour the food below.

A bamboo steamer placed on a wok is ideal for cooking fish and seafood. Oriental-style techniques and seasonings perfectly complement the taste and texture of seafood.

Free-standing electric steamers come and go; all the rage one day and not available the next. Depending on the shape of the steaming compartment, an electric steamer can be useful for cooking fish.

Improvising is not difficult and a wire rack placed in a roasting tin of water makes a good platform on which to steam small whole salmon trout, whole trout or a small curved whole salmon. A foil covering with a tightly crumpled edge will usually keep in the steam.

SELECTING FISH FOR STEAMING

Fish fillets are ideal for this cooking method. Plaice, Dover or lemon sole, portions of cod or haddock fillet and smoked fish fillets are all suitable. Thin fillets may be rolled or folded, with herbs or other flavourings placed inside for flavour.

Shellfish, such as scallops, mussels and oysters, are excellent steamed.

Oily fish, on the other hand, do not benefit from being cooked by this method; mackerel, herring and sardines are better baked or grilled.

Size imposes restrictions on the choice of fish for this cooking method: whole fish do not fit well into the majority of steamers but it is worth improvising – curling a whole fish or steaming a fish in sections for later assembly – especially when it comes to fish like salmon and trout that benefit from being steamed.

FLAVOURING AND SEASONING

The choice of flavouring ingredients for any dish should be considered alongside the cooking method. Steaming produces fairly intense results, therefore strong ingredients (onion or garlic) can be rather overpowering in the finished dish.

Fresh Herbs There is a herb to flavour every food. Where fish is concerned the more delicate herbs are ideal. Dill and parsley are, of course, the classics; try fresh lemon thyme, basil, fennel, coriander leaves, lemon balm and lemon grass too. Fresh rosemary, savory, marjoram and oregano tend to be too strong for steamed fish; these herbs should be used judiciously with all seafood, however cooked.

Dried herbs can also be too intense with steamed fish and seafood; if you must use them, do so with caution.

Fresh Root Ginger Ginger's reputation as a robust flavouring is based on the dried and ground product; fresh root ginger has a citrus-like tang and a hint of heat in its make-up. The preparation of fresh ginger plays an important role in determining its eventual impact in a dish: for just a touch of flavour a few slices of ginger may be added to a dish, then removed before serving. At the other end of the spectrum, grated ginger may be used liberally with other spices to maximize its warming properties. Peeled, thinly sliced and shredded ginger, added in carefully measured quantities, is a compromise between the two, contributing plenty of zest with some of the heat.

Combine ginger with spring onions, soy sauce, carrots and celery to flavour strips of plaice, chunks of cod or mussels. Add a little ginger and lemon to scallops, lemon sole rolls or squid rings.

Lemon or Lime Lemon is another favourite flavouring for fish. The rind (grated, cut in strips or shredded), the juice or just a slice or two of fruit may be used when steaming fish.

Lime also goes well with all types of fish and seafood. Use rind, juice and slices for steaming.

Soy Sauce Combined with spring onions and fresh root ginger, soy sauce gives steamed fish a wonderful Oriental flavour that is the perfect foil to plain cooked rice. Whole fish such as plaice, grey mullet, bass or snapper may be cooked with this strong seasoning.

Vegetables Celery, fennel, carrots and spring onions are useful for flavouring and adding colour to steamed fish. Cut the vegetables finely so that they give up their flavour and cook perfectly in the same time as the seafood.

STEAMING METHODS

Little by way of special preparation is needed for fish steamed between two plates. Lay fillets flat and add the chosen flavouring; a sprinkling of lemon juice, some chopped parsley or dill, seasoning and knob of butter produces excellent results.

If the fish is placed in a perforated, saucepan-top steamer or in a bamboo steamer, there are several options to consider. The cooking juices may be saved and served as a sauce or allowed to drip away into the water below. The flavouring ingredients may be placed on the fish or, in the plainest possible style of cooking, in the water to scent the steam. The seafood may be put in a covered container or left uncovered so that some moisture collects to yield extra cooking liquor.

Allowing the cooking juices from white fish fillets or pieces to drip away tends to give bland results, unless the juices are absorbed by rice or couscous placed below the fish. Whole fish such as trout, salmon and bass cooked this way are protected from loss of flavour by their skin. In addition, flavouring ingredients may be tucked into the body cavity of whole fish.

Wrapping Seafood Fish may be wrapped before being placed in a perforated steamer. Foil and roasting bags are ideal for retaining all the juices and flavourings. Greaseproof paper and cooking parchment may also be used but tend to become soft and allow loss of liquor and some flavour.

Leaves may be used to wrap seafood, imparting their own flavour as well as helping to retain the fish juices. Iceberg or cos lettuce leaves and vine leaves may be blanched to soften them before use as a wrapping for whole trout or red mullet. Herbs and other flavourings may be placed inside the fish or on the leaves before wrapping.

Cooking in Dishes The seafood may be placed in a suitable dish with the chosen flavouring ingredients. The dish may be covered or left open, in which case condensed steam will collect in it. The uncovered method is ideal when very brief cooking is required and when flavourings such as soy sauce are added, resulting in just the right amount of full-flavoured, thin sauce. Thinly cut strips of fish or shellfish may be cooked this way.

Cooking Directly on Other Food Fish can be steamed directly on other moist food with which it is being served. For example, fillets of smoked haddock may be laid on two-thirds cooked rice when making kedgeree. When the pan is covered the fish will cook in the steam from the rice. The fillets should be lifted off carefully at the end of cooking.

Similarly, fish may be laid on vegetables – a bed of spinach is ideal – and steamed gently in the cooking vapour.

POACHING

This is probably one of the most popular cooking methods for cooking fish and seafood. Poaching means cooking very gently in liquid. It is ideal for tender fish, allowing additional flavouring ingredients to be cooked with the fish to produce liquor, which may be thickened or reduced then served as a sauce.

Poaching is also the preferred method for cooking fish roes. Cod's roe is usually bought freshly boiled or smoked. Herring roes (soft roes, from the male fish) are not sold cooked. Poach them in Court Bouillon (page 263) for 15 minutes, then drain and press until cold, when they may be sliced and fried or grilled.

Very fresh trout may be cooked 'au bleu'. In this classic cooking method the natural slime on the skin of the fish is not rinsed off but is retained to give a soft slate blue covering to the lightly simmered fish.

FLAVOURING POACHED FISH

Poaching is often just one step in the overall cooking process. For example, fillets may be poached until barely cooked and the flesh flaked off them for adding to rice, pasta, pie fillings, croquettes and fish cakes. The poaching liquor is frequently saved and used to flavour the dish.

If poaching is to be the sole method of cooking used for the seafood, flavourings should be carefully chosen. Herbs and vegetables may be added to the poaching liquid. If the liquid is discarded or strained after poaching, these ingredients may be roughly cut and briefly simmered in the liquid before the fish is added. If the poaching liquid is reduced or thickened, then served without being strained, ingredients such as onion should be par-cooked in a little oil or butter to ensure they are completely cooked in the finished dish.

POACHING LIQUID

Fish Stock (page 289) or Court Bouillon (page 263) are used for poaching whole fish such as salmon, when the liquid is discarded after cooking and cooling.

Wine is usually combined with water or stock for poaching fish and seafood, with the resultant liquor thickened and served as a sauce. Dry cider may also be used in place of wine. Milk is used for poaching fish which is to be served in a creamy sauce or for cooking white fish for fish cakes.

Canned or fresh tomatoes may also be used for poaching or braising.

MAKING SEAFOOD CASSEROLES AND STEWS

Casseroles and stews are chunky and colourful compared to braised or sauced seafood, and they may be rich in the use of vegetables, herbs and spices. Vegetables, such as onion, celery and carrot, should be cooked in a little oil or butter before the seafood is added. Garlic, bay leaves and tomatoes are also excellent for flavouring mixed seafood casseroles. The cooking liquor may be derived from tomatoes or sautéed vegetables with a little added stock, wine or water. Cream, soured cream or yogurt may be swirled in before serving.

OVERCOOKING

Overcooking fish, particularly when steaming or poaching, ruins both flavour and texture. The plainer the cooking, the more important it is to ensure that the fish is cooked to perfection. The flesh should be just firm, still moist and just cooked. When steaming fish, always check part-way through the time to make sure that it is neither cooking too rapidly nor for too long.

When poaching fish the liquid should barely simmer. Boiling liquid will break delicate fillets and toughen seafood such as scallops or squid. The crucial words are time and temperature. Keep the cooking time short and the temperature low and check the fish frequently.

Poached fish which is to be served cold should be removed from the heat when it is three-quarters cooked, then allowed to cool in the liquid. The residual heat completes the cooking and ensures that the fish is moist.

MICROWAVE COOKING

The microwave produces results comparable with those achieved by steaming. It is a very quick cooking method which may be used successfully for fish. Mussels and scallops may be cooked in the microwave but take care not to overcook them or they will become rubbery.

It is most important to follow the microwave manufacturer's instructions and suggested timings for cooking fish.

GRILLING

Grilling is a quick cooking method, particularly well suited to oily fish, such as mackerel and herring. The practicalities of grilling as a cooking method mean that the choice of fish is limited to the more sturdy cuts and varieties. Thus cod fillet is more suitable than plaice fillets which tend to break more easily, and cod steaks are even better since they are thicker and less likely to break up.

Fillets should be firm and fairly thick for cooking on the grill rack; otherwise they may be grilled in a flameproof dish. All fish steaks are ideal for grilling. Similarly, small whole fish cook well by this method but larger fish may not cook through sufficiently. Chunks of firm fish (monkfish, huss, thick end of cod fillet) may be skewered.

Shellfish such as Mediterranean prawns and lobster are good grilled; other varieties – scallops, mussels and oysters – need protection. Grilled small squid can be delicious

MARINATING

Marinating is the process of soaking food before cooking. Its purpose is to flavour and to moisten food, also to tenderize meat. Fish is marinated before cooking principally for flavour, but also to moisten certain types.

Swordfish, tuna, shark, halibut and turbot all benefit from being marinated briefly before grilling. Cubed monkfish and peeled uncooked prawns may also be marinated to keep them moist when skewered.

Oil is an important ingredient in marinades for fish – sunflower, grapeseed and groundnut oils are all light; olive oil contributes its own distinctive flavour. Fresh herbs, garlic, grated citrus rind, grated fresh root ginger, ground coriander, cumin and other curry spices may be used. Tomatoes, chopped onion, olives and capers are also worth remembering.

Unlike meat, fish does not require lengthy marinating for tenderizing. A couple of hours is usually sufficient.

TURNING AND BASTING

During cooking the fish should be basted to keep it moist. A marinade may be drained and used for this purpose; otherwise oil may be used. Melted butter is another option but it tends to burn easily so should be reserved for seafood such as boiled lobster which grills very quickly. A mixture of melted butter and oil may be used.

Handle fish carefully to prevent it from breaking up. Check the cooking progress often and regulate the heat so that the fish is only turned once. Use a fish slice and palette knife or slotted spoon, or two slices to avoid the fish breaking. Turn skewered fish carefully.

USING FOIL

Fish often benefits from being cooked on foil. Fillets stay moist, but it is wise to be aware of the possible danger of flaming. Using foil to support the fish, but pricking holes all over the foil to drain the fat, is a good compromise.

TOPPINGS FOR GRILLED FISH

Flavoured butters are by far the easiest topping – have neat pats ready to place on each portion of cooked fish.

Other toppings can be placed on the fish before cooking. Here are a few ideas.
Cheese One of the simplest toppings and delicious on cod steaks. Cook the steaks on one side in a flameproof dish. Turn them over and partially cook the second side, then top each steak with a slice of cheese such as creamy mozzarella. Cook under moderate heat until golden.
Tomatoes Sliced peeled tomatoes are good under cheese. If they are added on their own, place them on top towards the end of grilling and baste them with oil.
Peppers Thin rings of red or green pepper are tasty and colourful – good with olive oil, garlic and chopped marjoram on meaty fish.
Breadcrumbs – gratin style Fresh breadcrumbs may be added to make a gratin topping on fish which is almost cooked. Trickle melted butter over or mix the crumbs with grated cheese first – Parmesan is robust. Chopped walnuts and herbs are other tasty additions.

All three methods of frying may be used for seafood – deep, shallow and stir frying.

DEEP FRYING

Fish for frying must be coated, either in breadcrumbs, flour or batter. It is important to follow the rules of frying if results are to be crisp and light.

Temperature Vegetable oil used for frying should be heated to 180°C/350°F. Check the temperature by using a sugar thermometer or by dropping a small cube of bread into the oil. The bread should brown in 30–60 seconds. If the oil is hot enough, it seals the coating on the food rapidly to give crisp, light results. If the oil is too cool, some of it is absorbed by the food before the outside becomes crisp and sealed. If the oil is too hot, the outside will brown before the inside of the food is cooked.

When the oil is heated and the food added, the heat should be kept at a fairly high level for about a minute before it is reduced to prevent the oil from overheating. The cold food cools down the oil when it is added and a common mistake is to reduce the heat under the pan at this stage. The time taken for the oil to come back to temperature will, of course, vary with the amount of food added.

By far the best way to deep fry is in an electric deep-fat fryer which automatically controls the temperature of the oil.

Draining Once fried, the food should be lifted from the pan and held over it for a few moments so that excess oil drips off. Then it should be placed on a plate or dish covered with a double thickness of absorbent kitchen paper. The paper absorbs the excess oil, leaving the fried food crisp. Deep fried food should be served freshly cooked.

If you must keep fried fish hot for a short time, perhaps while you are cooking subsequent batches, place it on a thick pad of absorbent kitchen paper under a grill on low heat.

Choice of Seafood Options include thick fish fillets coated in batter, cooked mussels or prawns in batter, squid rings in batter, whitebait coated in seasoned flour, fish cakes or croquettes in egg and breadcrumbs and white fish fillets coated in egg and breadcrumbs.

Oily fish, such as mackerel and herring, are not at their best when deep fried.

SHALLOW FRYING

Most fish may be cooked by this method but the choice of cooking fat is important.

Fat There are two options: either the cooking fat is discarded or it is served with the fish. For example, fish shallow fried in oil is drained before serving, whereas butter used for cooking may be poured over the fish as an accompaniment. Although it is not practical to check the exact temperature of the fat before adding the fish, it is important that it is hot enough to prevent absorption. Remember that butter overheats at a lower temperature than oil. A combination of oil and butter may be used for flavour, as when olive oil and butter is used as a basis for a sauce.

Turning and Draining The fish should be turned once during shallow frying. A large spatula or slice should be used along with a palette knife, fork or slotted spoon to prevent the fish from breaking.

Choice of Fish and Coating Small whole fish (trout, mackerel, red mullet and sardines), fillets or portions of fillets, steaks and cutlets are all suitable for shallow frying. Batter is not a good coating as it should be submerged completely in hot oil for successful cooking. Egg and breadcrumbs or seasoned flour are both suitable coatings for shallow-fried fish.

Draining and Serving Fish coated in egg and breadcrumbs should be drained on absorbent kitchen paper. Fish coated in seasoned flour should be drained over the pan and absorbent kitchen paper used if it is very crisp. Butter used in cooking may be flavoured with lemon juice, herbs or chopped capers and poured over the fish.

STIR FRYING

This is a quick method of moving food around in a large pan containing a small amount of very hot oil. All the ingredients should be cut to a similar size and should be of a type that will cook quickly.

Fish is usually stir fried with vegetables. Onions, carrots and celery, for example, should quickly be stirred around in the pan before the fish is added.

Choice of Fish Strips of whiting, plaice and other thin fillets are suitable. You might also like to try shellfish or squid. If using strips of fish, avoid stirring them so vigorously that they disintegrate.

COATING FOR FRYING

Egg and breadcrumbs

The fish or seafood should be trimmed and dry. Coat it first in seasoned flour, then in beaten egg and lastly in fine, dried, white breadcrumbs. Use two forks to lift the food. Make sure the egg is in a wide dish which allows room to hold the fish. The breadcrumbs are best placed in a thick layer on a sheet of greaseproof paper or foil. The paper can be lifted and used to tease the crumbs over the egg-coated fish. Press a thick layer of crumbs on the fish, then gently shake off any excess.

Batter

Recipes for suitable batters are on page 216. The batter should be freshly made. The fish or seafood is first coated in seasoned flour, then dipped in the batter just before being submerged in the hot oil. Use two forks to turn the food in the batter, taking care not to knock the air out of a very light mixture. Have the container near the pan, then lift the food and allow excess batter to drip off. Give the food a twist to catch the drips of batter, then lower it carefully into the hot oil.

BAKING

Baking is an easy, versatile cooking method for fish. Most types of seafood may be baked in some way or other, either very simply, with herbs and lemon juice or mixed with a sauce, layered with vegetables topped with breadcrumbs or made into a pie. Baking is one of the easiest cooking methods because, to a large extent, it takes care of itself. As with other methods, it is important to avoid overcooking the fish. Here are a few simple suggestions.

USING FOIL

Individual portions of fish cook well in closed foil packages. Steaks and small whole fish are ideal for baking by this method, and portions of thick fillet (from cod or monkfish) are also suitable.

Cut pieces of foil large enough to hold the fish. Brush the middle of the foil with oil or melted butter and place the fish on it. Add herb sprigs – parsley, thyme or bay – and a trickle of oil or knob of butter. Sprinkle salt and pepper over the fish and fold the foil around it. Fold the edges of the foil over to seal in the fish, then bake the package on a baking sheet. To check whether the fish is cooked open a very small gap in the foil and test with a thin skewer.

Serve the foil packages on individual plates to be opened at the table.

COOKING EN PAPILLOTE

A traditional method of baking in paper, this works well for fish. Cut neat pieces of double thick greaseproof paper, large enough to hold the fish. The paper may be cut in various ways; oblong or square shapes, circles or heart-shaped pieces may be used.

Brush the paper with oil or melted butter and lay the fish in the middle. Bring the paper up over the fish and crumple the edges together firmly to seal in the contents. The edges of the paper must be closed over the top of the fish so that the package may be opened easily on the plate, revealing the contents ready to eat. Once cooked the paper becomes very brittle. Non-stick baking parchment may be used instead of greaseproof paper for strength.

COOKING IN FILM

Roasting bags and film may be used for enclosing fish in sealed packages for baking. The large bags make practical containers for larger whole fish – redfish, grey mullet or a curved salmon trout. Several smaller fish (red mullet or mackerel) may be arranged in the same bag placed in a dish or roasting tin. This is useful if you do not have a suitable baking dish large enough to hold the fish.

BAKING IN SHELLS

Scrubbed scallop shells may be used for baking fish and seafood in sauce or with gratin toppings. The deep shells should be saved, thoroughly scrubbed, boiled, rinsed and dried. Some fishmongers sell the cleaned shells.

Smaller shells are also useful. Mussels may be 'stuffed' in their shells. Larger deep oyster shells and clam shells are suitable both for holding fish and seafood during baking and as attractive serving vessels, particularly for appetizers.

FLAVOURING BAKED FISH

Whether the fish is enclosed in a package or placed in a covered dish, the choice of seasonings and flavourings is important. Herbs, pared or grated lemon rind and cloves of garlic (whole, chopped or crushed) are typical additions. A moistening agent of some kind is usually added. This may be butter or margarine, a little oil or a squeeze of lemon juice. A couple of spoonfuls of milk or single cream may be used with white fish fillets, while a little white wine, dry cider or dry white vermouth can contribute flavour and moisture.

Vegetables should be selected with care. Onion added to a sauce can taste raw even after baking unless it is quickly cooked in oil or butter first. Carrots and celery also benefit from brief pre-cooking before being baked with fish. Cooked chopped spinach makes an excellent base on which to bake skinned fish fillets or steaks.

TOPPINGS

Baked fish is often finished off with a gratin topping of breadcrumbs. Chopped parsley, grated cheese (Cheddar or Parmesan) and a little melted butter may be mixed with the crumbs.

Other toppings include chopped nuts mixed with breadcrumbs, sliced boiled potatoes, diced boiled potatoes tossed with melted butter or sliced mozzarella cheese.

Creamy mixtures of yogurt or fromage frais with beaten egg also make good toppings, but care must be taken not to bake these mixtures at too high a temperature or for too long or they may curdle.

The stage at which the topping is added depends on the ingredients and the cooking time. Fish and seafood which bakes very quickly may be topped when first placed in the oven. If the main part of the dish requires slightly longer, and the topping is light, as when a sprinkling of breadcrumbs is added, it is often best to add the topping halfway through cooking.

POULTRY

Poultry is the term used for domestic birds specially bred for food, as opposed to birds caught in the wild, which are game. Except at small country markets, when birds may be 'rough-plucked', all poultry is sold ready for cooking; plucked and drawn. If you do have to carry out any such basic preparation, follow the information given for game birds. Unlike game, poultry should be plucked and drawn when freshly killed and the birds are not hung for lengthy periods.

CHICKEN

Chicken is lean, tender and easy to digest. The majority of the fat content is found in or under the skin, so trimming and skinning renders chicken meat ideal for low-fat meals. The vast majority of chickens are roasting birds, under a year old; birds over this age are referred to as boiling fowl but these are no longer popular. Although they taste good, boiling fowl require 1½–2 hours boiling to tenderize the meat, after which time they have to be sauced for pies or similar recipes or used in soup.

Chickens are sold ready for cooking, most often without their giblets. If the giblets are included, they will be sealed in a packet in the body cavity of the bird; this will be clearly marked on the outside of the packaging.

Corn Fed Chicken This has a distinct yellow tinge when raw and the skin browns to a golden colour when roasted. The meat has a fine flavour, due to the high proportion of corn in the birds' feed.

Poulet Noir A popular French breed of black-feathered bird. Poulet noir has a mild gamey flavour.

Poussins Young birds, 4–8 weeks old, these are ideal for grilling, steaming or speedy roasting. They are usually served as individual portions, but larger birds (up to 675 g / 1½ lb) may be split to provide two servings.

Spring Chickens Small chickens, weighing 900 g–1.4 kg/2–3 lb, these are 8–12 weeks old.

Chicken Portions There is a good choice of prepared portions, including skinned boneless breasts or thin fillets of breast meat, chicken quarters, drumsticks, thighs and wings.

TURKEY

Uncooked turkey portions, whole birds and turkey products are available throughout the year. Significantly larger than other poultry, weighing 2.25–11.3 kg/5–25 lb, turkey has a high meat yield for the carcass. The white, tender, delicately flavoured breast meat is the prized portion. Leg meat is dark and tougher, also veined with sinews. Like chicken, whole birds are sold ready for cooking, with or without giblets. Larger birds are not as popular as they were when turkey was reserved as a Christmas speciality.

In addition to whole birds, whole breast fillets are sold boned and tied into neat joints. These are usually barded with a thin coating of fat, or rolled so that the skin forms a neat covering. Breast fillets and a variety of white-meat products are also available. Drumsticks are also sold separately; these are useful for casseroling.

Cubed and diced turkey (trimmed of all skin) is sold in many larger supermarkets. It is economical and useful for braised dishes, pies and risottos. Minced turkey is also available.

DUCKS AND DUCKLINGS

Although larger than chickens, ducks do not have a high yield of meat for their carcass size. They range in weight from 1.5 kg/3¼ lb to 2.5 kg/5½ lb and yield 2–4 servings. Duck has a higher fat content than either turkey or chicken. However, birds are now reared to have far less fat so this once off-putting characteristic of duck is no longer as relevant as it once was. It is, however, advisable to prick the skin on a whole bird all over before roasting to release the fat.

As well as whole birds, which are mainly sold frozen (usually with giblets), legs, quarters and breast portions are available.

GOOSE

Goose is probably the most expensive of the poultry birds. Available all year, most often to order, goose yields little meat and a large quantity of fat for its carcass size of 3–7 kg/6½–15¼ lb. The main area of meat is on the breast, where it is dark and flavoursome. The high fat content means that goose requires long roasting to render the fat; small birds are therefore not the best buy.

GUINEAFOWL

Although guineafowl is a domestic bird, originally from West Africa, it does have a hint of game to its flavour. Available all year, the birds range from 675 g/1½ lb to 2 kg/4½ lb, depending on maturity. Sold ready for cooking, guineafowl should be treated in the same way as chicken.

FREEZING AND THAWING POULTRY

Poultry for freezing should be absolutely fresh. Never buy poultry and allow the use-by date to expire before freezing it; when buying from a butcher always check that the bird is suitably fresh for freezing, or that portions have not previously been frozen. NEVER RE-FREEZE UNCOOKED POULTRY ONCE IT HAS BEEN THAWED.

Prepare birds as for cooking and pack them in heavy-quality airtight bags, labelled with the date and weight or number of portions. Breasts, drumsticks, fillets or other portions may be individually wrapped in freezer film before being packed in bags. Cubed meat or strips of meat should be loosely packed in sealed bags. The bags should then be spread out thinly on a baking sheet until the meat is hard. When hard the meat may be shaken down in the bag and any extra air extracted – this method creates a 'free-flow' pack, permitting some of the meat to be used as required and the rest replaced in the freezer without thawing. If available, use the fast freeze facility on your freezer to process the poultry as speedily as possible. Follow the freezer manufacturer's instructions.

Always allow sufficient time for thawing poultry in the refrigerator before cooking. It is also possible to thaw poultry in the microwave oven; for more information, consult your handbook. Both chicken and turkey must be cooked through before serving; if the whole bird or portions are not thoroughly thawed before cooking, thick areas of meat may not cook through. Due to its size, whole turkey is the most difficult poultry to thaw.

Always unwrap poultry and place it in a covered deep dish in the refrigerator, preferably on a low shelf, ensuring that it will not drip on any other food. Occasionally, drain off the liquid which seeps from the poultry as it thaws. Allow several hours or up to 24 hours for portions and smaller birds to thaw. Large poultry such as turkeys are usually purchased fresh; when buying frozen birds always read and follow the recommendations listed on the wrapping. The following is a guide to recommended thawing times by weight in the refrigerator: these times are not exact and they can only act as a guide. As soon as it is possible to do so, remove the giblets, and cook them to make stock. Cool the stock and freeze it until required. This is preferable to storing the stock in the refrigerator for several days while the turkey continues to thaw.

Weight of turkey	2.5–3.5 kg/ 5½–8 lb	3.5–5.5 kg/ 8–12 lb	5.5–7.25 kg/ 12–16 lb	7.25–9 kg/ 16–20 lb
Thawing time in refrigerator	up to 2 days	2½–3 days	3–4 days	4–4½ days

The majority of poultry is sold ready for cooking. Check the bird to make sure that it is free from any small feathers or hairs. If necessary, singe the bird to remove hairs: use long matches or a taper and allow the flame to burn for a few seconds until it has stopped smoking. Trim away any lumps of fat from the body cavity. Rinse the bird inside and out under cold water and dry it well on absorbent kitchen paper.

If any special preparation is required, a good butcher will almost certainly do this willingly, given sufficient notice, but it is useful to know the basics of trussing and jointing poultry. Detailed instructions for trussing are given under Game, see page 57.

PREPARING POULTRY FOR COOKING

Always thoroughly wash surfaces, the sink and all utensils that come in contact with raw poultry immediately after use. Scrub cutting boards after use. Wash your hands well, paying attention to nails; dry them thoroughly before preparing other food.

HYGIENE NOTE

Never stuff a bird more than an hour before cooking it. The stuffing may be made in advance and kept separately in a covered container in the refrigerator. Stuffing may be placed in the body cavity of the bird or under the skin covering the breast.

To insert stuffing under the skin, first loosen the skin by inserting the point of a knife between it and the flesh at the neck end of the bird. Once the skin has been loosened, wash and dry your hands, then work your fingers up between the flesh and skin to form a pocket over the breast meat. Take care not to split the skin. Thoroughly clean your hands.

Use a spoon to insert the stuffing into the prepared pocket, easing it in place by moulding it with the skin on the outside. When the stuffing is in place, use a skewer to secure the end of the skin to the bird.

STUFFING POULTRY

BONING A BIRD

1 Have ready a sharp, pointed cook's knife. A pair of kitchen scissors is also useful for snipping flesh and sinew free from joint ends. Lay the bird breast down. Cut through the skin and flesh right in to the bone along the length of the back. Beginning at one end of the slit, slide the point of the knife under the flesh and skin. Keeping the knife close to the bone, cut the meat off the bone..

2 Work all the meat off the bone on one side of the carcass, going down the rib cage as far as the breast. Leave the breast meat attached to the soft bone.

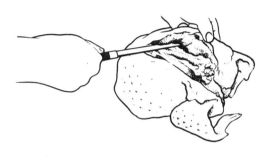

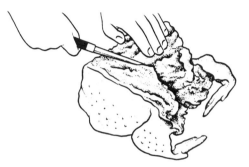

3 Cut off the wing ends, leaving only the first part of the joint in place. To free the flesh from the wing joint, carefully scrape the meat off the first part, using scissors or the point of the knife to cut sinews.

4 Pull the bones and meat apart as though removing an arm from a sleeve. Again use the point of a knife or scissors to cut sinew and skin attached at the bone end. This leaves the flesh and skin turned inside-out and the bones free but attached to the carcass. Turn the flesh and skin back out the right way. Repeat the process with the leg.

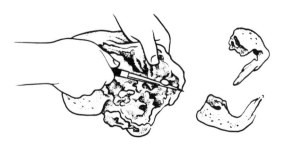

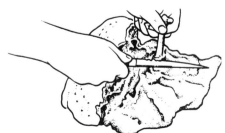

5 Turn the bird around and repeat the process on the second side, again leaving the breast meat attached to the soft bone.

When all the meat is removed from the second side, and the joints have been boned, the carcass will remain attached along the breast bone. Taking care not to cut the skin, lift the carcass away from the meat and cut along the breast bone, taking the finest sliver of soft bone to avoid damaging the skin.

6 Spread out the boned bird. It is now ready for stuffing.

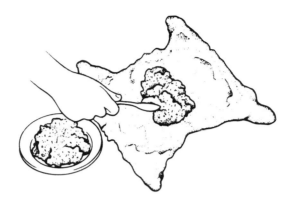

7 To reshape the bird simply fold the sides over the stuffing and sew them with a trussing needle and cooking thread. Turn the bird over with the seam down and plump it up into a neat shape, tucking the boned joint meat under.

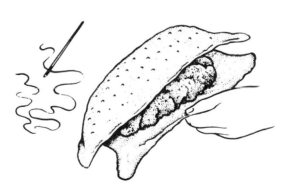

SPATCHCOCK

Turn the bird breast down. Cut off the parson's nose. Using a heavy cook's knife, cut through the skin, flesh and bone down the length of the bird to open the carcass. Do not cut right through to the breast. Open the carcass out and turn it over so that the breast is uppermost.

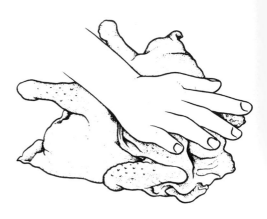

Place the palm of your hand on the top of the breast and flatten the bird by pressing down firmly with your other hand. The spatchcocked bird may be kept flat by threading two metal skewers through it.

SKINNING RAW POULTRY

It is occasionally necessary to skin a whole chicken. The technique is sometimes used to allow the full flavour of a marinade to permeate the flesh, notably when spicing a whole chicken for baking covered and serving cold. The technique is not difficult and there are no hard and fast rules about how it should be done. The method described below, however, is an organized and practical approach to the task, which avoids damaging the meat.

Use a sharp knife to slit the skin down the back of the bird. Pull it off, using a pointed knife to separate the skin from the membrane covering the flesh. Use scissors to cut the skin free around the joints. Turn the bird over and loosen the skin at the neck end, then pull it away from the breast meat, easing it off and cutting it free around the joints and at the parson's nose.

Skin the drumsticks individually with the help of scissors or a sharp pointed knife. Do the same with the first part of the wing joint, nearest the body. It is not easy to remove the skin from the wing ends, and they are best removed. The parson's nose may be left in place or cut off as required.

The cooking time should be calculated according to the weight of the prepared bird, with stuffing, if used. Place the bird in a roasting tin, using a rack or trivet if liked. A goose should always be cooked on a rack over a deep tin so that the large amount of fat drips away. Brush the bird with a little melted butter or oil if required and sprinkle with seasoning (see individual recipes for more detailed information). A large chicken or turkey may have its breast covered with streaky bacon to prevent the meat from drying out. Turkey should be covered with foil for part of the cooking time to prevent overbrowning.

Chicken does not usually require turning during cooking. Duck may be turned once or twice but this is not essential. Goose and turkey should be turned several times, depending on size, to promote moist, even cooking. All poultry should be basted during cooking. The following times are a general guide but may vary according to the exact ingredients used and the oven temperature, as when a bird is marinated and coated with seasonings that affect the browning.

Chicken and Guineafowl Allow 20 minutes per 450 g/1 lb plus 20 minutes at 180°C/350°F/gas 4.

Duck Prick the duck all over with a fork or skewer to release the fat. Roast on a rack, allowing 15–20 minutes per 450 g/1 lb at 190°C–200°C/375–400°F/gas 5–6.

Goose Allow 20–25 minutes per 450 g/1 lb at 180°C/350°F/gas 4.

Turkey This requires long, slow roasting to ensure that the meat is thoroughly cooked. This is particularly important if the body cavity of the bird is stuffed. The following times are at 180°C/350°F/gas 4. Keep the bird covered with foil until the final 30–45 minutes of cooking. These times are a guide only, based upon the bird's weight excluding stuffing, since it is not easy to weigh a stuffed turkey. Birds without stuffing will take slightly less time to cook.

ROASTING POULTRY

WEIGHT (BEFORE STUFFING)	2.5 kg/ 5½ lb	2.75–3.5 kg/ 6–8 lb	3.5–4.5 kg/ 8–10 lb	4.5–5.5 kg/ 10–12 lb	5.5–11.4 kg/ 12–25 lb
ROASTING TIME AT 180°C/350°F/ GAS 4	2½–3 hours	3–3¾ hours	3¾–4½ hours	4½–5 hours	20 minutes per 450 g/1 lb plus 20 minutes

Microwave Cooking Lean, tender poultry cooks well in the microwave, although whole chickens and ducks benefit from being partially cooked by this method, then placed in a conventional oven to crisp the skin.

TESTING FOR COOKING PROGRESS

It is essential that chicken and turkey are thoroughly cooked right through. With large birds, increasing the cooking temperature will not necessarily speed up the process as lengthy cooking must be allowed to ensure the thick areas of meat and the body cavity reach a high temperature.

To test, pierce the meat at a thick point – for example on the thigh behind the drumstick. Check for any signs of blood in the juices and for any meat that appears pink or uncooked. When the bird is cooked, the juices will run clear and the meat will be firm and white right through to the bone. On a large bird test in at least two places to ensure that all the meat is well cooked.

CARVING

The same rules apply to all poultry: the breast meat is carved in neat slices, working at an angle to the carcass to yield several slices of a similar size from each side. The wings and legs are then removed. To make it easier to carve the breast meat on chickens and smaller birds, the wings and legs are usually cut off first and served as individual portions. This is not necessary when carving larger birds, such as turkey, as the breast meat can easily be sliced off with the joints still in place.

GAME

Game refers to wild birds and animals which are hunted for sport as well as for food. The hunting, killing and selling of game is strictly controlled in Great Britain and the majority of game is protected by law, the exceptions being rabbits and woodpigeons.

There are certain times of the year when game cannot be shot. These 'seasons' vary slightly according to the nesting and mating patterns of the individual species. Outside of the season, not only is it illegal to kill game but it is also an offence to sell game unless it has been imported into the country when already dead. Only licensed butchers and poulterers are allowed to deal in game and it can be offered for sale up to 10 days after the end of the season. The restrictions on the sale of home-reared game apply to frozen animals as well as to fresh ones. However, there are companies that specialize in importing game for out-of-season sale. Some game, notably venison, is now farmed. Certain birds must not be killed and these include wild geese, Garganey teal, Long-tailed duck and Scaup duck.

A note of the season for each type of game is given in the following pages, along with advice on identifying birds and the best cooking methods to use. In the section which follows, the details of preparing and cooking game are outlined; however you will find that game is readily available dressed for the oven, not only from specialist butchers but also from good supermarkets where it is often sold frozen.

Season: October 1st to January 31st.

The capercaillie is a member of the grouse family, originating from Scandinavia. It is found today in small numbers in the northern areas of Scotland where it has been re-introduced following previous extinction from Britain. It is not a common game bird but when available it should be treated in the same way as grouse, and grouse can be substituted for it in recipes. This is a large bird which can weigh up to 4 kg/9 lb. It should be hung for 3–4 days, depending on conditions and personal preference.

Season: August 12th to December 10th.

In addition to the capercaillie (above) there are several other members of the grouse family, including the blackcock (also known as the heathpoult or black grouse) and the ptarmigan which comes from Europe and North America. However, the smaller Scottish grouse or red grouse (weighing about 675 g/1½ lb each) is considered to have the finest flavour.

Young grouse shot early in the season are the most tender. They can be slightly tough at the beginning of December, just before the season ends. Look for birds with pointed flight feathers and soft pliable feet, also a downy breast. Hang for about 3–4 days, depending on conditions and preference. The young birds are ideal for roasting or grilling and the older ones can be casseroled. An average-sized grouse serves 1–2.

Season: September 1st to February 1st.

This bird is related to the pheasant. There are two main varieties: the grey partridge which is the most common and considered to be the better bird and the red-legged, or French, partridge. When selecting birds, look for pliable, yellow-brown feet as they turn grey when the bird is older. The flight feathers should have pointed tips and the under feathers should be rounded. The beak of a young bird is fairly sharp. The best birds are obtained in October and November.

As a guide, partridges should be hung for about a week. Young birds can be roasted, older ones should be casseroled. It is usual to serve one partridge per person or one bird can be split before cooking to serve 2. The average weight for a partridge is 350–400 g/12–14 oz.

Season: October 1st to February 1st.

The pheasant is probably the best known and most readily obtainable of the game birds. Pheasants are sold dressed, ready for the oven, or they can be purchased in the traditional brace, consisting of a male and female bird. The male bird is easily distinguished by its bright plumage but the hen pheasant is rather dull by comparison, with pale brown feathers. However, the hen pheasant is the most tender and has the best flavour; the cock pheasant can be rather dry and slightly tough.

When looking for a bird, notice the feet which should be fairly smooth on a young bird. They tend to become scaly in appearance as the pheasant ages. The breast of a young bird should still be downy. Pheasants can be hung for some time, anything from a few days to two weeks, but this is a matter of taste and a source of great controversy among gourmets and cooks alike. The best months for buying pheasant are November and December.

The younger birds or tender hen pheasants can be roasted but if they are older or likely to be tough, they should be braised or casseroled. An average weight for pheasant is about 1.4 kg/3 lb and the hen is smaller than the cock. A smaller bird will serve 3; a larger one can be made to serve 4, depending on the way in which it is prepared and served.

PIGEON *Season:* Available all year.

There are two types of pigeon: the woodpigeon which is larger and has dark flesh and the stronger flavour, and the tame pigeon which has pale flesh and resembles young chicken more than game. The average weight for a pigeon is just over 450 g/1 lb and they are at their best from August to October. Look for birds with pink legs as they tend to be younger. Pigeons are best cooked by moist methods.

QUAIL *Season:* Available all year.

Quail are protected by law in Britain and are not shot in the wild; however, they are farmed and are therefore available all year round, both fresh and frozen. They are very small birds, weighing about 150 g/5 oz, and are often sold – and served – in pairs.

They are tender and delicate in flavour and much esteemed by gourmets. Suitable for grilling or roasting, quails are not hung. They are usually cooked whole, without being drawn.

SNIPE *Season:* August 12th to January 31st.

Small birds, not widely available in shops, and best killed when plump, in November. Related to woodcock, snipe live only in marshy land.

Weighing about 100 g/4 oz each, snipe are considered a delicacy. They are cooked whole, trussed with their long, pointed beaks skewered through their legs. Hang the birds for a few days, or up to a week. The gizzard can be removed before roasting or grilling. Serve 1 snipe per person.

WILD DUCK *Season:* September 1st to January 31st.

There are many varieties of wild duck. The mallard is the most common and is also the largest. Other common varieties include the pintail, teal and widgeon; the teal being the smallest. The best months for wild duck are November and December. They should be eaten fresh, without hanging. A mallard will serve 2–3; the teal serves 1.

Season: October 1st to January 31st.

A relative of the snipe, the woodcock is found in woodland as well as marshy land. Seldom available in the shops, this bird is prized for its flavour. Weighing about 150 g/5 oz, each woodcock serves 1. Hang these birds for up to a week, then cook them by roasting or braising.

Season:

ENGLAND AND WALES	SCOTLAND
Red deer –	*Red deer –*
stags: August 1st to April 30th.	stags: July 1st to October 20th.
hinds: November 1st to February 28/29th.	hinds: October 21st to February 15th.
Fallow deer –	*Fallow deer –*
bucks: August 1st to April 30th.	bucks: August 1st to April 30th.
does: November 1st to April 30th.	does: October 21st to February 15th.
Roe deer –	*Roe deer –*
bucks: April 1st to September 30th.	bucks: April 1st to October 20th.
does: November 1st to February 28/29th.	does: October 21st to March 31st.

WOODCOCK

VENISON

The red deer is the largest and most splendid-looking beast; the meat of the roe deer is paler and the least gamey; and the fallow deer is considered to have the best flavour. The meat of any type should be fine-grained and dark, with firm white fat. Young animals or fawns up to 18 months old produce delicate meat which should not be marinated before cooking. The meat of the male is preferred to that of the female and older venison is usually marinated, larded or barded before cooking as it is dry.

Venison is always hung, otherwise it would have little flavour. The whole carcass is hung for 10–14 days, depending on the weather and the strength of flavour required. Small cuts need hanging for about a week; however, if you buy the meat from a butcher, it will have been hung in advance. If you prefer well-hung venison, ask your butcher if he advises hanging the meat for a while longer before cooking.

If you have fresh venison, inspect the meat thoroughly before hanging it. If there is any musty smell, the meat should be washed in lukewarm water and dried thoroughly. Rub the meat with a mixture of ground ginger and black pepper, then hang it in a cool, dry, well-ventilated place. Check the venison daily and wipe off any moisture. To test if the meat is ready, run a sharp knife into the flesh near the bone. If it smells very strong, cook the meat at once or wash it with warm milk and water, then dry it and cover it with plenty of ginger and pepper. Wash the spices off before cooking. Haunch, saddle and loin are the prime cuts for roasting, or they can be cut into cutlets or steaks for grilling. Shoulder is a fairly tender cut which can be roasted or braised. The neck and other pieces of meat are either stewed, minced or made into sausages. The fat should always be removed from venison before cooking as it has an unpleasant flavour.

HARE Two types of hare are fairly common in Britain, the English or brown hare and the Scottish or blue hare; the brown hare is considered to have the best flavour. An animal under a year old is known as a leveret. It is distinguished by a small bony knot near the foot, a short neck, long joints, smooth sharp claws, a narrow cleft in its lip and soft ears.

Hare should be hung, whole, for 7–10 days, depending on the weather. It should hang from the back legs in a cool, dry, well-ventilated place. Catch its blood in a dish. Add one or two drops of vinegar to the blood to prevent clotting; store, covered, in the refrigerator if intending to jug the hare. The back, saddle and the hind legs can be roasted; the shoulders or forelegs are better cooked by braising or casseroling, or they can be jugged.

RABBIT Wild and tame (farmed) rabbit are closely related but the difference in flavour is derived from the diet and habitat.

The meat of wild rabbit is darker and it has a more gamey flavour. A freshly killed rabbit is treated in the same way as hare but it must be paunched (gutted) as soon as it is killed. There is no need to hang the animal for any length of time. Although the skin of the rabbit is usually left on once it is paunched, there is opinion which suggests skinning the animal immediately will eliminate the slightly musty taste which is often associated with wild rabbit.

Three-to-four-month-old rabbit is best, with thick foot joints, smooth claws, a flexible jaw and soft ears. The eyes should be bright, the fat whitish and the liver bright red. Average weight is 2–2.25 kg/4½–5 lb but can be up to 4 kg/9 lb.

Most game is sold ready for cooking and a good game butcher will happily prepare special cuts given sufficient notice. It is, however, useful to have an understanding of techniques like trussing and barding.

Birds are trussed to keep them in a neat shape while they are cooking and to secure any stuffing. The technique is the same for poultry and game birds. The easiest method is with a large needle and strong thread or fine string. Special, long, thick trussing needles are available from cook's shops. There are several ways of trussing birds, using one or two pieces of string inserted through the thighs, then wrapped back around the wings. Tying the legs neatly in place is adequate trussing for small game birds. If one piece is used, longer ends must be left and the string taken from the legs around the wings, then back to the legs.

PREPARING GAME FOR COOKING

TRUSSING GAME BIRDS AND POULTRY

1 Put the bird on its back and hold the legs together forming a 'V' shape pointing towards the neck end. Insert the trussing needle into one leg, then push it through the body and out through the other leg. The string should pass through just above the thigh bone. Leave good lengths of string to tie the legs firmly in place.

2 Tie the leg ends neatly, then re-thread the needle and thread it through the wings. Leave a long end of string and secure the flap of skin at the wing end of the bird to keep it neatly in place.

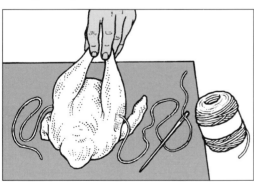

3 Take the string around underneath the body and towards the leg end of the bird. Tie off the ends to keep the whole body in a neat, secure shape.

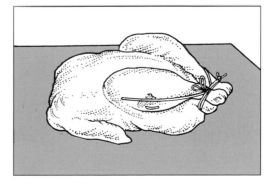

BARDING

Barding is the term used for wrapping or covering game birds (or a joint) with pieces of fat. This prevents the breast meat from drying out during cooking. It is used for birds which have dry meat, containing little fat. Pork fat, from the belly, is usually used. Alternatively use fatty streaky bacon.

1 For barding cut thin, even and neat slices of fat from belly of pork. The bird should be ready trussed. Lay the fat over the breast side of the bird, using as many slices as necessary to cover the breast completely.

2 Tie the fat neatly in place. The bird is now ready for cooking: the fat should be removed shortly before the end of the cooking time so as to brown the skin.

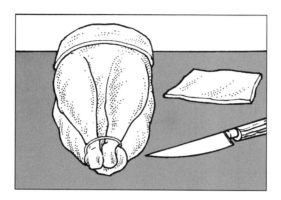 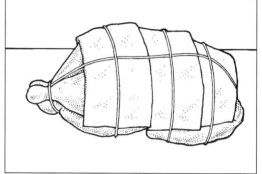

ROASTING TIMES FOR GAME BIRDS

The following times are a guide for roasting unstuffed birds. For a small stuffed bird up to 375 g/13 oz in weight allow up to 10 minutes extra; for a larger stuffed bird allow between 15–18 minutes extra cooking time.

Blackcock 40–50 minutes
Grouse 25–30 minutes
Pheasant 45–60 minutes
Partridge 20–30 minutes
Teal 15–20 minutes
Widgeon 25–30 minutes

Pintail 20–30 minutes
Mallard 30–45 minutes
Tame pigeon 30–40 minutes
Squab 15–25 minutes
Woodpigeon 35–45 minutes
Other small birds 10–15 minutes

Larding is the term used for threading strips of fat through meat before cooking. The fat is cut from belly of pork in neat slices, then the slices are cut into strips. A special larding needle is available, with a grip to hold a strip of fat at one end. Larding is used for very lean cuts of meat that tend to become dry on cooking. The strips of fat moisten the meat as it cooks.

LARDING VENISON

1 Cut neat strips of fat: they do not have to be too long but they should be fairly even in thickness. Larding is made easier if a fine skewer is first used to pierce the meat; this helps to prevent the fat from breaking as you pull it through with the larding needle. Pierce the meat as though sewing running stitches, inserting a fine skewer, then pushing it out about 2.5–5 cm/1–2 inches along.

2 Put a piece of fat in the larding needle, then thread it through the meat, following the line cut by the skewer. Leave a short piece of fat protruding at each end of the stitch, then continue to lard the piece of meat all over, keeping the spaces between the fat even.

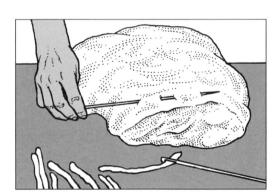
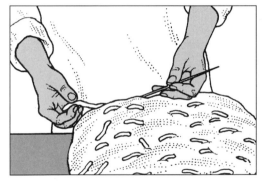

The following is a guide to cooking at 180°C/350°F/gas 4. Allow 15 minutes per 450 g/1 lb for large joints. Increase the time to 20 minutes per 450 g/1 lb for smaller joints weighing 1.5 kg/3¼ lb or less.

ROASTING TIMES FOR VENISON

PREPARING A HAUNCH OF VENISON FOR COOKING

A haunch of venison can be boned out completely, then tied neatly in place before cooking. The butcher will usually do this for you but should you want to attempt the task yourself, it is not very difficult but it is time-consuming. You will need a very sharp pointed knife.

Start from the wide end, cutting the meat off the bone. Work very closely to the bone, easing the meat away with your fingers. Alternatively, split the haunch down one side, then cut out the bone.

1 If the butcher has not already done so, chop off the bone end close to the meat and pull away any tendons. Trim all fat off the meat, cutting it away thinly using a sharp knife.

2 Once the meat is trimmed it should be larded, then marinated. Place the joint in a suitable dish, one which is large enough to hold the venison and deep enough to hold the marinade. A large gratin dish, lasagne dish or similar is ideal. During marinating the meat should be turned frequently and basted.

CARVING

Carving some types or cuts of game presents particular problems which are easily overcome by following the step-by-step instructions that follow.

CARVING A HAUNCH OF VENISON

A haunch of venison on the bone is not as difficult to carve as a saddle joint. The meat is taken off the sides, working on both sides of the joint to cut away large, even slices. The remaining small pieces of meat can be sliced off in small pieces but these are not prime portions. A boned haunch can be cut across into slices. Venison differs from beef in that the meat should be cut into fairly thick slices.

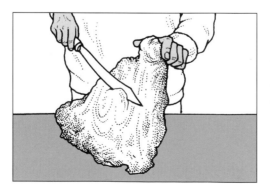

1 Holding the joint firmly by the bone end, cut neat slices off one side, then turn the leg slightly to carve the meat off the other side. The remaining meat can be cut off in small slices.

1 Carve the hare before arranging it on a plate for serving. Make short cuts across the spine in two or three places, then cut through down the length of the spine, from head to tail.

2 Cut across the spine towards the hindquarters, then cut between the legs to make two serving portions. This releases any stuffing in the body cavity and it can be scooped out at this stage.

CARVING HARE OR RABBIT

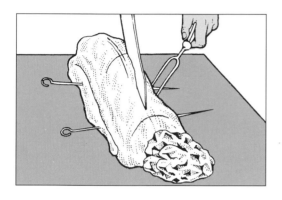

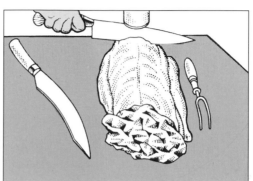

3 Divide the thigh and lower leg from the body meat to cut each of the two hind portions into two separate pieces.

4 Cut across the spine just behind the shoulders to separate the saddle from the forequarters. The saddle can be cut across into two or three portions. Cut off the head and cut forelegs into two further portions if preferred.

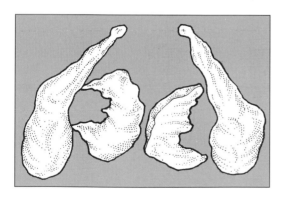

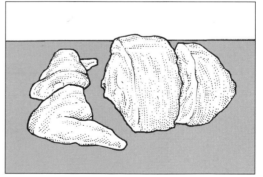

CARVING ROAST PHEASANT

1 Remove the legs by cutting between the breast and the point where the legs join the body. The bones should be cleanly cut and a pair of stout kitchen scissors may be useful. The legs can be cut into 2 portions, the thigh and the lower leg, although they are best left whole.

2 Next the wings should be removed, cutting them off close to the body and again using a pair of kitchen scissors to snip through awkward bones.

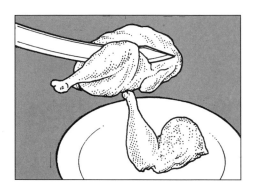

3 Lastly the breast meat should be carved off, first one side, then the other. Cut the meat into neat, even slices, as thinly as possible.

CARVING A SADDLE OF VENISON

The easiest way to prepare and serve saddle of venison is to ask the butcher for a boned and rolled joint which will include the tender fillet. Boned and rolled joints can be obtained in a variety of sizes, to cater for individual requirements. However, joints on the bone tend to be far larger and they may have the fillets left on. The fillets should be cut off in one piece and sliced. A rolled joint can be cut across into thick slices. The following steps are a guide to the more difficult process of carving the whole, unboned, saddle joint.

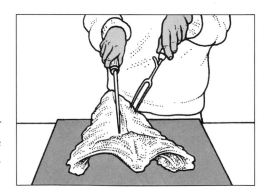

1 First carve the meat off the top, or loin, of the saddle. Starting in the middle to one side of the bone, cut downwards as near to the bone as possible.

2 The next cut should be at a slight angle but down to meet the base of the first cut and release the first slice of meat.

3 When one slice has been removed the carving is simplified and the rest of the same side of the haunch should be carved in neat, long slices. Carve the opposite side of the saddle of venison in the same way.

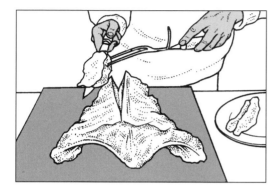

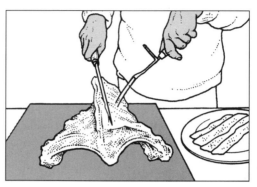

4 If the fillets were not removed before cooking, remove each in one piece: to do this, first slice down as near to the bone as possible, then cut outwards from the base to remove the fillet in one piece. Remove the fillet from the second side in the same way.

5 Cut the fillets into neat slices and serve them with the long slices taken from the top of the saddle.

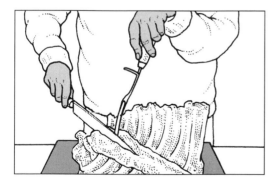

ACCOMPANIMENTS FOR GAME

The traditional accompaniments for roast game are the same for all types. Fried breadcrumbs may be served with large birds. Small to medium birds may be served on a croûte of fried bread.

- Thin gravy or giblet gravy.
- Bread Sauce (page 229) for grouse, pheasant and partridge.
- Sharp fruit jelly such as redcurrant or crab apple jelly.
- Watercress sprigs for garnish.
- Green vegetables, particularly Brussels sprouts, or a crisp salad.
- Game chips. These are made by thinly slicing potatoes, rinsing and patting dry, then frying in hot deep fat until golden. Before serving, drain game chips thoroughly on absorbent kitchen paper.

MEAT

Always buy meat from a reputable supplier to ensure that it has been properly handled and prepared before sale. Local butchers offer a personal service and expert advice. They will prepare exactly the amount or cut you want, or offer advice on the best buy if you are not sure what you need, and trim, truss or bone the meat for you, often more economically than the pre-packed product.

All meat should look moist and fresh. Fat should be firm and pale. There should be no unpleasant smell, slimy texture, softening or wet feel or appearance to the fat, nor any tinge of green or yellow to either meat or fat. Beef ranges from bright red to a darker colour when well hung. Lamb is neither as bright nor as dark as beef and it tends to be slightly drier. Its skin should look clean and pale and any fat should be creamy-white. Pork is a paler meat and the fat is softer and creamier in appearance. Liver, kidney and heart should all be firm, moist and evenly coloured and they should smell fresh without any hint of a strong or 'off' smell.

Bacon and ham should be firm and even in colour, with pale, creamy, firm fat. Avoid any fat which is yellowing, soft or slightly slimy in appearance; and meat which has a yellow-green tint or sheen.

Remember that meat should be kept chilled until sold either in a butcher's cold room or refrigerator or in a refrigerated display cabinet. It should not be displayed unchilled (pre-packed or otherwise).

Chill meat as soon as possible after purchase. Leave sealed packs closed; transfer wrapped meat to a large covered container. Place the meat on a low shelf in the refrigerator, making sure that it does not drip over the edges of the container. Cook the meat before the date on the packet, or within 1–2 days if bought loose. Use minced meat and offal within a day of purchase.

The selection of meat depends on the cooking method; some methods are suitable for certain cuts and not appropriate to others.

Roasting This is a dry cooking method for tender cuts. Originating from roasting on a spit over an open fire, the traditional method is to cook the joint uncovered on a rack in a tin. Modern cooks may dispense with the rack, placing the meat directly in the tin. It may be loosely covered for part of the cooking time to prevent over-browning.

Grilling A quick cooking method for tender, small cuts such as steak and chops.

Frying Shallow, deep or stir frying are all suitable methods for tender cuts. Deep frying, like stir frying, is used only for meat which has been cut into small pieces. Chops and steaks are typical candidates for shallow frying, whereas tender pork, trimmed and cut into small pieces, is perfect for stir frying.

Pot Roasting This is a form of roasting, usually on a bed of vegetables, in a tightly covered container. A little liquid may be added to the container. This is not strictly necessary; the condensation from the ingredients will be retained in the cooking pot. This method is suitable for less tender cuts but it is not a moist method and will not be successful with tough cuts.

Braising This is a part-moist method. The meat is cooked with some liquid, usually on a bed of vegetables, but is not submerged in liquid. It is suitable for less tender cuts as well as chops and steak but not for tough meats.

Stewing This is a moist cooking method for tough cuts of meat. The meat should be submerged in liquid and the container covered. Stews may be cooked on the hob or in the oven but it is important that the process is slow and lengthy, allowing time for the meat to become perfectly tender.

Casseroling This is a slightly ambiguous term used for moist cooking. It is similar to braising, but usually has more liquid; however it is not usually used to denote cooking periods as long as for stewing.

Microwave Cooking The majority of meat does not cook particularly well in the microwave oven. Sauces, such as Bolognese, which are based upon minced meat, can be cooked by this method, but microwave cooking is not suitable for any of the cuts that require long, slow cooking.

A wide variety of cuts is available, including the traditional portions listed here and Continental-style cuts which are cut quite differently, often with the grain of the meat instead of across it. Most supermarkets and butchers also offer a range of trimmed meats which are ready for grilling, frying or baking. These include skewered meats, rolled portions, thin escalopes or slices of meat and fine strips or cubes.

The value of becoming familiar with different cuts is in learning how best to cook them. Meat is muscle tissue: if it is taken from the most active part of the animal, for example the leg, it will have more connective tissue and be tougher than meat

COOKING METHODS

CUTS OF MEAT

65

from less active muscles on the back and around the rib areas. Long, moist cooking is necessary to soften connective tissue and make the meat tender. Tender cuts which do not have much connective tissue may be cooked by the quicker, fiercer and dry methods.

BEEF

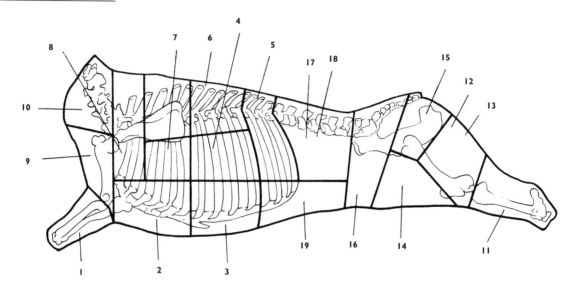

I Shin A tough cut with much gristle, this must be cooked by a slow moist method. It is ideal for flavoursome stews, soups and stocks, particularly on the bone, when it will yield stock which sets well on chilling.

2 Brisket Usually sold boned and rolled. This used to be a fatty cut, but modern breeding methods have reduced the fat content considerably. Suitable for pot roasting or braising, brisket may also be casseroled or boiled. It has good flavour.

3 Flank A comparatively fatty joint which requires long, slow cooking, by boiling, stewing or braising.

4 Flat Rib Taken from between the flank and forerib, this is not commonly available. If found it should be pot roasted or braised, as it is not a tender cut.

5 Wing Rib Cut from between the rib and sirloin, this is a succulent cut which is used for roasting.

6 Forerib A roasting joint, at its best cooked on the bone. A well-hung joint, roasted fairly slowly will yield full-flavoured, tender results. Since a joint on the bone has to be large in order to be practical, forerib is often sold boned and rolled.

7 Top Rib With back rib, this is also known as middle rib, thick rib or, traditionally, leg-of-mutton cut. Top rib and back rib may be sold separately, the former being an excellent cut for braising to soften the gristle which runs through the meat.

8 Chuck and Bladebone Both braising cuts, also used for making succulent stews. Chuck steak may also be purchased in one piece and pot roasted to give excellent results. In some areas chuck may also be known as chine. In Scotland chuck and blade combined are known as shoulder.

9/10 Clod or Front Chest and Sticking or Neck of Beef Although these inexpensive cuts do not have a lot of connective tissue, they contain significant amounts of gristle. Use for boiling or stewing.

11 Leg Suitable for long slow stewing and boiling, leg has good flavour and yields tender results when cooked correctly. Leg may be sliced across the muscle in large round nuggets of meat. It may be stewed in this form, or cut into cubes before cooking.

12 Topside This is taken from the inside of the leg. It is lean and boneless and the rolled joint is usually wrapped in a thin sheet of fat (barded) to keep it moist during cooking. Although topside is often regarded as a roasting joint, it is best pot roasted.

13 Silverside From the thigh and buttock, this is suitable for roasting, but benefits from pot roasting or braising. Silverside is also suitable for boiling; salted silverside is an excellent boiling joint.

14 Top Rump or Thick Flank Although this is generally regarded as a braising joint (whole or in slices) it may be pot roasted to give full-flavoured results.

15 Aitchbone This is a large joint on the bone lying over the rump. An old-fashioned cut, it can be boned and rolled and prepared in smaller joints. It may be roasted or braised.

16 Rump Next to the sirloin, this is a popular cut for grilling and frying, but it is not the most tender of steaks. Rump has a thin covering of fat but it is free of gristle.

17 Sirloin The prime, traditional roasting joint, sirloin includes the fillet. Tender and flavoursome, sirloin is one of the most expensive cuts of beef. A well-hung rib of beef is less expensive and offers equal if not better flavour when cooked with care.

18 Fillet Tucked underneath the bone, the fillet is a long, slim piece of very tender meat with a good flavour. As it is expensive it is usually reserved for special dishes, such as Beef Wellington, or it may be sliced into small, thick steaks for grilling or frying.

19 Hindquarter Flank The belly of the animal. A braising and stewing cut which has a high fat content and is therefore often trimmed and minced.

BEEF STEAKS

Fillet Small steaks off the fillet which cook quickly to give succulent, tender results.

Tournedos A 2.5 cm/1 inch thick slice off the fillet, trimmed and tied neatly.

Chateaubriand A thick centre cut from the fillet, weighing about 250 g/9 oz and measuring about 5 cm/2 inches thick, this may be served as a portion for two.

Rump Flavoursome steak for grilling, frying, or braising, this is not the most tender steak but it is economical with good texture.

Sirloin Large tender steak on the bone, this may be cut in several ways and served under several names.

Porterhouse A 2.5 cm/1 inch thick steak from the thick end of the sirloin, this is tender and ideal for grilling.

T-bone On the T-shaped bone, this large steak cut through the sirloin includes a slice each of the loin meat and of the fillet.

Entrecôte A boneless steak consisting of the eye of the loin meat from the sirloin, but without fillet. Usually cut 2.5–4 cm/1–1½ inches thick.

Minute Steak A thin slice of steak of good quality which may be fried or grilled very quickly. This may be taken from the sirloin, or even from the fillet. It is trimmed of all fat and may be beaten out very thinly.

VEAL

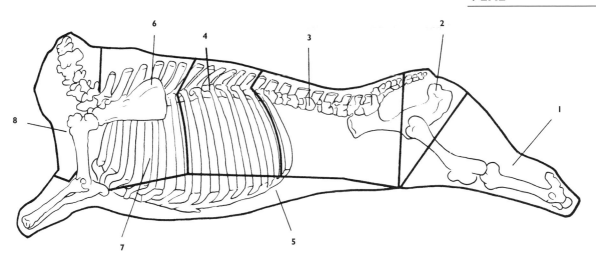

1 Leg The lower part of the leg, the knuckle or shin, this is jointed on the bone for stewing or boned and cubed to be sold as pie veal. The upper part of the leg provides a large roasting joint. Continental escalopes are cut along the muscle on the topside area of the joint; however British escalopes may be cut across the grain of the meat on the fleshy part of the leg in the form of steaks which are beaten out thinly to make escalopes.

2 Fillet The most expensive and tender cut, this is either sliced into steaks or cooked whole.

3 Loin For roasting on the bone or boned, this may be cut into chops for grilling or frying. The leg end of the loin may be referred to as the chump end.

4 Best End of Neck For roasting or braising, this is also chopped into cutlets for grilling and frying.

5 Breast Usually boned for stuffing, rolling and roasting. An economical cut with a good flavour.

6 Shoulder On the bone or boned and rolled, for roasting. If the fore knuckle is removed, this is called the oyster of veal.

7/8 Middle Neck and Scrag For stewing and braising, these have a high proportion of bone to meat.

9 Cutlets Cut from the best end of neck, providing 6 per carcass, each weighing about 175 g/6 oz.

10 Chops Cut from the loin, these may have a slice of kidney included. The chops may be cut in various ways; they usually weigh about 225 g/8 oz each.

LAMB

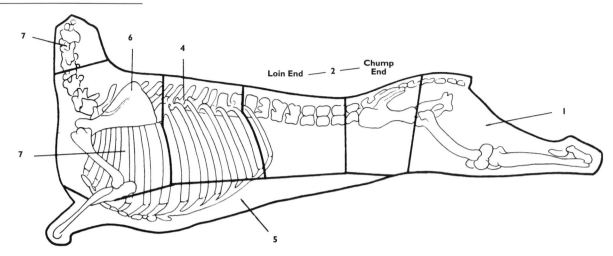

I Leg Known as gigot in Scotland, the leg may be divided into fillet and shank end. Leaner than shoulder, the leg may be roasted whole or boned and stuffed. Slices chopped off the leg are known as lamb steaks.

2 Loin A roasting joint for cooking on the bone or boned and rolled. Divided into loin and chump ends, the joint may be separated into loin and chump chops.

3 Saddle The whole loin from both sides of the lamb, with a central bone.

4 Best End of Neck This may be boned and rolled, then sliced into noisettes. The individual bones may be separated with their eye of meat to make cutlets or the whole rack roasted on the bone. Two racks may be interlocked to make a guard of honour, or they may be trussed into a circular crown roast.

5 Breast One of the most economical cuts of meat, the breast may be separated into riblets on the bone for treating like pork spare ribs. More commonly, the boned joint is stuffed and rolled for slow roasting, pot roasting or braising.

6 Shoulder An economical roasting joint which may be separated into the blade end or best end and the knuckle end. Shoulder may be roasted on the bone or the whole joint may be boned and trussed neatly. Boned shoulder is an excellent joint for stuffing.

7 Middle Neck Usually chopped into portions for stewing; however 2–3 chops of grilling quality may be taken from the meat closest to the best end of neck.

8 Scrag End of Neck Economical for stews and casseroles.

9 Chops Each carcass yields 4–6 chump chops, 6 loin chops and 4–6 neck chops (cutlets with the rib bone removed). Leg chops or cutlets, also known as steaks, may be cut from the fillet end of the leg.

PORK

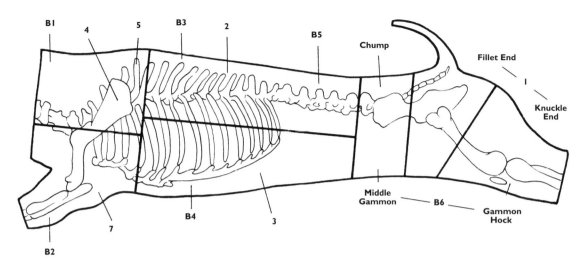

The majority of pork meat is tender and therefore suitable for quick cooking as well as braising. The important differences between the cuts is in the proportion of fat to lean and the presence of sinews, gristle or skin which must be trimmed before the meat is subjected to quick or dry cooking methods.

1 Leg Divided into the fillet end, from the top of the leg, or knuckle end, from the lower half of the leg. Popular for roasting, on the bone or boned and rolled.

2 Loin A popular roasting cut, either on the bone or boned and rolled (in which case the joint may be stuffed). Tenderloin is the meat from the inside of the loin bone, also known as the fillet.

3 Belly Also known as flank or draft of pork, this used to be regarded as a very fatty cut. Animals bred for leaner meat yield belly that has a better proportion of lean to fat. The flat joint may be roasted or sliced into rashers for grilling.

4 Bladebone Boned and stuffed or roasted on the bone.

5 Spare Rib A cut which is equivalent to the middle neck of lamb. This is marbled with fat, but overall it provides a lean roasting joint or slices (known as spare rib chops) for grilling and frying.

6 Spare Ribs These are cut from the belly once the main joint has been removed to include only the bones with their covering of meat. The amount of meat left on the bone can vary considerably, so always look for meaty ribs when buying.

7 Hand and Spring A large, economical cut which yields a generous amount of meat. Ideal for slow roasting, it can be divided into hand which may be boned and stuffed, and spring which may be trimmed and cubed for braising. With careful trimming of sinews, the joint provides a large quantity of meat which may be used for different purposes: a fair-sized portion for roasting, cubes for braising and strips or small cubes for frying and stir frying.

8 Head The head contains a considerable quantity of meat, notably the cheeks which are traditionally boiled and crumbed to be sold as Bath Chaps, small hams on the bone. The whole head may be boiled and cleaned for making brawn, or a prepared half head purchased from butchers.

9 Trotters or Pettitoes These may be boiled, skinned and the meat removed. The meat is flavoursome and the stock sets to a firm jelly. Unskinned trotters may be boned and stuffed, then roasted.

10 Chops Taken from the loin or spare rib. Chump chops are the first 2–3 chops from the leg-end of the loin. They are large and meaty. Middle loin chops are sometimes sold with the kidney, whereas foreloin chops have a curved shape and no kidney.

Bacon, gammon and ham are produced by curing fresh pork in brine. Gammon and ham are the terms used for the prime cuts from the hind leg of the pig. Gammon refers to uncooked cuts; traditionally, ham is used to describe both cooked and uncooked cuts. The term cooked ham' clearly distinguishes cooked from uncooked meat.

There are many variations on curing methods, including traditional techniques giving full-flavoured bacon and modern methods for milder, less-salty cuts.

The most popular curing method, based on an old Wiltshire technique, involves injecting the meat with brine, then soaking it in brine. It is matured for two to four days.

Modern quick-cure methods may be used on some cuts of meat such as gammon. In this case the various parts of the carcass are cured separately.

Sweet, tender and mild cure bacon has had sugar or other sweetening added during curing, and a fruit-based tenderizing agent is often added, particularly to 'tender-sweet' or 'tender-cure' cuts.

Smoked Bacon and Gammon

The meat is smoked over wood sawdust or oak chippings after curing.

Cured Ham for Serving Raw

Ham which is cured and air-dried is usually served raw, cut into very thin slices. This type of ham may be served as a first course, with lemon wedges and freshly ground black pepper or with fruit, such as melon or fresh figs. It may also be used in cooked dishes, as when chicory is wrapped in ham before braising or with lightly scrambled eggs to serve with pasta.

The method is an International one; the Italian prosciutto crudo is one of the best known types, particularly Parma ham; from France comes Bayonne ham; Germany produces Westphalian ham, which is smoked, and Britain also offers some regional equivalents, such as Cumberland ham.

The position of the following cuts is illustrated on page 71.

B1 Collar The collar joint is excellent for boiling or braising and it may be sold as rashers which are usually cut fairly thick. Collar is also good diced or cubed for pie fillings, pasta and rice dishes. A collar joint may need soaking before cooking, traditionally for several hours or overnight.

B2 Forehock Sometimes referred to as gammon hock. The forehock may be boiled as a base for soups, stews and casseroles. The meat is flavoursome and excellent for dicing and mincing. The butt end of the forehock is the meaty part which is suitable for cooking whole and slicing. The thinner end of the hock joint is ideal for making excellent stock and soup. The meat should be cut off the bone,

BACON, GAMMON AND HAM

CURING METHODS

CUTS OF BACON AND HAM

trimmed of fat and rind and diced. When well prepared, hock provides flavour-some inexpensive meat for a variety of dishes.

B3 Back Rashers and Chops Back rashers may also be cut from the portion of meat between the middle rashers and the middle gammon. These are prime bacon rashers with a good nugget of lean tender meat and they are ideal for grilling or frying.

Chops are cut thicker than bacon rashers, each providing an individual portion. They may be served plain grilled or fried. Alternatively, they can be browned, then braised.

B4 Streaky Streaky is a tasty cut which is striped with fat as well as lean. Streaky rashers are ideal for chopping and using in cooked dishes and they yield the best crispy bacon bits for garnishing soups or tossing into salad. Streaky bacon may also be bought as a joint for boiling, and it is excellent when pressed and served cold.

B5 Middle Rashers These are economical and meaty. They may be cooked by grilling or frying.

Throughcut Rashers These are rashers cut from the complete side of bacon, including the streaky and the middlecut or back rashers.

B6 Gammon This is the prime, lean and tender cut for boiling or baking, or cooking by a combination of both methods. The gammon may be purchased whole, as a large joint on the bone including the middle gammon down to the hock end of the joint. The whole joint is ideal for a large party or gathering, such as a wedding. Some butchers boil their own gammons (or hams) and will provide a whole joint to order.

However, the gammon is usually boned and rolled, then cut into smaller joints or steaks.

Middle Gammon The large round of meat; the prime joint for serving hot or cold.

Gammon Steaks These large, round slices, usually sliced about 1 cm/½ inch thick, are cut from the middle gammon joint. They are ideal for grilling or frying. Since they provide large individual portions, many butchers sell the steaks cut in half.

Gammon Slipper and Corner Gammon Small lean joints of prime meat cut from the hock.

Gammon Hock A meaty, well-shaped joint which may be cooked on the bone. This is the end of the gammon and, when cooked on the bone, it provides an impressive joint of practical size for small gatherings, Christmas or other festive occasions.

Bacon Offcuts These are the trimmings and bits left from cutting joints and slicing bacon rashers. They usually consist of a mixture of bits from all parts of the carcass and they can include a lot of fat. However, provided that there is not too much fat in the pack or tray of offcuts, they are an excellent, economical buy for dicing and chopping. The offcuts may also be trimmed and minced, then combined with breadcrumbs, egg, herbs and seasoning to make delicious burgers.

Bacon Rind Pre-packed bacon is often sold with the rind removed and many prime cuts which are sold loose are trimmed of rind.

Frying For rashers, steaks and chops. Remove the rind, if liked, and snip the fat to prevent the rashers from curling up during cooking. Lay the bacon in a heavy-bottomed frying pan and place over medium heat. As the bacon heats and the fat runs, turn the rashers over and cook for 1–2 minutes on each side, until lightly browned. Drain; serve on heated plates.

Grilling For rashers, steaks and chops. Lay the rashers on a rack in the grill pan, then place them under a hot grill for 2–3 minutes on each side, turning once, until lightly browned.

Boiling For joints. Weigh the joint and allow 20 minutes per 450 g/1 lb, plus 20 minutes. This timing applies whether the joint is cooked completely by boiling or boiled for half to three quarters of the time, then baked. The rind may be removed and the fat scored and glazed or browned in the oven.

Baking For joints, usually in combination with boiling. However, gammon joints may be baked from raw, allowing 20 minutes per 450 g/1 lb, plus 20 minutes. Very large joints, over 4.5 kg/10 lb, require 15 minutes per 450 g/1 lb, plus 15 minutes.

OFFAL

Offal is the term used for internal organs and other, less valuable, edible parts of the carcass. The term embraces brains, tongue, head, sweetbreads, heart, liver, kidneys, lights, tripe, melts, caul, marrow bones, tail and feet. Most offal is highly nutritious and low in fat, and many types cook quickly.

Liver Calf's liver is considered to have the best and most delicate flavour, followed by lamb's, pig's and ox liver, in that order. Calf's liver and lamb's liver are both suitable for grilling, frying or braising. Although pig's liver has a fine texture, its flavour is strong, so it is usually used in pâtés or combined with other ingredients in mixed dishes. Ox liver is the least popular since it is both strongly flavoured and coarse-textured. It is seldom used except in casseroles which include plenty of other ingredients.

Liver is covered with a fine membrane which should be removed before cooking. When rinsed and dried on absorbent kitchen paper, the liver may be sliced, cut in strips or diced. All sinews and any blood vessels should be removed. Before frying or grilling, liver is usually coated in well-seasoned flour.

Kidneys These have a distinct flavour, strongest in ox and pig's kidneys. Lamb's kidneys are milder. Lamb's, pig's and calf's kidneys may be grilled, fried or braised; ox kidney is suitable for stewing and for adding to pies and savoury puddings.

Kidneys are usually sold with the outer covering of fat removed. The fine membrane surrounding them should be removed and they should then be cut open so that the core, tubes and sinews may be cut out. A pair of kitchen scissors is the best implement for this.

Hearts Ox, calf's, lamb's and sheep's hearts are all lean and firm. They require careful preparation to remove all tubes, then long, slow cooking. The outer covering of fat and any membrane should be removed, then the tubes, fat and tough tissue should be cut away to leave only the trim, dark meat. The heart may be split and stuffed, then neatly sewn to enclose the stuffing before long slow braising.

Sweetbreads The thymus gland. Sweetbreads from British cattle are banned at present; however, imported sweetbreads are available from larger butchers offering a wide range of offal. Ox, calf's and lamb's sweetbreads are sold in pairs, each pair serving two people. Sweetbreads should be soaked in cold water for 15 minutes, then thoroughly washed in several changes of cold water. They must be simmered gently until firm – 2–5 minutes, depending on type – then drained and rinsed in cold water. The outer membrane should be removed and the sweetbreads pressed by placing in a dish, covering with scalded muslin and placing a weight on top. Chill until firm – this takes several hours. The sweetbreads will then be ready for cooking: they may be cut into pieces or sliced and coated in egg and breadcrumbs for frying. Alternatively, they may be coated in well-seasoned flour, browned in butter and served in a creamy sauce.

Oxtail This is sold ready jointed. Excess fat should be trimmed off and the joints stewed with vegetables and stock or water for several hours, until tender. The meat may be served on the bone or the joints may be picked over for meat and the bones discarded. Oxtail has a rich, beefy flavour and is ideal for winter stews and soups.

Tongue Lamb's, ox and calf's tongues require boiling, skinning and trimming. Ox tongue may be purchased pickled in brine or unsalted, the former requiring soaking before cooking. Tongue should be simmered gently with vegetables, bay leaves, mace and other herbs in plenty of water to cover until tender. This will take about 45 minutes for lambs' tongues, 1 hour for a calf's tongue and 2 or more hours for an ox tongue. Pressed tongue may be served with mustard. Hot Béchamel sauce flavoured with mustard is the ideal accompaniment for a freshly boiled tongue.

Tripe This is the lining of the stomach. Smooth, or blanket tripe comes from the first stomach cavity and honeycomb tripe comes from the second stomach cavity. The latter has a distinct honeycomb texture. Tripe is usually sold prepared, blanched and cleaned, or dressed, ready for cooking in a sauce. The preparation process is long, involving much washing, scrubbing, blanching and rinsing. The prepared tripe is white with a glutinous texture. It should be further cooked for anything from 30 minutes to 2 hours, depending on the dish.

Brains Brains from British cattle are banned at present; however imported brains are available from larger butchers offering a wide range of offal. Lamb's and calf's brains have a delicate flavour, although they are not a popular food. Their preparation is similar to that of sweetbreads, involving soaking and rinsing, blanching and removing all the covering membrane, then pressing and chilling before coating or cooking as required.

Heads Pig's head is used for making brawn and is the only head sold with the animal carcass to the butcher. They are easily obtainable from proper butchers (as opposed to meat sellers). The boiled head is used to make brawn, although a half head may be a more practical buy in view of its size.

Feet Pig's and calf's trotters and cow heel are all traditionally boiled for their jellied stock. Pig's trotters, both fresh or smoked, are more readily available than calf's. They are delicious for making soups and stews and yield a good portion of tasty meat.

Bones and Other Offal Marrow bones should be chopped by the butcher ready for baking and boiling at home to make stock.

In various countries and regions many other animal parts are eaten, including the lungs (lights) and melts (spleen) or even the testicles, ears and intestines. However, these are not popular for home cooking, even though they may be encountered as well-seasoned specialities at Continental charcuteries. Perhaps the nearest British equivalent is the Scottish haggis, although the modern version makes less use of offal than the old-fashioned stuffed sheep's stomach did.

Internal fat from carcasses also has a number of uses. Beef suet is taken from fat surrounding kidneys. Lard is derived from fat deposits inside the carcass of a pig. Caul is a fatty membrane which covers and supports internal organs as well as the head of the foetus. The fatty deposits distributed over it give it a lacy appearance. Traditionally, caul is used as a casing for lean joints, pâtés, faggots and their French equivalent, crepinette. It requires careful preparation, including soaking in warm water with a little vinegar added, and thorough rinsing several times before use.

Sausages are a familiar food which use offal as a casing. Natural sausage skins are prepared from the intestines of animals. They are cleaned and salted. Before use the skins have to be soaked and rinsed several times. Synthetic alternatives are now commonly used.

Availability of Offal Greater awareness of food safety has resulted in separate preparation of offal and meat products. The process varies according to the animal; however, the retail butcher no longer receives a whole carcass. Pig carcasses are bought complete with heads, so most independent butchers will provide a prepared head at a few days' notice. Less-popular offal is sometimes sold frozen. Unprocessed internal fat, such as caul, is difficult to obtain.

ROASTING TIMES FOR MEAT

The following times are a guide for roasting meat at 180°C/350°F/gas 4. Weights and timings are for oven-ready joints, including any stuffing. Small joints weighing less than 1 kg/2¼ lb may need an extra 5 minutes per 450 g/1 lb.

Personal preferences play an important role when roasting, and there are many methods. For example, the joint may be placed in an oven preheated to a higher temperature than that recommended for general roasting. The temperature may be reduced immediately or after the first 5–15 minutes. This method is popular for pork (to crisp the rind) and for sealing and browning the outside of larger joints of beef or lamb. Small to medium joints may need less time than that calculated below, if they are started off at a high temperature, but thick or large joints will still require the full calculated time to ensure they are cooked.

Attitudes towards roasting pork have changed considerably, based on professional guidance on food safety. Pork is usually served cooked through, not rare or medium; however, the meat may be roasted until it is succulent rather than very dry; hence the choice of two recommended timings.

BEEF
Rare – 20 minutes per 450 g/1 lb plus 20 minutes
Medium – 25 minutes per 450 g/1 lb plus 25 minutes
Well Done – 30 minutes per 450 g/1 lb plus
    30 minutes

PORK
Medium – 20–25 minutes per 450 g/1 lb plus
    25–30 minutes
Well Done – 25–30 minutes per 450 g/1 lb plus
    25–30 minutes

LAMB
Medium – 20–25 minutes per 450 g/1 lb plus
    20–25 minutes
Well Done – 25–30 minutes per 450 g/1 lb plus
    25–30 minutes

VEAL
Well Done – 30 minutes per 450 g/1 lb plus
    30 minutes

USING A MEAT THERMOMETER

A meat thermometer may be inserted into the joint before cooking, ready to register the internal temperature and indicate the extent of cooking. Preheat the thermometer in the oven from cold. Pierce the meat at the thickest point with a skewer and insert the hot thermometer into it. At any stage during cooking the reading on the thermometer may be checked to assess cooking progress (see chart below). When the meat is cooked, remove the thermometer and place it on a plate to cool.

BEEF
Rare – 60°C/140°F
Medium – 70°C/158°F
Well Done – 80°C/176°F

PORK
Medium – 75–80°C/167–176°F
Well Done – 80–85°C/176–185°F

LAMB
Medium – 70–75°C/158–167°F
Well Done – 75–80°C/167–176°F

VEAL
Well Done – 80–85°C/176–185°F

A sharp, long-bladed knife is essential for carving and a two-pronged carving fork is useful but not vital.

CARVING MEAT

Remove any trussing string and skewers. Holding the joint with the fork, use a sawing action to slice across the grain of the meat. Cutting across the grain is important as it makes the meat more tender to eat. If the joint has an 'L' shaped bone (such as in a rib of beef), then cut between the meat and bone, as close to the bone as possible, on the shortest side of the bone. Carve the meat in slices down towards the bone, either straight down or at an angle, whichever is best for giving large, neat slices. When the majority of the meat is removed from one side, turn the joint, if necessary, and remove meat from the other side. Any remaining small areas of meat should be cut in small neat pieces.

Carving Sirloin on the Bone

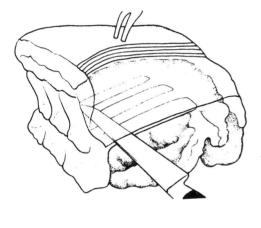

Carving Leg of Lamb

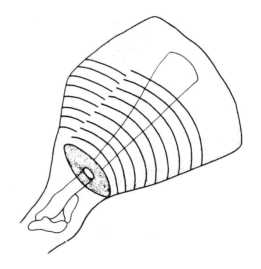

Carving Loin of Pork

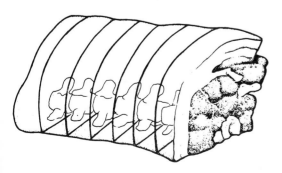

Carving Saddle of Lamb

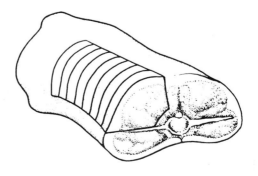

VEGETABLES

Variety and quality are all-important in the selection and use of vegetables.

BUYING VEGETABLES

Although most vegetables are on sale all year, it is still worth taking advantage of locally grown produce in season, both for flavour and economy. Look out for home-grown produce in supermarkets and take advantage of any local market gardens and farms. Remember, too, that markets are an excellent place to shop for value – in some rural areas they can be the best place to buy really fresh produce.

Whatever and wherever you buy, always look for good-quality produce. Vegetables should look fresh – firm, crisp and bright. Avoid limp, yellowing and wrinkled produce; onions that are soft or sprouting; and items that have been excessively trimmed. Do not buy green potatoes as they are inedible; this should be brought to the attention of the seller.

The fact that vegetables have been cleaned before being offered for sale is not necessarily an indication of their quality – for example, vegetables that have a certain amount of earth on them or retain their leaves are often better quality than thoroughly washed, trimmed and prepacked items.

When buying packs of vegetables always check that they are not sweating, with moisture inside the bag causing rapid deterioration in quality. Turn items over, feel them and inspect them for soft spots or bad patches.

STORING

Vegetables should be used as fresh as possible. The majority of vegetables should be stored in the refrigerator: salad vegetables should be polythene-wrapped or stored in the salad drawer. Carrots, parsnips and similar vegetables will soon deteriorate if they are stored in polythene bags, so thick paper bags are the best wrapping in the salad drawer. Similarly, mushrooms go off quickly if they are stored in polythene. Green vegetables and cauliflower should be stored in polythene bags.

Potatoes should be stored only if suitable conditions are available, that is a cool, dry place where the tubers may be kept in a thick brown paper bag to exclude all light. They should not be stored in warm, light, moist conditions for any length of time. So only buy large polythene bags of potatoes if you can use them within a few days.

As a general rule, buy little and often for best quality and food value.

FROZEN VEGETABLES

Frozen vegetables are excellent quality, in terms of food value as well as flavour. They are also easy to prepare at home. Take advantage of pick-your-own farms or farm shops if you do not grow your own vegetables, and freeze only good quality produce which is freshly picked and processed as quickly as possible.

British cooking has been given a bad name in the past by the characteristic over-boiling of vegetables, rendering high-quality produce unpalatable and lacking in nutrients. Happily, attitudes are changing and a broader range of cooking methods is now commonly used, with shorter cooking times and greater appreciation of the value of raw vegetables, for their texture and flavour as well as for their food value. Flavourings have become more adventurous and salt, which was once added automatically to every pan of boiling vegetables, is now very much a matter of personal choice.

Boiling

This is an easy, practical cooking method for many vegetables including potatoes, carrots, swedes, parsnips, beans, cauliflower and cabbage. However, it is important that the boiling process is only long enough to make the vegetables tender.

There are two methods of boiling. The first involves covering vegetables with water, which is then brought to the boil. The heat is then reduced and the pan covered so that the water just boils. For the second method, a comparatively small amount of water is brought to the boil, the vegetables are added and are cooked more fiercely with or without a lid on the pan. This takes less time but vigilance is needed to ensure that the pan does not boil dry.

The first method is used for potatoes, swedes and similar vegetables which require to be covered with liquid to make them tender in the shortest possible time. The liquid from cooking may be used for sauces, such as gravy, or in soups.

The second method is suitable for quick-cooking vegetables such as cabbage, green beans, Brussels sprouts and cauliflower. Once the vegetables are added to the pan, the liquid should be brought back to the boil quickly, then the heat controlled so that the cooking is fairly rapid. Cooking times will vary, depending on the vegetables.

Salt may be added to the cooking water. This is a matter for personal choice but the water should not be heavily salted.

Never add bicarbonate of soda to the cooking water for green vegetables. In the days when vegetables were regularly overcooked, this was regarded as a good way of preserving the colour; however it destroys the vitamin C content of the food and should be avoided.

Stewing and Braising

Ratatouille is one of the best-known, classic vegetable stews. Stewing and braising are used for vegetables which require moderate to lengthy cooking. or which benefit from a moist cooking method. They are also used to combine vegetable flavours and create a mixed vegetable dish.

Celery, fennel, cucumber and carrots are typical examples of vegetables that respond well to braising, with the addition of a little onion, some stock or wine and herbs. The braising process should be fairly slow so that the vegetables are tender throughout. The cooking juices are either reduced or thickened, then poured over the vegetables to serve.

Steaming

This is a good, plain method which gives results similar to boiling. Nutrients are lost from the vegetables by seepage via the steam into the water below. To conserve as much food value as possible steam vegetables over a main dish such as a stew so that the nutrients are retained.

Although a perforated container is usually used, vegetables that require light cooking, such as courgettes, may be steamed in a dish, on a plate over a saucepan of water or wrapped in foil.

The flavour of some vegetables is heightened by steaming rather than boiling. Cauliflower, broccoli and cabbage are all examples.

Frying

Shallow frying, under the guise of sautéing, is a popular method for vegetables that require little cooking. Courgettes are often cooked by this method. The thinly cut vegetables are tossed in a little butter or oil over moderate to high heat.

Deep frying is not a practical way of cooking many vegetables but it is used for potato chips and for making fritters or vegetable croquettes. In the latter case, the portions of vegetable are protected by a coating, such as batter.

Stir Frying

A comparatively modern method for Western cooks, this is suitable for most vegetables. The results are crisp, flavoursome and colourful. Many stir-fried vegetables are ideal for grilled dishes but are not the best accompaniment for casseroles or roasts.

Grilling

This method is not often used for vegetables other than mushrooms or tomatoes. However, courgettes, aubergines and peppers may be grilled.

Roasting

This is a method of cooking prepared vegetables in a little fat in the oven. The classic British roast vegetable is, of course, the potato with its golden, crisp coating and fluffy white centre. Parsnips are roasted in the same way as potatoes, in the same tin as a joint of meat or in a separate tin but coated with dripping from the joint. Potatoes may be roasted from raw or they may be parboiled and floured before being placed in the hot fat and basted. Parsnips may be parboiled and coated in seasoned flour to give a thick, crisp crust around a soft centre; roasting from raw gives a less thick crust and more even texture. Small whole aubergines and peppers may also be roasted in olive oil or butter.

Baking

Unlike roast vegetables, baked vegetables are usually cooked in their skins. The other difference between the cooking method is that baked vegetables are not cooked in fat. Potatoes are probably the most popular example. Aubergines, peppers and squashes, particularly small butternut squash, are all delicious when baked. Even though they are not cooked in fat, the vegetables may be brushed with a little oil to crisp their skins. Whole onions may be baked in their skins until tender, then their soft flesh eaten with butter.

Microwave Cooking

Microwave cooking is excellent for the majority of vegetables, particularly when small to medium quantities are cooked. Consult your handbook for more information. Here are a few reminders:

- Never add salt before cooking.
- Cook vegetables with a small amount of water or liquid.
- Use a covered microwave-proof container or roasting bag, closed loosely to allow steam to escape.
- Arrange tougher areas, such as stalks, towards the outside of a dish, where they receive most energy.
- Turn and rearrange vegetables at least once during cooking.
- Spinach, peas, French beans, cauliflower florets, new potatoes, Jerusalem and globe artichokes are just a few examples of vegetables which cook very well in the microwave.
- Less successful vegetables include celery (unless as part of a dish), old carrots in chunks, large quantities of 'boiled' potatoes – particularly for mashing – and larger quantities of green cabbage.

A GUIDE TO VEGETABLES

Globe

At their best and least expensive during late summer, these are the flower buds of a large thistle. They should be thoroughly washed and drained. Trim off loose leaves around the base of the head. Snip off the ends of the leaves and the top of the head. Place in acidulated water to prevent discoloration and cook promptly in boiling salted water with lemon juice added. Allow 25–45 minutes, depending on size. To check if the artichokes are cooked, pull off one of the base leaves: it should come away easily. Drain well and cool.

Separate the leaves slightly to reveal the group of leaves that form the central part of the artichoke. Pull these out to reveal the 'choke', a cushion of fine hairs

ARTICHOKES

seated in the centre of the vegetable. Use a teaspoon to scrape the choke away carefully, leaving a pad of pale, tender flesh known as the bottom, base or fond. Trim off the stalk so that the artichoke sits neatly and fill the centre with an oil and vinegar dressing or a stuffing.

Like asparagus, artichokes are eaten with the fingers. Each leaf is pulled off individually and the small portion of pale flesh at the base dipped in dressing before being eaten. The rest of the tough leaf is discarded.

Artichoke bottoms (or fonds) are regarded as a delicacy and frequently form the basis of more sophisticated dishes. If only the artichoke bottoms are required, the leaves, chokes and stalks may be removed and the artichoke bottoms carefully peeled before being cooked in boiling water until tender.

Jerusalem

These look like small, knobbly new potatoes, but have a delicate nutty flavour. They should be scrubbed and peeled or cooked with the peel left on. Jerusalem artichokes discolour quickly, so should be placed in acidulated water. Boil them for 10–15 minutes until tender or cook by steaming.

They may be served gratinéed, with a crumb topping, mashed, coated in sauce, tossed in melted butter or sliced and topped with cheese, then grilled. They also make good soup.

Asparagus

Although greengrocers have supplies throughout the year, home-grown asparagus is a summer vegetable, ready in May and June. Look for bright, firm but slim spears that are not woody. On larger spears, make sure that there is a good length of tender green stalk once the tougher end is trimmed. Allow 6–8 spears per portion.

Strip off the woody ends and scrape or peel any remaining tough spear ends. Tie the asparagus in bundles. Cook them in a special asparagus pan or stand them in a saucepan of boiling water, with the tender tips exposed. Tent with foil and simmer for about 15 minutes, or until tender. The tips will steam while the stalks cook in the simmering water.

Alternatively, asparagus may be steamed over boiling water on a rack in a wok or on a wire rack over boiling water in a roasting tin, with the tips towards the outside of the wok or tin so that they do not overcook.

Serve with melted butter poured over. The trimmings may be used to flavour soups or sauces.

Aubergines

Also known as eggplants (in America) and brinjals (in India), these vegetables have pale, tender but firm flesh. The shiny skins are usually purple, although white varieties are also available. They should be firm and shiny outside, with a bright green calyx. Aubergines are cooked in a wide variety of ways: they may be stewed in ratatouille; cubed and grilled on skewers; braised with meat or poultry; roasted and mashed to make a dip; stuffed and baked; sliced, fried and layered with meat in moussaka; or spiced in a variety of Indian or Mediterranean dishes.

Since the flesh can be rather bitter, aubergine flesh should be salted and allowed to stand in a colander or sieve over a bowl for 15–30 minutes before use. This process, which is also sometimes used for cucumbers, is known as *degorging*.

Broad

Available from spring through to autumn, broad beans are best when young and small. Allow about 225 g/8 oz pods per person, selecting firm plump pods with a good green colour. Shrivelled, blackened or largely empty pods are not a good buy. Equally, very large hard pods yield tough old beans.

Shell the beans and cook them in boiling water for 5–15 minutes, depending on their age and your personal taste. Add a sprig of summer savory to the cooking water if liked.

Serve the beans with butter and pepper. They are excellent with diced cooked ham or crisp grilled bacon, or they may be sauced with Hollandaise sauce or soured cream.

French

These require little preparation. Buy bright, firm beans which are not damaged or shrivelled. Trim off their ends and wash them well. Add to a pan of boiling water and cook for 2–10 minutes, depending on size and use. A crunchy result can quickly be achieved if the beans are very slim.

Serve French beans topped with butter or fried breadcrumbs. Chopped hard-boiled egg and chopped parsley is another popular topping.

Lightly cooked and cooled, these beans are good in salads. They may be stir fried.

Runner

These are best freshly picked. It is usually necessary to remove the strings, or trim these beans down both sides, before cooking. Some varieties do not need stringing. Avoid very large beans or any that have shrivelled.

Slice the beans at an angle into long thin pieces, add these to a saucepan of boiling water and cook for 3–10 minutes, depending on taste. About 5 minutes is average; any longer and the beans become soft. Toss with butter and serve freshly cooked.

BEANS

BEAN SPROUTS

These are usually mung beans, although a variety of dried beans may be sprouted. Bean sprouts provide a useful amount of protein and are therefore ideal for adding to vegetable stir fries which contain little meat or fish.

The bean sprouts should be rinsed and drained, then cooked very briefly – stir frying for 3 minutes or less is the best method. The bean sprouts may be added to sauced mixtures and braised for 1–2 minutes, but avoid overcooking them or they will become limp and unpleasant.

BEETROOT

Do not peel raw beetroot before boiling. Simply wash away dirt and twist off the leaves above stalk level. Put the beetroot in a large saucepan with water to cover. Add some salt, if liked. Bring to the boil, lower the heat and simmer, covered, for 45–60 minutes for small to medium young beetroot. Larger, older vegetables can take up to 1½–2 hours to cook but these are not often sold. Beetroot is cooked when it feels tender and the skin rubs off easily.

Drain off the cooking water and replace it with cold water to cover the beetroot. Working under water while the beetroot is still hot, rub off the skins. These should slip off easily with their stalks. Place the peeled beetroot in a dish, cover and leave until cool.

Beetroot may be served hot with fried breadcrumbs and chopped onion. It combines well with other vegetables in hot bakes, or it may be allowed to cool before being used in salads or served with soured cream or fromage frais.

Beetroot may be sliced or preserved whole in vinegar. It is traditionally served with cold roast meats. The uncooked vegetable is also used to make a delicious soup, known as Borsch (page 226).

BROCCOLI

The two main types are sprouting broccoli, with long stalks, a few leaves and small heads in purple or pale green, and calabrese with larger heads and shorter stalks. The stalks on young sprouting broccoli are tender when cooked and may be included as part of the vegetable; discard slightly older stalks.

Broccoli should be washed and trimmed, then broken if the heads are large. Cook in a saucepan of boiling water. Tender young sprouting broccoli cooks quite quickly and it will be tender after 3–5 minutes but larger heads may require 10–15 minutes. Broccoli may also be steamed or stir fried, and makes an excellent soup.

Serve plain with butter or coated with a sauce, such as cheese sauce. Broken into small florets, broccoli may be cooked in a little olive oil with garlic and onion for tossing with pasta and serving with grated Parmesan cheese.

Broccoli is useful as a filling for pies, with chicken or fish, and it also makes a first class pancake filling.

BRUSSELS SPROUTS

This winter vegetable is one of the traditional accompaniments to roast turkey. Look for small firm sprouts which are slightly shiny and green. Avoid very loose, yellowing or insect-nibbled sprouts.

Wash the vegetables thoroughly. Cut a cross in the stalk of larger ones so that they cook evenly. Add to a saucepan of boiling water and cook for 5–10 minutes.

Small, young sprouts may be steamed; halved sprouts may be stir fried. Cooked sprouts may be served plain or tossed with cooked chestnuts (see page 231) or browned blanched almonds.

There are many varieties, the key differences being that they may be hard or loose-packed. The following are some of the varieties most commonly sold in Britain:

White Cabbage
A hard creamy-white to pale green cabbage with tightly packed leaves.

Red Cabbage
Resembles white cabbage but has dark red leaves.

Savoy Cabbage
A large cabbage with a neat firm heart and slightly crinkly leaves.

Winter Cabbage
A term used for cabbage with a firm heart and looser outer leaves, similar to Savoy but without the characteristic crinkly, deeply veined leaves.

Spring Green
The new growth of loose leaves which do not have a heart. There are many cooking methods for cabbage; all types may also be eaten raw. For salads, white and red cabbage are the most popular; they are also ideal for stir frying or braising. Red cabbage is also suitable for pickling in vinegar and white cabbage is traditionally salted to make sauerkraut.

Green cabbages may be boiled, steamed or stir fried. Individual leaves may be blanched until soft, then stuffed and braised. Shredded green cabbage may be blanched, drained, then deep fried and tossed in sugar and soy sauce to be served Chinese style as 'seaweed'.

Wedges of cabbage heart may be steamed or braised. Shredded cabbage may be combined with rice in risottos or added to soups.

To boil cabbage, add the trimmed leaves to the minimum of boiling water. Press them down well. Cover the pan tightly and cook quickly for 3–7 minutes, according to taste. Drain and roughly chop the cabbage before tossing it with butter and pepper.

Steaming times vary according to the method of preparation: if the cabbage is cut in chunks allow up to 15 minutes. Braised cabbage may be cooked for anything from 15 minutes to 1½ hours (for red cabbage cooked with onions and apples).

Young, or baby, carrots have the best flavour. Look out for firm, unblemished carrots, preferably sold in bundles with leaves. If you do buy carrots prepacked in polythene, check that they are not wet from condensation; in damp conditions, they deteriorate very rapidly.

Young carrots do not require peeling; a good scrub or scrape is sufficient. Whether older carrots are peeled or scrubbed is a matter of taste. Small carrots are best cooked whole by boiling or steaming briefly. Medium and large carrots may be halved, quartered, cut in sticks or slices. Boil, steam or stir fry them. To glaze carrots, cut them into fine strips and cook them in a little water with a knob of butter. By the time the carrots are just tender the water should have evaporated, leaving the vegetables coated in a glossy glaze. A little sugar may be added when cooking old carrots. The carrots should be stirred or the pan shaken often to prevent them burning.

Small new carrots take about 5–7 minutes to boil until tender; older carrots take 10–15 minutes, depending on size. Carrots may be cooked for slightly longer, then mashed with swede or potatoes. Well cooked carrots may also be rubbed through a sieve or puréed in a food processor, then enriched with a little butter and cream.

Carrots are an essential flavouring vegetable for soups, stocks and stews. They are also valuable in mince dishes and they make delicious soup. Grated carrot is a useful salad ingredient and this versatile vegetable may also be used in preserves and sweet dishes, such as carrot cake or a lightly spiced Indian dessert. Carrot marmalade was a clever wartime invention as a substitute for orange preserve: the finely cut carrots were flavoured with orange rind and juice and cooked in syrup.

CAULIFLOWER

Green and purple cauliflowers are now available in addition to the more familiar white-headed vegetables, and very small cauliflowers are cultivated as individual portions.

Look for firm, white unblemished vegetables that are neatly packed with a small amount of green leaves. Avoid soft, rubbery cauliflowers or any that have very long stalks and loose heads. Cauliflowers that are not perfectly white are not necessarily inferior in flavour, provided that they are good quality in other respects. It is as well, however, to avoid any that have softening brown patches or have been trimmed.

Cauliflowers may be cooked whole or divided into florets. Boiling, steaming or stir frying are the most common cooking methods. Used raw or briefly blanched, cauliflower florets make very good additions to salads, and they may be coated in cheese-flavoured choux pastry, then deep fried to make delicious savoury fritters.

Overcooked cauliflower is soft, watery and tasteless. About 5–7 minutes is quite sufficient boiling time for florets and a whole cauliflower should not be boiled for more than 10–15 minutes. Steaming is a particularly good cooking method for cauliflower. For florets allow the same time as for boiling; when steaming a whole cauliflower increase the cooking time to 20–30 minutes, depending on size.

Serve cauliflower plain, with a little butter; coated with a cheese sauce; or topped with fried breadcrumbs. Cauliflower is excellent in vegetable curry, it makes good soup (particularly topped with cheese) or it may be puréed and enriched with cream or fromage frais.

CELERIAC

This is a cream-coloured root vegetable, about the same size as a swede and with a similarly thick skin. It has a delicate flavour reminiscent of celery. To prepare celeriac, peel and trim it, then plunge it straight into a bowl of acidulated water as it discolours quickly.

Cut celeriac into neat cubes or sticks and cook in a saucepan of boiling water until tender, about 8–10 minutes for small pieces. If preferred, the vegetable may be cut into large chunks and boiled for 15–20 minutes, then mashed with butter and pepper. Boiling is a better option than steaming, although finely cut celeriac may be steamed in packets of mixed vegetables or used as a flavouring for fish and poultry.

Celeriac may also be served raw, usually coarsely grated or finely shredded. If adding it to long-cooked soups and stews, put it in towards the end of the cooking time or it may become very soft. It also makes good soup. Plain cooked celeriac (in chunks or slices) is delicious coated with cheese sauce.

CELERY

A versatile vegetable for serving raw or cooked, or using as a flavouring ingredient. Look for firm, unblemished heads of celery with leaves that are bright and crisp. Stalks with large ribs may be stringy. Trimmed celery hearts are also available for braising whole. Canned celery hearts are a useful storecupboard standby for wrapping in cooked ham and coating in cheese sauce as a supper dish.

The top of the head and stalk ends should be cut off but not discarded. The leaves and stalk tops may be used as part of a bouquet garni or they may be reserved for garnish. Cut up small, they are perfectly good in salads, soups and stews, as are the chopped stalks.

Remove stalks from the celery as required, scrub them well and cut off any blemished parts. Slice the celery or cut it into lengths for cooking. If a recipe calls for diced or chopped celery, cut the stalks into thin strips lengthways before slicing them across into small pieces. Cut into very thin strips, about 5 cm/2 inches long, then soaked for about 30 minutes in iced water, celery is excellent in salads.

Serve lengths of raw celery with dips or cheese. Braise lengths or hearts with a small amount of sautéed onion and diced carrot in a little stock or wine. Cook for about 40–60 minutes, depending on size and age, until the celery is tender. The cooking juices may be thickened with beurre manié to serve as a sauce.

Stir frying is a good cooking method for celery. The sticks should be sliced thinly or cut into fine strips. Slicing at an angle is an Oriental technique which is popular for stir fries.

Celery may also be cooked by boiling and steaming. Boil for 10–20 minutes, depending on size and age; or allow up to 30 minutes' steaming time.

CHICORY

Small oval heads of pale, closely packed leaves tipped with yellow, chicory has a slightly bitter flavour. It may be used raw in salads or braised until tender.

Trim off the stalk end of each head and wash well. Cut the head across into slices for mixing into salads or separate the leaves and use them as a base for serving a variety of dishes. The whole leaves may also be served with dips.

Chicory may be boiled in a saucepan of acidulated water until tender – about 15–20 minutes – but the preferred cooking method is braising. Cook a small amount of finely chopped onion in butter or oil, then turn the chicory heads in the fat. Pour in stock or wine to come about a third to halfway up the heads. Cover and braise for 30–60 minutes depending on the size of the chicory heads, until tender throughout. Turn once or twice. The cooking juices may be thickened and poured over the chicory heads.

The American name for chicory is endive.

CHINESE LEAVES

Also known as Chinese cabbage. A tall, fairly loosely packed vegetable consisting mainly of tender crunchy stalks edged by pale green-yellow leaves. The vegetable has a mild, cabbage-like flavour. It may be shredded for use in salads or stir fries. Thicker slices may be added to sauced dishes, usually well-seasoned Chinese braised mixtures, and cooked very briefly.

Overcooking gives limp, tasteless results.

COURGETTES

Both green and yellow varieties are available. Look for firm, unblemished vegetables. Trim off the ends and peel the courgettes if liked, although they may be cooked with the peel on. Cut courgettes into slices, chunks or sticks, or grate them. They may be halved and baked with a topping, or their centres scooped out and a stuffing added.

Basic cooking methods include steaming, braising, baking, sautéing, stir frying and shallow frying. Although courgettes may be boiled, this cooking method does not do them justice as even brief boiling tends to oversoften the delicate flesh. Coated in batter or breadcrumbs, courgettes are also delicious deep fried. In Italy and America, where the vegetable is known as zucchini, the flowers are regarded as a delicacy and are frequently coated in light batter and deep fried.

For steaming, wrap sliced courgettes in foil; cook for about 10 minutes. Sautéing and stir frying are excellent methods. Thinly cut vegetables require 2–5 minutes. Baking is a practical method when the courgettes are served with a baked dish; simply dot them with butter, sprinkle them with salt and pepper and cook in a covered dish for 15–30 minutes at 180°C/350°F/gas 4. Braise courgettes with onions and tomatoes or other vegetables, allowing about 20 minutes' cooking, or up to 45 minutes depending on the way in which the vegetables are cut and the other ingredients.

CUCUMBER

Although they are usually eaten raw in salads, cucumbers are also good braised. Buy firm, bright green medium-sized cucumbers. Avoid any which have very dark, thick-looking skins, as these may have large seeds, poor texture and a strong unacceptable flavour.

Cucumbers may be peeled, partially peeled or served with the peel on for salads. The classic preparation is to slice the cucumber very thinly, sprinkle it with a little salt and allow it to drain in a colander for 10 minutes before use. This extracts the excess liquid from the vegetable. Having been prepared in this way, the cucumber slices may be rinsed, dried on absorbent kitchen paper and used to make delicious sandwiches. They may also be topped with a little chopped mint or snipped chives for serving as a plain salad. An oil and vinegar dressing, or cider vinegar, are classic additions.

Grated or diced cucumber may be mixed with plain yogurt to make a dip or side dish for spicy food. Add garlic and a little chopped onion to make tzatziki, a Greek starter served with plenty of crusty bread.

Peel cucumber before cooking, then cut it into 5 cm/2 inch lengths. The seeds are usually scooped out. Braise trimmed cucumber in stock for about 20 minutes. Dill or mint may be added before serving and the sauce may be enriched with soured cream. Sticks of cucumber may be stir fried briefly.

ENDIVE

This resembles a curly lettuce. It has firm leaves which are usually pale yellow-green with darker green tips. To prepare endive, trim off the stalk, wash well and use in salads. The American term for endive is chicory.

FENNEL

Florence fennel is a bulbous vegetable with a texture like that of celery and an aniseed flavour. There are usually a few fronds of feathery leaves attached to the trimmed stalks at the top of the bulbs — these may be reserved for garnishing or used in cooking.

Trim away tough stalk ends, then thoroughly wash and slice fennel for use in salads. Fennel discolours easily when cut, so always use a stainless steel knife and use the vegetable as soon as possible after cutting. The bulbs may be braised as for celery, either whole or as halves and cook in about 1–1¼ hours.

KOHLRABI

This is the swollen stem of a member of the cabbage family. It has a flavour slightly similar to swede. Either purple or green skinned, and ranging in size from that of a large potato to a small swede, kohlrabi may be served raw or cooked.

Peel the vegetable and place it in a bowl of acidulated water. For serving raw, kohlrabi should be grated or cut into small pieces. Small kohlrabi may be boiled whole; larger vegetables should be sliced or cut into chunks. Cook in boiling water for 15–45 minutes or until tender. Follow the longer time if cooking kohlrabi whole.

Sticks of kohlrabi may be stir fried with other vegetables, such as leeks or onions. Diced or cubed kohlrabi may be added to soups, stews or casseroles.

LEEKS

These vary considerably in size. Look for firm, well-formed vegetables with a good ratio of white to green. Trim off the ends and slice, then wash in a colander, separating the slices into rings. Alternatively, slit the leeks three-quarters through down their length, then open each one out and hold it under cold running water to wash away all the grit.

Leeks may be boiled, steamed, fried, stewed, braised or baked. Allow 10–20 minutes for boiling or steaming, the longer time for large lengths or small whole vegetables. Drain well and serve coated with cheese sauce. Alternatively, top with grated cheese and breadcrumbs and grill until brown.

Fry sliced leeks in butter until tender but not soft – about 15 minutes – or stir fry them with other vegetables. Add leeks to soups and stews or use them to flavour stocks.

LETTUCE

There is a wide variety of lettuces on offer all year. These are the most common types:

Round
The traditional British salad leaf; a loosely packed bright vegetable with a small heart. Flavour and texture are not particularly interesting.

Cos Lettuce
A tall, dark-leafed lettuce with crisp firm leaves and a good flavour.

Webb's Wonderful
A round lettuce with slightly wrinkled, crisp dark leaves, and a firm heart.

Iceberg
A tightly packed, pale green lettuce with very crisp leaves and a good flavour.

Lamb's Lettuce
Small oval-leafed plants, resembling immature round lettuce but darker.

Lollo Rosso/Lollo Biondo
A frilly, firm-textured lettuce which is loosely packed. The lollo rosso variety has dark leaves fringed with deep red, whereas the biondo type has pale-edged leaves.

Wash all lettuce well and discard any tough or damaged stalks. It is traditional to shred lettuce by hand rather than to cut it with a knife, but this is a matter for personal taste. Never prepare lettuce a long time before serving.

Although lettuce is usually served raw, it is also delicious braised with a little finely chopped onion in stock or wine. Fresh peas braised with lettuce is a classic French dish. Allow about 30 minutes' gentle cooking in a small amount of liquid and use a covered pan or dish.

MARROW

From the same family as courgettes and pumpkin, marrow has a tough skin and soft, fibrous centre with lots of seeds surrounded by firm flesh. Cut the vegetable in half or slice it into rings, then remove the soft flesh and seeds before peeling thickly.

Marrow may be baked, braised, steamed, stir fried or boiled, the latter being the least interesting cooking method. Overcooked marrow is watery and mushy, particularly when boiled. Baking or braising with onions and herbs are the best methods. Chunks of marrow (about 5 cm/2 inches in size) take about 40 minutes to bake at 180°C/350°F/gas 4, depending on the other ingredients added. They may also be braised for about 30 minutes with onions and herbs, either in their own juice or with the addition of tomatoes or a little wine or cider.

Stuffings for marrow range from meat mixtures to rice or breadcrumb fillings. Rings or halves may be stuffed, or the vegetable may be laid on its side and a thick slice removed from the top as a lid. The hollowed-out marrow may then be stuffed and the 'lid' replaced. Bake the stuffed marrow until tender, then remove the 'lid' to allow the stuffing to brown. At 180°C/350°F/gas 4, a medium-sized whole marrow will require 1¼–1½ hours to bake, whereas stuffed rings cook in 45 minutes–1½ hours, depending on size and filling.

Marrow may also be used as a key ingredient for making chutney. It is usually combined with fruit, such as apples, and lots of onions for flavour. It may also be cooked with ginger and used to add bulk to jam.

MOOLI

See Radish.

MUSHROOMS

Most of the mushrooms available in greengrocers and supermarkets are the same variety, differing only in the stage of development at which they have been harvested. Fully open or flat mushrooms traditionally known as field mushrooms are the most mature. They may be recognized by their dark gills and large heads. Flat mushrooms have good flavour but tend to discolour dishes to which they are added, so are usually used for grilling and stuffing.

Wild mushrooms are a separate issue from cultivated varieties. Before they are gathered, a specialist source of information should be consulted to avoid any danger of consuming a poisonous species. Some specialist stores sell wild mushrooms but they are most commonly available dried from delicatessens.

Cultivated mushrooms do not require peeling. Trim tough stalks from shiitake or oyster mushrooms. Rinse mushrooms, gills down under slowly running cold water, rubbing them gently. Alternatively, simply wipe them with dampened absorbent kitchen paper. Never leave mushrooms to soak as they will absorb water, ruining both texture and flavour.

Mushrooms may be brushed with a little fat and grilled, flat or on skewers. They may also be poached in a little milk, stock or wine for a few minutes. Alternatively, whole or cut-up mushrooms may be shallow fried or stir fried in oil or butter, either whole or cut up. Coated with egg and breadcrumbs, dipped in choux pastry or batter, button mushrooms are delicious deep fried. They are also excellent baked – particularly when topped with breadcrumbs and cheese.

For frying or poaching, allow about 5–15 minutes' cooking time. Allow 15–30 minutes for baking, depending on the topping or stuffing. Grill mushrooms briefly for about 5 minutes, gills uppermost.

Pale mushrooms may be added to sauces and soups; all types are suitable for flavouring stews, the choice depending on the colour of the stew.

Cup mushrooms or open mushrooms are slightly paler in colour and they have a lip around the edge. Useful for stuffing.

Button mushrooms may be fully closed or partially closed, with little of the gill area showing. They vary in size; very small buttons are perfect for adding whole to casseroles and sauces. Button mushrooms are ideal for sauces and pale dishes which require a delicate colour and flavour.

In addition to the grades of cultivated mushroom described above, at least three other types of fresh mushroom are commonly available.

Chestnut mushrooms have a darker skin than ordinary mushrooms and a more pronounced flavour. They are usually sold as large buttons.

Oyster mushrooms are flat and pale creamy-yellow in colour with a soft texture and delicate flavour. They break easily and require very little cooking.

Shiitake are strongly flavoured mushrooms from China and Japan. They are popular in Oriental cooking. They are usually sold dried in delicatessens and Oriental super-markets, when their flavour is very pronounced, but are also available fresh. The fresh mushrooms are darker than cultivated British field mushrooms and they tend to have a firmer, slightly more rubbery texture.

OKRA

Also known as ladies' fingers, these pale green ridged pods vary in size, the smaller ones being the most tender. Look for unblemished whole vegetables with the stalks intact. Trim off the stalk ends and wash well. The okra pods may be cooked whole or sliced before cooking. Do not prepare the vegetable too far in advance of cooking as slices may discolour.

Okra contains a gum-like substance that seeps out of the pods during long cooking to thicken stews and braised dishes. Typical dishes with okra include *gumbo*, a classic Creole stew, and spiced okra with onions, which is often served as a side dish in Indian restaurants. Okra may also be stuffed and braised or baked.

Cooking times for okra should either be brief, using fierce heat, or long enough to tenderize the pods. Sliced okra may be coated in flour and seasonings or spices, then shallow or deep fried for a few minutes until browned. Slices may also be braised briefly or added to casseroles and stews towards the end of cooking; however, the vegetable quickly becomes slimy when sliced and long-cooked by moist methods. Whole pods may be braised with onions, tomatoes and garlic until tender – about 15–30 minutes, depending on the size and age of the pods.

ONIONS

Large Spanish onions are the mildest variety. These are ideal for boiling whole and serving with butter or a sauce, or for stuffing. The medium-sized common onions, most often used in cooking, are stronger in flavour. Small, pickling or button onions have a strong flavour. They may be boiled and coated with sauce or peeled and added whole to casseroles. Cocktail, or silverskin, onions are tiny. They are some-times available fresh but are most often sold pickled in vinegar. Spring- or salad onions have not formed bulbs. They have a dense white base leading to hollow green ends. Once trimmed, the whole of the onion may be used raw or in cooking. Shallots and Welsh onions are small onions. Each shallot consists of two or three cloves, similar in shape to garlic cloves, clumped together inside the papery skin. They are mild in flavour and may be peeled and chopped or used whole. The tops from fresh young shallots may also be used in cooking, rather like chives.

Onions are often fried briefly as a preliminary cooking stage in more complicated dishes. The aim is to soften the onion but not brown it, and the cooking process will only be completed when the onion has been incorporated with other ingredients and cooked until tender. Browning onions by frying requires significantly longer cooking, depending on the number cooked. Onions shrink significantly when fried until brown, and this should be done over moderate heat, turning occasionally, for about 20–30 minutes until the onions are golden and evenly cooked. If fried by this method they will be tender and flavoursome. Onions that are browned quickly over too high a heat will not be cooked through, but simply scorched outside.

Onions may also be boiled or steamed. Allow 30 minutes for small onions or up to 1¼ hours for large ones. Large onions may be baked whole, washed but unpeeled, until very tender, then split and filled or topped with butter.

PARSNIPS

Look for firm, unblemished parsnips. To prepare them, peel, then cut them in half, in chunks or slices. They may be boiled, steamed or roasted.

Chunks of parsnip will be tender when boiled for 10 minutes; larger pieces require about 20 minutes. When tender, drain well and serve with a soured cream sauce, or mash with butter and pepper.

To roast whole parsnips arrange them around a joint of meat or in a separate dish and brush with fat. Allow about 45 minutes–1¼ hours at 180–190°C/ 350–375°F/gas 4–5, until tender and golden.

Parsnips are delicious in mixed vegetable curry and may also be added to soups and stews. Parsnip fritters may be made by coating par-boiled vegetables in batter and deep frying them until golden.

PEAS

Fresh peas are in season from May to September. Look for bright, fresh plump pods. The peas inside should not be bullet-hard nor very large as they can become very dry in texture and particularly dull in flavour. Allow about 350–400 g/12–14 oz per person as a good deal of weight is lost to the pods.

Split the pods over a colander and slide the peas out using a fingertip. Wash well, then add to a small amount of just boiling water. Cook for 7–10 minutes, until the peas are tender. Alternatively, peas may be steamed for 15–20 minutes. It is traditional to add a sprig of mint to the water when cooking peas which are to be served with lamb.

Mange Tout

The name means 'eat all', a fitting description. Mange tout are flat pea pods with tiny peas just forming inside. The entire pod is edible, excluding the stalk, which is trimmed. Mange tout may be cooked in boiling water for 2–3 minutes, or steamed for up to 5 minutes, but are at their best when stir fried for 3–5 minutes.

Sugar Snaps

These are small peas enclosed in edible pods. They have an excellent flavour. Everything is edible except the stalk, which should be trimmed. Cook sugar snaps in a saucepan of boiling water for 3–5 minutes, or by steaming for about 5 minutes. They are a more substantial and flavoursome vegetable than mange tout.

PEPPERS

Large sweet or bell peppers come from the capsicum family. They are also known as pimento (or pimientos when bottled). The most common type is the green pepper, which changes colour as it ripens, first to yellow and then to red. A variety of other colours is also available, including white and purple-black.

To prepare a pepper, remove the stalk end and cut out the core from the inside. Discard the ribs, pith and seeds. The pepper shell may then be rinsed free of seeds and drained.

Peppers are used in a variety of ways: they may be eaten raw in salads or crudités; lightly cooked in stir fries; stuffed and baked or braised; grilled on skewers; or stewed slowly with meat, poultry or other vegetables.

When raw they have a crunchy texture and fresh flavour, but when cooked they soften and their flavour mellows. Some salad recipes require peppers to be charred, then skinned.

POTATOES

These may be loosely divided into new and old, the former being the thin-skinned, spring crop for immediate consumption and the latter being the second crop of thicker-skinned potatoes grown for winter storage. The choice is always changing, with imported varieties and new strains constantly being developed.

Avoid buying or eating potatoes that have turned green. Cut out any eyes and sprouting areas from potatoes in preparation. Store potatoes in a cool, dry place in thick brown paper bags that exclude all light.

Although new potatoes are now available all year, Jerseys are the traditional 'first' new potatoes in the shops. Imported early in the year, from Christmas or even before, these have a fine flavour but are expensive. Small, waxy and firm, they are ideal for steaming or boiling. Small, waxy 'salad' potatoes are also available all year at a price.

The following are good all round, old potatoes for boiling, mashing, baking and frying: King Edward, Redskin, Maris Piper, Pentland Hawk, Pentland Ivory and Desirée. Majestic tend to break up easily when boiled, so they are better for baking and frying. Pentland Squire are floury and good for baking, as are Cara, because they are large and even in size and shape.

Boiling

Peel the potatoes, if liked, or scrub them well. Remove all eyes and blemishes and any green areas. Cut large potatoes in half or into quarters and place in a saucepan. Cover with cold water, add salt if wished, and bring to the boil. Reduce the heat, partly cover the pan and cook for about 20 minutes. Small chunks cook in about 10–15 minutes (useful for mashing); larger, unpeeled, potatoes take somewhat longer. New potatoes cook more quickly, in 10–15 minutes.

Baking

An easy cooking method, this is discussed, with serving suggestions, on page 212. Floury potatoes – the sort that do not boil well – give best results for baking. Scrub the potatoes well and prick them all over to prevent them from bursting. Potatoes may be brushed with oil if wished. Sliced potatoes may be baked with butter, cheese, cream or stock, as for Potatoes Savoyarde (page 363).

Roasting

Peeled potatoes, cut in halves or quarters, may either be roasted from raw or parboiled for 5–10 minutes, dusted with plain flour, and then added to the hot fat in the roasting tin. They should be coated in hot fat and turned once or twice during cooking. For crisp results, raw potatoes will take 1–1½ hours, depending on the size of the potatoes and the oven temperature. Parboiled potatoes require about 1 hour at 190°C/375°F/gas 5.

Chipped Potatoes

Cut the thoroughly scrubbed, or washed and peeled, potatoes into thick fingers and deep fry in oil at 190°C/375°F until just beginning to brown. Lift the chips out of the oil and drain them well. Bring the oil back to the original cooking temperature. Lower the chips into the oil again and cook for a couple of minutes more, until crisp and golden. Drain well on absorbent kitchen paper and serve at once.

Fried Potatoes

Cold boiled potatoes, cut into chunks or slices, are delicious when shallow fried until crisp and golden.

PUMPKIN

Pumpkin belongs to the same family as marrow. Pumpkins vary enormously in size. Small ones may be sold whole, but you are more likely to encounter wedges cut from a large vegetable.

The central soft core of seeds should be removed and the orange-coloured flesh thickly peeled. The flesh is firmer than marrow and is delicious roasted, baked or braised with onions, herbs and bacon and a cheese topping for about an hour. Pumpkin may also be boiled and mashed or steamed for 30–45 minutes and puréed for use in savoury and sweet dishes, particularly the American sweet and spicy pumpkin pie. Pumpkin also makes good soup.

RADISHES

These are usually eaten raw in salads or as crudités; however, large white radishes are also combined with other ingredients in stir fries and steamed Oriental-style dishes.

Small round red radishes are the most common, but the long white radish known as mooli or daikon (in Japanese cooking) is becoming increasingly popular. Red radishes require no preparation other than washing, topping and tailing. Large white radishes must be peeled. Very large, old white radishes can be fibrous, stringy and unpleasant even when cut finely.

SALSIFY AND SCORZONERA

These root vegetables are in season from October to May. Salsify is a creamy colour and scorzonera is black. Although both have a delicate flavour, scorzonera is considered to be salsify's superior.

Do not use a carbon steel knife to prepare these vegetables and cook them as soon as possible after preparation, or they may discolour. The moment the vegetables have been trimmed and peeled, put them into acidulated water. To cook, cut into lengths or fingers and add to a saucepan of salted boiling water to which a little lemon juice has been added. Cook for 20–30 minutes, or until tender. Drain and serve with butter or with a coating sauce such as Béchamel or Hollandaise.

Salsify or scorzonera which is three-quarters cooked by boiling, may be drained and fried in butter before serving or coated in a light batter and deep fried to make fritters.

SEAKALE

Resembling celery stalks surrounded by dark green, tough, frilly leaves, seakale grows wild on the beaches of South East England between December and May and is also found in Western Europe. Although it is also cultivated, it is seldom available in the shops. To prepare seakale, wash it thoroughly and trim off the thick, tough stalk. It should be freshly cooked in a small amount of boiling water for about 15 minutes, or until tender, then thoroughly drained and used like spinach.

SORREL

Sorrel is used both as a vegetable and a herb. There are many varieties, some quite bitter. It should be treated as spinach, with a little sugar added to taste during cooking to counteract the natural acidity.

SPINACH

There are winter and summer varieties of this versatile, easy-to-cook vegetable. Since it shrinks considerably on cooking, allow about 225 g/8 oz fresh spinach per portion.

Wash the leaves well and trim off any tough stalk ends. Pack the wet leaves into a large saucepan and cover with a tight-fitting lid. Place over moderate to high heat and cook for about 3 minutes, shaking the pan often, until the spinach has wilted. Lower the heat slightly, if necessary, and cook for 3–5 minutes more, or until the spinach is tender. Drain well in a sieve, squeezing out all the liquid if the vegetable is to be chopped.

Serve spinach tossed with butter and pepper or a little nutmeg. It may be used in a variety of pasta dishes, pies, quiches, soufflés and soups. Spinach is delicious topped with scrambled or poached eggs, poached fish or grilled chicken.

SQUASHES

Squash is an American term applied to marrow and a wide variety of vegetables of the same family. Availability in Britain and Europe is somewhat unpredictable; however these are a few of the main types:

Butternut Squash
A small vegetable with pale, beige-peach coloured skin and deep orange-coloured flesh. The halved vegetable has a small central hollow for seeds, so that it resembles a large avocado. The whole or halved squash is usually baked or roasted.

Crookneck
This is a large, rough-skinned, long-bodied yellow squash. As its name suggests it has a long narrow, curved neck. The flesh may be treated as marrow.

Custard Marrow
A pale, flat, fluted squash.

Hubbard Squash
A melon-shaped gourd with rough green skin, this may be treated as marrow once peeled.

Spaghetti Squash
Oval, yellow-skinned squash about the size of a large yellow melon. It gets its name from the flesh, which resembles spaghetti when cooked. The squash should be boiled or steamed whole, or halved and wrapped in foil, for 20–50 minutes, depending on size. When cooked, halve the squash if necessary, discard the seeds from the middle and use a fork to scoop out the strands of flesh. These are at their best when still slightly crunchy. They have plenty of flavour and are delicious topped with butter and cheese or any sauce suitable for pasta.

SWEDES

Large, inexpensive root vegetables with thick skin and pale orange flesh. Wash, trim and peel thickly, then cut into chunks for cooking. Boil for 20–30 minutes, or until tender, then drain thoroughly and mash with butter and pepper. This is the traditional accompaniment for haggis. Swedes may also be mashed with carrots or potatoes.

The diced vegetable is excellent in soups and stews. Puréed cooked swede may be used in soufflé mixtures.

SWEETCORN

Corn cobs are surrounded by silky threads and an outer covering of leafy husks, which must be removed before cooking unless the corn is to be cooked on a barbecue. The kernels are pale when raw, becoming a more intense yellow colour on cooking.

Place the corn cobs in a pan with water to cover and bring to the boil. Do not add salt as this toughens the kernels. Simmer for about 10 minutes, or until the corn kernels are tender and come away easily from the cob. Drain well and serve topped with a little butter. Corn holders – pronged utensils inserted at either end of the cob – make it possible to eat these tasty vegetables without burning your fingers.

For using in salads or other dishes, the cooked kernels may be scraped off the cobs using a kitchen knife. It is usually simpler, however, to use frozen or canned sweetcorn kernels, both of which are of excellent quality.

Whole cobs may be baked in their husks or barbecued. Carefully fold back the husks and remove the silky threads, then wash well and drain. Fold the husks back over the corn. Cook over medium coals or roast in the oven at 190°C/375°F/gas 5 for about 40 minutes, or until the kernels are tender.

SWEET POTATOES

In spite of their name, these are not potatoes at all, but are red-skinned, large vegetables with pale orange flesh and a slightly sweet flavour.

Sweet potatoes may be baked or boiled in their skins. To boil, allow about 30–40 minutes, depending on size. Bake as for ordinary potatoes (page 212). Once cooked, peel and cut into cubes, then toss with butter and a little nutmeg. Alternatively, mash with butter and nutmeg or a little mace.

Sweet potatoes are used in a variety of sweet and savoury dishes.

SWISS CHARD

The leaves of this vegetable may be cooked exactly as for spinach, giving very similar results. The tender stalks, which resemble thin, wide celery sticks, are delicious when lightly cooked in boiling water and served with butter. Allow about 5 minutes to cook tender stalks. Serve them as a separate vegetable or starter, perhaps with Hollandaise or with some grated Parmesan cheese.

TOMATOES

Although tomatoes are technically fruit, they are used as a vegetable. Of the many varieties available, all may be used raw and many are ideal for cooking. Freshly picked sun-ripened tomatoes are delicious, but it is worth investigating some of the other forms.

Canned tomatoes, whole or chopped, are an invaluable storecupboard item, while sun-dried tomatoes make a useful contribution to a wide variety of dishes. Packed in oil, or sold in packets ready to be reconstituted in a sauce or marinade, sun-dried tomatoes are relatively expensive but have a concentrated flavour.

Cherry Tomatoes
Very small tomatoes, these can have an excellent sweet flavour when ripe.

However, some purchased tomatoes can be sharp and lacking in flavour. Cherry tomatoes are ideal for salads or for skewering with other ingredients for kebabs.

Marmande, Beef or Beefsteak Tomatoes

Very large tomatoes that are ideal for stuffing. They should be a good deep red when ripe. Sun-ripened large tomatoes have an outstanding flavour. Sadly this is seldom found in purchased fruit, which is usually picked well before it is ripe.

Plum Tomatoes

Deep red, oval, small to medium-sized fruit. Plum tomatoes have a good flavour and are valued for cooking and as the prime ingredient in tomato purée. They are also good in salads.

Yellow Tomatoes

Large or cherry-sized, these tomatoes are sweet when ripe but can lack flavour when picked too early. They should be a rich yellow colour. Used mainly raw, yellow tomatoes may be cooked with yellow peppers, yellow courgettes and white aubergines in a pale version of ratatouille.

Cooking methods for tomatoes include grilling and frying. They are usually cut in half – or in slices for speed – and are traditionally served with grilled meat or fish, mixed grill or as part of a traditional cooked breakfast. Grilled or fried tomatoes on toast make a good snack or light meal.

Baked tomatoes are usually scooped out and filled with a rice- or breadcrumb-based stuffing or a minced meat mixture.

TURNIPS

Small, round summer turnips have delicate flavour. They are ideal for cooking whole and serving as a vegetable accompaniment. Tender young turnips may also be grated for use in salads. Larger main crop turnips are better suited to dicing or cutting into chunks and using in soups and stews or casseroles.

To prepare turnips, trim off the ends and remove the peel; small young vegetables need only be peeled thinly. Cook small whole turnips in a saucepan of boiling acidulated water for about 15 minutes, or until tender. Drain well and toss with butter and parsley or serve generously coated with cheese, Béchamel or Hollandaise sauce.

Larger turnips may be boiled, drained and mashed or puréed. Matchstick sticks of turnip are suitable for stir frying or baking in foil with parsnips and carrots cut to a similar size. Small, young turnips may also be parboiled, then glazed with the minimum of liquid and a little butter as for carrots.

The leaves of fresh young turnips may be trimmed from their stalks and cooked as for cabbage.

YAMS These tubers resemble large potatoes, with white, floury flesh. Scrub and boil yams in their skin.

There are a number of vegetables available which belong to the yam and cassava family, including small dark and hairy eddoes. These vegetables must not be eaten raw as they contain natural toxins: in fact, prepared cassava should be soaked in water for about 30 minutes before cooking.

NOTE

More information and methods of cooking, including microwave instructions are listed, where appropriate, under individual recipes.

BEANS AND PULSES

Whether you prepare them yourself, or save time by using a canned variety, beans and pulses are nutritious and inexpensive. In many diets they are a valued protein food (along with most nuts and some seeds) and soya beans in particular compare well with animal foods (fish, poultry, meat and dairy produce) as a source of protein. Tofu, or bean curd, is produced from soya beans, so it too is a valuable protein food, especially in a vegetarian diet.

As well as their essential role in a vegetarian diet, beans and pulses feature in many traditional meat and poultry soups and stews. They are also used extensively in ethnic cooking, often to extend small amounts of more expensive meat or to balance spicy seasonings.

Apart from hot dishes, the cooked pulses are used to make tempting dips. Puréed and combined with other ingredients, they may be formed into patties or loaves to serve hot and cold, for main meals, picnics, buffets and nutritious snacks.

SOYA MILK Soya milk, as its name suggests, is produced from soya beans. Available in long-life packs, it may be used instead of cow's milk in drinks, on cereals and in cooking. It is a useful product for anyone who is allergic to dairy produce as it gives excellent results and its flavour is very mild, making it an ideal substitute for cow's milk in sauces, custards and so on. Soya milk is not as rich as whole cow's milk, so results may be slightly 'weaker', as with skimmed milk.

COOKING BEANS AND PULSES The majority of dried beans and pulses should be soaked for several hours or overnight before cooking. Lentils and many brands of dried peas do not require soaking before cooking; however, the following notes apply to other pulses.

- Rinse the pulses, then leave them in plenty of cold water to soak, preferably in a cool place and never for longer than 24 hours.
- Drain, then transfer to a large saucepan and cover with fresh cold water.
- Do not add salt – this toughens the pulses if added before they are thoroughly tender, and they cannot be tenderized once seasoned.
- Bring to the boil and boil rapidly for 10 minutes. This is important as it destroys natural toxins in the pulses.

- Lower the heat, cover and keep the water just boiling.
- The cooking time varies but is usually between 40–60 minutes. Some pulses take longer, up to 1½ hours, and soya beans take 2½ hours or slightly longer.
- Make sure the pulses are covered with water all the time they cook. Drain when tender and use as required.
- When pulses are parboiled, then added to a stew to finish cooking, the stew must not be highly salted or the pulses will toughen.
- Pulses may be added to soups for cooking after the initial boiling period.

Pressure cooking

The pressure cooker is excellent for cooking dried beans and pulses. First soak the beans in boiling water, allowing 15 minutes for aduki beans, butter beans, mung beans or similar; 1 hour for kidney beans, soya beans or yellow split peas; and 2–3 hours for chick peas. Drain and put in the pressure cooker with plenty of water to cover. Cook at 15 lb pressure, allowing 12–15 minutes for aduki, mung and kidney beans, and split peas; chick peas and soya beans take about 15 minutes. Lentils cook without soaking in 8 minutes.

Microwave cooking

Not an ideal method for pulses which require large quantities of cooking liquid; however, lentils cook well in the microwave, particularly the red type which absorb all the cooking liquid. A quantity of 225 g/8 oz lentils will take about 15–20 minutes to cook.

Aduki Small, round red beans with a nutty flavour. Cooking time: 30 minutes.
Black-eyed Beans Small kidney-shaped whole beans with a prominent black spot. Cooking time: 30 minutes.
Borlotti Beans Mottled pink beans, often used in Italian cooking. Cooking time: 45 minutes.
Brown Beans Medium, oval beans, often used in Mediterranean cuisines. Cooking time: 30 minutes.
Butter Beans Large white beans which cook comparatively quickly when soaked and become mushy if overcooked. Cooking time: 40 minutes.
Chick-peas Also known as garbanzos. They resemble small, light brown nuts and have an affinity for spices. Cooking time: 1 hour.
Flageolet Beans Small, oval, pale green beans with a delicate flavour. Cooking time: 30 minutes.
Haricot Beans There are many varieties and sizes, but the name is generally used for small, oval white beans. Cooking time: 40 minutes.
Lentils Several different varieties are available. Unlike most other pulses, lentils do not need to be soaked before being cooked. Cooking time: 20–45 minutes.

TYPES OF BEANS AND PULSES

Peas Dried green peas are not as popular as they once were, but make a tasty soup or purée, especially when flavoured with onion and bacon or ham. Cooking time: 35–45 minutes.

Pinto Beans Mottled, pink beans often confused with borlotti beans from the same family. Cooking time: 40 minutes.

Processed Peas Bright green in colour and slightly sweet, they are usually sold in cans. Mushy peas are processed marrowfat peas.

Red Kidney Beans Dark red, oval beans, an essential ingredient of Chilli con Carne. Also delicious when cooked with Indian spices, onions and tomatoes. Cooking time: 50 minutes.

Soya Beans Creamy-beige small beans, rounded in shape. They require long soaking and cooking. Highly nutritious. Cooking time: 2–2½ hours.

Split Peas The basis of pea soup and pease pudding. They require less cooking time than whole dried peas. Although both yellow and green varieties are available, the former are most widely used. Like split lentils, they lose their shape when cooked. Cooking time: 20 minutes.

RICE, CEREALS AND OTHER GRAINS

Rice, grains and cereals have had an enormous impact on savoury dishes in the British diet as there has been a move away from traditional meat-and-two-veg meals. These ingredients make a wide variety of dishes, from traditional kedgeree to polenta and buttery gnocchi.

TYPES OF RICE

There are many types available in most good supermarkets and even more on offer in specialist stores.

Long-grain White Rice The most basic rice, found even in the smallest shop. White rice has had all the outer husk removed to leave white grains. Price is a good indication of quality, with some very cheap packets holding broken grains.

Easy-cook Rice There are many brands of easy-cook rice, both white and brown. This type of rice has been treated and partially cooked. The grains cook quickly and remain separate and whole. Always follow the packet instructions closely.

Pudding Rice Also known as short-grain or round-grain rice, pudding rice is an unprocessed grain which breaks down when cooked in milk to give a soft, creamy result (see also page 373).

Brown Rice Brown rice retains some of the outer covering on the grain. The types vary according to the brand; the cooking time varies too. Brown rice usually takes nominally longer to cook than white rice; however overcooking is a common fault with this grain. When cooked, brown rice should be nutty in flavour and slightly chewy (not soft). The grains should be separate – more so than with a fluffy white rice (such as Basmati). Brown rice is overcooked if the grains have burst and softened.

Basmati Rice Both brown and white are now available, the latter being more traditional and providing marginally more flavour. Most often served with Indian dishes, Basmati rice is a delicious grain with a distinct, very delicate, aroma and flavour. Open a new packet of good Basmati rice and take the trouble to smell the delicate scent of the grains. It is far superior to the easy-cook and plain types of rice and well worth buying. However, to overcook Basmati is a crime because the flavour is diminished.

Risotto Rice Italian risotto rice has rounder, shorter grains than other types of rice used for savoury cooking. When cooked, the grains should be creamy rather than separate. This type of rice is essential for making authentic risotto.

Sushi Rice or Japanese Rice A short-grained rice which is similar to risotto rice. The grains become quite sticky when cooked, a useful characteristic when shaping sushi.

Glutinous Rice Short-grain Chinese rice which becomes very sticky on cooking. It is also used for making congee, a cross between soup and porridge.

Convenience Types Frozen cooked rice, canned rice and a broad range of flavoured rice or rice mixtures are available (in cans, packets or frozen). The best advice is to sample and decide for yourself – frozen cooked rice and canned cooked rice are undeniably quick and easy, but rather mean on flavour.

CEREALS AND GRAINS

Barley Pot barley is whole grain and pearl barley is the husked, polished grain. Both are cooked by boiling and are traditionally added to soups or stews. However, they may be served or used in place of rice. Barley flakes are also available and are used in muesli.

Buckwheat The seed of a plant which is thought to have originated in China, buckwheat is nutritious and high in fibre. Commonly sold hulled and roasted, the grain must be cooked very gently to avoid reducing it to mush. Dark, buckwheat flour is made from the ground grain. It is used in some Eastern European puddings and pancakes known as blini.

Corn/Maize The familiar vegetable is also cultivated as a cereal crop. When ground, it is sold as maize flour, corn meal or polenta.

Couscous See Semolina.

Rye This grain is cultivated extensively, especially in Northern Europe. It is milled to make rye flour, which is used in breadmaking; also for crackers and crispbreads.

Millet Fine yellow grain which is available from wholefood shops. It cooks quickly and rapidly overcooks to a porridge, so it should be treated like buckwheat. Not particularly popular but may be used instead of rice as an accompaniment.

Oats The whole grain is not used in the same way as rice, barley or wheat in cooking. Hulled and ground grain is known as oatmeal and it ranges from fine ground (pinhead) oatmeal to coarse meal. Used in baking and for coating savoury food before frying or cooking. Oatmeal may also be used for porridge, although processed rolled oats are more popular.

Sago Is derived from the starchy pith of several varieties of palm. The starch extracted from the pith is dried, then made into granules. It is used in puddings, some soups, and as a general thickener.

Tapioca Similar to sago in terms of usage, this cereal is derived from the cassava root.

Wheat A widely distributed cereal crop, the basis of most of the flour used in the West for baking. The whole wheat grain requires lengthy boiling to tenderize it. Cracked wheat is the uncooked grain which has been split. It is added to breads for its texture or may be cooked by boiling or by adding to moist dishes. Burghul (or bulgar) is a hulled and cooked wheat-grain product which must not be confused with cracked wheat. It may be softened by soaking, then used in salads or it may be briefly cooked for hot dishes. Wheatgerm, the embryo of the wheat, is highly nutritious. It is used as a thickener and as a dietary supplement.

Semolina is a cereal derived from hard (durum) wheat. It is used as a thickener, especially in milk puddings, and is the basis of a type of porridge. A form of soaked semolina, couscous, is very popular in North Africa. The pearl-like pellets are steamed, traditionally over a pan of stew. Sold ready prepared, couscous cooks and swells quickly when soaked in boiling water.

Wild Rice Not a rice at all, but a species of aquatic grass, this consists of dark, long, thin grains (almost black in colour) which do not become soft on cooking, but remain firm and chewy. Packets often contain a mixture of different types of wild rice, or wild rice mixed with brown, cultivated grain. Wild rice is good when mixed with other ingredients (for example, in a stuffing) or scented with herbs and lemon as an accompaniment. Served solo, wild rice is satisfying; you will not need as much as if you were serving white or brown rice.

COOKING RICE

SERVES FOUR

225 g/8 oz long-grain rice
salt and pepper

If using Basmati rice, plain, untreated long-grain rice or wild rice, start by placing the grains in a bowl. Wash the rice in several changes of cold water, taking care not to swirl the grains vigorously as this may damage them. Pour off most of the water each time, then add fresh water and swirl the rice gently with your fingertips. Finally drain the rice in a sieve and turn it into a saucepan.

Add cold water: 600 ml/1 pint for white rice; 750 ml/1¼ pints for brown or wild rice. Add a little salt and bring to the boil. Stir once, then lower the heat and put a tight-fitting lid on the pan. Cook very gently until the grains are tender: 15–20 minutes for easy-cook varieties and white rice; 20 minutes for Basmati rice; 25–35 minutes for brown rice; 40–50 minutes for wild rice.

Remove the pan from the heat and leave, covered, for 5 minutes, then fork up the grains, add salt and pepper if liked, and serve the rice.

variations

SAFFRON RICE Add 3 green cardamom pods and a bay leaf to the rice. Reduce the amount of water by 50 ml/2 fl oz. Pound 2.5–5 ml/1 tsp saffron strands to a powder in a mortar with a pestle. Add 50 ml/2 fl oz boiling water and stir well until the saffron has dissolved. Sprinkle this over the rice after it has been cooking for 15 minutes, then replace the lid quickly and finish cooking. Fork up the rice before serving, removing the bay leaf and cardamoms.

PILAU RICE Cook 1 chopped onion in a little butter or ghee in a large saucepan, then add 1 cinnamon stick, 1 bay leaf, 4 green cardamoms and 4 cloves. Stir in 225 g/8 oz Basmati rice and 600 ml/1 pint water and cook as in the main recipe. In a separate pan, cook a second onion, this time thinly sliced, in 50 g/2 oz butter or ghee until golden brown. Add 30 ml/2 tbsp cumin seeds (preferably black seeds) when the onion has softened and before it begins to brown. Add half the sliced onion mixture to the rice and fork it in. Pour the remaining onion mixture over the top of the rice before serving. Saffron may be added to pilau.

BROWN AND WILD RICE Mix different grains for an interesting texture. Start by cooking the wild rice for 10 minutes, then add the brown rice and continue cooking until the brown rice is tender.

WALNUT RICE Cook the chosen rice; add 100 g/4 oz chopped walnuts and 30 ml/2 tbsp chopped parsley before serving.

LEMON RICE Add the grated rind of 1 lemon to the rice: if it is added at the start of cooking it gives a deep-seated flavour; added just before serving it adds a fresh, zesty tang to the rice.

RICE WITH HERBS Add bay leaves, sprigs of rosemary, thyme, savory or sage to the rice at the beginning of cooking. Alternatively, sprinkle chopped parsley, fresh tarragon, dill, mint or marjoram over the rice at the end of cooking. Match the herb to the flavouring in the main dish, with which the rice is to be served.

TOMATO RICE Add 1 finely chopped onion, 1 bay leaf and 30 ml/2 tbsp tomato purée to the rice before cooking.

RICE MOULDS

A rice mould may be large or small and it may be served hot or cold. Making a rice ring is the popular form of moulding rice so that the middle may be filled with a hot sauced mixture or cold dressed salad. Typical fillings are salmon, tuna, or mixed seafood in a white sauce, or chicken in sauce. Salads of seafood or poultry, dressed with mayonnaise, soured cream or fromage frais, turn a rice ring into a rich main dish; light vegetable mixtures, such as tomato or courgette salad, are ideal for moulds which are intended as a side dish.

For best results, and particularly when making large moulds, avoid easy-cook rice and mixtures with a high proportion of wild rice as the grains tend not to cling together well. The basic recipe on page 106 or any of the flavoured variations may be used to make the moulds and rings that follow.

Mrs Beeton's Rice Mould Here is a slight adaptation of the original recipe (referred to as a rice casserole) which suggested beating the overcooked (by our standards) rice until it formed a paste. Use plain rice and cook a double quantity of the basic recipe, using stock if liked instead of water. While the rice is cooking, set the oven at 230°C/450°F/gas 8 and thoroughly butter an 18 cm/7 inch round tin. Prepare a pad of absorbent kitchen paper, about 13 cm/5 inches across and 5 cm/2 inches (or slightly less) shallower than the tin. Wrap this completely in foil and grease it well with oil.

Stir the cooked rice well, then allow to cool for 5 minutes. Beat in an egg, then press a layer of mixture firmly into the base of the tin. Line the sides of the tin with about a 2.5 cm/1 inch thickness of mixture, then put the foil pad in the middle, filling around it with rice. Cover the top of the foil thickly with rice and press down well. Bake for 15 minutes. Grease a baking sheet, then invert the mould on it. Use a knife to cut a circle inside the top of the mould, for a lid, then bake for a further 15 minutes, until lightly browned and firm. Carefully cut out the lid and use a palette knife to remove it. Remove the foil pad and the rice mould is ready for filling.

Hot Ring Mould Cook 1 quantity of the rice. Set the oven at 180°C/350°F/gas 4. Meanwhile, thoroughly grease a 1.1 litre/2 pint metal ring mould with either butter or oil. Stir 45 ml/3 tbsp single cream or milk into the rice, then press it into the mould and cover the top with foil. Bake for 30 minutes. Turn out on a warmed serving dish.

Cold Rice Ring Cook 1 quantity of rice. Grease a 1.1 litre/2 pint ring mould with oil. Press the cooked rice into it, cover and cool. Chill lightly before inverting the mould on a serving dish.

Individual Moulds These may be either hot or cold, using tins or individual oven-proof basins for hot moulds. Grease the moulds well, using oil for cold rice. Dariole moulds, individual basins and ramekin dishes are all ideal. Follow the instructions for ring moulds, reducing the cooking time to 20 minutes for a hot mould.

Multi-layered Moulds With contrasting layers which are visually pleasing, the shape of the mould can be extremely simple, such as a plain round tin or soufflé dish. Combine two or three layers, remembering that the layer in the base of the dish will be on top when the rice is unmoulded. For example, begin by placing a layer of Lemon Rice in the mould, then add a layer of Tomato Rice and finally add a layer of Rice with Herbs, mixing in plenty of chopped parsley after cooking. This combination is excellent with plain grills, such as barbecued foods.

As versatile as the British potato, pasta is an International food with origins in many countries and favoured all over the world. Although Italy is usually the country that comes to mind when pasta is mentioned, many other nations have developed some form of pasta dough, and the ways in which this versatile food is used are legion. Oriental pasta dough is utilized to make noodles, popular in both Chinese and Japanese cooking, and small filled dumplings which are served as dim sum, or snacks, in the Chinese tradition. Filled dumplings from Poland and other European countries share more in common with their Italian relatives, ravioli, than they do with the suet dumplings of British fame.

SAUCES FOR PASTA

Sauces are the natural partners for pasta, whether you choose a plain tomato or rich meat sauce to serve Italian style; or toss a succulent, sauced stir fry with Chinese egg noodles to produce a tempting chow mein.

Simple milk-based sauces, such as cheese, mushroom or egg sauce, are sufficient to turn a bowl of cooked pasta into a meal. Tossed together, topped with cheese, then grilled until golden and bubbling, the combination is deliciously satisfying. Seafood, poultry and meat sauces take pasta beyond the realms of snack and supper cookery to dinner-party status. Meat-free dishes are quickly conjured up by combining braised vegetable mixtures with fresh cooked pasta.

PASTA SIMPLICITY

One of the most appealing aspects of pasta cookery is that it can be ultra simple, extremely stylish and absolutely mouthwatering. One classic Italian snack is a dish of piping hot pasta, generously dressed with olive oil in which a few crushed cloves of garlic have been lightly cooked. Sprinkled with some shredded basil or chopped parsley, topped with several grindings of black pepper and a few spoonfuls of freshly grated Parmesan cheese, this is indeed a snack to set before the hungriest gourmet. Here are a few equally simple combinations to toss into freshly cooked pasta.

- Flaked canned tuna, chopped spring onion and chopped black olives.
- Diced tomato, shredded fresh basil, a few chopped capers and crisp grilled bacon bits.
- Chopped hard-boiled egg with peeled cooked prawns, a knob of butter and pepper.
- Diced and sautéed courgettes with grated Gruyère cheese.

FILLED PASTA

Raw fillings may be used for small pasta shapes and dumplings. The rolled dough is filled, sealed and cooked. Enough time must be allowed for the filling to cook through. The drained cooked pasta is then tossed with a simple sauce; oil or butter and Parmesan cheese may be offered with Italian dishes.

On occasion, as when preparing cannelloni, the pasta and filling are cooked separately, then combined and coated with sauce for the final baking.

SWEET PASTA

The popularity of pasta as a savoury food outshines interest in its potential as an ingredient in sweet dishes; however, there are many traditional, International sweet pasta recipes, including macaroni pudding.

TYPES OF PASTA

Fresh Pasta Available chilled or frozen, this has the best flavour. It cooks very quickly (except when filled). Fresh pasta is also easy to make (for recipe, see page 352) and it freezes well. It may be flavoured and coloured with a variety of ingredients, such as spinach, tomato or beetroot.

Dried Pasta The shapes and forms of dried pasta are too numerous to mention; the list is always increasing. In addition to the traditional shapes, there are large shapes for stuffing and novelty shapes for children. Dried pasta is manufactured in many colours and flavours.

Quick-Cook Dried Pasta There are several forms, including shapes which require brief boiling and lasagne sheets which do not require any pre-cooking before they are layered with a sauce for baking. Quality varies enormously. In general, these products are inferior to more traditional forms of pasta as their texture tends to be softer and slightly more 'jellied', lacking the bite which is characteristic of pasta (fresh or dried), which is cooked 'al dente'.

USES FOR PASTA

Serving with Sauce Shapes, noodles, spaghetti, Chinese egg noodles.

Layering and Baking or Grilling Lasagne, medium-sized shapes, cut macaroni.

Filling Fresh pasta dough, cannelloni, large shells, large elbow shapes or other large shapes with a pocket or hollow for stuffing.

Soups Very small shapes, cut macaroni, vermicelli, Oriental rice noodles.

As a Stuffing For filling scooped out tomatoes and other vegetables, such as peppers, soup pasta, macaroni and small shapes are all suitable.

Eggs play many vital roles in cooking. They are used to enrich, set or lighten mixtures, both sweet and savoury. In some recipes, where a high proportion of eggs are used, they are the only raising agent; for example in baked soufflés or whisked sponge cakes. Eggs may be fully cooked, partially cooked (as used in custards) or used raw (for mayonnaise or mousse).

The eggs can be used whole or they may be separated before they are added to a mixture. Whisked with sugar, they may form the basis for a sweet mixture and the other ingredients will be folded into them. For some recipes the egg yolks are incorporated first, then the whisked whites are folded in; this is typical of soufflés or continental-style cake mixtures. In this case a little of the white should be stirred in first to soften the bulk of the mixture before the remainder is folded in.

In some recipes just the whites or yolks are used; for example, mayonnaise can be made with yolks alone, meringues require the whites only and biscuits often use just yolks. Other recipes may call for more whites than yolks in order to produce a very light mixture.

Eggs come in different sizes and they are also categorized by quality. Two quality grades of whole eggs are sold, either A or B quality, and this is clearly stated on the box. There are regulations that have to be observed for the sale of pre-packed eggs, and certain information has to be included on the outside of the box.

BUYING EGGS

Firstly, the class of eggs must be clearly marked and the number of eggs must also be shown along with the registered number of the packing station, the name and address of those responsible for packing and the date on which the eggs were packed. In addition there may be a sell-by-date, although this is optional – always look out for this and make sure that it has not expired if it is included.

It makes sense to buy eggs from a reputable supplier. Particular care should be taken if eggs are to be used raw, as in mayonnaise or chocolate mousse.

Class A eggs are graded in sizes from 1–7. The sizes most commonly available are 2–4. Size 3 are the most suitable for baking unless otherwise stated; for example if large eggs are called for, then size 2 should be used.

EGG SIZES

> Size 1 – 70 g and over
> Size 2 – 65 g and under 70 g
> Size 3 – 60 g and under 65 g
> Size 4 – 55 g and under 60 g
> Size 5 – 50 g and under 55 g
> Size 6 – 45 g and under 50 g
> Size 7 – under 45 g

Storing Eggs Eggs should be stored in the refrigerator, preferably in their box, and the pointed end of each egg should be kept downwards to help to prevent breakages, to reduce evaporation and to help to prevent any odours being absorbed through the shell.

Using Eggs For many recipes it is best if eggs are used at room temperature so they should be removed from the refrigerator about 30 minutes before they are to be used. However this is not essential. It is very important that eggs are clean and they should be washed under cool water and dried before they are cracked, taking care not to break them, of course. It is best to crack eggs individually into a mug, cup or small basin before adding them to mixtures and any traces of broken shell should be removed.

Eggs are a protein food and they should be treated with the same standards of hygiene that are adopted for all raw meat, fish and poultry. All utensils must be thoroughly clean before use and hands should be washed before and after breaking eggs, particularly if cooked food is handled after raw eggs. Any unused beaten egg should be kept in a tightly covered container and placed in the refrigerator. It should be used within 24 hours. Egg whites can be frozen in a clean, airtight, rigid container. Remember to label the container with the number of whites which it contains. Whole eggs (yolk and white; not in shells) or yolks may be frozen if beaten with a little salt or sugar but they are not as successful as whites alone. Once thawed, egg should always be used immediately.

COOKING EGGS

Boiling Bring the eggs to room temperature before cooking to avoid cracking the shells if they are very cold. If an egg does crack, add 15 ml/1 tbsp vinegar or lemon juice to the cooking water to set the white quickly as it escapes.

Bring a small saucepan of water to the boil, allowing enough water to cover the eggs. Place an egg on a spoon and lower it into the water. Begin timing the cooking as soon as the egg is in the water. Regulate the heat so that the water is just boiling. Timing for boiled eggs is very personal but the following provides a guide when cooking average-sized eggs (sizes 3–4):
Soft boiled (soft set white) 3¼ minutes. Medium (soft yolk, firm white) 4–4¾ minutes. Hard (firm white, just firm yolk) 10 minutes.

Poaching Pour 5 cm/2 inches water into a pan – a frying pan is ideal. Add 15 ml/1 tbsp cider vinegar and bring just to simmering point. Crack a fresh egg on to a saucer. Use a draining spoon to swirl the water in the pan, then slide the egg into the middle of the gentle swirl. (The swirling water gives the egg a good shape.) Simmer for about 3 minutes, or until the egg is set. Spoon the simmering water over the egg to set it evenly. Up to four eggs may be cooked at the same time in a frying pan. Use a slotted spoon to drain the eggs as they are cooked. Trim the edges of the whites and serve at once.

Scrambled Eggs Allow two eggs per person. Put the requisite number of eggs in a bowl. Add 15–30 ml/1–2 tbsp milk for each pair of eggs. Sprinkle in salt and pepper to taste and beat lightly.

Melt a little butter in a small saucepan. There should be just enough butter to cover the bottom of the pan; do not allow it to become too hot. Pour in the eggs. Cook gently, stirring or whisking all the time, until the eggs are lightly set and creamy. Remove from the heat and serve at once. If the eggs are allowed to stand in the hot pan or left on the heat, they set firmly and separate into curds and a thin liquid.

A variety of flavourings may be stirred into the cooked eggs. They may be enriched by using single cream instead of milk or by stirring in a little extra cream as the eggs begin to thicken. Diced smoked salmon or a little grated cheese may be added just before serving.

Fried Eggs Heat a thin layer of oil or half oil and half butter in a frying pan. Bacon fat may be used instead or this may be combined with oil. Crack an egg into a saucer, then slide it into the hot fat. Cook over moderate heat, spooning fat over the egg, until the white is set and the yolk is covered with a lightly set white film. For a firmer set use a fish slice to turn the egg over as soon as the white is set firmly underneath. Cook for a further 30–60 seconds before serving this gives a yolk which is partially set. A soft fried egg is usually ready in 2–3 minutes, slightly sooner if basted often.

Baking Plain baked eggs should be cooked in individual ovenproof dishes, such as ramekins or the slightly deeper, rounded cocotte dishes. Eggs which are baked with additional ingredients also cook successfully in a large dish; for example, eggs may be baked in hollows among vegetables such as spinach or ratatouille.

Deep Fried Eggs These are well puffed, crisp and golden outside, with a soft centre. Heat oil for deep frying to 180°C/350°F or until a cube of day-old bread browns in 30 seconds. Crack an egg into a mug or saucer. Standing back, slide the egg into the hot oil – it will bubble and spit. Use a slotted spoon to gently move the egg off the bottom of the pan if it does not rise to the surface quickly. The egg will quickly turn brown and crisp outside, and will be cooked with a soft centre in less than a minute. Drain well on the slotted spoon.

CUSTARDS

Many custards, especially those thickened solely by the addition of eggs, are notoriously delicate and require a little extra care in the preparation and cooking. If you have experienced problems when making custards, the following notes may be of some help.

It is most important that all dairy foods are perfectly fresh. Eggs, in particular, should be purchased from a reputable source as they are only lightly cooked. Dishes that are to be served chilled should be covered and cooled quickly, then stored in the refrigerator.

A common problem when making custard is that the mixture curdles. Follow a few simple rules to ensure this does not happen. Custard may be baked or cooked in a bowl over hot water to make a pouring custard. When cold and chilled a pouring custard may set, for example on the top of a trifle. The eggs in a custard curdle when the mixture has been overcooked. This may be due to cooking the custard for too long or at too high a temperature.

Pouring custards may be cooked in a double saucepan or in a heatproof bowl over a pan of water. The water should only just simmer; if it boils, the custard may well curdle. Stir the mixture all the time it cooks, until it thickens enough to coat the back of a spoon. A common mistake is to expect the custard to look thicker when it is cooked; remember that it will thicken on cooling and become creamy on chilling (depending on the number of eggs used).

Rich custards are made by using cream instead of milk. Single cream is the most common option; double is used for very rich desserts.

When the custard is cooked it should be removed from over the water and allowed to cool. To prevent the formation of a skin, the custard may be stirred as it cools or the surface may be covered with dampened greaseproof paper or microwave cling film. Alternatively, a little caster sugar may be sprinkled all over the surface to prevent a skin from forming.

USING A BAIN MARIE

A bain marie is simply a container of water in which to stand the dish of custard (or any other delicate mixture that requires careful cooking). A roasting tin or any fairly deep ovenproof dish that is large enough to hold the container of custard will do. Very hot, not boiling, water should be poured into the outer container. Ideally, the water in the outer container should come halfway up the outside of the dish of custard.

The bain marie protects the custard from overcooking; the water barrier moderates the heat which reaches the outside of the dish. If the recipe requires very lengthy cooking the water must be topped up.

SWEET CORNFLOUR CUSTARD

An easy alternative to custard thickened solely with egg is one with a little cornflour added. When cornflour and egg yolks are combined the custard may be brought to the boil in a saucepan. The resulting custard is significantly thicker and, with sufficient cornflour, it sets to a more creamy, or even firm, consistency when chilled, for example when used as a topping for trifle. This type of mixture (using plain flour in place of cornflour) and method is used for making crème pâtissière, a thick custard enriched with cream which is used as a filling for flans or gateaux. It also provides a quick alternative for topping trifles or as a basis for a variety of desserts.

PRESSURE COOKING

Surprisingly, set custards cook very well in the pressure cooker and far more quickly than when baked. Consult your handbook for more information. See also Baked Custard (page 212).

Set and pouring custards both cook successfully in the microwave. Individual set custards cook more evenly than large ones. Stand the custards in a microwave-proof bain marie.

To prevent it from curdling, a pouring custard must be frequently stirred or whisked during cooking. With care, custards cooked in the microwave are less likely to curdle than conventionally-cooked custards that are not watched constantly when cooking.

MICROWAVE COOKING

Custards and desserts thickened or lightened with eggs do not freeze successfully as they tend to separate and curdle on thawing.

FREEZING

A batter is made by combining flour with egg and liquid, usually milk or milk and water. Some savoury coating batters are a simple combination of flour and liquid; however the majority of recipes are enriched by the addition of eggs. These also serve to lighten the mixture.

BATTER

SMOOTH BATTERS

A good batter should be perfectly smooth and light. To achieve this, a whole egg is added to a well in the flour and a little of the milk (or liquid) is poured in. A wooden spoon is used to combine the egg with the milk and the flour is gradually worked in to make a smooth, thick mixture. This mixture should be thoroughly beaten to get rid of any lumps. When the thick batter is perfectly smooth, the remaining liquid is stirred in. The batter should be used immediately for baked puddings.

Alternatively, all the ingredients may be combined in a blender or food processor and processed until smooth.

If the batter is to be used for coating fritters, the eggs are separated. The yolks are combined with the flour and liquid to make a smooth, fairly thick batter. The egg whites are whisked until stiff, then folded in. The batter should be used at once. When fried this type of batter is very crisp and light.

A thin batter should be used for pancakes; it should be allowed to stand for at least 30 minutes so that all the air may escape. The batter may thicken slightly on standing and a little extra liquid may have to be added halfway through making the pancakes.

A good pan is essential for making successful pancakes. A heavy non-stick pan usually gives good results if the base is in good condition. The best pan is a heavy, cast-iron pan that has become well seasoned with years of use. It is a good idea to set aside a pan specifically for pancakes. It is possible to buy a heavy flat, non-stick pan with a shallow rim for just this purpose.

PERFECT PANCAKES

To prevent the batter from sticking, stir in a little cooking oil – about 15 ml/ 1 tbsp per 600 ml/1 pint of batter is sufficient. The pan should be hot and greased with oil or a mixture of butter and oil in equal proportions. Have a small bowl of oil or melted butter and oil to one side. Spoon a little into the pan and heat it, then pour out the excess and heat the pan again for a few seconds before pouring in the batter.

Use a ladle to pour the batter into the hot pan. Tilt the pan as your pour in the batter to coat the base thinly and evenly. The pan should be hot enough to set the batter immediately. Place the pan over moderate heat until the pancake has completely set and is browned underneath. Check that it is cooked underneath by lifting the edge with a palette knife or slice.

When the base of the pancake has browned and the edges are just beginning to turn crisp, slide a palette knife or slice under it and turn it over. To toss a pancake, first loosen it all around the edge, then give the pan a firm jolt upwards to flip the pancake up and over in one movement. Practice makes perfect!

As the pancakes are cooked, stack them, sprinkling each sweet pancake with a little caster sugar. Absorbent kitchen paper may be layered between savoury pancakes to prevent them from sticking.

FREEZING PANCAKES

Stack cold pancakes on a double thickness of foil, layering freezer film between each one. Pack tightly, label and freeze. They keep for up to 6 months. Individual pancakes thaw quickly; if you want to thaw the whole stack quickly separate them and spread them on a clean board. Keep the pancakes covered while they are thawing. See also individual recipes.

MAKING WAFFLES

Unlike pancake batter, the mixture for waffles is made from self-raising flour. As it cooks and sets, the batter rises in the waffle iron to give a crisp, slightly spongy result.

Batter for making waffles should be the consistency of thick cream and it should be cooked as soon as it is prepared. Serve waffles freshly cooked.

WAFFLE IRONS

To shape the waffles you will need a special utensil known as a waffle iron. This is a hinged metal mould which should be greased and heated over a gas flame or electric ring. Plug-in electric waffle cookers are also on sale, usually with non-stick plates that may be removed for easy cleaning. Always follow the manufacturer's instructions when using an electric appliance.

When using a hand-held waffle iron, pour enough batter into one side of the greased mould to cover it. Close the iron and cook the waffle on both sides until it has stopped steaming. Open the iron carefully if the waffle is cooked it should come away from the metal plate quite easily. If you have to keep waffles hot, place them in a single layer on a wire rack in a low oven. Do not stack them or they will become soggy.

SOUFFLES AND MOUSSES

The principles involved in making cold soufflés and mousses are the same. The difference between the two dishes is mainly in the way in which they are set and served.

Soufflés and mousses are mixtures that are lightened with egg. Hot soufflés rely on whisked egg whites to make the mixture rise and set; cold soufflés and mousses are lightened with egg whites and set with gelatine.

HOT SOUFFLES

A hot soufflé ought to make an impressive entrance at the end of a meal, so to ensure success you must be confident and well organized. The flavoured base mixture for the soufflé should be prepared in advance, ready for the egg whites to be whisked and folded in just before cooking. Timing is crucial, so work out a timetable and plan exactly when you intend to finish preparing the soufflé and place it in the oven. The cooked soufflé should be taken immediately to the table and served.

You will need an ovenproof, straight-sided soufflé dish or individual soufflé or ramekin dishes. These should be buttered. For sweet soufflés, dishes may be sprinkled with a little caster sugar, according to the recipe. This helps the mixture to cling to the sides of the dish as it rises.

For easy removal from the oven, stand individual dishes on a baking sheet once they are prepared. As soon as the dish, or dishes, have been filled with mixture, quickly wash and dry your hands and run your thumb around the inside edge of the dish, cleaning away the mixture, to create a gutter. This ensures that the mixture rises evenly and high instead of sticking to the top edge of the dish, which would make it dome and crack.

Creating a gutter to ensure soufflé rises evenly.

Adding a branded decoration (see page 118).

Adding the finishing touches to hot sweet soufflés

Hot soufflés may be dredged with a thick covering of icing sugar before serving. The icing sugar may be caramelized with a hot skewer in a criss-cross pattern. The best way to do this is to preheat two metal skewers under the grill until they are red hot. Alternatively, hold the skewers in a gas flame or on a solid electric hot plate. As soon as the soufflé has been thickly dredged with icing sugar, mark it by pressing the hot skewer into it; remove the skewer quickly. Having a second hot skewer in reserve means the decoration may be finished swiftly and the soufflé will be served speedily. For illustration see page 117.

COLD SOUFFLES

Cold soufflés are easier to make than hot ones and may be prepared in advance. The basic flavouring mixture is usually enriched with cream, lightened with whisked egg whites and set with gelatine. The egg yolks may be creamed with sugar or mixed with a savoury sauce base. The dissolved gelatine is usually stirred into the mixture just before any whipped cream is added. The egg whites are folded in last, just before the mixture is poured into the prepared dish.

When the cold soufflé mixture is poured into the dish it should come over the top of the rim. Level the mixture gently and keep the dish level in the refrigerator while the soufflé sets.

When the soufflé has set, untie the string that holds the paper. Carefully peel the paper from the set soufflé, at the same time gently running the blade of a knife between the soufflé mixture and the paper. This ensures that the soufflé mixture standing above the side of the dish keeps its shape.

Individual soufflés

Small soufflés may be set in ramekin dishes, using the same method as for a large soufflé. Alternatively, the soufflé mixture may be set in fruit shells. For example, lemon or orange shells or halved small melon shells may be used. The fruit shells should be trimmed at the base so that they stand level. Securing a band of paper around the fruit is more difficult. Adhesive tape should be used on the outside of the paper. Savoury mixtures may be set in avocado halves, artichokes or tomato shells.

PREPARING A SOUFFLE DISH

This method is used for all cold, set mixtures which stand above the rim of the dish. Although it is not necessary to prepare dishes in this way for baked soufflés, some cooks prefer to do so. In the event, the inside of the paper should be well greased.

1 Using a piece of string, measure the height of the dish and its circumference.

2 Cut a strip from two thicknesses of greaseproof paper or non-stick baking parchment that exceeds the height of the dish by 7.5 cm/3 inches and is long enough to go right around the dish with an overlap.

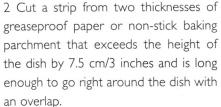

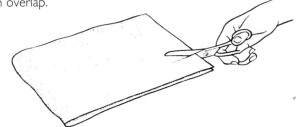

3 Tie the paper around the dish with string. If the dish has sloping sides or a projecting rim, secure the paper above and below the rim with gummed tape or pins. Make sure the paper has no creases and forms a neat round shape.

SWEET FINISHING TOUCHES FOR COLD SOUFFLÉS

Chopped nuts, grated chocolate or other fine ingredients are usually pressed against the side of the soufflé mixture that stands above the dish. Piped whipped cream may be used to decorate the top edge of the soufflé and fresh or glacé fruit, chocolate decorations, frosted flowers or other suitable ingredients may be added for decoration.

Light and creamy cold soufflé mixtures freeze well to make a dessert which is a cross between a soufflé and an ice cream. Individual soufflés are particularly practical for freezing as they soften to a pleasant eating consistency fairly quickly and are easy to serve. Prepare the soufflé as usual, then place it in the freezer, making sure that it is level. Freeze for several hours or overnight. Allow to soften for about 45 minutes in the refrigerator.

ICED SOUFFLES

CHEESE

Cheese is one of our most nourishing foods. Full-fat cheese contains almost all the nourishment of whole milk except the milk sugar (lactose), and a few vitamins and minerals. It consists of the solid parts of the milk solidified into clots or curd, separated from the whey, which is drained off. The curd is usually pressed or heated, or both, to expel more whey, and as it dries becomes firm and will keep for some time without spoiling.

Depending on how much whey is removed from it, cheese may be classed as hard, semi-hard, semi-soft or soft.

Cheese of any type is most valuable for its protein content. It contains more protein, weight for weight, than prime raw beef. It is a good source of calcium, and contains vitamins A and D, and some B vitamins. Most cheeses, certainly the hard and semi-hard ones, are also rich in fat. A hard cheese like Cheddar is made up of about one-third fat, one-third protein, and one-third water. Cheese made from skimmed or defatted milk contains less fat and therefore a higher proportion of protein.

Cheese does not contain any carbohydrate, but is generally eaten with foods which supply carbohydrate, eg bread and biscuits, vegetables or pasta.

BUYING AND STORING CHEESE

It is much easier to assess the quality of cheese in the block, free of wrappings, as both the texture and condition can be seen.

The cut surface of any cheese is a good guide to its quality and condition. A hard or semi-hard cheese for eating raw (or for grating) should be firm, even slightly flaky in a cheese such as Cheddar, but must not have cracks in the surface. Equally, it must not be sweaty or show beads of fat, which indicate it has been kept too long in a warm place, uncovered. It should be more or less the same colour throughout; a darker colour near the rind may be a sign that the cheese is old; any white specks or blue sheen indicate mould and a musty flavour. Even a strong cheese should not taste harsh or acidic.

A milder cheese for eating or cooking should be firm or crumbly and still have a definite cheesy taste; it should not be soapy.

The blander semi-soft cheeses such as Edam or Port Salut should be velvety when cut, neither moist nor flaky, and should have the same creamy colour throughout. They should yield slightly when pressed with the finger.

Soft cheeses such as Camembert and Brie can quickly ripen and spoil but are tasteless when under-ripe. The crust of Brie should be white and even with signs of red at the edges; the curd pale yellow and creamy throughout, although not spilling out. If it is running when purchased, it may well be inedible by the time it is needed. A hard cake-like white strip in the centre is unlikely to ripen before the outer cheese goes bad. The same applies to soft-paste cheeses, such as the creamy French cheeses. Like soft fresh cheeses, they spoil within a few days. They should be clean and well-shaped, neither discoloured nor dented, and the inside should be even in texture, without seeping moisture but soft enough to cut with a spoon.

Blue cheeses should also be even-coloured, without greyish patches, and with clear-cut veins of colour. They should be crumbly or moist, not grainy. Milder ones such as Dolcelatte may look creamy. All blue cheeses are fairly pungent, and may become unpleasantly harsh with age, so that colour and texture should be noted carefully before buying.

None of these pointers to quality can be checked in the case of prepacked cheeses. There are, however, one or two ways of telling whether they are good value and have been well cared for:

On any cheese counter, or in a chilled cabinet, cheeses should be on their own shelf or rack, separate from other foods, so that cross-flavouring cannot occur. Ideally, each cheese should have its separate place; strong and mild cheeses should not be stacked together.

Any semi-soft cheese should yield to the touch. It should always fill its box or wrapping, and never be sunken in the middle. All cheese wrappings should be fresh and clean. Sticky, stained or torn wrappings are always a warning not to buy.

Whenever possible, cheese should be bought in a compact block, not a long, thin slice or section. A thin slice is less easy to package, and keeps less well.

Cheese should be bought in small quantities, preferably just enough for 1 or 2 servings. Although the harder cheeses keep well, and it is tempting to keep a quantity in stock, any cheese tends to lose surface texture and flavour in storage, especially in a refrigerator. If it must be stored in a refrigerator, it should be kept in the least cold part, wrapped in greaseproof or waxed paper, and enclosed in a moisture-proof outer container or polythene bag. Cheeses should be removed and unwrapped at least 1 hour before use, to let them regain their full flavour. Any refrigerator-stored hard or semi-hard cheese should be used within 2 weeks, semi-soft and blue cheeses within 1 week. Soft cheeses must be used as soon as possible. To prevent ripe, soft, crusted cheeses oozing when a wedge has been cut out, wrap closely.

Any blue mould which develops on the surface of a hard or semi-hard cheese may be cut off; the cheese itself is unharmed; the flavour, especially of mature cheeses, will however become stronger the longer they are kept.

Most cheeses can be frozen successfully but tend to crumble after being frozen. Cream cheese tends to separate on thawing; it is best blended with double cream before freezing, to be used as a dip. Freeze cheeses in small quantities, wrapped in greaseproof or waxed paper and overwrapped in polythene.

COOKING CHEESE

Cheese must always be cooked gently and as briefly as possible. Even if cooked with extra fat, it should never spit, or bubble quickly.

Gentle cooking prevents the cheese becoming rubbery or ropey. If fat globules melt due to quick or fierce heating, the fat runs off, leaving a stringy mass of curd and separate fat instead of a creamy mass.

Hard and semi-hard cheeses are most often used for cooking. Cheeses with a high fat content and well-aged, mature cheeses melt and blend better with other ingredients than low-fat or less ripened cheeses. Less is needed too, since they are richer and better flavoured. Matured Cheddar and Parmesan cheeses are good for this reason. Processed cheeses melt easily but their flavour is usually very bland.

Most cheese will retain its creamy texture if it is first grated and mixed with breadcrumbs, flour or extra fat. This coats the fat globules and will absorb some of the cooking heat, thereby preventing the fat from melting too soon.

A good way to melt cheese by itself is to place it in a bowl over a pan of simmering water. Another way is to add it to a hot mixture after the main cooking is completed, eg to sprinkle it into a cooked omelette just before folding and serving.

When grilling cheese, it should be kept about 10 cm/4 inches below the heat, which should be as low as possible. Cheese used for a topping should be grated; it can be mixed with breadcrumbs before being sprinkled on the dish.

When cheese is mixed into a casserole or similar dish, whether cooked over heat or in the oven, the heat should also be kept as low as possible throughout the cooking time.

Types of British cheese

Caerphilly is a mild, white, close-textured, slightly salty cheese. The new cheese is lightly brined, then dried, and allowed to ripen for about 14 days. Caerphilly is good with salads and in packed meals and sandwiches, but is not an ideal cooking cheese. It can be crumbled instead of grated.

Cheddar is the best known and most widely used British cheese, and is copied in many parts of the world. Its flavour varies in strength a great deal. British Cheddar is of two main kinds: farmhouse and creamery. Farmhouse Cheddar is still made by individual families and small dairies, usually from a single herd of cows, although creameries do produce it also. It is of high quality, is matured slowly for at least 6 months, preferably much longer, and is slightly more expensive than creamery Cheddar. This may be a quickly ripened, quite mild cheese; or it may be sold as mature, having been allowed to ripen for 6–8 months. Like most British cheese, Cheddar is a full-fat, hard cheese made from cows' milk only. All Cheddar should be close in texture, with a clean, nutty flavour. It is a first-class eating cheese, but is also excellent for grating and cooking.

Cheshire may also be farmhouse or creamery-made. It is more salty than Cheddar, due to the salt in the Cheshire soil where most of it is still made. It is also slightly more acid, and more crumbly. It is naturally white, but a reddish type, dyed with a harmless vegetable dye, is also popular. There is also a fuller-flavoured, creamy-textured **Blue Cheshire**, which is yellow with broad blue streaks. Modern Cheshire cheese has a 33% fat content, and is usually medium-ripened for 4–8 weeks. It is a good eating cheese, especially with gingerbread, cake or apples. It is also widely used for cooking.

Derby is a pale honey-coloured, smooth-textured cheese, mild when young but with a certain tang when mature at 4–6 months old. It is good with biscuits, as a lunch cheese, and with fruit. **Sage Derby** has green threads or a broad band of green through it, and a flavour of the sage leaves which provide the colouring.

Double Gloucester is akin to Cheddar. It is straw-coloured or light red, close in texture, and mellow or pungent in flavour when mature; it ripens in 3–4 months as a rule. It is good after a meat meal or with beer, and is also good for cooking.

Dunlop is a Cheddar-style cheese from Scotland; so are the small **Orkney** and **Islay** cheeses.

Lancashire is a semi-hard cheese which may be farmhouse-made. It has the strongest flavour of the farmhouse cheeses, although the creamery-made cheese is mild. Both are white and crumble easily, and are good for toasted dishes (it was once called the 'Leigh Toaster'). It is also good crumbled into stews, or eaten, uncooked, with sharp salads or with sweet fruits. It is traditionally eaten with oatcakes.

Leicester This rich orange-red cheese is fairly mild in flavour, but with a tang when mature at about 2 months old. It is soft and crumbly, and may be slightly flaky. It makes a good cooking as well as an eating cheese.

Stilton is considered the king of British cheeses. It is rich and creamy, and slowly matured to let the blue veins develop properly. It is best eaten with bread or plain biscuits, and is an excellent accompaniment to wine, especially Madeira or port. The rind is wrinkled and crusty, and the creamy interior is slightly darker near the crust. Top-quality Stilton is still made, as a rule, in cylindrical hoops, although jars of Stilton are widely available; it is sold too in film-wrapped or vacuum-packed wedges. Aged Stilton, past its prime, can be potted for storage, and used later as a spread.

If you buy a whole Stilton or part of a round, do not scoop the cheese out of the centre or pour port into the cheese. It will be difficult to store and may go sour. The correct way to care for a Stilton is to cut off the top crust in a thin layer; keep this aside. When serving the cheese, cut wedges of equal depth from all round the cheese so that it keeps a flat top. To store the cheese, replace the top crust, wrap in greaseproof or waxed paper, put in a polythene bag or box and keep in a cool place.

The younger **White Stilton** is crumbly, with a strong aroma, and a mild, slightly sour flavour.

Wensleydale is a white, softish, close-textured cheese, not unlike Caerphilly in taste when young, being mild and slightly salty. It matures in 12–14 days. It is better for eating than for cooking. **Blue Wensleydale** has finer, more diffuse threads of blue veining than blue Cheshire and, as a rule, is less creamy and more salty than either blue Cheshire or Stilton.

Soft Cheeses of various kinds are made on farms, at home and in creameries. Colwick cheese and York cheese are both made only on farms, for private use. **Caboc** and **Crowdie** are creamery cheeses. They differ in appearance, flavour, and texture according to the area in which they are made, the type of moulds used, and the method of making. They may be lactic (sweet milk) or acid-curd cheeses, and are normally graded according to their butterfat content as follows:

skimmed milk soft cheese (less than 2% fat)
low-fat soft cheese (2–10% fat)
medium-fat soft cheese (10–20% fat)
full-fat soft cheese (20–45% fat)
cream cheese (46–65% fat)
double cream cheese (at least 65% fat)

Curd cheeses of various types which are often made in the home, may be low, medium or full-fat. Like cream cheese, they have a closer texture than cottage cheese which contains about 4% butterfat but also more whey.
All these cheeses keep for only about 4 days chilled.

Other cheeses available include **Red Windsor** which is based on Cheddar and flavoured with an English red wine. It has a creamier taste and a slightly more acid flavour than mature Cheddar. **Ilchester**, another Cheddar-based cheese, flavoured with beer and garlic, is a soft-textured cheese with a full flavour; the garlic is well subdued. **Walton** is a softer cheese based on Cheddar mixed with Stilton, with walnuts added; the taste of Stilton is mild. **Cotswold** is based on Double Gloucester and is flavoured with chives. **Sherwood** is another cheese based on Double Gloucester. It is flavoured with sweet pickle. **Blue Shropshire** cheese has a deep golden taste and clear-cut blue veining. It is lighter in flavour than blue Cheshire or Stilton, but fuller than blue Wensleydale, with its own character. **Melbury** is a mild soft cheese with a white surface mould coat.

Traditional hard cheeses are also available with a reduced fat content. Additionally, there are vegetarian hard cheeses; these are made with rennet of microbial origin.

POPULAR INTERNATIONAL CHEESES

Bel Paese is one of the best known Italian cheeses. It is a full-fat, ivory-coloured cheese, semi-soft and bland. It is used mostly as a table cheese although it melts easily, and is therefore useful in cooked dishes and for toasted sandwiches.
Boursin is French fresh cheese. The basic light-flavoured cheese can have either garlic added or a coat of crushed black peppercorns.
Brie, with a recorded history from 1217, is the most famous French cheese. It is often sold in prepacked wedges, so that its quality cannot be checked; it is best

to buy it cut to order, from a whole 35 cm/14 inch wheel, since Brie must be eaten in peak condition. Brie varies widely in flavour, depending on how long it is ripened. **Brie du Coulommiers** for instance, generally has a delicate, mild flavour whereas **Brie de Melun** is well-ripened and tastes much stronger, more like Camembert.

Camembert is France's most plentiful and popular cheese. It is widely sold prepacked, in whole or half rounds, or in small sections. One has to take a chance on its quality, since it is usually kept very cool in a store and is firmer than it will be when eaten. An unwrapped Camembert should have an even, light brownish crust level with the rim, with no sunken centre. Inside, it should be creamy-yellow throughout, like Brie. Its aroma and flavour is, however, a good deal stronger. Camembert matures and becomes inedible even more quickly than Brie, and is distinctly unpleasant when over-ripe.

Chèvre is the term for small, rich, French goats' milk cheeses, often shaped like small cylinders. Unless the words *pur chèvre* appear on the label, the cheese may be made from a mixture of goats' and cows' milk. Goats' milk cheeses vary in flavour with their type and area of origin; but they should all have a pale crust with only a light mould, and should be crumbly or creamy inside, not grainy.

Danish Blue is of two types; the usual type, sometimes called Danablu, is white with bluish-green veins; Mycella, which is less common, is yellowish with green veins, more aromatic and subtle. Both are rich in cream, buttery in texture, and are table cheeses. Danablu is sometimes over-salted for export.

Demi-sel and Petit-Suisse are two of the family of French soft cream cheeses. Rich and mild in flavour, all these cream cheeses should be eaten as soon as possible after purchase.

Dolcelatte is a mild, creamy, Italian cheese using milk from valley herds, and made in a similar way to Gorgonzola.

Edam is Holland's most widely exported cheese. It is made from partly skimmed cows' milk, and has a cannonball shape and a bright red rind or wax coating. Its texture is smooth, and its flavour bland. It is not good for cooking, but is popular for eating, especially with slimmers. It tastes fuller when cut in thin slivers or slices.

Emmental is Swiss in origin, and the best Emmental cheese still comes from Switzerland. It is one of the most difficult cheeses to make, requiring high-quality raw milk and considerable skill in manufacture. It has a hard golden-brown rind, and a yellow-ivory curd with cherry-sized holes. It has a sweet, dry flavour, and an aroma like hazelnuts. Famous as a cooking cheese, it is often used with Parmesan; and it is one of the cheeses traditionally used for a classic cheese fondue. It takes 7–10 months to mature fully.

Esrom, Havarti and Samsøe are hard Danish cheeses, all versatile, with a pale or golden-yellow taste, mild when young but gaining piquancy with age. All have tiny holes, yet are distinctly different; Esrom is the sweetest and most fragrant.

Feta is a Greek fresh sheeps' milk cheese or mixed milk cheese. It ripens in its own whey mixed with brine, so tastes piquant and salty. It should be eaten as soon as it is purchased, with salads, cold meats or black olives.

Gorgonzola is an ancient Italian blue cheese, widely exported. The curd varies from cream to straw-yellow with blue-green veining, and it should be elastic rather than crumbly. It is used mainly as a table cheese although its mildness makes it suitable for a number of cooked dishes.

Gouda is a full-fat Dutch cheese, made in both farmhouses and creameries. There is a good deal of difference between the two products, although both are good. Factory-made Gouda is relatively bland, not unlike Edam, although cartwheel in shape with a yellowish rind. Farmhouse Gouda has a noticeably variable flavour depending on where it comes from. An old one has a hard rind, a firm paste, and a full flavour. A farmhouse Gouda may be matured for as much as 12–14 months.

Gruyère is another Swiss cheese, although it is now widely copied because it is so popular. It is a classic cooking cheese, used for fondues and quiches. Wheel-shaped, with a warm brown rind, its curd is ivory-yellow, pocked with small holes, moister than that of Emmental, and therefore still better for hot dishes.

Jarlsberg is an old Norwegian full-fat cheese, revived and popularized in modern times. Its curd is pale and smooth with large, cherry-sized holes; its flavour is slightly sweet, mild, and nutty.

Monterey Jack is an American Cheddar-type cheese. It ranges from mild to mature in flavour.

Mozzarella is a soft, fresh cheese, originally made from buffalo milk, now more usually from cows' milk. Its shape varies, but the commonest is an oval ball. It should be very moist and yield slightly when bitten; it should be eaten as soon as possible after purchase.

Parmesan is the most famous and widely used Italian cheese. It is piquant, hard, and grainy due to long, slow maturing, although a milder, elastic, younger Parmesan is sold for table use in Italy. The Parmesan which reaches foreign markets, either in the block or ready-grated for cooking use, is at least 2–3 years old. The flavour of Parmesan bought ungrated is very much better than that of the factory-grated product.

Pipo Crème is a mild, creamy, fairly modern French blue cheese.

Pont l'Eveque is a semi-hard French cheese from Normandy, with a fat content of 50%. The cheese has a smooth, creamy consistency, golden rind, a savoury taste and some bouquet.

Port Salut is a small, round, French cheese with a pale yellow rind and a mild flavour. It is closely related to St Paulin. Both are mild table cheeses, not generally well suited to cooking.

Roquefort is easily the best known French blue cheese, with an old and noble history. Originally a sheeps' milk cheese, it is not always so today. Genuine Roquefort cheeses still come from the same Tarn area and are matured in mountain caves where the bacteria *penicillium roqueforti* give them their particular mould veining and flavour. The rind of a Roquefort cheese is wrinkled, its paste white and fairly crumbly, its veining dark blue-green and delicate. Matured in a thin coating of salt, its high but fine flavour can only be tasted fully when it is mature. Exported Roquefort cheeses, sometimes prepacked in wedges, are often too young and salty.

PASTRY

Good pastry should be light in texture. A few simple rules will help to ensure success with all types. Always weigh ingredients accurately as it is important that the correct proportions of fat, flour and liquid are used. Keep all the ingredients, utensils and your hands as cool as possible.

RUBBING IN

The first stage in making several types of pastry is to rub the fat into the flour. This basic technique is used for other purposes in cookery so it is worth getting it right. Cut the fat into small pieces; mix it with the flour. Using just the tips of your fingers, lift a little of the mixture and rub the fat with the flour once or twice. Let the mixture fall back into the bowl before lifting another small portion and rubbing again. Continue in this way until the mixture has the texture of fine breadcrumbs.

It is important that you lift the mixture and rub it lightly to incorporate air into it. If you pick up too much mixture and push it back into the palms of your hands, air will not mix with it and the pastry will be heavy. Once you have mastered the technique you will find it quick and easy to perform; in fact, the quicker the process is completed, the lighter the pastry.

ADDING LIQUID TO SHORT PASTRIES

The term 'short' is used to describe pastry that is not made heavy by the addition of too much liquid. The 'melt-in-your-mouth' texture that is characteristic of good 'short' pastry is the result of using the right proportion of fat to flour and just enough liquid to hold the pastry together as it is rolled.

When making sweet pastry dishes, various types of short pastry may be used and the difference may be in the liquid added to bind the ingredients. Plain short crust pastry is bound with a little water. The water should be very cold (preferably iced) and just enough should be added to bind the rubbed in mixture into lumps. The lumps are gently pressed together so that the pastry just holds its shape. It should not be sticky.

Sweet short crust or richer pastry for making flans may be bound with egg yolk instead of, or as well as, a little water. Egg yolk contains a high proportion of fat so the resulting pastry will be very short. Adding sugar to pastry also tends to give a short and crumbly texture. Some rich pastry is made very short by adding extra fat, usually butter, to give a good flavour as well as a short texture.

ADDING LIQUID TO PUFF PASTRY OR FLAKY PASTRY

The dough for this type of pastry has only a small proportion of the fat rubbed in, with the majority of the fat incorporated by rolling it with the pastry. A little extra liquid is added to make a dough that is just slightly sticky. This type of dough holds the fat which is added in lumps or a block during rolling. The resulting pastry is not short; it is crisp and it forms distinct layers. Puff pastry is lighter and has more layers than flaky pastry.

The layers in puff and flaky pastry trap air to make the pastry rise during cooking. A strengthening substance called 'gluten' is naturally present in flour; this is developed by rolling the pastry. The process of rolling and folding actually serves to toughen the basic dough. Adding the fat each time the pastry is rolled means that the dough does not form into a solid mass but retains very fine layers. The air trapped between these layers expands as the dough is heated and so the pastry rises. Because the dough itself is toughened by the gluten, the layers set and give the finished pastry its characteristic crisp texture.

ROLLING OUT

Whatever type of pastry you are handling, you should always roll it out very lightly. Use a very light dusting of flour on the work surface. There should be just enough to prevent the pastry from sticking; short pastries usually require less than puff or flaky pastries. Too much flour at this stage may spoil the balance of ingredients.

Never turn pastry over during rolling. The pastry should be lifted occasionally and turned around to prevent it from sticking to the surface. Push the rolling pin away from you in short, quick strokes. Keep the rolling pin lightly dusted with flour.

When rolling out pastry, try to establish the shape as soon as you begin. For example, if you are lining a round flan dish start with a ball of pastry which is flattened into a roughly circular shape. If you want to end up with an oblong sheet of pastry, form the pastry into an oblong lump and flatten it slightly before rolling it.

LIFTING ROLLED-OUT PASTRY

To lift a sheet of pastry, dust the rolling pin lightly with flour and place it in the middle of the pastry. Fold half the pastry over it, then use the rolling pin to lift the pastry into position.

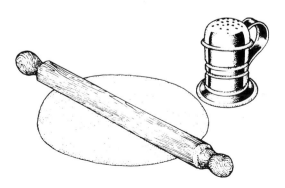

Paella (page 348)

Kedgeree (page 315)

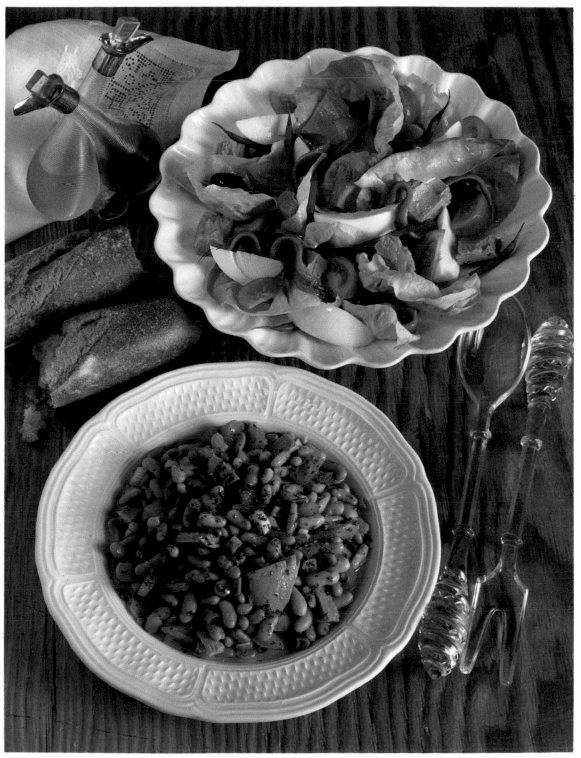

Salad Niçoise (page 385) and Bean Salad with Tuna (page 217)

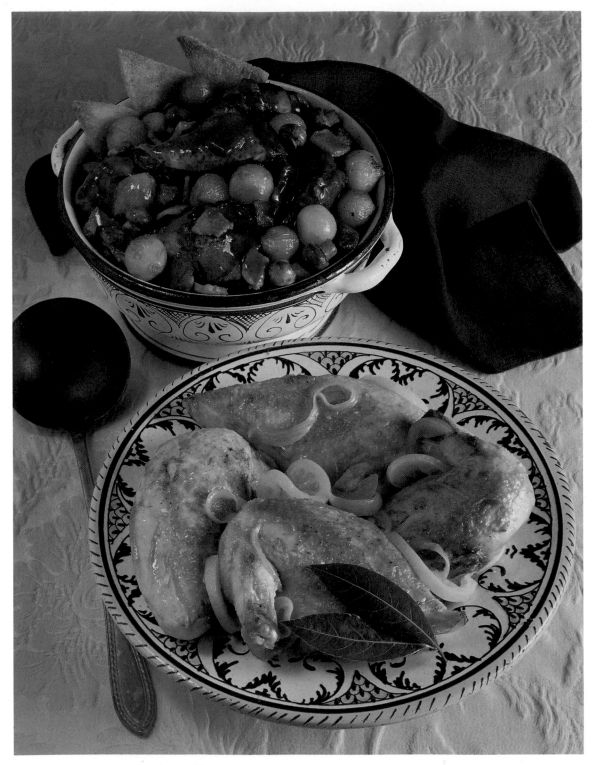

Coq au Vin (page 259) *and Lemon Chicken* (page 319)

Roll the pastry out to a size that will cover the base and come up the sides of the dish with a little extra to spare. Lift the pastry on the rolling pin, then lower it loosely over the tin or dish.

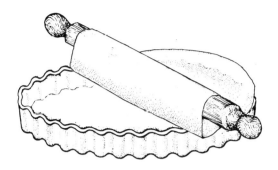

Quickly work around the dish, lifting the edge of the pastry with one hand and pressing it down into the corner of the dish with the forefinger and knuckle of the other hand. When the pastry is pressed neatly all around the base of the dish, press the excess around the edge of the dish so that it falls backwards slightly.

Roll the rolling pin across the top of the dish to trim off excess pastry. If you are lining a tin its edge will cut off the pastry; if using a dish you will have to pull away the excess pastry edges gently.

Pastry cases that are cooked and cooled before they are filled have a sheet of greaseproof paper and baking beans placed in them to prevent the base of the pastry from puffing up. This is known as baking blind. The paper and baking beans are usually removed once the pastry has cooked enough to set, and the pastry case returned to the oven to allow it to brown slightly.

In some recipes, the pastry case is partially baked before it is filled, and the cooking is completed with the filling. The technique of baking blind would be used for this preliminary baking of the pastry case.

Clear instructions are given in individual recipes. Ceramic baking beans may be purchased for baking blind, or ordinary dried peas or beans may be used. These are sprinkled over the greaseproof paper to weight the pastry slightly. Dried peas or beans used for this purpose may be cooled and stored in an airtight container and used over and over again. However, they may not be cooked to be eaten in another recipe.

MAKING TURNOVERS

Turnovers may be cut in circles or squares. The size to which the pastry should be rolled depends on the quantities given in the recipe.

Use a saucer or plate to mark out circles; small turnovers are made by using large round biscuit cutters. When using a saucer or plate, place it on the pastry and cut around it with a small pointed knife.

Put the filling on one half of the pastry. Dampen all around the pastry edge, then fold the pastry over the filling. Press the pastry edges together well to seal in the filling and to give a neat semi-circular turnover.

To make triangular turnovers, roll out the pastry into a large square. Use a large, clean ruler and a small, pointed knife to trim off the pastry edges. Cut the pastry into four squares of equal size. Place some filling on one half of each pastry square, in a corner, and dampen the edges. Fold the corner of pastry opposite the filling over to enclose it completely and to make a neat triangle. Press the edges together to seal in the filling.

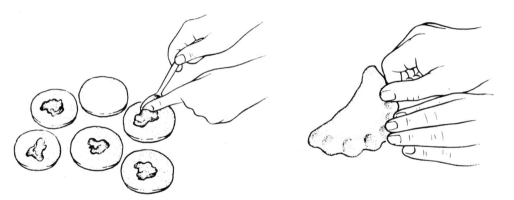

PASTRY PIES

Roll out the pastry about 5 cm/2 inches larger than the top of the dish. Cut off a strip from the edge of the pastry. Dampen the edge of the dish and press the strip of pastry on to it. Fill the dish, dampen the pastry edge and lift the pastry lid over the top. Press the edges of the pastry to seal in the filling. Holding the pie dish slightly raised in one hand, use a sharp knife to trim all around the edge of the dish. Keep the knife pointing outwards so that only the excess pastry is trimmed off.

KNOCKING UP

Knocking up is the term used for neatly sealing the pastry edges together. Press down and outwards on the pastry edge with the knuckle and forefinger of one hand, at the same time knocking the pastry edge inwards with the blunt edge of a round-bladed knife.

SCALLOPED EDGES

The traditional edge for a sweet pie is small scallops (large ones are used for savoury pies). Use the blunt edge of a knife to pull the pastry inwards as you push the edge out towards the rim of the dish with the finger of your other hand.

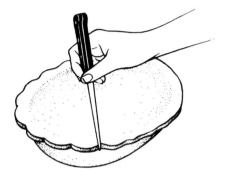

FORKED EDGE

A simple edging technique is to press all around the pastry with a fork. However, the edge does sometimes tend to become slightly too brown if the pastry is pressed very thin.

PLAITED EDGE

Re-roll leftover pastry and cut out three long, thin strips. Plait these together all around the edge of the pie.

DECORATIONS USING CUTTERS

Use small cocktail cutters to cut out pastry shapes. Dampen these and overlap them around the edge of the pie.

PASTRY LEAVES

Roll out a strip of pastry – the wider the strip, the longer the leaves – and cut it into diamond shapes. Mark veins on the leaves and pinch one end of each into a stalk.

IMAGINATIVE DESIGNS

Roll out pastry trimmings and cut out apples, pears, cherries or strawberry shapes to decorate the top of the pie. Dampen the pastry to keep the decorations in place. Alternatively, cut out letters to spell 'apple', 'pear' or whichever fruit is appropriate for the filling and press them on the pie. A message, or the name of the recipient may be applied in the same way.

SUET CRUST PASTRY

Suet crust pastry is quick and easy to make. Shredded suet is combined with self-raising flour and the ingredients mixed to a soft dough with cold water. The quantity of water should give a soft but not sticky dough which may be kneaded very lightly into a smooth shape. The pastry rises to give a light texture that is slightly spongy. Suet pastry is cooked by steaming, boiling or baking.

CHOUX PASTRY

Although many people shy away from making choux pastry, it is not difficult. However, it is important that all the ingredients are accurately measured and that a few rules are observed. The water and fat must be heated together gently until the fat melts, and the mixture brought to the boil as quickly as possible. Do not bring the water to the boil before the fat melts. The flour must be tipped into the liquid all at once, the pan removed from the heat and the mixture stirred to make a smooth paste that comes away from the sides of the pan in a clean ball. Do not beat the mixture at this stage or it will become greasy. If the mixture is too wet put the pan back on the heat and stir gently until the paste comes away from the sides of the pan. This paste must be cooled slightly before the eggs are added.

Lastly, eggs are beaten into the paste. At this stage the mixture should be thoroughly beaten until it is smooth and glossy. The paste should be soft enough to pipe but it should not be runny. Use the choux pastry at once.

This Greek pastry contains little fat. It is made with a strong flour. It is available both chilled and frozen, ready rolled in very thin sheets.

Two or three sheets are layered together before they are wrapped around a filling. Each sheet is brushed with melted butter. The pastry is very delicate to handle as it rapidly becomes brittle once unpacked. Always keep the pastry covered with cling film or under dampened tea-towels when you are not working with it as it dries rapidly if exposed to the air. Make sure the work surface is perfectly dry before unrolling the pastry. Any dampness will cause the pastry to stick, soften and break up.

FILO PASTRY

TIPS FOR SUCCESS WITH PASTRY

- Work in a cool place; keep hands, utensils and all ingredients cool.
- Weigh and measure all ingredients accurately.
- Handle pastry as lightly as possible, and work as quickly as you can, at all stages.
- Use the minimum amount of flour for rolling out.
- Chill short crust, flaky and puff pastry for 20–30 minutes before rolling it out.
- Chill finished short crust, puff or flaky pastry goods for 15 minutes before baking.

PASTRY PROBLEMS AND HOW TO AVOID THEM

SHORT CRUST PASTRY (OR SIMILAR PASTRIES)

Hard, tough pastry
- Too little fat used
- Too much liquid added
- Pastry handled too much or too heavily
- Too much flour used for rolling out

Pastry too short, very crumbly (collapses)
- Too much fat used
- Fat overworked into flour
- Too little liquid used

Grainy, flaky or blistered pastry
- Fat not rubbed in sufficiently
- Water not mixed in well
- Pastry rolled out twice
- Too much flour used for rolling

PUFF OR FLAKY PASTRY

Pastry Hard and Tough

- Warm fat used
- Too much water used
- Dough overkneaded
- Oven temperature too low during cooking

Soggy Pastry with a Hard Crust

- Oven too hot; pastry browned and hardened before it had time to rise

Unevenly Risen

- Fat not mixed in evenly during rolling
- Unevenly folded and rolled
- Pastry not chilled before use
- Pastry flat, not light
- Warm fat used
- Dough not folded and rolled sufficiently

SUET CRUST PASTRY

Hard and Tough

- Too much water added
- Cooked in a low oven for too long

Solid, Lumpy Pastry

- Plain flour used in a recipe that stipulated self-raising flour or plain flour plus a raising agent
- Pastry cooked too quickly (suet has not melted)
- Pastry became wet during steaming
- Home-grated suet was lumpy

HOT WATER CRUST PASTRY

By comparison with other pastries, hot water crust is a heavy dough. Plain flour is bound to a dough with a mixture of water and lard, heated together until boiling.

Hot water crust pastry should be mixed, then lightly kneaded until smooth. If it is overworked it becomes greasy. Once mixed, the pastry should be kept warm in a bowl placed over hot (not simmering) water. To prevent the surface from drying, the dough should be closely covered with a polythene bag.

Hot water crust pastry is usually used for moulding pies, both large and small. When hot it is malleable and the surface of the dough is easily smoothed. Also, while hot the edges of the dough seal together easily and they may be pinched into a neat border.

As the pastry cools it becomes more difficult to manage and tends to crack on the surface. When moulding pie cases around the outside of a container, the pastry has to be cooled before it may be filled and covered; during this time the pastry for the lid should be kept just warm over hot water. The method which gives a better finish is to line a mould with pastry, then fill and cover it at once.

If the sides of a mould are removed so that the pastry may brown, it is important to work quickly once the mould is no longer supporting the pie, otherwise the soft pastry may collapse. Before removing the sides of the mould, have beaten egg ready to brush the pastry. Brush the pastry quickly and put the pie back into the oven. The egg helps to strengthen and seal the pastry quickly.

If the sides of a moulded pie begin to bulge, quickly wrap a double-thick band of foil around the pie, placing it halfway up the depth. Return the pie to the oven until the pastry sets.

SHORT CRUST PASTRY

MAKES ABOUT 225 G/8 OZ

225 g/8 oz plain flour

2.5 ml/½ tsp salt

100 g/4 oz margarine (or half butter, half lard)

flour for rolling out

Sift the flour and salt into a bowl, then rub in the margarine until the mixture resembles fine breadcrumbs. Add enough cold water to make a stiff dough.

Press the dough together with your fingertips. If time permits, wrap in greaseproof paper and rest in the refrigerator for 30 minutes. To use, roll out on a lightly floured surface.

variation

WHOLEMEAL SHORT CRUST PASTRY Although wholemeal flour may be used on its own, this does tend to create a rather chewy pastry. Using 100 g/4 oz each of plain and wholemeal flour gives a very satisfactory result.

COMMON SWEET SHORT CRUST

This old-fashioned sweet pastry is firm, not crumbly – a sweet equivalent of hot water crust.

MAKES ABOUT 350 G/12 OZ

225 g/8 oz plain flour
45 g/1 ½ oz butter
25 g/1 oz caster sugar
150 ml/¼ pint milk

Put the flour into a bowl. Rub in the butter until the mixture resembles fine breadcrumbs, then stir in the sugar.

Bring the milk to the boil in a small saucepan. Add the boiling milk to the flour mixture and knead until smooth. Use at once by rolling out thinly on a lightly floured surface. This pastry may be used as a topping for fruit pies.

BUTTER CRUST PASTRY

This excellent pastry forms crisp layers when cooked. It does not rise as high as puff or flaky pastry but it has a pleasing, filo-like texture to the separate flakes.

MAKES ABOUT 350 G/12 OZ

225 g/8 oz plain flour, plus extra for rolling and dredging
75 g/3 oz butter

Put the flour in a bowl. Using a round-bladed knife for mixing, add enough water (about 150 ml/¼ pint) to make a smooth, soft dough.

Roll out the dough on a lightly floured surface into an oblong measuring 30 x 15 cm/12 x 6 inches. Mark roughly into thirds. Dot the middle third with the butter and dredge the fat lightly with flour.

Fold top and bottom thirds over the fat to enclose it completely, then roll it out again. If time permits, wrap in polythene and rest in the refrigerator for 15 minutes. Repeat the rolling and folding three times, so that the butter is evenly distributed. To use, roll out on a lightly floured surface. This pastry is ideal for topping savoury or sweet pies; for pasties or small items like sausage rolls and for plaits or slices.

PATE SUCREE

MAKES ABOUT 350 G/12 OZ

200 g/7 oz plain flour
1.25 ml/¼ tsp salt
90 g/3½ oz butter
50 g/2 oz caster sugar
1 egg yolk
flour for rolling out

Sift the flour and salt into a bowl. Cut the butter into small pieces and rub into the flour until the mixture resembles fine breadcrumbs. Mix in the sugar, then the egg yolk, and add enough cold water to make a stiff dough. Roll out on a lightly floured surface and use as required for sweet flans, tarts and tartlets.

PUFF PASTRY

MAKES ABOUT 450 G/1 LB

225 g/8 oz plain flour
1.25 ml/¼ tsp salt
225 g/8 oz butter, chilled
5 ml/1 tsp lemon juice
flour for rolling out

Sift the flour and salt into a bowl. Rub in 50 g/2 oz of the butter. Add the lemon juice and enough cold water to mix the ingredients to a smooth, fairly soft dough. The mixture should take about 125 ml/4 fl oz water but this must be added by the spoonful to avoid making the dough too wet. Wrap the dough in cling film and chill briefly.

Shape the remaining butter into a rectangle measuring about 10 x 7.5 cm/4 x 3 inches, then chill again. On a lightly floured surface, roll out the dough into an oblong measuring about 25 x 15 cm/10 x 6 inches, or slightly smaller. Place the butter in the middle of the dough, then fold the bottom third over it and fold the top third down to enclose the butter completely. The technique is illustrated below.

Press the edges of the dough together with the rolling pin. Give the dough a quarter turn in a clockwise direction. Roll out the dough into an oblong as before, fold it again, then wrap in cling film. Chill for 30 minutes. Roll and fold the pastry 6 times in all, chilling well each time. To remember the number of rollings, mark dents in the dough with your fingertips – 1 dent after the first rolling, 2 after the second and so on.

After the process of rolling and folding is complete, chill the pastry again before using it as required.

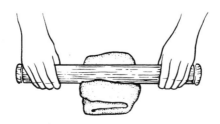

ROUGH PUFF PASTRY

A slightly easier version of puff pastry; all the fat must be well chilled for success.

MAKES ABOUT 450 G/1 LB

175 g/6 oz butter, cut in chunks and chilled

225 g/8 oz plain flour

1.25 ml/¼ tsp salt

5 ml/1 tsp lemon juice

flour for rolling out

Chill the fat (and the flour if possible). Sift the flour and salt into a bowl. Add the butter and mix in lightly using a round-bladed knife. Mix in the lemon juice and enough ice-cold water to make a soft dough. The mixture should take about 125 ml/4 fl oz (or very slightly more) but add the water a spoonful at a time to avoid making the dough too wet. The dough should be soft and very lumpy.

Make sure your hands are very cold by holding them under cold running water before handling the dough. On a lightly floured surface, roll out the dough into an oblong, keeping the corners square. Mark the oblong of dough into thirds, then fold and roll it as for flaky pastry below. Repeat the process four times in all, chilling the dough between each rolling or as necessary.

The rolled dough should be smooth. Wrap it in cling film and chill well before rolling it out to use as required.

FLAKY PASTRY

Flaky pastry does not have as many layers as puff pastry. It contains less fat to flour and the dough is rolled and folded fewer times.

MAKES ABOUT 450 G/1 LB

225 g/8 oz plain flour

1.25 ml/¼ tsp salt

175 g/6 oz butter or 75 g/3 oz each butter and lard, chilled

5 ml/1 tsp lemon juice

flour for rolling out

Sift the flour and salt into a bowl. If using butter and lard, mix them together roughly. Rub in a quarter of the fat, keeping the remaining fat chilled. Stir in the lemon juice and enough cold water to mix the ingredients to a soft dough. The mixture should take about 125 ml/4 fl oz water but this should be added by the spoonful to avoid making the dough too wet.

On a lightly floured surface, roll out the dough into an oblong measuring about 25 × 15 cm/10 × 6 inches. Mark the dough into thirds. Cut the fat into 3 equal portions. Dot one portion of fat over the top two-thirds of the dough, in neat lumps.

Fold the bottom third of the dough up over the middle portion, then fold the top third down so that the lumps of fat are enclosed completely. Press the edges of the dough together with the rolling pin. Give the dough a quarter turn in a clockwise direction, then roll out as before.

Repeat the process of dotting the dough with fat, folding and rolling it, twice more. Chill the dough briefly between each rolling. Finally, fold and roll the pastry once more, without any fat, then chill again before using it as required.

SUET CRUST PASTRY

MAKES 200 G/7 OZ

200 g/7 oz plain flour
5 ml/1 tsp baking powder
pinch of salt
75 g/3 oz shredded suet
flour for rolling out

Sift the flour, baking powder and salt into a mixing bowl. Stir in the suet, then add enough cold water (about 150–175 ml/5–6 fl oz) to make a soft but not sticky dough. Roll out on a lightly floured surface and use the suet crust pastry at once.

CHOUX PASTRY

MAKES ABOUT 175 G/6 OZ

100 g/4 oz plain flour
50 g/2 oz butter or margarine
pinch of salt
2 whole eggs plus 1 yolk

Sift the flour on to a sheet of greaseproof paper. Put 250 ml/8 fl oz water in a saucepan and add the butter or margarine with the salt. Heat gently until the fat melts.

When the fat has melted, bring the liquid rapidly to the boil, then add all the flour at once. Immediately remove the pan from the heat and stir the flour into the liquid to make a smooth paste which leaves the sides of the pan clean. Set aside to cool slightly.

Add the egg yolk and beat well. Add the whole eggs, one at a time, beating well after each addition. Continue beating until the paste is very glossy. Use at once as indicated in recipes.

HOT WATER CRUST PASTRY

This pastry is used for pork, veal and ham, and raised game pies. It must be moulded while still warm.

MAKES 350 G/12 OZ

200 g/7 oz plain flour
2.5 ml/½ tsp salt
75 g/3 oz lard
100 ml/3½ fl oz milk or water

Sift the flour and salt into a warm bowl and make a well in the centre. Keep the bowl in a warm place.

Meanwhile, heat the lard and milk or water until boiling. Add the hot mixture to the flour, mixing well with a wooden spoon until the pastry is cool enough to knead with the hands. Knead thoroughly and mould as required.

Bake at 220°C/425°F/gas 7 until the pastry is set, then reduce the oven temperature to 180°C/350°F/gas 4 until fully baked.

STEAMED SWEET PUDDINGS

Steamed puddings are perfect for winter days, from Newcastle Pudding to traditional Christmas Pudding. Treat the family to a delicious Chocolate Sponge Pudding or surprise them with a steamed sponge pudding cooked in minutes in the microwave.

Traditional steamed puddings take a while to cook and there are a few points to remember for safety and success. In Mrs Beeton's day steaming was a popular cooking method for both savoury and sweet puddings, fish and fowl. The food would be allowed to steam over a pot of boiling water on the kitchen fire or coal-burning stove. When gas and electric cookers became popular, these led to a decline in the use of long, hob-top cooking methods.

Recent trends in healthy eating and cooking have brought steaming right back into fashion, although this method of cooking is used primarily for savoury foods. There are many types of steamer available in the shops, from the metal saucepan-top steamer to the oriental-style bamboo steamer to fit over a wok. Here are a few key features to look out for if you are buying a steamer:

The steamer should have a large base, enabling it to hold plenty of water without needing constant topping up, and it should fit neatly on top of the base to prevent steam escaping around the sides. The top of the steamer should have a tight-fitting lid to keep the steam in during cooking. The following notes outline the types of steamers available and their usefulness for cooking puddings.

SAUCEPAN AND STEAMER SET

This usually comprises a double-handled saucepan base with one, two or more steamers that fit on top. The steaming sections have perforated bases to allow the steam to pass through and they are slightly smaller in diameter at the bottom to fit neatly into the base. Usually made of stainless steel, this type of steamer may be built up to include several cooking tiers. This is ideal for cooking puddings, and the main course or vegetables for the meal may be cooked in separate tiers at the same time.

BAMBOO STEAMERS

Bamboo steamers with tight-fitting lids are available in different sizes. These are designed to fit in a wok. They are perfect for cooking vegetables, oriental-style dishes and any suitable food which can be placed in a fairly shallow container. Some bamboo steamers are deep enough to hold pudding basins; however most woks will only hold sufficient water for comparatively short periods of steaming and need to be topped up frequently with boiling water. This type of steamer is not recommended for puddings that require hours of steaming.

EXPANDING STEAMERS

This type of steamer is made from small stainless steel plates that fold up into a compact shape for storage. The steamer opens out as large as is necessary to hold the food. It stands on short legs in the base of a saucepan. The boiling water must be kept below the level of the steamer and the saucepan must have a tight fitting lid. This type of steamer is ideal for vegetables and it may be used for puddings. Since only a small amount of water may be placed in the pan beneath the steamer it is not suitable for cooking puddings that require many hours of steaming.

ALUMINIUM STEAMERS WITH GRADUATED BASES

These are very common and are designed to fit on top of saucepans of different sizes. Ensure that the steamer has a tight-fitting lid and that it sits neatly on top of the pan.

ELECTRIC STEAMER

This is a plug-in, work-top appliance. A heating element in the base is controlled thermostatically to keep the water boiling or steaming at the right temperature. One or two tiers are supplied to fit over the base, with a tight-fitting lid for the top. In comparison with the other types of steamers, this is an expensive option. However, if you intend to steam a lot of foods it may be a worthwhile purchase. Depending on the individual steamer, this type may lose a lot of steam during cooking, creating puddles on the work surface or condensation on surrounding fittings. Check the steaming layers on the base to make sure they fit neatly. Follow the manufacturer's instructions closely.

IMPROVISING

If you do not own a steamer it is possible to steam puddings by standing them in a saucepan and adding boiling water to come part of the way up the outside of the container. Place a suitable saucer or cereal bowl upside down in the bottom of the pan as a base on which to stand the pudding, allowing for a greater depth of water. Make sure that the saucepan has a tight-fitting lid and follow the instructions in individual recipes.

MICROWAVE COOKING

The microwave oven may be used to make excellent steamed puddings. For more information, and a recipe, see Sponge Pudding (page 404). Here are some hints for safety and success:

- Never use a metal container or dish with metal trimmings.
- Sponge puddings rise rapidly and to a considerable height, so make sure the basin used is not more than half full before microwave steaming.
- When cooked, sponge puddings should be slightly sticky on top.
- Use microwave cling film or a suitable plate to cover the pudding during cooking.

PRESSURE COOKING

A pressure cooker may be used to cook steamed puddings quickly and very successfully. It may also be used to cook certain other puddings, for example set custards, and notes are given where applicable.

Always read and follow the manufacturer's instructions for your cooker. In particular, check information on the minimum volume of water to use in the cooker, notes about pressure levels and specific advice on cooking sponge-type puddings in the pressure cooker. Selected recipes have been tested in a pressure cooker and timings are given in Pressure Cooker Tips. The following rules should be followed when pressure cooking sponge puddings.

- Traditional large steamed puddings should be cooked on Low (5 lb) pressure.
- Small puddings and individual puddings may be cooked on High (15 lb) pressure.
- Add at least 900 ml/1½ pints of water to allow for the pre-steaming time before the cooker is brought to pressure.
- The basin used for the pudding should withstand the temperature reached in the pressure cooker; it should be watertight and not cracked or chipped.
- Thoroughly grease the pudding basin and half or two-thirds fill it.
- Tie down the cover on the basin securely.
- Before bringing to pressure, all sponge puddings must be pre-steamed in boiling water with the lid on but without using weights. This allows the raising agent to work.
- Reduce the pressure slowly after cooking, following the manufacturer's instructions.

Plain milk puddings fit very well into a day-to-day diet as they are inexpensive, satisfying and nutritious. You may always use semi-skimmed or skimmed milk if you are following a low-fat diet. Although white rice is the traditional ingredient for making puddings, brown rice may be used to provide a certain amount of fibre. Varieties of rice that are popular for savoury dishes are not necessarily suitable for making puddings. Unprocessed long-grain rice, Patna rice, pudding rice or flaked rice should be used. Short-grain or round-grain are other terms for pudding rice. Processed, or easy-cook, rice is not suitable for making puddings as the grains do not break down to give a creamy result. Other popular ingredients used to make milk puddings include semolina, macaroni, tapioca and sago.

Baked milk puddings are easy to prepare but they require slow cooking (for recipe, see page 373). For a creamy result stir in the skin which forms on the top of the pudding after the first two-thirds of the cooking time has elapsed. It is possible to cook rice pudding by simmering it very gently on the hob. The heat must be on the lowest setting and the pudding should be stirred often.

PRESSURE COOKING

Milk puddings may be cooked in a pressure cooker. This gives good, creamy results in a fraction of the time needed for baking or simmering. Do not use less than 600 ml/1 pint of milk and keep the heat at a steady temperature which is low enough to prevent the milk from rising too high in the cooker and blocking the vent. For the same reason the cooker should not be more than a quarter full when cooking a milk pudding.

MICROWAVE COOKING

Milk puddings may be cooked in the microwave oven. Semolina cooks particularly well; however puddings using rice, tapioca, macaroni or semolina boil over very readily. For this reason a medium or low microwave power setting should be used and the pudding should be cooked in a very large dish – a mixing bowl covered with a suitable dinner plate or very deep casserole is ideal. The advantage of cooking milk puddings thickened with rice in the microwave is a matter of personal opinion. Since a low power setting has to be used the time saving is not enormous and this cooking method demands attention to ensure that the pudding does not boil over. As an alternative to traditional recipes, the following is an excellent microwave method for making an extravagant, deliciously creamy rice pudding.

Put 50 g/2 oz short-grain rice in a covered dish. Add 600 ml/1 pint water and cook on High for 20–25 minutes. At the end of the cooking time all the water should have been absorbed and the grains of rice should be swollen and sticky. Immediately stir in sugar to taste and 300 ml/½ pint double or single cream. The pudding may be dotted with butter and sprinkled with a little grated nutmeg, then lightly browned under a moderate grill.

FRUIT DESSERTS AND JELLIES

A wide variety of fruit is now available throughout the country all year round, including many exotics that were unheard of in Mrs Beeton's day. Fruit salads may be as simple or as exciting as you please, offering just two or three fresh fruits, a combination of exotic fresh fruits (described below), or some familiar fresh fruits with exotic canned fruits. A fruit salad always looks good, especially when served in an ice bowl or a container made from the shell of one of the component fruits. Pineapple and Kirsch Salad (page 358), served in pineapple half-shells, looks spectacular, as would the Red Fruit Salad (page 372), served in a hollowed-out watermelon.

The diet-conscious may prefer an unsweetened fruit salad, or a little honey may be used in place of the traditional syrup. Serve cream, yogurt or fromage frais with fruit salad and offer some plain biscuits to complete the dessert.

EXOTIC FRUITS

New fruits appear on the supermarket shelves regularly. Some sell well and soon become familiar, others are only seen once or twice. The following is a brief guide to some of the unusual fruits that are available.

Apple Bananas These are very small bananas with thin skins. Their flesh is quite dry but they taste similar to a banana with a hint of apple. They are grown in Kenya and Malaysia. Their size and good flavour make apple bananas ideal dessert fruit, for topping with vanilla ice cream or serving flamed with brandy.

Carambola The carambola is known as star fruit because of its ridged shape. The slices resemble stars. The pale yellow, waxy-looking skin may be left on unless the fruit is particularly tough. The flesh has a very delicate flavour, making the fruit ideal for decorating a wide variety of desserts, including cheesecakes, trifles and gateaux.

Figs Purple-skinned figs should be just soft when ripe. They have a deep red-coloured flesh with lots of small pale seeds. When the skin is removed thinly, the flesh will be found to have a sweet flavour. Whole figs may be quartered and served with a small scoop of orange sorbet or good ice cream to make a tempting dessert. Figs are also exceedingly good with creamy goat's cheese.

Guava An oval, pale yellow-skinned fruit, pear or plum-shaped. The guava has a slightly scented, tangy flesh with lots of small seeds in the middle. The peel should be removed before the fruit is sliced. It is best lightly poached in syrup, after which the slices may be added to cool fruit salads or used in a variety of desserts.

Kiwi Fruit A green fruit with a brown, slightly furry skin that is quite thin. When cut across, the small oval fruit has a pale core, surrounded by small dark seeds and bright green flesh. The fruit should be peeled before being sliced. It is often used for decorating desserts or for adding to fruit salads.

Kumquats These look like tiny oranges. They are citrus fruit with a slightly bitter, orange flavour. They may be poached and eaten whole but they do contain pips. If sliced, the pips may be removed before the fruit is cooked. Kumquats may be eaten raw but they are quite sharp; their skin resembles fine orange peel.

Mango The mango is oval and about the size of a medium potato. The skin is red when the fruit is fully ripe, by which time the mango should feel slightly soft. There is a large, thin, oval stone in the centre of the juicy orange flesh. The mango has a flavour reminiscent of peaches but it is slightly more scented and a little tangy. The fruit should be peeled and the flesh cut off the stone in long wedges or slices.

Papaya An oval fruit with a deep yellow skin which is slightly green before the fruit ripens. Cut open, the papaya has seeds in the middle and sweet apricot-coloured flesh. It is very good in fruit salads.

Passion Fruit Small, round, dimpled fruit with a hard, purple skin. When cut in half the passion fruit reveals a soft, orange-coloured, juicy flesh with small, dark, edible seeds. The flesh is scooped out with a teaspoon, and may then be sieved and used to flavour desserts or sweet sauces.

Persimmon A small, round, orange-coloured fruit with a large stalk end. The skin is thin but tough. The soft flesh is evenly coloured and it has a slightly bitter flavour.

STEWED FRUIT

Stewed fruit may be served hot or cold. A common mistake is to overcook stewed fruit until it is reduced to a pulp. Perfectly stewed fruit should consist of large pieces of tender fruit in a small amount of syrup.

The fruit should be washed, dried and prepared according to its type.

Apples Peel, core and quarter or cut into thick slices.

Blackberries Pick over, wash and drain.

Blackcurrants String both redcurrants and blackcurrants.

Gooseberries Top and tail.

Peaches Place in a bowl, cover with boiling water and leave for 1 minute, then skin. Halve and remove stones.

Pears Peel, core and halve, quarter or slice.

Plums Leave whole or halve and stone.

Rhubarb Trim and slice into 2.5–5 cm/1–2 inch lengths. If rhubarb is old, peel it thinly to remove any tough strings.

Fruits that discolour should be sprinkled with lemon juice or added to a brine solution as they are prepared. Drain and thoroughly rinse fruit soaked in brine. Prepare a syrup, allowing 50–175 g/2–6 oz sugar to 150 ml/¼ pint water, depending on the fruit and on personal taste. This quantity is sufficient for 450 g/1 lb fruit. Sharp fruits, such as blackcurrants or rhubarb, may require extra sugar. Dissolve the sugar in the water over low heat, then bring the syrup to the boil. Reduce the heat before adding the fruit, then cover the pan and allow the liquid to simmer very gently so that the fruit yields its syrup to come about one-third of the way up the fruit, although this depends on the size of the pan. Cook the fruit until tender but not mushy, turning large pieces occasionally so that they cook evenly.

Medium or dry cider, or fruit juice, may be used to make the syrup instead of water. Honey may be added instead of sugar, in which case extra liquid should be used. The cooking syrup may be flavoured with a strip of lemon or orange rind, or with whole spices such as cloves or cinnamon.

Use a large spoon to transfer the fruit to a heatproof serving dish or individual dishes and coat with the cooking syrup. Alternatively, leave the fruit to cool in the covered pan and lightly chill it before serving.

MICROWAVE STEWED FRUIT

Most types of fruit cook well in the microwave. Use a large lidded dish or mixing bowl with a plate as a cover. Prepare the syrup first, allowing about 2–3 minutes on High for 150 ml/¼ pint of liquid. The more sugar, the longer the cooking time. Stir the syrup well so that the sugar has dissolved before the fruit is added. Make sure that the fruit is well coated with syrup and cover the dish. Cook the fruit on High, stirring once or twice during cooking. The following is a guide to cooking times for 450 g/1 lb fruit:

apples – 4–6 minutes
blackcurrants – 8–10 minutes
blackberries – 3–5 minutes
gooseberries – 5–7 minutes
peaches (4) – 4–5 minutes
pears – 6–8 minutes
plums – 3–5 minutes
rhubarb – 6–8 minutes

The exact cooking times depend on the size and ripeness of the fruit. Allow the fruit to stand for 2 minutes before serving.

JELLIES

Home-made fruit jelly makes a refreshing, healthy dessert, whether set in individual dishes or in a mould. Always check the size of the mould before pouring the jelly into it. The mould should be full but not overflowing; if it is only half full the turned out jelly will not look attractive.

Allow plenty of time for a jelly to set. Stand the mould on a small baking sheet. When cool place the jelly in the refrigerator. If the jelly has a strong scent of fruit cover the mould with cling film to prevent the flavour of the jelly from tainting other foods in the refrigerator. The jelly may be set in a cool place other than the refrigerator but this usually takes longer. Cover the mould to prevent any dust or dirt from falling on to the jelly.

A small amount of jelly may be set quickly by placing the mould in the freezer. Check that the mould is freezerproof before doing this. A larger volume of jelly may be placed in the freezer for 10 minutes to speed up the chilling process before transferring it to the refrigerator to set completely. Never place hot jellies in the refrigerator or freezer.

Pour in just enough jelly to cover the base and sides of the mould. Rotate the mould in your hands until it has a thin, even coating of jelly, then place it in the refrigerator to set completely. For speed, the jelly may be placed in the freezer to set. Keep the remaining jelly in a warm place so that it does not set.

If canned fruit is being added for decoration, drain this thoroughly before putting it into the mould. Cut pieces of fruit to fit the shape of the mould and make a decorative pattern on top of the set jelly. It is a good idea to dip each piece of fruit in the remaining liquid jelly before arranging it in the mould. When the pattern is complete, spoon a little more liquid jelly over it, taking care not to disturb the arrangement of the fruit.

Allow the lined mould to set before adding the filling. When the filling is added, it should come to the top of the mould so that when the jelly or jellied dessert is turned out, the shape is perfect. If a creamed filling is used which does not fill the mould completely, allow it to set lightly, then spoon liquid jelly on top.

COATING A MOULD WITH JELLY

This section explains all-important basic methods and techniques, from preparing tins to storing and freezing cakes.

CAKES

There is nothing quite as frustrating as battling unsuccessfully to release a beautifully cooked cake in one piece from an ill-prepared tin. Difficulties with turning cakes out of tins can often be avoided if the tin is properly prepared in the first instance. Each recipe featured in this book offers guidance on the size and shape of tin required and the method by which it should be prepared before the mixture is turned into it. Good cake tins are those to which the cooked mixture is not supposed to stick but this is little consolation when the tin fails to live up to its promise and you end up with the cake firmly stuck to it. So, if you have doubts about whether a specific tin is going to release the cake easily, do plan ahead and at least line the bottom of the tin. There are four main ways to prepare tins:

PREPARING TINS FOR BAKING

1 Bun tins, patty tins and baking sheets should be greased. In some instances the sheets should be dusted with flour after greasing.

2 For rubbed-in cakes each tin should be greased and the base should be lined. The lining paper should be greased before the mixture is placed in the tin.

3 For creamed mixtures it is best to line the base of each tin and in some cases, where the cake requires lengthy cooking, the sides of the tin should also be lined. The lining paper should be greased. The same preparation applies to cakes made by the melted method, for example gingerbread.

4 For whisked sponge cakes each tin should be greased and dusted with a little flour. If the tin is one to which the cake may stick on the base, then a circle of paper should be used to line the base of the tin. The floured sides of the tin provide a surface to which very light sponge mixtures may adhere as they rise during cooking.

Non-stick Tins

Many non-stick tins do not have to be lined before they are used. Follow the manufacturer's instructions carefully when preparing this type of tin.

Fat for greasing

The most convenient fat for greasing is oil. A special 'oil well' gadget is designed to hold a small amount of oil with a suitable brush ready for greasing tins. Alternatively, a few drops of oil can be tipped into the tin and brushed evenly over its surface. Lard or other white cooking fat is suitable for greasing tins but butter and margarine are not recommended. If butter or margarine is used it should be clarified first to remove all excess moisture and salt which it contains.

The purpose of greasing is obvious – to prevent the cake from sticking to the tin or to the lining paper. The process of lining tins is made easy if the tin itself is lightly greased first. The lining paper clings to the greased surface, allowing it to be pushed neatly up against the sides. Where the lining paper overlaps slightly, the under-piece should be lightly greased so that the top piece clings to it and stays in place.

Choice of lining paper

Greaseproof paper is the most common form of lining which is used when preparing tins. However, non-stick baking parchment can be used instead. Follow the manufacturer's instructions when using this product as, in many cases, it does not require greasing before the cake mixture is placed on it. Heavy, re-usable non-stick baking paper is also available and this is particularly useful if you want to make a semi-permanent lining for a frequently used tin. The tin should of course be washed and the paper wiped clean between uses. Again, the manufacturer's instructions should be followed for using this type of paper.

For making small cakes, paper cake cases can be used, either by standing them on a baking sheet or placing them in patty tins. If the cases are fairly flimsy, it is best to place them in tins for support. It is also possible to purchase large fluted paper cases that can be used to line full-sized cake tins. This is particularly useful if the cake is to be frozen once it is cooked.

When making rich fruit cakes, the tins are best lined with a double thickness of greaseproof paper. To protect the outside of the cake, near the sides and base of the tin, a thick piece of brown paper or newspaper can be tied securely around the outside of the tin, or a piece can be placed on a baking sheet underneath the tin. This is really only necessary when large cakes are baked for several hours and there may be a danger of the outside crust becoming dry.

1 Place the tin flat on a single or double thickness of lining paper and draw all around the outside of the bottom. Cut out the shape, cutting slightly inside the pencil mark to allow for the thickness of the tin.

2 Measure a strip of paper for the sides of the tin as for lining a round tin. Make sure that there is enough to go all the way around the inside of the tin and that the strip is wide enough for a 2.5 cm/1 inch fold all around the bottom as well as allowing at least 2.5 cm/1 inch to stand above the rim of the tin.

3 Lightly grease the tin and place one square of paper in the base if a double thickness is used; grease this lightly. Make a 2.5 cm/1 inch fold all along one side of the strip of paper.

4 Carefully lift the strip of paper into the sides of the tin. Have a pair of scissors ready to snip and fit the corners of the paper into the tin. The overlap in the strip of paper should be positioned on one side of the tin, not at a corner.

5 Press the paper against the sides of the tin and into the first corner. Snip into the corner of the strip of paper sitting in the base of the tin.

6 Overlap the paper in the base of the tin in the first corner, to make a neat squared lining. Continue to press the paper smoothly against the side of the tin up to the next corner, then cut and fit the paper as before. Fit the paper into all four corners in this way.

7 Place the square of lining paper in the base of the tin and brush all the inside evenly with a little oil.

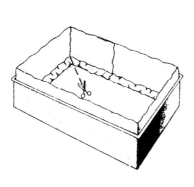

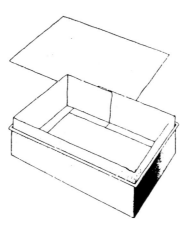

LINING A ROUND TIN

1 Place the tin on a single or double piece of lining paper and draw around the outside edge of the bottom in pencil. Remove the tin and cut out the circle of paper, cutting slightly inside the drawn circle to allow for the thickness of the tin and to ensure that the paper will fit neatly inside the base of the tin.

2 Cut out a strip of paper which is long enough to go around the outside of the tin and overlap by 5 cm/2 inches. The paper should be at least 5 cm/2 inches wider than the depth of the tin, to allow for 2.5 cm/1 inch to sit neatly in the bottom of the tin and at least 2.5 cm/1 inch to stand above the rim of the tin.

3 Make a 2.5 cm/1 inch fold all along one side of the strip of paper. Open out the fold and snip diagonally from the edge in as far as the foldline at 1–2.5 cm/½–1 inch intervals all along the length of the paper.

4 Very lightly grease the inside of the tin. If you are using a double thickness of paper, then place one circle in the base of the tin and grease it very lightly. If you are using a single thickness, then put the lining paper around the sides first. Carefully lower the strip of paper into the tin, placing the snipped folded edge downwards. The fold in the base of the strip should tuck neatly all around the inside of the bottom of the tin and the pieces of snipped paper should be overlapped. Place the circle of lining paper in the base of the tin.

5 Lightly grease the lining paper all over, making sure that it is pressed well into the shape of the tin.

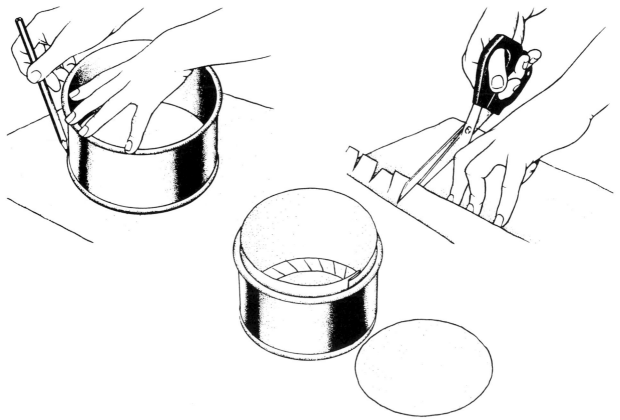

1 Stand the tin on a sheet of greaseproof paper and draw all around the outside of the bottom. Remove the tin.

2 Cut out the shape, about 5 cm/2 inches outside of the drawn shape. This is to allow enough paper to line the sides of the tin and to stand about 2.5 cm/1 inch above the rim of the tin. The paper should not stand more than 2.5 cm/1 inch above the rim as this may impair the process of browning.

3 Cut from each outer corner of the paper into the corner of the drawn shape of the tin.

4 Lightly grease the inside of the tin. Turn the paper over so that the pencil mark is facing downwards, into the tin. Press the paper into the tin, overlapping it at the corners to make a neatly squared lining.

5 The paper will stay in place at the corners if it is greased between the overlap. Grease the lining paper evenly.

LINING A SWISS ROLL TIN

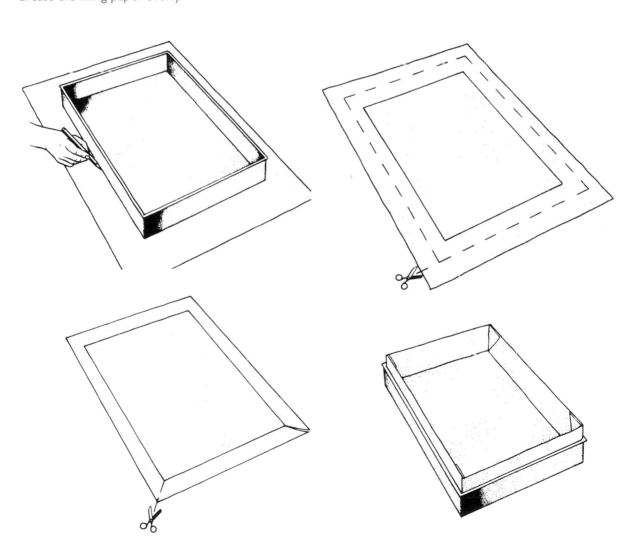

LINING A LOAF TIN

1 Cut a piece of paper large enough to cover the bottom of the tin, to come up both sides and the ends and to stand at least 2.5 cm/1 inch above the tin.

2 Stand the tin in the middle of the paper and draw all around the outside of the bottom.

3 Cut in from each outer corner of the piece of paper to the corner of the drawn shape.

4 Lightly grease the tin, then turn the paper over so that the pencil marks are downwards; lift the paper into the tin.

5 Press the paper neatly into the tin, overlapping the cut corners to make neat squares. Grease lightly between the overlap so that the paper clings together.

6 Grease the lining paper well.

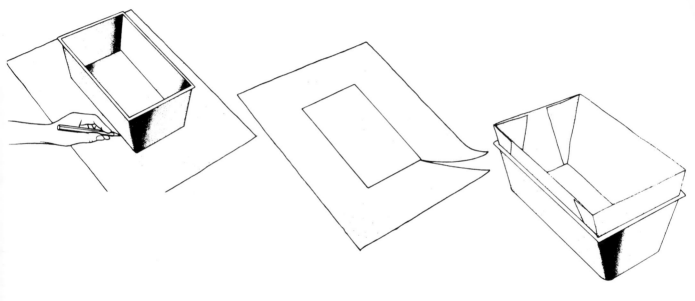

BASE LINING TINS

If the recipe suggests that the base of the tin should be lined, then simply place the tin on a piece of paper, draw around the outside edge and cut out the shape. Lightly grease the base of the tin so that the paper will stay firmly in place. Place the piece of paper in the base of the tin, then grease both paper and sides of the tin.

GREASING AND FLOURING TINS

Lightly grease the inside of the tin. Place a spoonful of flour on the base. Hold the tin at an angle and turn it around and around, tapping the sides as you turn the tin, so that the flour evenly coats the inside. Tip out any excess flour. A little cocoa may be added to the flour for a chocolate cake.

MIXING CAKES

There are several basic methods for mixing cakes, from the simple one-stage method to creaming, whisking, rubbing the fat into the dry ingredients or using a melted mixture.

CREAMED METHOD

For this method, the fat and sugar are creamed together until they are very soft, pale in colour and light. If brown sugar is used the mixture will not become very pale in colour but it should turn paler than it was when you started.

The fat should be warmed to room temperature if necessary so that it creams easily. Butter or margarine are the most common fats to use. Soft margarine can be creamed straight from the refrigerator.

When the creaming stage is complete the eggs are added. They should be beaten first so that they can be added gradually. The eggs should be lightly beaten in and a little of the measured flour sprinkled in if the mixture looks as though it may curdle.

When the eggs are incorporated the flour is folded in. It is important that this process is carried out correctly. A large metal spoon should be used and the mixture must not be beaten. The flour is folded in – it is sprinkled over the mixture and the spoon is used to lift the mixture and to cut the flour through it. Rather than stirring, a figure of eight action is used. The aim is to incorporate the flour with the creamed ingredients without knocking out all the air that was beaten in during the first stage.

Dried fruit or other flavouring ingredients are folded in with the flour or straight afterwards. Sometimes a little extra liquid is added to soften the mixture.

RUBBED-IN METHOD

The flour is sifted into a bowl and the fat is rubbed into it in the same way as for making short crust pastry.

For this method the fat should be chilled and all the other ingredients should be kept cool. When rubbing fat into flour it is important to use just the tips of the fingers. Lift the mixture up and lightly rub it together, letting it fall back into the bowl. By lifting the mixture and rubbing it lightly you are incorporating air. This keeps it light.

Once the fat is incorporated the sugar and other dry ingredients are added and stirred in. The liquid is added last to bind the ingredients.

WHISKED METHOD

The whisked method is used for making very light sponges. The eggs should be allowed to warm to room temperature. They are combined with the sugar in a bowl which is placed over a saucepan of barely simmering water. The water must not be boiling. An electric whisk can be used. It is hard work if an ordinary hand whisk of the balloon or spiral type is used. Whisking can take a very long time with these simple utensils.

The eggs and sugar are whisked together until they are very thick, very pale and quite creamy. A common mistake with this method is to consider that the mixture is whisked sufficiently as soon as it is slightly thickened. The mixture should be thick enough to hold the trail of the whisk for at least 30 seconds. Once it is whisked sufficiently, remove the bowl from the pan of water and continue whisking for a further 5 minutes, until the mixture has cooled.

At this stage the other ingredients are folded in. Flour and a small amount of fat can be added. The fat is usually butter which is melted before it is dribbled slowly over the whisked mixture and folded in. The folding in process is vital to the success of whisked mixtures – a figure of eight action should be used as for creamed mixtures and the whisked mixture should be gently lifted over the flour. On no account should the mixture be stirred or whisked as the air will be knocked out by the rapid movement. This type of cake relies on the air content to rise; if the air is knocked out the cake will not rise.

MELTED METHOD

For this type of mixture the fat and sugar are melted together, usually with some form of flavouring. Treacle or syrup is often used, either in place of the sugar or with it.

Once all the fat is melted the mixture should be allowed to cool very slightly before the beaten eggs are added. Do not overheat the melted ingredients, use low heat and stir the mixture frequently. Any crystals of sugar on the sides of the saucepan may be brushed down into the mixture with a pastry brush.

Lastly, the dry ingredients are beaten in. The majority of melted mixtures should be quite soft when all the ingredients are mixed and some may have the consistency of a thick batter.

ONE-STAGE METHOD

This is a modern method of cake mixing, popularized by margarine manufacturers to promote soft margarine in the early days of its availability. As well as the development of soft margarine which requires less creaming than hard fats, the growth in the ownership of electric food mixers has also helped to make this method an easy and convenient alternative to the creaming method.

All the ingredients are placed in a bowl and are beaten together until thoroughly combined, pale and creamy. A little extra raising agent is usually added to ensure a good rise and all the ingredients should be at room temperature, the best fat to use being soft margarine.

BAKING CAKES AND TURNING THEM OUT

For good results it is important that the oven has an even heat distribution, that it heats correctly to the temperature selected and holds that temperature steadily. The oven should stand evenly; most cookers, whether built in or free standing, have adjustable feet to compensate for any uneven floors. If the oven is not level, the cake mixture will rise unevenly, giving a lopsided result.

One of the most difficult areas of cake making is deciding exactly when the cake is cooked. Firstly, follow the timing given in the recipe as a guide, checking the cake at the first suggested time.

Open the oven door carefully – if you can see that the cake still looks raw, shut the door quickly. Do not bang it and cause the oven to jerk as the cake is cooking.

The appearance of the cooked cake will vary slightly according to its type. Most cakes will be well risen, the exception being very rich fruit cakes which are not intended to rise during cooking. Sponge cakes should have risen to the top of the tin; about doubled in volume. The cake should be evenly browned, not too light and not too dark. The cake should have shrunk away from the sides of the tin very slightly and when pressed lightly it should feel springy on top and the cake should bounce back. If the surface feels at all wet and if the impression of a finger-print remains on top, then the sponge cake is not cooked.

Fruit cakes should not feel spongy; they should be firm and quite well browned. For deep cakes and fruit cakes the skewer test is a good way of determining whether the cake is cooked through.

Take a clean metal skewer and insert it into the middle of the cake. Leave it for a few seconds, then take it out. If the cake is cooked the skewer should not have any mixture adhering to it. The skewer will be slightly greasy and there may be sticky marks on it, particularly if the cake contains a lot of fruit. However, there should not be crumbs or any wet mixture sticking to it. Instead of a skewer, the blade of a slim knife can be inserted into the middle of the cake.

THE SKEWER TEST

Some cakes that require fairly long cooking may begin to look slightly too dark on top before the middle is cooked. This may be due to the type of mixture, in which case the recipe should warn you to check the cake during cooking, or it may be due to the oven. To prevent the surface of the cake from burning while the middle of the cake cooks through, a piece of foil should be placed loosely over the top the cake, shiny side up. This will prevent the upper crust from burning.

PROTECTING THE TOP OF A CAKE

It is important that the tin is well prepared because this stage can be disastrous if the cake is stuck to the base of the tin.

Some fruit cakes should be allowed to cool in the tin for a while before being turned out and the recipe will suggest this if necessary. If this is the case, drape a clean tea-towel over the top of the tin to absorb steam and to prevent the cake from being exposed to dust or dirt.

To turn a cake out of a tin which is not fully lined, first slide a round-bladed knife gently around the inside of the tin, between it and the cake. Place a wire rack over the top of the tin and use an oven glove to hold both rack and tin firmly. Then invert the tin on to the rack and place it on the work surface. Lift the tin off the cake and remove any lining paper. To turn the cake back up the right way, place a second rack on it and invert it yet again.

If the tin has a loose bottom, then prepare some form of stand on which to place the cake in its tin, allowing the side to fall down, away from the cake. A suitable

RELEASING CAKES FROM TINS AND COOLING

storage jar or large upturned basin is ideal. Carefully lower the side of the tin off the cake, then lift the cake and its base to a wire rack. Slide the cake off the base of the tin on to the rack and remove any lining paper. Alternatively, simply invert the cake and tin on to the rack as before and lift off the sides and base of the tin.

Certain cakes may require special treatment, for example Swiss roll. Light sponge cakes mark very easily and they can be turned on to a wire rack covered with a clean tea-towel, or on to a piece of greaseproof paper which is sprinkled with caster sugar.

The cake should be allowed to cool completely before it is stored or wrapped, unless the recipe states otherwise.

STORING CAKES

The keeping quality of cakes depends on the individual mixtures. Some cakes, particularly fruit cakes, improve with keeping. Light fruit cakes often taste better a few days after they are baked and very rich fruit cakes should be allowed to mature for at least a month in order to let all the individual flavours mingle.

Fatless sponge cakes do not keep well and they quickly become very dry. Ideally they should be eaten on the same day or at least the day after they are baked.

Victoria sandwich type cakes keep quite well in an airtight container and they can be stored for about a week, although the time depends on the flavouring ingredients and any filling, covering or decoration which is added. Cakes covered in soft icings do not keep as well as plain cakes.

Most cakes should be stored in an airtight container in a cool, dry place. Fruit cakes which are to be kept for long periods are best stored with the lining paper from cooking left on. The underside is usually pierced all over and sprinkled with a little brandy or rum, then the cake is wrapped in two or three layers of greaseproof paper. To introduce the liquor, the base lining paper should be peeled back and then replaced. The cake can be stored in a clean cardboard cake box or wrapped in foil. Foil must not be placed directly on the cake as it reacts with the fruit acids and may disintegrate in places, causing the surface of the cake to be dusted with foil particles. Rich cakes of this type should not be stored in plastic containers as they may sweat. It is important to keep a rich cake in a cool, dry place and to check it occasionally during storage.

Extra brandy or rum can be used to 'feed' the cake occasionally if it is stored for a long period but it is important not to overdo the liquor feeding as the cake can become soggy.

FREEZING CAKES

Most cakes that are not decorated freeze well. There is no point in freezing a rich fruit cake as it will improve on keeping as described above. Light fruit cakes can be frozen successfully; also cakes made by the creamed or melted methods. Fatless sponges, or those with little fat added, made by the whisked method freeze very well and they also thaw quickly at room temperature. Cakes covered with royal icing, glacé icing or the softer moulding icings should not be frozen as the icing will not thaw successfully.

Packing Plain Cakes The cake should be allowed to cool completely before it is packed for freezing. When it is completely cold, pack the cake in a polythene bag, extracting all the air from the bag, and close it tightly. Label the cake with its type and date, then place it safely in the freezer, where it will neither be crushed nor damaged by other items.

Layers of cake should be separated by placing double thicknesses of greaseproof paper or special interleaving freezer film between them. The layers can then be packed together in one bag and frozen.

Undecorated cakes which are sandwiched together with a filling such as jam can be frozen as one plain cake, but it is best to freeze them unfilled, ready to be sandwiched together when thawed.

Cakes which are filled and covered with fresh cream, buttercream or frosting can be frozen successfully. Although the cake can be frozen with its filling and this type of icing, no decorations should be added before freezing. Decorated cakes should not be frozen for long periods and it is best to keep them for just two to four weeks. It is sometimes useful to be able to make a decorated cake in advance of an occasion and freeze it, provided that the icing is of an appropriate type.

The technique for packing these cakes is to open freeze them. The decorated cake should be placed on freezer film or foil on a baking sheet and frozen uncovered until it is firm. Remember that the icing will not freeze hard and that it can be easily damaged during storage, particularly if there are any piped decorations. Once the cake is frozen it can be packed loosely in a polythene bag (it is best to support the cake on a piece of card first) or, better still, it can be placed in a large rigid container. Place a little crumpled absorbent kitchen paper around the side of the cake to prevent it from slipping against the sides of the container when moved.

The cake should be unpacked and transferred to a serving plate before being allowed to thaw in the refrigerator, preferably overnight or for several hours.

FREEZING DECORATED CAKES

It can be useful to have slices of cake in the freezer, to be removed one piece at a time as required. Either plain or decorated cakes can be packed in this way.

The cake should be cut into slices or wedges. A piece of interleaving film should be placed carefully between each slice and the cake re-shaped. Plain cakes can be packed as before or decorated cakes should be open frozen.

The required number of slices can be removed as they are wanted – this is very useful for lunch boxes or hasty family teas. A piece of plain cake can be packed still frozen in a lunch box first thing in the morning and it will have thawed in time for the midday break.

PACKING INDIVIDUAL SLICES

**FREEZING
SMALL CAKES**

Small cakes cooked in paper cases can be packed neatly in rigid containers or poly-thene bags for freezing. Tray cakes can be cut into squares or portions and frozen in rigid containers, or interleaved with freezer film and packed in bags. They can be removed and thawed a few at a time, as required.

**STEPS TO
SUCCESS**

- Check that all the ingredients and equipment are ready before you begin to mix the cake.
- Weigh and measure correctly, and prepare the tins as suggested in the recipe.
- Follow the recipe carefully, heating the oven when necessary.
- For cakes made by the creamed method make sure that the fat is soft before beginning to beat it with the sugar – this makes the task much easier. Have the other ingredients at room temperature.
- When making a cake by the melting method do not overheat the ingredients. Melt them over low heat until the fat is just melted. Do not let it become too hot. Leave the melted ingredients to cool slightly, if necessary, before adding any eggs.
- Do not open the oven door when the cake is cooking until you think it is ready for checking. Opening the door in the early stages of cooking intro-duces colder air and can cause the cake to sink.
- Test the cake to check if it is cooked before fully removing it from the oven. Use a pair of oven gloves and slide the shelf out slightly. Check the colour and texture of the cake, and use a skewer to test if the middle is cooked if necessary.
- Allow the cake to stand for a few minutes in the tin and there is less chance of it breaking around the edges as it is being turned out. A rich cake should be allowed to cool in the tin until warm; a very rich cake is best left to cool completely in the tin.

Cake sunk in the centre

- Too much raising agent used.
- The fat and sugar were beaten for too long or the fat was too soft (almost runny when creamed).
- The mixture was too soft before baking – this could be due to too little flour or too much liquid.
- The oven door was opened too early or the cake removed from the oven before the mixture had time to set.
- The cake was removed from the oven before it was fully cooked, in which case it would have sunk on cooling slightly.

Cake has risen to a peak and cracked on top

- Fat and sugar not creamed enough.
- Oven too hot or uneven heat distribution in oven and cake cooked too near to the top of the oven, or in too hot an area of the oven.
- The tin was too small for the amount of mixture.

Cake has risen unevenly

- The mixture was not levelled out before baking.
- The oven was not prepared before the cake was put in – this does depend on the type of oven and the time it takes to heat up.
- The oven was not level. This could be because the floor of the kitchen is uneven. Most appliances have adjustable feet to compensate for this.
- The cake was placed on a far corner or to one side of the shelf.
- Too much raising agent was used.

Cake is very dry

- Not enough liquid was added to the mixture.
- The cake was baked for too long.
- Far too much raising agent was used.

Cake has a coarse, open texture

- If the mixture is a rubbed-in type, then the fat was not rubbed in enough. Alternatively, the fat may have been of poor quality.
- The fat and sugar were not creamed together for long enough.
- The oven temperature was too high.
- Too much raising agent was used.

Fruit sunk to the bottom of the cake

- The mixture was too soft and would not support the fruit. Cherries are the most common offender in this example. If the cherries are added to a light fruit cake they must be washed and dried first, then dusted with a little of the measured flour. If they are left coated in syrup they will sink. The dusting of flour helps them to adhere to the surrounding mixture and this prevents them from sinking.

Cake has a sugary crust

- Fat and sugar were not creamed together long enough.
- Too much sugar was used.
- The sugar was too coarse.

YEASTED BREADS

The choice of ingredients for making yeast mixtures is important. Strong flour is used because of its high gluten content. Gluten is the strengthening agent which forms the elastic dough during kneading, to trap the bubbles of gas given off by the yeast during proving. This makes the dough rise and gives the light result.

YEAST

There are various options and all work well.

Fresh Yeast Available from bakers who cook on the premises, small bread shops, hot bread shops or the hot bread counters at larger supermarkets.

Fresh yeast should be pale, firm and slightly crumbly in texture. It should smell fresh. Yeast that is very broken, dark, soft or sour-smelling is old and should not be used. Wrapped in polythene, fresh yeast will keep for several days in the refrigerator or it may be frozen. Freeze 25 g/I oz portions ready for use.

Cream fresh yeast with a little sugar and lukewarm liquid to make a paste. Add a little extra liquid, then place the mixture in a warm place until it becomes frothy. This process gives the yeast a good start so that it is very active when mixed with other ingredients. It is also a way of checking that the yeast is fresh and working.

There has been some controversy over whether the yeast should be creamed with sugar or just with water. The addition of sugar was thought by some to give an unacceptably strong 'yeasty' flavour to the finished baking but as long as the quantities in recipes are followed, and the liquid is not left too long, the results using sugar are better than without.

Other methods of starting the yeast include sponging it – mixing it to a paste, then adding all the liquid and enough flour to make a batter. This is left to rise and bubble before extra ingredients are added and the mixture mixed to a dough.

Sometimes the yeast liquid may be poured into a well in the dry ingredients and allowed to ferment, usually sprinkled with a little flour.

Dried Yeasts There are two types, so always read the manufacturer's instructions and follow them carefully.

The first is a granular product that is sprinkled over warm liquid and left to dissolve, then ferment until frothy before being stirred and mixed with the remaining ingredients. Usually the granules contain enough food for the yeast to work without having to add extra sugar. The second, newer and now more popular type is a finer-grained dried yeast which should be added to the dry ingredients. Slightly hotter liquid is used to mix the dough and only one rising, or proving, is necessary.

TECHNIQUES

Kneading The kneading is important as it mixes the yeast evenly with the other ingredients and it develops the gluten in the flour to make the dough elastic. Once the dough is toughened, it traps the bubbles of gas produced by the yeast and rises.

Proving This is the process of rising. The dough must be left in a warm place until it has doubled in bulk. It must be covered to keep in moisture and prevent a skin forming on the dough (polythene, cling film or a damp cloth may be used). The

Cornish Pasties (page 261)

Cottage Pie (page 262)

Bolognese Sauce (page 225)

Mixed Grill (page 335)

covering is removed after proving, before baking. The warmer the place, the faster the rising but if the dough becomes hot the yeast will be killed. Dough may be left overnight in the refrigerator to rise slowly, or in a cool place for many hours. In a warm room dough will rise in a couple of hours.

Except when using fast-action dried yeast (the type which is combined with dry ingredients), most doughs are proved twice.

Knocking Back After the first proving, the dough is very lightly kneaded to knock out the gas, then it is shaped and allowed to prove for a second time. The second kneading is known as knocking back.

STORING

Breads should be stored in a clean airtight container. If kept in a polythene bag, they should be placed in a cool place (but not the refrigerator which tends to promote staling) to prevent them from sweating.

FREEZING

Yeasted goods freeze well. They should be cooked and cooled, then packed and frozen promptly. Most breads freeze well for up to 2 months. Loaves should be left to thaw for several hours at room temperature; rolls and small items thaw within a couple of hours at room temperature.

BASIC WHITE BREAD

MAKES TWO 800 G/1¾ LB LOAVES

fat for greasing

800 g/1¾ lb strong white flour

10 ml/2 tsp salt

25 g/1 oz lard

25 g/1 oz fresh yeast or 15 ml/
 1 tbsp dried yeast

2.5 ml/½ tsp sugar

flour for kneading

beaten egg or milk for glazing

Grease two 23 x 13 x 7.5 cm/9 x 5 x 3 inch loaf tins. Sift the flour and salt into a large bowl. Rub in the lard. Measure 500 ml/17 fl oz lukewarm water. Blend the fresh yeast to a thin paste with the sugar and a little of the warm water. Set aside in a warm place until frothy – about 5 minutes. Alternatively, sprinkle dried yeast over all the warm water and set aside. When frothy, stir well.

Add the yeast liquid and remaining water to the flour mixture and mix to a soft dough. Turn on to a floured surface and knead for about 8 minutes or until the dough is smooth, elastic and no longer sticky. Return to the bowl and cover with cling film. Leave in a warm place until the dough has doubled in bulk – this will take up to 2 hours, or longer.

Knead the dough again until firm. Cut into two equal portions and form each into a loaf shape. Place the dough into the prepared loaf tins and brush the surface with beaten egg or milk. Place the tins in a large, lightly oiled polythene bag. Leave in a warm place for about 45 minutes or until the dough has doubled in bulk. Set the oven at 230°C/450°F/gas 8.

Bake for 35–40 minutes, until the loaves are crisp and golden brown, and sound hollow when tapped on the bottom.

NOTE

Wheatmeal Bread may be found in the A–Z recipes.

SHAPING YEAST
DOUGH

Yeast doughs of all types may be shaped in many ways to make attractive breads. The following ideas may be used for making two loaves from the Basic White Bread dough recipe on page 169.

Twist Divide the dough in half and roll each piece into a strip. Pinch the two ends of the strips together on a greased baking sheet, then twist the strips together, tucking the ends under neatly and pinching them in place.

Ring Make a long, fairly slim twist, then shape it in a ring on a greased baking sheet.

Cottage Loaf Shape two-thirds of the dough into a round loaf and place on a greased baking sheet. Shape the remaining dough into a ball. Make an indentation in the middle of the round loaf, then dampen the dough in the middle and place the ball on top. Make a deep indentation with your fingers or a wooden spoon handle down through the ball of dough and the round base. Before baking, score several slits down the side of the base of the loaf.

Plait Divide the dough for one loaf into three equal portions and roll them into long strips. Pinch the ends of the strips together on a greased baking sheet, then plait the strips neatly. Fold the ends under at the end of the plait, pinching them underneath to secure the plait.

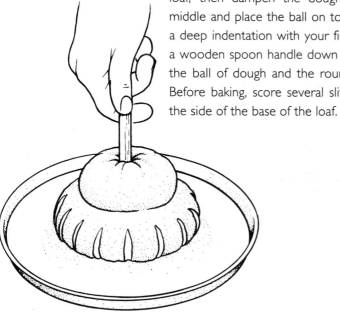

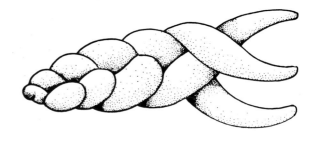

FANCY ROLL SHAPES

Divide the risen Basic White Bread dough (page 169) into 24 × 50 g/2 oz pieces and shape as below:

Small Plaits Divide each piece of dough into three equal portions; then shape each of these into a long strand. Plait the strands together, pinching ends securely.

Small Twists Divide each piece of dough into two equal portions, and shape into strands about 12 cm/4½ inches in length. Twist the strands together, pinching ends securely.

'S' Rolls Shape each piece of dough into a roll about 15 cm/6 inches in length, and form it into an 'S' shape.

Cottage Rolls Cut two-thirds off each piece of dough and shape into a ball. Shape the remaining third in the same way. Place the small ball on top of the larger one and push a hole through the centre of both with one finger, dusted with flour, to join the two pieces firmly together.

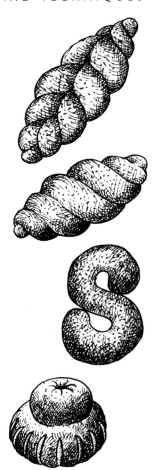

TOPPINGS FOR BREADS

Before baking, the risen dough may be glazed with beaten egg or milk for a golden crust. Brushing with water makes a crisp crust. Then the dough may be sprinkled with any of the following: Poppy seeds – dark or white; Sesame seeds – black or white, for flavour as well as texture and appearance; Cracked wheat – good on wholemeal loaves; Caraway, fennel or cumin seeds – when used generously these all contribute flavour.

DINNER ROLLS

MAKES 24

fat for greasing
800 g/1¾ lb strong white flour
10 ml/2 tsp sugar
400 ml/14 fl oz milk
25 g/1 oz fresh yeast or 15 ml/
  1 tbsp dried yeast
10 ml/2 tsp salt
50 g/2 oz butter or margarine
1 egg
flour for kneading
beaten egg for glazing

Grease two baking sheets. Sift about 75 g/3 oz of the flour and all the sugar into a large bowl. Warm the milk until lukewarm, then blend in the fresh yeast or stir in the dried yeast. Pour the yeast liquid into the flour and sugar and beat well. Leave the bowl in a warm place for 20 minutes.

Sift the remaining flour and the salt into a bowl. Rub in the butter or margarine. Beat the egg into the yeast mixture and stir in the flour mixture. Mix to a soft dough. Turn on to a lightly floured surface and knead for about 5 minutes or until the dough is smooth and no longer sticky. Return to the bowl and cover with cling film. Leave in a warm place until the dough has doubled in bulk – this will take up to 2 hours, or longer.

Knead the dough again until firm. Cut into 50 g/2 oz pieces, then shape each piece into a ball. Place on the prepared baking sheets 5–7.5 cm/2–3 inches apart. Brush with beaten egg. Cover with sheets of lightly oiled polythene. Leave in a warm place for about 20 minutes or until the rolls have doubled in bulk. Set the oven at 220°C/425°F/gas 7.

Bake for 12–15 minutes until the rolls are golden brown.

ENRICHED BREAD

MAKES TWO 800 G/1¾ LB LOAVES

fat for greasing

900 g/2 lb strong white flour

10 ml/2 tsp sugar

400 ml/14 fl oz milk

25 g/1 oz fresh yeast or 15 ml/
   1 tbsp dried yeast

10 ml/2 tsp salt

100 g/4 oz butter or margarine

2 eggs

flour for kneading

milk for glazing

Grease two 23 × 13 × 7.5 cm/9 × 5 × 3 inch loaf tins. Sift about 75 g/3 oz of the flour and all the sugar into a large bowl. Warm the milk until luke-warm, then blend in the fresh yeast or stir in the dried yeast. Pour the yeast liquid into the flour and sugar and beat well. Leave the bowl in a warm place for 20 minutes.

Sift the remaining flour and the salt into a bowl. Rub in the butter or margarine. Beat the eggs into the yeast mixture and stir in the flour mixture. Mix to a soft dough. Turn on to a lightly floured surface and knead for about 6 minutes or until the dough is smooth and no longer sticky. Return to the bowl and cover with cling film. Leave in a warm place until the dough has doubled in bulk – this will take up to 2 hours, or longer.

Knead the dough again until firm. Cut into two equal portions and form each into a loaf shape. Place the dough in the prepared loaf tins. Place the tins in a large, lightly oiled polythene bag. Leave in a warm place for about 30 minutes or until the dough has doubled in bulk. Set the oven at 220°C/425°F/gas 7.

Brush the surface of the dough with milk. Bake for 35–40 minutes until the loaves sound hollow when tapped on the bottom.

variations

BREAD PLAIT Make as for Enriched Bread. Cut the risen dough into two equal portions. Cut one of these into three equal pieces. Roll each piece into a strand 25–30 cm/10–12 inches long and plait the strands together. Repeat, using the second portion. Place the plaits on a greased baking sheet. Cover, leave to rise and bake the plaits as for Enriched Bread.

CHEESE BREAD PLAIT Make as for Bread Plait but add 200 g/7 oz grated Cheddar cheese to the dry ingredients.

CARAWAY BREAD Make as for Enriched Bread but add 10 ml/2 tsp dried sage, 5 ml/1 tsp grated nutmeg and 15 ml/1 tbsp caraway seeds to the dry ingredients.

FRUIT BREAD Make as for Enriched Bread but add 200 g/7 oz sultanas, currants or raisins to the dough when kneading for the second time.

NUT BREAD Make as for Enriched Bread but add 200 g/7 oz chopped nuts, such as walnuts or peanuts, to the dough when kneading for the second time.

POPPY SEED BREAD Make as for Enriched Bread but sprinkle poppy seeds thickly over the dough before baking.

Sweet yeast doughs differ from plain breads in that they are enriched as well as sweetened.

Even more so than when making plain breads, patience plays a vital role when handling rich yeasted mixtures. Although a little sugar is used to speed up the initial action of yeast, when it is added to doughs in quantity, it tends to have the opposite effect, so sweet doughs usually take longer to rise.

The addition of extra fat and eggs to enrich the dough also tends to slow down the action of the yeast. Therefore it is important to allow plenty of time for sweet breads to rise. As well, some of the very rich mixtures (for example, Danish pastries) are best left in a cool place to rise over a long period so that their high butter content does not melt.

Sweet yeast doughs may be used as the basis for making many exciting breads. Ready-to-eat dried fruits such as apricots, apples and peaches, as well as raisins, sultanas and dates, are ideal for kneading into sweet breads. Nuts may be added too – chopped walnuts, hazelnuts, Brazils or pistachios make loaves or buns quite different. With imagination, sweet doughs can be swirled with rich fillings – grated chocolate, ground almonds and icing sugar combine well; cinnamon, brown sugar, chopped walnuts and butter may be used; or chopped candied citron peel mixed with honey and chopped almonds makes a tempting combination. Roll out the dough, spread the filling in the middle, then roll it up and place it in a tin. Or flatten small pieces of dough and fill them, then shape them into buns.

Place shaped round buns in a square tin, slightly apart, so that they rise together into a bubbly loaf. Drizzle with melted butter and sprinkle with sugar for a golden glaze when the loaf is baked.

Allow the breads to cool on a wire rack before storing them in airtight containers. When cool, most sweet breads freeze well. However, remember not to add any icing or glaze before freezing; apply this after the bread has thawed.

If sweet breads do become stale they may be toasted and served hot and buttered. Stale bun loaves make good bread and butter pudding. Soak other sweet breads in eggs and milk, then bake them slowly before topping with jam and meringue and browning (rather like Queen of Puddings).

SWEET YEAST DOUGHS

UNDERSTANDING RICH DOUGHS

ADAPTING BASIC RECIPES

STORING AND FREEZING

SWEET PRESERVES

There are few areas of culinary craft more satisfying than making sweet preserves – a row of pots full of glistening jam, jelly or marmalade is reward in itself for the effort involved. You only have to sample the excellent flavour of your produce to understand why preserving is an annual treat as much as a task.

The majority of sweet preserves may be roughly grouped into two categories: those that set and those that are runny. Jams, jellies and marmalades are all set preserves, whereas conserves have a syrupy texture. Mincemeat is a combination of ingredients preserved by combining uncooked dried fruits, sugar and alcohol. It is thick rather than set. A third category comprises butters and cheeses which are thickened by cooking. Fruit curd is not strictly speaking a preserve, but is used in the same way as jam and is regarded as a related product.

ACHIEVING A SET

Three elements are essential for a good set – pectin, sugar and acid. When these are correctly balanced the mixture will set.

Pectin Naturally present in some fruit, this is the glue-like ingredient found in the cell walls of the fruit. It is extracted by cooking, assisted by the presence of acid.

Sugar Sugar is added in proportion, depending on the pectin content of the fruit, then dissolved and boiled down to the right concentration for producing a set.

Acid Some fruits contain acid, those that have a low acid content require the addition of lemon juice for making a good preserve. Lemon juice not only promotes pectin extraction but it also helps to give the preserve a good colour and sparkle.

INGREDIENTS

Fruit Fruit contains the maximum amount of pectin before it ripens; however in this state its flavour is not at its best. For a good preserve, the ideal is to use some fruit which is not quite ripe along with ripe fruit for flavour. Overripe fruit is not suitable for set preserves, although it may be used for butters and cheeses.

It is important to know or to check the pectin content of the fruit. Fruits with a low pectin content may be combined with others which have a high pectin content, thus ensuring that the preserve sets well.

Acid If the fruit does not have a good acid content, this should be added in the form of lemon juice. It should be added in the initial stages of cooking to assist in pectin extraction.

Sugar Sugar should be measured carefully: too much will cause the jam to be syrupy, not set; too little and the jam will require long boiling to give a set at all, making it dark and overcooked.

Any sugar can be used; however special preserving sugar gives the best results as the large crystals dissolve slowly and evenly, producing less scum and giving a sparkling preserve. This said, granulated sugar is probably the more frequently used type and it is perfectly acceptable.

The practice of warming the sugar before adding it to the cooked fruit helps to make it dissolve evenly and quickly.

Special sugar with pectin and acid added in the correct proportions for setting should be used according to the manufacturer's instructions. The boiling time is usually significantly shorter than with traditional ingredients. This type of sugar is very useful with low-pectin fruits or with exotic fruits.

Pectin Bottled pectin is also available for use with fruits that do not contain a good natural supply. Again, this should be used exactly according to the manufacturer's instructions.

Alternatively, fruit with a good pectin content such as apples, redcurrants and gooseberries may be cooked to a purée and used to set preserves made with fruit which does not have enough pectin. The purée is known as pectin stock. The whole, washed fruit (trimmed of bad parts, stalks and leaves) should be cooked to a pulp with water, then strained through muslin. Pectin stock may be combined with fruit such as strawberries, cherries or rhubarb to make a set preserve.

EQUIPMENT

Cooking Pan Do not use aluminium, copper, uncoated iron or zinc pans as these metals react with the fruit, adding unwanted deposits to the preserve and, in some cases, spoiling both colour and flavour.

A stainless steel pan is best. Alternatively, a heavy, well-coated (unchipped) enamel pan may be used. Good-quality non-stick pans are also suitable.

Although a covered pan is used for long cooking of fruit which needs tenderizing (particularly citrus fruit for marmalade), for boiling with sugar a wide, open pan is best. The wider the pan, the larger the surface area of preserve and the more efficient will be the process of evaporating unwanted liquid to achieve a set. Whatever the shape of pan, it is essential that it is large enough to hold both cooked fruit and sugar without being more than half to two-thirds full, so that the preserve does not boil over when it is brought to a full rolling boil.

Knife Use a stainless steel knife for cutting fruit. A carbon steel implement reacts with the fruit, causing discoloration.

Sugar Thermometer This is invaluable for checking the temperature of the preserve.

Saucer For testing for set (not essential).

Jelly Bag and Stand For making jellies and jelly marmalades you need a jelly bag and stand to strain the cooked fruit. You also need a large bowl to collect the juice. If you do not have a stand you can improvise by tying the four corners of the jelly bag to the legs of an upturned traditional kitchen stool by means of elastic. Instead of a jelly bag a large, double-thick piece of muslin may be used.

Jars Use sturdy, heatproof jars that have been thoroughly cleaned, rinsed in hot water and dried. Unless they are exceedingly dirty or have food deposits, there is no need to sterilize jars. However they must be washed in very hot soapy water (use rubber gloves to withstand the heat), then rinsed in hot or boiling water. Turn the jars upside down on folded clean tea-towels placed on a baking sheet or in a roasting tin, then put in a warm oven about 15 minutes before use.

Alternatively, wash the jars in a dishwasher just before use and leave them undisturbed to avoid contamination. They will be hot and perfectly clean.

Jam Funnel A wide metal funnel, this fits into jars and makes filling them far easier.

Small Jug This comes in handy for ladling the preserve into the jars.

Covers and Lids The surface of the potted preserve should be covered with discs of waxed paper. Airtight lids should be plastic-coated as bare metal will react with fruit acids in the jam and corrode. Cellophane discs may be used with elastic bands; they are not ideal for long-term storage but are useful under lids which may not be well coated in plastic.

Labels It is important to label each pot with the type of preserve and date.

PREPARATION TECHNIQUES

All fruit should be trimmed of bad parts, stalks and leaves. Then it should be prepared according to type – peeled, cored, stoned, cut up and so on. All these trimmings including any pips, should be tied in a piece of scalded muslin and cooked with the fruit, as they contain valuable pectin.

Make sure you have enough clean and warm jars, covers and labels.

COOKING TECHNIQUES

Cooking the Fruit The prepared fruit should be cooked with acid and a little water if needed. Soft fruits and others that yield a good volume of juice need only a little water to prevent them from drying out in the first stages of heating. The fruit must initially be cooked until it is thoroughly softened, preferably in a covered pan to prevent excessive evaporation. It is at this stage that the pectin is extracted. Undercooking not only results in tough pieces of fruit in the preserve but also in insufficient pectin for a good set.

Adding Sugar When the fruit is thoroughly cooked the sugar may be added. If possible warm the sugar first, then add it to the fruit. Keep the heat low and stir until the sugar has dissolved completely. This is important – if the preserve boils before all the sugar has dissolved, this may encourage the sugar to crystallize.

Boiling until Set Once the sugar has dissolved, the preserve should be brought to a full, or rolling, boil. This must be maintained until setting point is reached. This rapid boiling concentrates the sugar to the level needed to balance with the pectin.

Skimming At the end of cooking any scum which has collected on the surface of the preserve should be removed with a metal spoon. Sometimes a small knob of butter is added to disperse this scum or any remaining scum which cannot be removed.

Removing Stones If fruit is not stoned before cooking, the stones may be removed with a slotted spoon or small sieve as the preserve boils.

TESTING FOR SETTING

It is important to turn the heat off or take the pan off the heat when testing for setting. If the preserve continues to cook it may boil beyond the setting point, then it will not set.

Flake Test The least reliable. Lift a mixing spoon out of the preserve and allow the mixture to drip off it. When setting point is reached the preserve does not drip off cleanly but tends to fall off, leaving small drips of flakes building up on the edge of the spoon.

Saucer Test A reliable method: have a cold saucer ready in the refrigerator, spoon a little preserve on it and set it aside in a cool place for a few minutes. Push the sample of preserve with your finger; it should have formed a distinct skin which wrinkles. If the sample does not have a skin, the preserve will not set.

Temperature Test The best test: when the correct sugar concentration is reached the boiling preserve should achieve a temperature of 105°C/220°F. Do not let the temperature go any higher.

POTTING

Before potting, warm the jars and spread clean tea-towels or paper on the surface where the jars will stand. Have ready a tea-towel to hold or steady the jars (an oven glove is too bulky) and a dry tea-towel or absorbent kitchen paper for wiping up any bad spills on the jars. Never wipe the sides of very hot jars with a damp dish cloth.

Most preserves should be put into jars as soon as they are cooked. The jars should be full but not overfilled. There should be just a small space below the rim of the jar to prevent the preserve from touching the lid. Cover the surface of the hot preserve immediately with a disc of waxed paper, wax-side down, then put on lids at once.

Preserves with pieces of fruit or rind which tend to float should be left to stand for 15 minutes after cooking and before potting. This allows the preserve to set just enough to hold the fruit or rind in position. The preserve should be stirred and potted, covered with waxed discs, then left to cool completely before being covered with lids.

STORING

Store preserves in a cool, dark cupboard. They will keep from 6–12 months or longer in the right conditions. Since most modern homes have central heating, preserves tend to dry out during storage by slow evaporation. This can be averted if the rims of lids are sealed with heavy freezer tape.

BASIC FRUIT JAMS

To make a fruit jam you should know the pectin content. Fruits which have a good pectin content require an equal weight of sugar. Fruit with an excellent pectin content – currants, gooseberries or apples – can take up to 1.25/1¼ times their weight in sugar. Fruit with medium or poor pectin content will only set 0.75/¾ their weight in sugar. If the pectin content is poor, add pectin stock (page 175), plenty of lemon juice or commercial pectin.

PECTIN TEST Place a little methylated spirits in a clean, old jar. Add a spoonful of the thoroughly cooked fruit pulp (before sugar is added) and gently swirl the mixture. Allow the pulp to settle. If it forms a large lump, the fruit has a good pectin content. If there are a few lumps, then the fruit has a moderate pectin content. If the pulp is separated in lots of small lumps, it has little pectin and more should be added for a good set. These lumps are known as clots. Discard jar and contents after testing.

YIELD Although it is possible to estimate the yield of most jams and many marmalades, jellies rely on the volume of juice which is extracted from the fruit for the weight of sugar which has to be added. In the recipes in this book, it has therefore not always been possible to estimate yields accurately.

PICKLES Vinegar is the main preserving agent used in pickles, sometimes with sugar. Since vinegar is a strong preservative, preparing pickles is comparatively easy with none of the pitfalls involved in achieving a good jam or marmalade.

PREPARING PICKLES Vegetables should be prepared according to type, then salted for several hours or overnight. Sprinkle salt over every layer of vegetables. This extracts excess liquid and any bitter juices or very strong flavours. The salt should be rinsed off before pickling and the ingredients dried with absorbent kitchen paper. Brine solution may be used instead of salting vegetables.

Packing in Jars Thoroughly clean and dry jars must be well filled without squashing the vegetables or other ingredients. Unless the jars have been stored in dirty conditions (for example in a shed or outhouse) it is not necessary to sterilize them: a very hot wash and rinse with very hot or boiling water is adequate. If, however, the jars have been neglected for a long period and have become mouldy or very dirty, sterilize them as follows: Wash the jars in hot, soapy water, rinse them, then stand them on slats of wood, a rack or pad of paper in a deep pan. Pour in cold water to cover the jars completely. Put any lids into the pan. Heat gently until the water boils, then boil the jars for 5 minutes. Turn the heat off and leave the jars submerged until they are to be used, when they should be drained upside down on clean tea-towels. Alternatively, wine-making sterilizing products may be used to sterilize jars.

Vinegar White or distilled vinegar, cider vinegar or white wine vinegar gives pickles the best colour. Dark vinegars discolour the vegetables or fruit. The vinegar may be spiced, flavoured or sweetened as required.

Spiced vinegar may be used hot, immediately after straining, or cold. Opinions differ as to the best method but as a rule cold vinegar is always safest and should always be used for eggs and fruit whose texture may suffer from having boiling vinegar poured over them.

Pour the vinegar into the jars, shaking them gently to free any trapped air bubbles. Check the vinegar level about 24 hours after bottling the pickles, and add extra to cover the pickles if necessary.

Maturing Leave the pickles to mature for 1–3 weeks before using. Pickled eggs (hard-boiled eggs which are simply shelled and packed in jars promptly after cooking) should be left for a week; onions and other vegetables for at least 2–3 weeks.

Cover with airtight lids, making sure that the lids do not have any exposed metal which will react with the vinegar. Label and store in a cool, dark cupboard.

Pickled eggs and fruit keep for up to 3 months. Properly stored, most vegetables keep for 6–9 months. Red cabbage should be eaten within 3 months as it tends to soften and become limp with prolonged storage.

STORING PICKLES

Chutneys, long-cooked and rich in colour are ideal for sandwiches or serving with a ploughman's lunch. Ketchups are full-flavoured preserves and relishes are ideal for adding zest to plain meats or poultry.

CHUTNEYS, KETCHUPS AND RELISHES

As usual, the way in which ingredients are prepared depends on type. They should be chopped or even minced so that they eventually cook down to a thick pulp.

Peel, cores and pips should be removed. Tomatoes are best peeled but this is not necessary if they are minced or very finely chopped.

Spices Ground or whole spices may be added; usually a combination of both is used. Whole spices should be tied in a small piece of scalded muslin so that they may be removed after cooking and before potting. Cinnamon sticks are usually easy to spot in the cooked preserve, so these do not have to be tied in muslin.

Sugar Brown sugar gives chutneys a good flavour and rich colour. For lighter fruit chutneys, granulated sugar may be preferred.

PREPARING INGREDIENTS

Long slow cooking is the secret of success. A stainless steel pan is ideal (the information on saucepans to use for making sweet preserves, page 175, is also relevant to chutneys) and it must be large enough to hold all the ingredients and allow room for them to simmer steadily.

Stir the mixture occasionally until the sugar dissolves, then bring the chutney to the boil and lower the heat so that it simmers. Cover the pan and cook for the time recommended in the recipe or until the chutney has darkened and become thick and pulpy. Stir the mixture occasionally during cooking to prevent it from sticking to the bottom of the pan.

If the chutney is too liquid at the end of the recommended cooking time, or when all the ingredients are well reduced, allow it to boil, without a lid on the pan,

COOKING CHUTNEYS

until some of the excess liquid has evaporated. Stir frequently to prevent the mixture burning on the base of the pan.

POTTING

Have thoroughly clean, hot jars ready on a large sheet of paper or folded tea-towel. You also need a tea-towel to hold or steady the jars, a jam funnel and a small jug. The jars must have airtight lids which will not react with the metal and you should have sufficient waxed paper discs to top each preserve.

Pot the chutney as soon as it is cooked, cover with waxed paper and put on airtight lids at once. Seal the lids in place with freezer tape. If for any reason the chutney is allowed to stand before potting, lids should not be put on the jars until preserve is cold.

STORING

Store as for other preserves, in a cool, dark cupboard. Most chutneys will keep well for up to a year.

MICROWAVE COOKING

If you are completely new to microwave cooking, take care to read and follow the manufacturer's instructions supplied with your appliance. This is most important – probably more so than with any other appliance – as individual microwave ovens vary in terms of performance even if they are based on the same power output.

All microwave information given in this book is based on an oven with an output of 650–700 watts. If your oven has a lower power rating, the food will take longer to cook; for a higher output, the cooking times should be shortened.

The following terms have been used for the microwave settings: High, Medium, Defrost and Low. For each setting, the power input is as follows: High=100% power, Medium=50% power, Defrost=30% power and Low=20% power. Throughout the book, microwave notes and timings are for guidance only, and manufacturer's instructions should be consulted for basic cooking times as far as possible, or for the purpose of comparison.

CHOICE OF MICROWAVE OVEN

It is not practical to provide detailed information about appliances as choice and performance are continuously under review. However, here are a few points which may prove helpful.

Siting the Microwave The majority of microwave ovens are work-top appliances. Built-in, wall-mounted and combination models in the form of full-size cookers are available. Apart from full-size combination models which are wired into a cooker point, the majority of microwave ovens have to be located near a 13amp socket.

Ideally, the microwave should be sited near an area of work surface so that heavy dishes and similar items can be transferred to a safe standing place with ease. If there is plenty of space above the microwave, and the appliance has a suitable top surface, it is usually possible to make use of the top of the appliance as a resting place for dishes and utensils.

Combination or Standard Microwave A combination microwave oven, whether a work-top appliance or full-size cooker, offers the facility for cooking with microwave energy at the same time as using conventional heat. There are several different options available, including a fan oven and microwave combination, grill and microwave option or rotisserie and microwave combined.

The choice of appliance depends on your requirements as a cook, the budget available and your adaptability. The combination models provide versatility and excellent cooking results with a broader range of foods; however, they are more expensive than microwave-only cookers.

The range of facilities on microwave-only appliances varies considerably, from simple cooking options according to power setting and time, through to models which allow thawing, cooking and standing to be preprogrammed.

Personal Preferences When you have evaluated the potential in each appliance, give careful consideration to whether you are likely to find the facilities useful. It is easy to fall into the trap of buying an appliance with the widest possible choice of settings, gadgets and extras when a simpler model offers all you need at less cost. Simpler appliances can be quicker and easier to use and it can make sense to invest in a better-quality, less complicated cooker than to compromise on quality and durability for gimmickry.

Safety Standard Whatever type or style of microwave oven you intend buying, always look for the current official safety standard mark of approval.

BASICS OF MICROWAVE COOKING

Read the manufacturer's instructions for guidance on cooking utensils and techniques as well as for cooking times. Specific information on the use of metal depends on the particular appliance. Consult your handbook for more information.

Generating Heat Microwaves cook food by causing the molecules, or chemical particles, to vibrate to such an extent that the internal friction generates heat. This heat cooks the food. The amount of heat generated and the speed with which the food heats depends on the composition and quantity of the food.

Volume and Composition The greater the volume, the longer the food takes to get hot and cook. Foods which have a high water content take longer to cook than dry foods; for example, water takes a long time to boil in the microwave. So, adding boiling water to some dishes, such as soup, or adding the liquid in stages rather than all at once at the beginning of cooking, reduces the overall cooking time.

Foods with a low water content but high fat or sugar content heat very quickly and can therefore overcook speedily.

Dense foods take longer to cook or reheat than lighter foods. For example, potato takes longer to cook than egg. Mashed potato takes longer to reheat than cooked rice.

Microwave Penetration The microwaves penetrate food to a depth of up to 5 cm/2 inches, depending on the composition, shape and quantity of food. The remainder of the food, towards the centre, is cooked by conduction of the heat as during conventional cooking.

Food Preparation Food which is evenly shaped cooks more evenly. Examples of such foods include boneless chicken breasts; similar-sized cubes of poultry or vegetables; similar-sized new or old potatoes; similar-sized cauliflower or broccoli florets; and fish steaks.

If pieces of food have thin or narrow areas, these should be arranged to receive less microwave energy than thicker or larger areas. For example, place the pointed ends of poultry breasts together towards the centre of the cooking dish and overlap thin ends of fish fillets or fold them under.

Areas that require little cooking should be treated as for thin areas, for example, broccoli florets should be placed in the dish so that the tender heads are towards the centre and the tougher stalks are around the outside.

Do not add salt to food before cooking unless there is a significant quantity of sauce. Never sprinkle salt over vegetables, meat or poultry as this results in dark, dehydrated patches. Sauces may be seasoned before cooking.

Pricking Foods Any food which has a skin or membrane covering must be pricked before cooking, otherwise a build-up of heat within the food may cause it to burst during cooking. Whole potatoes, the skin on poultry and halved kidneys are typical examples. If you cook shelled eggs in the microwave, prick the yolks with a cocktail stick to prevent them from bursting; eggs in shells must never be cooked in the microwave as they are liable to explode.

Chicken livers must be cut up, otherwise they pop and splatter as heat builds up within the membranes which cover them. The heat build-up can happen between cooked areas and the membrane, so large pieces of food are just as prone to splattering as whole food items.

Stirring and Rearranging Food During microwave cooking, food should be stirred or rearranged to promote even cooking, preventing some areas from being under-cooked while others overcook.

As a general rule, the larger the quantity of food, the more often it has to be stirred or rearranged. However, the shape and size of container can influence the heating pattern. When heating liquid mixtures in small but deep vessels or in containers such as basins, bowls or wide casseroles, it is vital to stir frequently to avoid having fierce hot spots which tend to froth over when the liquid is stirred at the end of cooking. If the heat is allowed to build up in the lower area of a coffee pot or similar container filled with liquid, the liquid can froth out through a spout or narrow opening. This also applies when heating a mug of liquid: if the liquid is not stirred a hot spot can froth over at the end of heating. Stirring prevents this prob-lem from occurring.

Covering Many foods are covered during microwave cooking to retain moisture and heat, therefore promoting quick and even cooking. This applies to foods that are likely to dry out on the surface – fish or vegetables – as well as to items like rice, in which the moisture retained from the steam is necessary for successful cooking.

Lidded, microwaveproof dishes are ideal; however, suitable plates may be used instead of a lid. See also Paper (page 185).

When removing a cover, always take care to protect your hand and wrist, and, if possible, to lift the cover so that the escaping steam is directed away from you.

Shielding Some areas which are prone to overcooking may be shielded with small pieces of smooth cooking foil. Typical examples include the wing tips on poultry and the tail end of a whole salmon. This technique should only be used where there is large portion of food exposed, so that the majority of the microwave energy is absorbed, and for part of the cooking time. Consult your manufacturer's handbook to make sure that this is recommended for your appliance.

Standing Time During standing time, the heat generated by the microwaves is evenly conducted throughout the food. Standing time is important as it allows the food to cook evenly through to the centre. It ensures that heat is evenly distributed within the food, avoiding hot spots.

EQUIPMENT

Microwaves pass through glass, crockery and paper but are reflected by metals. Some materials (unglazed earthenware, for instance) absorb microwave energy in the same way as food does. The extent to which crockery absorbs microwave energy varies – some dishes or basins do absorb a certain amount but this does not make them unsuitable for use in the microwave. Even unglazed earthenware may be used. If in doubt, check first with the microwave manufacturers.

Metal Do not use metal utensils or containers with any metal trimming, including designs with metallic paint. The metal reflects the microwaves, causing them to arc and spark within the cooking cavity. Microwaves reflected back to the power source, the magnetron, may damage the appliance (with repeated misuse).

The general rule about avoiding metal does not necessarily apply to all containers, ovens and foods. Certain manufacturers have designed the shelving and oven cavity in such a way that shallow foil containers which are well filled with fairly dense food can be used in the appliance. However, the guidelines on the use of metal containers vary and the instructions with your oven should be followed closely.

Ovenproof Glass This is the most practical material for cooking containers. It is also suitable for use in the conventional oven and certain types are flameproof or suitable for use in the freezer too.

The thinner glass dishes absorb the least energy and give the best results; however all ovenproof glass is suitable and practical for use in the microwave. Remember to make use of suitable bowls, basins and jugs as well as casseroles, cake dishes and roasting dishes.

Although inexpensive drinking glasses may be used for brief heating purposes (warming a glass of mulled wine or milk, for instance), drinking glasses are not suitable for cooking or boiling liquids. Do not use cut glass or lead crystal as this causes sparking.

Crockery Crockery which will withstand the heat of the food is suitable for use in the microwave. Plates are useful for thawing or brief cooking as well as for covering dishes. Mugs and jugs may be used with care. See Stirring and Rearranging Food (page 183). Some crockery absorbs microwave energy, slowing down the cooking process. Highly glazed crockery can cause sparking. Delicate china is not suitable for use in the microwave.

Paper Absorbent kitchen paper, non-stick baking parchment and greaseproof paper are all useful for microwave cooking. Also, look for special browning paper, which has a coating to absorb microwave energy and brown food. Roasting bags and wrap are also suitable for microwave cooking. Boilable cooking bags may be used for moist dishes; however, they tend to melt under conditions of dry heat.

Plastics Polystyrene is not suitable for microwave cooking. Boilable plastic basins may be used for short heating or thawing, as may some freezer containers; however, in general these plastics are not suitable as they melt when the food becomes hot. Some plastics also absorb sufficient microwave energy to cause softening, or even melting.

Cling film or plastic wrap should not be used as a covering directly on food. Special microwave-covering may be used to cover bowls or basins containing a comparatively small amount of food but the wrap itself should never touch the food. Prick wrap or leave a small space for steam to escape.

Microwave Cookware There is a vast range of microwave utensils and containers on offer – many items are expensive and/or flimsy. These are not essential adjuncts to the microwave oven. Some are useful; many are gadgets which you may or may not find helpful, depending on the type of food you cook. It is best to get to know your microwave oven and to decide on the use you intend to make of the appliance before investing in specialist equipment which may prove unnecessary; evaluate these items carefully before buying.

The quality of the basic material used in specialist utensils varies enormously and some of the flimsy, inexpensive containers do not withstand extensive use. Flimsy containers can be useful if you want a particular shape of dish to cook an occasional recipe; for example a ring dish for making a pudding or chocolate cake.

The plastics used for microwave cookware are specifically manufactured to allow the maximum transfer of energy, so cooking times may be shorter when using these containers.

Browning Dishes and Wrap These have a coating which absorbs microwave energy and becomes hot. The hot surface browns the food as in traditional cooking methods. Wrap is usually designed for browning the base of items such as pizza or imparting some crispness to pastries when reheating them.

The use of a browning dish usually involves preheating it according to the instructions, for a given length of time at a certain setting. The food is then seared in the dish. In many cases, the heat of the browning surface is sufficient only to brown one side of food such as chicken joints lightly. The efficiency varies according to the particular container and the type of food, but for traditional browned results with foods such as meat, the browning dish may disappoint. Browning utensils include items such as burger makers. The range of browning gadgets is always changing – some give good results, others are less successful.

SUCCESSFUL MICROWAVE COOKING

The microwave may be used to cook a variety of foods successfully, with results as good as those achieved by traditional methods. Other foods cooked by microwave energy may be less satisfactory, usually in terms of texture. In a combination microwave oven the failures are fewer than when using microwave energy alone, as the appliance includes a traditional heat source.

Microwave Cooking: Moist and Rapid Microwave cooking is a moist method, best compared to boiling or steaming. It is also rapid. Therefore foods which cook well by steaming or boiling often yield successful results in the microwave oven. However, tough foods which require long slow cooking do not cook well in the microwave – braising or stewing meat does not have sufficient time to tenderize. A special microwave pressure cooker does give tender results with tough foods, when used according to the manufacturer's instructions.

Texture and Browning Food cooked in the microwave does not become crisp and, on the whole, it does not brown. Some joints of meat brown slightly if large enough for the fat content to become hot enough and for long enough to cause some surface browning.

Foods which rely on a crisp crust for success are not suitable for microwave cooking. Choux pastry is a prime example: the paste rises and puffs dramatically while the microwave oven is operating; as soon as the power is cut off the paste sinks. This is because the paste has to form a crisp outer shell to keep the shape of the baked item.

Other forms of pastry do not cook well in the microwave either – short crust dough is soft with a 'raw' flavour and puffed or layered pastries do not form a crisp crust to set the light texture. With these types of pastry, the layers set only when the dough is so overcooked as to be dehydrated and unpalatable.

Traditional bread dough is too dense to cook well by microwave energy; however, a yeasted batter will give reasonable results and can be useful for making small loaves or items such as a savarin. However, the results do not brown nor do they have a crusted surface.

Flavour The microwave oven acts in the same way as a steamer to intensify, or bring out the best of, some flavours. Vegetables usually have a good flavour when cooked by microwave and the natural flavour of fish is brought out to the full.

As when steaming or boiling, herbs and spices and other strongly flavoured ingredients should be used in moderation, depending on the balance of the dish, as they can come through strongly to dominate. Onions and garlic should be cooked first with or without a little fat, otherwise they will have a 'raw' flavour which is too strong for the majority of dishes– again, the same is true for traditional moist cooking methods.

Microwave-cooked meat does not develop the same flavour as grilled, baked or roast meat; instead it has a steamed or boiled flavour. Only the most succulent cuts are sufficiently tender for microwave cooking and the quality is not nearly as good as expected of traditional methods.

Minced meat is suitable for microwave cooking, for meat loaves, burgers made with added breadcrumbs and seasonings and meat sauces. All give perfectly acceptable results, although a microwave-cooked meat sauce cannot be compared for richness with a long-braised one.

Here is a checklist of some foods which cook well in the microwave.

FOODS TO COOK BY MICROWAVE

Apples puréed or stewed

Artichokes both globe and Jerusalem

Asparagus when spears are small and tender; avoid woody spears

Aubergines for example in ratatouille

Bacon rashers rolls or chopped

Bananas for a quick pudding, cook with a knob of butter and a little orange juice

Battenburg cake as the mixture is cooked in two portions, then trimmed

Beetroot when young and tender

Broccoli with short, tender stalks

Brussels sprouts, small whole or halved

Cabbage for a result similar to stir-frying, particularly white or red

Carrots when young and finely cut but not when older or in large pieces

Celeriac cut up small

Chicken especially in sauce

Chicken livers – must be cut up

Chocolate ring cake or cup cakes

Courgettes are better than when cooked by some traditional methods

Duck cook, then drain and brown well in a very hot oven or under the grill

Eggs scrambled only

Fish especially in sauce

Fruit most types poach well or cook perfectly for purées

Lentils particularly red

Liver cut small in sauces

Potatoes both small new and whole old but not for mashing or purées

Rice all types

Sauces savoury and sweet of all types

Steamed sponge puddings cook very quickly and taste wonderful

Turkey especially in small portions

Vegetables other types in addition to those listed

FOODS TO AVOID IN MICROWAVE COOKING

These are some of the foods that are either inferior or unsuccessful when cooked in the microwave.

Batters including Yorkshire pudding and pancakes

Bread dough is tough and unpleasant. Yeast batter cooks reasonably well

Cakes (with a few exceptions, mainly chocolate or well-flavoured mixtures and cup cakes)

Choux pastry does not form a crust so will not set in shape

Eggs baked, fried or omelettes (the exception is scrambled). Never attempt to cook eggs in shells in the microwave

Deep-fried foods are unsuitable. It is dangerous to heat large quantities of oil in the microwave

Fish fingers and other foods coated in egg and breadcrumbs

Fruit cake is too dense

Game the majority benefits from traditional roasting or long slow cooking, depending on type

Hamburgers traditional all-meat burgers are far better when grilled

Meat roasts can be partially cooked by microwave energy to shorten the final, traditional roasting time

Omelettes are rubbery

Pancakes have to be fried

Pasta

Pastry except suet crust

Preserves except very small quantities

Sausages except frankfurters and other tender boiling types

Sponge cakes made by the whisked method

Stews of meat, game or less tender offal, except when cooked in a pressure cooker designed specifically for the microwave

Tougher cuts of meat, offal and game

GENERAL GUIDELINES FOR THAWING FOOD

The microwave is undoubtedly an invaluable companion to the freezer as it makes possible speedy thawing without loss of quality. For good, safe results always remember the following points.

- Follow the microwave manufacturer's instructions regarding settings and timings.
- In the absence of a defrost setting or suggested alternative, use medium-low or low.
- Unwrap frozen food; place it in a suitable container. Most foods that benefit from retaining moisture should be covered during thawing; otherwise they may dry out on the surface.
- To make it easier to remove foods from their wrapping, it may be helpful to partially thaw them. Remove any metal tags or ties from the wrapping first,

and do not put any wrappings with metal coating or foiled labels in the microwave. As soon as it is possible to do so, unwrap the food and return it to the microwave in a suitable container to complete thawing.

- Baked goods, such as bread, should be unwrapped and placed on double-thick absorbent kitchen paper. The paper absorbs excess moisture.
- Turn and rearrange food occasionally during thawing, breaking up blocks of food as soon as possible.
- Check on thawing progress and allow standing time halfway through and/or at the end of thawing. It is only necessary to allow standing time during the thawing process when handling large food items, such as joints or large birds.
- Thawed foods should be cold, not unevenly warm or cooked in parts.
- When reheating frozen cooked food, such as a casserole, increase the setting when the food is just thawed to reheat it thoroughly and without delay.
- Small items or foods which thaw quickly may be speedily thawed by using a higher setting; however this is only useful when the food can be thoroughly thawed without any risk of cooking in parts.
- Pay particular attention to poultry, especially whole birds, ensuring that it is thoroughly thawed before cooking to avoid any risk of having undercooked areas when the poultry is served.
- Read and follow instructions on frozen convenience foods – most offer guidance on thawing and reheating or cooking by microwave when appropriate.
- Finally, always use or cook food promptly after thawing.

In the absence of the microwave manufacturer's cooking instructions and timings, the following information may be useful. All timings are for cooking on a High setting unless otherwise stated.

Fish can be cooked whole, in steaks or cutlets, in fillets or in chunks.

PREPARATION

Trim the fish, slitting the skin on whole fish to prevent it from bursting. Put into a suitable container and dot with butter or margarine or moisten with lemon juice, wine or water. Steaks, individual portions of fillet or chunks can be cooked in a sauce. Do not season with salt. Cover the dish.

COOKING NOTES

Thicker parts of the fillet, or the thick end of a steak, should be placed towards the outside of the dish. When cooking two or more large fish fillets, arrange them in a dish with head ends next to tail ends; tuck the thin tail pieces underneath to prevent overcooking. Chunks of fish should be placed as far apart as possible. Turn or rearrange halfway through cooking.

GUIDE TO COOKING TIME

FISH

189

COOKING TIMES

The cooked fish should flake easily but it should still be very slightly translucent at the base of the flakes or towards the centre of the cutlet or steak. By the time the fish is removed from the microwave and served the residual heat will have completed the cooking process.

White or Smoked Fish

Fillets
100 g/4 oz – 1½–2 minutes
225 g/8 oz – 4–6 minutes
450 g/1 lb – 8–10 minutes

Cutlets or Steaks
1 medium – 2–4 minutes
2 medium – 4–6 minutes
3 medium – 5–7 minutes
4 medium – 8–10 minutes

Plaice

Fillets
2 fillets – 1–2 minutes
4 fillets – 3–5 minutes
6 fillets – 4–6 minutes
8 fillets – 7–9 minutes

Mackerel

Whole Fish
1 – 2–4 minutes
2 – 4–6 minutes
3 – 5–7 minutes
4 – 7–9 minutes

Rolled Fillets (2 from each fish)
2 – 2–3 minutes
4 – 3–5 minutes
6 – 5–6 minutes
8 – 6–8 minutes

NOTE
For even results when cooking 6 or more fillets roll the fillets and secure them in place with wooden cocktail sticks.

Mullet

1 grey mullet (about 1–1.5 kg/2–3 lb)
    – 9–11 minutes
2 medium red mullet – 8–10 minutes
4 medium red mullet – 12–15 minutes

NOTE
If the red mullet are very small reduce the above times by 1–2 minutes in each case.

Herring

Whole Fish	*Kippers*
2 – 2–3 minutes	**1** – about 1 minute
4 – 4–6 minutes	**2** – 1–3 minutes
	3 – 2–4 minutes
	4 – 4–6 minutes

Frozen Boil-in-the-bag Kippers

Pierce the bag and lay it on a plate or dish. Cook on High for 4–6 minutes. Leave for 1–2 minutes before snipping the bag. Look out for instructions on the packet as many brands of frozen foods provide microwave cooking instructions which relate to tests carried out on the product to give best results.

Whole Salmon

A whole fish weighing up to 2.25 kg/5 lb can be cooked successfully in the microwave. Prepare the fish as usual, then slit the skin in several places. Curl the fish into a large flan dish. Cover the fish with special microwave film, wrapping two layers over the dish to keep the salmon firmly in place. As the fish skin is discarded, it does not matter that the film lays directly on it.

Cook on High for 2–3 minutes per 450 g/1 lb. A 2.25 kg/5 lb fish will need 10–15 minutes. Leave the salmon to stand for 5 minutes before checking that it is cooked by piercing the flesh at the thickest point. The cooked salmon should be moist and the flesh should flake easily.

Salmon Steaks

Weigh the steaks. Secure the flaps of flesh neatly in the middle of the steaks with wooden cocktail sticks. Arrange as far apart as possible in a dish, with the thicker sides towards the edge of the dish. Dot with butter and sprinkle with 15 ml/1 tbsp water. Cover and cook on High for 4–5 minutes per 450 g/1 lb. Turn the steaks halfway through cooking.

Trout

Prepare the trout, leaving heads on. Slit the skin in two or three places and sprinkle with 30 ml/2 tbsp water. Cover and cook on High for the following times:

1 trout – 2–3 minutes
2 trout – 4–6 minutes
3 trout – 5–7 minutes
4 trout – 8–10 minutes

NOTE

It can be more practical, depending on dish and microwave oven size, to cook four fish in pairs. When the first pair is cooked, wrap them in foil to keep hot while the second pair cook.

POULTRY   Chicken and turkey both cook well in the microwave as they are tender meats, although turkey drumsticks are less successful. Duck cooks extremely well; for delicious results, drain off excess fat occasionally and at the end of microwave cooking, then brown the whole bird or portions thoroughly in a very hot oven or under the grill before serving.

PREPARATION

For whole birds, complete the essential preparation and trimming as for conventional cooking, then truss neatly, keeping the joints tied firmly as close to the body as possible. Prepare duck by pricking the skin all over to allow the fat to escape. Boned birds cook particularly well, with or without stuffing.

COOKING NOTES

Cover the poultry during cooking. Whole birds may be placed in a roasting bag which should be partially closed with a microwaveproof tie. Stand the bird in its bag in a dish to catch juices.

When cooking portions, arrange thin parts or bone ends together towards the middle of the dish, with thicker areas around the perimeter. Rearrange the poultry during cooking, turning portions and whole birds over at least once.

Having prepared duck as described above, cook it in a fairly deep dish; drain off fat as necessary.

Place whole birds breast down for about two-thirds of the cooking time as this keeps the breast meat moist. When cooking large birds, such as turkey, shield the joint ends with small pieces of foil if they begin to overcook. Check in your manufacturer's handbook that this is permitted for your appliance.

STANDING TIMES AND CHECKING COOKING PROGRESS

Allow poultry portions to stand for 3–5 minutes at the end of cooking; whole birds should stand for 5–10 minutes, depending on size.

After standing times have been observed, test the poultry to make sure that it is cooked. The meat behind the thigh is thick and shielded, so always ensure it is done by piercing the meat with the point of a knife; look for any traces of blood in the cooking juices or pink flesh both indicate that the poultry is undercooked. If this occurs, return the poultry to the microwave and continue cooking until the juices run clear and the flesh is firm.

COOKING TIMES

Whole chicken – 7–9 minutes per 450 g/1 lb
Whole turkey – 6–8 minutes per 450 g/1 lb

Chicken Quarters

1 – 5–7 minutes
2 – 10–12 minutes
3 – 15–18 minutes
4 – 21–25 minutes

Chicken Thighs or Drumsticks

1 – 2–3 minutes
2 – 4–6 minutes
3 – 5–7 minutes
4 – 7–10 minutes
6 – 14–16 minutes
8 – 18–22 minutes

**Boneless Chicken Breasts
or Turkey Fillets**

1 – 2–4 minutes
2 – 5–8 minutes
3 – 9–11 minutes
4 – 12–15 minutes

Duck Quarters

1 – 4–6 minutes
2 – 7–9 minutes
3 – 12–15 minutes
4 – 17–20 minutes

Boneless Duck Breasts

1 – 4–6 minutes
2 – 8–10 minutes
3 – 12–15 minutes
4 – 16–18 minutes

MEAT

Some microwave ovens have automatic cooking programmes for meat, usually set according to the weight of the joint. Follow the manufacturer's instructions when using an automatic programme – the pre-programmed settings usually give best results as they are thoroughly tested by the manufacturer.

Avoid the tougher cuts of meat which would require slow stewing or braising if cooked by conventional energy. If a joint is cooked completely in the microwave, the result will not be as good as if it were roasted conventionally. A better method is to partially cook the meat in the microwave, then complete the cooking in a conventional oven. Similarly, to speed up the cooking of small cuts, such as thick pork chops, cook them briefly in the microwave, then flash them under a hot grill to complete the cooking.

PREPARATION

Boneless cuts are a better shape for microwave cooking, particularly if the microwave is the main or only cooking appliance used.

Meat which is cut up for cooking – for example to make a stir-fry style dish – is best cut across the grain into thin pieces. Slices or fine strips are more tender than cubes. Marinating meat before cooking it imparts flavour and helps to tenderize it.

Joints should be tied into a neat shape – remember to avoid metal skewers. When cooking or partially cooking an unevenly shaped joint, shield any thin areas which begin to overcook by covering them with small pieces of smooth foil, provided this is permitted in your appliance.

Chops, cutlets and other small cuts should be arranged with any thin or small parts close together in the centre of the dish; failing this, keep thin areas together or overlapping as far as possible.

Do not sprinkle salt over meat; cover or partially cover the meat while cooking.

COOKING NOTES

The High setting may be used to partially cook a joint or for small joints or cuts and cut-up meat; however on larger joints, the outside tends to overcook before the middle is done. Medium is therefore the recommended setting. If you intend to start the meat off in the microwave, before completing the cooking process in a conventional oven, use High.

Turn or rearrange the meat during cooking, stirring cubed or diced meat and breaking up mince.

Leave the meat to stand after cooking, allowing 5 minutes for small cuts, up to 15–25 minutes for joints.

MEAT THERMOMETER

A conventional meat thermometer may be used to check the internal temperature of the meat after it has been removed from the microwave. Heat the thermometer in readiness by standing it in hot water. Insert it into the centre of the joint, cover with foil and allow to stand, then check the temperature. If further cooking is necessary, remove the thermometer before returning the meat to the microwave.

Alternatively, if you often cook meat in the microwave, it may be worth buying a microwave thermometer. This is designed for use in the microwave oven and is free from metal. A skewer is used to make a hole in the meat and the thermometer is then inserted. Some cookers have a temperature probe which may be used for the same purpose.

COOKING TIMES

Times given are for complete cooking in the microwave.

Beef and Lamb Joints
Cooking times per 450 g/1 lb on Medium
rare – 10–12 minutes
medium – 13–15 minutes
well-done – 14–16 minutes

Cooking times per 450 g/1 lb on High
rare – 5–6 minutes
medium – 6–8 minutes
well-done – 8–9 minutes

Minced Meat (including pork or veal)

Cooking time per 450 g/1 lb on High
10–15 minutes

NOTE
Timing for mince may vary depending on other ingredients added.

Lamb Chops or Cutlets

Trim chops of excess fat before cooking and arrange them as far apart as possible on a shallow dish. Cover with absorbent kitchen paper. If the chops are cooked in a sauce, arrange the chops and sauce in a dish. Cover and cook on High, rearranging the chops halfway through cooking.

Cooking times on High
1 – 2–4 minutes
2 – 5–7 minutes
3 – 6–8 minutes
4 – 8–10 minutes

Pork

Small cuts are best cooked in a sauce so that the lack of browning is less obvious. *The following times are a guide to cooking on High.*
Joints – 7–10 minutes per 450 g/1 lb
Small cuts – 6–8 minutes per 450 g/1 lb

Liver

Trim and slice the liver, then arrange the slices in a dish and dot with butter. Season with pepper. Cover the dish.
Cook on High.
225 g/8 oz – 2–3 minutes
450 g/1 lb – 4–6 minutes

Bacon Rashers

Lay the rashers on a microwave cooking rack or large plate. Cover loosely with absorbent kitchen paper.
Cook on High.
2 rashers – 1½–2 minutes
4 rashers – 2–3 minutes
6 rashers – 3½–4½ minutes
8 rashers – 5–6 minutes

VEGETABLES Microwave cooking is excellent for small to medium quantities of vegetables; however large quantities are best split into two batches for cooking

PREPARATION

With the exception of frozen produce, the majority of vegetables should have a small amount of water added before cooking. Prepare the vegetables as usual, following the general information instructions in A Guide to Vegetables on page 83 if in any doubt, then place them in a covered container with a little water. Do not add salt.

In some cases a knob of butter may be added instead of water, for example with courgettes which are naturally moist, or wine or citrus juice may be used with or without a little butter.

When cooking large whole potatoes, arrange them as far apart as possible on a large plate, dish or double-thick absorbent kitchen paper. Prick potatoes before cooking them so that they do not burst.

Arrange cauliflower and broccoli so that the tender heads are close together in the middle of the dish. The stalks, which are tougher and denser, should be spaced around the rim of the dish so that they receive the maximum microwave energy. This principle should be applied to all vegetables in which some parts are more tender than others. When cooking florets in a deep dish, arrange them with the stalks pointing outwards and upwards so that the tender heads are together in the middle.

COOKING NOTES

Stir or rearrange vegetables once or twice during cooking, bringing small pieces from the outside towards the middle. The following times and notes are for cooking on High.

COOKING TIMES

Artichokes, Globe
1 – 6–8 minutes
2 – 9–11 minutes
3 – 12–14 minutes
4 – 15–18 minutes

Size and age affects cooking time. Leave the cooked vegetables to stand, still in their cooking container, for about 5 minutes, after cooking. To test that they are tender, pull off one of the outer leaves – it should come away easily.

Asparagus
Frozen asparagus does not take much longer than fresh but do not add water. Older spears which may be tough are best boiled.
225 g/8 oz – 4–6 minutes
450 g/1 lb – 7–9 minutes

Beans

Broad Beans
100 g/4 oz shelled fresh – 3–4 minutes
225 g/8 oz shelled fresh – 6–7 minutes
450 g/1 lb shelled fresh – 9–10 minutes
100 g/4 oz frozen – 4–5 minutes
225 g/8 oz frozen – 7–8 minutes
450 g/1 lb frozen – 11–12 minutes

Runner Beans
100 g/4 oz fresh – 2–3 minutes
225 g/8 oz fresh – 4–5 minutes
450 g/1 lb fresh – 6–7 minutes
100 g/4 oz frozen – 3–6 minutes
225 g/8 oz frozen – 6–8 minutes
450 g/1 lb frozen – 8–10 minutes

NOTE
Home-frozen runner beans that are in a block should be broken as they thaw. They take longer to thaw and cook than purchased frozen beans.

French Beans
100 g/4 oz fresh – 3–4 minutes
225 g/8 oz fresh – 5–7 minutes
450 g/1 lb fresh – 7–10 minutes
100 g/4 oz frozen – 4–5 minutes
225 g/8 oz frozen – 7–9 minutes
450 g/1 lb frozen – 12–14 minutes

Broccoli
100 g/4 oz fresh – 2–4 minutes
225 g/8 oz fresh – 5–6 minutes
450 g/1 lb fresh – 7–9 minutes
225 g/8 oz frozen – 7–8 minutes
450 g/1 lb frozen – 12–14 minutes
Leave for 2 minutes before draining and serving.

Brussels Sprouts
100 g/4 oz fresh – 2–3 minutes
225 g/8 oz fresh – 4–6 minutes
450 g/1 lb fresh – 8–10 minutes
100 g/4 oz frozen – 3–5 minutes
225 g/8 oz frozen – 7–8 minutes
450 g/1 lb frozen – 11–12 minutes

Carrots
100 g/4 oz – 2–3 minutes
225 g/8 oz – 4–5 minutes
450 g/1 lb – 6–8 minutes

NOTE
Frozen carrots need very little cooking once they have thawed so follow the above timings but do not add extra water.

Cabbage
Timing depends on personal taste. The following guide gives tender, crunchy results:
100 g/4 oz – 3–5 minutes
225 g/8 oz – 6–8 minutes
450 g/1 lb – 9–11 minutes

Cauliflower
small whole – 10–12 minutes cauliflower
large whole – 13–16 minutes cauliflower
100 g/4 oz florets – 4–5 minutes
225 g/8 oz florets – 6–8 minutes
450 g/1 lb florets – 10–12 minutes

NOTE
Frozen florets need very little cooking once they have thawed, so follow the above timings but do not add extra water. For best results, florets should be even in size and not too large.

Corn-on-the-cob

1 fresh – 3–5 minutes
2 fresh – 6–8 minutes
3 fresh – 8–10 minutes
4 fresh – 11–13 minutes
1 frozen – 5–7 minutes
2 frozen – 8–10 minutes
3 frozen – 12–14 minutes
4 frozen – 15–17 minutes

NOTE
There is no need to add water to frozen corn.

Leeks

225 g/8 oz fresh sliced – 4–6 minutes
450 g/1 lb fresh sliced – 8–10 minutes
450 g/1 lb fresh whole – 6–8 minutes
225 g/8 oz frozen sliced – 5–7 minutes
450 g/1 lb frozen sliced – 10–12 minutes

NOTE
There is no need to add water to frozen leeks.

Mushrooms

Whole Button Mix with olive oil or butter.
225 g/8 oz – 2–4 minutes
450 g/1 lb – 4–6 minutes

Sliced Mushrooms Heat 25–50 g/1–2 oz butter in a dish on High for 30–60 seconds. Add the mushrooms and cook on High.
100 g/4 oz – 1–2 minutes
225 g/8 oz – 2–4 minutes
350 g/12 oz – 3–5 minutes
450 g/1 lb – 4–6 minutes

Courgettes

225 g/8 oz – 2–4 minutes
450 g/1 lb – 4–6 minutes

NOTE
Courgettes should be evenly sliced or cut in neat sticks. They cook well in a loosely closed roasting bag.

Marrow The following times are for the prepared vegetable, cut into 2.5–5 cm/1–2 inch cubes.
225 g/8 oz – 3–5 minutes
450 g/1 lb – 7–10 minutes

Parsnips The following times are for prepared vegetables cut into chunks. Cook with water in a covered dish on High.
450 g/1 lb – 7–10 minutes
675 g/1½ lb – 12–15 minutes
Leave to stand, still covered, for 3 minutes, then drain. Mash the parsnips or toss them in butter.

Peas Frozen peas do not require liquid; canned peas should be heated in the liquid from the can.
225 g/8 oz fresh – 4–6 minutes
450 g/1 lb fresh – 7–10 minutes
50 g/2 oz frozen – 2–3 minutes
100 g/4 oz frozen – 3–4 minutes
225 g/8 oz frozen – 4–6 minutes
350 g/12 oz frozen – 5–7 minutes
450 g/1 lb frozen – 7–10 minutes

Potatoes

Whole Potatoes The following times are for potatoes weighing about 350 g/ 12 oz each and cooking on High.

1 – 6–8 minutes
2 – 10–12 minutes
3 – 14–16 minutes
4 – 20–22 minutes

New Potatoes Select even-sized new potatoes. Scrub, then place in a dish with 45 ml/3 tbsp water. Do not add salt. Cover and cook on High, rearranging once or twice.

450 g/1 lb – 5–7 minutes
675 g/1½ lb – 6–9 minutes
1 kg/2¼ lb – 8–11 minutes

Spinach Place the trimmed, wet leaves in a bowl or large roasting bag. Cover or close the opening with a microwave-proof tie. Cook on High, rearranging halfway through cooking. Allow 5–7 minutes per 450 g/1 lb on High. Drain well and use or serve as required.

Turnips The following times are for prepared vegetables, cut into even-sized chunks. Very small whole turnips or halved small to medium vegetables may be cooked in the same way.

225 g/8 oz – 5–7 minutes
450 g/1 lb – 9–11 minutes
Leave, closely covered, for 5 minutes, then drain and toss in butter, adding a good grinding of black pepper.

Old Potatoes Cut potatoes into large chunks, dice or slice; it is important to make sure the pieces of potato are fairly even in size. Place in a dish and add 45 ml/3 tbsp water. Do not add salt. Cover and cook on High, rearranging the potatoes once or twice during cooking.

450 g/1 lb – 6–8 minutes
675 g/1½ lb – 7–10 minutes
1 kg/2 lb – 12–14 minutes

NOTE
Small new potatoes take slightly less time than evenly cut old potatoes.

Sweetcorn

100 g/4 oz frozen – 2–4 minutes
225 g/8 oz frozen – 4–6 minutes
350 g/12 oz frozen – 6–7 minutes
450 g/1 lb frozen – 7–10 minutes

A–Z OF RECIPES

Mrs Beeton set out to provide her contemporaries with useful and practical information, from guidance on setting up home and employing staff to preparing everyday meals as well as organising dinner parties for special occasions. This section provides the same level of useful, everyday recipes, organised in alphabetical order according to title, making it easy to find your favourite dish. Additionally, all the recipes are listed in the index at the end of the book.

Basic cooking methods and techniques are found in the first part of the book and page numbers are given where there is a reference back to any of that information. Throughout this recipe collection, you will also find lists of foods which fall into the same category, such as breads, custards and pickles, or which use the same key ingredients, such as chicken, for inspiration or as an at-a-glance guide to the alternatives.

ALMOND MACAROONS

MAKES 16 TO 20

fat for greasing

2 egg whites

150 g/5 oz caster sugar

100 g/4 oz ground almonds

10 ml/2 tsp ground rice

split almonds or halved glacé
    cherries

Grease two baking sheets and cover with rice paper. Set the oven at 160°C/325°F/gas 3.

In a clean dry bowl, whisk the egg whites until frothy but not stiff enough to form peaks. Stir in the sugar, ground almonds, and ground rice. Beat with a wooden spoon until thick and white.

Put small spoonfuls of the mixture 5 cm/2 inches apart on the prepared baking sheets or pipe them on. Place a split almond or halved glacé cherry on each macaroon and bake for 20 minutes or until pale fawn in colour. Cool slightly on the baking sheets; finish cooling on wire racks.

variation

RATAFIAS Ratafias are used in trifles, to decorate desserts, and as petits fours. Follow the recipe above, but reduce the size of the biscuits so that when cooked they are only 2 cm/¾ inch in diameter. Omit the split almond or glacé cherry topping.

AMERICAN FROSTING

SUFFICIENT TO COVER THE TOP AND SIDES
OF ONE 18 CM/7 INCH CAKE

225 g/8 oz granulated sugar

pinch of cream of tartar

1 egg white

2.5 ml/½ tsp vanilla essence or a
    few drops of lemon juice

MRS BEETON'S TIP

Both bowl and whisk must be free from grease, or the frosting will not whisk up well.

Combine the sugar and cream of tartar in a small saucepan. Add 60 ml/4 tbsp water. Place over low heat, stirring occasionally until the sugar has melted. Heat, without stirring, until the syrup registers 115°C/240°F on a sugar thermometer or until a small amount of the syrup, dropped into a bowl of iced water, forms a lump which you can mould with your fingers to a soft ball. Remove from the heat.

In a large grease-free bowl, whisk the egg white until stiff. Pour on the syrup in a thin stream, whisking continuously. Add the flavouring and continue to whisk until the frosting is thick and glossy and stands in peaks.

Quickly spread over the cake. As the frosting cools, it may be swirled with a knife.

ANCHOVY TOAST

SERVES 4 TO 6

1 (50 g/2 oz) can anchovy fillets

100 g/4 oz butter, softened

cayenne pepper

prepared mustard

6–8 slices of toast

Pound the anchovies and their oil to a paste, then mix with the butter, adding a little cayenne and mustard to taste. Spread on hot toast, cut into pieces and serve at once.

ANNA POTATOES

SERVES 6

fat for greasing

1 kg/2¼ lb even-sized potatoes

salt and pepper

melted clarified butter (page 316)

Grease a 20 cm/8 inch round cake tin and line the base with greased greaseproof paper. Set the oven at 190°C/375°F/gas 5.

Trim the potatoes so that they will give equal-sized slices. Slice them very thinly using either a sharp knife or a mandolin. Arrange a layer of potatoes, slightly overlapping, in the base of the tin. Add salt and pepper to taste, then spoon a little clarified butter over them. Make a second layer of potatoes and spoon some more butter over them. Complete these layers until all the potatoes have been used. Cover the tin with greased greaseproof paper and foil.

Bake for 1 hour. Check the potatoes several times during cooking and add a little more clarified butter if they become too dry. Invert the tin on to a warm serving dish to remove the potatoes. Serve at once.

APPLE AND CELERY STUFFING

SUFFICIENT FOR 1 (4–5 K G/9–11 LB) GOOSE,
2 (2.5 KG/5½ LB) DUCKS OR
1 BONED PORK JOINT

3 rindless streaky bacon rashers

1 onion, finely chopped

1 celery stick, finely sliced

3 large cooking apples

75 g/3 oz fresh white breadcrumbs

15 ml/1 tbsp grated lemon rind

salt and pepper

Chop the bacon, fry it gently in a frying pan until the fat runs, then increase the heat and fry until browned, stirring frequently. Using a slotted spoon, transfer the bacon to a bowl. Add the onion and celery to the fat remaining in the frying pan and fry over moderate heat for 5 minutes. Remove with a slotted spoon, add to the bacon and mix lightly.

Peel, core and dice the apples. Add them to the pan and fry until soft and lightly browned. Add to the bacon mixture with the breadcrumbs and lemon rind. Mix well, adding salt and pepper to taste.

APPLE BATTER PUDDING

SERVES 4

25 g/1 oz cooking fat

450 g/1 lb cooking apples

50 g/2 oz sugar

grated rind of ½ lemon

BATTER

100 g/4 oz plain flour

1.25 ml/¼ tsp salt

1 egg, beaten

250 ml/8 fl oz milk, or half milk
and half water

Make the batter. Sift the flour and salt into a bowl, make a well in the centre and add the beaten egg. Stir in half the milk (or all the milk, if using a mixture of milk and water), gradually working in the flour.

Beat vigorously until the mixture is smooth and bubbly, then stir in the rest of the milk (or the water).

Set the oven at 220°C/425°F/gas 7. Put the fat into a 28 × 18 cm/ 11 × 7 inch baking tin and heat in the oven for 5 minutes.

Meanwhile peel, core and thinly slice the apples. Remove the baking tin from the oven and swiftly arrange the apples on the base. Sprinkle with the sugar and lemon rind. Pour the batter over the top and bake for 30–35 minutes until brown and risen.

Cut into 4 pieces and serve at once, with golden syrup or a rich Lemon Sauce if liked.

variations

APRICOT BATTER PUDDING Put 100 g/4 oz dried apricots in a bowl and add just enough water to cover. Soak until soft, preferably overnight. Transfer the apricots and soaking liquid to a saucepan and simmer for 15 minutes. Drain. Make the batter as in the main recipe, heat the fat, and layer the apricots on the base of the baking tin. Proceed as in the main recipe. Serve with an apricot jam sauce.

DRIED FRUIT BATTER PUDDING Make the batter and heat the fat as in the main recipe, then spread 50 g/2 oz mixed dried fruit over the base of the tin. Sprinkle with 2.5 ml/½ tsp mixed spice or cinnamon. Proceed as in the main recipe.

BLACK CAP PUDDINGS Make the batter as in the main recipe. Grease 12 deep patty tins and divide 50 g/2 oz currants between them. Pour in enough batter to half fill each tin and bake for 15–20 minutes. Turn out to serve.

APPLE CHARLOTTE

SERVES 5 TO 6

butter for greasing

400 g/14 oz cooking apples

grated rind and juice of 1 lemon

100 g/4 oz soft light brown
  sugar

pinch of ground cinnamon

50–75 g/2–3 oz butter

8–10 large slices of white bread,
  about 5 mm/¼ inch thick

15 ml/1 tbsp caster sugar

MRS BEETON'S TIP
The mould or tin may be lined
with slices of bread and butter,
placed buttered side out.

Generously grease a 1 litre/1¾ pint charlotte mould or 15 cm/6 inch cake tin with butter. Set the oven at 180°C/350°F/gas 4. Peel and core the apples. Slice them into a saucepan and add the lemon rind and juice. Stir in the brown sugar and cinnamon and simmer until the apples soften to a thick purée. Leave to cool.

Melt the butter in a saucepan, then pour into a shallow dish. Cut the crusts off the bread, and dip 1 slice in the butter. Cut it into a round to fit the bottom of the mould or tin. Fill any spaces with extra butter-soaked bread, if necessary. Dip the remaining bread slices in the butter. Use 6 slices to line the inside of the mould. The slices should touch one another to make a bread case. Fill the bread case with the cooled apple purée. Complete the case by fitting the top with more bread slices. Cover loosely with greased greaseproof paper or foil. Bake for 40–45 minutes. To serve the charlotte turn out and dredge with caster sugar. Serve with bramble jelly and cream.

APPLE CHUTNEY

MAKES ABOUT 5 KG/11 LB

3 kg/6½ lb apples

2 litres/3½ pints vinegar

1.5 kg/3¼ lb sugar

25 g/1 oz salt

10 ml/2 tsp ground allspice

300–400 g/11–14 oz preserved
  ginger, chopped

1 kg/2¼ lb sultanas, chopped

Peel and core the apples; chop them into small pieces. Combine the vinegar, sugar, salt and allspice in a saucepan or preserving pan. Bring to the boil, add the apples, lower the heat and simmer for 10 minutes.

Add the ginger and sultanas to the pan and simmer the mixture until fairly thick. Pour into warm clean jars and cover with vinegar-proof lids. When cool, wipe the jars, label and store in a cool dry place.

MRS BEETON'S TIP
Make chutney in stainless steel pans if possible. Keep a long-handled
heat-resistant plastic spoon for stirring pickles and chutneys.

APPLE CRUMBLE

SERVES 6

fat for greasing

675 g/1½ lb cooking apples

100 g/4 oz granulated sugar

grated rind of 1 lemon

150 g/5 oz plain flour

75 g/3 oz butter or margarine

75 g/3 oz caster sugar

1.25 ml/¼ tsp ground ginger

Grease a 1 litre/1¾ pint pie dish. Set the oven at 180°C/350°F/gas 4.

Peel and core the apples. Slice into a saucepan and add the granulated sugar and lemon rind. Stir in 50 ml/2 fl oz water, cover the pan and cook until the apples are soft. Spoon the apple mixture into the prepared dish and set aside.

Put the flour into a mixing bowl and rub in the butter or margarine until the mixture resembles fine breadcrumbs. Add the caster sugar and ginger and stir well. Sprinkle the mixture over the apples and press down lightly. Bake for 30–40 minutes until the crumble topping is golden brown.

variations

Instead of apples, use 675 g/1½ lb damsons, gooseberries, pears, plums, rhubarb or raspberries.

MICROWAVE TIP

Put the apple mixture in a large bowl, adding only 30 ml/2 tbsp water, cover and cook for 7 minutes on High. Add the crumble topping and cook for 4 minutes more, then brown the topping under a hot grill.

APPLE DUMPLINGS

SERVES 4

6 cooking apples

1.25 ml/¼ tsp cinnamon

50 g/2 oz soft light brown sugar

12 cloves

15 ml/1 tbsp milk

25 g/1 oz caster sugar

SHORT CRUST PASTRY

175 g/6 oz plain flour

1.25 ml/¼ tsp salt

75 g/3 oz margarine (or half butter, half lard)

flour for rolling out

Set the oven at 200°C/400°F/gas 6. To make the pastry, sift the flour and salt into a bowl, then rub in the margarine until the mixture resembles fine breadcrumbs. Add enough cold water to make a stiff dough. Press the dough together with your fingertips.

Divide the pastry into 6 portions. On a lightly floured surface roll out each portion to a round. Peel and core the apples and put one on each round of pastry. Mix the cinnamon and sugar together in a bowl and fill each apple cavity with some of the mixture. Press 2 cloves in the top of each apple. Work the pastry around each apple to enclose it, moisten the edges and press well together.

Place the dumplings on a baking sheet, brush with milk and dredge with caster sugar. Bake for 30–35 minutes or until the apples are tender. Serve with cream or custard.

APPLE FRITTERS

SERVES 4

450 g/1 lb apples
5 ml/1 tsp lemon juice
oil for deep frying
caster sugar for sprinkling
single cream to serve

BATTER
100 g/4 oz plain flour
1.25 ml/¼ tsp salt
15 ml/1 tbsp vegetable oil
60 ml/4 tbsp milk
2 egg whites

Make the batter. Sift the flour and salt into a bowl. Make a well in the centre of the flour and add the oil and milk. Gradually work in the flour from the sides, then beat well until smooth. Stir in 75 ml/5 tbsp cold water. The mixture may be left to stand at this stage, in which case it should be covered and stored in the refrigerator.

Peel and core the apples. Cut them into 5 mm/¼ inch slices and place in a bowl of cold water with the lemon juice added. Whisk the egg whites in a clean, grease-free bowl until stiff. Give the batter a final beat, then lightly fold in the egg whites.

Set the oven at 150°C/300°F/gas 2. Put the oil for frying in a deep wide saucepan. Heat the oil to 185°C/360°F or until a bread cube immersed in the oil turns pale brown in 45 seconds. If using a deep-fat fryer, follow the manufacturer's instructions.

Drain the apples thoroughly and dry with soft absorbent kitchen paper. Coat the apple slices in batter and fry 5 or 6 pieces at a time for 2–3 minutes until golden. Lift out the fritters with a slotted spoon and dry on absorbent kitchen paper. Keep hot on a baking sheet in the oven while cooking the next batch.

When all the fritters have been cooked, sprinkle them with caster sugar and serve with cream.

variations

APRICOT FRITTERS Prepare batter as above. Sprinkle drained canned apricot halves with rum and leave for 15 minutes. Coat in batter, then fry. Dredge with caster sugar and serve with custard or cream.

BANANA FRITTERS Prepare batter as above. Peel 4 small bananas, cut in half lengthways, then in half across. Coat in batter, then fry. Serve with custard or liqueur-flavoured cream.

ORANGE FRITTERS Prepare batter as above. Remove the peel and pith from 4 oranges. Divide them into pieces of about 2 or 3 segments each. Carefully cut into the centre to remove any pips. Coat in batter, then fry. Serve with custard or cream.

PEAR FRITTERS Prepare batter as above. Peel and core 4 pears. Cut into quarters, sprinkle with sugar and kirsch and leave to stand for 15 minutes. Finely crush 4 almond macaroons and toss the pear pieces in the crumbs. Coat in batter, then fry. Serve with a lemon sauce.

PINEAPPLE FRITTERS Prepare batter as above. Drain 1 (556 g/19 oz) can pineapple rings, pat dry on absorbent kitchen paper, and sprinkle with 20 ml/4 tsp kirsch. Leave to stand for 15 minutes. Coat in batter, then fry. Serve with the pineapple juice, thickened with arrowroot.

APPLE PIE

SERVES 6

675 g/1 ½ lb cooking apples

100 g/4 oz sugar

6 cloves

caster sugar for dredging

SHORT CRUST PASTRY

350 g/12 oz plain flour

pinch of salt

175 g/6 oz margarine (or half
butter, half lard)

flour for rolling out

Set the oven at 200°C/400°F/gas 6. To make the pastry, sift the flour and salt into a bowl, then rub in the margarine until the mixture resembles fine breadcrumbs. Add enough cold water to make a stiff dough. Press the dough together with your fingertips.

Roll out the pastry on a lightly floured surface and use just over half to line a 750 ml/1 ¼ pint pie dish. Peel, core and slice the apples. Place half in the pastry-lined dish, then add the sugar and cloves. Pile the remaining apples on top, cover with the remaining pastry and seal the edges. Brush the pastry with cold water and dredge with caster sugar.

Bake for 20 minutes, then lower the oven temperature to 180°C/350°F/gas 4 and bake for 20 minutes more. The pastry should be golden brown. Dredge with more caster sugar and serve hot or cold.

variations

APRICOT PIE Use two 375 g/15 oz cans apricots, drained, instead of apples. Omit the sugar and cloves.

BLACKBERRY AND APPLE PIE Use half blackberries and half apples and replace the cloves with 2.5 ml/½ tsp grated lemon rind.

DAMSON PIE Use damsons instead of apples, increase the sugar to 150 g/5 oz and omit the cloves.

GOOSEBERRY PIE Use cleaned, topped and tailed gooseberries instead of apples. Omit the cloves.

REDCURRANT AND RASPBERRY PIE This is a winning combination. Use 450 g/1 lb redcurrants and 225 g/8 oz raspberries instead of apples. Reduce the sugar to 30 ml/2 tbsp and omit the cloves.

RHUBARB PIE Use rhubarb cut into 2 cm/¾ inch lengths instead of apples. Increase the sugar to 150 g/5 oz.

APPLE SAUCE

MAKES ABOUT 350 ML/12 FL OZ

450 g/1 lb apples

4 cloves

15 g/½ oz butter

pared rind and juice of ½ lemon

sugar (see method)

Peel, core and slice the apples. Put them in a saucepan with 30 ml/2 tbsp water, add the cloves, butter and lemon rind. Cover and cook over low heat until the apple is reduced to a pulp. Remove the cloves. Beat until smooth, rub through a sieve or process in a blender or food processor. Return the sauce to the clean pan, stir in the lemon juice and add sugar to taste. Reheat gently, stirring until the sugar has dissolved. Serve the sauce hot or cold.

APRICOT GLAZE

SUFFICIENT TO COAT THE TOP AND SIDES
OF ONE 20 CM/8 INCH CAKE

225 g/8 oz apricot jam

Warm the jam with 30 ml/2 tbsp water in a small saucepan over a low heat until the jam has melted. Sieve the mixture and return the glaze to the clean pan. Bring slowly to the boil. Allow to cool slightly before use.

APRICOT JAM

Using dried fruit and flaked almonds from the pantry, this delectable jam can be made at any time of year.

MAKES ABOUT 2 KG/4½ LB

575 g/1¼ lb dried apricots
2 lemons
1.5 kg/3¼ lb sugar
50 g/2 oz flaked almonds

Wash the apricots and cut up each fruit in two or three pieces. Put them into a large bowl, cover with 1.5 litres/2¾ pints water and leave to soak for 24 hours.

Transfer the fruit and soaking liquid to a preserving pan. Squeeze the juice from the lemons. Chop one shell and tie it in scalded muslin. Add the juice and muslin bag to the apricots. Bring to the boil, lower the heat and simmer for about 30 minutes or until tender, stirring occasionally. Remove the muslin bag, squeezing it to extract all juice. Stir in the sugar and almonds. Stir over low heat until the sugar is dissolved, then bring to the boil. Boil rapidly until setting point is reached. Remove from the heat, skim, pot, cover and label.

ASPARAGUS SOUP

SERVES 6

450 g/1 lb fresh asparagus
salt and white pepper
1.4 litres/2½ pints chicken stock
50 g/2 oz butter
1 small onion, chopped
50 g/2 oz plain flour
1 egg yolk
150 ml/¼ pint double cream

Cut off the asparagus tips and put them in a saucepan. Add salted water to cover, bring to the boil, then simmer for about 5 minutes or until tender. Drain and set aside.

Slice the asparagus stalks and cook them in 600 ml/1 pint of the stock for about 15 minutes or until tender. Purée in a blender or food processor, or rub through a sieve into a bowl or large jug.

Melt the butter in a large saucepan, add the onion and fry over gentle heat for about 10 minutes until soft but not coloured. Stir in the flour and cook for 1 minute, stirring constantly. Gradually add the remaining stock, stirring until the mixture boils and thickens. Stir in the asparagus purée, with salt and pepper to taste. Reheat.

In a small bowl, mix the egg yolk with the cream. Stir a little of the hot soup into the egg mixture, mix well, then add the contents of the bowl to the soup, stirring over low heat until the mixture thickens slightly. Add the reserved asparagus tips and heat through without boiling. Serve at once.

AUBERGINE DIP

SERVES 8

2 small aubergines

75 ml/3 fl oz olive oil

1 large onion, finely chopped

2 garlic cloves, crushed

100 g/4 oz mushrooms, chopped

1 small green pepper, seeded and chopped

1 (397 g/14 oz) can chopped tomatoes with herbs

250 ml/8 fl oz tomato juice

15 ml/1 tbsp red wine vinegar

5 ml/1 tsp caster sugar

salt and pepper

Cut the aubergines in half lengthways. Scoop out the flesh, leaving the shells intact. Pack the shells on top of each other. Wrap closely in cling film. Refrigerate until required.

Make the dip. Cube the aubergine flesh. Heat the oil in a large frying pan. Add the onion and aubergine and fry for 5 minutes over moderate heat. Stir in the garlic, mushrooms and green pepper. Stir fry for 5 minutes.

Purée the chopped tomatoes, with their juices, in a blender or food processor. Alternatively, press them through a sieve into a bowl. Add the puréed tomatoes to the pan with the tomato juice, vinegar and sugar. Bring to the boil, lower the heat and simmer, uncovered, for 20–30 minutes, stirring occasionally. Add salt and pepper to taste. When the mixture is very thick, remove it from the heat. Cool, then chill.

To serve, unwrap the aubergine shells and arrange them on a serving platter. Fill each shell with the aubergine mixture, piling it in the centre. Serve with Melba toast, crackers or chunks of French bread.

AUBERGINES WITH ONION

SERVES 6

2 aubergines

salt and pepper

50 g/2 oz plain flour

cayenne pepper

oil for frying

1 onion, finely chopped

30 ml/2 tbsp chopped parsley to garnish

Cut the ends off the aubergines, slice them thinly and put them in a colander. Sprinkle generously with salt. Set aside for 30 minutes, then rinse, drain and dry thoroughly on absorbent kitchen paper.

Mix the flour with a pinch each of salt and cayenne. Add the aubergine slices, toss until lightly coated, then shake off excess flour.

Heat a little oil in a large frying pan, add the onion and cook over moderate heat for about 10 minutes until golden. Using a slotted spoon, transfer to a small bowl and keep hot. Add the aubergine slices, a few at a time, to the hot oil in the pan. Fry until soft and lightly browned, turning once during cooking. As the slices brown, remove them from the pan with a fish slice, arrange on a heated serving dish and keep hot. Add extra oil and heat it as necessary between batches of aubergine slices.

When all the aubergine slices have been fried, sprinkle them with the fried onion and the chopped parsley. Serve at once.

AVOCADO VINAIGRETTE

SERVES 2 TO 4

2 ripe avocados

60 ml/4 tbsp Vinaigrette
Dressing

Prepare the avocados just before serving. Cut in half lengthways; remove the stones. Arrange the halves on individual plates or in avocado-shaped dishes. Spoon a little dressing into each hollow and serve at once.

> ### MRS BEETON'S TIP
> The easiest way to remove the stone from an avocado is to spear it with a strong knife. Take care to avoid slipping the knife into your hand. Stab the blade down firmly into the stone, then lift the knife and the stone should come away cleanly.

BACON AND APPLE PATTIES

MAKES 8

225 g/8 oz rindless bacon
rashers, chopped (see Mrs
Beeton's Tip)

1 onion, finely chopped

75 g/3 oz fresh breadcrumbs

salt and pepper

5 ml/1 tsp chopped fresh thyme
or 2.5 ml/½ tsp dried thyme

15 ml/1 tbsp chopped fresh sage
or 5 ml/1 tsp dried sage

1 cooking apple, peeled, cored
and grated

15 ml/1 tbsp sugar

1 egg

oil for frying

In a bowl, mix the bacon, onion, breadcrumbs, a little salt and plenty of pepper, the thyme, sage, apple and sugar. When the ingredients are well combined, mix in the egg to bind the mixture. Wet your hands and shape the mixture into 8 small round patties. Heat a little oil in a frying pan and cook the patties fairly slowly so that they cook through. Allow 25–30 minutes, or until the patties are well browned on both sides. Serve freshly cooked, with baked potatoes and cabbage or a salad.

> ### MRS BEETON'S TIP
> This is a good recipe for inexpensive bacon offcuts or for turning a comparatively small amount of bacon into an interesting meal. An easy way of cutting bacon rashers into small pieces is by using kitchen scissors. Cut 2 or 3 rashers at a time, first into narrow strips, then across into small pieces.

BAKED APPLES — *Illustrated on page 302*

SERVES 6

6 cooking apples
75 g/3 oz sultanas, chopped
50 g/2 oz demerara sugar

Wash and core the apples. Cut around the skin of each apple with the tip of a sharp knife two-thirds of the way up from the base. Put the apples into an ovenproof dish, and fill the centres with the chopped sultanas. Sprinkle the demerara sugar on top of the apples and pour 75 ml/ 5 tbsp water around them.

Bake for 45–60 minutes, depending on the cooking quality and size of the apples. Serve with a vanilla custard, ice cream, Brandy Butter or with whipped cream.

variations
Fill the apple cavities with a mixture of 50 g/2 oz Barbados or other raw sugar and 50 g/2 oz butter, or use blackcurrant, raspberry, strawberry or apricot jam, or marmalade. Instead of sultanas, chopped stoned dates, raisins or currants could be used. A topping of toasted almonds looks effective and tastes delicious.

BAKED CHEESECAKE

SERVES 10

BASE
75 g/3 oz butter
150 g/5 oz fine dried white
    breadcrumbs
50 g/2 oz caster sugar
7.5 ml/3 tsp ground cinnamon

FILLING
3 eggs, separated
100 g/4 oz caster sugar
375 g/13 oz full-fat soft cheese
grated rind and juice of 1 lemon
125 ml/4 fl oz soured cream
icing sugar for dusting

Set the oven at 180°C/350°F/gas 4. Make the base. Melt the butter in a frying pan and stir in the breadcrumbs. Cook over gentle heat, stirring until the crumbs are golden. Remove from the heat; stir in the sugar and cinnamon. Press the crumbs over the base of a loose-bottomed 18 cm/ 7 inch cake tin.

Beat the egg yolks in a mixing bowl until liquid. Add the sugar to the egg yolks, beating until creamy. Rub the cheese through a sieve into the bowl, then work in lightly. Add the lemon rind and juice to the mixture with the soured cream.

In a clean, grease-free bowl, whisk the egg whites to soft peaks. Stir 30 ml/2 tbsp into the cheese mixture, then fold in the rest lightly. Turn the creamy mixture gently on to the prepared base in the tin. Bake for 45 minutes. Cover loosely with foil and bake for a further 15 minutes. Cool in the tin. Serve dusted with icing sugar.

> **MRS BEETON'S TIP**
> Use a pastry brush to brush all the lemon rind from a grater.

BAKED CUSTARD

SERVES 4

fat for greasing
600 ml/1 pint milk
3 eggs
25 g/1 oz caster sugar
grated nutmeg

Grease a baking dish. Set the oven at 140–150°C/275–300°F/gas 1–2.

In a saucepan, bring the milk to just below boiling point. Put the eggs and sugar into a bowl, mix well, then stir in the scalded milk. Strain the custard mixture into the prepared dish. Sprinkle the nutmeg on top. Stand the dish in a roasting tin and add enough hot water to come halfway up the sides of the dish. Bake for 1 hour or until the custard is set in the centre.

BAKED JACKET POTATOES

SERVES 4

4 large, even-sized baking potatoes
oil for brushing (optional)
butter or flavoured butter, to serve

Set the oven at 200°C/400°F/gas 6. Scrub the potatoes, dry them with absorbent kitchen paper and pierce the skin several times with a skewer. If you like soft jackets, brush the potatoes all over with oil.

Bake the potatoes directly on the oven shelf for 1–1½ hours. Test by pressing gently with the fingers. To serve, cut a cross in the top of each potato with a sharp knife. Squeeze the sides of the potato so that the top opens up. Add a pat of plain or flavoured butter and serve.

fillings
Make a meal of baked jacket potatoes by cutting them in half, scooping out the centres and mashing them with selected ingredients. Pile the fillings back into the potato shells and heat through, if necessary, in a 180°C/350°F/gas 4 oven for about 20 minutes.

Alternatively, reheat in the microwave oven or under a moderate grill.
CHEESE AND HAM Mash the potato. Grate in 100 g/4 oz Cheddar cheese, add 50 g/2 oz chopped ham (use trimmings for economy) and mix with 25 g/1 oz softened butter. Replace in oven until golden.
KIPPER Mash the potato with 75 g/3 oz flaked cooked kipper. Add 1 chopped hard-boiled egg, with salt and pepper to taste. Thin with a little milk, if necessary. Reheat.

toppings
The easy option. Cut the potatoes almost but not quite in half and open out. Top with either of the mixtures suggested below.
BLUE CHEESE AND YOGURT Mash 100 g/4 oz ripe Danish blue cheese. Mix with 150 ml/¼ pint Greek yogurt.
CHICK-PEA Mash 100 g/4 oz drained canned chick-peas. Mix with 1 crushed garlic clove and 15–30 ml/1–2 tbsp Greek yogurt. Top with chopped spring onion and sesame seeds.

BAKEWELL PUDDING

SERVES 4 TO 5

strawberry or apricot jam

50 g/2 oz butter

50 g/2 oz caster sugar

I egg

50 g/2 oz ground almonds

50 g/2 oz fine cake crumbs

few drops of almond essence

icing sugar for dusting

SHORT CRUST PASTRY

100 g/4 oz plain flour

1.25 ml/¼ tsp salt

50 g/2 oz margarine (or half
  butter, half lard)

flour for rolling out

Set the oven at 200°C/400°F/gas 6. To make the pastry, sift the flour and salt into a bowl, then rub in the margarine until the mixture resembles fine breadcrumbs. Add enough cold water to make a stiff dough. Press the dough together.

Roll out the pastry on a lightly floured surface and use to line an 18 cm/7 inch flan tin or ring placed on a baking sheet. Spread a good layer of jam over the pastry base.

In a mixing bowl, cream the butter with the sugar until pale and fluffy. Beat in the egg, then add the almonds, cake crumbs and essence. Beat until well mixed. Pour into the flan case, on top of the jam.

Bake for 30 minutes or until the centre of the pudding is firm. Sprinkle with icing sugar and serve hot or cold.

variations

BAKEWELL TART Make as above, but use raspberry jam and only 25 g/1 oz bread or cake crumbs and 25 g/1 oz ground almonds. Bake the tart for 25 minutes.

BANANA CUSTARD

SERVES 4

500 ml/17 fl oz milk

3 eggs plus 2 yolks

25 g/1 oz caster sugar

few drops of vanilla essence

3 bananas (about 400 g/14 oz)

DECORATION

30 ml/2 tbsp crushed
  butterscotch or grated
  chocolate or toasted flaked
  almonds

In a saucepan, bring the milk to just below boiling point. Put the eggs and sugar into a bowl, mix well, then stir in the scalded milk and vanilla essence. Strain the custard mixture into a heavy-bottomed saucepan or a heatproof bowl placed over a saucepan of simmering water. Alternatively, use a double saucepan, but make sure the water does not touch the upper pan.

Cook the custard over very gentle heat for 15–25 minutes, stirring all the time with a wooden spoon, until the custard thickens to the consistency of single cream. Stir well around the sides as well as the base of the pan or bowl to prevent the formation of lumps, especially if using a double saucepan. Do not let the custard boil or it may curdle. As soon as the custard thickens, pour it into a jug to stop further cooking. Peel and slice the bananas and stir them into the custard. Stand the jug in a bowl of hot water for 5 minutes to allow the flavours to blend. Spoon into a serving dish or individual dishes and decorate with butterscotch, grated chocolate or flaked almonds.

If the custard is to be served cold, pour it into a bowl and cover the surface closely. When cold, pour into a serving dish.

BARA BRITH

MAKES 12 SLICES

fat for greasing

450 g/1 lb strong plain flour

75 g/3 oz lard or butter

50 g/2 oz chopped mixed peel

150 g/5 oz seedless raisins

50 g/2 oz currants

75 g/3 oz soft light brown sugar

5 ml/1 tsp ground mixed spice

pinch of salt

25 g/1 oz fresh yeast

5 ml/1 tsp sugar

250 ml/8 fl oz lukewarm milk

1 egg, beaten

honey for glazing

Grease a 20 × 13 × 7.5 cm/8 × 5 × 3 inch loaf tin. Sift the flour into a bowl and rub in the lard or butter. Stir in the peel, raisins, currants, brown sugar, mixed spice and salt. Blend the fresh yeast to a thin paste with the sugar and milk. Set aside in a warm place until frothy – about 5 minutes.

Make a well in the centre of the dry ingredients and add the yeast mixture and the beaten egg. Mix to a soft dough, then cover the bowl with cling film. Leave in a warm place until the dough has doubled in bulk – this will take about 2 hours, or longer.

Turn out the dough on to a floured board and knead well. Place in the prepared loaf tin, pressing it well into the corners. Place the tin in a large, lightly oiled polythene bag. Leave for a further 30 minutes to rise. Set the oven at 200°C/400°F/gas 6. Bake for 15 minutes, then lower the oven temperature to 160°C/325°F/gas 3. Continue baking for about 1¼ hours. Turn out on to a wire rack and brush the top with clear honey.

BARBECUED CHICKEN DRUMSTICKS

SERVES 4

75 g/3 oz butter

12 chicken drumsticks

60 ml/4 tbsp vinegar

15 ml/1 tbsp Worcestershire sauce

15 ml/1 tbsp tomato purée

5 ml/1 tsp soy sauce

5 ml/1 tsp grated onion

5 ml/1 tsp paprika

2.5 ml/½ tsp salt

Melt the butter in a small saucepan. Brush a little of it over the chicken drumsticks to coat them thoroughly, then arrange on a rack in a grill pan.

Stir the remaining ingredients into the leftover butter in the pan. Simmer for 2 minutes, then brush a little of the mixture over the chicken. Grill or barbecue over medium coals, turning occasionally and brushing with more sauce until cooked through. Serve with rice or salad.

BARBECUED SPARE RIBS — *Illustrated on page 265*

SERVES 6 TO 8

2 kg/4½ lb pork spare ribs

1 lemon, cut in wedges

herb sprigs to garnish (optional)

BARBECUE SPICE MIXTURE

90 ml/6 tbsp soft light brown
    sugar

15 ml/1 tbsp grated lemon rind

15 ml/1 tbsp paprika

salt and pepper

BASTING SAUCE

200 ml/7 fl oz tomato juice

45 ml/3 tbsp tomato ketchup

15–30 ml/1–2 tbsp
    Worcestershire sauce

30 ml/2 tbsp soft light brown
    sugar

5 ml/1 tsp mustard powder

1.25 ml/¼ tsp chilli powder

Cut the ribs into individual portions. Mix all the ingredients for the barbecue spice mixture and rub into the ribs.

Meanwhile make the basting sauce. Combine all the ingredients in a small saucepan. Add 100 ml/3½ fl oz water, bring to the boil, then lower the heat and simmer for 15 minutes. Spread out the ribs in a large shallow dish or roasting tin and brush generously with the basting sauce. Cover and set aside for 30 minutes at cool room temperature. Brush again and leave for a further 30 minutes.

Cook the ribs on a grid placed high over medium coals for 1–1½ hours, turning frequently and basting with the sauce. Alternatively, bake in a preheated 150°C/300°F/gas 2 oven for about 1 hour or until nearly cooked. Baste frequently. Finish by cooking under a hot grill or over the fire. Serve with lemon wedges, and garnish with fresh herbs.

BARBECUE SAUCE

MAKES ABOUT 150 ML/¼ PINT

30 ml/2 tbsp oil

1 onion, finely chopped

2 garlic cloves, crushed

1 (397 g/14 oz) can chopped
    tomatoes

45 ml/3 tbsp red wine vinegar

30 ml/2 tbsp soft dark brown
    sugar

30 ml/2 tbsp tomato ketchup

10 ml/2 tsp soy sauce

10 ml/2 tsp Worcestershire sauce

salt and pepper

Heat the oil in a saucepan. Add the onion and garlic and fry over gentle heat for 4–6 minutes, until the onion is soft but not coloured. Stir in the remaining ingredients and bring to the boil. Lower the heat and simmer for 30–45 minutes, until the sauce is thick and well flavoured. Use as a marinade, as a basting sauce for chicken portions, steaks, chops and similar foods being cooked on the barbecue grill, or as a side sauce to serve with grilled meats.

BATTER – LIGHT

This light, thin batter is ideal for delicate or sweet foods.

MAKES ABOUT 175 ML/6 FL OZ

100 g/4 oz plain flour
pinch of salt
15 ml/1 tbsp oil
2 egg whites

Sift the flour and salt into a bowl and make a well in the centre.

Pour 125 ml/4 fl oz cold water into the well in the flour and add the oil. Gradually beat the liquid into the flour to make a smooth, thick batter. Beat really well so that the batter is light.

Just before the batter is to be used, whisk the egg whites until stiff in a clean dry bowl. Fold the egg whites into the batter and use at once.

BATTER FOR COATING

This is a stiff batter, suitable for cod fillets, meat and poultry.

MAKES ABOUT 150 ML/¼ PINT

100 g/4 oz plain flour
pinch of salt
1 egg
125 ml/4 fl oz milk

Sift the flour and salt into a bowl and make a well in the centre. Add the egg and a little milk, then beat well, gradually incorporating the flour and the remaining milk to make a smooth batter.

BATTER PUDDING

SERVES 4

25 g/1 oz cooking fat or 30 ml/
   2 tbsp oil
caster sugar for sprinkling

BATTER
100 g/4 oz plain flour
1.25 ml/¼ tsp salt
1 egg, beaten
250 ml/8 fl oz milk, or half milk
   and half water

Make the batter. Sift the flour and salt into a bowl, make a well in the centre and add the beaten egg. Stir in half the milk (or all the milk, if using a mixture of milk and water), gradually working the flour down from the sides. Beat vigorously until the mixture is smooth and bubbly, then stir in the rest of the milk (or the water). Pour into a jug. The mixture may be left to stand at this stage, in which case it should be covered and stored in the refrigerator.

Set the oven at 220°C/425°F/gas 7. Put the fat or oil into a 28 × 18 cm/ 11 × 7 inch baking tin and heat in the oven for 15 minutes. Stir the batter and immediately pour it into the baking tin. Return to the oven and bake for 30–35 minutes, until the pudding is brown and well risen.

Cut into squares and serve at once, sprinkled with caster sugar or with a suitable sauce.

BEAN SALAD WITH TUNA — *Illustrated on page 131*

SERVES 4

450 g/1 lb dry flageolet beans, soaked overnight in water to cover

150 g/5 oz tomatoes, peeled, seeded and chopped

2 spring onions, finely chopped

1 (198 g/7 oz) can tuna, drained and flaked

DRESSING

90 ml/6 tbsp sunflower oil

45 ml/3 tbsp white wine vinegar

1 garlic clove, crushed

15 ml/1 tbsp chopped parsley

Drain the beans and put them into a saucepan with fresh cold water to cover. Boil briskly for at least 10 minutes, then lower the heat and simmer for about 1 hour or until tender.

Meanwhile make the dressing by mixing all the ingredients in a screw-topped jar. Close the jar tightly; shake vigorously until well blended.

Drain the beans and put them in a bowl. Add the tomatoes, spring onions and tuna and mix well. Pour the cold dressing over the hot beans and the other ingredients and serve at once.

MRS BEETON'S TIP

A variety of beans may be combined with tuna: haricot, borlotti, butter and red kidney beans are all suitable. Remember that canned beans are excellent for speedy, highly successful salads.

BEAN SPROUT SALAD

SERVES 4

225 g/8 oz bean sprouts

1 small orange, peeled and sliced

100 g/4 oz Chinese leaves, shredded

2 celery sticks, thinly sliced

salt and pepper

DRESSING

45 ml/3 tbsp olive oil or a mixture of olive and sunflower oil

15 ml/1 tbsp white wine vinegar

1 garlic clove, crushed

2.5 ml/½ tsp soy sauce

pinch of caster sugar

Pick over the bean sprouts, wash them well, then dry. Cut the orange slices into quarters. Make the dressing by mixing all the ingredients in a screw-topped jar. Close the jar tightly and shake vigorously. Combine the bean sprouts, Chinese leaves, celery and orange in a bowl. Pour over the dressing and toss lightly. Season to taste and serve at once.

MRS BEETON'S TIP

Bean sprouts are highly nutritious. To grow your own, place dried soya beans, mung beans or alfalfa seeds in a clean glass jar. The jar should be no more than one-sixth full. Cover the jar with a piece of muslin held in place by an elastic band. Fill the jar with cold water, then drain off the liquid. Store in a cool dark place. Rinse the beans in fresh water every day. They should start to sprout in 2–3 days and will be ready to eat in 5–6 days.

BECHAMEL SAUCE

MAKES ABOUT 600 ML/1 PINT

1 small onion, thickly sliced

1 small carrot, sliced

1 small celery stick, sliced

600 ml/1 pint milk

1 bay leaf

few parsley stalks

1 fresh thyme sprig

1 clove

6 white peppercorns

1 blade of mace

salt

50 g/2 oz butter

50 g/2 oz plain flour

60 ml/4 tbsp single cream
  (optional)

Combine the onion, carrot, celery and milk in a saucepan. Add the herbs and spices, with salt to taste. Heat to simmering point, cover, turn off the heat and allow to stand for 30 minutes to infuse, then strain.

Melt the butter in a saucepan. Stir in the flour and cook over low heat for 2–3 minutes, without browning. With the heat on the lowest setting, gradually add the flavoured milk, stirring constantly. Increase the heat to moderate, stirring until the mixture boils and thickens to a coating consistency. Lower the heat when the mixture boils and simmer the sauce for 1–2 minutes, beating briskly to give the sauce a gloss. Stir in the cream, if used, and remove the sauce from the heat at once. Do not allow the sauce to come to the boil again. Add salt if required.

BEEF AND POTATO PIE

This is simple country cooking with no frills. Salt and pepper are the only condiments used; the pie deriving its flavour from long slow cooking of meat and vegetables.

SERVES 6

675 g/1½ lb stewing steak,
  trimmed and cut into 2 cm/
  ¾ inch cubes

3 onions, sliced

3 large carrots, sliced

1 kg/2¼ lb potatoes, sliced

salt and pepper

hot beef stock (see method)

Set the oven at 160°C/325°F/gas 3. Layer the meat with the onion, carrot and potato slices in an ovenproof casserole, finishing with a neat layer of potatoes. Add salt and pepper. Pour in enough hot stock to three-quarters cover the contents of the casserole, reserving some stock for adding if the dish begins to dry out during cooking. Cover with a tight-fitting lid or foil and bake for 3–3½ hours, or until the beef is very tender.

About 30–40 minutes before the end of the cooking time, remove the casserole lid to allow the top layer of potato to brown. Serve straight from the casserole.

> **MRS BEETON'S TIP**
>
> If liked, the top layer of potato may be sprinkled with paprika before browning. Use a sweet Hungarian rose paprika if possible.

BEEF OLIVES

This makes an excellent main course for a casual dinner party and has the advantage that the meat is prepared in individual portions and needs little last-minute attention.

SERVES 4

450 g/1 lb rump or chuck steak, trimmed

45 ml/3 tbsp dripping or oil

1 large onion, sliced

45 ml/3 tbsp plain flour

600 ml/1 pint beef stock

1 tomato, peeled and sliced

1 carrot, sliced

15 ml/1 tbsp Worcestershire sauce

salt and pepper

30 ml/2 tbsp chopped parsley

fresh herb sprigs to garnish

STUFFING

50 g/2 oz margarine

100 g/4 oz fresh white breadcrumbs

pinch of grated nutmeg

15 ml/1 tbsp chopped parsley

5 ml/1 tsp chopped fresh mixed herbs

grated rind of 1/2 lemon

1 egg, beaten

Make the stuffing. Melt the margarine in a small saucepan. Add the breadcrumbs, nutmeg, herbs and lemon rind, with salt and pepper to taste. Add enough beaten egg to bind the mixture. Cut the meat into four slices and flatten each with a cutlet bat or rolling pin. Divide the stuffing between the meat slices, spreading it out evenly. Roll each piece of meat up tightly and tie securely with fine string or cotton.

Heat the dripping or oil in a large saucepan and fry the beef olives, turning them frequently until browned. Using a slotted spoon, transfer them to a plate. Add the onion slices to the fat remaining in the pan and fry until golden brown. Using a slotted spoon, transfer to the plate with the beef olives. Add the flour to the pan and cook until golden brown, stirring constantly. Gradually add the stock, stirring until the mixture boils, then lower the heat and simmer for 5 minutes.

Return the beef olives and onion slices to the pan. Add the tomato, carrot and Worcestershire sauce, with salt and pepper to taste. Cover the pan with a tight-fitting lid and simmer for 1–2 hours.

Having removed the strings from the beef olives, serve them on a bed of mashed potato or rice. Strain the sauce and pour it over the beef olives. Sprinkle with chopped parsley and garnish with fresh herbs (the same types as used in the stuffing). Serve at once.

variations

HANOVER ROULADEN Omit the stuffing. Instead lay a strip of gherkin on each portion of beef, with 15 ml/1 tbsp finely chopped onion, 15 ml/1 tbsp chopped ham and 5 ml/1 tsp capers. Proceed as in the recipe above but cook for 1 1/2 hours only.

MUSHROOM PAUPIETTES Use a mushroom stuffing instead of herb. Chop 1 rindless bacon rasher and fry without additional fat for 2 minutes. Add 100 g/4 oz finely chopped mushrooms and fry over gentle heat for 5 minutes, stirring. Stir in 100 g/4 oz fresh white breadcrumbs, a knob of butter and pinch of grated nutmeg. Add salt and pepper to taste. Bind with beaten egg. Prepare and cook the paupiettes as for the beef olives in the recipe above, but stir 250 ml/8 fl oz soured cream into the sauce just before serving.

BEEF For basic information on beef cuts, preparation and cooking methods, see pages 64–79. See also Boeuf à la Mode, Boiled Beef and Dumplings, Bolognese Sauce, Chilli con Carne, Cornish Pasties, Cottage Pie, Goulash, Hamburgers, Lasagne al Forno, Meatloaf, Osso Buco, Oxtail Hot Pot, Roast Ribs of Beef with Yorkshire Pudding, Rump Steak Pie, Steak and Kidney Pudding, Steak and Onions, Steak Pie, Stew with Savoury Herb Dumplings, Stuffed Cabbage Leaves, Stuffed Marrow and Stuffed Peppers.

BEEF RISSOLES

SERVES 4

450 g/1 lb cold lean roast beef

350 g/12 oz fresh white breadcrumbs

2.5 ml/½ tsp chopped fresh summer savory

2.5 ml/½ tsp chopped fresh thyme or 1.25 ml/¼ tsp dried thyme

grated rind and juice of ½ lemon

salt and pepper

1–2 eggs, beaten

oil for shallow frying

fried parsley (see Mrs Beeton's Tip), to garnish

Mince the beef finely. Put it in a bowl with the breadcrumbs, herbs, lemon rind and juice, with salt and pepper to taste. Add enough beaten egg to bind the mixture, then shape into balls or cones.

Heat the oil in a large deep frying pan and fry the rissoles until they are a rich brown colour. Garnish with fried parsley and serve with a rich gravy, creamed onions and Anna Potatoes.

MRS BEETON'S TIP

Fried parsley makes a colourful garnish. Select perfectly fresh parsley sprigs, wash swiftly and lightly and dry thoroughly on absorbent kitchen paper. Heat oil for deep frying to 180–190°C/350–365°F. Put a double layer of absorbent kitchen paper on a plate. Drop the parsley carefully into the hot oil and cook for a few seconds until bright green and crisp. Drain on the paper and serve at once.

BEEF STROGANOFF

SERVES 4

675 g/1½ lb thinly sliced rump steak, trimmed

45 ml/3 tbsp plain flour

salt and pepper

50 g/2 oz butter

225 g/8 oz onions, thinly sliced

225 g/8 oz mushrooms, thinly sliced

250 ml/8 fl oz soured cream

Beat the steak slices with a cutlet bat or rolling pin, then cut them into thin strips. Put the flour in a shallow bowl, season with plenty of salt and pepper and coat the beef strips.

Melt half the butter in a large heavy-bottomed saucepan, add the onion slices and fry for about 10 minutes until golden. Stir in the mushrooms and continue cooking for a further 2–3 minutes. Using a slotted spoon, transfer the vegetables to a dish. Set aside.

Melt the remaining butter in the pan, add the meat and fry rapidly for 2–3 minutes, turning frequently. Return the vegetables to the pan and heat through for 1 minute. Pour in the soured cream, stir once or twice, and heat for 1–2 minutes until all the ingredients are heated through (see Mrs Beeton's Tip). Serve at once, with noodles, boiled new potatoes or rice.

MRS BEETON'S TIP

Do not allow the sauce to approach boiling point after the soured cream has been added, or it will curdle.

> **BISCUITS** See also Almond Macaroons, Brandy Snaps, Chocolate Chip Cookies, Flapjacks, Florentines, Ginger Snaps, Melting Moments, Meringues, Piped Almond Rings, Rubbed-in Biscuits, Shortbread and Sponge Fingers. Savoury biscuits include Cheese Straws and Oatcakes.

BISCUITS – CREAMED MIXTURE

MAKES 26 TO 30

fat for greasing

200 g/7 oz plain flour

1.25 ml/¼ tsp salt

100–150 g/4–5 oz butter or margarine

100–150 g/4–5 oz caster sugar

1 egg yolk

flour for rolling

caster sugar for dredging (optional)

Thoroughly grease two or three baking sheets. Set the oven at 180°C/350°F/gas 4. Mix the flour and salt in a bowl.

In a mixing bowl, beat the butter or margarine until soft, add the sugar and continue to beat until light and fluffy. Beat in the egg yolk. Fold in the flour, first using a knife and then the fingers. Knead the dough lightly on a floured surface, then roll out to a thickness of 5 mm/¼ inch. Cut into rounds with a 6 cm/2½ inch cutter. Re-roll and re-cut any trimmings.

Place the biscuits on the prepared baking sheets, pricking the top of each in several places. Bake for 12–15 minutes, until golden. Leave to stand for 5 minutes, then cool on a wire rack. Dredge with caster sugar, if liked.

BISCUITS – SIMPLE

The mixture for these plain biscuits is simply rolled into balls, which are then flattened slightly on the baking sheet.

MAKES 25 TO 30

fat for greasing

100 g/4 oz butter

100 g/4 oz soft light brown sugar

1 egg, beaten

grated rind of 1 lemon

225 g/8 oz self-raising flour

Grease two or more baking sheets. Set the oven at 160°C/325°F/gas 3. Cream the butter and sugar together until soft and creamy. Beat in the egg and lemon rind, then stir in the flour to make a soft dough.

Roll small pieces of dough into balls about the size of walnuts. Wet your hands under cold running water to prevent the mixture from sticking to them. Place the balls well apart on the baking sheets and flatten them slightly with a fork.

Bake for 20–25 minutes, until the biscuits are spread, risen and brown. Leave the biscuits on the baking sheets for a minute or so, then transfer them to a wire rack to cool.

BLACK FOREST GATEAU

SERVES 10 TO 12

fat for greasing

150 g/5 oz butter or margarine

150 g/5 oz caster sugar

3 eggs, beaten

few drops of vanilla essence

100 g/4 oz self-raising flour or
plain flour and 5 ml/1 tsp
baking powder

25 g/1 oz cocoa

pinch of salt

FILLING AND TOPPING

250 ml/8 fl oz double cream

125 ml/4 fl oz single cream

1 (540 g/18 oz) can Morello
cherries

kirsch (see method)

25 g/1 oz plain chocolate, grated

Line and grease a 20 cm/8 inch cake tin. Set the oven at 180°C/350°F/gas 4.

In a mixing bowl, cream the butter or margarine with the sugar until light and fluffy. Add the eggs gradually, beating well after each addition. Stir in the vanilla essence. Sift the flour, cocoa, salt and baking powder, if used, into a bowl. Stir into the creamed mixture, lightly but thoroughly, until evenly mixed. Spoon into the tin and bake for 40 minutes. Cool on a wire rack. When quite cold, carefully cut the cake into three layers, brushing all loose crumbs off the cut sides.

Make the filling. Combine the creams in a bowl and whip until stiff. Place half the whipped cream in another bowl. Drain the cherries, reserving the juice. Set aside 11 whole cherries and halve and stone the remainder. Gently fold the halved cherries into one of the bowls of cream. Set aside.

Strain the reserved cherry juice into a measuring jug and add kirsch to taste. Prick the cake layers and sprinkle with the cherry juice and kirsch until well saturated. Sandwich the layers together with the whipped cream and cherries. When assembled, cover with the remaining plain cream and use the cherries to decorate the top. Sprinkle the grated chocolate over the cream.

BLANCMANGE MOULD

Blancmange may be made using ground rice or arrowroot instead of the cornflour given below. The quantities will be the same.

SERVES 6

75 g/3 oz cornflour

1 litre/1¾ pints milk

50 g/2 oz sugar

a little almond essence

In a bowl, blend the cornflour to a smooth paste with a little of the cold milk. Bring the remaining milk to the boil in a saucepan.

Pour the boiling milk on to the cornflour mixture, stirring all the time. Pour the mixture back into the pan and heat gently, stirring all the time until the mixture simmers and thickens. Allow to simmer for 5–10 minutes, stirring occasionally. Remove the pan from the heat and stir in the sugar. Add almond essence to taste, stir, then pour the blancmange into a wetted 1.1 litre/2 pint mould. Press dampened greaseproof paper or microwave cooking film on to the surface of the blancmange and cool.

Chill the cooled blancmange for at least 2 hours, or until set. Unmould the blancmange just before serving.

flavourings

To keep the mould a creamy colour, vanilla, grated lemon rind or a good knob of butter with 125 ml/4 fl oz sherry may be added instead of the

BLANCMANGE MOULD — *continued*

almond essence. However, the mixture may also be flavoured with ingredients that add colour although the result is not strictly a blancmange.

CHOCOLATE Either add 30 ml/2 tbsp cocoa to the cornflour and mix it to a paste or add 175 g/6 oz plain chocolate, broken into squares, to the cooked mixture. Stir the mixture until the chocolate has melted before pouring it into the wetted mould.

COFFEE Dissolve 15 ml/1 tbsp instant coffee in 15 ml/1 tbsp boiling water, then stir in 30 ml/2 tbsp rum. Stir this essence into the cooked mixture before pouring it into the mould.

STRAWBERRY Substitute 300 ml/½ pint fresh strawberry purée for the same volume of milk, adding it to the cornflour mixture before stirring in the boiling milk.

BOEUF A LA MODE

SERVES 4 TO 6

2 rindless back bacon rashers

1 kg/2¼ lb thick flank of beef

100 ml/3½ fl oz red wine vinegar

25 g/1 oz butter

1 onion, sliced

2 celery sticks, sliced

1 carrot, chopped

½ turnip, chopped

75 ml/5 tbsp port

salt and pepper

SEASONING MIXTURE

1 clove

4 black peppercorns

3 allspice berries

3 parsley sprigs, finely chopped

1 fresh thyme sprig, leaves finely chopped or 1.25 ml/¼ tsp dried thyme

1 bay leaf, finely crumbled

Cut the bacon crossways into 2 cm/¾ inch strips, including fat and lean in each strip. Trim the meat and, using a sharp knife, make sufficient deep slits in the flesh to accommodate all the bacon strips.

Make the seasoning mixture. Pound the clove, peppercorns and allspice in a mortar with a pestle. Add all the remaining ingredients and mix well.

Pour the vinegar into a shallow bowl. Dip the bacon strips into the vinegar and then into the spice mixture. Insert a bacon strip into each slit in the meat. Rub any remaining spice mixture over the surface of the meat, then tie the beef into a neat shape.

Melt the butter in a flameproof casserole large enough to hold the piece of beef. Add the onion and fry gently until golden brown, then stir in the celery, carrot and turnip. Place the meat on the vegetables. Gently pour in the vinegar, with 250 ml/8 fl oz water, and cover the pan closely. Heat to boiling point, lower the heat and simmer very gently for about 1¾ hours, turning the meat over after 40 minutes' cooking time, and again after a further 30 minutes.

When cooked, transfer the meat to a warmed serving dish and keep hot. Strain the cooking liquid into a pan, skim off the fat, and add the port. Bring to the boil over gentle heat. Add salt and pepper if required. Remove the strings from the meat and pour a little of the sauce over. Serve the remaining sauce in a warmed sauceboat.

BOILED BEEF AND DUMPLINGS

SERVES 8 TO 10

1–1.25 kg/2¼–2¾ lb beef
  brisket or silverside, trimmed

5 ml/1 tsp salt

3 cloves

10 peppercorns

1 bouquet garni

3 onions, quartered

4 potatoes, halved or quartered

4 large carrots, cut lengthways in
  quarters, then in thick slices

4 small turnips, halved

1 small swede, cut in chunks

DUMPLINGS

225 g/8 oz self-raising flour

2.5 ml/½ tsp salt

100 g/4 oz shredded beef suet

Weigh the meat and calculate the cooking time, allowing 25 minutes per 450 g/1 lb plus 20 minutes over. Tie the meat to a neat shape with string, if necessary. Put it into a large heavy-bottomed saucepan, cover with boiling water and add the salt. Bring to the boil and boil for 5 minutes to seal the surface of the meat. Lower the heat to simmering point, skim, then add the cloves, peppercorns and bouquet garni. Cover and simmer for the rest of the calculated cooking time.

About 45 minutes before the end of the cooking time, add the onions; 15 minutes later add the potatoes and carrots. Make the dumplings by sifting the flour and salt into a mixing bowl. Stir in the suet and add enough cold water to make a firm elastic dough. Divide the dough into walnut-sized pieces, shaping each into a neat ball.

Twenty minutes before the end of the cooking time, add the turnips and swede, and bring the stock around the beef to boiling point. Drop in the dumplings. Lower the heat, half cover the pan and simmer until the dumplings are cooked, turning them over once with a slotted spoon during this time.

To serve, remove the dumplings from the pan and arrange them as a border on a large heated serving dish. Remove and discard the bouquet garni, then lift out the vegetables with a slotted spoon and arrange them with the dumplings, placing excess vegetables in a separate dish. Remove any strings from the meat, skewer it if necessary to retain the shape, and set it in the centre of the dish. Serve some of the cooking liquid separately in a sauceboat.

BOILED VEGETABLE SALAD

SERVES 6 TO 8

1 head of celery, trimmed

1 small onion, chopped

½ cauliflower, broken into
  florets

350 g/12 oz French beans,
  trimmed

1 lettuce heart, shredded
  (optional)

mayonnaise

Cut the celery into 5 cm/2 inch lengths. Bring a large saucepan of water to the boil. Add the celery and onion, bring back to the boil and cook for 2 minutes. Add the cauliflower, bring back to the boil again and cook for a further 2 minutes.

Meanwhile, cut the French beans into 5 cm/2 inch lengths. Add the beans to the other vegetables. Bring back to the boil, cook for 2 minutes, then drain the vegetables and cool until just warm. Arrange the lettuce in a salad bowl and top with the boiled vegetables. Pour the mayonnaise over and serve at once.

BOLOGNESE SAUCE — *Illustrated on page 167*

SERVES 4

15 g/½ oz butter

15 ml/1 tbsp olive oil

75 g/3 oz unsmoked rindless streaky bacon rashers, diced

1 onion, finely chopped

2 garlic cloves, crushed

1 carrot, finely diced

½ celery stick, thinly sliced

225 g/8 oz lean minced beef

100 g/4 oz chicken livers, trimmed and cut into small shreds

1 (397 g/14 oz) can chopped tomatoes

200 ml/7 fl oz beef stock

15 ml/1 tbsp tomato purée

125 ml/4 fl oz dry white or red wine

5 ml/1 tsp dried marjoram

salt and pepper

pinch of grated nutmeg

Melt the butter in the oil in a saucepan. Add the bacon and cook it gently until brown. Add the onion, garlic, carrot and celery. Cook over gentle heat for about 10 minutes until the onion is soft and just beginning to brown.

Add the beef and cook, stirring, until browned and broken up. Add the chicken livers to the pan and cook for 3 minutes, turning the livers over gently to brown them on all sides.

Stir in the tomatoes, stock, tomato purée, wine and marjoram. Add salt, pepper and nutmeg to taste. Bring to simmering point and cook, covered, for about 1 hour, stirring occasionally.

Remove the lid for the final 20 minutes of the cooking time to allow some of the liquid to evaporate. Taste and add extra salt and pepper if necessary. Serve with pasta, rice or baked potatoes.

MRS BEETON'S TIP
Many delicatessens and deli counters in supermarkets sell packets of bacon bits – the trimmings left after slicing. These are ideal for a recipe such as this, and may also be used in quiches, on pizzas and to flavour soups and stews.

BORSCH

SERVES 6

30 ml/2 tbsp oil

1 garlic clove, sliced

1 each onion, carrot, turnip and
    swede, diced

2 tomatoes

350 g/12 oz raw beetroot

1 bay leaf

2 litres/3½ pints rich strong
    stock

30 ml/2 tbsp tomato purée

salt and pepper

225 g/8 oz cabbage, sliced

225 g/8 oz potatoes, cubed

5 ml/1 tsp cider vinegar

150 ml/¼ pint soured cream

chopped dill to garnish

Heat the oil in a large saucepan. Add the garlic, onion, carrot, turnip and swede and cook for 10 minutes, stirring frequently to prevent the vegetables from sticking to the base of the pan.

Cut a small cross in the top of each tomato and place them in a heat-proof bowl. Pour on freshly boiling water. Leave for about about 45 seconds, then drain. Peel back and remove the skins, then chop the tomato flesh. Grate the beetroot.

Stir the tomatoes and beetroot into the vegetable mixture and add the bay leaf. Add the stock and tomato purée, with salt and pepper to taste. Bring to the boil, lower the heat, cover and simmer for 1 hour.

Add the sliced cabbage and cubed potato. Stir in the vinegar and simmer for 15 minutes more or until the potato cubes are tender. Taste the soup and add more salt and pepper, if required.

Leave to stand for 5 minutes. Serve topped with soured cream and garnished with dill.

BRAISED CELERY

SERVES 4

15 ml/1 tbsp dripping or
    margarine

2 rindless bacon rashers,
    chopped

2 onions, finely chopped

1 carrot, finely chopped

½ turnip, finely chopped

chicken stock (see method)

4 celery hearts, washed but left
    whole

15 ml/1 tbsp chopped fresh
    coriander or parsley

Melt the dripping or margarine in a large heavy-bottomed saucepan. Add the bacon and fry for 2 minutes, then stir in the onions, carrot and turnip. Cook over gentle heat, stirring occasionally, for 10 minutes.

Pour over enough chicken stock to half cover the vegetables. Place the celery on top and spoon over some of the stock. Cover the pan tightly with foil and a lid and cook over very gentle heat for 1½ hours or until the celery is very tender. Baste the celery occasionally with the stock.

Using a slotted spoon, transfer the celery to a heated serving dish. Drain the cooking liquid into a small pan, reserving the chopped vegetables in a small heated serving dish.

Boil the cooking liquid rapidly until it is reduced to a thin glaze, then pour it over the celery. Sprinkle the chopped vegetables with the chopped coriander or parsley and serve separately.

BRANDY BUTTER

MAKES ABOUT 150 G/5 OZ

50 g/2 oz butter

100 g/4 oz caster sugar

15–30 ml/1–2 tbsp brandy

In a bowl, cream the butter until soft. Gradually beat in the sugar until the mixture is pale and light. Work in the brandy, a little at a time, taking care not to allow the mixture to curdle. Chill before using. If the mixture has separated slightly after standing, beat well before serving.

variations

SHERRY BUTTER Make as for Brandy Butter but substitute sherry for the brandy. Add a stiffly beaten egg white, if a softer texture is preferred.

VANILLA BUTTER Make as for Brandy Butter but substitute 5 ml/1 tsp vanilla essence for the brandy.

ORANGE OR LEMON BUTTER Cream the grated rind of 1 orange or lemon with the butter and sugar, then gradually beat in 15 ml/1 tbsp orange juice or 5 ml/1 tsp lemon juice. Omit the brandy.

BRANDY SNAPS

Fill these traditional treats at the last moment with fresh whipped cream or Confectioners' Custard.

MAKES 14 TO 18

fat for greasing

50 g/2 oz plain flour

5 ml/1 tsp ground ginger

50 g/2 oz margarine

50 g/2 oz soft dark brown sugar

30 ml/2 tbsp golden syrup

10 ml/2 tsp grated lemon rind

5 ml/1 tsp lemon juice

Grease two or three 25 x 20 cm/10 x 8 inch baking sheets. Also grease the handles of several wooden spoons, standing them upside down in a jar until required. Set the oven at 180°C/350°F/gas 4.

Sift the flour and ginger into a bowl. Melt the margarine in a saucepan. Add the sugar and syrup and warm gently, but do not allow to become hot. Remove from the heat and add the sifted ingredients with the lemon rind and juice. Mix well.

Put spoonfuls of the mixture on to the prepared baking sheets, spacing well apart to allow for spreading. Do not put more than 6 spoonfuls on a baking sheet. Bake for 8–10 minutes.

Remove from the oven and leave to cool for a few seconds until the edges begin to firm. Lift one of the biscuits with a palette knife and roll loosely around the greased handle of one of the wooden spoons. Allow to cool before removing the spoon handle. Repeat with the remaining biscuits. Alternatively, make brandy snap cups by moulding the mixture in greased patty tins or over oranges.

BREAD AND BUTTER PICKLES

MAKES ABOUT 3.25 KG/7 LB

1.5 kg/3¼ lb large cucumbers

1.5 kg/3¼ lb small onions, thinly sliced

75 g/3 oz cooking salt

375 ml/13 fl oz white wine vinegar or distilled vinegar

300 g/11 oz soft light brown sugar

2.5 ml/½ tsp turmeric

2.5 ml/½ tsp ground cloves

15 ml/1 tbsp mustard seeds

2.5 ml/½ tsp celery seeds

Wash the cucumbers but do not peel them. Slice thinly. Layer with the onions and salt in a large bowl (see Mrs Beeton's Tip). Cover with a plate weighted down with a jar filled with water. Leave for 3 hours.

Rinse the vegetables thoroughly, drain and place in a large saucepan. Add the vinegar and bring to the boil. Lower the heat and simmer for 10–12 minutes or until the cucumber slices begin to soften.

Add the remaining ingredients, stirring over low heat until the sugar has dissolved. Bring to the boil, then remove from the heat. Turn the contents of the pan carefully into a large heatproof bowl. Leave until cold. Spoon into clean jars, seal with vinegar-proof covers, label and store in a cool dark place.

> ### MRS BEETON'S TIP
> To make the pickle especially crisp and crunchy, cover the final layer of cucumber with about 600 ml/1 pint crushed ice before leaving the salted mixture to stand.

BREAD AND BUTTER PUDDING

When the weather is dull and dreary, lift the spirits with this comforting old favourite.

SERVES 4

butter for greasing

4 thin slices of bread (about 100 g/4 oz)

25 g/1 oz butter

50 g/2 oz sultanas or currants

pinch of ground nutmeg or cinnamon

400 ml/14 fl oz milk

2 eggs

25 g/1 oz granulated sugar

Grease a 1 litre/1¾ pint pie dish. Cut the crusts off the bread and spread the slices with the butter. Cut the bread into squares or triangles and arrange in alternate layers, buttered side up, with the sultanas or currants. Sprinkle each layer lightly with nutmeg or cinnamon.

Warm the milk in a saucepan to about 65°C/150°F. Do not let it approach boiling point. Put the eggs in a bowl. Add most of the sugar. Beat with a fork and stir in the milk. Strain the custard mixture over the bread, sprinkle some nutmeg and the remaining sugar on top, and leave to stand for 30 minutes. Set the oven at 180°C/350°F/gas 4. Bake for 30–40 minutes until the custard is set and the top is lightly browned.

> ### PRESSURE COOKER TIP
> Use a dish that fits in the pressure cooker. Cover the pudding with foil or greased greaseproof paper, tied down securely. Cook at 15 lb pressure for 9 minutes. Reduce pressure slowly, then brown the pudding under the grill.

BREADS For basic information on yeasted breads and rolls, plus standard recipes, see pages 164–173. See also Bara Brith, Chelsea Buns, Hot Cross Buns, Malted Brown Bread, Pizza and Wheatmeal Bread.

BREADCRUMB OMELETTE

Some people find this more digestible than a conventional omelette as it is less rich.

SERVES 1

25 g/1 oz fresh white
   breadcrumbs
250 ml/8 fl oz milk
4 eggs, separated
salt and pepper
20 ml/4 tsp butter

Put the breadcrumbs in a bowl, add the milk and leave to stand for 10 minutes. Stir in the egg yolks, with salt and pepper to taste. In a clean, dry bowl, whisk the egg whites until stiff; fold them into the breadcrumb mixture.

Place a frying pan or omelette pan over gentle heat. When it is hot, add the butter or margarine, tilting the pan so that the whole surface is lightly greased. Without drawing the pan off the heat, add the egg mixture. Leave to stand for 10 seconds. Preheat the grill.

Using a spatula, gently draw egg mixture from the sides to the centre as it sets, allowing the uncooked egg mixture to run in to fill the gap. Do not stir or the mixture will scramble. When the omelette is set and browned underneath, but still moist on top, remove it from the heat. Place under the hot grill for a few seconds to cook the top. Fold the omelette over in half and slide it out of the pan on to a heated plate.

BREAD SAUCE

MAKES ABOUT 900 ML/1½ PINTS

600 ml/ 1 pint milk
1 large onion studded with
   6 cloves
1 blade of mace
4 peppercorns
1 allspice berry
1 bay leaf
100 g/4 oz fine fresh white
   breadcrumbs
15 ml/1 tbsp butter
salt and pepper
freshly grated nutmeg
30 ml/2 tbsp single cream
   (optional)

Put the milk in a small saucepan with the studded onion, mace, peppercorns, allspice and bay leaf. Bring very slowly to boiling point, then remove from the heat, cover the pan and set it aside for 30 minutes.

Strain the flavoured milk into a heatproof bowl, pressing the onion against the strainer to extract as much of the liquid as possible. Stir in the breadcrumbs and butter, with salt, pepper and nutmeg to taste.

Set the bowl over simmering water and cook for 20 minutes, stirring occasionally until thick and creamy. Stir in the cream, if using, just before serving the sauce.

MICROWAVE TIP

There is no need to infuse the onion in the milk. Simply put the clove-studded onion in a deep bowl, cover and cook on High for 2 minutes. Add the spices, bay leaf and milk, cover loosely and cook on High for 6–6½ minutes. Stir in the remaining ingredients, except the cream, and cook for 2 minutes more. Remove the studded onion, whole spices and bay leaf. Whisk the sauce, adding the cream if liked.

BREAD SOUP

SERVES 4

40 g/1½ oz butter

2 onions, chopped

100 g/4 oz fresh white
    breadcrumbs

2 carrots, diced

1 bay leaf

1.1 litres/2 pints chicken stock

60 ml/4 tbsp chopped parsley

salt and pepper

grated nutmeg

Melt the butter in a large saucepan. Add the onions and fry for 10 minutes without browning. Add the breadcrumbs and cook, stirring, for 5 minutes, then add all the remaining ingredients. Bring to the boil, reduce the heat and cover the saucepan. Simmer for 45 minutes. Taste for seasoning, then serve piping hot.

BROWN BETTY

SERVES 6

fat for greasing

1 kg/2¼ lb cooking apples

150 g/5 oz dried wholewheat
    breadcrumbs

grated rind and juice of 1 lemon

60 ml/4 tbsp golden syrup

100 g/4 oz demerara sugar

Grease a 1 litre/1¾ pint pie dish. Set the oven at 160°C/325°F/gas 3.

Peel and core the apples. Slice them thinly into a bowl. Coat the prepared pie dish with a thin layer of breadcrumbs, then fill with alternate layers of apples, lemon rind and breadcrumbs.

Put the syrup, sugar and lemon juice into a saucepan. Add 30 ml/2 tbsp water. Heat until the syrup has dissolved, then pour the mixture over the layered pudding.

Bake for 1–1½ hours until the pudding is brown and the apple cooked. Serve with single cream or a custard.

BROWN SAUCE

MAKES ABOUT 300 ML/½ PINT

25 g/1 oz dripping or lard

1 small carrot, sliced

1 onion, sliced

25 g/1 oz plain flour

600 ml/1 pint rich strong stock

salt and pepper

Melt the dripping or lard in a saucepan. Add the carrot and onion and fry over gentle heat for 10–15 minutes, until the onion is golden brown. Stir in the flour, lower the heat and cook, stirring, until the flour is also brown. Gradually add the stock, stirring constantly until the sauce boils and thickens. Add salt and pepper to taste. Strain and serve hot.

> ### MRS BEETON'S TIP
> This is often referred to as Foundation Brown Sauce, as it forms the basis of a number of classic sauces.

BRUSSELS SPROUTS WITH CHESTNUTS

This is a classic accompaniment to the Christmas turkey. The slightly sweet flavour of the chestnuts is the perfect foil for the Brussels sprouts.

SERVES 6

225 g/8 oz chestnuts, shelled (see Microwave Tip)

1 kg/2¼ lb Brussels sprouts

75 g/3 oz cooked ham, finely chopped

60 ml/4 tbsp single cream

salt and pepper

Set the oven at 180°C/350°F/gas 4. Place the cleaned nuts in a saucepan, just cover with water and bring to the boil. Cover the pan, lower the heat, and simmer for about 20 minutes or until the nuts are tender. Drain, then cut each chestnut into quarters.

Trim the sprouts, pulling off any damaged leaves. Using a sharp knife, cut a cross in the base of each. Cook the sprouts in a saucepan of salted boiling water for 5–10 minutes until just tender. Drain well.

Combine the sprouts, chestnuts and ham in a small casserole. Stir in the cream and season with salt and pepper. Cover and bake for 15 minutes.

MICROWAVE TIP

Shelling chestnuts is made a lot easier by using the microwave. Make a slit in the shell of each nut, then rinse them thoroughly but do not dry them. Put the damp nuts in a bowl, cover loosely and cook on High for 5 minutes. When cool enough to handle, remove the shells.

BUNS

These small buns may be baked in paper cases or greased patty tins if preferred, in which case the consistency should be softer than when the buns are put on a baking sheet.

MAKES 12 TO 14

fat for greasing

200 g/7 oz self-raising flour

1.25 ml/¼ tsp salt

75 g/3 oz margarine

75 g/3 oz sugar

1 egg

milk (see method)

Glacé Icing, to decorate (optional)

Thoroughly grease two baking sheets. Set the oven at 200°C/400°F/ gas 6.

Sift the flour and salt into a mixing bowl. Rub in the margarine until the mixture resembles fine breadcrumbs. Stir in the sugar. Put the egg into a measuring jug and add enough milk to make up to 125 ml/4 fl oz. Add the liquid to the dry ingredients and mix with a fork to a sticky stiff mixture that will support the fork.

Divide the mixture into 12–14 portions. Form into rocky heaps on the prepared baking sheets, allowing about 2 cm/¾ inch between each for spreading. Bake for 15–20 minutes or until each bun is firm to the touch on the base. Cool on a wire rack, then coat with glacé icing, if liked.

variations

CHOCOLATE BUNS Add 50 g/2 oz cocoa to the flour and 5 ml/1 tsp vanilla essence with the milk.

CHOCOLATE CHIP BUNS Add 100 g/4 oz of chocolate chips with the sugar.

COCONUT BUNS Add 75 g/3 oz desiccated coconut with the flour and an extra 10 ml/2 tsp milk.

FRUIT BUNS Add 75 g/3 oz mixed dried fruit with the sugar.

SEED BUNS Add 15 ml/1 tbsp caraway seeds with the sugar.

BUTTERCREAM

SUFFICIENT TO FILL AND COAT THE TOP OF
ONE 20 CM/8 INCH CAKE

100 g/4 oz butter, softened

15 ml/1 tbsp milk or fruit juice

225 g/8 oz icing sugar, sifted

FREEZER TIP

Buttercream can be frozen successfully, unless the recipe contains egg, in which case it may curdle. The buttercream can be flavoured before or after freezing.

In a mixing bowl, cream the butter with the milk or juice and gradually work in the icing sugar. Beat the icing until light and fluffy. Alternatively, work all the ingredients in a food processor.

variations

LEMON OR ORANGE Beat the finely grated rind of 1 lemon or orange with the butter and icing sugar. Use lemon or orange juice instead of the milk.

COFFEE Dissolve 15 ml/1 tbsp instant coffee in 30 ml/2 tbsp boiling water. Allow to cool, then beat this into the buttercream when all the sugar has been added.

CHOCOLATE Dissolve 15–30 ml/1–2 tbsp cocoa powder in 30 ml/2 tbsp boiling water. Stir well until smooth, then allow to cool slightly. Beat this into the buttercream when all the sugar has been added.

BUTTERFLY CAKES

MAKES 12 TO 14

fat for greasing

100 g/4 oz self-raising flour

pinch of salt

100 g/4 oz butter or margarine

100 g/4 oz caster sugar

2 eggs, beaten

DECORATION

150 ml/¼ pint double cream

5 ml/1 tsp caster sugar

1.25 ml/¼ tsp vanilla essence

icing sugar for dusting

Grease 12–14 bun tins. Set the oven at 180°C/350°F/gas 4. Mix the flour and salt in a bowl.

In a mixing bowl, cream the butter or margarine with the sugar until light and fluffy. Beat in the eggs, then lightly stir in the flour and salt. Divide the mixture evenly between the prepared bun tins, and bake for 15–20 minutes until golden brown. Cool on a wire rack.

In a bowl, whip the cream with the caster sugar and vanilla essence until stiff. Transfer to a piping bag fitted with a large star nozzle.

When the cakes are cold, cut a round off the top of each. Cut each round in half to create two butterfly 'wings'. Pipe a star of cream on each cake, then add the 'wings', placing them cut side down, and slightly apart. Dust with icing sugar.

Butterscotch brownies

MAKES 20

fat for greasing

75 g/3 oz butter

175 g/6 oz soft light brown
    sugar

1 egg, beaten

5 ml/1 tsp vanilla essence

75 g/3 oz plain flour

5 ml/1 tsp baking powder

1.25 ml/¼ tsp salt

50 g/2 oz dates, chopped

50 g/2 oz blanched almonds,
    chopped

Line and grease an 18 cm/7 inch square tin. Set the oven at 160°C/325°F/gas 3. Combine the butter and brown sugar in a large heavy-bottomed saucepan; heat gently until all the sugar has dissolved, stirring occasionally. Remove from the heat, cool slightly, then blend in the egg and vanilla essence.

Sift the flour, baking powder and salt into a bowl. Add the dates and mix to coat in flour. Stir the flour mixture into the pan with the almonds and mix well.

Spoon the mixture into the prepared tin and bake for 20–30 minutes. Cool in the tin. When cold, cut into squares.

Cabbage soup

C

Cabbage and bacon go wonderfully well together, a fact that is celebrated in this hearty soup.

SERVES 8

15 ml/1 tbsp oil

175 g/6 oz rindless streaky
    bacon rashers

2 carrots, thinly sliced

1 large onion, thinly sliced

1 large cabbage, shredded

1.1 litres/2 pints white stock

pepper to taste

croûtons to serve (optional)

Heat the oil in a large heavy-bottomed saucepan or flameproof casserole. Add the bacon and cook, stirring, for 5 minutes. Add the carrots and onion, then cook gently for 10 minutes. Stir in the cabbage and add the stock. Bring to the boil, lower the heat and cover the pan. Simmer for 45 minutes, until the vegetables are tender and the soup well flavoured.

Taste the soup for seasoning and add pepper. The bacon usually makes the soup sufficiently salty, depending on the stock. Skim off any excess surface fat, then serve the soup very hot, with croûtons, if liked.

CAKES For basic information on cake making see pages 151–163. For a complete list of cake recipes see entries in index under Cakes, large, and Cakes, small.

CANNELLONI WITH SPINACH STUFFING

SERVES 4

butter for greasing

12–16 cannelloni

15 ml/1 tbsp olive oil

300 g/11 oz frozen chopped
   spinach

salt and pepper

1.25 ml/¼ tsp grated nutmeg

150 g/5 oz ricotta cheese

50 g/2 oz cooked ham

600 ml/1 pint Cheese Sauce

25 g/1 oz Parmesan cheese

25 g/1 oz dried white
   breadcrumbs

Butter an ovenproof dish. Cook the cannelloni in a saucepan of boiling salted water with the oil for 10–15 minutes until tender but still firm to the bite. Drain well.

Place the spinach in a saucepan. Cook over low heat for about 10 minutes or until the spinach has thawed completely. Raise the temperature and heat the spinach thoroughly. Drain. Mix the spinach, salt, pepper, nutmeg and ricotta in a bowl. Chop the ham finely and stir it into the mixture, then spoon the stuffing into the cannelloni. Place in the prepared ovenproof dish. Pour the sauce over the cannelloni.

Bake for 15–20 minutes. Grate the Parmesan. Mix together the crumbs and Parmesan, then sprinkle over the dish. Place under a hot grill for 2–3 minutes to brown the top.

CARAMEL

SERVES 4

200 g/7 oz caster sugar

Put the sugar in a heavy-bottomed saucepan. Add 125 ml/4 fl oz water and stir over low heat for 3–4 minutes until the sugar has dissolved. Increase the heat and boil, without stirring, until the syrup is a light golden brown. Do not allow it to darken too much or it will taste bitter. Immediately plunge the bottom of the pan into warm water to prevent further cooking.

Allow the caramel mixture to cool slightly, then carefully add a further 75 ml/3 fl oz water. Return the pan to a low heat and stir constantly until the mixture becomes smooth. Remove from the heat, cool slightly, then use as required.

CARAMEL CUSTARD CUPS

SERVES 4

100 g/4 oz lump or granulated
   sugar

300 ml/½ pint milk

100 ml/3½ fl oz single cream

2 whole eggs and 2 yolks

25 g/1 oz caster sugar

few drops of vanilla essence

Warm four 150 ml/¼ pint ovenproof moulds by placing them in boiling water or heating them in the oven.

Make the caramel by heating the lump sugar with 150 ml/¼ pint water in a heavy-bottomed saucepan. Stir constantly until the sugar dissolves and the mixture comes to the boil. Continue to boil, without stirring, until the mixture is golden brown. Pour a little of the caramel on to a metal plate and set aside. Immediately pour the remaining caramel into the warmed moulds, twisting and turning each mould in turn until the sides and the base are evenly coated and protecting your hand with an oven glove. Leave until cold and set. Set the oven at 140–150°C/ 275–300°F/gas 1–2.

In a saucepan, bring the milk and cream to just below boiling point. Put the eggs and caster sugar into a bowl, mix well, then stir in the scalded milk. Add a few drops of vanilla essence. Strain the custard mixture into the prepared moulds. Stand the moulds in a roasting tin and add hot water to come halfway up the sides of the moulds. Bake for 30 minutes or until the custard is set.

Remove the cooked custards and leave to stand for a few minutes, then invert each on an individual dessert plate. The caramel will run off and serve as a sauce. Break up the reserved caramel by tapping sharply with a metal spoon, and decorate the top of each custard with the pieces of broken caramel.

CARROT SOUP

SERVES 4

600 ml/1 pint chicken or
   vegetable stock

3 carrots, grated

1 onion, finely chopped

1 potato, grated

25 g/1 oz butter

25 g/1 oz plain flour

300 ml/½ pint milk

salt and pepper

grated nutmeg

Combine the stock, carrots, onion and potato in a saucepan. Bring to the boil, lower the heat and simmer for about 15 minutes or until all the vegetables are tender.

Meanwhile melt the butter in a separate saucepan, add the flour and cook for 1 minute. Gradually stir in the milk, then add the stock and vegetables. Heat, stirring constantly, until the mixture boils and thickens. Add salt, pepper and nutmeg to taste. Serve at once, with triangles of hot toast, if liked.

variation

CARROT AND ORANGE SOUP Cut the carrot into matchstick strips and use 1 parsnip, cut into similar strips, instead of the potato. Use 900 ml/1½ pints stock and add 60 ml/4 tbsp fresh orange juice. Omit the milk and do not thicken the soup.

CAULIFLOWER CHEESE

SERVES 4

salt and pepper

1 firm cauliflower

25 g/1 oz butter

25 g/1 oz plain flour

200 ml/7 floz milk

125 g/4 oz Cheddar cheese, grated

pinch of dry mustard

pinch of cayenne pepper

25 g/1 oz dried white breadcrumbs

Bring a saucepan of salted water to the boil, add the cauliflower, cover the pan and cook gently for 20–30 minutes until tender. Drain well, reserving 175 ml/6 fl oz of the cooking water. Leave the cauliflower head whole or cut carefully into florets. Place in a warmed ovenproof dish, cover with greased greaseproof paper and keep hot. Set the oven at 220°C/425°F/gas 7 or preheat the grill.

Melt the butter in a saucepan, stir in the flour and cook for 1 minute. Gradually add the milk and reserved cooking water, stirring all the time until the sauce boils and thickens. Remove from the heat and stir in 100 g/4 oz of the cheese, stirring until it melts into the sauce. Add the mustard and cayenne, with salt and pepper to taste.

Pour the sauce over the cauliflower. Mix the remaining cheese with the breadcrumbs and sprinkle them on top. Brown the topping for 7–10 minutes in the oven or under the grill. Serve at once.

variations

A wide variety of vegetables can be cooked in this way. Try broccoli (particularly good with grilled bacon); small whole onions; celery, celeriac; leeks or chicory (both taste delicious if wrapped in ham before being covered in the cheese sauce) and asparagus. A mixed vegetable gratin – cooked sliced carrots, green beans, onions and potatoes – also works well, and makes a simple vegetarian supper dish.

CAULIFLOWER SOUP

SERVES 4

1 large cauliflower

25 g/1 oz butter

1 onion, finely chopped

900 ml/1½ pints milk

salt and pepper

2 egg yolks

150 ml/¼ pint single cream

50 g/2 oz flaked almonds, toasted

Steam the cauliflower whole for 20–30 minutes until tender. Cut it into florets, reserving any leaves or tender stem.

Melt the butter in a small frying pan. Add the onion and cook over gentle heat for about 10 minutes, until soft but not coloured. Purée the cauliflower and the onion mixture with 250 ml/8 fl oz of the milk in a blender or food processor, then rub through a fine sieve into a clean pan.

Stir the remaining milk into the pan, with salt and pepper to taste. Heat the soup to just below boiling point, then lower the heat so that it barely simmers. In a small bowl, mix the egg yolks with the cream. Stir a little of the hot soup into the egg mixture, mix well, then add the contents of the bowl to the soup, stirring over low heat until it thickens. Serve at once, topping each portion with toasted almonds.

CELERIAC PUREE

SERVES 4

15 ml/1 tbsp lemon juice

1 large celeriac root, about
    1 kg/2¼ lb

salt and white pepper

90 ml/6 tbsp single cream

15 ml/1 tbsp butter

60 ml/4 tbsp pine nuts

Have ready a large saucepan of water to which the lemon juice has been added. Peel the celeriac root fairly thickly so that the creamy white flesh is exposed. Cut it into 1 cm/½ inch cubes. Add the cubes to the acidulated water and bring to the boil over moderate heat. Add salt to taste, if desired, and cook for 8–10 minutes or until the celeriac is tender.

Drain the celeriac and purée it with the cream and butter in a blender or food processor. Alternatively, mash until smooth, then press through a sieve into a bowl. Reheat the purée if necessary, adjust the seasoning, stir in the nuts and serve at once.

variation

CELERIAC AND POTATO PUREE Substitute potato for half the celeriac. Cook and purée as suggested above.

MICROWAVE TIP

The celeriac can be cooked in the microwave. Toss the celeriac cubes in acidulated water, drain off all but 60 ml/4 tbsp, and put the mixture in a roasting bag. Close the bag lightly with an elastic band and cook on High for 15 minutes. Shake the bag once during cooking. It will be very hot, so protect your hand in an oven glove. Drain by snipping an end off the bag and holding it over the sink. Purée as above.

CELERY SOUP

SERVES 4

45 g/1½ oz butter

1 head of celery, finely sliced

2 leeks, trimmed, sliced and
    washed

1 litre/1¾ pints white stock

salt and pepper

grated nutmeg

2 egg yolks

150 ml/¼ pint single cream

Melt the butter in a large saucepan. Add the celery and leeks and cook over gentle heat for 10 minutes until soft.

Add the stock. Bring to the boil, then lower the heat and simmer for 15–20 minutes or until the vegetables are tender. Purée the soup in a blender or food processor, or rub through a sieve into a clean pan. Add salt, pepper and nutmeg to taste. Return the soup to the heat and simmer for 10 minutes.

In a small bowl, mix the egg yolks with the cream. Stir a little of the hot soup into the egg mixture, mix well, then add the contents of the bowl to the soup, stirring over low heat until heated but do not allow to boil. Serve at once.

CHARLOTTE RUSSE

SERVES 6

45 ml/3 tbsp icing sugar, sifted

24 sponge fingers

15 ml/1 tbsp gelatine

500 ml/17 fl oz single cream

45 ml/3 tbsp any sweet liqueur

1 (15 cm/6 inch) round sponge cake, 1 cm/½ inch thick

In a small bowl, mix 30 ml/2 tbsp of the icing sugar with a little water to make a thin glacé icing. Cut 4 sponge fingers in half, and dip the rounded ends in the icing. Line a 15 cm/6 inch soufflé dish with the halved fingers, placing them like a star, with the sugared sides uppermost and the iced ends meeting in the centre. Dip one end of each of the remaining biscuits in the icing; use to line the sides of the dish, with the sugared sides outward and the iced ends at the base. Trim the biscuits to the height of the soufflé dish.

Place 45 ml/3 tbsp water in a small heatproof bowl and sprinkle the gelatine on to the liquid. Set aside for 15 minutes until the gelatine is spongy. Stand the bowl over a saucepan of hot water and stir the gelatine until it has dissolved completely.

Combine the cream, liqueur and remaining icing sugar in a bowl. Add the gelatine and whisk until frothy. Stand the mixture in a cool place until it begins to thicken, then pour carefully into the charlotte. Cover the flavoured cream with the sponge cake, making sure it is set enough to support the cake. Chill for 8–12 hours, until firm. Loosen the biscuits from the sides of the dish with a knife, carefully turn the charlotte out on to a plate and serve.

CHEESE AND POTATO PIE

SERVES 4

fat for greasing

675 g/1½ lb potatoes, halved

175 g/6 oz Cheddar cheese, finely grated

salt and pepper

milk (see method)

Grease a pie dish. Cook the potatoes in a saucepan of boiling water for about 20 minutes or until tender. Drain thoroughly and mash with a potato masher, or beat with a hand-held electric whisk until smooth. Add 150 g/5 oz of the grated cheese, with salt and pepper to taste, then beat well with enough milk to make a creamy mixture. Spoon into the dish, sprinkle with the remaining cheese and brown under a moderate grill for 3–5 minutes. Serve at once.

CHEESE For basic information on varieties, plus instructions for making simple soft cheeses, see pages 120–127.

CHEESE FONDUE – MRS BEETON'S

Mrs Beeton's fondue has little in common with the Swiss variety. It is baked in the oven, in much the same way as a soufflé. See also Swiss Cheese Fondue.

SERVES 4

fat for greasing

4 eggs, separated

50 g/2 oz Parmesan cheese, finely grated

50 g/2 oz butter, finely grated

salt and pepper

Set the oven at 180°C/350°F/gas 4. Grease a soufflé dish.

Beat the egg yolks until pale in colour. Stir in the grated cheese and butter, with salt and pepper to taste. In a separate, grease-free bowl, whisk the egg whites to soft peaks. Fold them into the cheese mixture.

Scrape the mixture into the prepared dish or tin, which should be no more than half full as the mixture will rise considerably. Bake for about 45 minutes. Serve at once, as the fondue will sink if allowed to stand.

> **MRS BEETON'S TIP**
> Serve this type of fondue with slices of French bread, and follow with a crisp lettuce, cucumber and fresh herb salad.

CHEESE PUDDINGS

SERVES 4

75 g/3 oz butter, melted

50 g/2 oz fresh breadcrumbs

60 ml/4 tbsp milk

4 eggs, separated

salt and pepper

100 g/4 oz Cheshire cheese, finely grated

100 g/4 oz Parmesan cheese, grated

Set the oven at 190°C/375°F/gas 5. Grease 4 individual soufflé dishes or an ovenproof dish with some of the butter. Place the bread in a bowl and sprinkle the milk over. Leave for 5 minutes, then beat in the egg yolks, salt and pepper and both types of cheese.

Whisk the egg whites until stiff. Stir the remaining melted butter into the cheese mixture, then fold in the egg whites. Turn into the dishes and bake for about 30 minutes for individual puddings or 40–45 minutes for a large pudding. Serve at once.

CHEESE SANDWICHES – BAKED

SERVES 4

8 slices of bread

butter

4 large thick slices of Cheshire or Cheddar cheese

Set the oven at 200°C/400°F/gas 6 and heat a baking sheet. Spread the bread with the butter and make 4 cheese sandwiches.

Spread the top of each sandwich very lightly with butter, then invert them on the hot baking sheet. Spread the top of each sandwich very lightly with butter. Bake for 5 minutes, turn the sandwiches and bake for a further 5 minutes, until golden. Serve at once.

CHEESE SAUCE

MAKES 750 ML/1¼ PINTS

50 g/2 oz butter

45 g/1½ oz plain flour

600 ml/1 pint milk

100 g/4 oz Cheddar or Red
  Leicester cheese, grated

2.5–5 ml/½–1 tsp made
  mustard

salt and pepper

Melt the butter in a saucepan. Stir in the flour and cook over low heat for 2–3 minutes, without browning.

With the heat on the lowest setting, gradually add the milk, stirring constantly until smooth. Raise the heat to moderate and bring the sauce to the boil, stirring until it thickens.

Remove the sauce from the heat and add the grated cheese, with mustard, salt and pepper to taste. Stir until the cheese has melted into the sauce, returning the pan to the heat if necessary.

variation
For a thicker coating sauce, ideal for vegetables like courgettes or leeks, which yield liquid, use 50 g/2 oz flour.

CHEESE SOUFFLE

Individual hot soufflés make a very good starter, light main course or savoury finish to a meal. The quantity of mixture below will make 6 individual soufflés in 200 ml/7 fl oz dishes, and will take 20 minutes to bake.

SERVES 4

fat for greasing

50 g/2 oz butter

25 g/1 oz plain flour

250 ml/8 floz milk

100–150 g/4–5 oz Cheddar
  cheese, grated, or 75–100 g/
  3–4 oz mixed grated
  Parmesan and Gruyère cheese

2.5 ml/½ tsp dry mustard

pinch of cayenne pepper

salt and pepper

4 eggs, separated, plus 1 egg
  white

Grease a 1 litre/1¾ pint soufflé dish. Set the oven at 190°C/375°F/gas 5. Melt the butter in a saucepan, stir in the flour and cook over low heat for 2–3 minutes without colouring, stirring all the time. Over very low heat, gradually add the milk, stirring constantly. Bring to the boil, stirring, then lower the heat and simmer for 1–2 minutes more until smooth and thickened. Remove from the heat and beat hard until the sauce comes away cleanly from the sides of the pan. Cool slightly and put into a bowl. Stir in the cheese, mustard, cayenne, salt and pepper. Beat the yolks into the mixture one by one.

In a clean, grease-free bowl, whisk the egg whites until stiff. Using a metal spoon, stir one spoonful of the whites into the mixture to lighten it, then fold in the rest until evenly distributed. Spoon the mixture into the prepared dish and bake for 30–35 minutes, until well risen and browned. Serve the soufflé immediately with hot buttered toast.

variations
CHEESE AND ONION SOUFFLE Add 50 g/2 oz very finely chopped onion cooked in the butter for 2–3 minutes until transparent, to the grated cheese.
CHEESE AND WATERCRESS SOUFFLE Chop the leaves from half a bunch of watercress and add to the cheese.
LAYERED CHEESE SOUFFLE Put half the soufflé mixture into the dish and add a layer of 75 g/3 oz sautéed mushrooms, or 100 g/4 oz cooked

CHEESE SOUFFLE — *continued*

flaked fish, or 45 ml/3 tbsp spinach purée and then top with the remaining mixture.

OEUFS MOLLETS EN SOUFFLE Soft boil 4 small eggs. Put one-third of the soufflé mixture into the dish. Arrange the eggs on top. Add the remainder of the mixture and bake.

CHICKEN SOUFFLE Add 200 g/7 oz cooked minced chicken, 25 g/1 oz chopped sautéed onion, 30 ml/2 tbsp lemon juice and 5 ml/1 tsp chopped parsley.

CHEESE STRAWS

MAKES 48 TO 60

fat for greasing

100 g/4 oz plain flour

pinch of mustard powder

pinch of salt

pinch of cayenne pepper

75 g/3 oz butter

75 g/3 oz grated Parmesan cheese

1 egg yolk

flour for rolling out

Grease four baking sheets. Set the oven at 200°C/400°F/gas 6. Sift the flour, mustard, salt and cayenne into a bowl. In a mixing bowl, cream the butter until soft and white, then add the flour mixture with the cheese. Stir in the egg yolk and enough cold water to form a stiff dough.

Roll out on a lightly floured surface to a thickness of about 5 mm/¼ inch and cut into fingers, each measuring about 10 × 1 cm/4 inches × ½ inch. From the pastry trimmings make several rings, each about 4 cm/1½ inches in diameter. With a palette knife, transfer both rings and straws to the prepared baking sheets and bake for 8–10 minutes or until lightly browned and crisp. Cool on the baking sheets.

To serve, fit a few straws through each ring and lay the bundles in the centre of a plate with any remaining straws criss-crossed around them.

CHELSEA BUNS

MAKES 16

fat for greasing

400 g/14 oz strong white flour

5 ml/1 tsp sugar

200 ml/7 fl oz milk

25 g/1 oz fresh yeast or 15 ml/
 1 tbsp dried yeast

5 ml/1 tsp salt

50 g/2 oz butter plus 15 ml/
 1 tbsp

1 egg

flour for kneading

150 g/5 oz currants

50 g/2 oz chopped mixed peel

100 g/4 oz soft light brown
 sugar

honey for glazing

Grease a baking sheet. Sift about 75 g/3 oz of the flour and the sugar into a large bowl.

Warm the milk until lukewarm. Blend in the fresh yeast or sprinkle on the dried yeast. Pour the yeast liquid into the flour and sugar, then beat well. Leave the bowl in a warm place for 20 minutes.

Sift the remaining flour and the salt into a bowl. Rub in the 50 g/2 oz butter. Beat the egg into the yeast mixture and add the flour and fat mixture. Mix to a soft dough. Turn on to a lightly floured surface; knead for about 6 minutes or until the dough is smooth and no longer sticky. Return to the bowl and cover with cling film. Leave in a warm place until the dough has doubled in bulk.

On a floured surface, roll out the dough to a 50 cm/20 inch square. Melt the remaining butter and brush it all over the surface of the dough. Sprinkle with the dried fruit and sugar. Roll up the dough like a Swiss roll. Cut the roll into 16 equal pieces. Place the buns, about 2.5 cm/1 inch apart, on the prepared baking sheet with the cut side uppermost. Place the baking sheet in a large, lightly oiled polythene bag. Leave in a warm place for about 30 minutes or until the buns have joined together and are light and puffy.

Set the oven at 220°C/425°F/gas 7. Bake for 15–20 minutes, until golden brown. While still hot, brush with honey.

CHERRY CAKE — *Illustrated on page 303*

MAKES ONE 15 CM/6 INCH CAKE

fat for greasing

200 g/7 oz plain flour

1.25 ml/¼ tsp salt

2.5 ml/½ tsp baking powder

100 g/4 oz glacé cherries,
 washed, dried and quartered

150 g/5 oz butter or margarine

150 g/5 oz caster sugar

4 eggs, beaten

15 ml/1 tbsp milk (optional)

Line and grease a 15 cm/6 inch cake tin. Set the oven at 180°C/350°F/gas 4. Sift the flour, salt and baking powder into a bowl. Add the cherries and mix well. Set aside.

Place the butter or margarine in a mixing bowl and beat until very soft. Add the sugar and cream together until light and fluffy. Add the beaten eggs gradually, beating well after each addition. If the mixture shows signs of curdling, add a little of the flour mixture. Fold in the dry ingredients lightly but thoroughly, adding the milk if too stiff.

Spoon into the prepared tin, level the surface and make a slight hollow in the centre. Bake for 30 minutes, then reduce the oven temperature to 160°C/325°F/gas 3 and bake for 50 minutes more until cooked through and firm to the touch. Cool on a wire rack.

CHESTNUT AND ONION STUFFING

SUFFICIENT FOR 1 (2.5 KG/5 LB DUCK) – USE DOUBLE THE QUANTITY LISTED BELOW WHEN STUFFING THE NECK END OF A 5–6 KG/11–13 LB TURKEY.

1 large onion, thickly sliced

125 ml/4 fl oz chicken stock or water

450 g/1 lb chestnuts, prepared and cooked (see Mrs Beeton's Tip) or 300 g/11 oz canned chestnuts

salt and pepper

1 egg, beaten

Combine the onion and stock or water in a small saucepan. Bring the liquid to the boil, lower the heat and simmer for about 10 minutes until the onion is tender; drain and chop finely.

Meanwhile mince the chestnuts or chop them finely. Combine the chestnuts and onion in a bowl, stir in salt and pepper to taste and add enough of the egg to bind the stuffing.

MRS BEETON'S TIP

To prepare chestnuts, make a slit in the rounded side of each nut, then bake them in a preheated 180°C/350°F/gas 4 oven for 30 minutes or cook them in boiling water for 20 minutes. Remove the shells and skins while still hot. Put the shelled nuts in a saucepan with just enough stock to cover. Bring the liquid to the boil, lower the heat and simmer for 45–60 minutes or until the nuts are tender.

CHICKEN AND BACON CASSEROLE

SERVES 4 TO 6

25 g/1 oz plain flour

salt and pepper

1 (1.6 kg/3½ lb) chicken, cut in serving portions

30 ml/2 tbsp cooking oil

100 g/4 oz rindless streaky bacon rashers, cut into strips

100 g/4 oz mushrooms, sliced

1 onion or 100 g/4 oz shallots, finely chopped

500 ml/17 fl oz chicken stock

Mix the flour, salt and pepper in a sturdy polythene bag. Add the chicken portions and toss until well coated. Shake off and reserve excess flour.

Heat the oil in a flameproof casserole. Add the chicken pieces and fry them until golden on all sides, turning frequently. Remove from the casserole, then add the bacon, mushrooms and onion or shallots to the fat remaining in the casserole. Cook for 5 minutes, stirring frequently, then stir in the reserved flour and half the stock.

Replace the chicken in the casserole. Stir in enough stock to cover the chicken pieces. Bring to the boil, then lower the heat. Cover and simmer for 1–1½ hours or until the chicken portions are cooked through.

Taste and add more seasoning if required. Serve from the casserole, with Anna Potatoes and peas if liked. Alternatively, serve buttered noodles and plain green beans with the casserole.

CHICKEN For basic information on preparation, cooking methods and times, see pages 44–52. See also Barbecued Chicken Drumsticks, Coq au Vin, Couscous, Devilled Chicken, Lemon Chicken, Roast Chicken with Honey and Almonds and Tandoori Chicken.

CHICKEN AND HAM PIE

SERVES 6 TO 8

fat for greasing

1 (1.6 kg/3½ lb) chicken with giblets

1 onion, halved

salt and pepper

1 bouquet garni

1 blade of mace

2.5 ml/½ tsp grated nutmeg

2.5 ml/½ tsp ground mace

6 slices of lean cooked ham

3 hard-boiled eggs

flour for dredging

150 g/5 oz puff pastry, thawed if frozen

beaten egg for glazing

HERB FORCEMEAT

50 g/2 oz shredded beef suet or margarine

100 g/4 oz fresh white breadcrumbs

pinch of grated nutmeg

15 ml/1 tbsp chopped parsley

5 ml/1 tsp chopped fresh mixed herbs

grated rind of ½ lemon

1 egg, beaten

Lightly grease a 1.5 litre/2¾ pint pie dish. Make the herb forcemeat. Melt the margarine, if using. Mix the breadcrumbs with the suet or margarine in a bowl. Add the nutmeg, herbs and lemon rind. Add salt and pepper to taste, then bind with the beaten egg.

Skin the chicken and cut it into small serving joints. Put the leftover bones, neck and gizzard into a small pan with 250 ml/8 fl oz water. Add the onion to the pan with salt, pepper, bouquet garni and blade of mace. Half cover and simmer gently for about 45 minutes until the liquid is well reduced and strongly flavoured. Set the pan aside.

Set the oven at 220°C/425°F/gas 7. Put a layer of chicken joints in the bottom of the prepared dish. Sprinkle with salt, pepper, nutmeg and ground mace. Cover with a layer of ham, then with forcemeat; add salt and pepper to taste. Slice the eggs, place a layer over the forcemeat, and season again. Repeat the layers until the dish is full and all the ingredients are used, ending with a layer of chicken joints. Pour in 150–200 ml/5–7 fl oz water and dredge lightly with flour.

Roll out the pastry on a lightly floured surface to the same shape as the dish but 2.5 cm/1 inch larger all around. Cut off the outside 2 cm/¾ inch of the pastry. Lay the pastry strip on the rim of the dish. Dampen the strip and lay the lid on top. Knock up the edge, trim, then use any trimmings to decorate the crust with pastry leaves. Make a pastry rose and put to one side.

Brush the pastry with the beaten egg. Make a small hole in the centre of the pie. Bake for 15 minutes to set the pastry, then reduce the oven temperature to 180°C/350°F/gas 4, and cover the pastry loosely with greaseproof paper. Bake for 1–1¼ hours. Bake the pastry rose with – but not on – the pie for the final 20 minutes. Test whether the joints are cooked through by running a small heated skewer into the pie through the central hole. It should come out clean with no trace of blood. Just before the pie is cooked, reheat the stock and strain it. When the pie is cooked, pour the stock in through the central hole, then cover with the pastry rose.

MRS BEETON'S TIP

If the pie is to be served cold, substitute boneless chicken breasts for the jointed bird. Sausagemeat may be used instead of the forcemeat. In both cases increase the cooking time by about 30 minutes. Cover the pie crust loosely with foil if necessary.

CHICKEN MARENGO

SERVES 4

30 ml/2 tbsp plain flour

salt and pepper

1 (1.4 kg/3 lb) chicken, jointed

60 ml/4 tbsp oil

2 garlic cloves, crushed

100 g/4 oz small button
   mushrooms

2 tomatoes, peeled and
   chopped

15 ml/1 tbsp tomato purée

150 ml/¼ pint dry white wine

chopped parsley to garnish

Mix the flour with salt and pepper, then use to coat the chicken portions. Heat the oil in a large flameproof casserole, add the chicken and fry until golden on all sides. Stir in the garlic, mushrooms, tomatoes and tomato purée, with the wine.

Bring just to the boil, lower the heat so that the mixture simmers and cover with a tight-fitting lid. Cook over gentle heat for about 45 minutes until the chicken is cooked through. Sprinkle with parsley and serve.

CHICKEN STOCK

MAKES ABOUT 1.4 LITRES/2½ PINTS

4 chicken drumsticks or 1 meaty
   chicken carcass

1 small onion, sliced

1 carrot, roughly chopped

1 celery stick, sliced

1 bouquet garni

5 ml/1 tsp white peppercorns

Break or chop the carcass into manageable pieces. Put it in a large saucepan with 1.75 litres/3 pints cold water. Bring to the boil; skim the surface. Add the remaining ingredients, lower the heat and simmer for 3–4 hours. Cool quickly, then strain. Skim off surface fat. Season and use as required.

variation

RICH CHICKEN STOCK Use drumsticks and roast them at 200°C/400°F/gas 6 for 40 minutes. Drain off the fat. Continue as above, adding 225 g/8 oz cubed belly pork with the chicken.

GAME STOCK Use the carcasses of 1 or 2 game birds such as pheasant or grouse, with the giblets, instead of the chicken.

CHICKEN SUPREME

SERVES 4 TO 6

1 (1.4–1.6 kg/3–3½ lb) chicken

1 litre/1¾ pints chicken or
vegetable stock

chopped truffles or poached
mushrooms to garnish

SAUCE

50 g/2 oz butter

4 button mushrooms, finely
chopped

6 black peppercorns

4–5 parsley stalks

25 g/1 oz plain flour

salt and pepper

lemon juice (see method)

150 ml/¼ pint single cream

1 egg yolk

grated nutmeg

Truss the chicken neatly, put it into a large saucepan and pour over the stock. Bring the liquid to the boil, lower the heat, cover the pan and simmer for 1–2 hours or until tender.

After 1 hour, strain off 250 ml/8 fl oz of the chicken stock. Blot the surface with a piece of absorbent kitchen paper to remove excess fat, then set the stock aside for use in the sauce.

Melt half the butter in a saucepan. Add the mushrooms, peppercorns and parsley stalks. Cook gently for 10 minutes, then stir in the flour. Cook over gentle heat for 2–3 minutes. Gradually add the reserved stock, stirring well to prevent the formation of lumps. Raise the heat and cook the sauce, stirring constantly, until it thickens. Rub the sauce through a sieve into a clean pan, add salt, pepper and lemon juice to taste and stir in half the cream. Cool the sauce slightly.

Beat the egg yolk and remaining cream with a little of the cooled sauce in a bowl. Add the contents of the bowl to the sauce and stir over gentle heat until heated. The yolk and cream enrich, rather than thicken the sauce. Do not boil or the yolk and cream will curdle. Whisk in the remaining butter, adding a knob at a time. Add nutmeg to taste.

Drain the cooked chicken, joint it into serving portions and transfer these to a heated serving dish. Pour the sauce over, garnish with truffles or mushrooms and serve.

CHILLI CON CARNE

SERVES 4

225 g/8 oz red kidney beans, soaked overnight in water to cover

225 g/8 oz rindless smoked streaky bacon rashers, chopped

1 Spanish onion, chopped

2 garlic cloves, crushed

30 ml/2 tbsp ground coriander

15 ml/1 tbsp ground cumin

15 ml/1 tbsp chilli powder or to taste

450 g/1 lb minced beef

1 beef stock cube

30 ml/2 tbsp tomato purée

salt and pepper

30 ml/2 tbsp chopped fresh coriander or parsley

Drain the beans and put them in a large saucepan. Add plenty of water and bring to the boil. Boil vigorously for 10 minutes, then lower the heat, cover the pan and simmer gently for 30 minutes.

Put the bacon in a large heavy-bottomed saucepan. Heat gently until the fat runs. Add the chopped onion and fry, stirring frequently for about 5 minutes until the onion is soft but not browned. Stir in the garlic, ground coriander, cumin and chilli powder. Cook for 1 minute, stirring, then add the meat and cook until lightly browned. Crumble in the stock cube and pour in 600 ml/1 pint water. Stir in the tomato purée and add salt and pepper to taste. Bring to the boil.

Drain the beans. Add them to the saucepan and bring the stock back to the boil. Cover the pan, lower the heat and simmer gently for about 1 hour or until the beans are tender and the liquid has been absorbed. Stir in the coriander or parsley. Serve at once, with rice, crusty bread or as a filling for baked jacket potatoes.

CHOCOLATE CHIP COOKIES

MAKES 26 TO 30

fat for greasing

150 g/5 oz plain flour

1.25 ml/¼ tsp salt

2.5 ml/½ tsp bicarbonate of soda

100 g/4 oz butter or margarine

50 g/2 oz caster sugar

50 g/2 oz soft light brown sugar

1 egg, beaten

2.5 ml/½ tsp vanilla essence

75 g/3 oz chocolate chips

Thoroughly grease two or three baking sheets. Set the oven at 180°C/350°F/gas 4. Mix the flour, salt and bicarbonate of soda in a bowl. Beat the butter or margarine until soft, add the sugars and continue to beat until light and fluffy. Beat in the egg and vanilla essence. Stir in the flour and chocolate chips. Using a teaspoon, scoop up a little of the dough. Use a second teaspoon to transfer the dough to one of the prepared baking sheets. Repeat with the remaining dough, making the heaps about 5 cm/2 inches apart.

Bake the biscuits for 10–12 minutes, until golden. Leave to stand for 5 minutes, then cool on a wire rack.

CHOCOLATE FUDGE ICING

SUFFICIENT TO FILL AND COAT THE TOP OF
ONE 20 CM/8 INCH CAKE

100 g/4 oz plain chocolate,
  broken into pieces

50 g/2 oz butter, cut up

1 egg, beaten

175 g/6 oz icing sugar, sifted

MICROWAVE TIP

Melt the chocolate with the butter in a small bowl on Medium for 1–2 minutes.

Combine the chocolate and butter in a heatproof bowl. Set over hot water until the chocolate has melted. Beat in the egg, then remove the bowl from the heat and stir in half the icing sugar. Beat in the remaining sugar and continue beating until the icing is smooth and cold. Use the icing immediately.

variations

CHOCOLATE WALNUT FUDGE ICING Add 50 g/2 oz finely chopped walnuts to the icing just before spreading it on the cake.

CHOCOLATE RUM FUDGE ICING Add 30 ml/2 tbsp rum to the icing with the egg and continue as in the main recipe.

CHOCOLATE ORANGE FUDGE ICING Add the grated rind of 1 orange to the chocolate and butter. Continue as in the main recipe. This icing is excellent on a Victoria Sandwich Cake which has the grated rind of 1 orange added to the mixture.

CHOCOLATE LAYER CAKE

MAKES ONE 18 CM/7INCH CAKE

fat for greasing

150 g/5 oz butter or margarine

150 g/5 oz caster sugar

3 eggs, beaten

100 g/4 oz self-raising flour or
  plain flour and 5 ml/1 tsp
  baking powder

few drops of vanilla essence

25 g/1 oz cocoa

pinch of salt

Chocolate Buttercream (page
  232) for filling

caster sugar for dredging

Line and grease two 18 cm/7 inch sandwich tins. Set the oven at 180°C/350°F/gas 4.

In a mixing bowl cream the butter or margarine with the sugar until light and fluffy. Add the eggs gradually, beating well after each addition and adding a little of the flour if the mixture shows signs of curdling. Stir in the vanilla essence. Sift the flour, cocoa, salt and baking powder, if used, into a bowl. Stir into the creamed mixture, lightly but thoroughly, until evenly mixed.

Divide between the tins and bake for 25–30 minutes. Cool on a wire rack, then sandwich together with the buttercream. Sprinkle the top of the cake with caster sugar.

CHOCOLATE MOUSSE

SERVES 4

150 g/5 oz plain chocolate, grated

4 eggs, separated

vanilla essence

DECORATION

whipped cream

chopped walnuts

Put the grated chocolate into a large heatproof bowl with 30 ml/2 tbsp water. Stand over a saucepan of simmering water until the chocolate melts. Remove from the heat and stir the mixture until smooth.

Beat the egg yolks into the chocolate with a few drops of vanilla essence. In a clean, grease-free bowl, whisk the egg whites until fairly stiff, then fold gently into the chocolate mixture until evenly blended.

Pour into 4 individual dishes and refrigerate for 1–2 hours until set. Decorate with whipped cream and chopped walnuts just before serving.

variations

MOCHA MOUSSE Dissolve 5 ml/1 tsp instant coffee in 30 ml/2 tbsp hot water and stir this liquid into the chocolate with the egg yolks and vanilla essence.

CHOC-AU-RHUM Mousse Add 15 ml/1 tbsp dark rum to the mixture. Alternatively, use brandy, Grand Marnier or Tia Maria.

WHITE MOUSSE Use white chocolate, melting it in single cream instead of water.

CHOCOLATE ROLL

MAKES ONE 30 CM/12 INCH SWISS ROLL

fat for greasing

3 eggs

75 g/3 oz caster sugar

65 g/2½ oz plain flour

30 ml/2 tbsp cocoa

2.5 ml/½ tsp baking powder

pinch of salt

Chocolate Buttercream (page 232) for filling

caster sugar for dusting

Line and grease a 30 x 20 cm/12 x 8 inch Swiss roll tin. Set the oven at 220°C/425°F/gas 7.

Combine the eggs and sugar in a heatproof bowl. Set the bowl over a pan of hot water, taking care that the bottom of the bowl does not touch the water. Whisk for 10–15 minutes until thick and creamy, then remove from the pan and continue whisking until cold.

Sift the flour, cocoa, baking powder and salt into a bowl, then lightly fold into the egg mixture. Pour into the prepared tin and bake for 10 minutes.

When the cake is cooked, turn it on to a large sheet of greaseproof paper dusted with caster sugar. Peel off the lining paper. Trim off any crisp edges. Place a second piece of greaseproof paper on top of the cake and roll up tightly from one long side, with the paper inside. Cool completely on a wire rack.

When cold, unroll carefully, remove the paper, spread with the buttercream and roll up again. Dust the roll with caster sugar.

CHOCOLATE ROULADE

This cake is best baked the day before it is to be served.

SERVES 6

oil and butter for greasing

150 g/5 oz plain dessert
  chocolate, in squares

4 eggs, separated

100 g/4 oz caster sugar

icing sugar (see method)

about 175 ml/6 fl oz double
  cream

few drops of vanilla essence

MRS BEETON'S TIP

Do not worry too much if cracks appear in the roulade during rolling. The mixture does not include any flour so that the baked roulade is rich and sweet with a fragile texture. Dusting with icing sugar disguises the cracks.

Brush a 42 x 30 cm/17 x 12 inch Swiss roll tin with oil. Line with a piece of greaseproof paper, letting the paper overlap the edge a little. Cut out a second sheet of greaseproof paper to the same size, to cover the cooked roulade, and have ready a damp clean tea-towel with which to cover the paper-topped roulade. Set the oven at 190°C/375°F/gas 5.

Heat a saucepan of water. Place the chocolate in a heatproof bowl. When the water boils, remove the pan from the heat and set the bowl over it. Leave to melt, stirring occasionally.

Combine the egg yolks and caster sugar in a bowl and beat briskly until the mixture is pale and creamy. Add 45 ml/3 tbsp hot water to the melted chocolate and beat until well blended. Stir the chocolate into the egg yolk mixture, then whisk thoroughly.

In a clean, grease-free bowl, whisk the egg whites until fairly stiff. Using a metal spoon, fold them carefully into the chocolate mixture. Tip into the prepared Swiss roll tin and bake for 20 minutes until firm.

Butter the remaining sheet of greaseproof paper. Remove the tin from the oven and immediately cover the cake with the buttered paper and the damp tea-towel. Leave to stand for several hours or overnight.

Next day, remove the cloth. Turn the paper buttered side up, sprinkle with icing sugar and replace sugared side down. Grip the paper and tin and invert both together so that the roulade is upside-down. Lay it down on the paper and remove the tin. Peel off the lining paper.

In a bowl, whip the cream until very stiff, stir in the vanilla essence and spread evenly over the surface of the roulade. Roll the roulade up from one long side, using the paper as a guide. Place on a serving plate, with the join underneath, dust with extra icing sugar and chill for several hours before serving.

CHOCOLATE SAUCE

Plain ice cream becomes a party treat with this wickedly rich sauce. It also makes a very good topping for Chocolate Roulade.

MAKES ABOUT 500 ML/17 FL OZ

350 g/12 oz bitter-sweet dessert chocolate, roughly grated

45 ml/3 tbsp butter

30 ml/2 tbsp double cream

5 ml/1 tsp whisky

Put the grated chocolate in a saucepan with 200 ml/7 floz water. Heat gently, stirring all the time, until the chocolate melts. Do not let the sauce boil. Add the butter, 5 ml/1 tsp at a time, and continue stirring the sauce until it melts.

Remove the sauce from the heat and stir in the cream and whisky. Serve at once.

> ### FREEZER TIP
>
> The sauce may be poured into a heatproof container with a lid, cooled quickly and then frozen for up to 3 months. To use, thaw for 4 hours at room temperature, then stand the container in a saucepan of very hot water until warm.

CHOWDER

SERVES 4

25 g/1 oz butter

450 g/1 lb onions, chopped

½ green pepper, seeded and chopped

75 g/3 oz rindless streaky bacon rashers, chopped

450 g/1 lb huss fillets, skinned and cut into bite-sized pieces

450 g/1 lb tomatoes, peeled, seeded and roughly chopped

1 bay leaf

salt and pepper

125 ml/4 fl oz fish stock

chopped parsley to garnish

Set the oven at 180°C/350°F/gas 4. Melt the butter in a flameproof casserole. Add the onions, pepper and bacon and fry gently for 4–5 minutes. Add the fish to the casserole with the chopped tomatoes. Place the bay leaf on top and add plenty of salt and pepper.

Pour in the fish stock, cover and bake for 45 minutes. Remove the bay leaf. Serve hot, garnished with the parsley.

> ### MRS BEETON'S TIP
>
> Kitchen scissors are among the most useful items in any cook's collection. Not only do they make short work of chopping the bacon but they can also be used for the parsley. Simply place the parsley in a mug and snip it until finely chopped.

CHRISTMAS CAKE

MAKES ONE 20 CM/8 INCH CAKE

fat for greasing

200 g/7 oz plain flour

1.25 ml/¼ tsp salt

5–10 ml/1–2 tsp mixed spice

200 g/7 oz butter

200 g/7 oz caster sugar

6 eggs, beaten

30–60 ml/2–4 tbsp brandy or
    sherry

100 g/4 oz glacé cherries,
    chopped

50 g/2 oz preserved ginger,
    chopped

50 g/2 oz walnuts, chopped

200 g/7 oz currants

200 g/7 oz sultanas

150 g/5 oz seedless raisins

75 g/3 oz cut mixed peel

COATING AND ICING

almond paste

Royal Icing

Line and grease a 20 cm/8 inch round cake tin. Use doubled greaseproof paper and tie a strip of brown paper around the outside. Set the oven at 160°C/325°F/gas 3.

Sift the flour, salt and spice into a bowl. In a mixing bowl, cream the butter and sugar together until light and fluffy. Gradually beat in the eggs and the brandy or sherry, adding a little flour if the mixture starts to curdle. Add the cherries, ginger and walnuts. Stir in the dried fruit, peel and flour mixture. Spoon into the prepared tin and make a slight hollow in the centre.

Bake for 45 minutes, then reduce the oven temperature to 150°C/300°F/gas 2 and bake for a further hour. Reduce the temperature still further to 140°C/275°F/gas 1, and cook for 45–60 minutes more until cooked through and firm to the touch. Cool in the tin. Cover the cake with almond paste and decorate with royal icing.

MRS BEETON'S TIP

The quickest way to complete the decoration on a Christmas cake is to apply the royal icing in rough peaks, then add bought decorations. For a change, why not bake the cake mixture in a shaped tin, for example in the shape of a star or a bell. Shaped tins can be hired from kitchen shops and cake decorating suppliers. To work out how much mixture will fill an unusually-shaped tin, pour water into the tin until it is full to the brim. Measure the quantity of water as you are pouring it into the tin. Do the same with a 20 cm/8 inch round tin. Compare the volumes and adjust the weight of ingredients accordingly.

CHRISTMAS PUDDING

EACH PUDDING SERVES 6

fat for greasing

225 g/8 oz plain flour

pinch of salt

5 ml/1 tsp ground ginger

5 ml/1 tsp mixed spice

5 ml/1 tsp grated nutmeg

50 g/2 oz blanched almonds,
 chopped

400 g/14 oz soft dark brown
 sugar

225 g/8 oz shredded suet

225 g/8 oz sultanas

225 g/8 oz currants

200 g/7 oz seedless raisins

175 g/6 oz cut mixed peel

175 g/6 oz dried white
 breadcrumbs

6 eggs

75 ml/5 tbsp stout

juice of 1 orange

50 ml/2 fl oz brandy

125–250 ml/4–8 fl oz milk

Grease four 600 ml/1 pint pudding basins. Three-quarters fill four saucepans, each deep enough to hold a single pudding, with water.

Sift the flour, salt, ginger, mixed spice and nutmeg into a very large mixing bowl. Add the almonds, sugar, suet, dried fruit, peel and breadcrumbs.

In a second bowl, combine the eggs, stout, orange juice, brandy and 125 ml/4 fl oz milk. Mix well. Stir the liquid mixture into the dry ingredients, adding more milk if necessary to give a soft dropping consistency.

Divide the mixture between the pudding basins, covering each with greased greaseproof paper and a floured cloth or foil. Secure with string.

Carefully lower the basins into the pans of boiling water. Cover the pans and lower the heat so that the water is kept at a steady simmer. Cook the puddings for 6–7 hours, topping up each pan with boiling water as required. The pudding basins should be covered at all times with boiling water.

To store, cover each pudding with a clean dry cloth, wrap in greaseproof paper and place in an airtight container or seal in a polythene bag. Foil may be used as an outer covering, over paper, but it should not come in direct contact with the pudding as the fruit acid causes it to break down and disintegrate to a coarse foil powder which ruins the surface of the pudding. Kept in a cool dry place, Christmas pudding will remain excellent for up to a year. 'Feed' it occasionally with a little brandy.

To reheat, boil or steam each pudding for 1–2 hours. Serve with Brandy Butter.

PRESSURE COOKER TIP

Pour 1.5 litres/2¾ pints boiling water into the pressure cooker. Stand one pudding on the trivet and steam it, without weights, for 20 minutes. Bring to 15 lb pressure and cook for 1¾ hours. Allow the pressure to reduce slowly. To reheat, cook at 15 lb pressure for 20 minutes, reduce pressure slowly and serve.

| CHUTNEY | For basic information on making chutneys, ketchups and relishes, see pages 179–180. See also Apple Chutney, Green Tomato Chutney and Red Tomato Chutney. See also Raspberry Vinegar and Spiced Vinegar. |

COCK-A-LEEKIE

SERVES 6 TO 8

100 g/4 oz prunes

450 g/1 lb leeks, trimmed, sliced and washed

1 (1.4 kg/3 lb) chicken

3 rindless streaky bacon rashers, chopped

2.5 ml/½ tsp salt

1 bouquet garni

1.25 ml/¼ tsp pepper

Soak the prunes overnight in a small bowl of water, then drain them and remove the stones. Set aside, with about one-third of the drained leek slices.

Put the chicken, with its giblets if available, and bacon in a deep saucepan. Add cold water to cover (about 2 litres/3½ pints). Stir in the salt and bring slowly to simmering point.

Add the remaining leeks to the pan, with the bouquet garni and pepper. Cover, then simmer gently for about 3 hours or until the chicken is cooked through and tender.

Carefully remove the chicken, discard the skin, then carve off the meat and cut it into fairly large serving pieces. Return the chicken meat to the soup and add the reserved prunes and leeks. Simmer gently for about 30 minutes, until the prunes are cooked but not broken. Skim off surface fat and check seasoning before serving.

MRS BEETON'S TIP

Ready-to-eat dried prunes may be used. There is no need to presoak them.

COCONUT PYRAMIDS

MAKES 12

fat for greasing

2 egg whites

150 g/5 oz caster sugar

150 g/5 oz desiccated coconut

Grease a baking sheet and cover with rice paper. Set the oven at 140°C/275°F/gas 1. In a clean dry bowl, whisk the egg whites until stiff, then fold in the sugar and coconut, using a metal spoon. Divide the mixture into 12 portions and place in heaps on the rice paper. Using a fork, form into pyramid shapes. Bake for 45–60 minutes until pale brown in colour. Cool on the baking sheet.

COD AU GRATIN

SERVES 4

fat for greasing

4 (100 g/4 oz) portions of cod fillet

25 g/1 oz butter

2 large onions, finely chopped

100 g/4 oz mushrooms, sliced

salt and pepper

1 green pepper, seeded and diced

450 g/1 lb tomatoes, peeled, seeded and sliced

50 g/2 oz Cheddar cheese, grated

75 g/3 oz fresh white breadcrumbs

Grease a fairly deep ovenproof dish. Set the oven at 190°C/375°F/gas 5. Arrange the cod portions on the base of the dish.

Melt the butter in a frying pan, add the onions and fry gently for 4–5 minutes until slightly softened. Remove the onions with a slotted spoon and place on top of the fish. Cook the mushrooms in the same way.

Meanwhile bring a small saucepan of salted water to the boil, add the diced green pepper and blanch for 2 minutes. Drain and add to the fish, followed by the mushrooms. Top with the tomato slices, generously sprinkled with salt and pepper.

Combine the cheese and breadcrumbs in a bowl, mix well, then sprinkle over the fish and vegetables. Bake for 30 minutes. Serve at once.

COD WITH CREAM SAUCE

SERVES 6

6 (100 g/4 oz) cod steaks or portions

75 g/3 oz butter

250 ml/8 fl oz fish stock

milk (see method)

25 g/1 oz plain flour

30 ml/2 tbsp double cream

15 ml/1 tbsp lemon juice

salt and pepper

Rinse the fish and pat dry on absorbent kitchen paper. Melt half the butter in a frying pan, add the cod and fry quickly on both sides to seal without browning. Add the stock, cover the pan and simmer gently for 20 minutes. Drain the fish, reserving the cooking liquid in a measuring jug, place on a warmed dish and keep hot. Make the cooking liquid up to 300 ml/½ pint with milk.

Melt the remaining butter in a saucepan, add the flour and cook for 1 minute, stirring. Gradually add the reserved cooking liquid and milk mixture, stirring constantly. Bring to the boil, lower the heat and simmer for 4 minutes, stirring occasionally.

Remove the pan from the heat and stir in the cream and lemon juice. Add salt and pepper to taste and spoon a little sauce over each fish portion. Serve at once.

> ### MRS BEETON'S TIP
> The stock used as the basis for this recipe should be pale in colour. Avoid adding the skin of the fish when making it, as this would darken it.

COEUR A LA CREME AU CITRON

SERVES 6

150 ml/¼ pint double cream
pinch of salt
150 g/5 oz low-fat curd cheese
50 g/2 oz caster sugar
grated rind and juice of 1 lemon
2 egg whites

Line a 400 ml/14 fl oz heart-shaped coeur a la crème mould with grease-proof paper. In a bowl whip the cream with the salt until it holds soft peaks. Break up the curd cheese with a fork, and whisk it gradually into the cream with the sugar. Do not let the mixture lose stiffness. Fold the lemon rind and juice into the cream as lightly as possible.

In a clean, grease-free bowl, whisk the egg whites until they hold stiff peaks. Fold them into the mixture, then very gently turn the mixture into the mould, filling all the corners. Stand the mould in a roasting tin to catch the liquid which seeps from the mixture. Chill for at least 2 hours or overnight. Turn out and serve with single cream.

COFFEE GATEAU

SERVES 8 TO 12

fat for greasing
20 ml/4 tsp instant coffee
150 g/5 oz butter
150 g/5 oz caster sugar
3 eggs, beaten
150 g/5 oz self-raising flour

COFFEE BUTTERCREAM
30 ml/2 tbsp instant coffee
150 g/5 oz butter
450 g/1 lb icing sugar

DECORATION
50–75 g/2–3 oz walnuts,
   chopped
10–12 walnut halves

Line and grease two 20 cm/8 inch sandwich cake tins. Set the oven at 160°C/325°F/gas 3. In a cup, mix the instant coffee with 20 ml/4 tsp boiling water. Set aside to cool.

In a mixing bowl, cream the butter with the sugar until light and fluffy. Beat in the cooled coffee. Add the eggs gradually, beating well after each addition. If the mixture shows signs of curdling, add a little of the flour.

Sift the flour and fold it into the creamed mixture, using a metal spoon. Divide between the tins and bake for 35–40 minutes or until well risen, firm and golden brown. Leave in the tins for 2–3 minutes, then cool on a wire rack.

Make the buttercream. In a cup, mix the instant coffee with 30 ml/ 2 tbsp boiling water and leave to cool. Cream the butter with half the icing sugar in a bowl. Beat in the coffee, then the rest of the icing sugar.

Using about a quarter of the buttercream, sandwich the cake layers together. Spread about half the remaining buttercream on the sides of the cake, then roll in the chopped walnuts. Spread most of the remaining buttercream on top of the cake and mark with a fork in a wavy design. Spoon any remaining buttercream into a piping bag fitted with a small star nozzle and pipe 10–12 rosettes on top of the cake. Decorate each rosette with a walnut half.

COLESLAW

SERVES 4

450 g/1 lb firm white or Savoy cabbage, finely shredded

100 g/4 oz carrots, coarsely grated

2 celery sticks, thinly sliced

½ small green pepper, seeded and thinly sliced

150 ml/¼ pint mayonnaise or plain yogurt

salt and pepper

lemon juice (see method)

Mix all the ingredients in a salad bowl, adding enough lemon juice to give the mayonnaise or yogurt a tangy taste. Chill before serving.

variation

FRUIT AND NUT SLAW Core and dice, but do not peel, 1 red-skinned eating apple. Toss in 15 ml/1 tbsp lemon juice, then add to the slaw with 25 g/1 oz seedless raisins or sultanas and 25 g/1 oz chopped walnuts, almonds or hazelnuts.

MRS BEETON'S TIP

Remember that full-flavoured, firm-textured salads like Coleslaw make excellent fillings for piping-hot baked potatoes. Not only does the flavour of the salad complement potatoes but the textures also marry well. Coleslaw looks good in a natural cabbage bowl. Use a sharp knife to cut out the centre of a Savoy cabbage, using the cut portion for the coleslaw. Rinse the cabbage bowl under cold water, shake off excess moisture and dry between the leaves with absorbent kitchen paper. Trim the base of the cabbage bowl to stand neatly.

COLEY PROVENCALE

SERVES 4 TO 5

fat for greasing

15 ml/1 tbsp oil

2 onions, chopped

1 green pepper, seeded and chopped

3 large tomatoes, peeled, seeded and chopped

2 garlic cloves, crushed

salt and pepper

575 g/1¼ lb coley fillet, skinned and cut into 2 cm/¾ inch cubes

8 green olives, stoned

8 black olives, stoned, to garnish

Grease a shallow ovenproof dish. Set the oven at 180°C/350°F/gas 4.

Heat the oil in a large frying pan, add the onions and pepper and fry gently for 5 minutes, stirring frequently. Add the tomatoes and garlic, lower the heat and simmer for 10 minutes, stirring occasionally. Remove from the heat and add salt and pepper to taste.

Put the fish cubes in the prepared dish. Add the green olives, then pour the tomato mixture over the top. Cover loosely with greased greaseproof paper or foil and bake for 30 minutes.

Garnish with the black olives and serve at once.

MRS BEETON'S TIP

The finest green olives generally come from Spain. They should be large and firm, with a good colour. Greek black olives are considered to be the best, but it is always worth buying loose olives rather than the canned or bottled variety, so that you can try before you buy.

CONFECTIONERS' CUSTARD

MAKES ABOUT 300 ML/½ PINT

300 ml/½ pint milk

1 vanilla pod or a few drops of vanilla essence

2 egg yolks

50 g/2 oz caster sugar

25 g/1 oz plain flour

Place the milk and vanilla pod, if used, in a small saucepan and bring to the boil over low heat. Remove from the heat and leave to one side, adding the vanilla essence, if used. Whisk the egg yolks with the sugar in a bowl until thick and creamy, then add the flour.

Remove the vanilla pod and very gradually add the milk to the egg mixture, beating constantly until all has been incorporated. Pour the mixture back into the pan and stir over low heat for 1–2 minutes to cook the flour. The custard should thickly coat the back of the wooden spoon and be smooth and shiny.

Pour the custard into a clean bowl, cover and leave to cool. Beat well, then cover again and chill until required.

variations

CHOCOLATE CUSTARD Stir 25 g/1 oz grated chocolate into the custard while still hot.

CRÈME FRANGIPANE Omit the vanilla flavouring. Add 40 g/1½ oz finely chopped butter to final cooking. When cold, fold in 75 g/3 oz crushed almond macaroons or 50 g/2 oz ground almonds and a few drops of almond essence.

COQ AU VIN — *Illustrated on page 132*

The best coq au vin is made by marinating the chicken overnight in the red wine before cooking.

SERVES 4 TO 6

1 (1.6 kg/3½ lb) chicken with giblets

1 bouquet garni

salt and pepper

75 g/3 oz unsalted butter

15 ml/1 tbsp oil

150 g/5 oz belly of pickled pork or green (unsmoked) bacon rashers, rind removed and chopped

150 g/5 oz button onions or shallots

30 ml/2 tbsp brandy

175 g/6 oz small button mushrooms

2 garlic cloves, crushed

575 ml/19 fl oz burgundy or other red wine

15 ml/1 tbsp tomato purée

25 g/1 oz plain flour

croûtes of fried bread, to serve

Joint the chicken and skin the portions if liked. Place the giblets in a saucepan with 450 ml/¾ pint water. Add the bouquet garni, salt and pepper. Cook gently for about 1 hour, then strain.

Measure the stock and set aside 275 ml/9 fl oz. Set the oven at 150°C/300°F/gas 2. Melt 40 g/1½ oz of the butter in the oil in a flame-proof casserole. Add the pork or bacon, with the onions. Cook over gentle heat for about 10 minutes until the onions are lightly coloured. Using a slotted spoon, transfer the bacon and onions to a plate.

Add the chicken portions to the fat remaining in the casserole and brown lightly all over. Ignite the brandy (see Mrs Beeton's Tip). When the flames die down, pour it into the casserole.

Add the reserved bacon and onions, with the mushrooms and garlic. Stir in the wine, giblet stock and tomato purée. Cover and cook in the oven for 1–1½ hours or until the chicken is cooked through and tender.

Using a slotted spoon, transfer the chicken portions to a heated serving dish. Arrange the bacon, mushrooms and onions over them. Cover with buttered greaseproof paper and keep hot. Return the casserole to the hob and simmer the liquid until reduced by about one-third.

Meanwhile make a beurre manié by blending the remaining butter with the flour in a small bowl. Gradually add small pieces of the mixture to the stock, whisking thoroughly after each addition. Continue to whisk the sauce until it thickens. Pour it over the chicken. Garnish with croûtes of fried bread and serve.

MRS BEETON'S TIP

To flame the brandy, either pour it into a metal soup ladle and warm over low heat or warm it in a jug in the microwave for 15 seconds on High. Ignite the brandy (if warmed in a soup ladle it may well ignite spontaneously) and, when the flames die down, pour it into the casserole.

COQUILLES ST JACQUES MORNAY

Great care must be taken not to overcook the scallops. Their delectable flavour and texture is easily spoiled by high heat.

SERVES 4

fat for greasing

450 g/1 lb potatoes, halved

salt and pepper

50 g/2 oz butter

90 ml/6 tbsp single cream

8–12 large scallops, shelled, with corals

1 small onion, sliced

1 bay leaf

45 ml/3 tbsp dry white wine

juice of ½ lemon

25 g/1 oz plain flour

125 ml/4 fl oz milk

75 ml/5 tbsp single cream

45 ml/3 tbsp dried white breadcrumbs

60 ml/4 tbsp grated Parmesan cheese

watercress sprigs to garnish

Cook the potatoes in a saucepan of salted boiling water for about 30 minutes or until tender. Drain thoroughly and mash with a potato masher, or beat with a hand-held electric whisk until smooth. Beat in 25 g/1 oz of the butter and 15 ml/1 tbsp of the cream to make a creamy piping consistency.

Grease 4 scallop shells or shallow individual ovenproof dishes. Spoon the creamed potato into a piping bag fitted with a large star nozzle and pipe a border of mashed potato around the edge of each shell. Set the oven at 200°C/400°F/gas 6.

Combine the scallops, onion, bay leaf, wine and lemon juice in a saucepan. Add 75 ml/5 tbsp water. Bring to simmering point and poach the scallops gently for 5 minutes. Using a slotted spoon, remove the scallops and cut into slices. Strain the cooking liquid into a jug.

Melt the remaining butter in a saucepan, add the flour and cook for 1 minute, stirring constantly. Gradually add the reserved cooking liquid, stirring all the time until the sauce starts to thicken. Season to taste and stir in the milk. Bring to the boil, stirring, then lower the heat and simmer for 2–3 minutes. Remove from the heat and stir in the cream.

Divide the sliced scallops between the prepared scallop shells or dishes. Coat with the sauce and sprinkle lightly with the breadcrumbs and Parmesan.

Stand the scallop shells or dishes on a large baking sheet and bake for 10 minutes until the breadcrumbs are crisp and the potatoes browned. Garnish with the watercress sprigs and serve at once.

CORNISH PASTIES — *Illustrated on page 165*

MAKES 8

FILLING

1 large or 2 small potatoes

1 small turnip

1 onion, chopped

salt and pepper

300 g/11 oz lean chuck steak,
   finely diced

PASTRY

500 g/18 oz plain flour

5 ml/1 tsp salt

150 g/5 oz lard

60 ml/4 tbsp shredded suet

flour for rolling out

beaten egg for glazing

Set the oven at 230°C/450°F/gas 8. To make the pastry, sift the flour and salt into a bowl. Rub in the lard, then mix in the suet. Moisten with enough cold water to make a stiff dough. Roll out on a lightly floured surface and cut into eight 16 cm/6½ inch rounds.

To make the filling, dice the potatoes and turnip, then mix with the onion and add salt and pepper to taste. Add the meat and 30 ml/2 tbsp water, and mix well. Divide between the pastry rounds, placing a line of mixture across the centre of each round.

Dampen the edges of each pastry round. Lift them to meet over the filling. Pinch together to seal, then flute the edges. Make small slits in both sides of each pasty near the top.

Place the pasties on a baking sheet and brush with egg. Bake for 10 minutes, then lower the oven temperature to 180°C/350°F/gas 4. Continue baking for a further 45 minutes, or until the meat is tender when pierced by a thin, heated skewer through the top of a pasty.

CORNISH SPLITS

MAKES 14

fat for greasing

400 g/14 oz strong white flour

50 g/2 oz sugar

125 ml/4 fl oz milk

15 g/½ oz fresh yeast or 10 ml/
   2 tsp dried yeast

5 ml/1 tsp salt

50 g/2 oz butter

flour for kneading

Grease a baking sheet. Sift about 75 g/3 oz of the flour and 5 ml/1 tsp of the sugar into a large bowl. Warm the milk and 125 ml/4 fl oz water until lukewarm. Blend in the fresh yeast or sprinkle on the dried yeast. Pour the yeast liquid into the flour and sugar, then beat well. Leave the bowl in a warm place for 20 minutes.

Sift the rest of the flour and sugar and the salt together in a bowl. Rub in the butter. Stir into the yeast mixture and mix to form a soft dough. Turn on to a lightly floured surface and knead for about 6 minutes or until the dough is smooth and no longer sticky. Return to the bowl and cover with cling film. Leave in a warm place until the dough has doubled in bulk – this will take up to 2 hours, or longer.

Knead the dough again until firm. Divide into 50 g/2 oz pieces and form each into a round bun. Place the buns on the prepared baking sheet. Place the sheet in a large, lightly oiled polythene bag. Leave in a warm place for about 30 minutes or until the buns have doubled in size. Set the oven at 220°C/425°F/gas 7.

Bake for 15–20 minutes, until golden brown. Serve cold, split the buns and spread with cream and jam.

COTTAGE PIE — *Illustrated on page 166*

SERVES 4 TO 6

50 g/2 oz butter

575 g/1¼ lb minced beef

1 onion, chopped

2 carrots, finely chopped

100 g/4 oz mushrooms, chopped

30 ml/2 tbsp plain flour

300 ml/½ pint beef stock

5 ml/1 tsp Worcestershire sauce

salt and pepper

900 g/2 lb potatoes, halved

30 ml/2 tbsp milk

pinch of grated nutmeg

Melt half the butter in a saucepan and fry the minced beef until browned, stirring to break up any lumps. Add the chopped onion, carrots and mushrooms and cook for 10 minutes or until softened slightly.

Stir in the flour, then pour in the beef stock and Worcestershire sauce, with salt and pepper to taste. Bring to the boil, stirring, then lower the heat, cover the pan and simmer for 30 minutes.

Cook the potatoes in a saucepan of salted boiling water for about 20 minutes or until tender. Drain thoroughly and mash with a potato masher. Beat in the remaining butter and the milk until creamy. Add salt, pepper and nutmeg to taste.

Set the oven at 200°C/400°F/gas 6. Spoon the meat mixture into an ovenproof dish. Cover with the potato and mark the top with a fork. Bake for about 25 minutes until the potato topping is browned.

COURGETTES IN TOMATO SAUCE

SERVES 4

30 ml/2 tbsp olive or sunflower oil

450 g/1 lb courgettes, trimmed and sliced

6 spring onions, chopped

1 garlic clove, crushed

225 g/8 oz tomatoes, peeled, halved and seeded

15 ml/1 tbsp tomato purée

1 bay leaf

15 ml/1 tbsp dried basil

30 ml/2 tbsp dry white wine

salt and pepper

Heat the oil in a saucepan, add the courgettes, spring onions and garlic and cook over gentle heat for 5 minutes. Stir in the tomatoes, tomato purée, bay leaf, basil and wine, with salt and pepper to taste. Bring to the boil, lower the heat, cover and simmer for 15 minutes. Remove the bay leaf and serve.

variation
Use 1 (227 g/8 oz) can of chopped tomatoes instead of fresh tomatoes, if preferred. Alternatively, use 250 ml/8 fl oz passata. If fresh basil is available, use it instead of the dried herb. Shred the leaves and add them for the final 5 minutes' cooking.

COURGETTES WITH ALMONDS

SERVES 4 TO 6

25 g/1 oz butter

25 g/1 oz blanched almonds,
   split in half

450 g/1 lb courgettes, trimmed
   and thinly sliced

salt and pepper

30 ml/2 tbsp snipped chives or
   chopped parsley

Melt the butter in a large frying pan. Add the almonds and fry over moderate heat, stirring, until lightly browned. Tip the courgettes into the pan and cook, gently stirring and turning the slices all the time, for 3–5 minutes. The cooked courgettes should be firm and full flavoured, not overcooked and watery.

Tip the courgettes into a heated serving dish, add salt and pepper to taste and sprinkle the chives or parsley over them. Serve at once.

COURT BOUILLON

MAKES 1.5 LITRES/2¾ PINTS

500 ml/17 fl oz dry white wine
   or dry cider

30 ml/2 tbsp white wine vinegar

2 large carrots, sliced

2 large onions, sliced

2–3 celery sticks, chopped

6 parsley stalks, crushed

1 bouquet garni

10 peppercorns, lightly crushed

salt and pepper

Put the wine in a large stainless steel or enamel saucepan. Add 1 litre/1¾ pints water, with the remaining ingredients. Bring to the boil, lower the heat and simmer for 30 minutes. Set aside to cool, then strain the court bouillon and use as required.

MRS BEETON's TIP
This is the traditional cooking liquid for poached fish. Court bouillon is discarded after use.

Couscous

SERVES 8

50 g/2 oz chick-peas, soaked
  overnight in plenty of cold
  water

45 ml/3 tbsp olive oil

8 chicken thighs, skinned if
  preferred

2 garlic cloves, crushed

1 large onion, chopped

1 green pepper, seeded and
  sliced

1 green chilli, seeded and
  chopped (optional)

15 ml/1 tbsp ground coriander

5 ml/1 tsp ground cumin

100 g/4 oz carrots, sliced

100 g/4 oz turnips, cut into
  chunks

450 g/1 lb pumpkin, peeled,
  seeds removed and cut into
  chunks

450 g/1 lb potatoes, cut into
  chunks

1 bay leaf

2 (397 g/14 oz) cans chopped
  tomatoes

50 g/2 oz raisins

150 ml/¼ pint chicken stock or
  water

salt and pepper

225 g/8 oz courgettes, sliced

45 ml/3 tbsp chopped parsley

350 g/12 oz couscous

50 g/2 oz butter, melted

Drain the chick-peas, then cook them in plenty of fresh boiling water for 10 minutes. Lower the heat, cover the pan and simmer for 1½ hours, or until the chick-peas are just tender. Drain.

Heat the oil in a very large flameproof casserole or saucepan. Add the chicken pieces and brown them all over, then use a slotted spoon to remove them from the pan and set aside. Add the garlic, onion, pepper and chilli, if used, to the oil remaining in the pan and cook for 5 minutes, stirring frequently.

Stir in the coriander and cumin, then add the carrots, turnips, pumpkin, potatoes, bay leaf, tomatoes, raisins, stock or water with salt and pepper to taste. Stir in the drained chick-peas. Bring to the boil, then lower the heat. Replace the chicken thighs, tucking them in among the vegetables. Cover and simmer gently for 1 hour. Stir in the courgettes and parsley, cover the pan and continue to cook gently for a further 30 minutes.

There are two options for preparing the couscous. The first is to line a steamer with scalded muslin, then sprinkle the couscous into it. Place the steamer over the simmering stew for the final 30 minutes' cooking, covering it tightly to keep all the steam in. Alternatively – and this is the easier method – place the couscous in a deep casserole or bowl and pour in fresh boiling water from the kettle to cover the grains by 2.5 cm/1 inch. Cover and set aside for 15 minutes. The grains will absorb the boiling water and swell. If the couscous cools on standing, it may be reheated over a saucepan of boiling water or in a microwave for about 2 minutes on High.

To serve, transfer the couscous to a very large serving dish and pour the hot melted butter over it. Fork up the grains and make a well in the middle. Ladle the chicken and vegetable stew into the well, spooning cooking juices over the couscous.

MRS BEETON'S TIP
Cubes of boneless lamb may be used instead of the chicken. Vary the vegetables according to what is freshly available – marrow or green beans may be added or substituted for other ingredients. Couscous is usually accompanied by a hot, spicy condiment known as harissa. This paste, made from chillies, cumin, coriander, garlic, mint and oil, is deep red in colour and fiery of flavour. It is added to individual portions to taste but should be treated with respect.

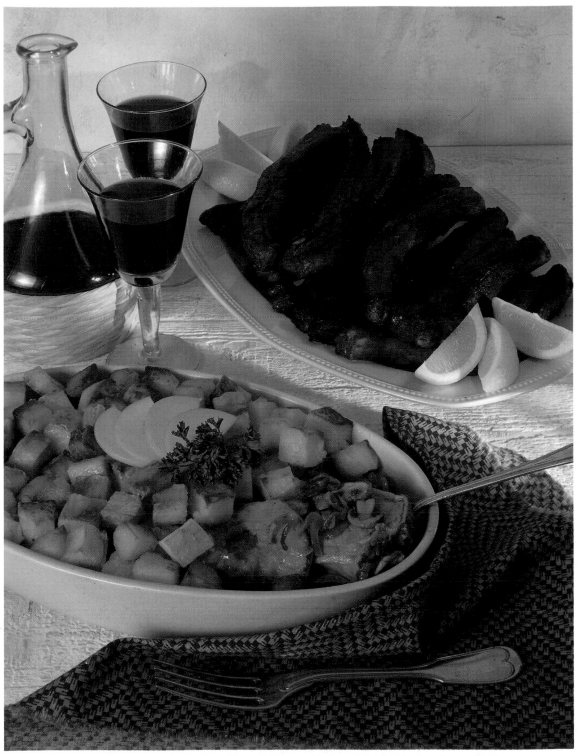

Barbecued Spare Ribs (page 215) *and Pork and Apple Hot Pot* (page 361)

Osso Buco (page 347) with Risotto Milanese (page 377)

Curried Eggs (page 275) *and Eggs Florentine* (page 284)

Gratin Dauphinois (page 300) **and Stuffed Cabbage Leaves** *(page 410)*

CRANBERRY SAUCE

MAKES ABOUT 300 ML/½ PINT

150 g/5 oz sugar
225 g/8 oz cranberries

Put the sugar in a heavy-bottomed saucepan. Add 125 ml/4 fl oz water. Stir over gentle heat until the sugar dissolves. Add the cranberries and cook gently for about 10 minutes until they have burst and are quite tender. Spoon into a bowl and leave to cool.

variation
CRANBERRY AND ORANGE SAUCE Use orange juice instead of water. Add 10 ml/2 tsp finely grated orange rind.

CREAM ECLAIRS

MAKES 10 TO 12

fat for greasing
250 ml/8 fl oz whipping cream
25 g/1 oz caster sugar and icing sugar, mixed
3–4 drops of vanilla essence

CHOUX PASTRY
100 g/4 oz plain flour
50 g/2 oz butter or margarine
pinch of salt
2 whole eggs plus 1 yolk

CHOCOLATE GLACÉ ICING
50 g/2 oz plain chocolate
10 ml/2 tsp butter
100 g/4 oz icing sugar, sifted

FREEZER TIP
Pack in sealed polythene bags. Thaw in wrappings for 1–1½ hours at room temperature, then place on baking sheets and crisp in an oven at 180°C/ 350°F/gas 4 for 5 minutes. Cool before filling.

Lightly grease a baking sheet. Set the oven at 220°C/425°F/gas 7.

To make the pastry, sift the flour on to a sheet of greaseproof paper. Put 250 ml/8 fl oz water in a saucepan and add the butter or margarine with the salt. Heat gently until the fat melts. When the fat has melted, bring the liquid rapidly to the boil and add all the flour at once. Immediately remove the pan from the heat and stir the flour into the liquid to make a smooth paste which leaves the sides of the pan clean. Set aside to cool slightly. Add the egg yolk and beat well. Add the whole eggs, one at a time, beating well after each addition. Continue beating until the paste is very glossy. Put the pastry into a piping bag fitted with a 2 cm/¾ inch nozzle and pipe it in 10 cm/4 inch lengths on the prepared baking sheet. Cut off each length with a knife or scissors dipped in hot water.

Bake for 10 minutes. Lower the oven temperature to 180°C/350°F/ gas 4. Bake for a further 20 minutes, or until risen and browned. Remove the éclairs from the oven and split them open. Cool completely on a wire rack.

Meanwhile, to make the glacé icing, break the chocolate into a heavy-bottomed pan. Add 15 ml/1 tbsp water and the butter. Warm gently, stirring until smooth and creamy. Stir in the icing sugar, a little at a time. Whip the cream until it holds its shape, adding the mixed sugars gradually. Add the vanilla essence while whipping.

Fill the éclairs with the cream and close neatly. Cover the tops with the glacé icing.

variation
CREAM BUNS Pipe the pastry in 5 cm/2 inch balls. Fill as above, and sift icing sugar over the tops instead of glacé icing.

CREAMED PASTA

SERVES 4

175 g/6 oz macaroni or
  tagliatelle

300 ml/½ pint milk

300 ml/½ pint chicken or
  vegetable stock

3 egg yolks

salt and pepper

60 ml/4 tbsp single cream

100 g/4 oz fresh Parmesan or
  Cheshire cheese, grated

25 g/1 oz butter

Place the pasta in a large saucepan with the milk and stock. Bring to the boil, stirring, reduce the heat so that the pasta simmers without boiling over and cover the pan. Simmer for 20 minutes, or until the pasta is tender. Stir occasionally to prevent the pasta from sticking.

Drain the pasta, reserving the cooking liquid, and place in a flameproof serving dish. Return the liquid to the pan. Beat the egg yolks, seasoning and cream, then pour this into the liquid in the pan. Heat gently without boiling. Stir in most of the cheese and pour over the pasta. Toss well, sprinkle with the remaining cheese and dot with butter. Brown under a hot grill and serve at once.

CREAM SLICES

MAKES 8

Puff Pastry (page 141), using
  100 g/4 oz flour

flour for rolling out

Glacé Icing, using 225 g/8 oz
  icing sugar

30 ml/2 tbsp smooth seedless
  jam

125 ml/4 fl oz sweetened
  whipped cream

Set the oven at 220°C/425°F/gas 7. Roll out the pastry 1 cm/½ inch thick on a lightly floured surface into a neat rectangle. Cut into 8 oblong pieces, each measuring 10 x 2 cm/4 x ¾ inch. Place on a baking sheet and spread the tops thinly with half of the icing.

Bake for 20 minutes or until the pastry is well risen and the icing is slightly browned. Leave to cool completely.

When cold, split each pastry in half crossways. Spread the top of each bottom half with jam, and the bottom of each top half with cream; then sandwich the halves together again. Spread a little icing on top of each slice, over the browned icing.

variation

VANILLA SLICES Make as for Cream Slices but without the baked icing. When the slices are cold, fill with Confectioner's Custard instead of cream. Ice the tops with Glacé Icing.

CREAMY MUSHROOM SAUCE

MAKES ABOUT 350 ML/12 FL OZ

50 g/2 oz butter

175 g/6 oz button mushrooms, sliced

25 g/1 oz plain flour

300 ml/½ pint milk

75 g/3 oz full fat soft cheese, cubed

salt and pepper

5–10 ml/1–2 tsp lemon juice (optional)

Melt 25 g/1 oz of the butter in a small saucepan. Add the mushrooms and fry over very gentle heat for 10 minutes until soft but not browned.

In a second saucepan, melt the remaining butter. Stir in the flour and cook for 1–2 minutes. Gradually add the milk, stirring constantly until the mixture boils and thickens. Remove the pan from the heat and beat in the cheese, a few cubes at a time. Fold in the mushrooms, with the pan juices, and add salt and pepper to taste. Stir in the lemon juice, if using, and reheat the sauce gently without boiling. Serve in a sauceboat.

CREME ANGLAISE

The classic egg custard sauce; and an essential ingredient of many desserts.

MAKES 300 ML/½ PINT

250 ml/8 fl oz milk

few drops of vanilla essence or a strip of lemon rind

3 egg yolks

50 g/2 oz caster sugar

Combine the milk and chosen flavouring in a saucepan. Warm gently but do not boil.

In a bowl, beat the egg yolks and sugar together until creamy. Remove the lemon rind, if used, from the saucepan and add the milk to the eggs. Strain the custard into a double saucepan or a heatproof bowl placed over a saucepan of simmering water. Cook, stirring constantly, until the custard thickens and coats the back of the spoon. Serve hot or cold.

variations

LIQUEUR SAUCE Stir 125 ml/4 fl oz lightly whipped double cream and 30 ml/2 tbsp orange-flavoured liqueur into the sauce.

CHOCOLATE CUSTARD SAUCE Use vanilla essence instead of lemon rind and add 100 g/4 oz coarsely grated plain chocolate to the milk. Warm until the chocolate melts, stir, then add to the egg yolks and proceed as in the main recipe.

CRÈME BRULÉE

An ideal dinner party dish. If serving cold, tap the caramel crust sharply with the back of a spoon to break it.

SERVES 4

250 ml/8 fl oz single cream or milk

250 ml/8 fl oz double cream

1 vanilla pod or a few drops of vanilla essence or 15 ml/1 tbsp brandy

6 egg yolks

about 75 g/3 oz caster sugar

Put the cream or milk and the double cream in a double saucepan or a bowl over a saucepan of hot water. Add the vanilla pod, if used, and warm very gently. Meanwhile mix the egg yolks with 25 g/1 oz of the caster sugar in a large bowl. Beat together thoroughly.

When the cream feels just warm to the finger, remove the pod, if used. Pour the cream on to the yolks, stir, and return to the double saucepan or bowl.

Continue to cook gently for about 40 minutes, stirring all the time with a wooden spoon, until the custard thickens to the consistency of single cream. Scrape down the sides of the pan or bowl frequently with a spatula to prevent lumps from forming. Do not let custard approach the boiling point. If a vanilla pod has not been used, add a few drops of vanilla essence or the brandy. Set the oven at 160°C/325°F/gas 3.

Strain the custard into a shallow 600 ml/1 pint flameproof dish, stand it on a baking sheet and bake for 5–10 minutes until a skin has formed on the top. Do not allow the custard to colour. Leave to cool, then refrigerate for at least 2–3 hours, or preferably overnight.

Heat the grill. Sprinkle enough of the remaining caster sugar over the surface of the custard to cover it entirely with an even, thin layer. Place the dish under the hot grill for 10–15 minutes or until the sugar melts and turns to caramel. Keep the top of the custard about 10 cm/4 inches from the heat. Serve hot or cold.

CROQUE MONSIEUR

These classic hot ham and cheese sandwiches may be grilled or baked, in which case the outside of the sandwiches should be spread with a little butter before cooking.

SERVES 4

8 slices of bread, crusts removed

butter

4 thin slices of lean cooked ham

4 slices of Gruyère cheese

Spread the bread with butter and make 4 ham and cheese sandwiches, pressing them together firmly. Heat a knob of butter in a large frying pan and fry the sandwiches for about 2 minutes on each side, until crisp and golden. Transfer to a platter and cut diagonally in half or into quarters.

variations
A little French mustard may be spread on the buttered bread when assembling the sandwiches. If a poached, baked or fried egg is served on top of the whole cooked sandwiches they become Croque Madame.

CUCUMBER IN YOGURT

SERVES 4 TO 6

1 large cucumber

salt and pepper

300 ml/½ pint plain or Greek
strained yogurt, chilled

15 ml/1 tsp vinegar (optional)

30 ml/2 tbsp chopped mint

pinch of sugar

Cut the cucumber into small dice and place it in a colander. Sprinkle with salt, leave for 3–4 hours, then rinse and drain thoroughly. Pat the cucumber dry on absorbent kitchen paper.

Stir the yogurt, vinegar (if used), mint and sugar together in a bowl. Add the cucumber and mix well. Taste and add salt and pepper if required. Serve within 1 hour of making, or the liquid in the cucumber may thin the yogurt and spoil the consistency of the salad.

variation

TZATZIKI The combination of cucumber and yogurt is an internationally popular one. This is a Greek-style variation. Grate the cucumber instead of dicing it. Omit the vinegar. The mint is optional but a crushed garlic clove and 15 ml/1 tbsp finely chopped onion are essential. Mix all the ingredients and serve with warm, fresh bread for a refreshing first course.

CUCUMBER SOUP

For extra piquancy, a little chopped sorrel may be added with the chervil.

SERVES 4

1 large cucumber
salt

15 g/½ oz butter

1.1 litres/2 pints well-flavoured
chicken stock

30 ml/2 tbsp chopped chervil

2 egg yolks

150 ml/¼ pint single cream

Peel the cucumber and cut it into quarters. Spoon out the seeds. Slice the cucumber thickly, put the slices in a colander and sprinkle with a little salt to draw out the excess liquid. Set aside for 20 minutes, then rinse the cucumber slices thoroughly and pat them dry with absorbent kitchen paper.

Melt the butter in a large saucepan. Add the cucumber slices and heat them through, turning frequently until well coated in butter. Stir in the stock and chervil. Simmer for 30 minutes or until the cucumber is tender.

In a small bowl, mix the egg yolks with the cream. Stir a little of the hot soup into the egg mixture, mix well, then add the contents of the bowl to the soup. Stir over low heat until heated but do not allow to boil. Serve at once.

variation

SMOOTH CUCUMBER SOUP For a smooth soup, purée the cooked cucumber with the stock before adding the yolks and cream.

CUMBERLAND SAUCE

MAKES ABOUT 250 ML/8 FL OZ

grated rind and juice of 1 orange
grated rind and juice of 1 lemon
75 ml/5 tbsp port
30 ml/2 tbsp red wine vinegar
100 g/4 oz redcurrant jelly
1.25 ml/¼ tsp prepared mustard
salt and cayenne pepper

Combine the orange and lemon rind in a small saucepan. Add 75 ml/ 5 tbsp water and heat to simmering point. Simmer gently for 10 minutes. Add the port, vinegar, redcurrant jelly and mustard, stirring until the jelly melts. Stir in the citrus juices and add salt and cayenne to taste. Simmer for 3–4 minutes, pour into a sauceboat and serve hot or cold with plain roast or grilled game.

CURRIED COD

SERVES 6

800 g/1¾ lb cod fillets, skinned
50 g/2 oz butter
1 large onion, sliced
15 ml/1 tbsp plain flour
10 ml/2 tsp curry powder
500 ml/17 fl oz fish stock
15 ml/1 tbsp lemon juice
salt and pepper
cayenne pepper

Rinse the fish and pat dry. Cut into pieces about 2.5 cm/1 inch square. Melt the butter in a saucepan and fry the cod lightly for 2–3 minutes. Using a slotted spoon, transfer the pieces to a warmed dish; keep hot.

Add the onion to the butter remaining in the pan and fry gently for 3–4 minutes until soft. Stir in the flour and curry powder and fry for 5 minutes. Stir constantly to prevent the onion from becoming too brown. Pour in the stock and bring to the boil, stirring constantly. Lower the heat and simmer for 15 minutes. Strain the sauce into a clean saucepan, adding lemon juice, salt and pepper and cayenne to taste. Carefully add the fish to the pan, stir gently and bring to simmering point.

Simmer for about 10 minutes, until the fish has absorbed the flavour of the sauce. Stir occasionally to prevent sticking. Serve at once, with boiled rice if liked.

variation
QUICK COD CURRY Use cold cooked fish, omitting the preliminary frying. Serve with Cucumber in Yogurt.

CURRIED EGGS — *Illustrated on page 267*

SERVES 4

60 ml/4 tbsp oil

2 onions, finely chopped

1 cooking apple

15–30 ml/1–2 tbsp mild curry
  powder

30 ml/2 tbsp plain flour

10 ml/2 tsp tomato purée

500 ml/17 fl oz vegetable stock

30 ml/2 tbsp mango chutney

15 ml/1 tbsp soft light brown sugar

30 ml/2 tbsp lemon juice

salt

6 eggs, hard boiled

30 ml/2 tbsp plain yogurt

Heat the oil in a saucepan, add the onions and sauté for 4–6 minutes until soft but not coloured. Peel, core and chop the apple. Add it to the onions, and continue cooking for 5 minutes.

Stir in the curry powder and flour and fry for 2–3 minutes, then add the tomato purée, vegetable stock, chutney, sugar, lemon juice and a pinch of salt. Bring to the boil, stirring constantly, then lower the heat, cover and simmer for 30 minutes, stirring occasionally.

Shell the hard-boiled eggs, cut them into quarters and add them to the curry sauce. Warm through over gentle heat. To serve, remove from the heat and gently stir in the yogurt, taking care not to break up the curried eggs.

MRS BEETON'S TIP
Cook some Basmati rice according to the instructions on page 106, adding a few frozen peas halfway through cooking. Serve the rice and peas with the eggs.

CUSTARD SAUCE

MAKES ABOUT 600 ML/1 PINT

30 ml/2 tbsp cornflour

500 ml/16 fl oz milk

2 egg yolks

30 ml/2 tbsp sugar

few drops of vanilla essence

Mix the cornflour with a little of the cold milk in a large bowl. Bring the rest of the milk to the boil in a saucepan, then stir into the blended mixture. Return the mixture to the clean pan.

Bring the cornflour mixture to the boil and boil for 3 minutes, stirring constantly to cook the cornflour. Remove from the heat.

When the mixture has cooled a little, stir in the egg yolks and sugar. Return to low heat and cook, stirring carefully, until the sauce thickens futher. Do not let it boil. Flavour with a few drops of vanilla essence and pour into a jug.

MICROWAVE TIP
Mix the cornflour with all the milk in a bowl. Cook on High for 4–6 minutes, whisking twice. Whisk well, then whisk in the yolks, sugar and vanilla. Cook for a further 30–45 seconds on High.

CUSTARDS For basic information on making custards, see pages 113–115. See also Baked Custard, Banana Custard, Caramel Custard Cups, Confectioners' Custard, Crème Anglaise, and Crème Brûlée.

CUSTARD SAUCE – CLASSIC

This sauce may be used as the basis for ice cream or for Vanilla Bavarois.

MAKES ABOUT 500 ML/17 FL OZ

500 ml/17 fl oz milk

few drops of vanilla essence or other flavouring

6 egg yolks

100 g/4 oz caster sugar

Put the milk in a saucepan with the vanilla or other flavouring. Warm gently but do not let the liquid boil. If a solid flavouring such as a strip of citrus rind is used, allow it to infuse in the milk for 5 minutes, then remove.

In a bowl, beat the egg yolks and sugar together until creamy. Add the warm milk to the egg mixture. Strain the mixture into a double saucepan or a heatproof bowl placed over a saucepan of simmering water. Cook, stirring constantly with a wooden spoon for 20–30 minutes, until the custard thickens and coats the back of the spoon. Take care not to let the custard curdle. Serve hot or cold.

variations

CLASSIC ORANGE CUSTARD Substitute orange rind for lemon rind.

CLASSIC LIQUEUR CUSTARD Add 15 ml/1 tbsp kirsch or curaçao at the end of the cooking time.

PRALINE CUSTARD Heat 100 g/4 oz sugar with 15 ml/1 tbsp water until dissolved, then boil until golden. Stir in 100 g/4 oz toasted blanched almonds and turn the mixture on to an oiled baking sheet to cool. Crush in a mortar with a pestle, or use a blender. Stir 50 g/2 oz of the crushed praline into the custard sauce just before serving.

CUSTARD TART

SERVES 4 TO 6

250 ml/8 floz milk

2 eggs

50 g/2 oz caster sugar

pinch of grated nutmeg

SHORT CRUST PASTRY

100 g/4 oz plain flour

1.25 ml/¼ tsp salt

50 g/2 oz margarine (or half butter, half lard)

flour for rolling out

Put an 18 cm/7 inch flan ring on a heavy baking sheet. Alternatively, line an 18 cm/7 inch sandwich cake tin with foil. Set the oven at 190°C/375°F/gas 5.

Make the pastry. Sift the flour and salt into a bowl, then rub in the margarine until the mixture resembles fine breadcrumbs. Add enough cold water to make a stiff dough. Press the dough together with your fingertips. Roll out on a lightly floured surface and use to line the flan ring or tin.

In a saucepan, bring the milk to just below boiling point. Put the eggs and caster sugar into a bowl, mix well, then stir in the scalded milk. Strain the mixture into the pastry case and sprinkle the top with grated nutmeg. Bake for 10 minutes.

Lower the oven temperature to 150°C/300°F/gas 2 and bake for 15–20 minutes more or until the custard is just set. Remove the tart from the ring or tin and serve hot or cold.

CUSTARD TARTLETS

MAKES 12

1 egg

15 ml/1 tbsp caster sugar

125 ml/4 fl oz milk

pinch of grated nutmeg

SWEET SHORT CRUST PASTRY

100 g/4 oz plain flour

1.25 ml/¼ tsp salt

50 g/2 oz margarine (or half
butter, half lard)

5 ml/1 tsp caster sugar

flour for rolling out

Set the oven at 180°C/350°F/gas 4. To make the pastry, sift the flour and salt into a bowl, then rub in the margarine until the mixture resembles fine breadcrumbs. Stir in the caster sugar. Add enough cold water to make a stiff dough. Press the dough together with your fingertips. Roll out and use to line twelve 7.5 cm/3 inch patty tins.

Beat the egg lightly in a bowl and add the sugar. Warm the milk in a saucepan, then pour it on to the egg. Strain the custard mixture into the pastry cases and sprinkle a little nutmeg on top of each.

Bake for about 30 minutes, until the custard is firm and set. Leave to cool before removing the tartlets from the tins.

variation

CUSTARD MERINGUE TARTLETS Make as above, but omit the nutmeg and bake for 15 minutes only. Lower the oven temperature to 140°C/275°F/gas 1. Whisk 2 egg whites in a clean, grease-free bowl until stiff. Fold in 75 g/3 oz caster sugar. Pile the meringue on to the tartlets. Bake for about 30 minutes.

DATE AND WALNUT CAKE

D

MAKES ONE 15 CM/6 INCH CAKE

fat for greasing

200 g/7 oz self-raising flour or
200 g/7 oz plain flour and
10 ml/2 tsp baking powder

pinch of grated nutmeg

75 g/3 oz margarine

75 g/3 oz dates, stoned and
chopped

25 g/1 oz walnuts, chopped

75 g/3 oz soft light brown sugar

2 small eggs

about 125 ml/4 fl oz milk

Line and grease a 15 cm/6 inch tin. Set the oven at 180°C/350°F/gas 4.

Mix the flour and nutmeg in a mixing bowl, and rub in the margarine until the mixture resembles fine breadcrumbs. Add the dates and walnuts with the sugar and baking powder, if used.

In a bowl, beat the eggs with the milk and stir into the dry ingredients. Mix well. Spoon the mixture into the cake tin and bake for 1¼–1½ hours or until cooked through and firm to the touch. Cool on a wire rack.

MICROWAVE TIP

Dried dates in a compact slab are often difficult to chop. Soften them by heating for 30–40 seconds on Defrost and the job will be made much easier.

DEVILLED CHICKEN

SERVES 4

4 chicken breasts

30 ml/2 tbsp oil

50 g/2 oz butter, softened

15 ml/1 tbsp tomato purée

2.5 ml/½ tsp mustard powder

few drops of Tabasco sauce

10 ml/2 tsp Worcestershire
  sauce

lemon or lime wedges to serve

Place the chicken breasts on a rack in a grill pan. Brush generously with oil and grill under moderate heat for 5 minutes on each side.

Meanwhile, prepare the devilled mixture. Beat the butter in a small bowl and gradually work in the tomato purée, mustard powder, Tabasco and Worcestershire sauce.

Spread half the mixture over the chicken and grill for 5 minutes more, then turn the breasts over carefully, spread with the remaining mixture and grill for a further 5 minutes or until the chicken is thoroughly cooked.

Transfer the chicken to plates or a serving dish and add lemon or lime wedges: the fruit juice may be squeezed over just before the chicken is eaten. Serve with baked jacket potatoes and a salad.

DEVILLED KIDNEYS

SERVES 4

8 lambs' kidneys

30 ml/2 tbsp oil

15 ml/1 tbsp chopped onion

2.5 ml/½ tsp salt

1.25 ml/¼ tsp cayenne pepper

5 ml/1 tsp Worcestershire sauce

10 ml/2 tsp lemon juice

2.5 ml/½ tsp prepared mustard

125 ml/4 fl oz beef stock

2 egg yolks

fresh white breadcrumbs

Skin, halve and core the kidneys, then chop them into small pieces. Heat the oil in a small saucepan, add the onion and cook gently for 4–6 minutes until softened but not browned.

Add the kidneys, salt, cayenne, Worcestershire sauce, lemon juice, mustard and stock. Bring to the boil, lower the heat and simmer for 15–20 minutes, until the kidneys are cooked. Cool slightly.

Beat the egg yolks lightly and stir them quickly into the kidney mixture. Sprinkle in enough of the breadcrumbs to give the mixture a soft consistency. Add more salt and pepper if required. The devilled kidneys are traditionally served on buttered wholemeal toast.

DEVIL'S FOOD CAKE

SERVES 8

fat for greasing

plain flour for dusting

100 g/4 oz butter

350 g/12 oz granulated sugar

5 ml/1 tsp vanilla essence

3 eggs, separated

250 g/9 oz plain flour

50 g/2 oz cocoa

7.5 ml/1½ tsp bicarbonate of soda

5 ml/1 tsp salt

FROSTING

100 g/4 oz soft light brown sugar

60 ml/4 tbsp golden syrup

1 egg white

pinch of cream of tartar

pinch of salt

5 ml/1 tsp vanilla essence

Grease and lightly flour three 20 cm/8 inch sandwich cake tins. Tap out excess flour. Set the oven at 180°C/350°F/gas 4.

In a mixing bowl, cream the butter with 225 g/8 oz of the sugar until light, then add the vanilla essence. Beat in the egg yolks, one at a time, alternately with 275 ml/9 fl oz cold water. Beat well after each addition. Beat in the flour, cocoa, soda and salt.

In a clean, grease-free bowl, whisk the egg whites to soft peaks, add the remaining sugar and continue whisking until stiff peaks form. Fold the egg whites into the chocolate mixture lightly but thoroughly. Gently pour one third of the mixture into each prepared tin. Bake for 30–35 minutes until each layer is firm in the centre and has shrunk from the sides of the tin. Cool lightly, then transfer to wire racks. Set aside until cold.

Meanwhile make the frosting. Combine all the ingredients except the vanilla essence in the top of a double saucepan. Set the pan over boiling water and cook, beating constantly with an electric whisk or rotary whisk until the mixture thickens and stands in peaks. Remove the pan from the heat and add the vanilla essence. Continue to beat until the mixture is thick and forms swirls. Use immediately to fill and cover the cake.

DIPS	See Aubergine Dip, Cucumber in Yogurt and Hummus.

DRIED FRUIT COMPOTE

SERVES 6

100 g/4 oz dried apricots

100 g/4 oz prunes

100 g/4 oz dried figs

50 g/2 oz dried apple rings

30 ml/2 tbsp liquid honey

2.5 cm/1 inch cinnamon stick

2 cloves

pared rind and juice of ½ lemon

50 g/2 oz raisins

50 g/2 oz flaked almonds,
   toasted

Combine the apricots, prunes and figs in a bowl. Add water to cover and leave to soak. Put the apples in a separate bowl with water to cover and leave both bowls to soak overnight.

Next day, place the honey in a saucepan with 600 ml/1 pint water. Add the cinnamon stick, cloves and lemon rind. Bring to the boil. Stir in the lemon juice. Drain both bowls of soaked fruit. Add the mixed fruit to the pan, cover and simmer for 10 minutes.

Stir in the drained apples and simmer for 10 minutes more, then add the raisins and simmer for 2–3 minutes. Discard the cinnamon, cloves and lemon rind.

Spoon the compote into a serving dish and sprinkle with the almonds. Serve warm or cold.

MICROWAVE TIP

There is no need to presoak the dried fruit. Make the honey syrup in a large bowl, using 450 ml/¾ pint water. Microwave on High for about 4 minutes, then stir in all the dried fruit with the cinnamon, cloves and lemon rind. Cover and cook on High for 15–20 minutes or until all the fruit is soft. Stir several times during cooking, each time pressing the fruit down into the syrup.

DUCHESSE POTATOES

SERVES 4

butter or margarine for greasing

450 g/1 lb old potatoes

salt and pepper

25 g/1 oz butter or margarine

1 egg or 2 egg yolks

grated nutmeg (optional)

beaten egg for brushing

Grease a baking sheet. Cut the potatoes into pieces and cook in a saucepan of salted water for 15–20 minutes. Drain thoroughly, then press the potatoes through a sieve into a large mixing bowl.

Set the oven at 200°C/400°F/gas 6. Beat the butter or margarine and egg or egg yolks into the potatoes. Add salt and pepper to taste and the nutmeg, if used. Spoon the mixture into a piping bag fitted with a large rose nozzle. Pipe rounds of potato on to the prepared baking sheet. Brush with a little beaten egg. Bake for about 15 minutes, until the potatoes are golden brown.

DUCK WITH RICH CHERRY DRESSING

Creamy mashed potatoes or plain cooked noodles and crisp, lightly cooked green beans are suitable accompaniments for this simple, yet rich dish.

SERVES 6

4 boneless duck breasts

salt and pepper

2.5 ml/½ tsp ground mace

4 bay leaves

4 fresh thyme sprigs

125 ml/4 fl oz red wine

60 ml/4 tbsp port

25 g/1 oz butter

15 ml/1 tbsp finely chopped onion

225 g/8 oz cherries, stoned

5 ml/1 tsp grated lemon rind

10 ml/2 tsp arrowroot

MRS BEETON'S TIP

For presentation purposes, cut each cooked duck fillet across into thick slices. Separate the slices slightly on individual plates before finishing with bay leaves, cherries and sauce.

Prick the skin on the duck breasts all over, or remove it, if preferred. Rub plenty of salt, pepper and mace into the breasts, then place them in a shallow dish, skin uppermost, with a bay leaf and thyme sprig under each. Pour the wine and port over the duck, cover and allow to marinate for at least 2 hours; the duck may be chilled overnight.

Melt the butter in a frying pan and add the onion with the herbs from the duck. Cook over low heat for 5 minutes. Meanwhile, drain the duck breasts, reserving the marinade. Place them skin down in the pan and increase the heat to moderate. Cook until the skin is well browned, then turn the breasts and cook the second side. Allow about 15 minutes on each side to cook the duck breasts.

Using a slotted spoon, transfer the cooked duck to a heated serving dish or individual plates. Keep hot. Leaving the herbs in the pan, add the cherries and lemon rind. Toss the cherries in the cooking juices for about a minute, until the heat causes them to begin to change colour.

Pour in the reserved marinade and heat gently until just boiling. While the sauce is heating, put the arrowroot in a cup and blend to a paste with 15–30 ml/1–2 tbsp cold water. Add it to the pan, stirring. Bring to the boil and remove the pan from the heat.

Discard the thyme sprigs but arrange the bay leaves on the duck. Use a slotted spoon to divide the cherries between the duck breasts, then pour the sauce over and serve at once.

variation

FILLETS OF DUCK BIGARADE Cut the pared rind from 1 Seville orange into fine strips and simmer these in water until tender; drain and set aside. Marinate the duck as above, adding the juice of the orange but omitting the port. Continue as above, stirring 30 ml/2 tbsp plain flour into the cooking juices from the duck, then add 250 ml/8 fl oz duck or chicken stock and 5 ml/1 tsp tomato purée. Bring to the boil, stirring, then add the reserved marinade. Lower the heat and simmer rapidly for 10 minutes. Stir in the juice of ½ lemon and 5 ml/1 tsp redcurrant jelly. Taste for seasoning and pour over the duck.

 DUCK For basic information on preparation, cooking methods and times, see pages 45–52. See also Roast Duck.

DUCK WITH ORANGE SAUCE

SERVES 4

1 (1.6–1.8 kg/3½–4 lb) oven-
   ready duck

salt and pepper

5 oranges

15 ml/1 tbsp caster sugar

15 ml/1 tbsp white wine vinegar

30 ml/2 tbsp brandy

15 ml/1 tbsp plain flour

Set the oven at 190°C/375°F/gas 5. Weigh the duck and calculate the cooking time at 20 minutes per 450 g/1 lb. Sprinkle the breast with salt. Put the duck on a wire rack in a roasting tin and prick the skin all over with a fork or skewer to release the fat. Roast for the required time, basting the duck occasionally with the pan juices and pouring away the excess fat as necessary.

Meanwhile, thinly peel the rind from one of the oranges, taking care not to include any of the bitter pith. Cut the rind into strips, then cook these in a saucepan of boiling water for 1 minute. Drain and set aside on absorbent kitchen paper. Slice one of the remaining oranges and set the slices aside for the garnish. Squeeze the rest of the oranges, including the one with the rind removed, and set the juice aside.

Put the sugar in a saucepan with the vinegar. Heat gently, stirring until the sugar has dissolved, then bring to the boil and boil rapidly without stirring until the syrup turns a golden caramel colour. Remove from the heat and carefully add the orange juice and brandy. Return to the heat and stir until just blended, then add the blanched orange rind strips.

When the duck is cooked, transfer it to a platter, remove the trussing string and cut it into serving portions. Transfer to a heated serving dish and keep hot. Pour off the fat from the roasting tin, sprinkle in the flour and cook, stirring, for 2 minutes. Blend in the orange mixture. Bring to the boil, then lower the heat and simmer, stirring, for 3–4 minutes. Add the salt and pepper to taste. Spoon the sauce over the duck, garnish with the reserved orange slices and serve.

DUMPLINGS

MAKES ABOUT 16

100 g/4 oz self-raising flour
50 g/2 oz shredded beef suet
salt and pepper

Mix the flour and suet in a bowl. Add salt and pepper to taste and bind with enough cold water to make a soft, smooth dough. With floured hands, divide the dough into 16 portions; roll into balls. Drop into simmering salted water, stock, soup or stew, lower the heat and simmer for 15–20 minutes. Serve with the liquid or with boiled meat, stew or vegetables.

variation

HERB DUMPLINGS Add 25 g/1 oz grated onion and 5 ml/1 tsp chopped fresh herbs to the flour and suet.

DUNDEE CAKE

MAKES ONE 18 CM/7 INCH CAKE

fat for greasing

200 g/7 oz plain flour

2.5 ml/½ tsp baking powder

1.25 ml/¼ tsp salt

150 g/5 oz butter

150 g/5 oz caster sugar

4 eggs, beaten

100 g/4 oz glacé cherries, quartered

150 g/5 oz currants

150 g/5 oz sultanas

100 g/4 oz seedless raisins

50 g/2 oz cut mixed peel

50 g/2 oz ground almonds

grated rind of 1 lemon

50 g/2 oz blanched split almonds

Line and grease an 18 cm/7 inch round cake tin. Set the oven at 180°C/350°F/gas 4. Sift the flour, baking powder and salt into a bowl.

In a mixing bowl, cream the butter and sugar together well, and beat in the eggs. Fold the flour mixture, cherries, currants, sultanas, raisins, mixed peel and ground almonds into the creamed mixture. Add the lemon rind and mix well.

Spoon into the prepared tin and make a slight hollow in the centre. Bake for 20 minutes, by which time the hollow should have filled in. Arrange the split almonds on top. Return the cake to the oven, bake for a further 40–50 minutes, then reduce the temperature to 160°C/325°F/gas 3 and bake for 1 hour more. Cool on a wire rack.

ECCLES CAKES

E

MAKES 12 TO 14

Rough Puff Pastry (page 142), using 200 g/7 oz flour

flour for rolling out

25 g/1 oz butter or margarine

15 ml/1 tbsp sugar

75 g/3 oz currants

25 g/1 oz chopped mixed peel

1.25 ml/¼ tsp ground mixed spice

1.25 ml/¼ tsp ground nutmeg

caster sugar for dusting

Set the oven at 200°C/425°F/gas 7. Roll out the pastry on a lightly floured surface to 3 mm/⅛ inch thick. Cut into rounds using a 10 cm/4 inch pastry cutter. Cream the butter or margarine and sugar in a bowl. Add the currants, peel and spices. Place spoonfuls of the mixture in the centre of each pastry round. Gather the edges of each round together to form a ball. With the smooth side uppermost, form into a flat cake. Make 2 cuts in the top of each cake with a sharp knife. Brush with water and dust with caster sugar. Put on a baking sheet and bake for 20 minutes or until golden brown.

EGGS FLORENTINE — *Illustrated on page 267*

SERVES 4

butter for greasing

1 kg/2¼ lb fresh spinach or
  2 (225 g/8 oz) packets
  frozen leaf spinach

15 ml/1 tbsp butter

salt and pepper

4 eggs

100 g/4 oz Fontina or Cheddar
  cheese, finely grated

Set the oven at 190°C/375°F/gas 5. Wash the fresh spinach several times and remove any coarse stalks. Put into a saucepan with just the water that clings to the leaves, then cover the pan with a tight-fitting lid. Place over moderate heat for about 3 minutes, shaking the pan often until the spinach has wilted. Lower the heat slightly and cook for 3–5 minutes more. (Cook frozen spinach according to the directions on the packet.)

When the spinach is tender, drain it thoroughly in a colander. Cut through the leaves several times with a knife to chop them roughly. Melt the butter in the clean pan, add the spinach with salt and pepper to taste, and heat through gently.

Spoon into a greased ovenproof dish and, using the back of a spoon, make 4 small hollows in the surface. Break an egg into each hollow, add salt and pepper to taste, then sprinkle the grated cheese over the eggs. Bake for 12–15 minutes until the eggs are lightly set. Serve at once.

EGGS MORNAY

SERVES 4

1 kg/2¼ lb potatoes, halved

salt and pepper

8 eggs

300 ml/½ pint Béchamel Sauce

75 g/3 oz Cheddar cheese,
  grated

2.5 ml/½ tsp French mustard

30 ml/2 tbsp butter

45 ml/3 tbsp milk

Cook the potatoes in a saucepan of salted boiling water for 20 minutes until tender.

Meanwhile bring a small saucepan of water to the boil, carefully add the eggs and cook them for 5 minutes. Plunge them into cold water, leave for 5 minutes, then remove their shells carefully under the water. Leave the shelled eggs under the water. Reheat the Béchamel sauce gently with most of the cheese and stir in the mustard.

Drain the cooked potatoes thoroughly and mash with a potato masher, or beat with a hand-held electric whisk until smooth. Beat in the butter and milk to make a creamy piping consistency. Spoon the creamed potato into a piping bag fitted with a star nozzle and pipe a border of mashed potato around the edge of a large shallow dish which can be used under the grill.

Using a slotted spoon, drain the shelled eggs well and arrange in the dish. Coat with the hot sauce. Sprinkle the remaining cheese over and grill until brown.

EGGS For basic information on buying, storing, using and cooking eggs, see pages 111–113. See also Breadcrumb Omelette, Curried Eggs, Omelette, Omelette Arnold Bennett, Scotch Eggs, Scotch Eggs with Bacon, Spanish Omelette and Sweet Soufflé Omelettes. Consult the index for soufflé recipes.

EGGY BREAD AND CHEESE

SERVES 4

8 thin slices of white bread,
   crusts removed

butter

175 g/6 oz Cheshire or Cheddar
   cheese, thinly sliced

3 eggs, beaten

salt

oil for shallow frying

Spread the bread thinly with butter. Top four of the slices with cheese, leaving a narrow border all around. Add the remaining slices of bread to make four sandwiches, then press the edges of each sandwich lightly with a rolling pin to seal in the filling.

Put the eggs with a little salt in a shallow dish large enough to hold all the sandwiches in a single layer. Add the sandwiches and soak for 20 minutes, turning them over carefully halfway through.

Heat the oil in a large frying pan, add the sandwiches and fry for 2–3 minutes on each side until crisp and golden. Drain on absorbent kitchen paper before serving.

ESPAGNOLE SAUCE

MAKES 300–450 ML/½–¾ PINT

50 g/2 oz butter

50 g/2 oz lean raw ham or
   bacon, chopped

1 small onion, sliced

1 small carrot, sliced

50 g/2 oz mushrooms, sliced

50 g/2 oz plain flour

600 ml/1 pint rich strong stock

1 bouquet garni

6 black peppercorns

1 bay leaf

150 ml/¼ pint puréed canned
   tomatoes or 15 ml/1 tbsp
   tomato purée

60 ml/4 tbsp sherry (optional)

Melt the butter in a saucepan and fry the ham or bacon for 2–3 minutes. Add the vegetables and fry very gently for 8–10 minutes, until golden brown.

Stir in the flour until smooth. Cook over gentle heat, stirring frequently until the flour is a rich brown colour. Gradually add the stock, stirring constantly until the mixture boils and thickens. Add the bouquet garni, peppercorns and bay leaf. Half cover the pan, lower the heat and simmer the sauce for 30 minutes. Stir in the tomatoes or tomato purée and simmer for 30 minutes more.

Rub through a fine nylon sieve into a clean saucepan and stir in the sherry, if using. Reheat before serving.

EVERYDAY CHOCOLATE PUDDING

SERVES 6

fat for greasing
200 g/7 oz plain flour
5 ml/1 tsp baking powder
pinch of salt
25 g/1 oz cocoa
100 g/4 oz butter or margarine
100 g/4 oz caster sugar
2 eggs
1.25 ml/¼ tsp vanilla essence
milk (see method)

Grease a 1 litre/1¾ pint pudding basin. Prepare a steamer or half fill a large saucepan with water and bring to the boil.

Sift the flour, baking powder, salt and cocoa into a mixing bowl. Rub in the butter or margarine and stir in the sugar.

In a second bowl, beat the eggs with the vanilla essence. Add to the dry ingredients with enough milk to give a soft dropping consistency.

Spoon the mixture into the prepared basin, cover with greased greaseproof paper and foil and secure with string.

Put the pudding in the perforated part of the steamer, or stand it on an old saucer or plate in the pan of boiling water. The water should come halfway up the sides of the basin. Cover the pan tightly and steam the pudding over gently simmering water for 1¾–2 hours.

Leave for 5–10 minutes at room temperature to firm up, then turn out on to a serving plate. Serve with Custard Sauce, Chocolate Sauce or single cream.

EVE'S PUDDING

SERVES 4

fat for greasing
450 g/1 lb cooking apples
grated rind and juice of 1 lemon
75 g/3 oz demerara sugar
75 g/3 oz butter or margarine
75 g/3 oz caster sugar
1 egg, beaten
100 g/4 oz self-raising flour

Grease a 1 litre/1¾ pint pie dish. Set the oven at 180°C/350°F/gas 4. Peel and core the apples and slice them thinly into a large bowl. Add the lemon rind and juice, with the demerara sugar. Stir in 15 ml/1 tbsp water, then tip the mixture into the prepared pie dish.

In a mixing bowl, cream the butter or margarine with the caster sugar until light and fluffy. Beat in the egg. Fold in the flour lightly and spread the mixture over the apples.

Bake for 40–45 minutes until the apples are soft and the sponge is firm. Serve with melted apple jelly and single cream or Greek yogurt.

variations
Instead of apples, use 450 g/1 lb apricots, peaches, gooseberries, rhubarb, raspberries or plums.

FAGGOTS

SERVES 4 TO 6

fat for greasing

800 g/1¾ lb pig's liver

2 onions, quartered

2.5 ml/½ tsp dried thyme

10 ml/2 tsp dried sage

generous pinch of grated
   nutmeg

2.5 ml/½ tsp ground mace

salt and pepper

1 egg, lightly beaten

100 g/4 oz fresh white
   breadcrumbs

caul fat, pork dripping, lard or
   butter

Remove the skin and any tubes from the liver and slice it thinly. Put it in a saucepan with the onions. Add just enough water to cover. Bring to the boil, lower the heat, cover and simmer for 30 minutes. Drain. Mince the liver and onions finely or process in a food processor. Add the herbs, spices, seasoning, egg and enough breadcrumbs to make a firm mixture.

Divide the mixture into 8 equal portions and shape into balls. Wrap in caul fat, if used. Lay the faggots side by side in a greased baking tin and dot with fat if caul is not used.

Cover the tin loosely with foil. Bake for 25 minutes, then remove the foil and bake for a further 10–15 minutes to brown the tops of the faggots. Serve hot, with a thickened gravy.

MRS BEETON'S TIP

Caul fat is a tough membrane laced with fat. Salted caul is seldom available; however should it be obtained, it must be soaked in cold water for 30 minutes, then thoroughly rinsed and soaked in fresh water with a little vinegar added. Finally, it should be rinsed and spread out on a perfectly clean tea-towel ready for use.

FISH CAKES

SERVES 4

350 g/12 oz cooked white fish

450 g/1 lb potatoes

25 g/1 oz butter

30 ml/2 tbsp milk

15 ml/1 tbsp finely chopped
   parsley

salt and pepper

50 g/2 oz plain flour

oil for shallow frying

Remove any bones from the fish and flake it finely. Cook the potatoes in a saucepan of salted boiling water for about 30 minutes or until tender. Drain well and mash with a potato masher, or beat with a hand-held electric whisk until smooth. Beat in the butter and milk. Add the flaked fish and parsley, with salt and pepper to taste. Set aside until cold.

Form the fish mixture into 8 portions, shaping each to a flat round cake. Spread out the flour in a shallow bowl, add salt and pepper and use to coat the fish cakes. Heat the oil in a frying pan, add the fish cakes and fry for 6–8 minutes, turning once. Drain on absorbent kitchen paper, arrange on a warmed serving dish and serve.

 FISH For basic information on varieties, preparation and cooking methods, see pages 13–43. See also recipes listed in index, under entries for Fish, Shellfish and individual types of fish and shellfish.

FISHERMAN'S HOT POT

SERVES 4

2 slices of white bread

25 g/1 oz butter

45 ml/3 tbsp oil

50 g/2 oz piece of white cabbage, shredded

2 leeks, trimmed, sliced and washed

1 large onion, chopped

225 g/8 oz white fish fillet, skinned and cut into 2.5 cm/ 1 inch cubes

150 ml/¼ pint Muscadet or other dry white wine

45 ml/3 tbsp tomato purée

1 chicken stock cube

1 bouquet garni

1 garlic clove, crushed

salt and pepper

chopped parsley to garnish

Remove the crusts from the bread, cut it into cubes and spread on a baking sheet. Dry out in a 150°C/300°F/gas 2 oven for 10–15 minutes, then set aside.

Melt the butter in the oil in a large saucepan. Add the vegetables, cover and cook gently for 7–8 minutes until soft. Do not allow the leeks and onions to colour. Add the fish cubes and fry for 3 minutes, turning occasionally, until firm on all sides.

Pour in the wine and add 1 litre/1¾ pints water. Stir in the tomato purée and crumble in the stock cube. Add the bouquet garni, crushed garlic and salt and pepper to taste.

Heat the stew to simmering point and cook for 20 minutes. Discard the bouquet garni. Pour into a serving dish and sprinkle with the chopped parsley. Serve with the toasted bread cubes.

FISH PIE WITH POTATO TOPPING

SERVES 4 TO 5

fat for greasing

450 g/1 lb potatoes, halved

salt and pepper

90 g/3 oz butter

30–45 ml/2–3 tbsp single cream

25 g/1 oz plain flour

300 ml/½ pint milk

450 g/1 lb cooked cod, skinned,
  boned and flaked

50 g/2 oz Cheddar cheese,
  grated

few grains of cayenne pepper

1 egg, beaten

pinch of grated nutmeg

Grease a 1 litre/1¾ pint pie dish. Cook the potatoes in a saucepan of salted boiling water for about 20 minutes or until tender. Drain and mash until smooth. Beat in 25 g/1 oz of the butter and the cream. Set aside until cold.

Set the oven at 190°C/375°F/gas 5. Melt 25 g/1 oz of the remaining butter in a saucepan. Stir in the flour and cook over low heat for 2–3 minutes, without allowing the mixture to colour. Gradually add the milk, stirring constantly until the sauce boils and thickens. Add salt and pepper to taste. Stir in the flaked cod, half the cheese and 15 g/½ oz of the remaining butter. Add the cayenne. Remove from the heat.

Set aside about 10 ml/2 tsp of the beaten egg for glazing. Stir the remaining egg into the cold mashed potato. Melt the remaining butter and stir it into the potato with the nutmeg. Line the prepared dish with half the potato mixture.

Heat the fish mixture until it bubbles. Pour it into the lined pie dish and cover evenly with the rest of the potato. Press the edge with the tines of a fork. Glaze with the reserved egg and sprinkle with the remaining cheese. Bake for 8–12 minutes until well browned.

FISH STOCK

Use fish bones and trimmings without gills, which cause bitterness.

MAKES ABOUT 1 LITRE/1¾ PINTS

5 ml/1 tsp salt

1 small onion, sliced

2 celery sticks, sliced

4 white peppercorns

1 bouquet garni

Break up any bones and wash the fish trimmings, if used. Put the bones, trimmings or heads in a saucepan and cover with 1 litre/1¾ pints cold water. Add the salt. Bring the liquid to the boil and add the vegetables, peppercorns and bouquet garni. Lower the heat, cover and simmer gently for 30–40 minutes. Do not cook the stock for longer than 40 minutes or it may develop a bitter taste. Strain, cool quickly and use as required.

variation
WHITE WINE FISH STOCK Add 100 ml/3½ fl oz dry white wine, 4–5 mushroom stalks and 1 sliced carrot. Simmer for 30 minutes only.

FLAPJACKS

MAKES ABOUT 20

fat for greasing

50 g/2 oz margarine

50 g/2 oz soft light brown sugar

30 ml/2 tbsp golden syrup

100 g/4 oz rolled oats

Grease a 28 × 18 cm/11 × 7 inch baking tin. Set the oven at 160°C/325°F/gas 3. Melt the margarine in a large saucepan. Add the sugar and syrup, and warm gently. Do not boil. Remove from the heat and stir in the oats. Press into the prepared tin, then bake for 25 minutes or until firm. Cut into fingers while still warm and leave in the tin to cool

variations

SULTANA FLAPJACKS Add 50 g/2 oz sultanas to the basic mixture, stirring them in with the oats.

SESAME FLAPJACKS Sesame seeds contribute their own, distinctive flavour to this traditional recipe. Press the flapjack mixture into the tin, then sprinkle a layer of sesame seeds over the top and press them down well with the back of a spoon. Do not use roasted sesame seeds.

HONEY FLAPJACKS Follow the main recipe, but use clear honey instead of golden syrup.

FLORENTINES

MAKES 20 TO 24

oil for greasing

25 g/1 oz glacé cherries, chopped

100 g/4 oz cut mixed peel, finely chopped

50 g/2 oz flaked almonds

100 g/4 oz chopped almonds

25 g/1 oz sultanas

100 g/4 oz butter or margarine

100 g/4 oz caster sugar

30 ml/2 tbsp double cream

100 g/4 oz plain or couverture chocolate

Line three or four baking sheets with oiled greaseproof paper. Set the oven at 180°C/350°F/gas 4. In a bowl, mix the cherries and mixed peel with the flaked and chopped almonds and the sultanas.

Melt the butter or margarine in a small saucepan, add the sugar and boil for 1 minute. Remove from the heat and stir in the fruit and nuts. Whip the cream in a separate bowl, then fold it in.

Place small spoonfuls of the mixture on to the prepared baking sheets, leaving room for spreading. Bake for 8–10 minutes. After the biscuits have been cooking for about 5 minutes, neaten the edges by drawing them together with a plain biscuit cutter. Leave the cooked biscuits on the baking sheets to firm up slightly before transferring to a wire rack to cool completely.

To finish, melt the chocolate in a bowl over hot water and use to coat the flat underside of each biscuit. Mark into wavy lines with a fork as the chocolate cools.

FORCEMEAT

MAKES ABOUT 350 G/12 OZ

100 g/4 oz gammon or rindless
   bacon, finely chopped

50 g/2 oz shredded beef suet

grated rind of 1 lemon

5 ml/1 tsp chopped parsley

5 ml/1 tsp chopped mixed herbs

salt and cayenne pepper

pinch of ground mace

150 g/5 oz fresh white
   breadcrumbs

2 eggs, lightly beaten

Combine the gammon or bacon, suet, lemon rind and herbs in a bowl. Add salt, cayenne and mace to taste, mix well with a fork, then stir in the breadcrumbs. Gradually add enough beaten egg to bind.

variation

FORCEMEAT BALLS Roll the mixture into 6–8 small balls. Either cook the forcemeat balls around a roast joint or bird, or fry them in a little oil until browned and cooked through.

FRENCH BEAN AND TOMATO SALAD

SERVES 4

salt and pepper

225 g/8 oz French beans,
   trimmed

3 tomatoes, peeled, seeded and
   quartered

15 ml/1 tsp snipped chives

DRESSING

45 ml/3 tbsp walnut or
   sunflower oil

10 ml/2 tsp white wine vinegar

5 ml/1 tsp lemon juice

pinch of caster sugar

pinch of mustard powder

1 garlic clove, crushed

Make the dressing by mixing all the ingredients in a screw-topped jar. Add salt and pepper to taste, close the jar tightly and shake vigorously until well blended.

Bring a small saucepan of salted water to the boil. Add the beans and cook for 5–10 minutes or until just tender. Drain, rinse briefly under cold water, drain again, then tip into a bowl. Immediately add the dressing and toss the beans in it. Leave to cool.

Add the tomatoes to the salad and toss lightly. Taste and add more salt and pepper if required. Turn into a salad bowl, sprinkle with the chives and serve.

MICROWAVE TIP

Wash the beans. Drain lightly, leaving some moisture on the pods. Place them in a roasting bag, tie the top loosely with an elastic band and microwave on High for 5 minutes. Shake the bag carefully, set it aside for 1 minute, then transfer the contents to a bowl and add the dressing and remaining ingredients.

FRENCH DRESSING

MAKES ABOUT 125 ML/4 FL OZ

salt and pepper

pinch of mustard powder

pinch of caster sugar

30 ml/2 tbsp wine vinegar

90 ml/6 tbsp olive oil or a
mixture of sunflower and
olive oil

Mix the salt and pepper, mustard and sugar in a small bowl. Add the vinegar and whisk until the sugar has dissolved. Whisk in the oil and check the dressing for salt and pepper before using.

variations
Almost every cook has his or her favourite way of preparing French dressing. Garlic, whole or crushed, is a favourite addition, while others swear that a few drops of soy sauce sharpen the flavour. Lemon juice frequently replaces all or part of the vinegar. The recipe above may be doubled or trebled, if liked, but the proportions should always remain the same.

> **MRS BEETON'S TIP**
>
> The ingredients for French Dressing may be mixed in a screw-topped jar and shaken but the result is not as good as when the sugar is dissolved in the vinegar before the oil is mixed in.

FRENCH ONION SOUP

SERVES 4

75 g/3 oz butter, plus extra for
toast

6 onions, about 575 g/1¼ lb,
thinly sliced

1 litre/1¾ pints consommé

30 ml/2 tbsp dry white wine

salt and pepper

6 slices of French bread

50 g/2 oz Gruyère cheese,
grated

Melt the butter in a large heavy-bottomed saucepan. Add the onions and cook slowly, turning occasionally, for at least 30 minutes, or until golden brown. Stir in the consommé and white wine. Bring to the boil, lower the heat and cover the pan, then simmer for about 1 hour, or until the onions are quite soft. Add salt and pepper to taste.

Toast the French bread, spread it with butter and top with grated cheese. Pour the soup into individual bowls, float a slice of toast on each, and brown the cheese under a preheated hot grill or in a very hot oven.

> **MRS BEETON'S TIP**
>
> Sprinkle 2.5 ml/½ tsp sugar over the onions while browning them in the butter. This will encourage the browning process. The wine may be omitted from the soup, and a little brandy added just before floating the toast on top.

FUDGE

MAKES ABOUT 450 G/1 LB

oil for greasing
400 g/14 oz sugar
125 ml/4 fl oz milk
50 g/2 oz butter
2.5 ml/½ tsp vanilla essence

Grease an 18 cm/7 inch square baking tin. Combine all the ingredients except the vanilla essence in a large saucepan. Heat gently until the sugar has dissolved, then bring to the boil.

Boil, stirring constantly, until the mixture registers 115°C/235° F on a sugar thermometer, the soft ball stage. When a small drop of the fudge is cooled in cold water, then rolled between the fingers it should form a soft ball if it has boiled sufficiently. Remove the pan from the heat and stir in the vanilla essence. Cool for 2 minutes, then beat the mixture until it becomes thick and creamy.

Pour into the prepared tin. When nearly set, score the surface of the fudge deeply with a knife, marking it into squares. When set, cut into squares as marked and store in an airtight tin lined with waxed paper.

MRS BEETON'S TIP

Fudge crystallizes if the sugar is not dissolved properly and if crystals are allowed to form on the sides of the saucepan. To prevent this either grease the pan lightly with a little butter or cover the saucepan with a lid as soon as the mixture comes to the boil. The steam will wash down the sides of the pan. Remove the lid after 2–3 minutes and boil without stirring until the soft ball stage is reached. The crystals may also be brushed down from the sides of the pan into the mixture, using a clean brush dipped in cold water.

GAME STOCK

G

MAKES ABOUT 1.5 LITRES/2½ PINTS

carcass of 1 game bird, with giblets
cleaned feet of bird (optional)
5 ml/1 tsp salt
1 onion, sliced
1 celery stick, sliced
4 white peppercorns
1 bouquet garni

Break or chop the carcass into manageable pieces. Put these, with the giblets and feet, if using, in a large saucepan. Add about 1.75 litres/3 pints water to cover the bones, then stir in the salt. Bring to the boil, skim the surface, then add the remaining ingredients. Simmer over very gentle heat for 3–4 hours. Cool quickly, then strain. Skim off surface fat. Season and use as required.

GAME For basic information on seasonal availability, preparation and cooking methods, see pages 52–64. See also Pheasant with Mushroom Stuffing, Pigeon Pie, Pigeons in Red Wine, Rabbit Casserole, Rabbit Pie and Venison Steaks with Red Wine Marinade.

GARAM MASALA

There are many versions of garam masala. The spice mix may be used in a wide variety of dishes, either added towards the end of the cooking time or combined with other spices in a paste. It may be sprinkled over the food during the final stages before serving.

MAKES ABOUT 75 G/3 OZ

60 ml/4 tbsp coriander seeds

30 ml/2 tbsp cumin seeds

15 ml/1 tbsp black peppercorns

10 ml/2 tsp cardamom seeds

3 cinnamon sticks

5 ml/1 tsp whole cloves

30 ml/2 tsp grated nutmeg

To make your own garam masala, toast the coriander seeds in a small ungreased frying pan, stirring all the time for a few minutes until they give off their aroma. Tip the seeds into a bowl and repeat the process with the cumin seeds, black peppercorns, cardamom seeds, cinnamon sticks and whole cloves, toasting each spice separately. When all the spices have been toasted and cooled, grind them to a powder in a coffee grinder (reserved for the purpose) or in a mortar with a pestle. Stir in the freshly grated nutmeg. Store in an airtight jar.

GARLIC BUTTER

MAKES 50–75 G/2–3 OZ

1 garlic clove, crushed

50–75 g/2–3 oz butter, softened

Put the crushed garlic in a bowl and add enough butter to give the desired flavour. Use at once or press into small pots, tapping the pots while filling to knock out all the air. Cover with foil and refrigerate until required. Use within 2 days.

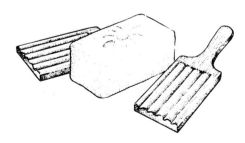

GAZPACHO

SERVES 4

2 thick slices of bread, cubed

1 litre/1¾ pints tomato juice

1 small onion, finely chopped

½ cucumber, finely chopped

1 green pepper, seeded and chopped

6 tomatoes, peeled and chopped

2 garlic cloves, crushed

75 ml/3 fl oz olive oil

30 ml/2 tbsp red wine vinegar

1.25 ml/¼ tsp dried oregano

1.25 ml/¼ tsp dried mixed herbs

salt and pepper

croûtons; diced cucumber; diced onion and black olives to serve

Put the bread cubes in a large bowl with the tomato juice. Leave to soak for 5 minutes, then add the chopped onion, cucumber, green pepper and tomatoes, with the crushed garlic. Stir in the olive oil, cover and leave to stand for 1 hour.

Purée the soup in a blender or food processor, then rub through a sieve into a clean bowl. Stir in the vinegar and herbs, with salt and pepper to taste. Cover the bowl closely and chill for 2–3 hours. Place the croûtons, diced cucumber, diced onion and black olives in separate bowls. Serve with the gazpacho.

MRS BEETON'S TIP

If you do not have a blender, strain the mixture, reserving the tomato juice, then pound the vegetables and bread to a paste in a mortar with a pestle; rub through a sieve into a clean bowl. Return the tomato juice to the bowl and add the vinegar, herbs and seasoning. Chill as suggested above.

GENOESE SPONGE

For an 18 cm/7 inch square or 25 × 15 cm/10 × 6 inch oblong cake, use 75 g/3 oz flour, pinch of salt, 50 g/ 2 oz clarified butter or margarine, 3 eggs and 75 g/3 oz caster sugar.

MAKES ONE 30 × 20 CM/12 × 8 INCH CAKE

fat for greasing

100 g/4 oz plain flour

2.5 ml/½ tsp salt

75 g/3 oz clarified butter or margarine

4 eggs

100 g/4 oz caster sugar

Line and grease a 30 × 20 cm/12 × 8 inch Swiss roll tin. Set the oven at 180°C/350°F/gas 4. Sift the flour and salt into a bowl and put in a warm place. Melt the clarified butter or margarine without letting it get hot.

Whisk the eggs lightly in a mixing bowl. Add the sugar and place the bowl over a saucepan of hot water. Whisk for 10–15 minutes until thick. Take care that the base of the bowl does not touch the water. Remove from the heat and continue whisking until at blood-heat. The melted butter should be at the same temperature.

Sift half the flour over the eggs, then pour in half the melted butter or margarine in a thin stream. Fold in gently. Repeat, using the remaining flour and fat. Spoon gently into the prepared tin and bake for 30–40 minutes. Cool on a wire rack.

GINGERBREAD

MAKES ONE 15 CM/6 INCH SQUARE CAKE

fat for greasing

200 g/7 oz plain flour

1.25 ml/¼ tsp salt

10–15 ml/2–3 tsp ground ginger

2.5 ml/½ tsp bicarbonate soda

75 g/3 oz lard

50 g/2 oz soft light brown sugar

50 g/2 oz golden syrup

50 g/2 oz black treacle

1 egg

milk (see method)

Line and grease a 15 cm/6 inch square tin. Set the oven at 160°C/325°F/gas 3.

Sift the flour, salt, ginger and bicarbonate of soda into a mixing bowl. Warm the lard, sugar, syrup and treacle in a saucepan until the fat has melted. Do not let the mixture become hot.

In a measuring jug, beat the egg lightly and add enough milk to make up to 125 ml/4 fl oz. Add the melted mixture to the dry ingredients with the beaten egg and milk mixture. Stir thoroughly; the mixture should run easily off the spoon.

Pour into the prepared tin and bake for 1¼–1½ hours until firm to the touch. Cool the gingerbread on a wire rack.

GINGER SNAPS

MAKES ABOUT 56

fat for greasing

200 g/7 oz self-raising flour

pinch of salt

5 ml/1 tsp ground ginger

100 g/4 oz soft light brown
   sugar

75 g/3 oz margarine

100 g/4 oz golden syrup

1 egg, beaten

Thoroughly grease several baking sheets. Set the oven at 160°C/325°F/gas 3. Sift together the flour, salt and ginger. Stir in the sugar.

Melt the margarine with the syrup in a large heavy-bottomed saucepan. When the fat has melted, add the dry ingredients and beaten egg alternately and beat until smooth and thick.

Using 2 teaspoons, place rounds of the mixture on to the prepared baking sheets, allowing plenty of room for spreading. Bake for 15 minutes. Leave to stand for a few minutes, then cool on a wire rack.

MRS BEETON'S TIP

If the biscuit mixture has to stand before baking perhaps because a shortage of baking sheets makes it necessary to batch-bake it will thicken. When this happens, simply shape the biscuit mixture into small balls and bake as above.

GLACE ICING

Glacé icing is mainly used as a covering for small cakes, sponge cakes or other light cakes. It is quick and easy to make and therefore ideal for simple, informal cakes. It gives a smooth, slightly crisp coating that complements piped buttercream edges.

SUFFICIENT TO COVER THE TOP OF ONE 18 CM/7 INCH CAKE

100 g/4 oz icing sugar, sifted
food colouring, optional

Place the icing sugar in a bowl. Using a wooden spoon gradually stir in sufficient water (about 15 ml/1 tbsp) to create icing whose consistency will thickly coat the back of the spoon. Take care not to add too much liquid or the icing will be too runny. At first the icing will seem quite stiff, but it will slacken rapidly as the icing sugar absorbs the water. Stir in 1–2 drops of food colouring, if required.

variations

LEMON OR ORANGE GLACE ICING Use 15 ml/1 tbsp strained lemon or orange juice instead of the water.

CHOCOLATE GLACE ICING Combine 50 g/2 oz plain chocolate, a knob of butter and 15 ml/1 tbsp water in a heatproof bowl. Set over hot water until the chocolate and butter melt. Stir the mixture, gradually adding 100 g/4 oz icing sugar. Stir in a little more water if required. This icing sets particularly quickly; use at once.

COFFEE GLACE ICING Dissolve 5 ml/1 tsp instant coffee in 15 ml/1 tbsp warm water and add instead of the water in the main recipe.

GLAZED CARROTS

SERVES 6

50 g/2 oz butter

575 g/1¼ lb young carrots, scraped but left whole

3 sugar cubes, crushed

1.25 ml/¼ tsp salt

beef stock (see method)

15 ml/1 tbsp chopped parsley to garnish

Melt the butter in a saucepan. Add the carrots, sugar and salt. Pour in enough stock to half cover the carrots. Cook over gentle heat, without covering the pan, for 15–20 minutes or until the carrots are tender. Shake the pan occasionally to prevent sticking.

Using a slotted spoon, transfer the carrots to a bowl and keep hot. Boil the stock rapidly in the pan until it is reduced to a rich glaze. Return the carrots to the pan, two or three at a time, turning them in the glaze until thoroughly coated. Place on a heated serving dish, garnish with parsley and serve at once.

GLAZED ONIONS

Glazed onions make a tasty accompaniment to grilled steak, baked ham or bacon chops. They are often used as a garnish.

SERVES 4

400 g/14 oz button onions

chicken stock (see method)

salt and pepper

15 ml/1 tbsp soft light brown
   sugar

25 g/1 oz butter

pinch of grated nutmeg

Skin the onions and put them in a single layer in a large saucepan. Add just enough stock to cover. Bring to the simmering point and cook for 15–20 minutes until the onions are just tender, adding a small amount of extra stock if necessary. By the time the onions are cooked, the stock should have reduced almost to a glaze.

Remove from the heat and stir in the remaining ingredients. Turn the onions over with a spoon so that the added ingredients mix well and the onions are coated in the mixture. Return the pan to the heat until the onions become golden and glazed. Serve at once, with the remaining syrupy glaze.

variation

CITRUS GLAZED ONIONS Melt 25 g/1 oz butter in a frying pan. Add 400 g/14 oz button onions. Sprinkle with 15 ml/1 tbsp soft light brown sugar. Add salt and pepper to taste and fry, turning the onions occasionally until golden brown. Stir in 150 ml/¼ pint orange juice and 10 ml/2 tsp lemon juice. Cover and simmer for 15 minutes.

GOOSEBERRY FOOL

When elderflowers are available, try adding 2 heads, well washed and tied in muslin, to the gooseberries while poaching. Discard the muslin bags when the gooseberries are cooked.

SERVES 6

575 g/1¼ lb gooseberries,
   topped and tailed

150 g/5 oz caster sugar

300 ml/½ pint whipping cream

Put the gooseberries in a heavy-bottomed saucepan. Stir in the sugar. Cover the pan and cook the gooseberries over gentle heat for 10–15 minutes until the skins are just beginning to split. Leave to cool.

Purée the fruit in a blender or food processor, or rub through a sieve into a clean bowl. In a separate bowl, whip the cream until it holds its shape. Fold the cream gently into the gooseberry Purée. Spoon into a serving dish or six individual glasses. Chill before serving.

variations

If a fruit is suitable for puréeing, it will make a creamy fool. Try rhubarb, apricots, red- or blackcurrants, raspberries or blackberries. Sieve the purée if necessary.

GOOSE For basic information on preparation, cooking methods and times, see pages 45–52. See also Roast Goose with Apples and Onions.

GOUJONS OF PLAICE

SERVES 6

12 (100 g/4 oz) plaice fillets

50 g/2 oz plain flour

salt and pepper

100 ml/3½ floz milk

oil for deep frying

Tartare Sauce to serve

GARNISH
lemon wedges

parsley sprigs

Cut the fish fillets lengthways into short strips about 4 cm/1½ inches wide. Mix the flour with salt and pepper and spread out in a shallow bowl. Pour the milk into a second bowl. Coat the strips of plaice first in milk and then in seasoned flour, shaking off any excess.

Put the oil for frying into a deep wide pan. Heat the oil to 180–190°C/350–375°F or until a cube of bread added to the oil browns in 30 seconds. If you are using a deep-fat fryer, follow the manufacturer's instructions.

Carefully add the strips of fish, a few at a time, to the hot oil. Fry for 2–3 minutes until golden brown. Drain on absorbent kitchen paper and keep hot on a warmed dish. Reheat the oil before putting in each fresh batch of goujons. Garnish and serve with tartare sauce.

GOULASH

SERVES 6

675 g/1½ lb chuck or blade
    steak, trimmed

50 g/2 oz dripping or lard

2 onions, sliced

30 ml/2 tbsp plain flour

125 ml/4 fl oz beef stock

125 ml/4 fl oz red wine

450 g/1 lb tomatoes, peeled and
    diced or 1 (397 g/14 oz) can
    chopped tomatoes

2.5 ml/½ tsp salt

15 ml/1 tbsp paprika

1 bouquet garni

450 g/1 lb potatoes

150 ml/¼ pint soured cream

Cut the steak into 2 cm/¾ inch cubes. Heat the dripping in a flameproof casserole and fry the meat until browned on all sides. Using a slotted spoon, remove the meat and set aside. Add the onions to the fat remaining in the casserole and fry gently until just beginning to brown.

Add the flour and cook, stirring until browned. Gradually add the stock and wine, with the tomatoes, salt, paprika and bouquet garni. Bring to the boil, stirring, then lower the heat and simmer for 1–2 hours or until the meat is tender. Alternatively, transfer the goulash to a casserole and bake at 160°C/325°F/gas 3 for 1–2 hours.

Thirty minutes before the end of the cooking time, peel the potatoes, cut them into cubes and add them to the goulash. When cooked they should be tender but not broken. Just before serving, remove the bouquet garni and stir in the soured cream.

GRAPEFRUIT COCKTAIL

SERVES 4

2 grapefruit

caster or soft brown sugar
   (optional)

30 ml/2 tbsp medium-dry sherry

mint leaves to decorate

Cut the grapefruit across in half; remove visible pips. Using a serrated stainless steel knife (preferably a grapefruit knife) cut around each half between the flesh and the pith, to loosen the flesh. Cut between the membranes which divide the segments, but leave the flesh in the halved skins as if uncut. Sprinkle with sugar, if required, and with sherry. Decorate with mint leaves.

GRATIN DAUPHINOIS — *Illustrated on page 268*

SERVES 6

25 g/1 oz butter

1 kg/2¼ lb potatoes, thinly sliced

1 large onion, about 200 g/7 oz,
   thinly sliced

200 g/7 oz Gruyère cheese, grated

salt and pepper

grated nutmeg

125 ml/4 fl oz single cream

Butter a 1.5 litre/2¾ pint casserole, reserving the remaining butter. Set the oven at 190°C/375°F/gas 5. Bring a saucepan of water to the boil, add the potatoes and onion, then blanch for 30 seconds. Drain.

Put a layer of potatoes in the bottom of the prepared casserole. Dot with a little of the butter, then sprinkle with some of the onion and cheese, a little salt, pepper and grated nutmeg. Pour over some of the cream. Repeat the layers until all the ingredients have been used, finishing with a layer of cheese. Pour the remaining cream on top.

Cover and bake for 1 hour. Remove from the oven and place under a hot grill for 5 minutes, until the cheese is golden brown and bubbling.

GRAVY

SERVES 4 TO 6

giblets, carcass bones or
   trimmings from meat, poultry
   or game

1 bay leaf

1 thyme sprig

1 clove

6 black peppercorns

¼ onion, sliced

pan juices from roasting (see
   Gravy notes on page 305)

25 g/1 oz plain flour (optional)

salt and pepper

Place the giblets, bones, carcass and/or trimmings (for example wing ends) in a saucepan. Pour in water to cover, then add the bay leaf, thyme, clove, peppercorns and onion. Bring to the boil and skim off any scum, then lower the heat, cover the pan and simmer for about 1 hour.

Strain the stock and measure it. You need 600–750 ml/1–1¼ pints to make gravy for up to six servings. If necessary, pour the stock back into the saucepan and boil until reduced. Pour off most of the fat from the roasting tin, leaving a thin layer and all the cooking juices.

Place the tin over moderate heat; add the flour if the gravy is to be thickened. Cook the flour, stirring all the time and scraping all the sediment off the tin, for about 3 minutes, until it is browned. If the gravy is not thickened, pour in about 300 ml/½ pint of the stock and boil, stirring and scraping, until the sediment on the base of the tin is incorporated.

Slowly pour in the stock (or the remaining stock, if making thin gravy), stirring. Boil for 2–3 minutes and check seasoning.

Leek Tart (page 318) *and* **Quiche Lorraine** *(page 369)*

Baked Apples (page 211)

Mixed Fruit Loaf (page 335) *and Cherry Cake* (page 242)

Summer Pudding (page 413)

Gravy notes

• The quality of the sediment on the base of the cooking tin determines the quality of the gravy. If the meat was well seasoned and roasted until well browned outside, the sediment should have a good colour and flavour. Any herbs (other than large stalks), onions or flavouring roasted under the meat should be left in the pan until the gravy is boiled, then strained out before serving.

• If making gravy for a meal other than a roast, for example to accompany sausages or toad-in-the-hole, use a little fat instead of the pan juices and brown the flour well over low to moderate heat. Meat dripping gives the best flavour but butter or other fat may be used.

• To make onion gravy, slowly brown 2 thinly sliced onions in the fat before adding the flour – this is excellent with grilled sausages or toad-in-the-hole.

• Gravy browning may be added if necessary; however, it can make the sauce look artificial and unpleasant. Pale gravy is perfectly acceptable, provided it has good flavour.

• Always taste gravy when cooked. It should be well seasoned. If it lacks flavour, or is rather dull, a dash of Worcestershire sauce, mushroom ketchup or about 5–15 ml/1–3 tsp tomato purée may be whisked in.

• Gravy may be enriched by adding up to half wine instead of stock.

• Add 60 ml/4 tbsp port or sherry, and 15 ml/1 tbsp redcurrant jelly to make a rich gravy.

• Add 2 chopped pickled walnuts and 15 ml/1 tbsp walnut oil to the pan juices to make a delicious walnut gravy.

• Use vegetable stock to make vegetable gravy. Cook a finely diced carrot and 2 thinly sliced onions in butter or margarine instead of using meat juices. Add 1.25 ml/¼ tsp ground mace and 30 ml/2 tbsp chopped parsley. Stir well.

• Add 100 g/4 oz thinly sliced mushrooms to the pan juices to make a mushroom gravy. The sauce may be further enriched by adding a little mushroom ketchup.

GREEN TOMATO CHUTNEY

MAKES ABOUT 3 KG/6½ LB

450 g/1 lb cooking apples

450 g/1 lb onions, chopped

2 kg/4½ lb green tomatoes, roughly chopped

450 g/1 lb sultanas

15 g/½ oz salt

1.25 ml/¼ tsp cayenne pepper

15 ml/1 tbsp mustard seeds

1 cm/½ inch fresh root ginger, bruised

750 ml/1¼ pints malt vinegar

450 g/1 lb demerara sugar

Peel, core and chop the apples. Put them in a large saucepan or preserving pan with the onions, tomatoes and sultanas. Stir in the salt and cayenne. Tie the mustard seeds and root ginger in a muslin bag and add to the pan with just enough of the vinegar to cover. Bring to simmering point and simmer for 20 minutes.

Meanwhile combine the remaining vinegar and the sugar in a second pan, stirring constantly over gentle heat until the sugar has dissolved. Add the vinegar mixture to the large saucepan or preserving pan and boil steadily until the chutney reaches the desired consistency. Remove the spice bag.

Pour the chutney into warm clean jars and cover with vinegar-proof lids. When cool, wipe the jars, label and store in a cool dry place.

HADDOCK FLORENTINE

SERVES 4

50 g/2 oz butter

1 kg/2¼ lb fresh spinach

salt and pepper

100 ml/3½ fl oz fish stock

100 ml/3½ floz dry white wine

1 kg/2¼ lb haddock fillets, skinned

1.25 ml/¼ tsp grated nutmeg

50 g/2 oz Parmesan cheese, grated

MORNAY SAUCE

1 small onion

1 small carrot

1 small celery stick

600 ml/1 pint milk

1 bay leaf

few parsley stalks

1 fresh thyme sprig

1 clove

6 white peppercorns

1 blade of mace

50 g/2 oz butter

50 g/2 oz plain flour

1 egg yolk

25 g/1 oz Gruyère cheese, grated

25 g/1 oz Parmesan cheese, grated

60 ml/4 tbsp single cream

pinch of grated nutmeg

Start by making the sauce. Combine the onion, carrot, celery and milk in a saucepan. Add the herbs and spices, with salt to taste. Heat to simmering point, cover, turn off the heat and allow to stand for 30 minutes to infuse. Strain into a measuring jug.

Melt the butter in a saucepan. Stir in the flour and cook over low heat for 2–3 minutes, stirring occasionally, without allowing the mixture to colour. Gradually add the flavoured milk, stirring constantly.

Continue to cook over moderate heat, stirring until the mixture boils and thickens to a thick coating consistency. When the mixture boils, lower the heat and simmer gently for 1–2 minutes, stirring occasionally to prevent the formation of a skin. Cool slightly.

Beat the egg yolk in a small bowl. Add a little of the sauce and mix well. Add the contents of the bowl to the sauce and heat gently, stirring. Do not allow the sauce to boil. Stir in the cheeses until melted. Add the cream and nutmeg. Cover the surface of the sauce closely with damp greaseproof paper and set aside.

Using 25 g/1 oz of the butter, grease a shallow ovenproof serving dish. Tear the spinach leaves from the stalks; place in a large saucepan with the remaining butter. Add salt and pepper to taste. Cover with a tight-fitting lid and cook gently for about 15 minutes, shaking the pan occasionally.

Meanwhile, combine the stock and white wine in a large saucepan. Bring to simmering point, add the fish and poach for 7–10 minutes. Drain the spinach thoroughly in a colander, pressing out all free liquid with the back of a wooden spoon. Put the spinach on the base of the prepared dish. Remove the fish fillets with a slotted spoon and arrange them on top of the spinach. Keep hot.

Boil the fish stock until reduced by half. Reheat the sauce, stirring frequently. Add reduced fish stock, season with salt, pepper and nutmeg and pour the sauce over the fish. Sprinkle with the grated Parmesan and brown under a hot grill. Serve at once.

HADDOCK IN CIDER

SERVES 4

fat for greasing

575 g/1¼ lb haddock fillet, skinned and cubed

225 g/8 oz tomatoes, peeled and sliced

150 g/5 oz mushrooms, sliced

125 ml/4 fl oz dry cider

salt and pepper

30 ml/2 tbsp chopped parsley

25 g/1 oz Cheddar cheese, grated

30 ml/2 tbsp fresh white breadcrumbs

Grease a large ovenproof baking dish. Set the oven at 230°C/450°F/gas 8. Spread out the fish cubes in an even layer on the base of the dish and top with the tomatoes and mushrooms. Pour the cider over the fish and sprinkle with salt and pepper.

Mix the parsley, cheese and breadcrumbs together in a small bowl. Scatter over the fish and bake for 20–25 minutes. Serve at once.

MRS BEETON'S TIP

If commercially soured cream is not available, stir 5 ml/1 tsp lemon juice into 125 ml/4 fl oz single cream. Set aside for 10–15 minutes before use.

HAM – BOILED

1 leg of ham

250 ml/8 fl oz cider or white wine (optional)

1 large onion, roughly chopped

3–4 celery sticks, roughly chopped

1 large turnip, roughly chopped

1 large carrot, roughly chopped

1 bouquet garni

GARNISH

browned breadcrumbs

demerara sugar

cloves

small bunches of watercress

Weigh the ham. Depending on how salty the ham is, it may be necessary to soak it in cold water for up to 12 hours. Soaking is not usually necessary with modern curing, however, since less salt is used. Check with your butcher.

Drain the ham if necessary. Place it in a large saucepan, cover with fresh water and bring to the boil. Skim off any scum that rises to the surface, lower the heat and simmer for 20 minutes per 450 g/1 lb, or until the bone at the knuckle end sticks out about 2.5 cm/1 inch and starts to feel loose.

Pour off the water from the pan and add the cider or wine, if used. Add fresh tepid water to cover, together with the prepared vegetables and bouquet garni. Bring the liquid to simmering point, half cover the pan and simmer gently for 10 minutes per 450 g/1 lb. When the ham is cooked, lift it out of the pan. Remove the rind and score the fat into a diamond pattern, using a sharp knife and making the cuts about 5 mm/¼ inch deep.

Cover the fat with equal quantities of browned breadcrumbs and demerara sugar. Press a clove into the centre of each diamond pattern. Place small bunches of watercress at either end of the ham and cover the knuckle with a pie frill. Serve hot or cold.

HAMBURGERS

If you intend serving the burgers less than well cooked, buy good-quality steak and mince it at home. Bought minced steak should be cooked through before serving.

SERVES 4

450 g/1 lb minced steak

2.5 ml/½ tsp salt

2.5 ml/½ tsp freshly ground
   black pepper

5–10 ml/1–2 tsp grated onion
   (optional)

Combine the meat, salt and pepper in a bowl. Add the onion, if used, and mix well. Shape the mixture lightly into four flat round cakes, about 2 cm/¾ inch thick.

Heat a frying pan or griddle until very hot, add the hamburgers and cook for 2 minutes on each side for rare meat; 4 minutes per side for well done meat. Alternatively, cook under a preheated grill or over coals on a barbecue grill for 6–8 minutes, turning once. Serve plain or in buns, with toppings or fillings as desired.

variations

Offer any or all of the following: lettuce leaves; sliced cucumber; sliced tomatoes; sliced gherkins; sliced raw or fried onions; hamburger relish; German or French mustard; tomato ketchup; mayonnaise; soured cream.
LAMB BURGERS Use good quality minced lamb instead of steak. Add 2.5 ml/½ tsp dried oregano to the mixture.
CHEESE BURGERS Top each hamburger with a slice of processed cheese during the final minute of grilling.
PITTA BURGERS Make 8 burgers instead of 4 and serve them in warm pitta bread pockets, with shredded lettuce, chopped cucumber and chopped tomatoes. Add a dollop of Greek yogurt, if liked.

HERB BUTTER

Herb butter may be prepared using one or more herbs. When mixing herbs, balance strong and mild types. Although dried herbs may be used, fresh ones give a superior flavour. Parsley and dill work well.

MAKES 100 G/4 OZ

100 g/4 oz butter, softened

45 ml/3 tbsp chopped parsley

5 ml/1 tsp chopped fresh thyme
   or 2.5 ml/½ tsp dried thyme

salt and pepper

Beat the butter until creamy in a small bowl. Add the herbs, beating until well combined. Add salt to taste and a small pinch of pepper. Use at once or press into small pots, tapping the pots while filling to knock out the air. Cover with foil and refrigerate until required. Use within 2 days.

MRS BEETON'S TIP
Whole hams vary considerably in size and in the relation of meat to bone. It is therefore difficult to give exact servings. As a general guide, a 4.5 kg/10 lb ham should feed 30 people.

HERB STUFFING

SUFFICIENT FOR 1 (1.5–2 KG/3¼–4½ LB)
CHICKEN, A BONED JOINT OF VEAL OR
8 (75 G/3 OZ) FISH FILLETS

50 g/2 oz butter or margarine

100 g/4 oz soft white or
　Granary breadcrumbs

pinch of grated nutmeg

15 ml/1 tbsp chopped parsley

5 ml/1 tsp chopped fresh mixed
　herbs

grated rind of lemon

salt and pepper

1 egg, beaten

Melt the butter or margarine in a small saucepan and stir in the bread-crumbs, nutmeg, herbs and lemon rind. Add salt and pepper to taste. Stir in enough of the beaten egg to bind the mixture.

> ## MRS BEETON'S TIP
>
> Keeping a stock of stuffing in the freezer means that chicken, fish fillets and boned joints can be prepared swiftly for the oven. Use double the quantity in the recipe to stuff the neck end of a 5–6 kg/ 11–13 lb turkey.
>
> A bird, joint of meat or fish should always be stuffed just before being cooked. If preferred, the stuffing may be shaped into 12 or 16 small balls and baked in a preheated 180°C/350°F/gas 4 oven for 15–20 minutes.

HERRINGS WITH APPLE STUFFING

SERVES 4

butter for greasing

4 large herrings

STUFFING

50 g/2 oz butter

225 g/8 oz onions, finely
　chopped

225 g/8 oz cooking apples

15 ml/1 tbsp cider or white wine
　vinegar

salt and pepper

Grease a flat ovenproof dish and a piece of foil large enough to cover it. Set the oven at 190°C/375°F/gas 5. Scale the herrings, cut off the heads and remove the bones without breaking the skin.

Make the stuffing. Melt the butter in a large frying pan, add the onions and fry gently for about 10 minutes until soft. Peel, core and grate the apples and add them to the pan. Mix well, then add the vinegar, with salt and pepper to taste.

Divide the stuffing between the herrings, filling the cavities and then reshaping the fish. Lay them on the prepared dish, cover loosely with the foil and bake for 25 minutes. Serve at once.

> ## MICROWAVE TIP
>
> Arrange the stuffed herrings in alternate directions in a suitable dish. Cover with microwave film and cook on High for 7–8 minutes.

HOLLANDAISE SAUCE

Serve this classic sauce with poached salmon or other firm fish.

MAKES ABOUT 125 ML/4 FL OZ

45 ml/3 tbsp white wine vinegar

6 peppercorns

1 bay leaf

1 blade of mace

3 egg yolks

100 g/4 oz butter, softened

salt and pepper

Combine the vinegar, peppercorns, bay leaf and mace in a small saucepan. Boil rapidly until the liquid is reduced to 15 ml/1 tbsp. Strain into a heatproof bowl and leave to cool.

Add the egg yolks and a nut of butter to the vinegar and place over a pan of gently simmering water. Heat the mixture gently, beating constantly until thick. Do not allow it to approach boiling point. Add the remaining butter, a little at a time, beating well after each addition. When all the butter has been added the sauce should be thick and glossy. If the sauce curdles, whisk in 10 ml/2 tsp cold water. If this fails to bind it, put an egg yolk in a clean bowl and beat in the sauce gradually. Add a little salt and pepper and serve the sauce lukewarm.

HONEYCOMB MOULD

SERVES 4 TO 6

2 eggs, separated

25 g/1 oz caster sugar

500 ml/17 fl oz milk

5 ml/1 tsp vanilla essence

20 ml/4 tsp gelatine

FILLING

375 g/13 oz chopped fresh fruit or 1 (425 g/15 oz) can fruit, well drained

In a bowl, combine the egg yolks, sugar and milk. Mix lightly. Pour into the top of a double saucepan and cook over simmering water until the custard coats the back of a spoon, stirring all the time. Do not allow the custard to boil. Stir in the essence.

Place 45 ml/3 tbsp water in a small bowl and sprinkle the gelatine on to the liquid. Set aside for 15 minutes until the gelatine is spongy. Stand the bowl over a saucepan of hot water and stir the gelatine until it has dissolved completely. Stir the gelatine mixture into the custard. Cool.

In a clean, grease-free bowl, whisk the egg whites until just stiff. When the custard is just beginning to set, fold in the egg whites. Pour the mixture into a wetted 1 litre/1¾ pint ring mould and refrigerate for 2–3 hours until set. Turn out on a serving plate; fill the centre with fruit.

HORSERADISH SAUCE

MAKES ABOUT 150 ML/¼ PINT

60 ml/4 tbsp grated horseradish

5 ml/1 tsp caster sugar

5 ml/1 tsp salt

2.5 ml/½ tsp pepper

10 ml/2 tsp prepared mustard

malt vinegar (see method)

45–60 ml/3–4 tbsp single cream
  (optional)

Mix the horseradish, sugar, salt, pepper and mustard in a non-metallic bowl. Stir in enough vinegar to make a sauce with the consistency of cream. The flavour and appearance will be improved if the quantity of vinegar is reduced, and the single cream added.

HOT CROSS BUNS

MAKES 12

flour for dusting

400 g/14 oz strong white flour

5 ml/1 tsp sugar

125 ml/4 fl oz milk

25 g/1 oz fresh yeast or 15 ml/
  1 tbsp dried yeast

5 ml/1 tsp salt

7.5 ml/1½ tsp ground mixed
  spice

2.5 ml/½ tsp ground cinnamon

2.5 ml/½ tsp grated nutmeg

50 g/2 oz butter

50 g/2 oz caster sugar

100 g/4 oz currants

50 g/2 oz chopped mixed peel

1 egg

flour for kneading

GLAZE

30 ml/2 tbsp milk

40 g/1½ oz caster sugar

Sift about 75 g/3 oz of the flour and the 5 ml/1 tsp sugar into a large bowl. Warm the milk and 75 ml/3 fl oz water until lukewarm. Blend in the fresh yeast or sprinkle on the dried yeast. Pour the yeast liquid into the flour and sugar, then beat well. Leave the bowl in a warm place for 20 minutes.

Sift the rest of the flour, the salt and spices into a bowl. Rub in the butter. Add the caster sugar and dried fruit. Beat the egg into the frothy yeast mixture and add the flour, fat and fruit mixture. Mix to a soft dough. Turn on to a lightly floured surface and knead for about 5 minutes. Return to the bowl and cover wih cling film. Leave in a warm place until the dough has almost doubled in bulk.

Knead the dough again until firm. Cut into 12 equal pieces and shape each into a round bun. Place on a floured baking sheet. With a sharp knife slash a cross on the top of each bun, or make crosses with pastry trimmings. Cover with oiled polythene. Leave for about 35 minutes, until the dough has doubled in bulk.

Set the oven at 220°C/425°F/gas 7. Bake for 15–20 minutes, until golden. Boil the milk, sugar and 30 ml/2 tbsp water in a saucepan for 6 minutes. Brush over the hot buns to glaze.

HUMMUS

Serve as a starter or snack, with French bread, pitta or crispbreads. Hummus also makes a delicious filling for baked potatoes. Add a crisp salad garnish for a contrast in texture.

SERVES 6 TO 8

150 g/5 oz chick-peas

1 garlic clove, chopped

salt

90ml/6tbsp olive oil

60 ml/4 tbsp tahini (bought or see Mrs Beeton's Tip)

60 ml/4 tbsp lemon juice

chopped parsley to garnish

Soak and cook the chick-peas, following the method given on pages 102–104. Drain thoroughly, then mash and sieve or crush in a mortar with a pestle to a smooth paste. An alternative, and much easier method, is to process the chick-peas in a blender or food processor.

Add the garlic and salt to taste. Stir briskly until well mixed, then work in the olive oil gradually, as when making mayonnaise. The chick-peas should form a creamy paste. Work in the tahini slowly, adding it a teaspoonful at a time at first. When the mixture is creamy work in lemon juice to taste. Transfer the hummus to a shallow serving bowl and sprinkle with chopped parsley.

MRS BEETON'S TIP

To make tahini, place 50 g/2 oz ground sesame seeds in a bowl. Add 1 crushed garlic clove, 1.25 ml/¼ tsp salt, 15 ml/1 tbsp lemon juice and a pinch of pepper. Stir in 75 ml/5 tbsp water. Press the mixture through a sieve into a clean bowl; alternatively, purée in a blender or food processor. Add more salt and pepper if required.

IRISH BAKE

SERVES 4

butter or margarine for greasing

450 g/1 lb potatoes, thinly sliced

450 g/1 lb firm white fish fillet, skinned and cut in 2 cm/ ¾ inch cubes

1 small onion, grated

50 g/2 oz mushrooms, sliced

salt and pepper

1 (298 g/11 oz) can ready-to-serve tomato soup

chopped parsley to garnish

Grease a shallow ovenproof dish. Set the oven at 200°C/400°F/gas 6. Cook the potatoes in a saucepan of boiling salted water for 10 minutes, then drain well.

Lay the fish in the prepared dish. Top with the grated onion and mushrooms, then add a layer of sliced potatoes. Pour the soup over the potatoes, then bake for 25–30 minutes, or until the fish is cooked and the mixture is bubbling hot. Sprinkle with chopped parsley and serve.

ICINGS   See American Frosting, Buttercream, Chocolate Fudge Icing, Glacé Icing and Royal Icing.

IRISH STEW

SERVES 4 TO 6

1 kg/2¼ lb middle neck or scrag
   end of neck of lamb

2 large onions, thinly sliced

1 kg/2¼ lb potatoes, thinly sliced

salt and pepper

well-flavoured lamb or chicken
   stock

30 ml/2 tbsp chopped parsley
   to garnish

Set the oven at 190°C/375°F/gas 5. Cut the meat into neat cutlets or pieces, trimming off any excess fat. Layer the meat, onions and potatoes in a casserole, sprinkling each layer with salt and pepper, and ending with potatoes.

Add enough stock to half fill the casserole. Cover with a lid and bake for about 2–2½ hours, removing the lid for the last 30 minutes of the cooking time, to allow the potato topping to brown. Sprinkle with chopped parsley to serve.

ITALIAN SPINACH

SERVES 4

25 g/1 oz sultanas

1 kg/2¼ lb spinach

30 ml/2 tbsp oil

1 garlic clove, crushed

salt and pepper

25 g/1 oz pine nuts

Put the sultanas in a small bowl or mug, pour on boiling water to cover and set aside for 2–3 minutes until plumped. Drain well and set the sultanas aside.

Wash the fresh spinach several times and remove any coarse stalks. Put into a saucepan with just the water that clings to the leaves, then cover the pan. Put the pan over high heat for 2–3 minutes, shaking it frequently. Lower the heat, stir the spinach and cook for a further 5 minutes, turning the spinach occasionally, until cooked to your liking. Drain thoroughly, then chop the spinach coarsely.

Heat the oil in a large frying pan. Add the spinach and garlic, with salt and pepper to taste. Turn the spinach over and over in the pan with a wide spatula to heat it thoroughly without frying. Turn into a heated serving bowl, add the sultanas and nuts and mix lightly. Serve at once.

MRS BEETON'S TIP

Pine nuts or pine kernels as they are sometimes known are produced inside the cones of a pine tree that grows in North America and in the southern Mediterranean. White and waxy in appearance, they are used extensively in the cooking of the Middle East and are also an important ingredient in the Italian sauce, pesto.

JAM SAUCE

Simple sauces can be highly successful. Try jam sauce on steamed or baked puddings.

MAKES ABOUT 300 ML/½ PINT

60 ml/4 tbsp seedless jam

lemon juice

10 ml/2 tsp arrowroot

few drops of food colouring
   (optional)

Put the jam in a saucepan with 250 ml/8 fl oz water and bring to the boil. Add lemon juice to taste.

In a cup, mix the arrowroot with a little cold water until smooth. Stir into the hot liquid and heat gently until the sauce thickens, stirring all the time. Add a little colouring if necessary. Pour into a jug and serve at once.

variation

MARMALADE SAUCE Substitute marmalade for jam and use orange juice instead of water.

JAM TART

SERVES 6

60–90 ml/4–6 tbsp firm jam

beaten egg for glazing

SHORT CRUST PASTRY

150 g/5 oz plain flour

2.5 ml/½ tsp salt

65 g/2½ oz margarine (or half
   butter, half lard)

flour for rolling out

Set the oven at 200°C/400°F/gas 6. To make the pastry, sift the flour and salt into a bowl, then rub in the margarine until the mixture resembles fine breadcrumbs. Add enough cold water to make a stiff dough. Press the dough together lightly.

Roll out the pastry on a lightly floured surface and use to line a 20 cm/8 inch pie plate. Decorate the edge with any trimmings. Fill with the jam and glaze the uncovered pastry with beaten egg. Bake for 15 minutes or until the pastry is cooked. Serve hot or cold.

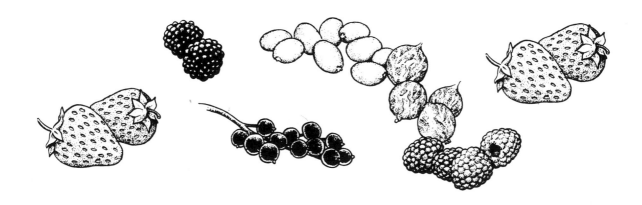

KEDGEREE — *Illustrated on page 130*

SERVES 4

salt and pepper

150 g/5 oz long-grain rice

125 ml/4 fl oz milk

450 g/1 lb smoked haddock

50 g/2 oz butter

15 ml/1 tbsp curry powder

2 hard-boiled eggs, roughly chopped

cayenne pepper

GARNISH

15 g/½ oz butter

1 hard-boiled egg, white and yolk sieved separately

15 ml/1 tbsp chopped parsley

Bring a saucepan of salted water to the boil. Add the rice and cook for 12 minutes. Drain thoroughly, rinse under cold water and drain again. Place the strainer over a saucepan of simmering water to keep the rice warm.

Put the milk in a large shallow saucepan or frying pan with 125 ml/4 fl oz water. Bring to simmering point, add the fish and poach gently for 4 minutes. Using a slotted spoon and a fish slice, transfer the haddock to a wooden board. Discard the cooking liquid.

Remove the skin and any bones from the haddock and break up the flesh into fairly large flakes. Melt half the butter in a large saucepan. Blend in the curry powder and add the flaked fish. Warm the mixture through. Remove from the heat, lightly stir in the chopped eggs; add salt, pepper and cayenne.

Melt the remaining butter in a second pan, add the rice and toss until well coated. Add salt, pepper and cayenne. Add the rice to the haddock mixture and mix well. Pile the kedgeree on to a warmed dish.

Dot the kedgeree with the butter, garnish with sieved hard-boiled egg yolk, egg white and parsley and serve at once.

KIDNEYS TURBIGO

SERVES 4

15 ml/1 tbsp oil

225 g/8 oz cocktail sausages

1 small onion, finely chopped

450 g/1 lb lambs' kidneys, halved and cored

salt and pepper

100 g/4 oz small button mushrooms

15 ml/1 tbsp plain flour

30 ml/2 tbsp tomato purée

150 ml/¼ pint dry white wine

150 ml/¼ pint chicken stock

45 ml/3 tbsp chopped parsley

Heat the oil in a large frying pan, add the sausages and cook them over moderate heat until evenly golden. Using a slotted spoon, transfer them to a dish and set aside.

Pour off any excess fat from the pan, leaving enough to cook the remaining ingredients. Add the onion and cook, stirring, for 10 minutes, until softened. Add the kidneys, with salt and pepper to taste. Cook them, turning often, until browned all over and just cooked.

Add the mushrooms to the pan and continue cooking for about 5 minutes, so that mushrooms are lightly cooked. Use a slotted spoon to transfer the kidneys and mushrooms to the dish with the sausages. Stir the flour into the fat remaining in the pan. Stir in the tomato purée, then gradually stir in the wine and stock. Bring to the boil, stirring all the time, then lower the heat and return the sausages, mushrooms and kidneys to the pan. Simmer gently for 5 minutes.

Add the parsley and seasoning to taste before serving with cooked pasta or rice.

KIPPER GRILL

SERVES 4

4 kippers

20 ml/4 tsp butter

4 pats of butter, chilled, to serve

chopped parsley to garnish

Lay the kippers flat, skin side up, in the base of the grill pan. Do not place on a rack. Grill under moderate heat for 3 minutes.

Turn the kippers over, dot each one with 5 ml/1 tsp butter and grill for 3 minutes more. Serve on individual warmed plates, topping each portion with a pat of chilled butter and a sprinkling of chopped parsley. Add a wedge of lemon, if liked.

LAMB CURRY

Marinating the lamb cubes in yogurt makes them particularly tender. Adjust the spices to taste.

SERVES 4 TO 6

1 kg/2¼ lb boneless leg or shoulder lamb, cut into 2.5 cm/1 inch cubes

60 ml/4 tbsp lemon juice

450 ml/¾ pint plain yogurt

salt and freshly ground black pepper

75 g/3 oz ghee (see Mrs Beeton's Tip)

2 onions, finely chopped

3 garlic cloves, crushed

5 cm/2 inch fresh root ginger, grated

5 ml/1 tsp chilli powder

10 ml/2 tsp each ground coriander and cumin

8 green cardamom pods

150 g/5 oz tomato purée

Put the lamb cubes into a large non-metallic bowl and sprinkle with the lemon juice. Stir in the yogurt and salt. Cover and marinate for 24 hours or for up to 3 days. Stir the mixture occasionally.

Heat the ghee in a large saucepan, add the onions, garlic and ginger and fry for 4–6 minutes until the onion is soft but not coloured. Add the chilli powder, coriander, cumin and black pepper and fry for 2 minutes, then stir in the lamb, with its marinade. Stir in the cardamom pods and tomato purée, with 300 ml/½ pint water. Bring to the boil, reduce the heat and simmer for about 1 hour or until the meat is tender. Serve with rice, chopped tomato and onion, and diced cucumber in yogurt.

MRS BEETON'S TIP

Ghee, or clarified butter, is widely used in Indian cooking. Unlike ordinary butter, it does not brown and burn as easily when used for frying. To clarify butter, melt it over gentle heat and continue to cook until the spluttering stops and a white sediment forms in the bottom of the pan. Cool slightly, then pour off the butter, leaving the sediment in the pan. The butter can be strained through muslin or a filter paper to remove all sediment.

 For basic information on lamb cuts, preparation and cooking methods, see pages 64–79. See also Lancashire Hot Pot, Moussaka, Shoulder of Lamb with Herbs and Stuffed Breast of Lamb with Pilaff.

LAMB SHASHLIK

SERVES 4

50 g/2 oz butter

450 g/1 lb boned leg of lamb,
    cut into 2 cm/¾ inch cubes

8 button onions

200 g/7 oz lean bacon, cut into
    1 cm/½ inch cubes

8 bay leaves

salt and pepper

Heat 25 g/1 oz of the butter in a large frying pan, add the lamb cubes and brown on all sides.

Bring a small saucepan of water to the boil, add the onions and cook for 3 minutes; drain thoroughly.

Divide the meat, bacon, onions and bay leaves into 4 portions. Thread each portion on to a long skewer. Season with salt and pepper. Melt the remaining butter in a small pan and brush the cubed meat and vegetables generously all over.

Cook the shashlik under a hot grill or over medium coals for 8–10 minutes, turning the skewers occasionally, until the meat is well browned. Serve with rice and Cucumber in Yogurt.

LANCASHIRE HOT POT

SERVES 6

fat for greasing

1 kg/2¼ lb potatoes

1 kg/2¼ lb middle neck of lamb
    or mutton, trimmed and cut
    into neat cutlets

3 lambs' kidneys, skinned, cored
    and sliced

2 large onions, sliced

salt and pepper

250 ml/8 fl oz hot lamb or
    vegetable stock

25 g/1 oz lard or dripping

Set the oven at 180°C/350°F/gas 4. Slice half the potatoes and cut the rest into chunks. Arrange half the sliced potatoes in the bottom of a greased large deep casserole. Layer the meat, kidneys, onions and potato chunks on top, seasoning each layer lightly with salt and pepper. Finish with the remaining potato slices.

Pour in the hot stock. Melt the lard or dripping and brush it over the top layer of potatoes. Cover the casserole with a tight-fitting lid and bake for about 2 hours or until the meat and potatoes are tender.

Remove the lid, increase the oven temperature to 220°C/425°F/gas 7 and cook for 20 minutes more or until the top layer of potatoes is brown and crisp. Serve from the casserole.

variation

LAMB AND OYSTER HOTPOT Add a central layer, consisting of 8 sliced flat mushrooms and 18 shelled fresh oysters. Proceed as in the recipe above.

LASAGNE AL FORNO

SERVES 6 TO 8

150 g/5 oz lasagne (7 sheets) or
   200 g/7 oz (12 sheets)
   no-precook lasagne

30 ml/2 tbsp oil

2 onions, finely chopped

2 garlic cloves, chopped

225 g/8 oz minced beef

225 g/8 oz minced pork

100 g/4 oz mushrooms, sliced

2 (397 g/14 oz) cans chopped
   tomatoes

2.5 ml/½ tsp each dried basil
   and oregano

150 ml/¼ pint red wine

salt and pepper

900 ml/1½ pints white sauce

50 g/2 oz Parmesan cheese

Cook the lasagne, if necessary, in plenty of boiling salted water. Add the lasagne a sheet at a time, then boil for about 12 minutes until tender but not soft. Drain well, rinse under cold water and lay out to dry on absorbent kitchen paper.

Heat the oil in a heavy-bottomed saucepan, add the onions and garlic and fry over medium heat for 10 minutes. Stir in the beef and pork. Cook, stirring, for 5–10 minutes.

Stir in the mushrooms, tomatoes, herbs and wine. Add salt and pepper. Bring just to the boil, stirring. Reduce the heat, then simmer the sauce steadily, uncovered, stirring occasionally. Allow 1¼–1½ hours until the meat is tender and the sauce thick when stirred.

Set the oven at 180°C/350°F/gas 4. Spread a thin layer of the white sauce over the base of a 30 × 20 cm/12 × 8 inch baking dish. Arrange a layer of lasagne in the dish. Top with a layer of meat sauce. Add a thin layer of white sauce, but do not worry too much about spreading the sauce perfectly; the next layer of lasagne will smooth it out. Repeat the layers, ending with white sauce. Grate the Parmesan and sprinkle it evenly over the top. Bake for 40–50 minutes, until golden brown. Allow the lasagne to stand for 10 minutes before serving.

LEEK TART — *Illustrated on page 301*

SERVES 8

175 g/6 oz Short Crust Pastry
   (page 139)

8 small leeks, trimmed

2 eggs

salt and pepper

grated nutmeg

25 g/1 oz Gruyère cheese

SAUCE

15 g/½ oz butter

15 g/½ oz plain flour

150 ml/¼ pint milk or milk and
   leek cooking liquid

Set the oven at 200°C/400°F/gas 6. Roll out the pastry and line an 18 cm/7 inch flan tin. Bake 'blind' for 20 minutes (page 133) then remove the paper and beans. Return to the oven for 5 minutes, then leave to cool. Reduce the oven temperature to 190°C/375°F/gas 5.

Using the white parts of the leeks only, tie them into two bundles with string. Bring a pan of salted water to the boil, add the leeks and simmer for 10 minutes. Drain, squeeze dry and slice thickly.

To make the sauce, melt the butter in a saucepan. Stir in the flour and cook over low heat for 2–3 minutes, without colouring. Gradually add the liquid, stirring constantly. Bring to the boil, stirring, then lower the heat and simmer for 1–2 minutes. Beat the eggs into the white sauce. Then add salt, pepper and nutmeg to taste. Grate in half the Gruyère. Put a layer of sauce in the cooled pastry case, cover with the leeks, then with the remaining sauce. Grate the remaining Gruyère on top. Bake for 20 minutes or until golden.

LEMON CHEESECAKE

SERVES 4 TO 6

BASE

100 g/4 oz digestive biscuits

50 g/2 oz butter

25 g/1 oz caster sugar

FILLING

200 g/7 oz full-fat soft cheese

75 g/3 oz caster sugar

2 eggs, separated

125 ml/4 fl oz soured cream

15 g/½ oz gelatine

grated rind and juice of 1 lemon

Make the base. Crumb the biscuits in a food processor. Alternatively, place them in a strong polythene bag and use a rolling pin to crush them. Melt the butter in a small saucepan and mix in the crumbs and sugar. Press the mixture on to the base of a loose-bottomed 15 cm/6 inch cake tin. Put in a cool place to set.

Make the filling. In a mixing bowl, beat the cheese and sugar together. Beat in the egg yolk. Stir in the soured cream. Place 45 ml/3 tbsp water in a small bowl. Sprinkle the gelatine on to the liquid. Set aside for 15 minutes until the gelatine is spongy. Stand the bowl over a pan of hot water and stir the gelatine until it has dissolved completely. Stir the lemon rind, juice and dissolved gelatine into the cheese mixture.

In a clean, grease-free bowl, whisk the egg whites until stiff and fold carefully into the mixture. Pour into the prepared tin and chill for 45–60 minutes until firm. When quite cold, remove from the tin, transfer to a plate and slice to serve.

LEMON CHICKEN — *Illustrated on page 132*

SERVES 6

6 chicken breasts

salt and pepper

50 g/2 oz butter

15 ml/1 tbsp oil

1 onion, sliced

1 lemon, sliced

60 ml/4 tbsp plain flour

300 ml/½ pint chicken stock

2–3 bay leaves

5 ml/1 tsp caster sugar

Set the oven at 190°C/375°F/gas 5. Season the chicken breasts with salt and pepper. Melt the butter in the oil in a large frying pan, add the chicken and fry until golden brown all over.

Using tongs or a slotted spoon, transfer to a casserole. Add the onion and lemon slices to the fat remaining in the pan and fry over very gentle heat for about 15 minutes. Using a slotted spoon, transfer the onion and lemon to the casserole.

Sprinkle the flour into the fat remaining in the pan. Cook for 1 minute, then blend in the stock. Bring to the boil, stirring all the time. Add the bay leaves and sugar, with salt and pepper to taste. Pour over the chicken breasts in the casserole, cover and bake for about 45 minutes or until the chicken is tender. Remove the casserole lid 5 minutes before the end of the cooking time. Remove the bay leaves before serving or reserve them as a garnish.

Lemon chiffon

SERVES 4

3 eggs, separated
150 g/5 oz caster sugar
125 ml/4 fl oz lemon juice
10 ml/2 tsp gelatine
grated rind of 2 lemons

Combine the egg yolks, sugar and lemon juice in a heatproof bowl. Stand over a saucepan of gently simmering water and whisk the mixture until frothy, pale and the consistency of single cream. Remove from the heat.

Place 45 ml/3 tbsp water in a small bowl and sprinkle the gelatine on to the liquid. Set aside for 15 minutes until the gelatine is spongy. Stand the bowl over a pan of hot water and stir the gelatine until it has dissolved completely. Cool for 5 minutes.

Whisk the gelatine into the egg yolk mixture. Cool the mixture, then refrigerate until beginning to set. Stir in the lemon rind. In a clean, grease-free bowl, whisk the egg whites until stiff. Fold into the lemon mixture. Spoon into 4 glasses. Return to the refrigerator until completely set.

Lemon curd

Lemon curd is not a true preserve but it keeps for a while in the refrigerator. Use very fresh eggs bought from a reputable source.

MAKES ABOUT 450 G/1 LB

2 lemons
225 g/8 oz sugar
75 g/3 oz butter, cut up
3 eggs

Wash, dry and grate the lemons. Squeeze out the juice and put it with the sugar in the top of a double saucepan or heatproof bowl set over boiling water. Stir occasionally until the sugar has dissolved. Remove from the heat and stir in the butter. Leave to cool.

Beat the eggs lightly in a bowl. Pour the cooled lemon mixture over them, mix well, then strain the mixture back into the pan or bowl. Place over gentle heat, stirring frequently until the mixture thickens enough to coat the back of a wooden spoon lightly.

Pour into warmed clean jars. Cover with waxed paper discs. Put on lids and label when cold. Leave for 24 hours to thicken; store the curd in the refrigerator. Use within 2–3 weeks.

LEMON MERINGUE PIE

SERVES 6

225 g/8 oz Short Crust Pastry
(page 139)

flour for rolling out

300 g/11 oz caster sugar

45 ml/3 tbsp cornflour

45 ml/3 tbsp plain flour

30 ml/2 tbsp butter

grated rind of 2 lemons

75 ml/5 tbsp lemon juice

3 eggs, separated

Set the oven at 200°C/400°F/gas 6

Roll out the pastry on a lightly floured surface. Line a 23 cm/9 inch pie plate. Line the pastry with greaseproof paper and fill with baking beans. Bake 'blind' for 15 minutes; remove paper and beans. Return to the oven for 5 minutes, then remove from the oven and reduce the oven temperature to 180°C/350°F/gas 4.

Meanwhile mix half the sugar with the cornflour and plain flour in the top of a double saucepan. In a separate saucepan, bring 300 ml/½ pint water to the boil. Stir the boiling water slowly into the dry mixture, then place the top of the double saucepan over gently simmering water. Cover and cook gently for 20 minutes.

Draw the pan off the heat and add the butter, lemon rind and juice. Beat the egg yolks in a bowl, add a little of the cooked mixture, then add to the mixture in the pan. Beat well, replace over the heat and cook, stirring constantly until thick. Remove the pan from the heat and set aside to cool.

In a clean, grease-free bowl, whisk the egg whites until stiff. Fold in the remaining sugar. Pour the lemon custard into the baked pastry case and cover the top with the meringue, making sure that it covers the top completely. Bake for 12–15 minutes until the meringue is lightly browned. Cool before cutting.

LEMON SAUCE

MAKES ABOUT 175 ML/6 FL OZ

thinly pared rind of 1 lemon or
other solid flavouring

100 g/4 oz sugar

lemon juice

10 ml/2 tsp arrowroot

125 ml/4 fl oz sherry

1 egg yolk

Put 125 ml/4 fl oz water in a saucepan. Add the lemon rind or other flavouring and bring to the boil. Lower the heat and simmer the sauce gently for 15 minutes.

Remove the lemon rind, if used, and stir in the sugar. Return the liquid to the boil and boil steadily for 5 minutes. Stir in lemon juice to taste.

In a cup, mix the arrowroot with 10 ml/2 tsp water until smooth. Stir into the hot liquid. Heat gently for 1–2 minutes, stirring constantly as the sauce thickens. Remove from the heat once the sauce has boiled. Mix the sherry with the egg yolk until thoroughly combined, stir in a little of the hot sauce, then pour the mixture into the pan. Heat gently for 1–2 minutes, without boiling, to cook the yolk slightly. Serve at once.

LEMON SORBET

Traditionally, sorbets were eaten between the entree and roast courses at a formal dinner, to cleanse the palate.

SERVES 6 TO 8

10 ml/2 tsp gelatine

150 g/5 oz caster sugar

2.5 ml/½ tsp grated lemon rind

250 ml/8 fl oz lemon juice

2 egg whites

Turn the freezing compartment or freezer to the coldest setting about 1 hour before making the sorbet.

Place 30 ml/2 tbsp water in a small bowl and sprinkle the gelatine on to the liquid. Set aside for 15 minutes until the gelatine is spongy. Stand the bowl over a pan of hot water; stir the gelatine until it has dissolved. Put the sugar in a heavy-bottomed saucepan with 200 ml/7 fl oz water. Dissolve the sugar over gentle heat, without stirring. Bring the mixture to the boil and boil gently for about 10 minutes. Stir the dissolved gelatine into the syrup, with the lemon rind and juice. Cover and cool.

Pour the cool syrup mixture into a suitable container for freezing. Cover the container closely and freeze until half-frozen.

In a clean, grease-free bowl, whisk the egg whites until stiff. Beat the sorbet mixture until smooth, scraping off any ice crystals. Fold in the egg whites, replace the cover on the bowl and freeze. The mixture should be firm enough to scoop; it will not freeze hard. Return the freezer to the normal setting. Serve straight from the freezer, in dishes, glasses or lemon shells.

LENTIL AND PARSLEY SOUP

SERVES 4

25 g/1 oz butter or margarine

2 carrots, diced

1 large leek, trimmed, finely sliced and washed

100 g/4 oz red lentils

300 ml/½ pint milk

1 bay leaf

salt and pepper

30 ml/2 tbsp chopped parsley

Melt the butter or margarine in a saucepan, add the carrots and leek and fry gently for about 5 minutes, stirring frequently, until the leek slices are soft but not coloured.

Add the lentils, milk, bay leaf and 600 ml/1 pint water. Heat gently to simmering point, cover and simmer for about 20 minutes or until the lentils are soft. Remove the bay leaf. Add salt and pepper to taste, stir in the chopped parsley and serve.

PRESSURE COOKER TIP

Having added the liquid, put the lid on the cooker and bring to 15 lb pressure. Cook for 15 minutes. Reduce pressure slowly, then remove the bay leaf and add the seasoning and parsley.

LETTUCE SOUP

SERVES 4

400 g/14 oz lettuce, shredded

600 ml/1 pint white stock

30 ml/2 tbsp butter

1 onion, finely chopped

1 garlic clove, crushed

225 g/8 oz potatoes, cubed

1 bouquet garni

salt and pepper

150 ml/¼ pint single cream

1 egg yolk

Put the lettuce in a large heatproof bowl. Bring the stock to the boil in a deep saucepan, pour over the lettuce and set aside.

Melt the butter in the clean pan, add the onion, garlic and potatoes and fry over gentle heat, turning the vegetables frequently, for 10 minutes. Add the lettuce and stock with the bouquet garni. Stir in salt and pepper to taste. Bring to the boil, then lower the heat and simmer for 2 minutes or until the lettuce is tender.

Remove the bouquet garni. Purée the soup in a blender or food processor, or rub through a sieve into a clean pan. Reheat to simmering point, then remove the pan from the heat. Mix the cream and egg yolk together in a small bowl, stir in a little of the hot soup and mix well.

Whisk the mixture into the remaining soup, return it to the heat and reheat without boiling, stirring all the time. Adjust the seasoning, if necessary. Serve hot.

MRS BEETON'S TIP
For a cheaper and less rich soup, substitute 125 ml/4 fl oz milk for the egg and cream mixture. Add the milk to the lettuce purée when reheating.

LIVER HOT POT

SERVES 6

fat for greasing

450 g/1 lb lamb's liver, sliced

45 ml/3 tbsp plain flour

salt and pepper

2 large onions, thinly sliced

800 g/1¾ lb potatoes, thinly sliced

500 ml/18 fl oz beef stock

6–8 rindless streaky bacon rashers

Set the oven at 180°C/350°F/gas 4. Remove the skin and any tubes from the liver. Mix the flour with salt and pepper in a shallow bowl. Coat the liver slices in the seasoned flour. Shake off excess flour.

Arrange layers of liver, onions and potatoes in a greased casserole, ending with a layer of potatoes. Heat the stock in a small saucepan and pour in just enough to cover the potatoes. Cover the casserole with a lid or foil and bake for 1 hour or until the liver is tender.

Remove the lid and arrange the bacon rashers on top of the potatoes. Return the casserole to the oven for about 15 minutes or until the bacon is browned. Serve immediately, straight from the casserole.

LIVER PATE

Serve this flavoursome pâté in the dish in which it was cooked, with hot dry toast, or cut into slices and serve with salad.

MAKES ABOUT 675 G/1½ LB

fat for greasing

75 g/3 oz butter

100 g/4 oz lean rindless bacon rashers, chopped

225 g/8 oz calf's or pig's liver, trimmed and chopped

225 g/8 oz chicken livers, trimmed and chopped

1 small onion, finely chopped

a few gherkins, chopped (optional)

12 hard-boiled eggs, chopped

salt and pepper

5–10 ml/1–2 tsp dried mixed herbs

melted clarified butter (page 316)

Grease an ovenproof terrine or similar dish. Set the oven at 180°C/350°F/gas 4. Melt the butter in a frying pan, add the bacon, livers and onion and fry gently for 5–6 minutes. Mince finely twice or process in a blender or food processor to a smooth paste. Add the chopped gherkins and hard-boiled eggs, with salt, pepper and herbs to taste. Stir well. Spoon into the prepared dish; cover with buttered greaseproof paper.

Stand the dish in a roasting tin and add enough hot water to come to within 2.5 cm/1 inch of the rim of the tin. Bake for 30 minutes.

When cooked, cover immediately with a layer of clarified butter. Leave to cool, then chill before serving. Alternatively, place under a light weight and cover with clarified butter when cold.

MACARONI CHEESE

SERVES 3 TO 4

fat for greasing

150 g/5 oz elbow macaroni

salt and pepper

600 ml/1 pint hot white sauce

100 g/4 oz Cheddar cheese, grated

Grease a 750 ml/1¼ pint pie dish. Set the oven at 200°C/400°F/gas 6. Cook the macaroni in a large saucepan of boiling salted water for 10–12 minutes or until tender but still firm to the bite.

Drain the macaroni thoroughly and stir it gently into the white sauce. Add three-quarters of the cheese, with salt and pepper to taste. Spoon the mixture into the prepared pie dish. Sprinkle with the remaining cheese and bake for 15–20 minutes. Alternatively, place under a pre-heated grill for 2–4 minutes to melt and brown the cheese topping.

MACARONI SAVOURY

Mrs Beeton served this simple dish as a savoury with the cheese course; however, today it is better classed as a quick, delicious but rich, supper dish. Good with a crisp green salad or a tomato salad.

SERVES 4

225 g/8 oz macaroni

salt and pepper

100–175 g/4–6 oz fresh
   Parmesan cheese, grated

75–100 g/3–4 oz butter, melted

50 g/2 oz fresh breadcrumbs

Cook the macaroni in a large saucepan of boiling salted water for 10–12 minutes or until just tender but still firm to the bite. Drain well and layer in a warmed flameproof dish, sprinkling each layer with pepper, Parmesan and a little butter. Top with the breadcrumbs and remaining butter, then brown under a hot grill. Serve at once.

variation

Cheshire cheese may be used instead of fresh Parmesan and a few shredded basil leaves may be added.

MACKEREL WITH GOOSEBERRY SAUCE

Gooseberry sauce is such a classic accompaniment to mackerel that in France the fruit is known as groseille à maquereau.

SERVES 4

50 g/2 oz plain flour

salt and pepper

8 mackerel fillets

50 g/2 oz butter

juice of 1 lemon

45 ml/3 tbsp chopped parsley

SAUCE

450 g/1 lb gooseberries, topped
   and tailed

45 ml/3 tbsp dry still cider

25 g/1 oz butter

15 ml/1 tbsp caster sugar

Make the sauce by combining the gooseberries, cider and butter in a small saucepan. Bring the liquid to simmering point and poach the fruit, stirring occasionally, until soft. Purée the mixture by passing it through a sieve set over a small pan. Stir in the sugar.

Spread out the flour in a shallow bowl, add salt and pepper, and coat the fish lightly all over. Melt the butter in a large frying pan, add the fish and fry gently for 5–7 minutes or until browned, turning once. Using a slotted spoon and a fish slice, transfer the fish to a warmed serving dish and keep hot.

Heat the gooseberry sauce. Continue to heat the butter remaining in the frying pan until it becomes light brown. Stir in the lemon juice and parsley and pour over the fish. Serve at once, with the gooseberry sauce in a jug or sauceboat.

MRS BEETON'S TIP

The gooseberries can be cooked in the microwave. Combine the cider and butter in a mixing bowl and heat for 1 minute on High. Add the fruit, stir, cover the bowl and cook for 5–7 minutes or until soft. Stir once or twice during cooking.

MADEIRA CAKE

MAKES ONE 15 CM/6 INCH CAKE

fat for greasing

150 g/5 oz butter or margarine

150 g/5 oz caster sugar

4 eggs, beaten

200 g/7 oz plain flour

10 ml/2 tsp baking powder

pinch of salt

grated rind of 1 lemon

caster sugar for dredging

1 thin slice of candied or glacé
   citron peel

Line and grease a 15 cm/6 inch round cake tin. Set the oven at 180°C/350°F/gas 4. In a mixing bowl, cream the butter or margarine with the sugar until light and fluffy. Gradually add the eggs, beating well after each addition.

Sift the flour, baking powder and salt together into a second bowl, then fold into the creamed mixture. Stir in the lemon rind and mix well.

Spoon into the prepared tin. Dredge the top with caster sugar. Bake for 20 minutes, then lay the slice of peel on top. Bake for a further 45–50 minutes or until cooked through and firm to the touch. Turn out on a wire rack to cool.

MADELEINES – ENGLISH

MAKES 10

fat for greasing

100 g/4 oz self-raising flour

pinch of salt

100 g/4 oz butter or margarine

100 g/4 oz caster sugar

2 eggs, beaten

DECORATION

45 ml/3 tbsp smooth apricot jam

25 g/1 oz desiccated coconut

glacé cherries, halved

20 angelica leaves

Thoroughly grease 10 dariole moulds. Set the oven at 180°C/350°F/gas 4. Mix the flour and salt in a bowl.

In a mixing bowl, cream the butter or margarine with the sugar until light and fluffy. Beat in the eggs, then lightly stir in the flour and salt. Divide the mixture evenly between the prepared moulds and bake for 15–20 minutes until golden brown. Cool on a wire rack.

Trim off the rounded ends of the cakes, if necessary, and stand upright. Warm the jam in a small saucepan, then brush the cakes all over. Toss in the coconut. Decorate the top of each madeleine with a glacé cherry or angelica leaves or both.

MAIDS OF HONOUR

MAKES 20

Puff Pastry (page 141), using
    200 g/7 oz flour
flour for rolling out
200 g/7 oz ground almonds
100 g/4 oz caster sugar
2 eggs, beaten
25 g/1 oz plain flour
60 ml/4 tbsp single cream
30 ml/2 tbsp orange flower
    water

Set the oven at 200°C/400°F/gas 6. Roll out the pastry on a lightly floured surface and use to line twenty 7.5 cm/3 inch patty tins.

Mix the ground almonds and sugar in a bowl. Add the eggs, then mix in the flour, cream and orange flower water. Put the mixture into the pastry cases. Bake for about 15 minutes or until the filling is firm and golden.

MAITRE D'HOTEL BUTTER

MAKES 100 G/4 OZ

100 g/4 oz butter
4–5 large parsley sprigs, finely
    chopped
salt and pepper
2.5 ml/½ tsp lemon juice

Beat the butter until creamy in a small bowl. Add the parsley, a little at a time, beating until well combined. Add salt to taste and a small pinch of pepper. Add a few drops of lemon juice to intensify the flavour. Use at once or press into small pots, tapping the pots while filling to knock out all the air. Cover with foil and refrigerate until required. Use within 2 days.

FREEZER TIP

A convenient way to freeze this butter is to shape it into a roll on a piece of foil or freezer paper. Roll it up in the paper, overwrap in a polythene bag, seal, label and freeze. The frozen butter can then be cut into slices as required, using a warm knife.

MALTED BROWN BREAD

MAKES TWO 800G/1¾ LB LOAVES

fat for greasing

800 g/1¾ lb wholemeal flour

15 ml/1 tbsp salt

25 g/1 oz fresh yeast or 15 ml/
1 tbsp dried yeast

2.5 ml/½ tsp sugar

30 ml/2 tbsp malt extract

flour for kneading

Grease two 23 x 13 x 7.5 cm/9 x 5 x 3 inch loaf tins. Mix the flour and salt in a large bowl. Measure 500 ml/17 fl oz lukewarm water. Blend the fresh yeast to a thin paste with the sugar and a little of the warm water. Set aside in a warm place until frothy – about 5 minutes. Alternatively, sprinkle the dried yeast over all the warm water and set aside until frothy.

Stir the malt extract into the yeast liquid and remaining water. Add to the flour and mix to a soft dough. Turn on to a lightly floured surface and knead for about 4 minutes or until the dough is smooth, elastic and no longer sticky. Return to the bowl and cover with cling film. Leave in a warm place until the dough has doubled in bulk – this will take 2 hours, or longer.

Knead the dough again until firm. Cut into two equal portions and form each into a loaf shape. Place the dough in the prepared loaf tins. Place the tins in a large, lightly oiled polythene bag. Leave in a warm place for about 45 minutes or until the dough has doubled in bulk. Set the oven at 230°C/450°F/gas 8.

Bake for 35–45 minutes, until the loaves are golden brown and crisp, and sound hollow when tapped on the bottom.

MARBLE CAKE

MAKES ONE 20 CM/8 INCH CAKE

fat for greasing

175 g/6 oz butter or margarine

175 g/6 oz caster sugar

3 eggs, beaten

few drops of vanilla essence

225 g/8 oz self-raising flour

pinch of salt

30 ml/2 tbsp milk

30 ml/2 tbsp strong black coffee

50 g/2 oz chocolate, broken into chunks

Chocolate Fudge Icing

15 ml/1 tbsp grated chocolate

Line and grease a 20 cm/8 inch round cake tin. Set the oven at 180°C/350°F/gas 4.

In a mixing bowl cream the butter or margarine with the sugar until light and fluffy. Add the eggs gradually, beating well after each addition. Stir in the vanilla.

Sift the flour and salt into a bowl. Stir into the creamed mixture, lightly but thoroughly, until evenly mixed. Place half the mixture in a second bowl and beat in the milk.

Combine the coffee and chocolate in a bowl set over a saucepan of simmering water. Heat gently until the chocolate melts. Stir thoroughly, then add to the cake mixture in the mixing bowl, beating well.

Put alternate spoonfuls of plain and chocolate mixture into the prepared cake tin. Bake for 45–60 minutes, until firm to the touch. Cool on a wire rack. Top with the chocolate fudge icing and grated chocolate.

MEATLOAF

SERVES 4

oil for greasing

450 g/1 lb minced beef or pork, or a mixture of both

50 g/2 oz fresh breadcrumbs

1 large onion, finely chopped

30 ml/2 tbsp chopped parsley

5 ml/1 tsp each chopped fresh thyme and sage

1 egg

15 ml/1 tbsp Worcestershire sauce

salt and pepper

Grease a 450 g/1 lb loaf tin. Set the oven at 180°C/350°F/gas 4. Place all the ingredients in a bowl, adding plenty of salt and pepper. Pound the ingredients with the back of a mixing spoon until thoroughly combined and well bound together.

Turn the mixture into the tin, press it down well and cover the top with a piece of greased greaseproof paper. Bake for 1 hour, until firm and shrunk away from the tin slightly. Turn out and serve hot or cold.

MELBA SAUCE

Although this sauce is principally used for Peach Melba, it is equally delicious when served with meringues, sorbet or any raspberry flavoured dessert.

MAKES ABOUT 125 ML/4 FL OZ

225 g/8 oz fresh raspberries

45 ml/3 tbsp icing sugar

white wine (optional)

Put the raspberries in a sieve over a heatproof bowl. Crush them lightly with the back of a wooden spoon, then add the icing sugar and rub the raspberries through the sieve into the bowl.

Place the bowl over a saucepan of simmering water, and stir for 2–3 minutes to dissolve the sugar.

Remove from the heat, and stir in a little white wine if a thinner consistency is preferred. The sauce should only just coat the back of a spoon. Pour into a bowl or jug and chill before use.

MICROWAVE TIP

Mix the fruit and sugar in a bowl. Cover the bowl and cook on High for 2 minutes, until the fruit is pulpy. Rub the sauce through a sieve. Continue as above, thinning the sauce with wine if liked.

MELTING MOMENTS

MAKES 16 TO 20

fat for greasing

100 g/4 oz margarine or half
   margarine and half blended
   white vegetable fat

75 g/3 oz caster sugar

30 ml/2 tbsp beaten egg

125 g/4 oz self-raising flour

pinch of salt

rolled oats for coating

4–5 glacé cherries, quartered

Grease two baking sheets. Set the oven at 180°C/350°F/gas 4.

In a mixing bowl, cream the margarine or mixed fats and sugar until pale and fluffy. Add the egg with a little flour and beat again. Stir in the remaining flour with the salt, mix well, then shape the mixture into 16–20 balls with the hands.

Place the rolled oats on a sheet of greaseproof paper and toss the balls in them to coat them evenly all over. Space the balls on the prepared baking sheets. Place a small piece of glacé cherry in the centre of each.

Bake for about 20 minutes until pale golden brown. Leave to stand for a few minutes on the baking sheets, then cool on a wire rack.

variation

Custard Treats Substitute 40 g/1½ oz of the flour with custard powder for a deliciously creamy biscuit with a rich buttery colour. Omit the rolled oats coating.

MERINGUES

This basic meringue mixture may be used for a wide variety of dishes, from the individual meringues of various sizes to shells, cases and toppings. Provided the cooked meringues are dried out thoroughly, they will keep for 2 weeks in an airtight tin.

MAKES 24 TO 30 MEDIUM MERINGUES

4 egg whites

pinch of salt

200 g/7 oz caster sugar, plus
   extra for dusting

1.25 ml/¼ tsp baking powder
   (optional)

whipped cream, to fill (optional)

Line a baking sheet with oiled greaseproof paper or with non-stick baking parchment. Set the oven at 110°C/225°F/gas ¼ .

Combine the egg whites and salt in a mixing bowl and whisk until the whites are very stiff and standing in peaks. They must be completely dry. Gradually add half the caster sugar, 15 ml/1 tbsp at a time, whisking well after each addition until the meringue is stiff. If the sugar is not thoroughly blended in it will form droplets of syrup which may brown, spoiling the appearance and texture of the meringues, and making them difficult to remove from the paper when cooked.

When half the sugar has been whisked in, sprinkle the rest over the surface of the mixture and, using a metal spoon, fold it in very lightly with the baking powder, if used. Put the meringue mixture into a piping bag fitted with a large nozzle and pipe into rounds on the paper. Alternatively, shape the mixture using two wet tablespoons. Take up a spoonful of the mixture and smooth it with a palette knife, bringing it up into a ridge in the centre. Slide it out with the other spoon on to the prepared baking sheet, with the ridge on top.

Dust the meringues lightly with caster sugar, then dry off in the oven for 3–4 hours, until they are firm and crisp but still white. If the meringues

MERINGUES — *continued*

begin to brown, prop the oven door open a little. When they are crisp on the outside, lift the meringues carefully off the sheet, using a palette knife. Turn them on to their sides and return to the oven until the bases are dry. Cool on a wire rack and, if liked, sandwich them together with whipped cream. Filled meringues should be served within 1 hour or they will soften.

variations

Meringue Fingers Pipe the meringue mixture into fingers instead of shaping rounds. Dip one end of each meringue in melted chocolate when cool, then leave to set on waxed paper. Alternatively, sandwich the fingers together with whipped cream; coat the top of each with melted chocolate.

MILANAISE SOUFFLE

SERVES 4

15 ml/1 tbsp gelatine

3 eggs, separated

grated rind and juice of
   2 lemons

100 g/4 oz caster sugar

125 ml/4 fl oz double cream

DECORATION

finely chopped nuts or cake
   crumbs

whipped double cream
   (optional)

crystallized lemon slices

angelica

Prepare a 500 ml/17 fl oz soufflé dish (see Mrs Beeton's Tip on page 332 and page 119) and stand it on a plate for easy handling.

Place 45 ml/3 tbsp water in a small bowl and sprinkle the gelatine on to the liquid. Set aside for 15 minutes until the gelatine is spongy. Stand the bowl over a pan of hot water and stir the gelatine until it has dissolved completely. Cool slightly.

Combine the egg yolks, lemon rind and juice, and sugar in a heatproof bowl and stand over a saucepan of hot water set over low heat. Do not let the water boil or touch the bowl. Whisk the mixture for 10–15 minutes until thick and pale, then remove from the heat and continue whisking until cool. Fold a little yolk mixture into the cooled gelatine, then whisk this into the rest of the yolk mixture. Put in a cool place until the mixture starts to set.

In a bowl, whip the cream to soft peaks. Using a large metal spoon, fold into the yolk mixture until evenly blended. Whisk the egg whites in a clean, grease-free bowl until stiff, then fold into the mixture. Tip the soufflé mixture gently into the prepared dish and refrigerate until set.

Carefully remove the paper from the crown of the soufflé and decorate the sides with chopped nuts or cake crumbs. Pipe whipped cream on top, if liked, and decorate with crystallized lemon slices and small pieces of angelica. *continues over*

MILANAISE SOUFFLE — *continued*

> ### MRS BEETON'S TIP
>
> The size of the soufflé dish is crucial, since the mixture must 'rise' above it. To check the capacity of the dish, measure by pouring in 500 ml/17 fl oz water. If the dish is slightly too small, do not worry, since the crown will merely be a little taller. A larger dish, however, will not be suitable.

variations

In each of the variations below, omit the lemon rind and juice.

COLD CHOCOLATE SOUFFLE Whisk the yolks with 30 ml/2 tbsp water and 75 g/3 oz caster sugar. Melt 75 g/3 oz grated plain chocolate over a pan of hot water. Add to the yolk mixture with the dissolved gelatine and whisk well.

COLD ORANGE SOUFFLE Whisk the yolks with the finely grated rind and juice of 2 oranges and use 75 g/3 oz caster sugar only. Add 30 ml/2 tbsp Grand Marnier or orange curaçao, if liked. Dissolve the gelatine in a mixture of 15 ml/1 tbsp water and 30 ml/2 tbsp lemon juice.

Decorate the soufflé with crystallized orange slices, nuts and cream.

COLD PRALINE SOUFFLE Make 75 g/3 oz Praline, following the instructions under Praline Custard on page 276, and crush it. Dissolve 5 ml/1 tsp instant coffee in 30 ml/2 tbsp hot water, and add 30 ml/2 tbsp cold water. Whisk the liquid with the yolks. Add 50 g/2 oz of the crushed praline to the mixture with the whipped cream. Decorate with the rest of the praline and additional cream.

COLD FRUIT SOUFFLE The recipe below uses raspberries but other fresh, frozen or canned soft fruits, such as strawberries, blackcurrants or blackberries, may be substituted to produce a strongly flavoured soufflé.

COLD RASPBERRY SOUFFLE Soften the gelatine in 45 ml/3 tbsp of strained fruit syrup from 1 (440 g/15 oz) can of raspberries. Add 15 ml/1 tbsp lemon juice and 150 ml/¼ pint sieved fruit to the yolk mixture (this can be made up with a little strained syrup, if necessary). Use only 75 g/3 oz sugar and 100 ml/3½ fl oz double cream. Decorate the sides of the soufflé with desiccated coconut, and the top with whipped cream and raspberries.

COLD APRICOT SOUFFLE Dried apricots make a delicious soufflé: Soak 50 g/2 oz overnight in enough water to cover. Tip into a saucepan and simmer for 15–20 minutes until tender, then purée the apricots and liquid in a blender or food processor. Soften the gelatine in a mixture of 15 ml/1 tbsp water and 30 ml/2 tbsp lemon juice. Add the apricot purée (made up to 150 ml/¼ pint with water, if necessary) and proceed as in the main recipe.

MINCEMEAT

MAKES ABOUT 1.8 KG/4 LB

200 g/7 oz cut mixed peel

200 g/7 oz seedless raisins

25 g/1 oz preserved stem ginger

200 g/7 oz cooking apples

200 g/7 oz shredded suet

200 g/7 oz sultanas

200 g/7 oz currants

200 g/7 oz soft light brown sugar

50 g/2 oz chopped blanched almonds

generous pinch each of mixed spice, ground ginger and ground cinnamon

grated rind and juice of 2 lemons and 1 orange

150 ml/¼ pint brandy, sherry or rum

Mince or finely chop the peel, raisins and ginger. Peel, core and grate the apples. Combine all the ingredients in a very large bowl, cover and leave to stand for two days in a cool place, stirring occasionally (see Mrs Beeton's Tip). Pot, cover and label. Store in a cool, dry place.

variations
Use a vegetarian 'suet' if you prefer a mincemeat which is free from animal products. If an alcohol-free mincemeat is desired, use apple juice instead of brandy and store the jars in the refrigerator if not using at once. Alternatively, freeze for up to 6 months.

> **MRS BEETON'S TIP**
> Observing the standing and stirring time helps to stop the mincemeat from fermenting later.

MINCE PIES

MAKES 12

350 g/12 oz mincemeat

25 g/1 oz icing or caster sugar for dredging

SHORT CRUST PASTRY

300 g/10 oz plain flour

5 ml/1 tsp salt

150 g/5 oz margarine (or half butter, half lard)

flour for rolling out

Set the oven at 200°C/400°F/gas 6. To make the pastry, sift the flour and salt into a bowl, then rub in the margarine until the mixture resembles fine breadcrumbs. Add enough cold water to make a stiff dough. Press the dough together with your fingertips.

Roll out the pastry on a lightly floured surface and use just over half of it to line twelve 7.5 cm/3 inch patty tins. Cut out 12 lids from the rest of the pastry. If liked, make holly leaf decorations from the pastry trimmings.

Place a spoonful of mincemeat in each pastry case. Dampen the edges of the cases and cover with the pastry lids. Seal the edges well. Brush the tops with water and add any pastry decorations. Dredge with the sugar. Make 2 small cuts in the top of each pie. Bake for 15–20 minutes or until golden brown.

MINESTRONE

SERVES 6

75 g/3 oz small haricot beans

15 ml/1 tbsp oil

2 rindless streaky bacon rashers, chopped

1 leek, trimmed, thinly sliced and washed

1 onion, chopped

1 garlic clove, crushed

2 carrots, thinly sliced

50 g/2 oz French beans, sliced

3 celery sticks, sliced

2 potatoes, diced

150 g/5 oz white cabbage, shredded

1 bay leaf

30 ml/2 tbsp tomato purée

1.25 litres/2¼ pints white stock

salt and pepper

50 g/2 oz small pasta shells or rings

Parmesan cheese to serve

Soak the beans overnight in water to cover. Next day, drain the beans. Put them in a saucepan with fresh water to cover. Bring to the boil, boil vigorously for 10 minutes, then drain thoroughly.

Heat the oil in a large saucepan, add the bacon, leek, onion and garlic and fry gently for about 10 minutes.

Add the remaining vegetables and cook, stirring frequently, for 2–3 minutes. Stir in the drained beans, with the bay leaf, tomato purée, stock and pepper. Do not add salt at this stage. Bring the soup to the boil, lower the heat, cover the pan and simmer for 45–60 minutes or until the haricot beans are tender. Add salt to taste.

Stir in the pasta and cook for 8–12 minutes or until tender but still firm to the bite. Remove the bay leaf. Grate the Parmesan cheese. Serve the soup at once, sprinkled with Parmesan cheese.

PRESSURE COOKER TIP

Minestrone can be made very successfully in the pressure cooker. Make the soup as suggested above, but do not add the cabbage with the other vegetables. Reduce the quantity of stock to 900 ml/1½ pints. Put the lid on and bring to 15 lb pressure. Cook for 10 minutes; reduce the pressure slowly. Add the cabbage and pasta, stirring well. Close the lid again, bring the soup back to 15 lb pressure and cook for 5 minutes more. Reduce the pressure slowly, remove the bay leaf and add salt to taste. Serve as suggested above.

MINT JELLY

1 kg/2¼ lb green apples

1 small bunch of mint

500 ml/17 fl oz distilled white vinegar

sugar (see method)

20 ml/4 tsp finely chopped mint

green food colouring (optional)

Wash the apples, cut into quarters and put in a preserving pan with the small bunch of mint. Add 500 ml/17 fl oz water, bring to the boil, lower the heat and simmer until the apples are soft and pulpy. Add the vinegar, bring to the boil and boil for 5 minutes.

Strain through a scalded jelly bag and leave to drip for several hours or overnight. Measure the juice and return it to the clean pan. Add 800 g/ 1¾ lb sugar for every 1 litre/1¾ pints of juice.

Heat gently, stirring until the sugar has dissolved, then boil rapidly until close to setting point. Stir in the chopped mint, with colouring, if used, and boil steadily until setting point is reached. Remove from the heat, pot and cover immediately.

MIXED FRUIT LOAF — *Illustrated on page 303*

MAKES ONE 23 X 13 X 7.5 CM/9 X 5 X 3 INCH
LOAF

fat for greasing

200 g/7 oz self-raising flour

pinch of salt

100 g/4 oz margarine

100 g/4 oz caster sugar

grated rind of 1 orange

225 g/8 oz mixed dried fruit, for
    example 25 g/1 oz glacé
    cherries, 25 g/1 oz cut mixed
    peel, 75 g/3 oz sultanas, 75 g/3
    oz seedless raisins

1 egg

milk (see method)

Line and grease a 23 x 13 x 7.5 cm/9 x 5 x 3 inch loaf tin. Set the oven at 180°C/350°F/gas 4.

Mix the flour and salt in a mixing bowl and rub in the margarine until the mixture resembles fine breadcrumbs. Stir in the sugar and orange rind. Wash and dry the cherries, if used, cut into 4–6 pieces each, depending on size, and add with the remaining fruit.

In a measuring jug, beat the egg lightly and add enough milk to make up to 125 ml/4 fl oz. Add to the flour mixture, stir in, then mix well. Spoon into the prepared tin and bake for about 1 hour or until firm to the touch. Cool the cake on a wire rack.

MICROWAVE TIP

The dried fruit may be cleaned and plumped in a single operation in the microwave. Place the fruit in a bowl with cold water to cover. Heat on High until the water boils, allow to stand until cool enough to handle, then drain the fruit, removing any stalks.

MIXED GRILL — *Illustrated on page 168*

SERVES 4

4 lamb cutlets

4 pork sausages

4 lambs' kidneys, skinned, cored
    and halved

a little oil

2 gammon rashers, rind
    removed and halved or
    8 rindless bacon rashers

salt and pepper

8 flat mushrooms

4 tomatoes

GARNISH (OPTIONAL)
fried bread

parsley sprigs

Trim excess fat from the cutlets. Place the sausages on the rack in the grill pan. Cook for 5 minutes, turning once, before adding the cutlets and lambs' kidneys to the rack. Brush with a little oil. If serving gammon, lay the steaks on the rack at the same time and brush with a little oil. If serving bacon, add after about 5 minutes.

Continue cooking, turning the sausages often and turning the cutlets, kidneys and gammon when browned on one side. Allow about 5 minutes on each side for the cutlets, depending on thickness. Brush occasionally with juices from the pan and rearrange the food so that it all cooks at the same rate, pushing the sausages to a cooler part of the grill when they are browned. Have a heated serving dish ready and transfer cooked items to it promptly.

Lastly, brush the mushrooms and tomatoes with cooking juices and sprinkle them with a little salt and pepper. Place them on the grill rack when the meats are almost cooked. Grill the mushrooms for 1–2 minutes on each side, so that they are very lightly cooked, and grill the tomatoes cut sides up for 2 minutes.

Arrange the grilled foods on a serving plate, adding fried bread and parsley sprigs if liked. Serve freshly cooked.

MOULES MARINIERE

SERVES 4 TO 6

1.6 kg/3½ lb mussels

1 onion, sliced

2 garlic cloves, cut in slivers

1 carrot, sliced

1 celery stick, sliced

1 bouquet garni

125 ml/4 fl oz white wine

25 g/1 oz butter

15 ml/1 tbsp plain flour

salt and pepper

chopped parsley to garnish

Wash, scrape and beard the mussels following the instructions on page 31. Put them in a large saucepan. Tuck the sliced vegetables among the mussels and add the bouquet garni.

Pour over 125 ml/4 fl oz water and the wine. Place over moderate heat and bring to the boil. As soon as the liquid begins to boil, shake the pan 2 or 3 times, cover it tightly and cook for about 5 minutes until the mussels have opened. Discard any that remain shut. With a slotted spoon transfer the mussels to a deep dish and keep hot.

Strain the cooking liquid through muslin or a very fine sieve into a smaller saucepan. In a cup, cream the butter with the flour. Place the small pan over moderate heat and add the butter and flour in small pieces, whisking thoroughly. Bring to the boil, whisking, then add salt and pepper.

Pour the thickened cooking liquid over the mussels, sprinkle with chopped parsley and serve with plenty of chunky bread.

MOUSSAKA

SERVES 4

fat for greasing

1 aubergine

salt and pepper

30 ml/2 tbsp olive oil

1 large onion, chopped

1 garlic clove, crushed

450 g/1 lb minced lamb or beef

10 ml/2 tsp chopped parsley

2 tomatoes, peeled, seeded and chopped

150 ml/¼ pint dry white wine

300 ml/½ pint milk

1 egg, plus 2 egg yolks

pinch of grated nutmeg

75 g/3 oz Kefalotiri or Parmesan cheese, grated

Grease a 20 x 10 x 10 cm (8 x 4 x 4 inch) baking dish. Set the oven at 180°C/350°F/gas 4. Cut the aubergine into 1 cm/½ inch slices, put them in a colander, and sprinkle generously with salt. Set aside.

Heat the olive oil. Gently fry the onion and garlic for about 10 minutes until the onion is soft. Add the mince and continue cooking, stirring with a fork to break up any lumps in the meat. When the meat is thoroughly browned, add salt, pepper, parsley and tomatoes. Mix well, then add the white wine.

In a bowl, beat the milk, whole egg, egg yolks, salt and a good pinch of grated nutmeg together. Add about half the cheese to the egg mixture, then beat again briefly.

Rinse and drain the aubergine slices and pat dry with absorbent kitchen paper. Place half in the bottom of the prepared dish and cover with the meat mixture. Lay the remaining aubergine slices on the meat and pour the milk and egg mixture over them. Sprinkle the remaining cheese on top. Bake for 30–40 minutes, until golden brown.

MULLET WITH TOMATOES

SERVES 4

25 g/1 oz butter

225 g/8 oz onions, thinly sliced

225 g/8 oz tomatoes, peeled, seeded and sliced

4 (225 g/8 oz) grey mullet, cleaned and trimmed

100 ml/3½ fl oz dry white wine

salt and pepper

15 ml/1 tbsp chopped fresh tarragon or 5 ml/1 tsp dried tarragon

1 lemon, sliced

sippets (see Mrs Beeton's Tip), to garnish

Use the butter to grease a shallow ovenproof baking dish and a sheet of greaseproof paper. Set the oven at 190°C/375°F/gas 5.

Spread out the onion rings on the base of the dish and top with the sliced tomatoes. Lay the fish on top of the vegetables and pour the wine over. Sprinkle with salt, pepper and tarragon.

Arrange the lemon slices on top of the fish and cover loosely with the buttered greaseproof paper. Bake for 30 minutes. Garnish with sippets and serve from the dish.

MRS BEETON'S TIP

To make sippets, toast white or Granary bread until golden. Cut into triangles, cubes or fancy shapes.

MULLIGATAWNY

SERVES 8

25 g/1 oz butter

30 ml/2 tbsp oil

1 chicken, skinned and jointed or 900 g/2 lb chicken portions

4 rindless back bacon rashers, chopped

3 onions, sliced

1 garlic clove, crushed

15 ml/1 tbsp mild curry powder

25 g/1 oz ground almonds

2 litres/3½ pints chicken stock

175 g/6 oz red lentils

salt and pepper

hot boiled rice to serve

Heat the butter and oil in a large, heavy-bottomed saucepan. Add the chicken and brown the joints all over, then remove them from the pan and set aside. Add the bacon, onions and garlic to the fat remaining in the pan and cook over gentle heat for 5 minutes, then stir in the curry powder and cook for 2 minutes more.

In a small bowl, mix the ground almonds to a paste with a little of the stock. Set aside. Add the remaining stock to the pan and return the chicken joints. Bring to the boil, lower the heat and simmer for 1 hour or until the chicken is tender.

Remove the chicken and cut the meat off the bones, then set aside. Skim any fat off the soup. Add the lentils and bring back to the boil. Reduce the heat, cover and simmer the soup for 30 minutes.

Stir the almond paste into the pan and replace the chicken meat. Simmer for a further 5–10 minutes. Taste for seasoning before serving very hot, with boiled rice.

MUSHROOMS IN CREAM SAUCE

SERVES 4 TO 6

50 g/2 oz butter

450 g/1 lb small button
   mushrooms

10 ml/2 tsp arrowroot

125 ml/4 fl oz chicken or
   vegetable stock

15 ml/1 tbsp lemon juice

30 ml/2 tbsp double cream

salt and pepper

30 ml/2 tbsp chopped parsley

Melt the butter in large frying pan, add the mushrooms and fry over gentle heat without browning for 10 minutes.

Put the arrowroot in a small bowl. Stir in 30 ml/2 tbsp of the stock until smooth. Add the remaining stock to the mushrooms and bring to the boil. Lower the heat and simmer gently for 15 minutes, stirring occasionally. Stir in the arrowroot mixture, bring to the boil, stirring, then remove the pan from the heat.

Stir in the lemon juice and cream, with salt and pepper to taste. Serve sprinkled with parsley.

MUSHROOM STUFFING

Although this stuffing is recommended for fish, it is also very good with all poultry and game birds.

SUFFICIENT FOR 8 (75 G/3 OZ) THIN FISH FILLETS OR 2 PHEASANTS

1 rindless streaky bacon rasher,
   chopped

100 g/4 oz button mushrooms
   with stalks, chopped

100 g/4 oz fresh white
   breadcrumbs

knob of butter or margarine

pinch of grated nutmeg

salt and pepper

1 egg

Put the bacon in a heavy-bottomed saucepan over moderate heat for about 2 minutes or until the fat runs.

Add the mushrooms and fry very gently for 3–5 minutes, stirring frequently. When the mushrooms soften, remove the pan from the heat and stir in the breadcrumbs, butter or margarine and nutmeg. Add salt and pepper to taste.

Beat the egg in a cup until it is just liquid, then stir enough of the beaten egg into the stuffing to bind it. Use as required.

MRS BEETON'S TIP

It is a good idea to keep a stock of breadcrumbs in a sealed polythene bag in the freezer. They thaw swiftly and can be used in a wide variety of sweet and savoury dishes.

MUSHROOMS WITH HAM STUFFING

SERVES 6

fat for greasing

12 large flat mushrooms

25 g/1 oz butter or margarine

1 onion, finely chopped

50 g/2 oz cooked ham, finely
  chopped

15 ml/1 tbsp fresh white
  breadcrumbs

10 ml/2 tsp grated Parmesan
  cheese

10 ml/2 tsp chopped parsley

white wine

salt and pepper

Generously grease an ovenproof dish. Set the oven at 190°C/375°F/
gas 5.

Clean the mushrooms and remove the stalks. Place the caps in the
prepared dish, gills uppermost. Chop the stalks finely.

Melt the butter or margarine in a pan and fry the mushroom stalks and
onion gently for 5 minutes. Add the ham to the onion mixture together
with the breadcrumbs, Parmesan and parsley. Add just enough white
wine to bind the mixture together. Add salt and pepper to taste.

Divide the stuffing mixture between the mushroom caps, heaping it up
in the centre. Cover and bake for 25 minutes.

NEWCASTLE PUDDING

SERVES 6

fat for greasing

25 g/1 oz glacé cherries, halved

100 g/4 oz butter or margarine

100 g/4 oz caster sugar

2 eggs, beaten

150 g/5 oz plain flour

pinch of salt

5 ml/1 tsp baking powder

about 45 ml/3 tbsp milk

single cream to serve

Grease a 1 litre/1¾ pint pudding basin. With the cherries, make a pattern on the base of the basin. Prepare a steamer or half fill a large saucepan with water and bring to the boil.

Cream the butter or margarine with the sugar in a mixing bowl. Gradually beat in the eggs, adding a little flour if the mixture begins to curdle.

Sift the flour with the salt and baking powder and stir into the pudding mixture with enough milk to give a soft dropping consistency. Spoon the mixture into the prepared basin, cover with greased greaseproof paper and foil and secure with string.

Put the pudding in the perforated part of the steamer, or stand it on an old saucer or plate in the pan of boiling water. The water should come halfway up the sides of the basin. Cover the pan tightly and steam the pudding over gently simmering water for 1½–2 hours.

Leave for 5–10 minutes at room temperature to firm up, then turn out on to a serving plate. Serve with single cream.

NOODLES WITH MUSHROOMS

SERVES 4

15 g/½ oz butter

30 ml/2 tbsp oil

2 rindless streaky bacon rashers, chopped

450 g/1 lb open mushrooms, sliced

salt and pepper

350 g/12 oz noodles

150 ml/¼ pint single cream

Melt the butter in the oil in a large frying pan. Add the bacon and fry for 2 minutes, then stir in the mushrooms. Add salt and pepper to taste and cook over moderately high heat, stirring occasionally, for 10 minutes.

Meanwhile cook the noodles in a large saucepan of boiling salted water for 8–10 minutes or until tender but still firm to the bite.

Stir the cream into the mushrooms and heat through over low heat. Drain the noodles thoroughly, pour the mushroom mixture over the top and toss lightly. Serve at once.

OATCAKES

MAKES ABOUT 16

fat for greasing

25 g/1 oz bacon fat or dripping

225 g/8 oz medium oatmeal

1.25 ml/¼ tsp salt

1.25 ml/¼ tsp bicarbonate of
  soda

fine oatmeal for rolling out

Grease two baking sheets. Set the oven at 160°C/325°F/gas 3.

Melt the bacon fat or dripping in a large saucepan. Remove from the heat and stir in the dry ingredients, then add 60–75 ml/4–5 tbsp boiling water to make a stiff dough.

When cool enough to handle, knead the dough thoroughly, then cut it in half. Roll out one portion of dough on a surface dusted with fine oatmeal, to a circle measuring about 18 cm/7 inch in diameter and about 5 mm/¼ inch thick. Cut into eight wedges and transfer to the prepared baking sheets. Repeat with the remaining dough. Bake for 20–30 minutes. Cool on a wire rack.

OKRA AND AUBERGINE BAKE

SERVES 6

1 aubergine

salt and pepper

400 g/14 oz okra

60 ml/4 tbsp olive oil

1 onion, finely chopped

2 garlic cloves, crushed

10 ml/2 tsp fennel seeds

3 tomatoes, peeled and sliced

10 ml/2 tsp chopped fresh
  marjoram

60 ml/4 tbsp wholemeal
  breadcrumbs

15 ml/1 tbsp butter

Set the oven at 190°C/375°F/gas 5. Cut the ends off the aubergine and cut it into cubes. Put the cubes in a colander and sprinkle generously with salt. Set aside for 30 minutes.

Meanwhile wash the okra in cold water. Pat dry on absorbent kitchen paper. Trim but do not completely remove the stems. Rinse the aubergines thoroughly, drain and pat dry.

Heat the oil in a flameproof casserole, add the onion, garlic, fennel seeds and aubergine and cook over gentle heat for about 20 minutes until the onion is soft but not coloured and the aubergine is tender. Stir in the okra, tomatoes and marjoram.

Sprinkle the breadcrumbs over the top of the casserole, dot with the butter and bake for 15–20 minutes. Serve at once.

MRS BEETON'S TIP

When preparing the okra, take care not to split the pods or the sticky juices inside will be lost and the okra will lose their shape during cooking.

OFFAL For basic information, see pages 75–77. See also Devilled Kidneys, Faggots, Kidneys Turbigo, Liver Hot Pot, Liver Pâté and Tripe and Onions.

OMELETTE

The secret of a light omelette is to add water, not milk, to the mixture, beating it only sufficiently to mix the yolks and whites. The mixture must be cooked quickly until evenly and lightly set, then served when still moist. Have everything ready before you start to cook, including the diner, so that the omelette can be taken to the table as soon as it is ready.

SERVES 1

2 eggs

salt and pepper

15 ml/1 tbsp unsalted butter or margarine

MRS BEETON'S TIP

In Mrs Beeton's day, most households would have a special omelette pan. When new, this would be 'seasoned' by melting a little butter in the pan, sprinkling it with salt, and rubbing vigorously with a soft cloth. This process helped to prevent the egg mixture from sticking. The omelette pan would not be washed after use; instead it would be rubbed all over with a soft cloth. Salt would be used, if necessary, to remove any egg still sticking to the pan.

Break the eggs into a bowl, add 15 ml/1 tbsp cold water, salt and pepper. Beat lightly with a fork. Thoroughly heat a frying pan or omelette pan. When it is hot, add the butter or margarine, tilting the pan so that the whole surface is lightly greased. Without drawing the pan off the heat, add the egg mixture. Leave to stand for 10 seconds.

Using a spatula, gently draw the egg mixture from the sides towards the centre as it sets, allowing the uncooked egg mixture to run in to fill the gap. Do not stir or the mixture will scramble.

When the omelette is golden and set underneath, but still slightly moist on top, remove it from the heat. Loosen the edges by shaking the pan, using a round-bladed knife or the edge of a spatula if the omelette sticks, then flip one-third of the omelette towards the centre. Flip the opposite third over towards the centre. Tip the omelette on to a hot plate, folded sides underneath.

Alternatively, the cooked omelette may be rolled out of the pan after the first folding, so that it is served folded in three. A simpler method is to fold the omelette in half in the pan, then slide it out on to the plate.

omelette fillings

CHEESE Add 40 g/1½ oz grated cheese to the beaten eggs. Sprinkle a further 15 g/½ oz over the omelette.

FINES HERBES Add 2.5 ml/½ tsp chopped fresh tarragon, 2.5 ml/½ tsp chopped fresh chervil, 5 ml/1 tsp chopped parsley and a few snipped chives to the beaten eggs.

HAM Add 50 g/2 oz chopped ham to the egg mixture.

FISH Add 50 g/2 oz flaked cooked fish to the omelette just before folding.

BACON Grill 2 rindless bacon rashers until crisp; crumble into the centre of the omelette just before folding.

MUSHROOM Fry 50 g/2 oz sliced mushrooms in butter. Spoon into the centre of the omelette just before folding.

SHRIMP OR PRAWN Sauté 50 g/2 oz shrimps or prawns in a little butter in a saucepan. Add a squeeze of lemon juice and spoon into the omelette before folding.

CHICKEN Chop 25 g/1 oz cooked chicken. Mix with 60 ml/4 tbsp white sauce. Heat gently in a small saucepan. Spoon into the centre of the omelette before folding.

Omelette Arnold Bennett

SERVES 2

150 g/5 oz smoked haddock

25 g/1 oz unsalted butter

60 ml/4 tbsp single cream

2 eggs, separated

salt and pepper

30 ml/2 tbsp grated Parmesan
  cheese

parsley sprigs to garnish

Bring a saucepan of water to simmering point, add the haddock and poach gently for 10 minutes. Using a slotted spoon transfer the fish to a large plate. Remove any skin or bones. Flake the fish into a large bowl and add half the butter and 15 ml/1 tbsp of the cream. Mix well.

In a separate bowl mix the egg yolks with 15 ml/1 tbsp of the remaining cream. Add salt and pepper to taste. Add to the fish mixture and stir in half the cheese.

In a clean dry bowl, whisk the egg whites until stiff. Fold them into the fish mixture.

Heat half the remaining butter in an omelette pan. Pour in half the fish mixture and cook quickly until golden brown underneath. Sprinkle over half the remaining cheese, spoon over 15 ml/1 tbsp of the remaining cream and brown quickly under a hot grill. Do not fold. Very quickly make a second omelette in the same way. Garnish and serve at once.

One-stage fruit cake

MAKES ONE 18 CM/7INCH CAKE

fat for greasing

225 g/8 oz self-raising flour

5 ml/1 tsp mixed spice
  (optional)

100 g/4 oz soft margarine

100 g/4 oz glacé cherries,
  chopped

100 g/4 oz currants

75 g/3 oz sultanas

25 g/1 oz cut mixed peel

100 g/4 oz soft light brown
  sugar

2 eggs

75 ml/3 fl oz milk

Line and grease an 18 cm/7 inch round cake tin. Set the oven at 180°C/350°F/gas 4. Mix the flour and spice, if used.

Put all the ingredients in a bowl, stir, then beat until smooth, allowing 2–3 minutes by hand or 1–1½ minutes with an electric mixer. Spoon the mixture into the prepared tin and bake for 2 hours. Cool on a wire rack.

MRS BEETON'S TIP

The cherries will be easy to chop if you use a pair of kitchen scissors and dip the blades in boiling water first.

ONE-STAGE VICTORIA SANDWICH

MAKES ONE 18 CM/7 INCH CAKE

fat for greasing
150 g/5 oz self-raising flour
pinch of salt
150 g/5 oz soft margarine
150 g/5 oz caster sugar
3 eggs

Line and grease two 18 cm/7 inch sandwich cake tins. Set the oven at 180°C/350°F/gas 4.

Put all the ingredients in a mixing bowl and stir. Beat until smooth, allowing 2–3 minutes by hand or 1–1½ minutes with an electric mixer.

Divide the mixture evenly between the tins; level each surface. Bake for 25–30 minutes. Turn out the cakes and cool on a wire rack, then fill and top as desired.

flavourings and fillings

The basic mixture for Victoria Sandwich Cake can be adapted to make a variety of cakes. For example, sweet spices or citrus rinds can be added to the mixture. Alternatively flavourings such as vanilla essence or almond essence can be added in small quantities to alter the result slightly.

There is a wide variety of commercial preserves and sweet spreads available and many of these are ideal for filling the sandwich cake. Try any of the following ideas:

CHOCOLATE SANDWICH CAKE Substitute 60 ml/4 tbsp of cocoa for an equal quantity of the flour. Sift the cocoa with the flour and continue as in the main recipe. Sandwich the cooled cakes together with chocolate spread and sift a little icing sugar over the top of the chocolate cake.

CINNAMON AND APPLE SANDWICH CAKE Add 10 ml/2 tsp ground cinnamon to the flour. Continue as in the main recipe. Peel, core and slice a large cooking apple, then cook it with a little sugar until it is reduced to a pulp. Press the pulp through a sieve, return it to the saucepan and add 10 ml/2 tsp of cornflour blended with 30 ml/2 tbsp of milk. Bring to the boil, stirring, and cook until thickened. Sweeten the Purée to taste, then leave it to cool. Gradually fold in 50 ml/2 fl oz of whipped double cream, then use this apple cream to sandwich the cooled cakes together.

COFFEE SANDWICH CAKE Dissolve 30 ml/2 tbsp of instant coffee in 30 ml/2 tbsp boiling water and leave to cool. Fold this into the mixture last. Whip 150 ml/¼ pint double cream with 5 ml/1 tsp of instant coffee dissolved in 15 ml/1 tbsp of boiling water and 30 ml/2 tbsp of icing sugar. Sandwich the cooled cakes with this coffee cream.

GINGER SANDWICH CAKE The combination of ground ginger and lemon rind makes a delicious cake. Add the grated rind of 1 lemon to the fat and sugar. Sift 15 ml/1 tbsp of ground ginger with the flour. Prepare and bake the cake as in the main recipe. When cool, sandwich the layers with ginger marmalade.

ONE-STAGE VICTORIA SANDWICH — *continued*

HARLEQUIN SANDWICH CAKE Make the cake mixture as in the main recipe, then put half in one sandwich cake tin. Add pink food colouring to the second portion of mixture, making it a fairly strong colour. Put the second portion in the other sandwich cake tin and bake the cake. When cool, cut both cakes into rings: cut a 5 cm/2 inch circle from the middle of each cake, then cut a 10 cm/4 inch circle around it. Either use plain pastry cutters or cut out circles of paper and use a pointed knife to cut around them. You should have three rings of each cake. Carefully put the rings of cake together alternating the colours to make two layers. Sandwich the layers together with raspberry jam. Spread warmed raspberry jam over the top of the cake and sift icing sugar over it. Alternatively, fill the cake with whipped cream and swirl more whipped cream over the top. When slices are cut the pattern will show.

LEMON SANDWICH CAKE Add the grated rind of 1 large lemon to the fat and sugar. Continue as in the main recipe, then sandwich the cooled cakes together with lemon curd.

MOCHA SANDWICH CAKE Substitute 30 ml/2 tbsp of cocoa for an equal quantity of flour and sift it with the flour. Prepare the mixture as in the main recipe. Dissolve 10 ml/2 tsp of instant coffee in 15 ml/1 tbsp of boiling water and add it to the mixture. Sandwich the cooled cakes together with chocolate spread.

ORANGE SANDWICH CAKE Add the grated rind of 1 large orange to the fat and sugar, then continue as in the main recipe. Sandwich the cooled cakes together with orange marmalade.

ONION SOUP

SERVES 4 TO 6

50 g/2 oz butter

4 large onions, finely chopped

50 g/2 oz plain flour

1.1 litres/2 pints white stock

salt and white pepper

1.25 ml/¼ tsp ground mace

2 egg yolks

150 ml/¼ pint double cream

Melt the butter in the top of a double saucepan. Add the onions and cook over gentle heat for 10 minutes until soft but not coloured.

Stir in the flour and cook for 1 minute, then gradually add the stock. Cook over moderate heat until the mixture boils and thickens. Season to taste with salt, pepper and mace.

Set over simmering water and cook the soup, stirring occasionally, for about 30 minutes or until the onions are very tender and the soup is creamy.

In a small bowl, mix the egg yolks with the cream. Stir a little of the hot soup into the egg mixture, mix well, then add the contents of the bowl to the soup, stirring over the simmering water until it thickens. Serve.

ORANGE MARMALADE

MAKES ABOUT 4 KG/9 LB

1.5 kg/3¼ lb Seville or bitter
 oranges

2 lemons

1 sweet orange

sugar (see method)

MRS BEETON'S TIP

If a very clear jelly is required,
do not squeeze the muslin bag;
instead tie it to the handle and
allow the liquid to drip slowly
back into the pan.

Wash the oranges and lemons. Squeeze the fruit and strain the juice into
a large bowl. Reserve the fruit shells, pulp and pips.

Scrape all the pith from the shells and put it in a large bowl with the
pulp and pips. Add 2 litres/3½ pints water and set aside. Shred the
orange and lemon peel finely and add it to the bowl of juice. Stir in
2 litres/3½ pints water. Leave both mixtures to soak for 24 hours if liked.

Line a strainer with muslin and strain the liquid containing the pips into
a preserving pan. Bring up the sides of the muslin and tie to make a bag
containing the pith, pips and pulp. Add the bag to the pan, with the contents of the second bowl. Bring the liquid to simmering point and simmer
for 1½ hours or until the peel is tender.

Remove from the heat. Squeeze the muslin bag between two plates
over the pan to extract as much of the pectin-rich juice as possible (see
Mrs Beeton's Tip).

Measure the liquid, return it to the pan and add 800 g/1¾ lb sugar for
every litre/1¾ pints of juice. Heat gently until the sugar has dissolved,
then bring to the boil and boil fast until setting point is reached. Remove
from the heat and skim quickly.

Leave to cool slightly until a skin forms on the surface, then pot and
top with waxed paper discs. Cover and label when cold.

Osso buco — *Illustrated on page 266*

SERVES 4

450 g/1 lb tomatoes, peeled, seeded and chopped

30 ml/2 tbsp tomato purée

200 ml/7 fl oz beef stock

salt and pepper

50 g/2 oz plain flour

4 veal knuckles or shank slices

60 ml/4 tbsp oil

1 onion, finely chopped

2 each garlic cloves, carrots and celery sticks, finely chopped

juice of 1 lemon

150 ml/¼ pint dry white wine

2 bay leaves

2 fresh thyme sprigs

GREMOLADA

45 ml/3 tbsp chopped parsley

1 garlic clove, chopped

grated rind of lemon

Set the oven at 180°C/350°F/gas 4. Put the tomatoes, with any juices, into a bowl. Stir in the tomato purée and stock, with salt and pepper to taste. Set the mixture aside.

Put the flour in a stout polythene or paper bag. Season with salt and pepper. Add the veal knuckles or shank slices and toss until well coated. Shake off excess flour. Heat the oil in a large flameproof casserole, add the meat and fry for about 8 minutes, turning once or twice, until browned all over. With tongs, transfer the meat to a plate and set aside.

Add the onion, garlic, carrots and celery to the fat remaining in the casserole. Fry over gentle heat for 6–8 minutes or until the onion is golden brown. Add the reserved tomato mixture and bring to the boil, scraping in any sediment on the base of the pan. Remove from the heat and add the lemon juice and wine, with the bay leaves and thyme.

Return the veal to the casserole, pushing the pieces well down so that they are completely covered by the sauce. Cover the dish tightly with foil and a lid and bake for 12 hours or until the meat is very tender. Remove the bay leaves and thyme sprigs. If necessary, place the casserole over moderate heat for 5–10 minutes, stirring occasionally, to reduce the sauce.

Make the gremolada by mixing all the ingredients together in a small bowl. Sprinkle over the osso buco just before serving.

Oxtail hot pot

SERVES 4

1 kg/2¼ lb oxtail, jointed

30 ml/2 tbsp plain flour

salt and pepper

2 large onions, thinly sliced

800 g/1¾ lb potatoes, sliced

5 ml/1 tsp dried mixed herbs

beef stock (see method)

6 rindless streaky bacon rashers, cut in small squares

Set the oven at 180°C/350°F/gas 4. Wash the oxtail, dry it thoroughly and trim off any excess fat. Mix the flour with salt and pepper, and use to coat the oxtail. Place alternate layers of onions, oxtail and potatoes in a pie dish or casserole, sprinkling each layer with salt, pepper and dried mixed herbs, and ending with a layer of potatoes.

Pour in just enough beef stock to cover the meat. Cover the casserole and bake for 2–3 hours, or until the meat is tender. Check the hot pot from time to time, and add more stock if necessary.

Remove the lid from the casserole, lay the bacon rashers over the top and bake for 30 minutes more. Serve.

PAELLA — *Illustrated on page 129*

Illustrated on page 129

SERVES 8

1 kg/2¼ lb mussels, washed, scraped and bearded

30 ml/2 tbsp plain flour

1 (1.5 kg/3¼ lb) roasting chicken, cut into portions

90 ml/6 tbsp olive oil

2 garlic cloves

675 g/1½ lb risotto rice

pinch of saffron threads

salt

GARNISH

450 g/1 lb cooked shellfish (prawns, crayfish, lobster or crab; see Mrs Beeton's Tip)

strips of canned pimiento

green or black olives

chopped parsley

Wash, scrape and beard the mussels, following the instructions on page 31. Put them in a large saucepan with 125 ml/4 fl oz water. Place over moderate heat and bring to the boil.

As soon as the liquid bubbles up over the mussels, shake the pan two or three times, cover, lower the heat and simmer until the mussels have opened. Discard any that remain shut. Remove the mussels with a slotted spoon and shell them, retaining the best half shells. Strain the mussel liquid through muslin into a large measuring jug, add the cooking liquid and make up to 1.25 litres/2¼ pints with water. Set aside.

Put the flour in a stout polythene bag, add the chicken portions and shake until well coated. Heat 45 ml/3 tbsp of the olive oil in a large frying pan, add the chicken and fry until golden brown on all sides. Using tongs, transfer the chicken to a plate and set aside.

Heat the remaining oil in a large deep frying pan or paella pan. Slice half a garlic clove thinly and add the slices to the oil. Fry until golden brown, then discard the garlic. Add the rice to the pan and fry very gently, turning frequently with a spatula. Crush the remaining garlic. Pound the saffron to a powder with a pestle in a mortar and sprinkle it over the rice with the garlic. Add salt to taste.

Add the reserved cooking liquid to the pan and heat to simmering point, stirring frequently. Cook for 5 minutes, still stirring. Add the chicken pieces, cooking them with the rice for 15–20 minutes until they are tender and the rice is cooked through.

Garnish with the shellfish, pimiento, olives and parsley. Replace the mussels in the half shells and arrange them on top of the rice mixture. Remove the pan from the heat, cover with a clean cloth and set aside for 10 minutes before serving. Serve from the pan.

MRS BEETON'S TIP

The weight of shellfish depends on the types included: increase the quantity if adding lots of crab claws or lobster.

PANCAKES

Pancakes are much too good to be reserved exclusively for Shrove Tuesday. Simple, versatile, and always popular, they lend themselves to a wide range of savoury and sweet fillings.

MAKES 8

100 g/4 oz plain flour

1.25 ml/¼ tsp salt

1 egg, beaten

250 ml/8 fl oz milk, or half milk and half water

oil for frying

Make the batter. Sift the flour and salt into a bowl, make a well in the centre and add the beaten egg. Stir in half the milk (or all the milk, if using a mixture of milk and water), gradually working the flour down from the sides. Beat vigorously until the mixture is smooth and bubbly, then stir in the rest of the milk (or the water), Pour into a jug. The mixture may be left to stand at this stage, in which case it should be covered and stored in the refrigerator.

Heat a little oil in a clean 18 cm/7 inch pancake pan. Pour off any excess oil, leaving the pan covered with a thin film of grease. Stir the batter and pour about 30–45 ml/2–3 tbsp into the pan. There should be just enough to thinly cover the base. Tilt and rotate the pan so that the batter runs over the surface evenly.

Cook over moderate heat for about 1 minute until the pancake is set and golden brown underneath. Make sure the pancake is loose by shaking the pan, then either toss it or turn it with a palette knife or fish slice. Cook the second side for about 30 seconds or until golden.

Slide the pancake out on to a warmed plate. Serve at once, with a sauce or filling, or keep warm over simmering water while making 7 more pancakes in the same way. Add more oil to the pan when necessary.

savoury pancake fillings

Reheat savoury pancakes in a 180°C/350°F/gas 4 oven for 30 minutes if they have a cold filling; 20 minutes if the filling is hot. Pancakes topped with grated cheese may be browned under the grill.

ASPARAGUS Add 30 ml/2 tbsp thawed frozen chopped spinach to the pancake batter, if liked. Place a trimmed slice of ham on each pancake, top with a large asparagus spear and roll up. Cover the rolled pancakes with 600 ml/1 pint Béchamel sauce, reheat, then sprinkle with grated Gruyère cheese and grill to brown.

CHICKEN AND MUSHROOM Sauté 175 g/6 oz sliced mushrooms in 45 ml/3 tbsp butter for 2–3 minutes. Stir in 15 ml/1 tbsp plain flour and cook for 1 minute, then gradually add 150 ml/¼ pint chicken stock. Bring to the boil, stirring. Add 5 ml/1 tsp mushroom ketchup, if liked. Stir in 75 g/3 oz chopped cooked chicken. Fill the pancakes and reheat.

SPINACH PANCAKES Cook 300 g/11 oz frozen spinach; drain well. Add 200 g/7 oz cottage cheese, 50 g/2 oz grated mature Cheddar cheese, 100 ml/3½ fl oz double cream, a pinch of nutmeg and seasoning. Fill the pancakes, sprinkle with 25 g/1 oz grated cheese and reheat.

continued over

PANCAKES — *continued*

sweet pancake fillings

Lemon juice and caster sugar share the honours with warmed jam as the most common fillings for pancakes. Here are a few more ideas: Spoon the chosen filling on to the pancakes and roll up. If liked, sprinkle the rolled pancakes with caster sugar, and glaze in a very hot oven or under a hot grill.

APPLE In a bowl, mix together 250 ml/8 fl oz sweetened thick apple pureé, 50 g/2 oz sultanas and a pinch of cinnamon.

APRICOT Add 15 ml/1 tbsp cinnamon to the pancake batter. Soak 50 g/2 oz dried apricots in 60 ml/4 tbsp water in a saucepan, then simmer with 50 g/2 oz sugar and a generous squeeze of lemon juice until soft and pulpy. Add 25 g/1 oz chopped toasted almonds.

BANANA In a bowl, mash 4 bananas with 50 g/2 oz softened butter, 30 ml/2 tbsp sugar and the grated rind and juice of 1 lemon.

CHOCOLATE AND WHIPPED CREAM Whip 150 ml/¼ pint double cream with 15–30 ml/1–2 tbsp icing sugar until it stands in soft peaks. Gently fold in 100 g/4 oz grated chocolate and 30 ml/2 tbsp finely chopped toasted hazelnuts. Swirl this on the pancakes, fold into quarters and serve at once.

CURD CHEESE In a bowl, beat 100 g/4 oz curd cheese with 45 ml/3 tbsp double cream, 30 ml/2 tbsp caster sugar and the grated rind of ½ lemon. Add 40 g/1½ oz sultanas.

DRIED FRUIT Put 100 g/4 oz chopped raisins, dates and cut mixed peel into a small saucepan with 100 ml/3½ fl oz apple juice. Simmer until syrupy.

GINGER AND BANANA Add 15 ml/1 tbsp ground ginger to the batter when making the pancakes, if liked. For the filling, mash 4 bananas in a bowl with 30 ml/2 tbsp double cream. Add a few pieces of chopped preserved ginger.

MAPLE SYRUP AND ICE CREAM Trickle about 10 ml/2 tsp maple syrup over each pancake and roll up. Arrange on serving plates and top with good-quality Cornish ice cream. Sprinkle with chopped walnuts.

PINEAPPLE Drain 1 (227 g/8 oz) can crushed pineapple. Combine the fruit with 250 ml/8 fl oz soured cream in a bowl. Fill the pancakes with this mixture and serve with a sauce made by heating the fruit syrup with a few drops of the lemon juice.

PARSNIP SOUP

SERVES 4

25 g/1 oz butter

1 onion, chopped

450 g/1 lb parsnips, sliced

1 litre/1¾ pints chicken or
    vegetable stock

salt and cayenne pepper

150 ml/¼ pint single cream

30 ml/2 tbsp pine nuts
    (optional)

Melt the butter in a large saucepan, add the onion and parsnips, and cook over gentle heat for 10 minutes, turning frequently to coat them in the butter. Add the stock, with salt and cayenne pepper to taste. Bring to the boil, lower the heat and simmer for 20 minutes until the parsnips are very soft.

Purée the soup in a blender or food processor, or rub through a sieve into a clean pan. Reheat it to just below boiling point, then stir in most of the cream, reserving about 30 ml/2 tbsp for the garnish.

Meanwhile spread out the pine nuts (if used) in a grill pan and toast them under a hot grill until golden. Ladle the soup into individual bowls and top each portion with a swirl of cream and a sprinkling of toasted pine nuts.

variation

SPICED PARSNIP SOUP Add 5 ml/1 tsp good-quality curry powder to the onion and parsnips when cooking in the butter. Substitute plain yogurt for the cream and use roughly chopped cashew nuts instead of the pine nuts. Sprinkle with a little chopped fresh coriander leaves, if liked.

PASTA

Home-made pasta dough may be used to make noodles, lasagne or stuffed pasta (such as ravioli). Alternatively, it may be cut into small squares for cooking.

MAKES ABOUT 450 G/1 LB

400 g/14 oz strong white flour

2.5 ml/½ tsp salt

30 ml/2 tbsp olive oil or
  40 g/1½ oz butter, melted

3 eggs, beaten

about 15 ml/1 tbsp oil for
  cooking

about 50 g/2 oz butter

freshly ground black pepper

FREEZER TIP

Roll out and cut up the pasta, then freeze it in practical quantities. Fresh pasta freezes very well and cooks from frozen, taking 2–3 minutes longer than usual.

Put the flour and salt in a large bowl and make a well in the middle. Add the oil or butter and the eggs, then gradually mix in the flour to make a stiff dough. As the mixture clumps together use your hands to knead it into one piece. If necessary add 15–30 ml/1–2 tbsp water, but take care not to make the mixture soft. It should be quite hard at this stage as it will become more pliable on kneading.

Knead the dough thoroughly on a very lightly floured surface for 10–15 minutes, or until it is very smooth and pliable. Ideally you should be able to work without dusting the surface with flour more than once, provided you keep the dough moving fairly fast all the time.

Cut the dough in half and wrap one piece in polythene to prevent it from drying out. Roll out the dough, adding a dusting of flour as needed, into a large thin oblong sheet.

To cut noodles, dust the dough with flour and fold it in half, dust it again and fold over once more. Cut the folded dough into 1 cm/½ inch wide strips, then shake them out and place on a floured plate. Cover loosely with polythene to prevent them from drying out until they are cooked. Repeat with the remaining dough.

Bring a very large saucepan of salted water to the boil. Add a little oil. Tip all the noodles into the pan and bring the water back to the boil rapidly, stir once, then regulate the heat so that the water boils but does not froth over. Cook for about 3 minutes. The pasta should be tender but not soft.

Drain the pasta and turn it into a heated bowl. Toss a knob of butter and plenty of freshly ground black pepper with the noodles, then serve piping hot.

variations

PASTA VERDE Cook 225 g/8 oz fresh spinach, or 100 g/4 oz frozen chopped spinach. Drain the spinach thoroughly and purée in a blender or food processor. When making the pasta, use an extra 50 g/2 oz plain flour. Add the spinach purée to the well in the flour and mix it in with the eggs. It will not be necessary to add any water.

TOMATO PASTA Mix 30 ml/2 tbsp tomato purée with the oil or butter, then stir in the eggs before incorporating the mixture with the flour.

PASTA For basic information on pasta types, see page 109–110.

PASTRIES For basic information on pastry making, plus standard recipes, see pages 127–143. See index entries under Pastries, savoury and Pastries, sweet for a complete list of recipes.

PASTRY HORNS

MAKES 8

Puff Pastry (page 141), using 100 g/4 oz flour

flour for rolling out

beaten egg and milk for glazing

Roll out the pastry 5mm/¼ inch thick on a lightly floured surface, then cut into strips 35 cm/14 inches long and 2 cm/¾ inch wide. Moisten the strips with cold water.

Wind each strip around a cornet mould, working from the point upward, keeping the moistened surface on the outside. Lay the horns on a dampened baking sheet, with the final overlap of the pastry strip underneath. Leave in a cool place for 1 hour.

Set the oven at 220°C/425°F/gas 7. Brush the horns with beaten egg and milk. Bake for 10–15 minutes or until golden brown. Remove the moulds and return the horns to the oven for 5 minutes. Cool completely on a wire rack. When cold, fill the horns with a sweet or savoury filling.

PATE MAISON

MAKES ABOUT 1 KG/2¼ LB

8–10 rindless back bacon rashers

100 g/4 oz pig's liver, trimmed and coarsely chopped

100 g/4 oz rindless boned belly of pork, coarsely chopped

225 g/8 oz sausagemeat

225 g/8 oz cold cooked rabbit, finely chopped

1 onion, finely chopped

25 g/1 oz fresh white breadcrumbs

1 egg, beaten

15 ml/1 tbsp milk

75 ml/3 fl oz brandy

salt and pepper

3 bay leaves, to garnish

Set the oven at 180°C/350°F/gas 4. Arrange the bay leaves on the base of 1.25 litre/2¼ pint rectangular ovenproof dish or terrine. Lay the bacon rashers flat on a board, one at a time, and stretch them with the back of a knife until quite thin. Set aside two or three rashers for the topping and use the rest to line the dish, overlapping them neatly.

Combine the chopped liver, pork, sausagemeat, rabbit, onion and breadcrumbs in a mixing bowl. Stir in the egg, milk and brandy, with salt and pepper to taste. Spoon the mixture into the lined dish, cover with the reserved bacon rashers and then with a lid or foil. Stand the dish in a roasting tin and add enough hot water to come to within 2.5 cm/1 inch of the rim of the tin.

When cooked, weight the pâté and leave to cool. Chill for 18–24 hours. To serve, remove the top bacon rashers and invert the pate on a platter.

MRS BEETON'S TIP
Depending on the size of the container, a house brick can be ideal for weighting pâté. Brush the brick well, wrap it in paper and seal it in a clean polythene bag to prevent any transfer of dust to the food. Place on top of the covered pâté.

| PATE | For basic information on making pâtés, terrines and savoury mousses, see pages 11–12. See also Liver Pâté, Potted Shrimps or Prawns, Salmon Mousse and Smoked Mackerel Pâté. |

PAVLOVA

SERVES 4

3 egg whites

150 g/5 oz caster sugar

2.5 ml/½ tsp vinegar

2.5 ml/½ tsp vanilla essence

10 ml/2 tsp cornflourg

glacé cherries and angelica to
    decorate

FILLING

250 ml/8 fl oz double cream

caster sugar (see method)

2 peaches, skinned and sliced

Line a baking sheet with greaseproof paper or non-stick baking parchment. Draw a 20 cm/8 inch circle on the paper and very lightly grease the greaseproof paper, if used. Set the oven at 150°C/300°F/gas 2.

In a large bowl, whisk the egg whites until very stiff. Continue whisking, gradually adding the sugar until the mixture stands in stiff peaks. Beat in the vinegar, vanilla and cornflour.

Spread the meringue over the circle, piling it up at the edges to form a rim, or pipe the circle and rim from a piping bag fitted with a large star nozzle.

Bake for about 1 hour or until the pavlova is crisp on the outside and has the texture of marshmallow inside. It should be pale coffee in colour. Leave to cool, then carefully remove the paper. Put the pavlova on a large serving plate.

Make the filling by whipping the cream in a bowl with caster sugar to taste. Add the sliced peaches and pile into the cold pavlova shell. Decorate with glacé cherries and angelica and serve as soon as possible.

PEASE PUDDING

SERVES 6

575 g/1¼ lb split peas, soaked
    overnight in cold water to
    cover

1 small onion, peeled but left
    whole

1 bouquet garni

salt and pepper

50 g/2 oz butter, cut into small
    pieces

2 eggs, beaten

Drain the peas, put them in a saucepan and add cold water to cover. Add the onion, the bouquet garni and salt and pepper to taste. Bring to the boil, skim off any scum on the surface of the liquid, then reduce the heat to very low and simmer the peas for 2–2½ hours or until tender.

Drain the peas thoroughly. Press them through a sieve or pureé in a blender or food processor. Add the pieces of butter with the beaten eggs. Beat well.

Spoon the mixture into a floured pudding cloth and tie tightly. Suspend the bag in a large saucepan of boiling salted water and simmer gently for 1 hour. Remove from the pan, take the pudding out of the cloth and serve very hot. Alternatively, bake the pudding in a greased casserole for 30 minutes at 180°C/350°F/gas 4.

PEA SOUP

SERVES 4

675 g/1½ lb peas in the pod

15 ml/1 tbsp butter

1 onion, chopped

1 litre/1¾ pints white stock

salt and pepper

3–4 fresh young spinach leaves, roughly chopped

1 mint sprig

2–3 parsley sprigs

pinch of sugar (optional)

60 ml/4 tbsp single cream

GARNISH

60 ml/4 tbsp young fresh or frozen peas

4 small mint sprigs

Shell the peas, reserving about half the pods (the youngest and most tender). Melt the butter in a large saucepan. Add the onion and cook over gentle heat for 3–4 minutes. Add the pea pods, turning them over until coated in the butter, and cook gently for 10 minutes.

Stir in the stock, with salt and pepper to taste. Bring to the boil, then lower the heat and add the peas, spinach leaves, mint and parsley. Simmer for 10–20 minutes or until the peas are just tender.

Purée the soup in a blender or food processor, or rub through a sieve into a clean pan. Check the seasoning and add more salt and pepper if required. A pinch of sugar may also be added to bring out the flavour of the peas.

Reheat the soup to just below boiling point. (Do not allow the soup to boil after the peas have been added, or you will spoil the colour.) In a separate pan, cook the peas for the garnish in salted boiling water until tender. Remove the soup from the heat, swirl in the cream and serve in individual bowls. Using a slotted spoon, ladle 15 ml/1 tbsp freshly cooked peas into each bowl. Complete the garnish by adding the mint.

PESTO GENOVESE

A little pesto goes a long way to flavour pasta. Put the pasta in a heated serving bowl or individual dishes, add the pesto and toss lightly.

SERVES 4

2 garlic cloves, roughly chopped

25–40 g/1–1½ oz fresh basil leaves, roughly chopped

25 g/1 oz pine nuts, chopped

juice of 1 lemon

salt and pepper

40 g/1½ oz Parmesan cheese

75–100 ml/3–3½ fl oz olive oil

Combine the garlic, basil leaves, nuts, lemon juice, salt and pepper in a mortar. Grate in the Parmesan cheese. Pound with a pestle until smooth. Alternatively, process in a blender or food processor.

While blending, trickle in the oil as when making mayonnaise, until the sauce forms a very thick paste.

MRS BEETON'S TIP
Basil has a particular affinity with Italian dishes and it is worth growing it in a large pot on the patio during summer. For a simple starter with a wonderful taste, try sliced tomatoes topped with mozzarella cheese, a drizzle of olive oil and shredded fresh basil leaves.

PHEASANT WITH MUSHROOM STUFFING

SERVES 6

2 pheasants

½ onion

Mushroom Stuffing

50 g/2 oz butter

watercress sprigs to garnish

Wash the pheasant giblets. Put them in a saucepan, and cover with cold water. Add the half onion and simmer gently for 40 minutes to make stock for the gravy.

Set the oven at 190°C/375°F/gas 5. Divide the stuffing between the birds, filling the body cavities only. Truss the birds neatly and put them in a roasting tin; spread with the butter.

Roast for 45–60 minutes, depending on the size of the birds. Baste occasionally while roasting.

Transfer the birds to a heated serving dish and remove the trussing strings. Garnish with watercress and serve with gravy made from the giblet stock. Wild mushrooms, tossed in butter, are good with this dish.

PICCALILLI

MAKES ABOUT 1 KG/2¼ LB

450 g/1 lb green tomatoes, diced

½ small firm cauliflower, broken into florets

1 small cucumber, peeled, seeded and cubed

2 onions, roughly chopped

100 g/4 oz firm white cabbage, shredded

50 g/2 oz cooking salt

750 ml/1¼ pints vinegar

12 chillies

225 g/8 oz sugar

25 g/1 oz mustard powder

15 g/½ oz turmeric

30 ml/2 tbsp cornflour

Combine all the vegetables in a large bowl, sprinkle with the salt, cover and leave to stand for 24 hours. Rinse thoroughly, then drain well.

Heat the vinegar in a saucepan with the chillies. Boil for 2 minutes, leave to stand for 30 minutes, then strain the vinegar into a jug and allow to cool.

Combine the sugar, mustard, turmeric and cornflour in a large bowl. Mix to a paste with a little of the cooled vinegar. Bring the rest of the vinegar back to the boil in a saucepan, pour over the blended mixture, return to the pan; boil for 3 minutes.

Remove from the heat, stir in the drained vegetables, pack into clean jars and seal at once with vinegar-proof covers.

MRS BEETON'S TIP

This colourful pickle is made from a variety of vegetables. In addition to the selection listed, chopped peppers (green, yellow and red), young broad beans, shallots or marrow may be used. The prepared mixed vegetables should weigh about 1 kg/2¼ lb.

PICKLED ONIONS

This is a recipe for onions without tears. Soaking the unskinned onions in brine makes them easy to peel.

MAKES ABOUT 1.4 KG/3 LB

450 g/1 lb salt

1.4 kg/3 lb pickling onions

2.25 litres/4 pints cold Spiced Vinegar

5 ml/1 tsp mustard seeds (optional)

Dissolve half the salt in 2 litres/3½ pints of water in a large bowl. Add the onions. Set a plate inside the bowl to keep the onions submerged, weighting the plate with a jar filled with water. Do not use a can as the salt water would corrode it. Leave for 24 hours.

Drain and skin the onions and return them to the clean bowl. Make up a fresh solution of brine, using the rest of the salt and a further 2 litres/3½ pints water. Pour it over the onions, weight as before and leave for a further 24 hours.

Drain the onions, rinse them thoroughly to remove excess salt, and drain again. Pack into wide-mouthed jars. Cover with cold spiced vinegar, adding a few mustard seeds to each jar, if liked. Cover with vinegar-proof lids. Label and store in a cool, dark place. Keep for at least 1 month before using.

PICKLED RED CABBAGE

Do not make too much of this pickle at one time, as it will lose its crispness if stored for longer than two or three months.

MAKES ABOUT 1.4 KG/3 LB

1 firm red cabbage

100–150 g/4–5 oz salt

2–3 onions, very thinly sliced

soft dark brown sugar (see method)

600–900 ml/1–1½ pints Spiced Vinegar

Remove any discoloured outer leaves from the cabbage, cut it into quarters and then into shreds. Layer the shreds in a large bowl, sprinkling each layer with salt. Cover the bowl and leave overnight. Next day, rinse the cabbage and drain it very thoroughly in a colander, pressing out all the surplus liquid.

Pack a 7.5 cm/3 inch layer of cabbage in a large glass jar. Cover with a layer of onion and sprinkle with 5 ml/1 tsp brown sugar. Repeat the layers until the jar is full, using additional jars if necessary. Fill the jar or jars with spiced vinegar. Cover with vinegar-proof lids. Label and store in a cool, dark place. Keep for at least 1 week before using.

PICKLES For basic information on preparing pickles, see pages 178–179. See also Bread and Butter Pickles.

PIGEONS IN RED WINE

SERVES 6

75 g/3 oz butter

3 woodpigeons

salt and pepper

1 large onion or 3 shallots, sliced

SAUCE

25 g/1 oz dripping or lard

1 small carrot, sliced

1 onion, sliced

25 g/1 oz plain flour

600 ml/1 pint game or chicken
  stock

salt and pepper

300 ml/½ pint red wine

Start by making the sauce. Melt the dripping or lard in a saucepan. Fry the vegetables slowly for about 10 minutes until the onion is golden brown. Stir in the flour and cook very gently until golden, then gradually add the stock, stirring constantly until the sauce boils and thickens. Lower the heat and simmer for 30 minutes, then strain the sauce into a large clean pan. Add salt and pepper to taste, stir in the red wine and bring the mixture slowly to simmering point.

Meanwhile melt two-thirds of the butter in a large frying pan and fry the pigeons, turning as required, until browned on all sides. Add the pigeons to the wine sauce and simmer with the pan half-covered for about 45 minutes, or until the birds are tender. Taste and season towards the end of the cooking time.

Melt the remaining butter in a frying pan and fry the onion or shallots. Drain well and keep hot. Split the cooked pigeons in half. Serve with the onions and the sauce poured over.

PINEAPPLE AND KIRSCH SALAD

SERVES 4

2 small pineapples

100 g/4 oz black grapes

1 banana

1 pear

15 ml/1 tbsp lemon juice

30–45 ml/2–3 tbsp kirsch

sugar

Cut the pineapples in half lengthways. Cut out the core from each, then scoop out the flesh, using first a knife, then a spoon, but taking care to keep the pineapple shells intact. Discard the core, and working over a bowl, chop the flesh.

Add the pineapple flesh to the bowl. Halve the grapes and remove the pips. Add to the pineapple mixture. Peel and slice the banana; peel, core and slice the pear. Put the lemon juice in a shallow bowl, add the pear and banana slices and toss both fruits before adding to the pineapple and grapes. Mix all the fruit together, pour the kirsch over and sweeten to taste with the sugar. Pile the fruit back into the pineapple shells and chill until required.

PIPED ALMOND RINGS

MAKES ABOUT 24

fat for greasing

175 g/6 oz butter

100 g/4 oz caster sugar

1 egg, beaten

225 g/8 oz self-raising flour

50 g/2 oz ground almonds

12 drops of vanilla essence

about 10 ml/2 tsp milk

Thoroughly grease two baking sheets. In a mixing bowl, cream the butter and sugar until light and fluffy. Add the beaten egg, beating thoroughly and adding a little of the flour if the mixture begins to curdle. Blend in the remaining flour and ground almonds gradually. Add the vanilla essence and enough milk to give a piping consistency. Leave the mixture to stand for about 20 minutes in a cool place.

Set the oven at 200°C/400°F/gas 6. Put the biscuit mixture into a piping bag fitted with a medium star nozzle, and pipe small rings on to the prepared baking sheets. Bake for 10 minutes or until golden. Leave to stand for a few minutes, then cool on a wire rack.

PIZZA

MAKES 4

fat for greasing

25 g/1 oz fresh yeast or 15 ml/ 1 tbsp dried yeast

5 ml/1 tsp sugar

450 g/1 lb strong white flour

5 ml/1 tsp salt

30 ml/2 tbsp olive oil

flour for rolling out

TOPPING

60 ml/4 tbsp olive oil

2 garlic cloves, crushed

1 large onion, chopped

15 ml/1 tbsp dried oregano or marjoram

1 (397 g/14 oz) can chopped tomatoes

30 ml/2 tbsp tomato pureé

salt and pepper

375 g/12 oz mozzarella cheese, sliced

Grease four large baking sheets. Measure 300 ml/½ pint lukewarm water. Blend the fresh yeast with the sugar and a little lukewarm water. Set aside until frothy. For dried yeast, sprinkle the yeast over all the water, then leave until frothy.

Sift the flour and salt into a bowl, make a well in the middle and add the yeast liquid, any remaining water and oil. Mix the flour into the liquid to make a firm dough. Turn out the dough on to a lightly floured surface and knead thoroughly until smooth and elastic – about 10 minutes. Place the dough in a clean, lightly floured bowl. Cover with cling film and leave in a warm place until doubled in bulk. This will take about 2 hours.

To make the topping, heat the oil in a saucepan and cook the garlic and onion until soft but not browned – about 15 minutes. Stir in the oregano, tomatoes and tomato pureé. Bring to the boil, reduce the heat and simmer for 15 minutes. Remove the pan from the heat and add salt and pepper to taste.

Set the oven at 240°C/475°F/gas 9. Knead the dough again, then divide it into four. Roll out each portion into a 25–30 cm/10–12 inch circle. Place a piece of dough on each prepared baking sheet. Top with the tomato mixture and mozzarella, then leave in a warm place for about 5 minutes, or until the dough bases begin to rise slightly.

Bake for about 15 minutes, or until the topping is well browned and the dough is crisp and bubbly. Serve freshly baked.

PLAICE MORNAY

SERVES 4

fat for greasing

350 ml/12 fl oz milk

1 onion, finely chopped

1 carrot, finely chopped

1 celery stick, finely chopped

1 bouquet garni

salt and pepper

8 plaice fillets

25 g/1 oz butter

25 g/1 oz plain flour

100 g/4 oz Gruyère cheese, grated

50 g/2 oz Parmesan cheese, grated

1.25 ml/¼ tsp mustard powder

fresh chervil sprigs to garnish

Grease a shallow flameproof dish. Combine the milk, vegetables and bouquet garni in a saucepan. Add salt and pepper to taste. Bring to the boil, lower the heat and simmer for 10 minutes. Set aside to cool.

Fold the plaice fillets in three, skin side inwards. Strain the flavoured milk into a deep frying pan and heat to simmering point. Add the fish and poach for 6–8 minutes or until the fish is cooked. Using a slotted spoon, transfer the fish to the prepared dish. Cover with buttered greaseproof paper and keep warm. Reserve the cooking liquid in a jug.

Melt the butter in a saucepan, add the flour and cook for 1 minute, stirring. Gradually add the reserved cooking liquid, whisking constantly until the sauce thickens.

Mix the cheeses. Stir half the mixture into the sauce, with the mustard. Remove the buttered paper from the fish, pour the sauce over the top and sprinkle with the remaining cheese mixture. Brown briefly under a hot grill. Garnish with chervil and serve.

PLAIN CAKE

MAKES ONE 15 CM/6 INCH CAKE

fat for greasing

200 g/7 oz self-raising flour or 200 g/7 oz plain flour and 10 ml/2 tsp baking powder

1.25 ml/¼ tsp salt

75 g/3 oz margarine or blended white cooking fat, diced

75 g/3 oz sugar

2 small eggs

about 125 ml/4 fl oz milk

Line and grease a 15 cm/6 inch cake tin. Set the oven at 180°C/350°F/gas 4.

Mix the flour and salt together in a mixing bowl. Rub in the margarine or cooking fat until the mixture resembles fine breadcrumbs. Add the baking powder, if used, and the sugar. In a bowl, beat the eggs with some of the milk and stir into the flour mixture. Add a little more milk if needed to give a consistency which just drops off the end of a wooden spoon.

Spoon the mixture into the prepared tin and bake for 1–1½ hours or until cooked through. Cool on a wire rack.

PORK For basic information on pork cuts, preparation and cooking methods, see pages 64–79. See also Barbecued Spare Ribs and Sweet and Sour Pork.

PORK AND APPLE HOT POT – *Illustrated on page 265*

SERVES 4

I cooking apple

45 ml/3 tbsp oil

I onion, thinly sliced

100 g/4 oz mushrooms, thinly sliced

4 pork loin chops, trimmed

2.5 ml/½ tsp dried sage or savory

450 g/I lb potatoes

salt and pepper

apple slices and parsley sprigs to garnish

Set the oven at 180°C/350°F/gas 4. Peel, core and slice the apple. Heat the oil in a large frying pan, add the apple and onion and fry over moderate heat until golden brown.

Put the mushrooms on the base of a large shallow greased casserole. Add the chops and cover with the apple and onion. Sprinkle the herbs over the top. Peel the potatoes and cut them into 2 cm/¾ inch cubes. Cover the chops with the potatoes, brushing them with the fat remaining in the pan. Sprinkle with salt and pepper to taste. Pour in enough water to come halfway up the meat and vegetables.

Cover the casserole with foil or a tight-fitting lid. Bake for I½ hours, removing the covering 30 minutes before the end of the cooking time to allow the potatoes to brown. Garnish with apple and parsley (if used), then serve from the casserole.

PORK CHOPS IN CIDER

SERVES 4

4 pork loin chops, trimmed

oil (optional)

60 ml/4 tbsp dry cider

I bouquet garni

2 cooking apples

2 onions, chopped

pinch of ground cinnamon

salt and pepper

100 g/4 oz flat mushrooms, thickly sliced

200 g/7 oz fresh peas

25 g/I oz butter

200 g/7 oz cooked small whole beetroot

225 g/8 oz tagliatelle, cooked

Set the oven at 160°C/325°F/gas 3. Heat a frying pan. Brown the chops on both sides, adding a little oil if the chops are very lean. Remove the chops and place them in a casserole. Pour the cider over the chops and add the bouquet garni. Cover the casserole and transfer it to the oven to start cooking.

Peel, core and chop the apples. Add them with the onions to the fat remaining in the frying pan and fry gently for 5 minutes. Stir in the cinnamon, with just enough water to cover the onion mixture. Cover the pan and simmer for about 15 minutes, until the onions and apples are soft. Rub the mixture through a sieve into a bowl, add salt and pepper to taste, then spoon the mixture over the chops in the casserole. Return to the oven for 45 minutes.

Add the mushrooms and peas to the casserole. Cook for 30 minutes more. Towards the end of the cooking time, melt the butter in a small saucepan, add the beetroot and heat gently, turning often. Arrange the tagliatelle and chops on a heated serving dish with the chops on top. Arrange the mushrooms, peas and beetroot around them.

PORK SAUSAGES WITH CABBAGE

SERVES 4

1 large hard white cabbage,
   about 1 kg/2¼ lb

75 g/3 oz butter

1 small onion, finely chopped

6 juniper berries, crushed

salt and pepper

50 ml/2 fl oz chicken stock

450 g/1 lb pork sausages

Trim the cabbage and cut it into quarters. Shred it finely lengthways. Melt the butter in a large saucepan, add the onion and fry over gentle heat for about 5 minutes until transparent.

Add the cabbage and juniper berries, with salt and pepper to taste. Pour in the stock, cover with a tight-fitting lid and cook gently for 1 hour. Stir occasionally and top up the liquid if it threatens to evaporate, leaving the cabbage dry.

Meanwhile grill, bake or fry the sausages until cooked through. Pile the cooked cabbage in a heated serving dish. Arrange the hot sausages on top and serve at once.

POTATOES DAUPHINE

SERVES 6

575 g/1¼ lb potatoes

salt and pepper

oil for deep frying

CHOUX PASTRY

100 g/4 oz plain flour

pinch of salt

50 g/2 oz butter or margarine

2 whole eggs, plus 1 yolk

MRS BEETON'S TIP

Potatoes Dauphine may also be baked. Place rounds of the mixture on to greased baking sheets. Bake in a preheated 220°C/425°F/ gas 7 oven for 10 minutes, then lower the heat to 180°C/ 350°F/gas 4 and bake for 20 minutes.

Scrub the potatoes, but do not peel them. Steam them or cook in a large saucepan of boiling water for 20–30 minutes, or until tender. Drain, peel and press through a sieve into a mixing bowl. Beat in salt and pepper to taste. Set aside.

Make the choux pastry. Sift the flour and salt on to a sheet of grease-proof paper. Put 250 ml/8 fl oz water in a saucepan and add the butter or margarine. Heat gently until the fat melts. When the fat has melted, bring the liquid rapidly to the boil and add all the flour at once. Immediately remove the pan from the heat and stir the flour into the liquid to make a smooth paste which leaves the sides of the pan clean. Set aside to cool slightly.

Add the egg yolk and beat well. Add the whole eggs, one at a time, beating well after each addition. Continue beating until the paste is very glossy. Add the potato pureé to the choux pastry mixture and beat well.

Put the oil for frying into a deep wide saucepan. Heat the oil to 180–190°C/350–375°F or until a cube of bread added to the oil browns in 30 seconds. If using a deep-fat fryer, follow the manufacturer's instructions. Drop small spoonfuls of the potato mixture, a few at a time, into the hot oil, and cook until they are puffed up and golden brown. Remove from the pan, drain on absorbent kitchen paper and keep hot while cooking successive batches. Serve freshly cooked.

POTATOES See also Anna Potatoes, Baked Jacket Potatoes, Duchesse Potatoes and Gratin Dauphinois.

POTATOES LYONNAISE

This is a very good way of using up leftover boiled new potatoes. A crushed garlic clove may be added to the onion, if liked.

SERVES 6

1 kg/2¼ lb potatoes, scrubbed but not peeled

75 g/3 oz butter or margarine

225 g/8 oz onions, thickly sliced

salt and pepper

15 ml/1 tbsp chopped parsley

Boil or steam the potatoes in their jackets until tender. When cool enough to handle, peel and cut into slices 5 mm/¼ inch thick.

Melt the butter or margarine in a large frying pan. Add the onions and fry over moderate heat until just golden. Using a slotted spoon, transfer the onions to a plate; keep warm.

Add the potatoes to the fat remaining in the pan and fry on both sides until crisp and golden. Return the onions to the pan and mix with the potatoes. Add salt and pepper to taste, turn into a serving dish; sprinkle with the parsley.

MRS BEETON'S TIP
Use an electric frying pan, if you have one, for this recipe. The size and depth means that the onions will be easy to cook, and the readily-controlled temperature will be an asset when frying the potatoes.

POTATOES SAVOYARDE

SERVES 6

1 small garlic clove, cut in half

75 g/3 oz Gruyère cheese, grated

1 kg/2¼ lb potatoes, thinly sliced

salt and pepper

freshly grated nutmeg

40 g/1½ oz butter

about 375 ml/13 fl oz chicken or vegetable stock

Set the oven at 190°C/375°F/gas 5. Rub the cut garlic all over the inside of a 2 litre/3½ pint baking dish. Set aside 30 ml/2 tbsp of the grated cheese.

Put the potatoes into a mixing bowl. Add salt, pepper and nutmeg to taste, then mix in the remaining cheese. Use a little of the butter to grease the baking dish generously, add the potato mixture and pour in just enough stock to cover the potatoes.

Dot the remaining butter over the potatoes and sprinkle with the reserved grated cheese.

Bake for 1¼ hours or until the topping is golden brown and all the potatoes are tender.

POTATO RISSOLES

MAKES ABOUT 10

50 g/2 oz butter

1 large onion, finely chopped

350 g/12 oz hot mashed potato

salt and pepper

10 ml/2 tsp chopped parsley

2 eggs, beaten

75 g/3 oz dried white
   breadcrumbs

oil for shallow frying

Melt half the butter in a frying pan. Cook the onion, stirring often, until soft but not browned. Season the mashed potato generously, then stir in the parsley and onion with all the butter from the pan. Allow the mixture to cool completely. When cold, shape the mixture into small balls.

Put the beaten egg in a shallow bowl and the breadcrumbs on a plate or sheet of foil. Dip the potato rissoles in the egg, then coat them well in breadcrumbs. Place on a baking sheet and chill for 15 minutes to firm the mixture.

Heat the remaining butter with the oil for frying in a deep frying pan. Put in the rissoles and turn them in the hot fat for 6–9 minutes until golden brown all over. Drain on absorbent kitchen paper and serve hot.

variation
Mrs Beeton suggests that these rissoles may be made very simply, without the onion, or that their flavour may be improved by adding a little chopped cooked tongue or ham or diced grilled bacon.

POTATO SALAD

SERVES 6

salt and pepper

6 large new potatoes or waxy
   old potatoes

150 ml/¼ pint mayonnaise

3 spring onions, chopped

30 ml/2 tbsp chopped parsley

Bring a saucepan of salted water to the boil, add the potatoes in their jackets and cook for 20–30 minutes until tender. Drain thoroughly. When cool enough to handle, peel and dice the potatoes. Put them in a bowl and add the mayonnaise while still warm. Lightly stir in the spring onions and parsley, with salt and pepper to taste. Cover, leave to become quite cold and stir before serving.

variations
FRENCH POTATO SALAD Substitute 100 ml/3½ fl oz French dressing for the mayonnaise. Omit the spring onions, increase the parsley to 45 ml/3 tbsp and add 5 ml/1 tsp chopped fresh mint and 5 ml/1 tsp snipped chives.
GERMAN POTATO SALAD Omit the mayonnaise and spring onions. Reduce the parsley to 5 ml/1 tsp and add 5 ml/1 tsp finely chopped onion. Heat 60 ml/4 tbsp vegetable stock in a saucepan. Beat in 15 ml/1 tbsp white wine vinegar and 30 ml/2 tbsp oil. Add salt and pepper to taste. Pour over the diced potatoes while still hot and toss lightly together. Serve at once, or leave to become quite cold.
POTATO SALAD WITH APPLE AND CELERY Follow the basic recipe above, but add 2 sliced celery sticks and 1 diced red-skinned apple tossed in a little lemon juice.

POTATO SALAD – MRS BEETON'S

This should be made two or three hours before it is to be served so that the flavours have time to mature. Cold beef, turkey or other poultry may be thinly sliced or cut into chunks and combined with the potato salad to make a light main course dish.

SERVES 6

10 small cold cooked potatoes

60 ml/4 tbsp tarragon vinegar

90 ml/6 tbsp salad oil

salt and pepper

15 ml/1 tbsp chopped parsley

Cut the potatoes into 1 cm/½ inch thick slices. For the dressing, mix the tarragon vinegar, oil and plenty of salt and pepper in a screw-topped jar. Close the jar tightly and shake vigorously until well blended.

Layer the potatoes in a salad bowl, sprinkling with a little dressing and the parsley. Pour over any remaining dressing, cover and set aside to marinate before serving.

variations

POTATO AND ANCHOVY SALAD Drain a 50 g/2 oz can of anchovy fillets, reserving the oil. Chop the fillets. Use the oil to make the dressing. Sprinkle the chopped anchovies between the layers of potato with the dressing.

POTATO AND OLIVE SALAD Thinly slice 50 g/2 oz stoned black olives. Chop 2 spring onions, if liked; mix them with the olives. Sprinkle the olives between the potato layers.

POTATO SALAD WITH PICKLES Dice 1 pickled gherkin and 1–2 pickled onions. Reduce the vinegar to 15–30 ml/1–2 tbsp when making the dressing. Sprinkle the pickles between the layers of potato with the dressing.

POTTED SHRIMPS OR PRAWNS

MAKES ABOUT 675 G/1½ LB

225 g/8 oz unsalted butter

450 g/1 lb peeled cooked shrimps or prawns

1.25 ml/¼ tsp ground white pepper

1.25 ml/¼ tsp ground mace

1.25 ml/¼ tsp ground cloves

dill sprigs to garnish

Melt the butter in a saucepan, add the shrimps or prawns and heat very gently, without boiling. Add the pepper, mace and cloves.

Using a slotted spoon, transfer the shrimps or prawns to small pots. Pour a little of the hot spiced butter into each pot.

Set the remaining spiced butter aside until the residue has settled, then pour over the shrimps or prawns. Chill until the butter is firm. Store in a refrigerator for no more than 48 hours. Garnish with dill.

MRS BEETON'S TIP

Look out for small brown shrimps, sold unshelled, particularly in good fishmongers or coastal towns. They have an excellent flavour which warrants the time and effort of peeling them. Buy double the quantity to allow for shell wastage.

PRAWN COCKTAIL

SERVES 4

4 lettuce leaves, shredded

225 g/8 oz peeled cooked prawns

75 ml/5 tbsp mayonnaise

15 ml/1 tbsp tomato pureé

few drops of Tabasco sauce

5 ml/1 tsp chilli vinegar or tarragon vinegar (optional)

4 whole cooked prawns to garnish

Place a little shredded lettuce on the base of 4 glass dishes. Put the prawns on top. Mix the mayonnaise with the tomato Pureé and add a few drops of Tabasco sauce. Stir in the vinegar, if liked. Spoon the mayonnaise mixture over the prawns and garnish each dish with a whole cooked prawn, preferably in the shell. Serve with brown bread and butter, if liked.

variations

AVOCADO RITZ Serve the prawns and mayonnaise on avocado halves. Cut the avocados in half and remove the stones just before topping and serving. If there is likely to be a short delay, brush the avocado flesh with lemon juice to prevent discoloration.

PRAWN AND HORSERADISH COCKTAIL Omit the Tabasco sauce and vinegar from the recipe above and add 5 ml/1 tsp grated fresh horseradish or 15 ml/1 tbsp creamed horseradish.

PRAWN CURRY

SERVES 4

15 ml/1 tbsp ground coriander

2.5 ml/½ tsp ground cumin

2.5 ml/½ tsp chilli powder

2.5 ml/½ tsp turmeric

1 garlic clove, crushed

250 ml/8 floz fish stock

30 ml/2 tbsp oil

1 large onion, finely chopped

45 ml/3 tbsp tomato pureé

2 tomatoes

450 g/1 lb peeled cooked prawns

juice of ½ lemon

10 ml/2 tsp coconut cream

fresh coriander sprigs, to garnish

Mix all the spices in a small bowl. Add the garlic and mix to a paste with a little of the stock. Set aside.

Heat the oil in a frying pan, add the onion and fry for 4–5 minutes until golden brown. Add the tomato purée and spice mixture, then cook for 1–2 minutes. Meanwhile cut a small cross in the top of each tomato and place them in a heatproof bowl. Pour on freshly boiling water. Leave for about 45 seconds, then drain. Peel back and remove the skins, then chop the flesh. Add it to the onion mixture with the remaining stock. Stir, cover the pan and simmer gently for 20 minutes.

Add the prawns and lemon juice to the pan, with the coconut cream. Stir until the coconut cream dissolves, then simmer for 5 minutes more. Garnish with fresh coriander sprigs and serve with Basmati rice.

> **PRESERVES** For general information on making preserves, see pages 174–178. See also Apricot Jam, Lemon Curd, Mint Jelly, Orange Marmalade, Raspberry Conserve, Strawberry Jam and Three Fruit Marmalade.

PROFITEROLES

SERVES 8

CHOUX PASTRY PUFFS
100 g/4 oz plain flour
50 g/2 oz butter or margarine
pinch of salt
2 whole eggs plus 1 yolk

FILLING
250 ml/8 fl oz double cream, chilled
25 g/1 oz caster sugar
vanilla essence

TOPPING
200 g/7 oz icing sugar, sifted
15 ml/1 tbsp cocoa

FREEZER TIP

When cool, the unfilled choux puffs may be packed in sealed polythene bags and frozen. Thaw in wrappings for 1–1½ hours at room temperature, then place on baking sheets and crisp in a 180°C/350°F/gas 4 oven for 5 minutes. Cool before filling and topping.

Lightly grease 2 baking sheets. Set the oven at 220°C/425°F/gas 7.

Make the choux pastry. Sift the flour on to a sheet of greaseproof paper. Put 250 ml/8 floz water in a saucepan and add the butter or margarine with the salt. Heat gently until the fat melts.

When the fat has melted, bring the liquid rapidly to the boil and add all the flour at once. Immediately remove the pan from the heat and stir the flour into the liquid to make a smooth paste which leaves the sides of the pan clean. Set aside to cool slightly.

Add the egg yolk and beat well. Add the whole eggs, one at a time, beating well after each addition. Continue beating until the paste is very glossy. Put it into a piping bag fitted with a 2 cm/¾ inch nozzle and pipe it in 2 cm/¾ inch balls on the baking sheets, leaving room for them to puff up. Bake for 10 minutes, then lower the oven temperature to 180°C/350°F/gas 4 and bake for 20 minutes more until crisp, golden and puffed.

Remove the puffs from the oven, slit them with a sharp knife, and remove any uncooked paste. If necessary, return them to the oven for a few minutes to dry out. Cool the puffs completely on a wire rack.

Just before serving, whip the cream lightly. Whip in the sugar with a few drops of vanilla essence to taste. Put into a piping bag and fill the choux puffs.

Make the chocolate topping by mixing the icing sugar and cocoa in a bowl with enough warm water (about 15–30 ml/1–2 tbsp) to form an icing that will coat the back of the spoon. Glaze the tops of the puffs with this mixture, reserving a little for assembling the dish. Let the icing on the puffs harden, then arrange them in a pyramid, sticking the buns together with small dabs of the remaining icing. Serve 3 or 4 buns per person, with a chocolate sauce, if liked.

variations
The filling may be varied to taste. Sweetened whipped cream, confectioners' custard or chocolate buttercream may be used. Instead of the icing, melted chocolate may simply be poured over the choux.

PUMPKIN SOUP

SERVES 6

25 g/1 oz butter

1 onion, finely chopped

1 garlic clove, crushed

1 kg/2¼ lb pumpkin, peeled, seeded and cubed

1.5 litres/2¾ pints chicken or vegetable stock

5 ml/1 tsp ground coriander seeds

5 ml/1 tsp ground cinnamon

2.5 ml/½ tsp ground cumin

salt and pepper

150 ml/¼ pint whipping cream or fromage frais

Melt the butter in a large saucepan, add the onion and garlic and cook over gentle heat for 10 minutes until soft but not coloured.

Add the pumpkin cubes, stock and spices, with salt and pepper to taste. Bring to the boil, lower the heat and simmer for about 30 minutes or until the pumpkin is tender.

Purée the soup in a blender or food processor, or rub through a sieve into a clean pan. Taste and add more salt and pepper if required. The soup should be quite spicy. Reheat without boiling.

Whip the cream, if using. Ladle the soup into individual bowls and top each portion with a spoonful of whipped cream or fromage frais.

variation
PUMPKIN AND APPLE SOUP Omit the coriander and cumin. Add 2 peeled, cored and sliced cooking apples with the pumpkin. Continue as above, then stir in a little sugar to taste when reheated. The sweetness should just balance the tang of the apples. Serve as above.

QUEEN OF PUDDINGS

Q

SERVES 4

butter for greasing

75 g/3 oz fresh white breadcrumbs

400 ml/14 fl oz milk

25 g/1 oz butter

10 ml/2 tsp grated lemon rind

2 eggs, separated

75 g/3 oz caster sugar

30 ml/2 tbsp red jam

MICROWAVE TIP

Warm the jam in a bowl for a few seconds on High.

Grease a 750 ml/1¼ pint pie dish. Set the oven at 160°C/325°F/gas 3. Spread the breadcrumbs out on a baking sheet and put into the oven to dry off slightly.

Warm the milk and butter with the lemon rind in a saucepan. Meanwhile put the egg yolks in a bowl and stir in 25 g/1 oz of the sugar. Pour on the warmed milk mixture, stirring thoroughly. Add the breadcrumbs, mix thoroughly and pour into the prepared pie dish. Leave to stand for 30 minutes.

Bake the pudding for 40–50 minutes until lightly set, then remove from the oven. Lower the oven temperature to 120°C/250°F/gas½. Warm the jam in a small saucepan until runny, then spread it over the top of the pudding.

In a clean, grease-free bowl, whisk the egg whites until stiff. Add half the remaining sugar and whisk again. Fold in all but 15 ml/1 tbsp of the remaining sugar. Spoon the meringue around the edge of the jam, drawing it up into peaks at regular intervals to resemble a crown. Sprinkle with the rest of the sugar. Return the pudding to the oven and bake for 40–45 minutes more, until the meringue is set.

QUICHE LORRAINE – *Illustrated on page 301*

SERVES 4 TO 6

225 g/8 oz rindless streaky
  bacon rashers

I onion, chopped

3 eggs

300 ml/½ pint single cream

2.5 ml/½ tsp salt

grinding of black pepper

pinch of grated nutmeg

25 g/I oz butter, diced

SHORT CRUST PASTRY

100 g/4 oz plain flour

2.5 ml/½ tsp salt

50 g/2 oz margarine (or half
  butter, half lard)

Set the oven at 200°C/400°F/gas 6. To make the pastry, sift the flour and salt into a bowl, then rub in the margarine until the mixture resembles fine breadcrumbs. Add enough cold water to make a stiff dough. Press the dough together.

Roll out the pastry on a lightly floured surface. Line an 18 cm/7 inch flan tin or ring placed on a baking sheet. Line the pastry with greaseproof paper and fill with baking beans. Bake 'blind' for 20 minutes until the rim of the pastry is slightly browned but the base is still soft. Remove the paper and beans. Reduce the oven temperature to 190°C/375°F/gas 5.

Cut the bacon in 2 cm × 5 mm/¾ × ¼ inch strips. Dry fry for a few minutes, until the fat runs, then add the onion to the bacon and cook for 5 minutes, stirring occasionally. Drain and scatter the strips over the pastry base. Press in lightly. Beat the eggs, cream, salt, pepper and nutmeg. Pour the mixture into the pastry case and dot with butter. Bake for 30 minutes. Serve at once.

RABBIT CASSEROLE

SERVES 4

I rabbit

salt and pepper

60 ml/4 tbsp plain flour

65 g/2½ oz butter

I onion, sliced

225 g/8 oz cooking apples,
  peeled, cored and sliced

I (213 g/7 oz) can prunes

I chicken stock cube

GARNISH

chopped parsley

crescents of fried bread

Set the oven at 180°C/350°F/gas 4. Joint the rabbit and discard the lower forelegs and rib-cage, or keep for stock. Put half the flour in a shallow bowl, season and coat the rabbit lightly. Melt 50 g/2 oz of the butter in a flameproof casserole and brown the rabbit on all sides; transfer to a plate. Add the onion to the casserole and fry until soft. Stir in the apples.

Drain the prunes and make the juice up to 250 ml/8 fl oz with water. Add the stock cube, crumbling it finely. Return the rabbit to the casserole with the prunes and stock. Cover and cook in the oven for 1½ hours, or until the rabbit is tender.

When the rabbit is cooked, arrange the joints on a warmed serving dish with the apples and prunes; keep hot. In a small bowl, blend the remaining butter with the remaining flour. Place the casserole over the heat. Gradually add small pieces of the mixture to the liquid, whisking thoroughly after each addition. Bring to the boil and stir all the time until the sauce thickens. Check the seasoning before pouring the sauce over the rabbit. Garnish and serve.

RABBIT PIE

SERVES 4

200 g/7 oz cooked rabbit

50 g/2 oz boiled bacon, without rinds

4 eggs

salt and pepper

beaten egg or milk for glazing

SHORT CRUST PASTRY

225 g/8 oz plain flour

2.5 ml/½ tsp salt

100 g/4 oz margarine (or half butter, half lard)

flour for rolling out

Set the oven at 200°C/400°F/gas 6. To make the pastry, sift the flour and salt into a bowl, then rub in the margarine or mixed fats until the mixture resembles fine breadcrumbs. Add enough cold water to make a stiff dough. Press the dough together with your fingertips.

Roll out half the pastry on a lightly floured surface and line a 20 cm/ 8 inch pie plate. Set the remainder aside for the lid.

Chop the rabbit meat and bacon finely and mix together in a bowl. Place the mixture on the pastry in the form of a cross, leaving the outside 1 cm/½ inch of pastry uncovered. Break an egg carefully into each uncovered pastry triangle, taking care not to break the yolks. Add salt and pepper to taste.

Roll out the remaining pastry and cut a lid for the pie. Dampen the edges of the pastry shell and cover with the lid. Brush with egg or milk. Bake for 30-40 minutes. Serve hot.

RASPBERRY CONSERVE

This conserve does not set firmly but it has a wonderful fresh flavour.

MAKES ABOUT 2.5 KG/5½ LB

1.5 kg/3¼ lb sugar

1.25 kg/2½ lb raspberries

Put the sugar in a heatproof bowl and warm in a preheated 150°C/300°F/gas 2 oven. Meanwhile wash the raspberries lightly but thoroughly and drain them very well. Put them in a preserving pan without any additional water, bring them gently to the boil, then boil rapidly for 5 minutes.

Draw the preserving pan off the heat and add the warmed sugar. Return the pan to the heat and stir well until all the sugar has dissolved. Bring to the boil and boil rapidly for 1 minute. Remove from the heat, skim quickly, pot at once and label.

RASPBERRY VINEGAR

raspberries

white wine vinegar

caster sugar

Clean the fruit thoroughly and measure it by volume. Put it in a bowl and add an equal quantity each of vinegar and water. Leave to stand overnight.

Next day, strain the liquid through a fine sieve or jelly bag and measure it again. To each 300 ml/½ pint liquid add 200 ml/7 floz caster sugar. Pour the mixture into a saucepan, bring to the boil; boil for 10 minutes. Pour the hot liquid into heated clean bottles and seal at once. Label the bottles when cold.

Ratatouille

SERVES 4 TO 6

2 aubergines

salt and pepper

125–150 ml/4–5 fl oz olive oil

2 large onions, finely chopped

2 garlic cloves, crushed

2 peppers, seeded and cut into thin strips

30 ml/2 tbsp chopped fresh marjoram or 10 ml/2 tsp dried marjoram

450 g/1 lb tomatoes, peeled and chopped

4 courgettes, thinly sliced

30 ml/2 tbsp finely chopped parsley or mint

Cut the ends off the aubergines and cut them into cubes. Put the cubes in a colander and sprinkle generously with salt. Set aside for 30 minutes, then rinse thoroughly, drain and pat dry on absorbent kitchen paper.

Heat some of the oil in a large saucepan or flameproof casserole, add some of the aubergine cubes and cook over moderate heat, stirring frequently, for 10 minutes. Using a slotted spoon, transfer the aubergine to a bowl; repeat until all the cubes are cooked, adding more of the oil as necessary.

Add the onions to the oil remaining in the pan and fry for 5 minutes, until slightly softened. Stir in the garlic, peppers and marjoram, with salt and pepper to taste. Cook, stirring occasionally for 15–20 minutes, or until the onions are thoroughly softened.

Stir the tomatoes and courgettes into the vegetable mixture. Replace the aubergines, heat until bubbling, then cover and simmer for a further 15–20 minutes, stirring occasionally. Serve hot, sprinkled with parsley, or cold, sprinkled with mint.

Red cabbage with apples

SERVES 6

45 ml/3 tbsp oil

1 onion, finely chopped

1 garlic clove, crushed

900 g/2 lb red cabbage, finely shredded

2 large cooking apples

15 ml/1 tbsp soft light brown sugar or golden syrup

juice of 1/2 lemon

30 ml/2 tbsp red wine vinegar

salt and pepper

15 ml/1 tbsp caraway seeds (optional)

Heat the oil in a large saucepan, add the onion and garlic and fry gently for 5 minutes. Add the cabbage. Peel, core and slice the apples and add them to the pan with the sugar or syrup. Cook over very gentle heat for 10 minutes, shaking the pan frequently.

Add the lemon juice and vinegar, with salt and pepper to taste. Stir in the caraway seeds, if used. Cover and simmer gently for 1–1 1/2 hours, stirring occasionally and adding a little water if the mixture appears dry. Check the seasoning before serving.

FREEZING TIP

Red cabbage freezes well. Cool quickly, then pack in a rigid container. Freeze for up to 3 months.

RED FRUIT SALAD

Choose small strawberries, if possible, for this dessert, since they are juicier when left whole. Do not strip the redcurrants from the stalks.

SERVES 6

225 g/8 oz redcurrants

6 red plums, stoned and quartered

225 g/8 oz strawberries, hulled

225 g/8 oz raspberries, hulled

100 g/4 oz slice watermelon, seeded and cubed

TO SERVE

Greek yogurt or clotted cream

caster sugar

Using a pair of kitchen scissors, neatly snip the redcurrants into small bunches.

Combine the plums, strawberries, raspberries and watermelon on a large platter. Arrange the redcurrants around or over the salad.

Serve as soon as possible, with yogurt or cream. Offer a bowl of caster sugar with the salad.

RED TOMATO CHUTNEY

If this chutney is to have a good red colour, it is essential to use white sugar and white vinegar.

MAKES ABOUT 3 KG/6½ LB

3 kg/6½ lb ripe red tomatoes

450 g/1 lb sugar

20 g/¾ oz salt

pinch of paprika

pinch of cayenne pepper

300 ml/½ pint Spiced Vinegar, made with white vinegar

To achieve the correct texture, the tomatoes should be processed in one continuous action from peeling to potting. Peel the tomatoes. Place them in a bowl and cover with freshly boiling water. Leave for 30–60 seconds, then drain and slit the skins. Rub them off.

Immediately cut up the tomatoes, removing the hard cores, and put them in a large saucepan. Add a very little water and bring slowly to the boil. Lower the heat and simmer until thick. Add the remaining ingredients, stirring well. Continue cooking over low heat until the mixture is thick. Test the consistency by spooning a little of the chutney on to a cold plate. When ready, pour the chutney into warm clean jars and cover with vinegar-proof lids. When cool, wipe the jars, label and store in a cool dry place.

RED WINE MARINADE

MAKES ABOUT 600 ML/1 PINT

1 each onion, carrot and celery stick, chopped

6–10 parsley sprigs, chopped

1 garlic clove, crushed

5 ml/1 tsp dried thyme

1 bay leaf

6–8 peppercorns

12 cloves

5 ml/1 tsp ground coriander

2.5 ml/½ tsp juniper berries, lightly crushed

salt and pepper

250 ml/8 fl oz rich strong stock

150 ml/¼ pint red wine

150 ml/¼ pint oil

Mix all the ingredients in a large bowl. Stir in 150 ml/¼ pint water. Use as required.

MRS BEETON'S TIP

Marinades are used to add moisture to dry meats before roasting. They also impart flavour and can help to tenderise meat. With its robust flavour, Red Wine Marinade is particularly suitable for beef and game.

RICE PUDDING

This basic recipe works equally well with flaked rice, sago or flaked tapioca.

SERVES 4 TO 5

butter for greasing

100 g/4 oz pudding rice

1 litre/1¾ pints milk

pinch of salt

50–75 g/2–3 oz caster sugar

15 g/½ oz butter (optional)

1.25 ml/¼ tsp grated nutmeg

Butter a 1.75 litre/3 pint pie dish. Wash the rice in cold water, drain and put it into the dish with the milk. Leave to stand for 30 minutes.

Set the oven at 150°C/300°F/gas 2. Stir the salt and sugar into the milk mixture and sprinkle with flakes of butter, if used, and nutmeg. Bake for 2–2½ hours or until the pudding is thick and creamy, and brown on the top. The pudding is better if it cooks even more slowly, at 120°C/250°F/gas for 4–5 hours.

PRESSURE COOKER TIP

Bring all the ingredients to the boil in the open cooker, stirring. Reduce the heat so that the milk just bubbles. Put the lid on and bring to 15 lb pressure without increasing the heat. Cook for 12 minutes. Reduce pressure slowly.

RICE For basic information on types of rice and cooking methods, see pages 104–108. See also Paella, Risotto Milanaise and Savoury Rice.

RICE SALAD

SERVES 4 TO 6

200 g/7 oz long-grain rice

salt

60 ml/4 tbsp olive oil

30 ml/2 tbsp white wine vinegar

2 spring onions, finely chopped

1 carrot, finely diced and blanched

1 small green pepper, seeded and finely diced

2 gherkins, finely diced

30 ml/2 tbsp snipped chives

watercress to serve

Place the rice in a saucepan. Pour in 450 ml/¾ pint cold water. Add a little salt, then bring to the boil. Cover the pan tightly and reduce the heat to the lowest setting. Leave the rice for 15 minutes, turn off the heat and leave for 15 minutes more without removing the lid. The rice should have absorbed all the liquid. Drain if necessary.

Stir in the oil and vinegar while the rice is still hot. Add the vegetables and chives; mix well. Pile on a dish and garnish with watercress. Serve

MRS BEETON'S TIP

This looks good in tomato shells. Cut the tops off 4–6 beefsteak tomatoes and reserve as lids. Hollow out the centres, saving the pulp for use in soup or another recipe. Turn the tomatoes upside down on absorbent kitchen paper to drain. When ready to serve the tomatoes, fill them with the rice mixture and replace the lids at an angle.

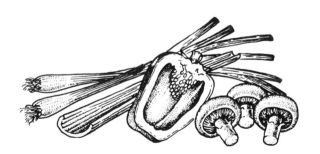

RICH FRUIT CAKE

ROUND SQUARE	15 cm/6 inch 13 cm/5 inch	18 cm/7 inch 15 cm/6 inch	20 cm/8 inch 18 cm/7 inch	23 cm/9 inch 20 cm/8 inch	25 cm/10 inch 23 cm/9 inch	28 cm/11 inch 15 cm/10 inch	30 cm/12 inch 28 cm/11 inch	33 cm/13 inch 30 cm/12 inch
Currants	225 g/8 oz	275 g/10 oz	400 g/14 oz	500 g/18 oz	575 g/1¼ lb	675 g/1½ lb	900 g/2 lb	1.25 kg/2½ lb
Raisins	100 g/4 oz	150 g/5 oz	200 g/7 oz	250 g/9 oz	300 g/11 oz	375 g/13 oz	450 g/1 lb	575 g/1¼ lb
Sultanas	100 g/4 oz	150 g/5 oz	200 g/7 oz	250 g/9 oz	300 g/11 oz	375 g/13 oz	450 g/1 lb	575 g/1¼ lb
Butter, softened	100 g/4 oz	150 g/5 oz	200 g/7 oz	250 g/9 oz	300 g/11 oz	375 g/13 oz	450 g/1 lb	575 g/1¼ lb
Moist dark brown sugar	100 g/4 oz	150 g/5 oz	200 g/7 oz	250 g/9 oz	300 g/11 oz	375 g/13 oz	450 g/1 lb	575 g/1¼ lb
Lemon, grated rind of	½	½	1	1	1½	1½	2	2
Almonds, shelled weight	25 g/1 oz	25 g/1 oz	40 g/1½ oz	65 g/2½ oz	75 g/3 oz	90 g/3½ oz	100 g/4 oz	100 g/4 oz
Candied peel, chopped	25 g/1 oz	25 g/1 oz	40 g/1½ oz	65 g/2½ oz	75 g/3 oz	90g/3½ oz	100 g/4 oz	100 g/4 oz
Glacé cherries	50 g/2 oz	50 g/2 oz	75 g/3 oz	90 g/3½ oz	100 g/4 oz	150 g/5 oz	175 g/6 oz	175 g/6 oz
Plain flour	100 g/4 oz	150 g/5 oz	200 g/7 oz	250 g/9 oz	300 g/11 oz	375 g/13 oz	450 g/1 lb	575 g/1¼ lb
Ground mixed spice	1.25 ml/¼ tsp	2.5 ml/½ tsp	2.5 ml/½ tsp	5 ml/1 tsp	5 ml/1 tsp	7.5 ml/1½ tsp	7.5 ml/1½ tsp	10 ml/2 tsp
Eggs, beaten	2	2	3	4	5	6	8	10
Black treacle	10 ml/2 tsp	10 ml/2 tsp	15 ml/1 tbsp	15 ml/1 tbsp	22.5 ml/4½ tsp	22.5 ml/4½ tsp	30 ml/2 tbsp	30 ml/2 tbsp
PORTION GUIDE: round	20	30	40	50	70	85	100	120
square	15	25	38	55	75	90	115	135

The traditional centre piece for a celebration is inevitably a rich fruit cake, whether served singly for a birthday, Christening or anniversary, or in tiers to celebrate a wedding. It is very useful, therefore, to have a reliable basic recipe, which can be adapted as required. The chart above gives quantities for cakes of different sizes and also provides a guide to portions.

Set the oven at 150°C/300°F/gas 2. Line and grease the appropriate tin. Mix the currants, raisins and sultanas. Cream the butter and sugar with the lemon rind until very soft. Beat in the almonds and the candied peel. Wash and dry the cherries, then roughly chop them and toss them with a little of the measured flour. Sift the remaining flour with the spice and toss a little with the mixed dried fruit. Beat the eggs and treacle into the creamed mixture, adding a spoonful of the flour occasionally to prevent the mixture curdling. Fold in the remaining flour. Lastly fold in the fruit and the cherries.

Turn the mixture into the tin and smooth the top with the back of a wetted metal spoon, hollowing out the centre slightly.

The cooking time depends on the size of the cake. The small cakes will take about 1–2 hours, cakes of 20–23 cm/8–9 inches about 4–5 hours and larger cakes about 7–8 hours.

Insert a clean metal skewer into the centre of the cake to test if it is cooked: it should come out clean when the cake is ready. If there is any sticky mixture on the skewer the cake is not cooked.

Leave the cake to cool in the tin for at least an hour, then transfer it to a wire rack to cool completely. Do not remove the lining paper. Wrap the cake, still in the lining paper, in fresh greaseproof paper and store it in an airtight tin.

RICH STRONG STOCK

MAKES ABOUT 5 LITRES/8¾ PINTS

675 g/1½ lb shin of beef on the
   bone

675 g/1½ lb knuckle of veal on
   the bone, or other stewing
   veal

450 g/1 lb beef marrow bones

1 chicken drumstick or poultry
   trimmings

1 onion, sliced

1 carrot, quartered

100 g/4 oz gammon or bacon,
   diced

1 small turnip, roughly chopped

2 celery sticks, quartered

2 open cup mushrooms,
   quartered

1 tomato, quartered

1 bouquet garni

4 white peppercorns

2 cloves

1 blade of mace

Set the oven at 200°C/400°F/gas 6. Put the bones in a roasting tin and roast for about 2 hours until browned. Transfer the bones to a large saucepan. Pour off the fat from the tin, add some boiling water and stir to scrape all the sediment off the tin. Then add to the bones in the pan. Add the onion and carrot.

Pour about 5.6 litres/10 pints water into the pan to cover the bones generously. Bring to the boil, skim the surface, then lower the heat and add the remaining ingredients. Simmer for about 5 hours.

Cool, then strain. Skim off surface fat. Season and use as required.

NOTE

For more information on making stock, see pages 9–10. This recipe makes a large quantity of meat stock which freezes well for future use. Although the quantities may be reduced, a large volume of liquid is required to cover marrow bones. It is more practical to invest in a large stockpot or saucepan and to boil a large quantity occasionally than to reduce the weight of ingredients in proportion to water to make a weaker meat stock.

Risotto milanese – *Illustrated on page 266*

SERVES 4

75 g/3 oz butter

30 ml/2 tbsp olive oil

1 onion, finely chopped

350 g/12 oz risotto rice

600 ml/1 pint vegetable stock

2.5 ml/½ tsp saffron threads

300 ml/½ pint dry white wine

salt and pepper

150 g/5 oz Parmesan cheese, grated

Heat 25 g/1 oz of the butter with the olive oil in a large saucepan. Add the onion and fry gently, stirring occasionally for 10 minutes. Add the rice and cook for a few minutes, stirring gently until all the rice grains are coated in fat. Meanwhile heat the stock to simmering point in a separate pan. Put the saffron threads in a mortar and pound them with a pestle. Stir in a little of the hot stock to dissolve the saffron, then set aside.

Add the wine and half the remaining stock to the rice, with salt and pepper to taste. Bring to the boil. Stir once, lower the heat and cover the pan tightly. Leave over low heat for 10 minutes. Pour in half the remaining hot stock, do not stir, then cover and cook for 5 minutes, shaking the pan occasionally to prevent sticking. Finally, add the remaining stock and saffron liquid. Stir once or twice, cover and cook for about 10 minutes, until the rice is cooked, creamy and moist.

Stir in the remaining butter and the cheese. Taste the risotto, adding more salt and pepper if required. Cover tightly and leave to stand for 5 minutes before serving.

Roast chicken with honey and almonds

SERVES 4 TO 6

1 (1.5–1.8 kg/3¼–4 lb) oven-ready roasting chicken

½ lemon

salt and pepper

45 ml/3 tbsp honey

50 g/2 oz flaked almonds

pinch of powdered saffron

30 ml/2 tbsp oil

watercress sprigs to garnish (optional)

Set the oven at 180°C/350°F/gas 4. Rub the chicken all over with the cut lemon, then sprinkle with salt and pepper. Line a roasting tin with a piece of foil large enough to enclose the bird completely.

Put the bird into the foil-lined tin, then brush it all over with the honey. Sprinkle the nuts and saffron over, then trickle the oil very gently over the top. Bring up the foil carefully, tenting it over the bird so that it is completely covered. Make sure that the foil does not touch the skin. Seal the package by folding the edges of the foil over.

Roast for 1½–2 hours or until the chicken is cooked through. Open the foil for the last 10 minutes to allow the breast of the bird to brown. Transfer the chicken to a heated serving dish and garnish it with sprigs of watercress if liked.

ROAST DUCK

SERVES 4

fat for basting

1 (1.8 kg/4 lb) oven-ready duck

salt and pepper

30 ml/2 tbsp plain flour

300 ml/½ pint duck or chicken
stock (see Mrs Beeton's Tip)

SAGE AND ONION STUFFING

2 onions, thickly sliced

4 young fresh sage sprigs or
10 ml/2 tsp dried sage

100 g/4 oz fresh white
breadcrumbs

50 g/2 oz butter or margarine,
melted

salt and pepper

Set the oven at 190°C/375°F/gas 5. Make the stuffing. Put the onions in a small saucepan with water to cover. Bring to the boil, cook for 2–3 minutes, then remove the onions from the pan with a slotted spoon. Chop them finely. Chop the sage leaves finely, discarding any stalk.

Combine the breadcrumbs, onions and sage in a bowl. Add the melted butter or margarine, with salt and pepper to taste. Mix well.

Spoon the stuffing into the duck and truss it. Weigh the duck and calculate the cooking time at 20 minutes per 450 g/1 lb. Sprinkle the breast with salt.

Put the duck on a wire rack in a roasting tin and prick the skin all over with a fork or skewer to release the fat. Roast for the required time, basting the duck occasionally with the pan juices and pouring away the excess fat as necessary. Test by piercing the thickest part of the thigh with the point of a sharp knife. The juices should run clear.

Transfer the duck to a heated platter, remove the trussing string and keep hot. Pour off most of the fat from the roasting tin, sprinkle in the flour and cook, stirring, for 2 minutes. Blend in the stock. Bring to the boil, then lower the heat and simmer, stirring, for 3–4 minutes. Add salt and pepper to taste. Serve in a gravy boat, with the duck.

MRS BEETON'S TIPS

If you have the duck giblets, use them as the basis of your stock. Put them in a saucepan with 1 sliced onion and 1 sliced carrot. Add 600 ml/1 pint water. Simmer, covered, for 1 hour, then strain.

The stuffing can be shaped into balls and cooked around the roast duck, if preferred. Bind it with a little beaten egg.

Roast goose with apples and onions

SERVES 6 (WITH MEAT TO SPARE, DEPENDING
ON THE SIZE OF THE GOOSE)

1 goose with giblets

salt and pepper

1 orange

1 lemon

13 small onions

7 bay leaves

1 large fresh thyme sprig

30 ml/2 tbsp dried sage

1 cinnamon stick

4 cloves

50 g/2 oz butter, cubed

12 Cox's Orange Pippin apples

5 ml/1 tsp lemon juice

45 ml/3 tbsp port

45 ml/3 tbsp crab apple or
   redcurrant jelly

25 g/1 oz plain flour

Remove the giblets from the goose and put them in a saucepan. Add 1.5 litres/2¾ pints water and bring to the boil. Lower the heat and simmer until the liquid is reduced by half. Strain and set aside.

Set the oven at 230°C/450°F/gas 8. Weigh the goose and calculate the cooking time at 20 minutes per 450 g/1 lb. Trim away excess fat and rinse the bird, then rub it all over with plenty of salt and pepper. Pare the rind from the fruit and place it in the body cavity with 1 onion, 2 bay leaves and the thyme sprig. Rub the sage over the outside of the bird and tuck a bay leaf behind each of the wing and leg joints.

Place the goose on a rack in a roasting tin. Place it in the oven and immediately reduce the heat to 180°C/350°F/gas 4. Cook for the calculated time, draining away fat from the roasting tin occasionally.

Meanwhile, peel the remaining onions but leave them whole. Place them in a saucepan and pour in boiling water to cover. Add a little salt. Simmer for 15 minutes, then drain well. Squeeze the juice from the orange and lemon, and mix together in a small saucepan. Add the cinnamon, cloves and remaining bay leaf, then heat gently until simmering. Cover and cook for 15 minutes. Off the heat, stir in the butter.

Peel and core the apples. As each apple is prepared, place it in a bowl of iced water to which the lemon juice has been added. This will prevent discoloration. Drain the apples, put them in an ovenproof dish and spoon the fruit juice and spice mixture over them to coat them completely. Add the onions, then toss them with the apples so all are coated in juices.

Place the dish of apples and onions in the oven 1 hour before the goose is cooked. Turn them occasionally during cooking so that they are evenly browned and tender. About 10 minutes before the goose is cooked, heat the port and jelly gently in a saucepan or in a bowl in the microwave until the jelly has melted. Spoon this over the apple and onion mixture for the final 5 minutes.

When the goose is cooked, transfer it to a heated serving platter and keep hot. Drain off the fat from the tin. Stir the flour into the cooking juices and cook over low heat for 5 minutes, scraping in all the sediment from the base of the pan. Pour in the reserved giblet stock and bring to the boil, stirring all the time. Taste for seasoning and pour or strain into a sauceboat. Serve the goose surrounded by the glazed apples and onions, with their juices.

ROAST RIBS OF BEEF WITH YORKSHIRE PUDDING

*This impressive joint is also known
as a standing rib roast. Ask the
butcher to trim the thin ends of the
bones so that the joint will stand
upright. The recipe uses clarified
dripping for cooking, but the roast
may be cooked without any
additional fat. There will be sufficient
fat from the meat for basting.*

SERVES 6 TO 8

2.5 kg/5½ lb forerib of beef

50–75 g/2–3 oz beef dripping

1 quantity Yorkshire Pudding
    batter

salt and pepper

vegetable stock or water

Set the oven at 230°C/450°F/gas 8. Wipe the meat but do not salt it.
Melt 50 g/2 oz of the dripping in a roasting tin, add the meat and quickly
spoon some of the hot fat over it. Roast for 10 minutes.

Lower the oven temperature to 180°C/350°F/gas 4. Baste the meat
thoroughly, then continue to roast for a further 1¾ hours for rare meat;
2¼ hours for well-done meat. Baste frequently during cooking.

Meanwhile make the Yorkshire pudding batter. About 30 minutes
before the end of the cooking time, spoon off 30 ml/2 tbsp of the
dripping and divide it between six 7.5 cm/3 inch Yorkshire pudding tins.
Place the tins in the oven for 5 minutes or until the fat is very hot, then
carefully divide the batter between them. Bake above the meat for
15–20 minutes.

When the beef is cooked, salt it lightly, transfer it to a warmed serving
platter and keep hot. Pour off almost all the fat from the roasting tin,
leaving the sediment. Pour in enough vegetable stock or water to make a
thin gravy, then heat to boiling point, stirring all the time. Season with salt
and pepper and serve in a heated gravy boat with the roast and
Yorkshire puddings.

ROAST TURKEY

*For information on thawing frozen
turkeys, plus tips for cooking and
carving, refer to the section on
Poultry at the start of this book.
Cooking times for birds of different
weights are on page 46.*

SERVES 14 TO 16

fat for basting

1 (5–6 kg/11–13 lb) turkey

450 g/1 lb Forcemeat

675 g/1½ lb seasoned
    sausagemeat

225 g/8 oz rindless streaky
    bacon rashers

Set the oven at 220°C/425°F/gas 7. Weigh the turkey. Trim it, and wash
it inside and out in cold water. Pat dry with absorbent kitchen paper.
Immediately before cooking, stuff the neck of the bird with forcemeat.
Put the sausagemeat inside the body cavity. Cover the breast of the bird
with the bacon rashers.

Place the prepared turkey in a roasting tin. Cover with foil and roast for
15 minutes. Lower the oven temperature to 180°C/350°F/gas 4 and
roast for 20 minutes per 450 g/1 lb (unstuffed weight) plus 20 minutes,
or until cooked through. Remove the foil for the last hour of cooking and
the bacon strips for the final 20 minutes to allow the breast to brown.
Serve with bacon rolls (see Mrs Beeton's Tip) and Bread Sauce.

MRS BEETON'S TIP
To make bacon rolls, roll up 16 rindless streaky bacon rashers,
threading them in pairs on short metal skewers. Grill the rolls for
about 5 minutes, turning frequently, until crisp.

ROAST TURKEY WITH CHESTNUT STUFFING

SERVES 14 TO 16

1 (4.5–5.5 kg/10–12 lb) turkey

salt and pepper

225 g/8 oz rindless streaky
  bacon rashers

HERB FORCEMEAT

50 g/2 oz margarine

100 g/4 oz fresh white
  breadcrumbs

pinch of grated nutmeg

15 ml/1 tbsp chopped parsley

5 ml/1 tsp chopped fresh mixed
  herbs

grated rind of ½ lemon

salt and pepper

1 egg, beaten

CHESTNUT STUFFING

1 kg/2¼ lb chestnuts

275 ml/9 fl oz turkey or chicken
  stock

50 g/2 oz butter

1 egg, beaten

single cream or milk (see
  method)

Make the chestnut stuffing first. Make a small slit in the shell of each chestnut, then place the nuts in a saucepan of boiling water. Cook for 5 minutes. Drain carefully and remove the shells and skins while the chestnuts are still hot. Transfer them to a clean pan, add the stock and simmer for 20 minutes or until tender. Drain the chestnuts and chop them finely, or press through a sieve into a clean bowl. Melt the butter in a small saucepan. Add to the bowl containing the chestnuts. Stir in the beaten egg, with enough cream or milk to moisten the mixture.

Make the forcemeat. Melt the margarine in a small saucepan. Add the breadcrumbs, nutmeg, herbs and lemon rind. Stir in salt and pepper to taste and sufficient beaten egg to bind the mixture.

Set the oven at 180°C/350°F/gas 4. Trim the turkey and wash it inside and out in cold water. Pat dry with absorbent kitchen paper and season inside with salt and pepper. Immediately before cooking, fill the neck end of the bird with chestnut stuffing and the body with the forcemeat. Truss if wished, and cover the bird with the bacon. Place the bird in a roasting tin and roast for 4½–5 hours or until cooked through, removing the bacon towards the end to allow the breast to brown. (For a larger bird, see the chart on page 46 for cooking times.) Serve with giblet gravy.

ideas for leftover roast turkey

HASHED TURKEY Make stock from turkey bones and trimmings, a sliced carrot, a diced turnip, a blade of mace and a bouquet garni. Cover with water and simmer for 1 hour. Strain. Cook 1 chopped onion in a knob of butter. Add 40 g/1½ oz plain flour and cook for 2 minutes. Pour in 600 ml/1 pint strained stock and bring to the boil. Add 30 ml/2 tbsp mushroom ketchup, 45 ml/3 tbsp port or sherry and salt and pepper. Gently poach sliced cooked turkey in the sauce, adding any leftover stuffing cut in neat portions, for 15 minutes until thoroughly heated.

TURKEY CROQUETTES Mince or finely chop cooked turkey – this is ideal for dark meat and small pieces which do not slice well. For every 225 g/8 oz turkey, allow 50 g/2 oz diced or minced cooked ham and ½ small finely chopped onion. Cook the onion in a little butter, stir in 15 ml/1 tbsp plain flour and 150 ml/¼ pint turkey gravy or stock. Bring to the boil. Off the heat add the turkey, ham, 1 egg yolk and plenty of seasoning. Cool, then chill. Shape the mixture into croquettes. Coat in flour, egg and breadcrumbs, then deep or shallow fry until golden. Originally, the mixture was shaped into small mounds by pressing it into a small, greased wine glass before coating.

ROCK CAKES

MAKES 12 TO 14

fat for greasing

200 g/7 oz self-raising flour

1.25 ml/¼ tsp salt

1.25 ml/¼ tsp grated nutmeg

75 g/3 oz margarine

75 g/3 oz sugar

75 g/3 oz mixed dried fruit
(currants, sultanas, mixed
peel, glacé cherries)

1 egg

milk (see method)

Thoroughly grease two baking sheets. Set the oven at 200°C/400°F/gas 6.

Sift the flour and salt into a mixing bowl. Add the nutmeg. Rub in the margarine until the mixture resembles fine breadcrumbs. Stir in the sugar and dried fruit. Put the egg into a measuring jug and add enough milk to make up to 125 ml/4 fl oz. Add the liquid to the dry ingredients and mix with a fork to a sticky stiff mixture that will support the fork.

Divide the mixture into 12–14 portions. Form into rocky heaps on the prepared baking sheets, allowing about 2 cm/¾ inch between each for spreading. Bake for 15–20 minutes or until each bun is firm to the touch on the base. Cool on a wire rack.

variation

COCONUT CAKES Omit the dried fruit. Stir in 50 g/2 oz desiccated coconut instead. Bake as above

ROYAL ICING

Royal icing cannot be applied directly to a cake because it would drag the crumbs and discolour badly, so rich fruit cakes are usually covered with a layer of almond paste or marzipan before the royal icing is applied.

SUFFICIENT TO COAT THE TOP AND SIDES
OF ONE 20 CM/8 INCH CAKE

2 egg whites

450 g/1 lb icing sugar, sifted

Place the egg whites in a grease free bowl and break them up with a fork. Gradually beat in about two-thirds of the icing sugar with a wooden spoon (kept solely for the purpose), and continue beating for about 15 minutes until the icing is pure white and forms soft peaks. Add the remaining icing sugar, if necessary, to attain this texture. Cover the bowl with cling film and place a dampened tea-towel on top. Place the bowl inside a polythene bag if storing overnight or for longer. Before use, lightly beat the icing to burst any air bubbles that have risen to the surface. Adjust the consistency for flat icing or piping.

> ### MRS BEETON'S TIP
> If the icing is to be used for a single cake, glycerine may be added to prevent it from becoming too brittle when dry. Add 2.5 ml/½ tsp glycerine during the final beating. Do not, however, use glycerine for a tiered cake where the icing must be hard in order to hold the tiers.

ROYAL ICING QUANTITIES

Quick guide to quantities required to cover cakes (sufficient for 3 coats)

ROUND	ROYAL ICING	SQUARE	ROYAL ICING
15 cm/6 inch	575 g/1¼ lb	15 cm/6 inch	675 g/1½ lb
18 cm/7 inch	675 g/1½ lb	18 cm/7 inch	800 g/1¾ lb
20 cm/8 inch	800 g/1¾ lb	20 cm/8 inch	900 g/2 lb
23 cm/9 inch	900 g/2 lb	23 cm/9 inch	1 kg/2¼ lb
25 cm/10 inch	1 kg/2¼ lb	25 cm/10 inch	1.25 kg/2¾ lb
28 cm/11 inch	1.25 kg/2¾ lb	28 cm/11 inch	1.4 kg/3 lb
30 cm/12 inch	1.4 kg/3 lb	30 cm/12 inch	1.5 kg/3¼ lb

RUBBED-IN BISCUITS

This simple method may be used for making a wide variety of biscuits.

MAKES 20 TO 26

fat for greasing

200 g/7 oz plain flour

1.25 ml/¼ tsp salt

75–100 g/3–4 oz butter or margarine

50 g/2 oz caster sugar

5 ml/1 tsp baking powder

1 egg yolk

flour for rolling out

Grease two baking sheets. Set the oven at 180°C/350°F/gas 4.

In a mixing bowl, mix the flour and salt. Rub in the butter or margarine until the mixture resembles fine breadcrumbs, then stir in the sugar and baking powder. Bind to a stiff paste with the egg yolk. Knead well and roll out to a thickness of just under 1 cm/½ inch on a lightly floured surface. Cut into rounds with a 5 cm/2 inch cutter. Re-roll any trimmings and cut more rounds.

Place the biscuits on the prepared baking sheets, pricking the top of each in several places. Bake for 12–15 minutes or until firm and pale golden brown. Leave for a few minutes, then cool on a wire rack.

variations
PLAIN MOCHA BISCUITS Add 50 g/2 oz powdered drinking chocolate with the flour and 10 ml/2 tsp instant coffee (dissolved in 7.5 ml/1 tsp boiling water) with the egg yolk.

PLAIN CINNAMON OR SPICE BISCUITS Add 5 ml/1 tsp ground cinnamon or mixed spice to the flour. When cold, sandwich the biscuits together in pairs with jam, and dredge with icing sugar.

PLAIN COCONUT BISCUITS Use 150 g/5 oz flour and 50 g/2 oz desiccated coconut. As soon as the biscuits are cooked, brush with warm Apricot Glaze and sprinkle with coconut.

RUMP STEAK PIE

SERVES 4

225 g/8 oz plain flour
75 g/3 oz beef dripping
900 g/2 lb rump steak
salt and pepper
1 egg yolk

Place the flour in a bowl. Gradually mix in enough water (about 150ml/ ¼ pint) to make a soft but not too sticky dough.

On a lightly floured surface, roll out the dough into a 28 x 15 cm (11 x 6 inch) oblong. Dot a third of the dripping over the top two-thirds of the dough, fold the bottom third of the dough over the middle portion of fat, then fold the top third over that. Give the dough a quarter turn to the right, roll it out and repeat the process twice more to incorporate all the fat. Roll and fold the dough a fourth time without fat, then wrap it in polythene and chill for 30 minutes.

Set the oven at 180°C/350°F/gas 4. Cut the steak into thin slices measuring about 7.5 x 5 cm/3 x 2 inches, then layer it in a 1.1 litre/2 pint pie dish, mounding it up in the middle and pressing down neatly. Season each layer very generously. Slowly pour in enough water to come just below the rim of the dish.

Roll out the dough thickly. Dampen the rim of the dish and press a strip of dough on it. Dampen the dough rim, then cover the pie and seal the edge well. Decorate the top with pastry trimmings. Beat the egg yolk with 5 ml/1 tsp water; brush it over the pie. Bake for about 2½ hours, covering loosely with foil after 1½–1¾ hours. Pierce the pie with a knife to check that the meat is tender.

See also Bean Salad with Tuna, Bean Sprout Salad, Boiled Vegetable Salad, Coleslaw, French Bean and Tomato Salad, Potato Salad, Ratatouille, Rice Salad, Tomato Salad, Veal and Tuna Salad, Waldorf Salad and Winter Salad.

SALAD NICOISE — *Illustrated on page 131*

SERVES 4 TO 6

225 g/8 oz French beans

salt and pepper

2 hard-boiled eggs

3 small tomatoes

1 garlic clove, crushed

1 (198 g/7 oz) can tuna, drained and flaked

50 g/2 oz black olives

60 ml/2 fl oz French Dressing

1 large lettuce, separated into leaves

1 (50 g/2 oz) can anchovy fillets, drained, to garnish

Top and tail the French beans. Bring a small saucepan of salted water to the boil. Add the beans and cook for 5–10 minutes or until just tender. Drain, refresh under cold water and drain again. Shell the eggs and cut them into quarters. Quarter the tomatoes.

Put the beans into a large bowl with the eggs, tomatoes, garlic, tuna and most of the olives. Pour over the dressing and toss lightly. Add salt and pepper to taste.

Line a large salad bowl with the lettuce leaves. Pile the tuna mixture into the centre and garnish with the remaining olives and the anchovy fillets. Serve at once.

SALAMI AND PORK SALAD

SERVES 4

100 g/4 oz boiled beetroot

1 lettuce, separated into leaves

200 g/7 oz each of diced cold roast pork and cold boiled potatoes

2–3 gherkins, sliced

15 ml/1 tbsp capers

salt and pepper

100 ml/3 fl oz mayonnaise

12 slices of salami

1 lemon, sliced

12 stoned green olives to garnish

Dice the beetroot. Wash the lettuce leaves and dry them thoroughly. Use them to line a salad bowl. mix the pork, potatoes, beetroot, gherkins and capers lightly. Add salt and pepper to taste. Then pile the mixture into the lined bowl.

Pour the mayonnaise over the top, and arrange alternate slices of salami and lemon around the rim. If the salami is sliced thinly, roll each slice into a neat cone shape; alternatively, overlap the slices as they are arranged flat. garnish with the olives. Serve at once.

SALMON MOUSSE

SERVES 6 TO 8

oil for greasing

450 g/1 lb salmon fillet or steak
  (a tail piece may be used)

1 litre/1¾ pints Court Bouillon

15 g/½ oz gelatine

50 g/2 oz butter, softened

45 ml/3 tbsp double cream,
  lightly whipped

15 ml/1 tbsp medium-dry sherry

BECHAMEL SAUCE

½ small onion

½ small carrot

1 small celery stick

300 ml/½ pint milk

1 bay leaf

few parsley stalks

1 fresh thyme sprig

1 clove

5 white peppercorns

1 blade of mace

salt

25 g/1 oz butter

25 g/1 oz plain flour

Brush a glass or metal fish mould with oil. Leave upside down to drain. Make the Béchamel sauce. Combine the onion, carrot, celery and milk in a saucepan. Add the herbs and spices, with salt to taste. Heat to simmering point, cover, turn off the heat and allow to stand for 30 minutes to infuse. Strain into a measuring jug.

Melt the butter in a saucepan. Stir in the flour and cook over a low heat for 2–3 minutes, without allowing the mixture to colour. Gradually add the flavoured milk, stirring constantly until the mixture boils and thickens. Remove the pan from the heat, cover the surface of the sauce with damp greaseproof paper and set aside until required.

Put the salmon in a large saucepan and cover with court bouillon. Bring to the boil, lower the heat and simmer for 15 minutes. Drain, cool and remove the skin and bones. Pound to a paste in a mortar or process in a blender or food processor until smooth.

Place 30 ml/2 tbsp water in a small bowl and sprinkle the gelatine on to the liquid. Set aside for 15 minutes until the gelatine is spongy. Stand the bowl over a pan of hot water and stir the gelatine until it has dissolved completely.

Tip the salmon into a large bowl and add the cold Béchamel sauce. Mix until thoroughly blended, then add the softened butter, whipped cream, sherry and dissolved gelatine. Mix well, then spoon into the prepared mould. Smooth the top, cover closely and chill for 2–3 hours until set. Turn out, garnish with cucumber and radish slices and serve.

variation
Canned salmon may be used instead of fresh fish. Use one 213 g/7 oz can. Drain the can liquid and use to sponge the gelatine instead of water.

SAUSAGEMEAT CAKES — MRS BEETON'S

Mrs Beeton's original recipe did not have any breadcrumbs but they do help to give the mixture a workable consistency, avoiding hours of hard pounding in a mortar.

MAKES 8

450 g/1 lb boneless belly of
    pork, skinned

350 g/12 oz rindless bacon

15 g/½ oz salt

freshly ground black pepper

1.25 ml/¼ tsp grated nutmeg

15 ml/1 tbsp chopped parsley

50 g/2 oz fresh breadcrumbs

flour for shaping

oil for frying

Finely chop the pork and bacon, then place them in a bowl. A food processor is ideal for this, otherwise use a large, very sharp knife or cleaver. Add the salt, plenty of pepper, nutmeg, parsley and bread-crumbs. Pound the mixture until the ingredients bind together.

Wet your hands and shape the mixture into 8 neat round cakes. Knead the mixture together so that it binds firmly, then dust the cakes with flour. Heat a very small amount of oil in a frying pan (just enough to stop the cakes from sticking), then cook the cakes fairly slowly so that they are thoroughly cooked through by the time they are well browned on both sides. Allow about 30 minutes' total cooking time. Serve at once.

> ### MRS BEETON"S TIP
> Bacon offcuts are ideal for this economical recipe. Finely chopped belly pork is traditionally combined with the bacon in these cakes but prepared pork sausagemeat could be used to save time.

SAUSAGEMEAT STUFFING

SUFFICIENT FOR 1 (1.5 KG/3¼ LB) CHICKEN

1 chicken or turkey liver,
    trimmed (optional)

450 g/1 lb pork sausagemeat

50 g/2 oz fresh white
    breadcrumbs

15 ml/1 tbsp chopped parsley

5 ml/1 tsp dried mixed herbs

1 egg, lightly beaten

salt and pepper

If using the liver, chop it finely and put it in a mixing bowl. Add the sausagemeat and breadcrumbs, with the herbs. Mix well, using a spoon or clean hands. Stir in enough of the beaten egg to bind the mixture. Add plenty of salt and pepper.

NOTE
If using the sausagemeat stuffing for a 5–6 kg/9–11 lb turkey, treble the quantity.

> SAUCES   See individual entries in alphabetical order according to recipe title; see also Custards and Haddock Florentine for Mornay Sauce. A complete list of sauce recipes is given in the index under the entries Sauces, savoury and Sauces, sweet.

SAVOURY RICE

SERVES 3 TO 4

200 g/7 oz long-grain rice

1 onion, chopped

salt and pepper

50 g/2 oz mature Cheddar
  cheese, grated

45 ml/3 tbsp Tomato Sauce

30 ml/2 tbsp chopped parsley

1.25 ml/¼ tsp dried mixed herbs

pinch of cayenne pepper

50 g/2 oz butter, chopped

25 g/1 oz Parmesan cheese,
  grated, to serve

Place the rice and onion in a saucepan and pour in 450 ml/¾ pint cold water. Add a little salt. Bring to the boil, cover the pan tightly and lower the heat to the lowest setting. Leave for 15 minutes, turn off the heat and leave for a further 15 minutes without removing the lid.

Mix in the Cheddar and the tomato sauce, with the parsley, herbs, cayenne and salt and pepper to taste. Stir in the butter.

Heat through, stirring, for 3–4 minutes, then pile on to a warmed serving dish. Sprinkle with Parmesan cheese and serve at once.

variations
Add chopped grilled bacon or hot sliced German-style sausages to the rice with the tomato sauce.

SCONES

MAKES 12

fat for greasing

225 g/8 oz self-raising flour

2.5 ml/½ tsp salt

25–50 g/1–2 oz butter or
  margarine

125–150 ml/4–5 fl oz milk

flour for kneading

milk or beaten egg for glazing
  (optional)

Grease a baking sheet. Set the oven at 220°C/425°F/gas 7. Sift the flour and salt into a large bowl. Rub in the butter or margarine, then mix to a soft dough with the milk, using a round-bladed knife. Knead very lightly on a floured surface until smooth.

Roll or pat out the dough to about 1 cm/½ inch thick and cut into rounds, using a 6 cm/2½ inch cutter. (Alternatively, divide into two equal portions and roll each piece into a round 1–2 cm/½–¾ inch thick. Mark each round into six wedges.) Re-roll the trimmings and re-cut.

Place the scones on the prepared baking sheet. Brush the tops with milk or beaten egg, if liked. Bake for 10–12 minutes. Cool on a wire rack.

other raising agents
Scones can be made using plain flour with raising agents: for 225 g/8 oz plain flour, use 5 ml/1 tsp bicarbonate of soda and 10 ml/2 tsp cream of tartar. Or use 20 ml/4 tsp baking powder as the raising agent.

SCOTCH BROTH

This economical soup was originally intended to furnish two meals: the meat was removed after cooking and served separately. Today it is more usual to cut up the meat and add it to the soup.

SERVES 4

25 g/1 oz pearl barley

450 g/1 lb middle neck of lamb, trimmed of excess fat

1.4 litres/2½ pints white stock or chicken stock

1 onion, chopped

1 leek, trimmed, sliced and washed

2 carrots, sliced

1 swede, cubed

salt and pepper

Put the barley in a small saucepan with water to cover. Bring to the boil, then drain off the water and transfer the barley to a large pan with the meat and stock. Bring the mixture to the boil, skim off any scum on the surface, then lower the heat and simmer gently for 2 hours.

Add the vegetables with plenty of salt and pepper. Simmer for a further 45–60 minutes. Lift out the meat, remove it from the bones, and roughly chop it. Skim off any fat from the broth, add more salt and if required, then replace the chopped meat. Serve very hot.

> ## PRESSURE COOKER TIP
>
> It is not necessary to blanch the barley. Simply combine the ingredients in the cooker, reducing the amount of stock to 900 ml/1½ pints. The cooker should not be more than half full. Put the lid on, bring to 15 lb pressure and cook for 10 minutes. Reduce the pressure slowly. Continue as above, reheating the soup in the open pan, and adding more stock if liked.

SCOTCH EGGS

MAKES 4

1 egg

50 g/2 oz dried white breadcrumbs

350 g/12 oz sausagemeat

15 ml/1 tbsp plain flour

salt and pepper

4 eggs, hard-boiled

oil for deep frying

Beat the egg with 10 ml/2 tsp water in a small bowl. Spread out the breadcrumbs in a second, shallow bowl. Divide the sausagemeat into four equal portions. Pat out each portion to a burger-like shape.

Mix the flour with salt and pepper, and use to coat the hard-boiled eggs. Place an egg in the centre of each circle of sausagemeat. Mould the sausagemeat evenly around each egg, pinching it together to seal the joins. Mould each Scotch egg to a good shape, roll in beaten egg, then roll in the breadcrumbs. Press the crumbs on well.

Put the oil for frying into a deep saucepan and heat to 160°C/325°F or until a cube of bread added to the oil browns in 2 minutes. If using a deep-fat fryer, follow the manufacturer's instructions. Add the eggs carefully and fry for about 10 minutes until golden brown. Lift out with a slotted spoon and drain on absorbent kitchen paper. Serve hot or cold, cutting each egg in half lengthways.

SCOTCH EGGS WITH BACON

This old-fashioned recipe for Scotch eggs uses a flavoursome bacon, breadcrumb and suet mixture instead of prepared sausagemeat.

SERVES 4

4 rindless back bacon rashers

50 g/2 oz shredded suet

75 g/3 oz wholemeal
  breadcrumbs

15 ml/1 tbsp grated lemon rind

5 ml/1 tsp finely chopped
  parsley

1.25 ml/¼ tsp dried oregano

pinch of ground mace

salt and cayenne pepper

Worcestershire sauce

2 eggs, beaten

75 g/3 oz fresh white
  breadcrumbs

15 ml/1 tbsp plain flour

salt and pepper

4 hard-boiled eggs

oil for deep frying

Chop the bacon finely. Combine with the suet, breadcrumbs, lemon rind, herbs and mace in a bowl. Add salt, cayenne and Worcestershire sauce to taste. Stir in enough of the beaten egg to make a forcemeat which can be shaped.

Beat the remaining beaten egg with 10 ml/2 tsp water in a small bowl. Spread out the breadcrumbs in a second, shallow bowl. Divide the forcemeat into 4 equal pieces. On a lightly floured surface, pat each piece into a circle about 13 cm/5 inches in diameter.

Mix the remaining flour with the salt and pepper in a sturdy polythene bag. Add the hard-boiled eggs and toss gently to coat evenly. Place an egg in the centre of each circle of forcemeat. Mould the forcemeat evenly round the egg, making sure it fits snugly. Seal the joins with a little of the beaten egg mixture and pinch well together. Mould each Scotch egg to a good shape, brush all over with beaten egg, then roll in the breadcrumbs until evenly coated. Press the crumbs well in.

Put the oil for frying into a deep saucepan and heat to 160°C/325°F or until a cube of bread added to the oil browns in 2 minutes. If using a deep fat fryer, follow the manufacturer's instructions. Carefully add the eggs and fry for about 10 minutes until golden brown. Lift out with a slotted spoon and drain on absorbent kitchen paper. Serve hot or cold.

MRS BEETON'S TIP

Scotch eggs will keep for a day if chilled when cold; however, do not freeze them as the cooked egg becomes unpleasant, watery and rubbery during freezing and thawing.

SCOTCH WOODCOCK

SERVES 4

1 (50 g/2 oz) can anchovy fillets

50 g/2 oz butter

freshly ground black pepper

150 ml/¼ pint single cream

3 egg yolks

4 slices of hot thick toast

Mash the anchovy fillets in a small bowl with the butter and pepper. Set aside. Heat the cream in a small heavy-bottomed saucepan but do not boil. Beat the egg yolks in a small bowl, then stir in the hot cream. Return the mixture to the pan. Cook over gentle heat, stirring until the sauce thickens. Do not boil or it will curdle. Spread the anchovy butter on the toast, pour the sauce over and serve at once.

SEED CAKE

MAKES ONE 15 CM/6 INCH CAKE

fat for greasing

200 g/7 oz plain flour

1.25 ml/¼ tsp salt

2.5 ml/½ tsp baking powder

15 ml/1 tbsp caraway seeds

150 g/5 oz butter or margarine

150 g/5 oz caster sugar

4 eggs, beaten

15 ml/1 tbsp milk (optional)

Line and grease a 15 cm/6 inch cake tin. Set the oven at 180°C/350°F/gas 4. Sift the flour, salt and baking powder into a bowl. Add the caraway seeds and mix well. Set aside.

Place the butter or margarine in a mixing bowl and beat until very soft. Add the sugar and cream together until light and fluffy. Add the beaten eggs gradually, beating well after each addition. If the mixture shows signs of curdling, add a little of the flour mixture. Fold in the dry ingredients lightly but thoroughly, adding the milk if too stiff.

Spoon the mixture into the prepared tin, smooth the surface and make a slight hollow in the centre. Bake for 30 minutes, then reduce the oven temperature to 160°C/325°F/gas 3 and bake for a further 50 minutes until firm to the touch. Cool the cake on a wire rack.

SEMOLINA GNOCCHI

Serve this Italian-style dish with a tomato sauce or spicy savoury meat sauce. Cook the gnocchi in the oven or under the grill.

SERVES 4

fat for greasing

500 ml/17 fl oz milk

100 g/4 oz semolina

salt and pepper

1.25 ml/¼ tsp grated nutmeg

1 egg

100 g/4 oz Parmesan cheese, grated

25 g/1 oz butter

Grease a shallow ovenproof dish. Bring the milk to the boil in a saucepan. Sprinkle in the semolina and stir over low heat until the mixture is thick. Mix in the salt, pepper, nutmeg, egg and 75 g/3 oz of the Parmesan. Beat the mixture well until smooth. Spread on a shallow dish and set aside to cool.

Set the oven at 200°C/400°F/gas 6, if using. Cut the cooled semolina mixture into 2 cm/¾ inch squares or shape into rounds. Place in the prepared ovenproof dish and sprinkle with the remaining Parmesan; dot with butter. Brown under the grill or in the oven for 8–10 minutes.

SEMOLINA PUDDING

Use coarsely ground rice, oatmeal, small sago or cornmeal instead of semolina, if preferred.

SERVES 6

1 litre/1¾ pints milk

flavouring (see Mrs Beeton's Tip)

75 g/3 oz semolina

pinch of salt

50–75 g/2–3 oz caster sugar

butter for greasing (optional)

Warm the milk in a heavy-bottomed saucepan. Add any solid flavouring, if used, to the milk and infuse for about 10 minutes; then remove. Sprinkle the semolina on to the milk, stirring quickly to prevent the formation of lumps. Bring to simmering point, stirring all the time. Continue stirring, and simmer for 15–20 minutes or until the grain is transparent and cooked through.

Stir in the salt, sugar, and any flavouring essence used. Serve the creamed semolina hot or cold or pour into a well-buttered 1.75 litre/3 pint pie dish, and bake at 180°C/350°F/gas 4, for 20–30 minutes until the top has browned.

MRS BEETON'S TIP

Grated citrus rind, ground cinnamon, allspice or grated nutmeg may be added to this pudding. Natural flavouring essences or liqueurs are also suitable.

SHEPHERD'S PIE

SERVES 4 TO 6

butter for greasing

50 g/2 oz butter

2 onions, roughly chopped

15 ml/1 tbsp plain flour

250 ml/8 fl oz well-flavoured lamb stock

575 g/1¼ lb lean cooked lamb, minced

salt and pepper

5 ml/1 tsp Worcestershire sauce

675 g/1½ lb potatoes, halved

15–30 ml/1–2 tbsp milk

pinch of grated nutmeg

Melt half the butter in a saucepan and fry the onions until softened but not coloured. Stir in the flour and cook gently for 1–2 minutes, stirring all the time. Gradually add the stock. Bring to the boil, stirring until the sauce thickens. Stir in the lamb, with salt and pepper and Worcestershire sauce to taste. Cover the pan and simmer for 30 minutes.

Meanwhile cook the potatoes in a saucepan of salted boiling water for about 30 minutes or until tender. Drain thoroughly and mash with a potato masher, or beat them with a hand-held electric whisk until smooth. Beat in the rest of the butter and the milk to make a creamy consistency. Add salt, pepper and nutmeg to taste.

Set the oven at 220°C/450°F/gas 7. Spoon the meat mixture into a greased pie dish or shallow oven-to-table dish. Cover with the potato, smooth the top, then flick it up into small peaks or score a pattern on the surface with a fork. Bake for 10–15 minutes until browned on top. Serve at once.

SHELLFISH For basic information on varieties, preparation and cooking methods, see pages 13–43. See also Coquilles St Jacques Mornay, Moules Marinière, Paella, Prawn Cocktail, Prawn Curry, Potted Shrimps or Prawns and Sweet and Sour Prawns.

SHORTBREAD

Shortbread should be handled as lightly – and as little – as possible; if the dough is worked too much, it will toughen. Wooden moulds, carved with an appropriate motif, such as a thistle, are sometimes used for this Scottish speciality but it is easier to shape the dough by hand.

MAKES 8 WEDGES

fat for greasing

100 g/4 oz plain flour

1.25 ml/¼ tsp salt

50 g/2 oz rice flour, ground rice or semolina

50 g/2 oz caster sugar

100 g/4 oz butter

Invert a baking sheet, then grease the surface now uppermost. Set the oven at 180°C/350°F/gas 4.

Mix all the dry ingredients in a mixing bowl. Rub in the butter until the mixture binds together to a dough. Shape into a large round about 1 cm/½ inch thick. Pinch up the edges to decorate. Place on the prepared baking sheet, and prick with a fork. Bake for 40–45 minutes. Cut the shortbread into wedges while still warm.

variations

SHORTBREAD BISCUITS Roll out the dough on a lightly floured surface to a thickness of just under 1 cm/½ inch. Cut into rounds with a 5–6 cm/ 2–2½ inch cutter. Place on 1–2 greased baking sheets, allowing room for spreading. Prick the surface of each biscuit in several places with a fork. Bake for 15–20 minutes. Leave to stand for a few minutes, then cool on a wire rack.

ORIGINAL SCOTCH SHORTBREAD Omit the salt and rice flour, and use 225 g/8 oz plain flour. The butter must be well softened in order to combine with the flour to make a dough. Reduce the sugar to 25 g/1 oz. Add 10 ml/2 tsp caraway seeds. Top the shortbread with strips of candied peel.

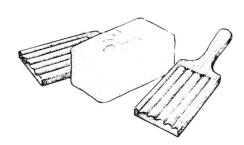

SHOULDER OF LAMB WITH HERBS

This recipe may be used for leg as well as for shoulder of lamb.

SERVES 6

1 shoulder of lamb, boned

4 garlic cloves, peeled and quartered lengthways

about 6 each small fresh rosemary and thyme sprigs

4 bay leaves

2 oranges

60 ml/4 tbsp olive oil

salt and pepper

300 ml/½ pint red wine

GARNISH

orange slices

fresh herbs

Trim any lumps of fat from the lamb, then tie it in a neat shape if the butcher has not already done this. Weigh the joint and calculate the cooking time at 30 minutes per 450 g/1 lb plus 30 minutes (see guide to cooking times, page 78). Use a small pointed knife to make short cuts into the lamb, at an angle running under the skin, all over the joint. Insert pieces of garlic and the rosemary and thyme sprigs into the cuts. Place the joint in a deep dish, with two bay leaves underneath and two on top.

Pare two long strips of rind off one orange and add them to the dish, next to or on top of the lamb. Squeeze the juice from the oranges, then mix it with the olive oil, salt and pepper. Pour this mixture over the lamb, cover and marinate for several hours or overnight. Turn the joint at least once during marinating.

Set the oven at 180°C/350°F/gas 4. Transfer the joint to a roasting tin, adding the bay leaves and orange rind but reserving the marinade. Cook for half the calculated time, brushing occasionally with the reserved marinade and basting with cooking juices from the tin. Pour the remaining marinade and the wine over the joint and continue roasting. Baste the lamb occasionally and add a little water to the juices in the tin if they begin to dry up – if the roasting tin is large the juices will evaporate more speedily.

Transfer the cooked joint to a serving dish, cover with foil and set aside. Pour 300 ml/½ pint boiling water or vegetable cooking water into the roasting tin. Boil the cooking juices rapidly, stirring and scraping the sediment off the base and sides of the pan, until they are reduced by half. Taste for seasoning, then strain the sauce into a heated sauceboat. Garnish the lamb with orange slices and fresh herbs and serve at once, carving it into thick slices. Offer the sauce separately.

MRS BEETON'S TIP

Once it has been reduced, the sauce may be thickened by whisking in small knobs of beurre manié, then boiling for 2 minutes, whisking all the time. To make beurre manié cream 25 g/1 oz butter with 30–45 ml/2–3 tbsp plain flour.

SIMNEL CAKE

MAKES ONE 18 CM/7 INCH CAKE

fat for greasing

200 g/7 oz plain flour

2.5 ml/½ tsp baking powder

1.25 ml/¼ tsp salt

150 g/5 oz butter

150 g/5 oz caster sugar

4 eggs

100 g/4 oz glacé cherries, halved

150 g/5 oz currants

150 g/5 oz sultanas

100 g/4 oz seedless raisins

50 g/2 oz cut mixed peel

50 g/2 oz ground almonds

grated rind of 1 lemon

DECORATION

450 g/1 lb marzipan

30 ml/2 tbsp apricot jam

1 egg, beaten

glacé icing using 50 g/2 oz icing
  sugar

Line and grease a 18 cm/7 inch round cake tin. Set the oven at 180°C/350°F/gas 4.

Sift the flour, baking powder and salt into a bowl. In a mixing bowl, cream the butter and sugar together well and beat in the eggs, adding a little of the flour mixture if necessary. Fold the flour mixture, cherries, dried fruit, peel and ground almonds into the creamed mixture. Add the lemon rind and mix well.

Spoon half the mixture into the prepared tin. Cut off one third of the marzipan and roll it to a pancake about 1 cm/½ inch thick and slightly smaller than the circumference of the tin. Place it gently on top of the cake mixture and spoon the remaining cake mixture on top.

Bake for 1 hour, then reduce the oven temperature to 160°C/325°F/gas 3 and bake for 1½ hours more. Cool in the tin, then turn out on a wire rack.

Warm, then sieve the apricot jam. When the cake is cold, divide the remaining marzipan in half. Roll one half to a round with a slightly smaller diameter than the top of the cake. Brush the top of the cake with apricot jam and press the marzipan lightly on to it. Trim the edge neatly.

Make 11 small balls with the remaining marzipan; place them around the edge of the cake. Brush the balls with the beaten egg and brown under the grill. Pour the glacé icing over the centre of the cake. Decorate with chickens and Easter eggs.

SKATE – FRIED

SERVES 4

50 g/2 oz plain flour

salt and pepper

1 egg, lightly beaten

50 g/2 oz dried white
  breadcrumbs

4 skate wings, total weight about
  575 g/1¼ lb

75 g/3 oz butter

Tartare Sauce

Mix the flour with salt and pepper and spread out in a shallow bowl. Put the egg in a second bowl and spread out the breadcrumbs on a sheet of foil. Coat each skate wing in flour, egg and breadcrumbs.

Melt the butter in a large frying pan, add the fish and fry gently for 5 minutes on each side or until golden and cooked through. Garnish with lemon slices and watercress sprigs, if liked. Serve with tartare sauce.

SMALL RICH CAKES

MAKES 12 TO 14

fat for greasing (optional)
100 g/4 oz self-raising flour
pinch of salt
100 g/4 oz butter or margarine
100 g/4 oz caster sugar
2 eggs, beaten

Grease 12–14 bun tins or support an equivalent number of paper cases in dry bun tins. Set the oven at 180°C/350°F/gas 4. Mix the flour and salt in a bowl.

In a mixing bowl, cream the butter or margarine with the sugar until light and fluffy. Beat in the eggs, then lightly stir in the flour and salt. Divide the mixture evenly between the prepared paper cases or bun tins, and bake for 15–20 minutes until golden brown. Cool on a wire rack.

variations
CHERRY CAKES Add 50 g/2 oz chopped glacé cherries with the flour.
CHOCOLATE CAKES Add 30 ml/2 tbsp cocoa with the flour and stir in 15 ml/1 tbsp milk.
COCONUT CAKES Add 50 g/2 oz desiccated coconut with the flour and 15–30 ml/1–2 tbsp milk with the eggs.
COFFEE CAKES Dissolve 10 ml/2 tsp instant coffee in 5 ml/1 tsp boiling water. Add with the eggs.
QUEEN CAKES Add 100 g/4 oz currants with the flour.

SMOKED HADDOCK CHOWDER

SERVES 4 TO 6

450 g/1 lb smoked haddock fillet, skinned
750 ml/1¼ pints milk
50 g/2 oz butter
1 small onion, finely chopped
100 g/4 oz mushrooms, finely chopped
40 g/1½ oz plain flour
250 ml/8 fl oz single cream
freshly ground black pepper

Put the haddock fillets into a saucepan with the milk. Heat to simmering point, then simmer for about 10 minutes until just tender. Drain the fish, reserving the cooking liquid, remove the skin and shred lightly.

Melt the butter in a clean pan, add the onion and mushrooms and fry gently for about 10 minutes until soft. Do not allow the onion to colour. Stir in the flour and cook for 1 minute, stirring constantly. Gradually add the fish-flavoured milk, stirring until smooth. Bring to the boil, lower the heat and simmer until thickened.

Off the heat, add the cream and the shredded haddock. Return the pan to the heat and warm through gently. Do not allow the soup to boil after adding the cream. Top with a generous grinding of black pepper and serve at once.

> **MRS BEETON'S TIP**
> Reserve a few perfect mushrooms for a garnish if liked. Slice them thinly and sprinkle a few slices on top of each portion of soup. It is not necessary to cook the mushrooms.

SMOKED MACKEREL PATE

MAKES ABOUT 450 G/1 LB

25 g/1 oz clarified butter, plus extra for sealing (page 316)

2 shallots, finely chopped

75 g/3 oz tomato purée

5 ml/1 tsp soft light brown sugar

juice of ½ lemon

8 crushed peppercorns

15 ml/1 tbsp shredded fresh basil

1.25 ml/¼ tsp dried tarragon

few drops of Tabasco sauce

450 g/1 lb smoked mackerel fillets, skinned

75 ml/5 tbsp double cream

Melt the clarified butter in a saucepan, add the shallots and cook over gentle heat for 2–3 minutes until soft. Add the tomato purée, sugar, lemon juice, peppercorns and herbs and cook gently for 4–5 minutes. Stir in the Tabasco sauce, then set aside to cool.

Roughly purée the shallot mixture, mackerel fillets and cream in a blender or food processor. Turn into a suitable dish or mould and cool. Cover with clarified butter and chill until firm. Serve with toast.

MRS BEETON'S TIP

Serve this pâté in tomato shells. Cut small tomatoes in half and remove the pulp, setting it aside for use in a soup or sauce. Invert the tomato shells on absorbent kitchen paper to drain thoroughly, then fill each shell with the mackerel pâté. The pâté may be put in a piping bag fitted with a large star nozzle and piped into the shells. Thin it down a little with additional cream, if necessary.

SODA BREAD

MAKES ONE 800 G/1¾ LB LOAF

fat for greasing

575 g/1¼ lb plain flour

5 ml/1 tsp bicarbonate of soda

5 ml/1 tsp salt

5 ml/1 tsp cream of tartar (if using fresh milk)

300 ml/½ pint buttermilk or soured milk or fresh milk

flour for dusting

Grease a baking sheet. Set the oven at 190–200°C/375–400°F/gas 5–6. Mix all the dry ingredients in a bowl, then make a well in the centre. Add enough milk to make a fairly slack dough, pouring it in almost all at once, not spoonful by spoonful. Mix with a wooden spoon, lightly and quickly.

With floured hands, place the mixture on a lightly floured surface and flatten the dough into a round about 2.5 cm/1 inch thick. Turn on to the prepared baking sheet. Make a large cross in the surface with a floured knife to make it heat through evenly.

Bake for about 40 minutes. Pierce the centre with a thin skewer to test for readiness; it should come out clean. Wrap the loaf in a clean tea-towel to keep it soft until required.

SOLE VERONIQUE

SERVES 4

4 large lemon sole fillets

2 shallots, chopped

50 g/2 oz mushrooms, finely chopped

2 parsley sprigs

1 bay leaf

salt and pepper

125 ml/4 fl oz dry white wine

25 g/1 oz butter

30 ml/2 tbsp plain flour

125 ml/4 fl oz milk

100 g/4 oz small seedless white grapes, halved

juice of ½ lemon

30 ml/2 tbsp single cream

GARNISH

puff pastry fleurons (see Mrs Beeton's Tip)

chopped parsley

Set the oven at 190°C/375°F/gas 5. Arrange the fillets in a shallow oven-proof dish. Sprinkle the shallots, mushrooms, herbs and salt and pepper over. Pour in the wine, with 125 ml/4 fl oz water. Cover the dish and bake for 15 minutes. Using a slotted spoon and a fish slice, carefully transfer the fish to a warmed serving dish and keep hot. Tip the cooking liquid into a pan; boil until reduced to about 125 ml/4 fl oz.

Meanwhile melt the butter in a clean pan and stir in the flour. Cook for 1 minute, stirring, then gradually add the reduced cooking liquid with the milk, stirring constantly until boiling.

Set aside a few grapes and stir the rest into the sauce. Remove the sauce from the heat and stir in the lemon juice and cream. Pour over the fish, garnish with the pastry fleurons, sprinkle with parsley and serve.

MRS BEETON'S TIP

To make pastry fleurons, roll out 215 g/7 oz puff pastry on a floured surface. Cut into rounds, using a 5 cm/2 inch cutter. Move the cutter halfway across each round and cut in half again, making a half moon and an almond shape. Arrange the half moons on a baking sheet, brush with beaten egg and bake in a preheated 200°C/400° F/gas 6 oven for 8–10 minutes. The almond shapes may either be baked as biscuits or re-rolled and cut to make more fleurons.

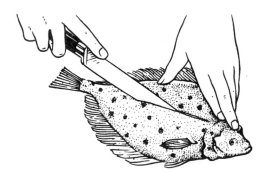

SOUP For basic information on making soups, see pages 9–10. For a complete list of soup recipes, see the entries under Soup in the index.

SOUSED HERRINGS

*Soused herrings make an excellent
starter or summer main course.
Serve them with potato salad and
radicchio or lollo rosso.*

SERVES 6

6 herrings, scaled, heads and
    tails removed, and boned

salt and pepper

150 ml/¼ pint malt vinegar

15 ml/1 tbsp pickling spice

4 bay leaves

2 small onions, sliced in rings

Set the oven at 150°C/300°F/gas 2. Season the herrings with salt and
pepper. Roll up the fillets, skin side in, from the tail end. Place neatly and
fairly close together in an ovenproof baking dish.

In a jug, mix the vinegar with 100 ml/3½ fl oz water. Pour over the
herrings, sprinkle with pickling spice and add the bay leaves. Lay the
onion rings on top. Cover the dish loosely with foil and bake for 1½
hours. Remove from the oven and leave to cool completely. Use a slotted spoon to lift the rolls from the cooking liquor when serving.

MRS BEETON'S TIP
Small mackerel or mackerel fillets can be soused in the same way as
herrings. Both are excellent served with a dish of soured cream
flavoured with plenty of chopped fresh dill.

SPAGHETTI ALLA CARBONARA

SERVES 4

450 g/1 lb spaghetti

salt and pepper

15 ml/1 tbsp oil

100 g/4 oz rindless streaky
    bacon rashers, cut into fine
    strips

4 eggs

30 ml/2 tbsp double cream

75 g/3 oz Pecorino or Parmesan
    cheese, grated

Cook the spaghetti in a large saucepan of boiling salted water for 8–10
minutes or until tender but still firm to the bite.

Meanwhile heat the oil in a large frying pan and fry the bacon until the
fat is transparent. Draw the pan off the heat. In a bowl, beat the eggs
with the cream, adding a little salt and a generous grinding of pepper.

Drain the cooked spaghetti thoroughly and mix it with the bacon.
Return to moderate heat for 1–2 minutes to heat through. Stir the egg
mixture rapidly into the pan. As it begins to thicken, tip in the cheese. Do
not stir it in. Serve immediately on hot plates.

MRS BEETON'S TIP
Use fresh pasta with this sauce, if preferred. It will cook in considerably less time than dried pasta and will be ready as soon as it rises to
the surface of the boiling water. Test after 1 minute.

SPANISH OMELETTE

Known as tortilla, a Spanish omelette is quite different from filled and folded omelettes or feather-light soufflé omelettes. It is a thick cake of potato and onion set in eggs, cut into wedges and served hot or cold.

SERVES 4 TO 6

675 g/1½ lb potatoes
225 g/8 oz onions, thinly sliced
salt and pepper
45 ml/3 tbsp olive oil
6 eggs, beaten

Cut the potatoes into 1 cm/½ inch cubes and mix them with the onions in a basin. Add plenty of seasoning and mix well.

Heat the oil in a heavy-bottomed frying pan which has fairly deep sides. Add the potatoes and onions, then cook, stirring the vegetables and turning often, until both potatoes and onions are tender. This takes about 25 minutes. Pour the eggs over the potatoes and cook over medium heat, stirring, until the eggs begin to set. Press the vegetables down evenly and leave to set. Lower the heat to prevent the base of the omelette from overbrowning before the eggs have set sufficiently.

Lay a large plate over the omelette and invert the pan to turn the omelette out on the plate. The base of the pan should be well greased but if it looks a little dry, then add a little extra olive oil and heat it. Slide the omelette back into the pan and cook over medium to high heat for 3–5 minutes, until crisp and browned. Serve hot, warm or cold.

variations
This classic potato omelette is quite delicious without any additional ingredients; however, the recipe is often varied to include red and green peppers or a mixture of vegetables, such as peas and green beans.

SPICED VINEGAR

MAKES 1 LITRE/1¾ PINTS

7 g/¼ oz each of the following spices: cloves, allspice berries, cinnamon sticks (broken into short lengths), fresh root ginger, bruised
1 litre/1¾ pints white or malt vinegar

Fold the spices in a clean cloth. Using a rolling pin, beat lightly to release all the flavour.

Combine the spices and vinegar in a large jug, mix well, then pour the liquid into a 1.1 litre/2 pint bottle. Seal the bottle tightly.

Shake the bottle daily for 1 month, then store in a cool dry place for at least 1 month more before straining out the spices and returning the vinegar to the clean bottle.

SPINACH AND BACON SALAD

SERVES 4

450 g/1 lb fresh young spinach

150 g/5 oz button mushrooms, thinly sliced

1 small onion, thinly sliced

15 ml/1 tbsp oil

6 rindless streaky bacon rashers, cut into strips

75 ml/5 tbsp French Dressing

Remove the stalks from the spinach, wash the leaves well in cold water, then dry thoroughly on absorbent kitchen paper. If time permits, put the leaves in a polythene bag and chill for 1 hour.

Tear the spinach into large pieces and put into a salad bowl with the mushrooms and onion. Heat the oil in a small frying pan and fry the bacon until crisp. Meanwhile toss the salad vegetables with the French dressing. Pour in the hot bacon and fat, toss lightly to mix and serve.

MRS BEETON'S TIP
If preferred, the bacon may be grilled until crisp and crumbled into the salad just before serving.

SPINACH SOUP

SERVES 4

25 g/1 oz butter

1 large onion, finely chopped

1.1 litres/2 pints chicken stock

2 potatoes, diced

900 g/2 lb spinach, washed, trimmed and roughly chopped

2.5 ml/½ tsp grated nutmeg

salt and pepper

150 ml/¼ pint single cream

2 rindless back bacon rashers, grilled and crumbled, to garnish (optional)

Melt the butter, add the onion and cook over gentle heat for 10 minutes until soft but not coloured. Add the stock and potatoes and cook for 15 minutes. Add the spinach and cook for 10 minutes more or until both potatoes and spinach are tender. Purée the soup in a blender or food processor, or rub through a sieve into a clean pan. Add the nutmeg, with salt and pepper to taste. Stir in the cream and reheat without boiling. Serve the soup in individual bowls, topping each portion with crumbled bacon, if liked.

variation

GREEN AND GOLD Fry the onion in the butter as described above. Meanwhile cook the spinach with just the water that clings to the leaves after washing. Drain thoroughly, pressing the spinach against the sides of the colander with a wooden spoon to extract as much liquid as possible, then mix the spinach with the onion mixture. Form into egg-sized balls. Bring the stock to the boil. Spoon a few spinach balls into each soup bowl, add the boiling stock and serve at once.

SPLIT PEA SOUP

SERVES 4 TO 6

100 g/4 oz yellow split peas

30 ml/2 tbsp oil

6 rindless streaky bacon rashers,
chopped

1 large onion, finely chopped

2 litres/3½ pints chicken or
vegetable stock

60 ml/4 tbsp chopped celery
leaves

2 parsley sprigs

2 bay leaves

5 ml/1 tsp chopped summer savory
or 2.5 ml/½ tsp dried savory

salt and pepper

Soak the split peas overnight in water to cover. Next day, heat the oil in a large saucepan. Add the bacon and onion. Fry for 10 minutes over gentle heat, until the onion is soft but not coloured.

Drain the split peas and add them to the pan with the stock, celery leaves, parsley, bay leaves and savory. Bring to the boil, lower the heat and simmer for about 2 hours, or until the peas are very tender. If the soup becomes too thick, add water or extra stock.

Remove the parsley sprigs and bay leaves. Add salt and pepper to taste. Serve the soup as it is, or purée in a blender or food processor. Alternatively, rub through a sieve into a clean pan. Reheat, stirring frequently to prevent the soup from sticking to the pan, and serve at once.

variation

PEA AND HAM SOUP Save the stock when boiling a joint of ham or bacon as it makes delicious split pea soup. Omit the streaky bacon and add seasoning, if needed, only after the soup is cooked.

PRESSURE COOKER TIP

It is not necessary to soak the split peas if the soup is to be made in a pressure cooker. Fry the bacon and onion in the oil in the open cooker. Add the split peas and herbs as in the recipe above, but reduce the amount of stock to 1 litre/1¾ pints. Put the lid on the cooker and bring to 15 lb pressure. Cook for 12 minutes. Reduce pressure slowly, then continue as described above, adding more stock to adjust the consistency as desired.

SPONGE CAKE

MAKES ONE 18 CM/7 INCH CAKE OR TWO
15 CM/6 INCH LAYERS

fat for greasing

flour for dusting

3 eggs

75 g/3 oz caster sugar

75 g/3 oz plain flour

pinch of salt

pinch of baking powder

MRS BEETON'S TIP

If an electric mixer is used there is no need to place the bowl over hot water. Whisk at high speed for about 5 minutes until thick. Fold in the flour by hand.

Grease an 18 cm/7 inch round cake tin or two 15 cm/6 inch sandwich cake tins. Dust with sifted flour, tapping out the excess. Set the oven at 180°C/350°F/gas 4.

Whisk the eggs and sugar together in a bowl over a saucepan of hot water, taking care that the base of the bowl does not touch the water. Continue whisking for 10–15 minutes until the mixture is thick and creamy. Remove the bowl from the pan. Whisk until cold.

Sift the flour, salt and baking powder into a bowl. Add to the creamed mixture, using a metal spoon. Do this lightly, so that the air incorporated during whisking is not lost. Pour the mixture into the prepared tin or tins.

Bake a single 18 cm/7 inch cake for 40 minutes; two 15 cm/6 inch cakes for 25 minutes. Leave the sponge in the tins for a few minutes, then cool on a wire rack. Fill and top as desired.

flavourings and fillings

Sponge cakes are light in texture, with a delicate flavour, and this should be reflected in the choice of flavouring ingredients or fillings that are added. Jams and other sweet preserves can be used to fill the cakes or whipped cream is ideal for this type of cake. Fresh fruit perfectly complements the lightness of these sponges.

CHOCOLATE CREAM SPONGE Make a layered plain sponge cake or substitute 15 ml/1 tbsp cocoa for an equal quantity of flour, sifting it in with the flour to flavour the cake. For the filling, melt 100 g/4 oz of milk chocolate with 50 g/2 oz of butter in a heatproof bowl over hot water. Stir well and leave to cool but do not allow to set. Carefully fold in 150 ml/¼ pint of whipped double cream, then use this chocolate cream to sandwich the layers together.

LEMON CREAM SPONGE Add the grated rind of 1 lemon to the eggs and sugar, then continue as in the main recipe. Whip 150 ml/¼ pint of double cream and fold in 60–90 ml/4–6 tbsp of lemon curd, to taste. Use this to sandwich the layers together.

PEACHES AND CREAM CAKE Make the cake as in the main recipe. Finely chop peeled and stoned fresh peaches or drained canned peaches and mix them with whipped cream or soft cheese. Sweeten with icing sugar and use this to sandwich the layers together.

STRAWBERRY CREAM CAKE Make the cakes as in the main recipe and leave to cool. Hull and halve 225 g/8 oz of strawberries. Whip 150 ml/¼ pint of double cream with icing sugar to taste, then fold in the halved strawberries. Sandwich the cooled layers together with the strawberry cream.

SPONGE PUDDING

SERVES 6

fat for greasing

150 g/5 oz butter or margarine

150 g/5 oz caster sugar

3 eggs, beaten

150 g/5 oz plain flour

grated rind of ½ lemon

5 ml/1 tsp baking powder

MICROWAVE TIP

To make a light sponge pudding in the microwave, use 50 g/ 2 oz each of butter or margarine, sugar and self-raising flour with 1 egg and 30 ml/ 2 tbsp milk. Prepare the pudding as above and put it into a greased 1.1 litre/2 pint basin. Cook on High for 3–5 minutes.

Grease a 1 litre/1¾ pint pudding basin. Prepare a steamer or half fill a large saucepan with water and bring to the boil.

Cream the butter or margarine with the sugar in a mixing bowl until light and fluffy. Beat in the eggs gradually, adding a little of the flour if the mixture begins to curdle. Add the lemon rind.

Sift the flour and baking powder together and fold lightly into the creamed mixture. Spoon the mixture into the prepared basin, cover with greased greaseproof paper and foil; secure with string. Put the pudding in the perforated part of the steamer, or stand it on an old saucer or plate in the pan of boiling water. The water should come halfway up the sides of the basin. Cover the pan tightly and steam the pudding over gently simmering water for 1¼ –1½ hours. Leave for 3–5 minutes at room temperature to firm up, then turn out on to a serving plate.

variations

DATE SPONGE PUDDING Add 150 g/5 oz chopped stoned dates. Substitute orange rind for lemon rind.

DRIED FRUIT SPONGE PUDDING Add to the basic recipe 150 g/5 oz mixed dried fruit. Serve with a vanilla custard.

CHOCOLATE SPONGE PUDDING Substitute 25 g/1 oz cocoa for the same quantity of the flour and stir 75 g/3 oz chocolate chips into the mixture.

GINGER SPONGE PUDDING Add 10 ml/2 tsp ground ginger with the flour and stir 50 g/2 oz chopped preserved ginger into the mixture.

STEAK AND KIDNEY PUDDING

The original recipe was contributed by a lady who lived in Sussex, a county renowned for its savoury puddings in Mrs Beeton's day. Prepared in a dish, rather than a basin, it would have contained more meat and ox kidney. Onion was not added and the suet pastry was mixed with milk. Apart from these minor variations, this classic British dish has survived generations of changing tastes to remain a firm favourite.

SERVES 6

fat for greasing

150 g/5 oz lamb's, pig's or ox kidney(s)

575 g/1¼ lb stewing steak, trimmed and cut into 1 cm/ ½ inch cubes

1 onion, chopped

45 ml/3 tbsp plain flour

5 ml/1 tsp salt

1.25 ml/¼ tsp freshly ground black pepper

45 ml/3 tbsp beef stock or water

SUET CRUST PASTRY

225 g/8 oz self-raising flour

2.5 ml/½ tsp salt

100 g/4 oz shredded beef suet

Grease a 1.1 litre/2 pint pudding basin. Make the pastry. Sift the flour and salt into a mixing bowl. Stir in the suet and add cold water (about 150 ml/¼ pint) to make a firm dough.

Wash the kidney(s) and remove the membrane and white core. Cut into 2.5 cm/1 inch chunks. In a bowl, mix the beef cubes, kidney and onion with the flour, salt and pepper. Set aside one quarter of the pastry for the lid. Roll out the remaining pastry on a lightly floured surface to a round 1 cm/½ inch larger than the rim of the prepared basin. The pastry should be about 5 mm/¼ inch thick. Press the pastry round well into the basin.

Half fill the lined basin with the steak mixture, add the stock or water, then spoon in the rest of the meat. Roll out the reserved pastry to make a lid. Put the lid on the pudding, tucking its edges down around the meat. Dampen the top edge of the lid, then fold the top of the lining pastry over it. Cut a large piece of greaseproof paper, fold a pleat in it and grease it. Cover the pudding with the pleated paper, top with pleated foil and tie down securely.

Prepare a steamer or half fill a large saucepan with water and bring to the boil. Put the pudding in the perforated part of the steamer, or stand it on an old saucer or plate in the saucepan of boiling water. The water should come halfway up the sides of the basin. Cover the pan tightly and steam the pudding over boiling water for about 5 hours, topping up the boiling water frequently to prevent the pan from boiling dry.

Serve the pudding from the basin. Fold a clean tea-towel or large table napkin in half or thirds, then wrap it neatly around the side and up to the rim of the basin. Beef gravy may be served with the pudding.

PRESSURE COOKER TIP

To save time, the steak and kidney mixture may be precooked with 300 ml/½ pint beef stock. Cook in a pressure cooker, allowing 15 minutes at 15 lb pressure. Cool the mixture, then fill the pastry-lined pudding basin, using only enough of the gravy to half cover the meat. Place the pudding basin on a trivet in the clean pressure cooker. Steam gently without weights for 10 minutes, bring to 5 lb pressure and cook for 35 minutes. Reduce the pressure slowly. Reheat the remaining gravy, add more salt and pepper if required, then pour it into the pudding through a hole cut in the crust.

STEAK AND ONIONS

Serve creamy mashed potatoes, fine potato chips or French fries or plain boiled potatoes sprinkled with a little parsley with this traditional dish of fried steak with onions.

SERVES 4

beef dripping for cooking

2 large onions, thinly sliced

I bay leaf

I fresh thyme sprig

4 (225–350 g/8–12 oz) slices of
   rump steak

salt and pepper

60 ml/4 tbsp plain flour

15 ml/I tbsp tomato purée

300 ml/½ pint beef stock

dash of Worcestershire sauce

GARNISH (OPTIONAL)

4 small tomatoes, halved or
   quartered

fresh herb sprigs

Melt a knob of dripping in a large frying pan. Add the onions, bay leaf and thyme, and cook the onions over moderate heat, stirring occasionally, until they are evenly browned. This takes up to 25 minutes – do not increase the heat to hurry the browning; the secret of a good flavour is the long cooking.

Meanwhile, trim any gristle and excess fat from the steak, then beat the pieces with a meat mallet or rolling pin to tenderize them. Avoid beating the meat in such a way that the steaks are thinned. Place the steaks on a plate. Add plenty of salt and pepper to the flour, then sprinkle half over the steaks, dusting them evenly. Turn the meat over and sprinkle with the remaining flour.

Use a slotted spoon to remove the onions from the pan. Drain them on absorbent kitchen paper and transfer to a heated serving dish or individual plates. Keep hot. Leave the bay leaf and thyme in the pan and add a little extra dripping if necessary. When the fat is hot, add the steaks and brown them quickly on both sides. Allow about 3 minutes on each side for rare steaks. For medium or well done steaks, lower the heat slightly once the meat is sealed and continue to cook for 4–7 minutes on each side. The exact time depends on the thickness of the meat.

Transfer the steaks to the dish or plates, cover loosely and keep hot. Stir any remaining flour into the juices in the pan, then stir in the tomato purée and the stock. Bring to the boil, stirring, and boil rapidly to reduce the sauce by about a third. Add a little Worcestershire sauce and taste for seasoning. Spoon the sauce and onion over the steaks. Garnish with tomatoes and herbs, if liked. Serve at once.

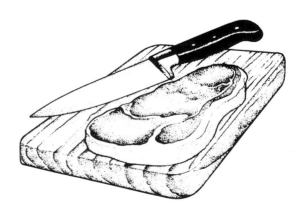

STEAK PIE

SERVES 6

575 g/1 ¼ lb chuck or blade
    steak, trimmed and cut into
    1 cm/½ inch cubes

45 ml/3 tbsp seasoned flour

2 onions, chopped

about 250 ml/8 fl oz beef stock

beaten egg or milk for glazing

ROUGH PUFF PASTRY

200 g/7 oz plain flour

1.25 ml/¼ tsp salt

150 g/5 oz butter or half butter,
    half lard, well chilled

2.5 ml/½ tsp lemon juice

flour for rolling out

Make the pastry. Sift the flour and salt into a bowl. If butter and lard are used, blend them together evenly with a round-bladed knife and chill. Cut the fat into pieces the size of walnuts and add to the flour. Make a well in the centre, mix in the lemon juice, then gradually add enough cold water to make an elastic dough. On a lightly floured surface, roll into a long strip, keeping the edges square. Fold the bottom third over the centre third, then fold the top third over. With the rolling pin, press to seal the edges. Turn the pastry so that the folded edges are on the left and right. Repeat the rolling and folding process three more times, allowing the pastry to rest in a cool place for 10 minutes between the second and third rollings. Wrap in foil and refrigerate until required.

In a stout polythene or paper bag, toss the beef cubes in seasoned flour until well coated. Shake off excess flour, then transfer the cubes to a 1 litre/1¾ pint pie dish, piling them higher in the centre than at the sides and sprinkling chopped onion between the layers. Pour in enough of the stock to quarter-fill the dish. Reserve the remaining stock.

Set the oven at 230°C/450°F/gas 8. Roll out the pastry on a lightly floured surface. Cut a strip of pastry from around the outside of the piece. Dampen the rim of the pie dish and press the pastry strip on it, trimming off any extra length. Use the remaining pastry to cover the dish. Trim the edge, knock up with the back of a knife and flute the edge. Make a small hole in the centre of the lid and surround it with pastry leaves made from the trimmings. Make a pastry tassel or rose to cover the hole after baking, if liked. Brush the pastry with the beaten egg or milk. Set the tassel or rose aside.

Place the pie on a baking sheet with the pastry tassel, if made, next to it. Bake for about 10 minutes until the pastry is risen and golden brown. Lower the oven temperature to 180°C/350°F/gas 4 and, if necessary, move the pie to a lower shelf. Cover loosely with foil to prevent over-browning and continue to cook for about 2 hours or until the meat is tender when tested through the crust with a skewer. Remove the tassel as soon as it is cooked, 10–15 minutes after lowering the oven temperature.

Heat the reserved beef stock in a small saucepan. Pour it into the pie through a funnel inserted in the hole in the crust. Cover the hole with the pastry tassel or rose, if made, and serve at once.

variation
STEAK AND KIDNEY Pie Add 2 sheep's or 150 g/5 oz ox kidneys. Skin, core and slice the kidneys before mixing with the steak and onions.

STEW WITH SAVOURY PARSLEY DUMPLINGS

SERVES 6

30 ml/2 tbsp dripping or oil

675 g/1½ lb chuck or blade
    steak, trimmed and cut into
    5 cm/2 inch cubes

3 onions, chopped

45 ml/3 tbsp plain flour

600 ml/1 pint beef stock

5 ml/1 tsp vinegar

salt and pepper

PARSLEY DUMPLINGS

175 g/6 oz self-raising flour

2.5 ml/½ tsp salt

75 g/3 oz shredded beef suet

15 ml/1 tbsp finely chopped
    parsley

Heat the dripping or oil in a large heavy-bottomed saucepan. Add the meat and fry until browned on all sides, then remove with a slotted spoon and set aside. Add the onions to the fat remaining in the pan and fry gently until golden brown. Stir in the flour and cook until lightly browned.

Gradually stir in the stock. Bring to the boil, stirring, then lower the heat to simmering point. Stir in the vinegar, with salt and pepper to taste. Return the beef cubes, cover the pan and simmer gently for 1½ hours, or until the meat is tender.

To make the parsley dumplings, sift the flour and salt into a mixing bowl and stir in the suet and parsley. Add about 90 ml/6 tbsp water and mix lightly to make a firm elastic dough.

Divide the dough into 12 equal pieces, shaping each into a ball. Bring the stew to boiling point and arrange the parsley dumplings on top. Lower the heat, half cover the pan and simmer for a further 20 minutes or until the dumplings are cooked. To serve, arrange the dumplings around a heated serving dish, then ladle the meat into the centre.

PRESSURE COOKER TIP

The stew can be made very successfully in a pressure cooker. Follow the recipe above, removing the pan from the heat before adding the stock. The pan should not be more than half full. Close the pressure cooker, bring to 15 lb pressure and cook for 20 minutes. Return the cooker – without the lid – to the heat and bring to the boil. Add the dumplings and lower the heat. Place the lid lightly on top to serve as a cover, but do not close or add weights. Simmer gently until the dumplings are cooked. Serve the stew as suggested above.

STRAWBERRY JAM

MAKES ABOUT 2.5 KG/5½ LB

1.5 kg/3¼ lb strawberries, hulled

juice of 1 lemon

1.5 kg/3¼ lb sugar

Combine the strawberries and lemon juice in a preserving pan. Heat gently for 10 minutes, stirring all the time, to reduce the volume. Add the sugar, stirring over low heat until it has dissolved.

Bring to the boil and boil rapidly until setting point is reached. Remove from the heat and skim. Leave the jam undisturbed to cool for about 20 minutes or until a skin forms on the surface and the fruit sinks. Stir gently to distribute the strawberries. Pot and top with waxed paper discs. Cover and label when cold. Do not use twist-topped jars; the jam will have cooled down too much before potting.

STUFFED BREAST OF LAMB WITH PILAFF

SERVES 6

1 breast of lamb, about 675 g/
  1½ lb

salt and pepper

350 g/12 oz pork sausagemeat

15 ml/1 tbsp oil

2 rindless streaky bacon rashers,
  chopped

1 large carrot, chopped

1 large onion, chopped

1 bouquet garni

250 ml/8 fl oz lamb or chicken
  stock

PILAFF

30 ml/2 tbsp olive oil

1 large onion, chopped

1 bay leaf

1 cinnamon stick

1 garlic clove, crushed

225 g/8 oz long-grain rice

750 ml/1¼ pints vegetable stock

50 g/2 oz sultanas

50 g/2 oz blanched almonds, cut
  into slivers and toasted

250 ml/8 fl oz Tomato Sauce

Set the oven at 180°C/350°F/gas 4. Remove all the bones from the meat and trim off any excess fat. Flatten it, if necessary, with a cutlet bat or rolling pin, season with salt and pepper and spread the sausagemeat over the surface. Roll up tightly and tie the meat neatly.

Heat the oil in a frying pan, add the bacon and cook until the fat runs. Add the vegetables and fry quickly until lightly browned, then place them in a large casserole. Add the bouquet garni, sprinkle with salt and pepper, and pour in just enough stock to cover the vegetables. Put the rolled breast of lamb on top of the vegetables and cover the casserole with a tight-fitting lid. Bake for 2–2½ hours, until tender.

Prepare the pilaff about 30 minutes before the lamb is ready. Heat the oil in a saucepan, add the onion, bay leaf, cinnamon stick and garlic, then fry gently for about 10 minutes until the onion is slightly softened but not browned. Add the rice, stir well, then pour in the stock. Add salt and pepper to taste, bring the stock to the boil and stir once. Cover, lower the heat and simmer for 15 minutes. Sprinkle the sultanas and almonds over the rice, replace the lid (without stirring) and cook for 5 minutes more. Turn the heat off and leave for 5 minutes. Heat the tomato sauce.

Turn out the pilaff on a warmed serving dish. Cut the lamb into thick slices and lay them on the pilaff, then pour the tomato sauce over the meat. Serve at once.

STUFFINGS See Apple and Celery Stuffing, Chestnut and Onion Stuffing, Forcemeat, Herb Stuffing, Mushroom Stuffing, Sausagemeat Stuffing and Wild Rice Stuffing. For Sage and Onion Stuffing, see Roast Duck.

STUFFED CABBAGE LEAVES — *Illustrated on page 268*

SERVES 4

fat for greasing

8 large cabbage leaves

STUFFING

15 ml/1 tbsp oil

1 onion, finely chopped

400 g/14 oz minced beef

1 (397 g/14 oz) can tomatoes

10 ml/2 tsp cornflour

15 ml/1 tbsp Worcestershire
   sauce

2.5 ml/½ tsp dried mixed herbs

15 ml/1 tbsp chopped parsley

salt and pepper

SAUCE

15 ml/1 tbsp tomato purée

20 ml/4 tsp cornflour

Remove the thick centre stems from the cabbage leaves, then blanch them in boiling water for 2 minutes. Drain well.

To make the stuffing, heat the oil in a saucepan and gently fry the onion for 5 minutes. Add the beef and cook, stirring, until the meat has browned. Drain the tomatoes and reserve the juice. Roughly chop the tomatoes and add them to the meat mixture. Mix the cornflour with the Worcestershire sauce in a cup; stir into the meat mixture with the herbs and salt and pepper. Cook for 20 minutes, stirring frequently.

Grease a shallow ovenproof dish. Set the oven at 190°C/375°F/gas 5. Divide the stuffing between the cabbage leaves and roll up, folding over the edges of the leaves to enclose the stuffing completely. Place in the prepared dish and cover with foil. Bake for 20 minutes.

Meanwhile make the sauce. Mix the reserved juice from the tomatoes with the tomato purée in a measuring jug; make up to 250 ml/8 fl oz with water. In a cup, blend the cornflour with 15 ml/1 tbsp of the sauce. Pour the rest of the sauce into a saucepan and bring to the boil. Stir in the blended cornflour. Boil, stirring all the time, until the sauce has thickened. Add salt and pepper to taste. Pour the sauce over the stuffed cabbage leaves just before serving.

STUFFED MARROW

SERVES 4 TO 6

fat for greasing

1 marrow

1 small onion

225 g/8 oz minced beef

100 g/4 oz pork sausagemeat or 100 g/4 oz extra minced beef

25 g/1 oz fresh white breadcrumbs

15 ml/1 tbsp each chopped parsley and snipped chives

5 ml/1 tsp Worcestershire sauce

salt and pepper

1 egg, beaten

SAUCE

25 g/1 oz butter

25 g/1 oz plain flour

300 ml/½ pint milk, stock or mixture (see method)

75–100 g/3–4 oz Cheddar cheese, grated

pinch of dry mustard

Generously grease a large, shallow casserole. Set the oven at 180°C/350°F/gas 4. Halve the marrow lengthways and scoop out the seeds. Lay the halves side by side in the prepared casserole.

Chop the onion finely and put it into a bowl with the beef, sausage-meat, if used, breadcrumbs, parsley, chives, Worcestershire sauce and salt and pepper. Mix well. Bind the mixture with beaten egg. Avoid making it too moist. Divide the stuffing between each marrow half. Cover the dish and bake for 1 hour.

Strain off most of the liquid in the casserole. Meanwhile make the sauce. Melt the butter in a saucepan. Stir in the flour and cook over low heat for 2–3 minutes, without colouring. Over very low heat, gradually add the liquid (the casserole juices may be used), stirring constantly. Bring to the boil, stirring, then lower the heat and simmer for 1–2 minutes until smooth and thickened. Add the cheese, mustard and salt and pepper to taste. Pour the cheese sauce over the marrow and bake, uncovered, for a further 20 minutes, until the sauce topping is golden brown.

variation
Instead of using the cheese sauce, the stuffed marrow can be topped with Tomato Sauce. Bake for 15 minutes, then sprinkle with freshly grated Parmesan or Cheddar cheese and bake for 5 minutes more.

STUFFED ONIONS

SERVES 6

salt and pepper

6 large onions

75 g/3 oz cooked ham, finely
chopped

30 ml/2 tbsp fresh white
breadcrumbs

2.5 ml/½ tsp finely chopped
sage

beaten egg for binding

30 ml/2 tbsp butter

100 g/4 oz Cheddar cheese,
grated (optional)

Bring a saucepan of salted water to the boil, add the unpeeled onions
and parboil for 45 minutes or until almost tender. Drain, skin and remove
the centres with a teaspoon.

Set the oven at 180°C/350°F/gas 4. Mix the ham, breadcrumbs and
sage in a small bowl. Add salt and pepper to taste and stir in enough of
the beaten egg to give a fairly firm mixture. Fill the centres of the onions
with the mixture.

Put the onions in a baking dish just large enough to hold them snugly.
Dot the tops with butter. Bake for 30–45 minutes or until tender, sprinkling the tops of the onions with the grated cheese, if used, 10 minutes
before the end of the cooking time.

MICROWAVE TIP

Peel the onions. Arrange them around the rim of a round shallow
dish, add 45 ml/3 tbsp water and cover. Cook on High for 10–12
minutes or until the onions are tender. When cool enough to handle,
scoop out the centres and fill as described above. Return the onions
to the dry dish and cook for 4–6 minutes. If a cheese topping is
required, sprinkle the grated cheese on top and brown under a grill
for 3–4 minutes.

STUFFED PEPPERS

SERVES 4

fat for greasing

4 green peppers

1 small onion, finely chopped

400 g/14 oz lean minced beef

100 g/4 oz cooked rice

salt and pepper

good pinch of dried marjoram

250 ml/8 fl oz tomato juice

strips of green pepper to garnish

Grease an ovenproof dish. Set the oven at 180°C/350°F/gas 4. Cut a
slice off the top of each pepper, then remove the membranes and seeds.
Blanch in a saucepan of boiling water for 2 minutes.

Mix the onion, beef, rice, salt, pepper and marjoram together in a bowl.
Stand the peppers upright in the prepared dish; if they do not stand
upright easily, cut a thin slice off the base. Divide the stuffing mixture
between the peppers.

Pour the tomato juice around the base of the peppers. Cover and bake
for 1 hour. Garnish with strips of pepper.

SUMMER PUDDING — *Illustrated on page 304*

This delectable dessert started life with the cumbersome name of Hydropathic Pudding. It was originally invented for spa patients who were forbidden rich creams and pastries. Vary the fruit filling if you wish — blackberries or bilberries make very good additions — but keep the total quantity of fruit at about I kg/2¼ lb.

SERVES 6

150 g/5 oz caster sugar

225 g/8 oz blackcurrants or redcurrants, stalks removed

225 g/8 oz ripe red plums, halved and stoned

1 strip of lemon rind

225 g/8 oz strawberries, hulled

225 g/8 oz raspberries, hulled

8–10 slices of day-old white bread, crusts removed

Put the sugar into a saucepan with 60 ml/4 tbsp water. Heat gently, stirring, until the sugar has dissolved. Add the black- or redcurrants, plums and lemon rind and poach until tender. Add the strawberries and raspberries to the saucepan and cook for 2 minutes. Remove from the heat and, using a slotted spoon, remove the lemon rind.

Cut a circle from 1 slice of bread to fit the base of a 1.25 litre/2¼ pint pudding basin. Line the base and sides of the basin with bread, leaving no spaces. Pour in the stewed fruit, reserving about 45–60 ml/3–4 tbsp of the juice in a jug. Top the stewed fruit filling with more bread slices. Cover with a plate or saucer that exactly fits inside the basin. Put a weight on top to press the pudding down firmly. Leave in a cool place for 5–8 hours, preferably overnight.

Turn out carefully on to a plate or shallow dish to serve. If there are any places on the bread shell where the juice from the fruit filling has not penetrated, drizzle a little of the reserved fruit juice over. Serve with whipped cream or plain yogurt.

FREEZER TIP

After the pudding has been weighted, pack the basin in a polythene bag, seal and freeze for up to 3 months. Thaw overnight in the refrigerator. Alternatively, line the basin completely with cling film before making the pudding. Thicker microwave cooking film is stronger than ordinary film, or use a double layer. Leave plenty of film overhanging the rim of the basin. Freeze the weighted pudding, then use the film to remove it from the basin. Pack and label before storing.

SWEET AND SOUR PORK

SERVES 4

675 g/1½ lb pork, trimmed and
    cut into 2 cm/¾ inch cubes

oil for deep frying

MARINADE

1 egg white

40 g/1½ oz cornflour

30 ml/2 tbsp soy sauce

30 ml/2 tbsp dry sherry

salt and pepper

BATTER

1 egg

45 ml/3 tbsp plain flour

45 ml/3 tbsp cornflour

45–60 ml/3–4 tbsp light beer

SAUCE

3 spring onions

1 small red pepper

3 canned pineapple rings

30 ml/2 tbsp oil

500 ml/17 fl oz chicken stock

30 ml/2 tbsp vinegar

45 ml/3 tbsp tomato ketchup

45 ml/3 tbsp soy sauce

25 g/1 oz caster sugar

30 ml/2 tbsp cornflour

Make the marinade. Beat the egg white in a bowl with the cornflour. Stir in the soy sauce and sherry, with salt and pepper to taste. Add the meat cubes and marinate for 15 minutes, turning frequently.

Meanwhile make the sauce. Chop the spring onions finely. Cut the red pepper in half, remove the core and seeds and cut the flesh into thin strips. Chop the pineapple rings. Heat the oil in a saucepan, add the spring onions, peppers and pineapple and fry for 2 minutes, stirring all the time. Add the chicken stock, vinegar, tomato ketchup and soy sauce, with sugar and salt to taste. Simmer for 5 minutes.

To make the batter, mix the egg, flour, cornflour and beer in a bowl. Add a pinch of salt and whisk the mixture.

Heat the oil for deep frying to 180–190°C/350–375°F or until a cube of bread added to the oil browns in 30 seconds. If using a deep-fat fryer, follow the manufacturer's instructions. Remove the meat cubes from the marinade and drain well. Dip them in the batter and fry a few at a time until golden brown. As each batch of cubes browns, remove them with a slotted spoon and keep warm on a serving dish.

Finish the sauce. Put the cornflour in a cup and mix to a paste with a little cold water. Stir the paste into the sweet and sour sauce and bring to the boil, stirring until it thickens. Pour the sauce over the pieces of pork and serve at once.

variation

SWEET AND SOUR PORK STIR FRY Mix the marinade as suggested in the main recipe, add the pork cubes and turn to coat in the mixture. Do not allow to stand. Heat 75 ml/5 tbsp oil in a wok. Add the pork cubes and stir fry over high heat until cooked and crisp. Transfer to a bowl with a slotted spoon and serve with the sweet and sour sauce.

SWEET SOUFFLE OMELETTES

Soufflé omelettes are quick and easy to make – the perfect finale for the busy cook. Fill simply with 30 ml/ 2 tbsp warmed jam or try any of the exciting fillings that follow.

SERVES 1

2 eggs, separated
5 ml/1 tsp caster sugar
few drops of vanilla essence
15 ml/1 tbsp unsalted butter
icing sugar for dredging

MRS BEETON'S TIPS

When folding the beaten egg whites into the omelette mixture, be very careful not to overmix, as it is the air incorporated in the frothy whites that causes the omelette to rise.

A little water is often added to omelette mixtures to lighten them. Never add milk or cream, which would make the texture of the omelette tough.

In a large bowl, whisk the yolks until creamy. Add the sugar and vanilla essence with 30 ml/2 tbsp water, then whisk again. In a clean, grease-free bowl, whisk the egg whites until stiff and matt.

Place an 18 cm/7 inch omelette pan over gentle heat and when it is hot, add the butter. Tilt the pan to grease the whole of the inside. Pour out any excess.

Fold the egg whites into the yolk mixture carefully until distributed, using a metal spoon (see Mrs Beeton's Tips). Heat the grill to moderate.

Pour the egg mixture into the omelette pan, level the top very lightly, and cook for 1–2 minutes over moderate heat until the omelette is golden brown on the underside and moist on top. (Use a palette knife to lift the edge of the omelette to look underneath.) Put the pan under the grill for 5–6 minutes until the omelette is risen and lightly browned on the top. The texture of the omelette should be firm yet spongy.

Remove the omelette from the heat as soon as it is ready, as overcooking tends to make it tough. Run a palette knife gently round the edge and underneath to loosen it. Make a mark across the middle at right angles to the pan handle but do not cut the surface. Put the chosen filling on one half, raise the handle of the pan and double the omelette over. Turn gently on to a warm plate, dredge with icing sugar and serve.

fillings
JAM OMELETTE Warm 45 ml/3 tbsp fruity jam and spread over the omelette.
LEMON OMELETTE Add the grated rind of lemon to the egg yolks. Warm 45 ml/3 tbsp lemon curd with 10 ml/2 tsp lemon juice, and spread over the omelette.
RASPBERRY OMELETTE Spread 30 ml/2 tbsp warm, thick, raspberry purée or Melba Sauce over the omelette.
STRAWBERRY OMELETTE Hull 5 ripe strawberries and soak in a bowl with a little kirsch. Mash slightly with icing sugar to taste. Put in the centre of the omelette.

special effect
BRANDED OMELETTES Heat the pointed ends of three metal skewers until red-hot. When the omelette is on the plate, dredge with icing sugar.

Protecting your hand in an oven glove, quickly press the hot skewers, one at a time, on to the sugar, holding them there until the sugar caramelizes. Make a diagonal criss-cross design. Each skewer should make two marks if you work quickly.

SWEET WHITE SAUCE

MAKES ABOUT 250 ML/8 FL OZ

20 ml/4 tsp cornflour

250 ml/8 fl oz milk

15–30 ml/1–2 tbsp sugar

vanilla essence or other
    flavouring

Put the cornflour in a bowl. Stir in enough of the cold milk to form a smooth, thin paste. Heat the remaining milk in a small saucepan. When it boils, stir it into the cornflour paste, then return the mixture to the clean pan and stir until boiling. Lower the heat and cook, stirring frequently, for 3 minutes. Stir in sugar to taste and add the chosen flavouring. Serve hot.

variations

ALMOND SAUCE Add 10 ml/2 tsp ground almonds to the cornflour when blending with the milk. When the sauce is cooked, stir in 2–3 drops of almond essence with vanilla essence to taste.

BRANDY SAUCE When the sauce is cooked, stir in 15–30 ml/1–2 tbsp brandy.

CHOCOLATE SAUCE When the sauce is cooked, stir in 15 ml/1 tbsp cocoa dissolved in 15 ml/1 tbsp boiling water.

COFFEE SAUCE To the cooked sauce add 10 ml/2 tsp instant coffee dissolved in 15 ml/1 tbsp boiling water.

GINGER SAUCE Stir in 10 ml/2 tsp ground ginger with the cornflour. For extra taste and texture, 50 g/2 oz crystallized ginger, finely chopped, can be added to the cooked sauce.

SWISS CHEESE FONDUE

SERVES 6 TO 8

1 garlic clove

300 ml/½ pint dry white wine

350 g/12 oz Emmental cheese,
    grated

450 g/1 lb Gruyère cheese,
    grated

10 ml/2 tsp cornflour or potato
    flour

15 ml/1 tbsp kirsch

white pepper and grated nutmeg

2 long French sticks, cubed

Cut the garlic clove in half; rub the cut sides over the inside of a fondue pan or flameproof casserole. Pour the wine into the pan or casserole and heat until steaming but not simmering.

Gradually add the grated cheese, a little at a time, stirring constantly. Allow each addition of cheese to melt before adding the next. Remove the pan from the heat.

Mix the cornflour or potato flour to a paste with the kirsch and stir this into the fondue. Return to the heat and cook, stirring constantly, until the mixture is smooth, thick and creamy. Add pepper and nutmeg to taste.

Set the pan over a burner or hotplate at the table. Serve at once, with the bread. Supply long-handled fondue forks for spearing the bread and dipping the cubes into the fondue.

Swiss roll

MAKES ONE 30 CM/12 INCH SWISS ROLL

fat for greasing

3 eggs

75 g/3 oz caster sugar

75 g/3 oz plain flour

2.5 ml/½ tsp baking powder

pinch of salt

about 60 ml/4 tbsp jam for filling

caster sugar for dusting

Line and grease a 30 x 20 cm/12 x 8 inch Swiss roll tin. Set the oven at 220°C/425°F/gas 7.

Combine the eggs and sugar in a heatproof bowl. Set the bowl over a pan of hot water, taking care that the bottom of the bowl does not touch the water. Whisk for 10–15 minutes until thick and creamy, then remove from the pan. Continue whisking until the mixture is cold.

Sift the flour, baking powder and salt into a bowl, then lightly fold into the egg mixture. Pour into the prepared tin and bake for 10 minutes. Meanwhile warm the jam in a small saucepan.

When the cake is cooked, turn it on to a large sheet of greaseproof paper dusted with caster sugar. Peel off the lining paper. Trim off any crisp edges. Spread the cake with the warmed jam and roll up tightly from one long side. Dredge with caster sugar and place on a wire rack, with the join underneath, to cool.

variations

The classic Swiss Roll is quick and easy to make once you have mastered the technique of rolling the hot cake. The basic recipe for the light, rolled sponge can be used as a base for making cakes that are just that little bit different. The following variations suggest suitable combinations of flavouring ingredients, fillings and coatings.

CHOCOLATE RUM ROLL Make this luscious, rich, rolled cake for special occasions. Prepare the Chocolate Roll, following the instructions for Chocolate Ice Roll, and allow it to cool. Soak 50 g/2 oz of seedless raisins in 60 ml/4 tbsp of rum for 30 minutes. Drain the raisins and add the rum to 150 ml/¼ pint of double cream. Add 15 ml/1 tbsp of icing sugar to the cream and lightly whip it. Fold in the raisins and 30 ml/2 tbsp of chopped maraschino cherries. Spread this cream over the unrolled cake and roll it up again.

EASTER ALMOND ROLL Make the Swiss Roll following the basic recipe. Leave to cool completely. Roll out 350 g/12 oz marzipan or almond paste into an oblong the same width as the length of the roll, and long enough to wrap around the roll. Brush the outside of the Swiss roll with warmed apricot jam and place it on the rolled out marzipan or almond paste. Wrap the paste around the roll, trimming off the excess and making sure that the join is underneath. Decorate the top of the roll with miniature chocolate Easter eggs.

ST CLEMENT'S ROLL Make a Swiss roll following the basic recipe, adding the grated rind of 1 orange to the eggs and sugar. Instead of jam, use lemon curd to fill the cake.

SYLLABUB

SERVES 4

50 ml/2 fl oz sweet red wine or
ruby port

250 ml/8 fl oz double cream

50 ml/2 fl oz medium dry sherry

juice of ½ orange

grated rind of ½ lemon

50 g/2 oz caster sugar

Divide the wine or port between 4 chilled stemmed glasses, and keep chilled. In a bowl, whip the cream, adding all the remaining ingredients gradually, in order, until the mixture just holds firm peaks. Pile the cream mixture into the chilled glasses (see Mrs Beeton's Tip). Serve as soon as possible.

MRS BEETON'S TIP
When adding the cream mixture to the chilled wine take care not to mix the two. The wine should clearly be seen in the bottom of each glass.

T

TANDOORI CHICKEN

SERVES 4

1 (1.4–1.6 kg/3–3½ lb) chicken

15 ml/1 tbsp cumin seeds

30 ml/2 tbsp grated fresh root
ginger

1 onion, grated

4 garlic cloves, crushed

5 ml/1 tsp salt

5 ml/1 tsp chilli powder

2.5 ml/½ tsp turmeric

5 ml/1 tsp Garam Masala

few drops of red food colouring
(optional)

juice of 2 lemons

150 ml/¼ pint plain yogurt

30 ml/2 tbsp oil

Skin the chicken. Keep it whole or cut it into 4 or 8 pieces. Toast the cumin seeds in a small ungreased frying pan over moderate heat for 1 minute. Grind them in a pepper mill, or use a pestle and mortar. Set the seeds aside.

Combine the ginger, onion, garlic, salt, chilli powder, turmeric and garam masala in a small bowl. Add the colouring, if used, then stir in the lemon juice and yogurt. Prick the chicken with a fork and cut a few slits in the legs and breast. Rub the bird with the paste, pressing it deeply into the slits. Place in a shallow dish, cover tightly with foil and a lid and marinate for 12 hours or overnight.

Set the oven at 180°C/350°F/gas 4. Transfer the chicken to a rack in a shallow roasting tin. Baste it with the oil and any remaining paste. Bake for 1½–2 hours, spooning over the oil and pan juices from time to time. When cooked, sprinkle with the toasted cumin seeds. Serve with rice and a tomato and onion salad.

TARTARE SAUCE

MAKES ABOUT 300 ML/½ PINT

2 hard-boiled egg yolks

2 egg yolks

salt and pepper

15 ml/1 tbsp white wine vinegar

300 ml/½ pint oil (olive oil or a
 mixture of olive with
 grapeseed or sunflower oil)

15 ml/1 tbsp each chopped
 capers, gherkin and snipped
 chives

30 ml/2 tbsp chopped parsley

Sieve the hard-boiled egg yolks into a bowl. Add one of the raw yolks and mix thoroughly, then work in the second raw yolk. Stir in salt and pepper to taste and mix to a paste with the vinegar.

Beating vigorously, gradually add the oil, drop by drop, as for making mayonnaise. When all the oil has been incorporated and the mixture is thick, stir in the capers, gherkin and herbs.

THREE FRUIT MARMALADE

One of the most popular forms of home-made marmalade, this combines the flavours of grapefruit, lemon and orange.

MAKES ABOUT 2.5 KG/5½ LB

1 grapefruit

2 lemons

1 sweet orange

1.5 kg/3¼ lb sugar

Wash the citrus fruit, peel it and shred the peel finely or coarsely as preferred. Scrape off the pith if very thick and chop the flesh roughly. Tie the pips and pith or coarse tissue in a muslin bag. Put the peel, chopped flesh and muslin bag in a large bowl, add 2 litres/3½ pints water and soak for 24 hours.

Next day, transfer the contents of the bowl to a preserving pan. Bring the liquid to the boil, lower the heat and simmer for 1½ hours or until the peel is tender and the contents of the pan are reduced by one third. Remove from the heat. Squeeze the muslin bag over the pan to extract as much of the juice as possible.

Return the pan to the heat, add the sugar and stir over low heat until dissolved. Bring to the boil, then boil rapidly until setting point is reached. Remove from the heat and skim quickly. Leave to cool slightly until a skin forms on the surface of the marmalade, then stir, pot and top with waxed paper discs. Cover and label when cold.

TOAD-IN-THE-HOLE

SERVES 4

450 g/1 lb pork sausages

BATTER

100 g/4 oz plain flour

1.25 ml/¼ tsp salt

1 egg, beaten

300 ml/½ pint milk, or milk and
  water

Make the batter. Sift the flour and salt into a bowl, make a well in the centre and add the beaten egg. Stir in half the milk (or all the milk, if using a mixture of milk and water), gradually working in the flour. Whisk until the mixture is smooth and bubbly, then stir in the rest of the milk (or the water). Pour the batter into a jug and set aside.

Set the oven at 220°C/425°F/gas 7. Arrange the sausages, like the spokes of a wheel, in a shallow 1.1 litre/2 pint circular dish. Stand the dish on a baking sheet and cook the sausages for 15 minutes. Pour the batter over the sausages and bake for 40–45 minutes more until golden brown and well risen. Serve at once with a rich gravy or tomato sauce.

TOMATO SALAD

Sun-warmed tomatoes, freshly picked, are perfect for this salad. In the classic Italian version, olive oil is the only dressing, but a little red wine vinegar may be added, if preferred.

SERVES 4 TO 6

450 g/1 lb firm tomatoes

salt and pepper

pinch of caster sugar (optional)

45 ml/3 tbsp olive oil

5 ml/1 tsp chopped fresh basil

fresh basil sprigs to garnish

Cut a small cross in the top of each tomato. Place them in a heatproof bowl. Pour on freshly boiling water and leave for about 45 seconds, then drain. Peel back and remove the skins, then slice tomatoes. Put them in a serving dish and sprinkle lightly with salt and pepper. Add the sugar, if used. Pour over the olive oil and sprinkle with the chopped basil. Garnish with basil sprigs.

variations

MOZZARELLA AND TOMATO SALAD Interleave the sliced tomatoes with sliced mozzarella cheese. Cover and leave to marinate for at least an hour before serving.

TOMATO AND ONION SALAD A popular salad to serve with cold meats. Omit the basil. Thinly slice 1 red or white onion and separate the slices into rings. Sprinkle these over the tomatoes. Sprinkle with sugar, salt and pepper, and a few drops of cider vinegar as well as the oil.

MINTED TOMATO SALAD WITH CHIVES Omit the basil. Sprinkle 15 ml/1 tbsp chopped fresh mint and 45 ml/3 tbsp snipped chives over the tomatoes before adding the oil. Garnish with sprigs of mint.

TOMATO SAUCE

MAKES ABOUT 600 ML/1 PINT

30 ml/2 tbsp olive oil

1 onion, finely chopped

1 garlic clove, crushed

1 bay leaf

1 rindless streaky bacon rasher, chopped

800 g/1¾ lb tomatoes, peeled and chopped

60 ml/4 tbsp stock or red wine

salt and pepper

generous pinch of sugar

15 ml/1 tbsp chopped fresh basil or 5 ml/1 tsp dried basil

Heat the oil in a saucepan and fry the onion, garlic, bay leaf and bacon over gentle heat for 15 minutes.

Stir in the remaining ingredients except the basil. Heat until bubbling, then cover the pan and simmer gently for 30 minutes or until the tomatoes are reduced to a pulp.

Rub the sauce through a sieve into a clean saucepan. Alternatively, purée it in a blender or food processor until smooth, then rub it through a sieve into a pan. Reheat the sauce. Stir in the basil. Add more salt and pepper if required before serving.

TOMATO SOUP

SERVES 6

25 g/1 oz butter

2 rindless back bacon rashers, chopped

1 small onion, chopped

1 carrot, chopped

900 g/2 lb tomatoes, chopped

600 ml/1 pint chicken stock or white stock

1 bouquet garni

salt and pepper

10 ml/2 tsp sugar

300 ml/½ pint double cream

chopped parsley or snipped chives to garnish

Melt the butter in a large saucepan, add the chopped bacon and fry for 2–3 minutes. Stir in the onion and carrot and fry over gentle heat for 5 minutes, then add the tomatoes and cook for 5 minutes more. Add the stock and bouquet garni, with salt and pepper to taste. Bring to the boil, lower the heat and simmer for 20 minutes, until the vegetables are soft.

Remove the bouquet garni. Purée the soup in a blender or food processor, then rub through a sieve to remove traces of skin and seeds. Return the soup to the rinsed-out pan. Stir in the sugar and reheat to just below boiling point. Stir in the cream, heat briefly but do not allow to simmer or the soup will curdle. Taste and adjust the seasoning, then serve at once, topped with chopped parsley or snipped chives.

TREACLE TART

SERVES 6

45 ml/3 tbsp golden syrup

50 g/2 oz soft white
   breadcrumbs

5 ml/1 tsp lemon juice

SHORT CRUST PASTRY

150 g/5 oz plain flour

2.5 ml/½ tsp salt

65 g/2 oz margarine (or half
   butter, half lard)

flour for rolling out

Set the oven at 200°C/400°F/gas 6. To make the pastry, sift the flour and salt into a bowl, then rub in the margarine until the mixture resembles fine breadcrumbs. Add enough cold water to make a stiff dough. Press the dough together with your fingertips.

Roll out the pastry on a lightly floured surface and use just over three quarters of it to line a 20 cm/8 inch pie plate, reserving the rest for a lattice topping.

Melt the syrup in a saucepan. Stir in the breadcrumbs and lemon juice, then pour the mixture into the prepared pastry case. Roll out the reserved pastry to a rectangle and cut into 1 cm/½ inch strips. Arrange in a lattice on top of the tart. Bake for about 30 minutes.

TRIFLE

SERVES 6

4 slices of plain cake or
   individual cakes

6 almond macaroons

12 ratafias

175 ml/6 fl oz sherry

30–45 ml/2–3 tbsp brandy

60–90 ml/4–6 tbsp raspberry or
   strawberry jam

grated rind of ½ lemon

25 g/1 oz flaked almonds

300 ml/½ pint double cream

30 ml/2 tbsp icing sugar

candied and crystallized fruit and
   peel to decorate

CUSTARD

25 g/1 oz cornflour

25 g/1 oz caster sugar

4 egg yolks

5 ml/1 tsp vanilla essence

600 ml/1 pint milk

Place the sponge cakes in a glass dish. Add the macaroons and ratafias, pressing them down gently. Pour about 50 ml/2 fl oz of the sherry into a basin and set it aside, then pour the rest over the biscuits and cake. Sprinkle with the brandy. Warm the jam in a small saucepan, then pour it evenly over the trifle base, spreading it lightly. Top with the lemon rind and almonds.

For the custard, blend the cornflour, caster sugar, egg yolks and vanilla to a smooth cream with a little of the milk. Heat the remaining milk until hot. Pour some of the milk on the egg mixture, stirring, then replace the mixture in the saucepan with the rest of the milk.

Bring to the boil, stirring constantly, then lower the heat and simmer for 3 minutes. Pour the custard over the trifle base and cover the surface with a piece of dampened greaseproof paper. Set aside to cool.

Add the cream and icing sugar to the reserved sherry and whip until the mixture stands in soft peaks. Swirl the cream over the top of the trifle and chill. Decorate with pieces of candied and crystallized fruit and peel before serving.

TRIPE AND ONIONS

SERVES 4

450 g/1 lb dressed tripe

600 ml/1 pint milk

salt and pepper

3 large onions, chopped

25 g/1 oz butter

30 ml/2 tbsp plain flour

GARNISH

15 ml/1 tbsp chopped parsley

toast triangles

Wash the tripe and cut it into 5 cm/2 inch squares. Put it in a heavy-bottomed saucepan. Add the milk, with salt and pepper to taste. Stir in the onions. Bring the milk to the boil, lower the heat, cover tightly and simmer for about 2 hours (see Mrs Beeton's Tip) or until the tripe is tender.

Knead the butter and flour together until evenly blended. Add it in small pieces to the contents of the pan. Stir until smooth, then continue cooking for a further 30 minutes. Serve on a heated dish, garnished with parsley and toast triangles.

MRS BEETON'S TIP

Honeycomb tripe is the most delicate type. It is usually sold blanched and parboiled. It is highly perishable and should always be cooked as soon as possible after purchase. Cooking time for tripe varies, depending on type and preliminary preparation. Ask the butcher's advice.

TROUT MEUNIERE

SERVES 4

4 trout

50 g/2 oz plain flour

salt and pepper

50 g/2 oz butter

juice of ½ lemon

10 ml/2 tsp chopped parsley

lemon twists to garnish

Dry the fish well with absorbent kitchen paper. Spread out the flour in a shallow bowl and add salt and pepper. Add the fish and coat well on all sides.

Melt the butter in a large frying pan. When it foams, add the trout. Fry gently for 6–7 minutes on each side or until the skin is golden and crisp. Using a slotted spoon and a fish slice, transfer the fish to a warmed serving dish. Keep hot. Add salt and pepper to the butter remaining in the pan and heat until it is nut brown. Add the lemon juice and chopped parsley and pour over the trout. Garnish with lemon twists and serve.

TROUT WITH ALMONDS

SERVES 4

100 g/4 oz butter

4 trout, cleaned and trimmed

salt and pepper

juice of ½ lemon

50 g/2 oz flaked almonds

125 ml/4 fl oz double cream

3 egg yolks

Melt the butter in a grill pan under moderate heat. Lay the trout in the pan and sprinkle with salt and pepper and lemon juice. Grill the trout for 5 minutes.

Carefully turn the trout over. Sprinkle most of the almonds over the fish, spreading out the rest at the side of the pan. Grill for 3–5 minutes more until the trout are tender and the almonds browned. Using a fish slice and slotted spoon, transfer the trout and almonds to absorbent kitchen paper to drain. Tip the grill pan juices into a small saucepan. Arrange the trout on a warmed serving platter and keep hot. Set the browned almonds aside.

Add the cream and egg yolks to the pan juices and mix well. Heat gently, stirring constantly until the sauce thickens. Do not let the mixture boil. Spoon the sauce over the trout, garnish with the reserved almonds and serve at once.

TUNA SAUCE

Serve the sauce over cooked pasta as a quick and easy starter before a light main course.

SERVES 4

25 g/1 oz butter or margarine

1 (200 g/7 oz) can tuna

1 onion, chopped

25 g/1 oz plain flour

450 ml/¾ pint milk

100 g/4 oz mushrooms, sliced

50 g/2 oz Cheddar cheese, grated

salt and pepper

30 ml/2 tbsp chopped parsley

Melt the butter in a saucepan. If the tuna is canned in oil, drain the oil into the pan with the butter. Drain and flake the tuna and set it aside. Add the chopped onion and cook gently, stirring occasionally, for about 15 minutes or until soft. Stir in the flour and cook for 1 minute, then reduce the heat to low and slowly pour in the milk, stirring constantly. Bring to the boil, lower the heat again and simmer for 3 minutes.

Stir the mushrooms and cheese into the sauce with salt and pepper to taste. Cook over low heat until the cheese melts, then add the parsley and flaked drained tuna. Stir for 1–2 minutes until the tuna is hot. Serve at once.

variations
The sauce may also be served with rice, ladled into split baked potatoes or into scooped-out crusty rolls for a simple snack supper.

TURKEY For basic information on preparation, cooking methods and times, see pages 44–52. See also Roast Turkey and Roast Turkey with Chestnuts.

VANILLA BAVAROIS

A bavarois, or Bavarian Cream, as it is sometimes known, consists of a cup custard combined with cream and flavouring, with gelatine as the setting agent.

SERVES 4 TO 6

oil for greasing

4 egg yolks or 1 whole egg and 2 yolks

50 g/2 oz caster sugar

250 ml/8 fl oz milk

2.5 ml/½ tsp vanilla essence

10 ml/2 tsp gelatine

150 ml/¼ pint double cream

150 ml/¼ pint single cream

Oil a 750 ml/1 pint mould. In a bowl, beat the eggs and sugar together until fluffy and pale. Warm the milk in a saucepan; do not let it boil. Slowly stir it into the egg mixture, then strain the custard back into the clean pan or into a double saucepan or heatproof bowl placed over hot water. Cook over very low heat until the custard thickens.

Strain the thickened custard into a bowl, stir in the vanilla essence and leave to cool. Place 15 ml/1 tbsp water in a small bowl and sprinkle the gelatine on to the liquid. Set aside for 15 minutes until the gelatine is spongy. Stand the bowl over a saucepan of hot water and stir the gelatine until it has dissolved completely. Cool until tepid and add to the custard. Leave in a cool place until the mixture thickens at the edges. Stir from time to time to prevent the formation of a skin.

Combine the creams in a bowl and whip lightly. Fold into the custard mixture, and pour into the prepared mould. Refrigerate for about 2 hours until set, then turn out on to a flat wetted plate to serve.

variations

CARAMEL BAVAROIS Dissolve 100 g/4 oz granulated sugar in 15 ml/1 tbsp water. Heat until the syrup turns a rich brown colour. Carefully add 60 ml/4 tbsp hot water, remove from the heat; stir until all the caramel dissolves. Stir into the warm custard.

CHOCOLATE BAVAROIS Grate 100 g/4 oz plain chocolate and add with the milk. It will melt in the warm custard. Add 5 ml/1 tsp vanilla essence.

COFFEE BAVAROIS Dissolve 15 ml/1 tbsp instant coffee in 15 ml/1 tbsp boiling water. Cool, then stir in 15 ml/1 tbsp rum. Add this essence with the milk.

CREME DIPLOMATE Soak 100 g/4 oz chopped crystallized fruit in 30 ml/2 tbsp kirsch. Pour the vanilla Bavarian cream into the mould to a depth of 2 cm/¾ inch and leave to set. Spread half the fruit over it and cover with a little of the cream. Leave to set. Continue alternating layers of fruit and cream, finishing with a layer of cream. Allow each layer to set before adding the next.

CREME TRICOLORE Divide the mixture into three portions. Flavour the first with vanilla essence, the second with chocolate, the third with strawberry purée. Line the mould with vanilla cream in the same way as when lining with jelly (page 151). When this is completely set, fill alternately with equal layers of the chocolate and strawberry creams, allowing each layer to set before adding the next.

VANILLA ICE CREAM

SERVES 6

30 ml/2 tbsp custard powder
500 ml/17 fl oz milk
100 g/4 oz caster sugar
125 ml/4 fl oz double cream
5 ml/1 tsp vanilla essence

Turn the freezing compartment or freezer to the coldest setting about 1 hour before making the ice cream. In a bowl, mix the custard powder to a cream with a little of the milk. Bring the remaining milk to the boil in a saucepan, then pour it into the bowl, stirring constantly. Return the custard mixture to the clean pan and simmer, stirring all the time, until thickened. Stir in the sugar, cover closely with dampened greaseproof paper and set aside to cool.

In a large bowl, whip the cream to soft peaks. Add the cold custard and vanilla essence. Spoon into a suitable container for freezing. Cover the container closely and freeze until half-frozen (when ice crystals appear around the edge of the mixture). Beat the mixture until smooth, scraping off any crystals. Replace the cover and freeze until firm. Return the freezer to the normal setting.

Transfer the ice cream to the refrigerator about 15 minutes before serving, to allow it to soften and 'ripen'. Serve in scoops in individual dishes or in a large decorative bowl.

VANILLA PARFAIT

This is a quick method of making a rich vanilla ice cream. It is important to use a good-quality natural vanilla essence and not one of the very strong flavourings.

50 g/2 oz icing sugar

10 ml/2 tsp natural vanilla
    essence

300 ml/½ pint double cream

300 ml/½ pint whipping cream

Place the icing sugar and vanilla essence in a large bowl. Pour in both creams. Stir with a whisk until the sugar has dissolved, then whip the creams until they stand in soft peaks.

Turn the mixture into a container suitable for freezing. Cover and freeze for several hours or overnight, until the mixture is solid. Depending on the freezer, the parfait may be scooped immediately it is removed from the freezer or it may be slightly too firm, in which case it should be allowed to stand in the refrigerator for 15 minutes.

flavourings for ice cream and parfait

The following flavourings can be added to either Vanilla Ice Cream or Vanilla Parfait.

CHOCOLATE Mix 60 ml/4 tbsp boiling water with 45 ml/3 tbsp cocoa powder, stirring until smooth. Add the cocoa mixture to the cold custard or to the icing sugar and vanilla mixture if making the parfait.

COFFEE Mix 30 ml/2 tbsp boiling water with 15 ml/1 tbsp instant coffee. When the coffee has dissolved, 30–60 ml/2–4 tbsp rum may be added, if liked. Stir the coffee mixture into the cold custard or into the icing sugar and vanilla mixture if making the parfait.

CHOCOLATE CHIP Coarsely grate 100 g/4 oz plain chocolate and mix it into the ice cream after the final beating, before the mixture is allowed to freeze until firm. Fold the grated chocolate into the whipped cream mixture for the parfait.

LEMON OR ORANGE Add the grated rind of 2 lemons or 2 oranges to the cooled custard or to the icing sugar and vanilla mixture if making the parfait.

PISTACHIO Finely chop 100 g/4 oz shelled pistachio nuts and fold them into the ice cream after the final beating. Fold them into the whipped cream for the parfait mixture.

RATAFIA Coarsely crush 100 g/4 oz ratafia biscuits and fold them into the ice cream after the final beating. Fold them into the whipped cream for the parfait mixture.

STRAWBERRY OR RASPBERRY RIPPLE Warm 225 g/8 oz good-quality strawberry or raspberry jam until it is softened but not too hot. Fold the jam through the ice cream after the final beating or into the whipped cream for the parfait mixture. Do not fold in the jam thoroughly – leave it streaked through the mixture.

Vanilla souffle

SERVES 4 TO 6

40 g/1½ oz butter

40 g/1½ oz plain flour

250 ml/8 fl oz milk

4 eggs, separated, plus 1 white

50 g/2 oz caster sugar

2.5 ml/½ tsp vanilla essence

caster or icing sugar for dredging

Grease a 1 litre/1¾ pint soufflé dish. Set the oven at 180°C/350°F/gas 4. Melt the butter in a saucepan, stir in the flour and cook slowly for 2–3 minutes without colouring, stirring all the time. Add the milk gradually and beat until smooth. Cook for 1–2 minutes more, still stirring. Remove from the heat and beat hard until the sauce comes away cleanly from the sides of the pan. Cool slightly and put into a bowl.

Beat the yolks into the flour mixture one by one. Beat in the sugar and vanilla essence. In a clean, grease-free bowl, whisk all the egg whites until stiff. Using a metal spoon, stir 1 spoonful of the whites into the mixture to lighten it, then fold in the rest until evenly distributed.

Spoon into the prepared dish and bake for 45 minutes until well risen and browned. Dredge with caster or icing sugar and serve immediately from the dish, with a jam sauce.

variations

ALMOND SOUFFLE Add 100 g/4 oz ground almonds, 15 ml/1 tbsp lemon juice and a few drops of ratafia essence to the mixture before adding the egg yolks. Reduce the sugar to 40 g/1½ oz. Omit the vanilla essence.

COFFEE SOUFFLE Add 30 ml/2 tbsp instant coffee dissolved in a little hot water before adding the egg yolks, or use 125 ml/4 fl oz strong black coffee and only 125 ml/4 fl oz milk. Omit the vanilla essence.

GINGER SOUFFLE Add a pinch of ground ginger and 50 g/2 oz chopped preserved stem ginger before adding the egg yolks. Omit the vanilla essence. Serve each portion topped with double cream and ginger syrup.

LEMON SOUFFLE Add the thinly grated rind and juice of 1 lemon before adding the egg yolks. Omit the vanilla essence. Serve with Lemon Sauce.

ORANGE SOUFFLE Thinly pare the rind of 2 oranges. Put in a saucepan with the milk and bring slowly to the boil. Remove from the heat, cover, and leave to stand for 10 minutes, then remove the rind. Make up the sauce using the flavoured milk. Reduce the sugar to 40 g/1½ oz and omit the vanilla essence. Add the strained juice of ½ orange.

PRALINE SOUFFLE Dissolve 30–45 ml/2–3 tbsp almond praline in the milk before making the sauce, or crush and add just before the egg yolks. Omit the vanilla essence.

SOUFFLE AMBASSADRICE Crumble 2 almond macaroons; soak in 30 ml/2 tbsp rum with 50 g/2 oz chopped blanched almonds. Stir into a vanilla soufflé mixture.

SOUFFLE ROTHSCHILD Rinse 50 g/2 oz mixed glacé fruit in hot water to remove any excess sugar. Chop the fruit and soak it in 30 ml/2 tbsp

VANILLA SOUFFLE — *continued*

brandy or kirsch for 2 hours. Make up 1 quantity vanilla soufflé mixture. Put half the vanilla soufflé mixture into the dish, add the fruit, and then the rest of the soufflé mixture.

hot fruit soufflés

For fruit-flavoured soufflés a thick, sweet purée is added to the basic vanilla soufflé. It is important that the purée should have a strong flavour, otherwise the taste will not be discernible. If extra purée is added, the soufflé will be heavy and will not rise.

APPLE SOUFFLE Add 125 ml/4 fl oz thick sweet apple purée, 15 ml/1 tbsp lemon juice, and a pinch of powdered cinnamon to the soufflé before adding the egg yolks. Dust the soufflé with cinnamon before serving.

APRICOT SOUFFLE Before adding the egg yolks, add 125 ml/4 fl oz thick fresh apricot purée and 15 ml/1 tbsp lemon juice. If using canned apricots – 1 (397 g/14 oz) can yields 125 ml/4 fl oz purée – use half milk and half can syrup for the sauce. A purée made from dried apricots makes a delicious soufflé.

PINEAPPLE SOUFFLE Before adding the egg yolks, add 125 ml/4 fl oz crushed pineapple or 75 g/3 oz chopped fresh pineapple, and make the sauce using half milk and half pineapple juice.

RASPBERRY SOUFFLE Before adding the egg yolks, stir in 125 ml/4 fl oz raspberry purée – 1 (397 g/14 oz) can yields 125 ml/4 fl oz purée – and 10 ml/2 tsp lemon juice.

VEAL AND TUNA SALAD

SERVES 6

1.8 kg/4 lb fillet of veal

1 carrot, cut into quarters

1 small onion, cut into quarters

1 celery stick, roughly chopped

4 black peppercorns

5 ml/1 tsp salt

SAUCE

1 (198 g/7 oz) can tuna, drained

4 anchovy fillets

125 ml/4 fl oz olive oil

2 egg yolks

black pepper

15–30 ml/1–2 tbsp lemon juice

Trim the veal. Tie it into a neat shape, if necessary. Place in a large saucepan with the carrot, onion, celery, peppercorns and salt. Pour over enough water to cover the meat. Bring to the boil, lower the heat, cover the pan and simmer for 1½ hours or until the meat is very tender. Carefully lift it out of the liquid and set it aside on a plate to cool. Boil the cooking liquid quickly to reduce it by half, strain through a fine sieve and reserve.

Make the sauce. Put the tuna in a bowl with the anchovies. Add 15 ml/ 1 tbsp of the olive oil. Pound to a smooth paste by hand or use a blender or food processor. Blend in the egg yolks; season with pepper. Add half the lemon juice, then gradually add the remaining oil, as when making mayonnaise. When the sauce is thick and shiny, add more lemon juice to taste. Stir in about 30 ml/2 tbsp of the reserved cooking liquid from the veal to make a thin coating sauce.

Cut the cold veal into thin slices and arrange them in a dish. Coat completely with the sauce, then cover the dish and refrigerate for up to 24 hours. Before serving, garnish the salad with capers, sliced gherkins and fresh tarragon, if liked.

VEAL OR HAM LOAF

SERVES 3 TO 4

fat for greasing

200 g/7 oz cold roast veal or cooked ham

4 rindless streaky bacon rashers

175 g/6 oz fresh white breadcrumbs

250 ml/8 fl oz veal or chicken stock

2.5 ml/½ tsp grated lemon rind

2.5 ml/½ tsp ground mace

1.25 ml/¼ tsp cayenne pepper

30 ml/2 tbsp chopped parsley

salt

2 eggs, lightly beaten

Thoroughly grease a 450 g/1 lb loaf tin or 750 ml/1¼ pint ovenproof dish. Set the oven at 160°C/325°F/gas 3. Mince the veal or ham and bacon together finely or process in a food processor. Scrape into a bowl and add the breadcrumbs, stock and lemon rind, mace, cayenne and parsley with salt to taste. Mix in the eggs. Spoon the mixture into the prepared tin or dish and bake for 1 hour, or until the mixture is firm and lightly browned. Serve hot, with gravy or tomato sauce, if liked.

MRS BEETON'S TIP

If the loaf tin has a tendency to stick, line the base with baking parchment or greaseproof paper so that the loaf will turn out easily.

VEGETABLE SOUP

SERVES 6

30 ml/2 tbsp oil

1 onion, chopped

2 leeks, trimmed, sliced and
washed

3 celery sticks, sliced

2 potatoes, diced

2 carrots, diced

1 swede, diced

1 parsnip, diced

1.75 litres/3 pints chicken,
vegetable or rich strong stock

salt and pepper

Heat the oil in a large, heavy-bottomed saucepan. Add the onion and leeks, and cook gently for 10 minutes, stirring occasionally. Add the remaining vegetables, pour in the stock and add salt and pepper to taste. Bring to the boil, lower the heat and cover the pan. Simmer the soup for about 1 hour or until it is well flavoured and all the vegetables are tender.

If a clear soup with identifiable vegetables is preferred, serve at once. To thicken the soup, purée it in a blender or food processor, return to the pan and heat through before serving.

PRESSURE COOKER TIP

Put the vegetables in the cooker with only 1 litre/1¾ pints of stock; the cooker should not be more than half full. Put the lid on the cooker and bring to 15 lb pressure. Cook for 5 minutes. Reduce pressure quickly. Add more stock if liked.

VEGETABLE STOCK

MAKES ABOUT 1.75 LITRES/3 PINTS

2 onions

2 leeks

1 small turnip

2 tomatoes

4 celery sticks

1 bouquet garni

6 black peppercorns

2 cloves

a few lettuce and spinach leaves

a few watercress sprigs

2.5 ml/½ tsp yeast extract
(optional)

salt

Slice the onions and place them in a large saucepan. Trim, slice and wash the leeks, chop the turnip and tomatoes and add them all to the pan with the sliced celery. Tuck the bouquet garni among the vegetables and add the peppercorns and cloves. Pour in 2 litres/3½ pints water. Bring to the boil, lower the heat and simmer for 1 hour.

Add the lettuce, spinach and watercress and simmer for 1 hour more. Stir in the yeast extract, if using, and add salt to taste.

VEGETABLES For basic information on varieties, preparation and cooking methods, see page 80–102. See also individual entries.

VENISON STEAKS WITH RED WINE MARINADE

SERVES 6 TO 8

4 slices of venison (from haunch)

salt and pepper

25 g/1 oz plain flour

butter or dripping

1 small onion, chopped

6–8 juniper berries, crushed

150 ml/¼ pint game or chicken stock

chopped parsley to garnish

MARINADE

about 300 ml/½ pint red wine

1 bouquet garni

6 peppercorns

4 onion slices

30 ml/2 tbsp olive oil

10 ml/2 tsp red wine vinegar

Make the marinade. Mix all the ingredients in a saucepan. Bring to the boil and boil for 1 minute. Cool completely. Put the venison in a large dish. Pour the marinade over, cover the dish and marinate overnight in the refrigerator..

Set the oven at 180°C/350°F/gas 4. Drain the venison and pat dry. Reserve the marinade. Snip the edges of the venison steaks to prevent them from curling. Season the flour and rub it over the steaks.

Heat the fat in a flameproof casserole. Sear the steaks; add the onion when searing the second side. Pour off all but a film of fat from the pan. Sprinkle the steaks with the crushed juniper. Pour the stock and a little of the marinade around them, to a depth of about 1 cm/½ inch.

Cover the casserole tightly with foil and bake for 30 minutes, or until the steaks are tender. Drain and serve, sprinkled with parsley. Drain off the excess fat from the stock, pour it into a jug and serve with the steaks.

VICHYSSOISE

A simple soup which can be served hot, but tastes even better chilled.

SERVES 4 TO 6

25 g/1 oz butter

450 g/1 lb leeks, white parts only, trimmed, sliced and washed

2 onions, chopped

450 g/1 lb potatoes, cubed

900 ml/1½ pints chicken stock

salt and pepper

150 ml/¼ pint milk

150 ml/¼ pint single cream

snipped chives to garnish

Melt the butter in a saucepan, add the leeks, onions and potatoes and fry gently for 10 minutes without browning. Stir in the stock, with salt and pepper to taste. Bring to the boil, lower the heat and simmer for about 30 minutes or until the vegetables are soft.

Purée the mixture in a blender or food processor, or press through a sieve into a bowl. Cool quickly, then stir in the milk and cream. Add more salt and pepper if required. Cover and chill for 4–6 hours. Serve in chilled individual bowls, sprinkled with chives.

FREEZER TIP

Make the soup as above, but use only 1 onion and 600 ml/1 pint chicken stock. After puréeing the vegetables and stock, cool the mixture quickly and freeze in a rigid container. Thaw overnight in the refrigerator. Stir in the remaining stock with the milk and cream, then chill for at least 2 hours more before serving.

VICTORIA SANDWICH CAKE

MAKES ONE 18 CM/7 INCH CAKE

fat for greasing

150 g/5 oz butter or margarine

150 g/5 oz caster sugar

3 eggs, beaten

150 g/5 oz self-raising flour or plain flour and 5 ml/1 tsp baking powder

pinch of salt

raspberry or other jam for filling

caster sugar for dredging

Line and grease two 18 cm/7 inch sandwich tins. Set the oven at 180°C/350°F/gas 4.

In a mixing bowl cream the butter or margarine with the sugar until light and fluffy. Add the eggs gradually, beating well after each addition. Sift the flour, salt and baking powder, if used, into a bowl. Stir into the creamed mixture, lightly but thoroughly, until evenly mixed.

Divide between the tins and bake for 25–30 minutes. Cool on a wire rack, then sandwich together with jam. Sprinkle the top with caster sugar or spread with Glacé Icing.

VINAIGRETTE DRESSING

MAKES ABOUT 125 ML/4 FL OZ

90 ml/6 tbsp light olive oil

salt and pepper

pinch each of mustard powder and caster sugar

30 ml/2 tbsp white wine vinegar

10 ml/2 tsp finely chopped gherkin

5 ml/1 tsp each of finely chopped onion or chives, chopped parsley, finely chopped capers and finely chopped fresh tarragon or chervil

Mix all the ingredients in a screw-topped jar. Close the jar tightly and shake vigorously until well blended; then allow to stand for at least 1 hour. Shake again before using.

WAFFLES

Waffles are crisp fried wafers made from a leavened batter and cooked in a hinged electric or hob-top waffle iron. Follow the manufacturer's instructions, taking care not to overfill the iron.

SERVES 4 TO 8

75 g/3 oz butter

250 g/9 oz self-raising flour

1.25 ml/¼ tsp salt

5 ml/1 tsp baking powder

2 eggs, separated

375 ml/13 fl oz milk

butter and golden syrup, to serve

Melt the butter in a small saucepan. Set aside to cool. Sift the flour, salt and baking powder into a bowl. Make a well in the centre of the flour. Add the egg yolks, cooled butter and some of the milk. Gradually work in the flour from the sides and then beat well until smooth Beat in the rest of the milk.

In a clean, grease-free bowl, whisk the egg whites until stiff, and fold into the batter. It should be the consistency of thick cream.

Heat the waffle iron, pour in some of the batter, and cook the waffle for about 5 minutes, until the steaming stops. Remove the waffle and keep hot. Make more waffles in the same way. Serve hot with butter and golden syrup.

variations

BUTTERMILK WAFFLES Substitute buttermilk for the milk. Add the whole eggs to the batter instead of separating them.

NUT WAFFLES Sprinkle 15 ml/1 tbsp chopped nuts over the batter as soon as it has been poured into the iron.

WALDORF SALAD

SERVES 4

4 sharp red dessert apples

2 celery sticks, thinly sliced

25 g/1 oz chopped or broken walnuts

75 ml/5 tbsp mayonnaise

30 ml/2 tbsp lemon juice

pinch of salt

lettuce leaves (optional)

Core the apples, but do not peel them. Cut them into dice. Put them in a bowl with the celery and walnuts. Mix the mayonnaise with the lemon juice. Add salt to taste and fold into the apple mixture. Chill. Serve on a bed of lettuce leaves, if liked.

variation

WALDORF SALAD WITH CHICKEN Make as above, but use only 2 apples. Add 350 g/12 oz diced cold cooked chicken. For extra flavour and colour, add 50 g/2 oz small seedless green grapes.

WELSH RAREBIT

SERVES 4 TO 6

25 g/1 oz butter

15 ml/1 tbsp plain flour

75 ml/5 tbsp milk or 30 ml/2 tbsp milk and 45 ml/3 tbsp ale or beer

5 ml/1 tsp French mustard

few drops of Worcestershire sauce

175 g/6 oz Cheddar cheese, grated

salt and pepper

Melt the butter in a saucepan, stir in the flour and cook over gentle heat for 2–3 minutes, stirring constantly. Do not let the flour colour. Stir in the milk and blend to a smooth, thick mixture, then stir in the ale or beer, if used. Add the mustard and Worcestershire sauce.

Gradually add the cheese, stirring after each addition. Remove from the heat as soon as the mixture is smooth. Add salt and pepper to taste. Place in a covered container and chill when cool.

To use the rarebit, spread the mixture on buttered toast and place under a preheated hot grill for 2–3 minutes until bubbling and lightly browned. Serve at once.

variations

BUCK RAREBIT Make as for Welsh Rarebit, but top each slice with a poached egg.

YORKSHIRE RAREBIT Make as for Welsh Rarebit, but add 4 grilled rindless back bacon rashers.

WESTMORLAND PARKIN

This makes a dense, dark parkin with excellent keeping qualities.

MAKES TWO 20 CM/8 INCH CAKES (ABOUT 32 SQUARES)

fat for greasing

200 g/7 oz butter or clarified dripping

450 g/1 lb black treacle

450 g/1 lb fine oatmeal

200 g/7 oz plain flour

5 ml/1 tsp ground ginger

2.5 ml/½ tsp salt

10 ml/2 tsp baking powder

200 g/7 oz demerara sugar

100 ml/3½ fl oz milk

5 ml/1 tsp bicarbonate of soda

Line and grease two 20 cm/8 inch square tins. Set the oven at 160°C/325°F/gas 3.

Heat the butter or dripping and treacle gently in a saucepan, stirring until the fat has melted. Mix the dry ingredients, except the bicarbonate of soda, in a mixing bowl and make a well in the centre.

Warm the milk in a saucepan over low heat to hand-hot. Stir in the bicarbonate of soda until dissolved. Pour into the dry ingredients and mix well. Stir in the melted butter and treacle. Spoon the mixture into the prepared tins and bake for about 1½ hours or until cooked through and firm to the touch. Cool in the tins, then cut into squares.

WHEATMEAL BREAD

MAKES TWO 800 G/1¾ LB LOAVES

fat for greasing

400 g/14 oz wholemeal flour

400 g/14 oz strong white flour

10 ml/2 tsp salt

25 g/1 oz lard

25 g/1 oz fresh yeast or 15 ml/
 1 tbsp dried yeast

2.5 ml/½ tsp sugar

flour for kneading

salted water

Grease two 23 x 13 x 7.5 cm/9 x 5 x 3 inch loaf tins. Mix the flours and salt in a large bowl. Rub in the lard. Measure 450 ml/¾ pint lukewarm water.

Blend the fresh yeast to a thin paste with the sugar and a little of the warm water. Set aside in a warm place until frothy. Alternatively, sprinkle dried yeast over all the warm water and set aside until frothy, then stir well. Add the yeast liquid and any remaining water to the flour mixture and mix to a soft dough. Turn on to a floured surface and knead for about 4 minutes or until the dough is smooth and elastic. Replace in the bowl, cover and leave in a warm place until doubled in bulk.

Cut the dough into two equal portions and form each into a loaf shape. Place the dough in the prepared loaf tins, then brush the surface with salted water. Place the tins in a large, lightly oiled polythene bag. Leave the tins in a warm place for about 50 minutes or until the dough has doubled in bulk.

Set the oven at 230°C/450°F/gas 8. Bake for 30–40 minutes, until the loaves are golden brown and crisp, and sound hollow when tapped lightly on the bottom.

WHITEBAIT

SERVES 3 TO 4

50 g/2 oz plain flour

salt and pepper

125 ml/4 fl oz milk

100 g/4 oz whitebait

oil for deep frying

cayenne pepper

GARNISH

parsley sprigs

lemon wedges

Mix the flour, salt and pepper in a sturdy polythene bag. Pour the milk into a shallow bowl. Dip the whitebait into the milk, then toss them in the seasoned flour in the bag. Shake off excess flour and make sure that all the fish are separate.

Put the oil for frying into a deep wide pan. Heat the oil to 180–190°C/350–375°F or until a cube of bread added to the oil browns in 30 seconds. If you are using a deep-fat fryer, follow the manufacturer's instructions.

Carefully add the fish, a few at a time, in a chip basket to the hot oil and fry for 30 seconds to 1 minute. Drain on absorbent kitchen paper and keep hot in a warmed dish. Reheat the oil before putting in each fresh batch of fish. When all the fish are fried, pile them on a serving plate, sprinkle with salt and cayenne and serve, garnished with parsley and lemon wedges.

WHITE SAUCE

The recipe that follows is for a thick coating sauce. See Chart for variations.

MAKES 600 ML/1 PINT

50 g/2 oz butter

50 g/2 oz plain flour

600 ml/1 pint milk, stock or a mixture

salt and pepper

Melt the butter in a saucepan. Stir in the flour and cook over low heat for 2–3 minutes, without browning.

With the heat on the lowest setting, gradually add the liquid, stirring constantly. If lumps begin to form, stop pouring in liquid and stir the sauce vigorously, then continue pouring in the liquid when smooth. Increase the heat to moderate and cook the sauce, stirring, until it boils and thickens.

Lower the heat and simmer for 1–2 minutes, beating briskly to give the sauce a gloss. Add salt and pepper to taste.

variation

Pouring Sauce Follow the recipe above, but use only 40 g/1½ oz each of butter and flour.

MRS BEETON'S TIP

White Sauce can be made by the all-in-one method. Simply combine the butter, flour and liquid in a saucepan and whisk over moderate heat until the mixture comes to the boil. Lower the heat and simmer for 3–4 minutes, whisking constantly until the sauce is thick, smooth and glossy. Add salt and pepper to taste.

SIMPLE VARIATIONS ON BASIC SAUCES

Add the ingredients shown to the basic recipe, when the sauce is cooked.

	Cheese, grated (Cheddar)	Eggs, hard-boiled and chopped	Anchovy Essence	Parsley, chopped	Tomato purée	Mushrooms, sliced and cooked in butter	Mustard, made mild	Capers, chopped
White Sauce	100 g/4 oz	3–4	–	60 ml/4 tbsp	–	175 g/6 oz	45–60 ml/ 3–4 tbsp	–
Béchamel Sauce	–	3	30 ml/2 tbsp	–	30 ml/2 tbsp	100 g/4 oz	–	45 ml/3 tbsp
Hollandaise Sauce	–	–	–	–	15 ml/1 tbsp	–	–	15 ml/1 tbsp
Mayonnaise	–	–	15 ml/1 tbsp	30 ml/2 tbsp	15 ml/1 tbsp	–	10–15 ml/ 2–3 tsp	15 ml/1 tbsp

WHITE STOCK

1.4 kg/3 lb knuckle of veal on the bone, or other stewing veal

2 chicken drumsticks or poultry trimmings

1 onion, sliced

1 carrot, quartered

2 celery sticks, quartered

2 open cup mushrooms, quartered

1 bouquet garni

4 white peppercorns

1 blade of mace

Put the bones in a large saucepan. Add 900 ml/1½ pints water. Bring to the boil, skim the surface, then add the remaining ingredients. Lower the heat and simmer for 30 minutes. Add a further 900 ml/1½ pints water and simmer for about 3 hours more. Cool quickly, then strain. Skim off surface fat. Season and use as required.

WILD RICE STUFFING

SUFFICIENT FOR 2 PHEASANTS OR 1 LARGE GUINEAFOWL

350 ml/12 fl oz stock

150 g/5 oz wild rice

50 g/2 oz butter

2 shallots, finely chopped

½ small green pepper, finely chopped

1 small celery stick, finely sliced

100 g/4 oz mushrooms, chopped

30 ml/2 tbsp tomato purée

Bring the stock to the boil in a saucepan and add the wild rice. Lower the heat, cover and cook gently for 40 minutes until the rice is almost tender and the majority of the stock is absorbed. Cover and set aside.

Melt the butter in a saucepan, add the shallots, green pepper, celery and mushrooms and fry over gentle heat for 3 minutes. Remove from the heat, add to the wild rice with the tomato purée and mix well.

WINTER SALAD

Adding milk to an oil and vinegar dressing gives an unusual, slightly creamy mixture.

SERVES 6

1 head of endive, washed and shredded

1 punnet of mustard and cress

2 celery sticks, thinly sliced

4 hard-boiled eggs, sliced

225 g/8 oz cooked beetroot, sliced

DRESSING
5 ml/1 tsp French mustard

5 ml/1 tsp caster sugar

30 ml/2 tbsp salad oil

30 ml/2 tbsp milk

30 ml/2 tbsp cider vinegar

salt

cayenne

Arrange the endive, mustard and cress and celery in a salad bowl. Top with the eggs and beetroot, overlapping the slices or interleaving them with the endive but keeping them separate from each other.

For the dressing, put the mustard and sugar in a small basin. Add the oil gradually, whisking all the time. Add the milk very slowly, whisking vigorously to prevent the mixture curdling. Continue adding the vinegar in the same way – if the ingredients are added too quickly the dressing will curdle. Add salt and a hint of cayenne. Spoon this dressing over the salad just before serving.

variations
When making the dressing, the milk may be omitted, or mayonnaise thinned with single cream, yogurt or milk may be used instead.

YORKSHIRE PUDDING

Yorkshire pudding is traditionally cooked in a large tin below the joint, so that some of the cooking juices from the meat fall into the pudding to give it an excellent flavour. In a modern oven, this means using a rotisserie or resting the meat directly on the oven shelf. The pudding should be cooked in a large roasting tin, then cut into portions.

100 g/4 oz plain flour

1 egg, beaten

150 ml/¼ pint milk

Sift the flour into a bowl and add a pinch of salt. Make a well in the centre of the flour and add the beaten egg. Stir in the milk, gradually working in the flour. Beat vigorously until the mixture is smooth and bubbly, then stir in 150 ml/¼ pint water.

If the Yorkshire pudding is to be served with a joint which has been cooked on a rotisserie or directly on the oven shelf, remove the roasting pan placed under the joint to catch the drips and spoon off 30 ml/2 tbsp of the dripping into a large baking tin. Place the tin under the joint in the oven for 5 minutes until the fat is very hot, then carefully pour in the batter. Bake below the meat for 35–45 minutes.

Alternatively, bake the pudding in individual tins, following the method given for Roast Ribs of Beef with Yorkshire Pudding. The pudding may be served as a course on its own before the meat course. Gravy should be poured over the portions of pudding.

ZABAGLIONE

SERVES 4

4 egg yolks
40 g/1 oz caster sugar
60 ml/4 tbsp Marsala or Madeira

Put the egg yolks into a deep heatproof bowl and whisk lightly. Add the sugar and wine, and place the bowl over a saucepan of hot water. Whisk for about 10 minutes or until the mixture is very thick and creamy (see Mrs Beeton's Tip). Pour the custard into individual glasses and serve while still warm, with sponge fingers.

variation

ZABAGLIONE CREAM Dissolve 50 g/2 oz caster sugar in 60 ml/4 tbsp water in a saucepan and boil for 12 minutes until syrupy. Whisk with 4 egg yolks until pale and thick. Add 30 ml/2 tbsp Marsala or Madeira and 30 ml/2 tbsp single cream while whisking. The finely grated rind of ½ lemon can be added, if liked. Spoon into individual glasses. Chill before serving.

> **MRS BEETON'S TIP**
> When the whisk is lifted out of the bowl, the trail of the whisk should lie on top of the mixture for 2–3 seconds.

INDEX